THE PRESOCRATIC
PHILOSOPHERS

The Presocratic Philosophers

A CRITICAL HISTORY
WITH A SELECTION OF TEXTS

BY

G. S. KIRK
REGIUS PROFESSOR EMERITUS OF GREEK
IN THE UNIVERSITY OF CAMBRIDGE

J. E. RAVEN
FORMERLY FELLOW OF KING'S COLLEGE, CAMBRIDGE

M. SCHOFIELD
FELLOW OF ST JOHN'S COLLEGE, CAMBRIDGE

Second Edition

CAMBRIDGE UNIVERSITY PRESS

CAMBRIDGE

LONDON   NEW YORK   NEW ROCHELLE

MELBOURNE   SYDNEY

Published by the Press Syndicate of the University of Cambridge
The Pitt Building, Trumpington Street, Cambridge CB2 1RP
32 East 57th Street, New York, NY 10022, USA
296 Beaconsfield Parade, Middle Park, Melbourne 3206, Australia

First published 1957
Reprinted with corrections 1960, 1962, 1963
Reprinted 1964, 1966, 1969, 1971, 1973, 1975, 1976, 1977, 1979
Second edition 1983
Printed in Great Britain at the University Press, Cambridge

Library of Congress catalogue card number: 82-23505

British Library Cataloguing in Publication Data
Kirk, G. S.
The presocratic philosophers.—2nd ed
1. Philosophy, Ancient
I. Title II. Raven, J. E. III. Schofield, M.
180'.938   B171

ISBN 0 521 25444 2 hard covers
ISBN 0 521 27455 9 paperback

(First edition ISBNs
0 521 05891 0 hard covers
0 521 09169 1 paperback)

To

F. H. SANDBACH

CONTENTS

Preface to the second edition   *page* ix
Preface to the first edition   xi
Abbreviations   xiii
Introductory Note: The Sources for Presocratic Philosophy   1

   I   The Forerunners of Philosophical Cosmogony   7
     1. The naïve view of the world   9
     2. Okeanos   10
     3. Night   17
     4. Orphic cosmogonies   21
     5. The Hesiodic cosmogony, and the separation of
        sky and earth   34
     6. 'Mixed' theogonies: 47
        A. Alcman   47
        B. Pherecydes   50
     7. Toward philosophy   72

THE IONIAN THINKERS
   II   Thales of Miletus   76
  III   Anaximander of Miletus   100
  IV   Anaximenes of Miletus   143
   V   Xenophanes of Colophon   163
  VI   Heraclitus of Ephesus   181

PHILOSOPHY IN THE WEST
  VII   Pythagoras of Samos   214
VIII   Parmenides of Elea   239
  IX   Zeno of Elea   263
   X   Empedocles of Acragas   280
  XI   Philolaus of Croton and Fifth-Century
        Pythagoreanism   322

THE IONIAN RESPONSE

XII   Anaxagoras of Clazomenae   352
XIII Archelaus of Athens   385
XIV   Melissus of Samos   390
 XV   The Atomists: Leucippus of Miletus and Democritus
        of Abdera   402
XVI   Diogenes of Apollonia   434

Selective Bibliography   453
Index of Passages   461
General Index   475

PREFACE TO SECOND EDITION

It is now more than twenty-five years since *The Presocratic Philosophers* first appeared; it has been through many printings since, with minor corrections until 1963 and subsequently without change. During the last few years GSK and JER were conscious that a basically revised edition would soon be needed, if it was not overdue. JER's health was not good and his research interests had become exclusively botanical; he therefore asked GSK to gauge the moment and suggest a third member of the team. As it happened, the part of the book that was primarily JER's called for most revision because of the way scholarly interests had developed; but GSK, too, had been working in other fields and needed a collaborator in the thick of things. MS agreed in 1979 to become a partner in the enterprise, and there was complete accord between all three on how the work should be done.

There are major and important changes in this new edition. MS has completely rewritten the chapters on the Eleatics and Pythagoreans, principally because of work by analytic philosophers on the former and by Walter Burkert (in particular) on the latter – work which has called for some reassessment of the Cornford–Raven view on the interrelations between the two schools. Alcmaeon has been incorporated in these chapters. MS has likewise completely rewritten the chapter on Empedocles to take account of the reinterpretations of J. Bollack, G. Zuntz and others and the controversy these have provoked. It is hoped that the arrangement of the fragments of Empedocles in their probably original order will be found more useful by the reader. The chapter on Anaxagoras, on the other hand, remains largely as JER wrote it; MS has indicated in footnotes how his own solutions (for which see his *An Essay on Anaxagoras*, Cambridge, 1980) might differ here and there, but it was the wish of all three authors that this chapter should remain largely unchanged. Archelaus, too, remains unaltered, and Diogenes is expanded by a single footnote; on the Atomists MS has rewritten the sections on metaphysical principles, on atoms and the void and on the weight of atoms (to take account of the work of D. J. Furley, J. Barnes, D. O' Brien and others), also on epistemology and ethics – the ethics section being largely the work of Dr J. F. Procopé, to whom we express warm thanks.

The earlier part of the book has been revised throughout by GSK, but with little complete rewriting. Chapter 1, on Forerunners, has been rearranged, abbreviated and simplified in places, and has additional sections on the new Orphic material, on the Alcman cosmogonical fragment and on the movement from myths to philosophy. There has been a spate of publication on the Milesians, Xenophanes and Heraclitus over the last quarter-century, but the effects have been minor compared with those of work on the Pythagoreans and Eleatics and on Empedocles. Account has been taken of the contributions of, in particular, C. H. Kahn (on Anaximander and Heraclitus), J. Barnes and W. K. C. Guthrie, but the interpretation and presentation, despite numerous changes in detail, have not been very drastically altered. That reflects a general conviction that the book should not be radically changed in its approach and emphasis, except where necessary; and also the opinion of GSK, at least, that despite all the dust of battle the real advances, with respect to these earlier thinkers, have been quite small.

A definite improvement, especially for the many readers who use the translations rather than the Greek texts, has been to bring these up into the body of the text. The Bibliography has been brought up to date, and the new Index Locorum is the work of Mr N. O'Sullivan, to whom the authors are most grateful, as they also are to the publishers and printers for their help and their careful treatment of a relatively complicated text. But 'the authors' means, sadly, the surviving ones, for JER died in March 1980, aged 65; his remarkable gifts and lovable personality are well conveyed in *John Raven by his Friends* (published in 1981 by his widow, Faith Raven, from Docwra's Manor, Shepreth, Herts., England). On a happier note it is a pleasure to re-dedicate the book to Professor F. H. Sandbach, whose profound learning is even better appreciated now than it was then.

G.S.K.
M.S.

June 1983

PREFACE TO FIRST EDITION

This book is designed primarily for those who have more than a casual interest in the history of early Greek thought; but by translating all Greek passages, and confining some of the more detailed discussion to small-type notes at the end of paragraphs, we have also aimed to make the book useful for those students of the history of philosophy or science who have no previous acquaintance with this important and fascinating field.

Two points should be emphasized. First, we have limited our scope to the chief Presocratic 'physicists' and their forerunners, whose main preoccupation was with the nature (*physis*) and coherence of things as a whole. More specialized scientific interests were simultaneously developing throughout the sixth and fifth centuries B.C., especially in mathematics, astronomy, geography, medicine and biology; but for lack of space, and to some extent of evidence, we have not pursued these topics beyond the interests of the chief physicists. We have also excluded the Sophists, whose positive philosophical contribution, often exaggerated, lay mainly in the fields of epistemology and semantics. Secondly, we have not set out to produce a necessarily orthodox exposition (if, indeed, such a thing is conceivable in a field where opinion is changing so rapidly), but have preferred in many places to put forward our own interpretations. At the same time we have usually mentioned other interpretations of disputed points, and have always tried to present the reader with the main materials for the formation of his own judgement.

The part of the book dealing with the Ionian tradition, including its forerunners and also the atomists and Diogenes (i.e. chapters I–VI, XVII and XVIII), with the note on the sources, is by G. S. Kirk, while the part dealing with the Italian tradition, and also the chapters on Anaxagoras and Archelaus (i.e. chapters VII–XVI), are by J. E. Raven. The contributions of each author were of course subjected to detailed criticism by the other, and the planning of the book as a whole is by both.

The scale of different sections of the book is admittedly rather variable. Where the evidence is fuller and clearer – particularly where considerable fragments survive, as for example in the case of Parmenides – the commentary can naturally be shorter; where the evidence is sparser and more confusing, as for example in the case of Anaximander or the Pythagoreans, our own explanations must be longer and more involved. Chapter 1 in particular, which deals with a part of the subject which is often neglected, is perhaps more detailed in parts than its ultimate importance demands, and non-specialists are advised to leave it until last.

Only the most important texts have been quoted, and those in an inevitably personal selection. For a nearly complete collection of fragments and testimonies the reader should turn to H. Diels, *Die Fragmente der Vorsokratiker* (5th and later editions, Berlin, 1934–54, edited by W. Kranz). This fundamental work is referred to by the abbreviation DK. Where a DK number (e.g. DK 28A12) is appended to the reference of a passage quoted in the present work, this means that DK, in the section referred to, quotes more of the passage in question than we do. DK references are omitted where less, or no more, of the text is given, and also in the case of fragments (where the fragment-number, always in Diels' numeration, is the same as the number in the relevant B-section in DK). Where supplements occur in texts quoted, without further information, they are usually by Diels, and reference may be made to the textual notes in DK.

We are obviously indebted to many friends for suggestions and help; and also, as goes without saying, to previous writers like Zeller, Burnet, Cornford, Ross and Cherniss. Many of these debts are recorded in the text. For typographical advice and assistance we are indebted to the printing staff of the Cambridge University Press. H. Lloyd-Jones and I. R. D. Mathewson read the proofs and made many valuable suggestions. Another outstanding contribution was made by F. H. Sandbach, whose numerous acute and learned comments on the final draft were of the utmost value, and to whom, as an unworthy offering, we should like to dedicate this book.

G.S.K.
J.E.R.

Cambridge
May 1957

ABBREVIATIONS

The following abbreviations may be mentioned; others should be self-evident:

ACPA H. Cherniss, *Aristotle's Criticism of Plato and the Academy* (Baltimore, 1944).

AGP *Archiv für Geschichte der Philosophie.*

AJP *American Journal of Philology.*

ANET *Ancient Near Eastern Texts relating to the Old Testament*, ed. J. B. Pritchard (2nd ed., Princeton, 1955).

CP *Classical Philology.*

CQ *Classical Quarterly.*

DK *Die Fragmente der Vorsokratiker*, 5th to 7th eds., by H. Diels, ed. with additions by W. Kranz. (The 6th and 7th eds. are photographic reprints, 1951–2 and 1954, of the 5th, with Nachträge by Kranz.)

EGP John Burnet, *Early Greek Philosophy*, 4th ed., London, 1930 (a reprint with corrections of 3rd ed., 1920).

GGN *Nachrichten v. d. Gesellschaft zu Göttingen* (Phil.-hist. Klasse).

HGP W. K. C. Guthrie, *A History of Greek Philosophy*, in 6 vols. (Cambridge, 1962–81).

HSCP *Harvard Studies in Classical Philology.*

JHS *Journal of Hellenic Studies.*

J.Phil. *Journal of Philology.*

KR G. S. Kirk and J. E. Raven, *The Presocratic Philosophers* (Cambridge, 1957).

LSJ Liddell and Scott, *A Greek–English Lexicon*, 9th ed., 1925–40, revised by H. Stuart Jones and R. McKenzie.

PCPS *Proceedings of the Cambridge Philological Society.*

Rh. M. *Rheinisches Museum.*

Σ Scholion or scholiast.

SB Ber. *Sitzungsberichte d. preussischen Akademie d. Wissenschaft.*

SVF *Stoicorum Veterum Fragmenta*, ed. H. von Arnim (Leipzig, 1903–5).

ZPE *Zeitschrift für Papyrologie und Epigraphik.*

The Sources for Presocratic Philosophy

A. Direct quotations

The actual fragments of the Presocratic thinkers are preserved as quotations in subsequent ancient authors, from Plato in the fourth century B.C. to Simplicius in the sixth century A.D., and even, in rare cases, to late Byzantine writers like John Tzetzes. The date of the source in which a quotation occurs is not, of course, a reliable guide to its accuracy. Thus Plato is notoriously lax in his quotations from all sources; he often mixes quotation with paraphrase, and his attitude to his predecessors is frequently not objective but humorous or ironical. The Neoplatonist Simplicius, on the other hand, who lived a whole millennium after the Presocratics, made long and evidently accurate quotations, in particular from Parmenides, Empedocles, Anaxagoras and Diogenes of Apollonia; not for the sake of literary embellishment, but because in his commentaries on the *Physics* and *de caelo* of Aristotle he found it necessary to expound Aristotle's views on his predecessors by setting down their actual words. At times Simplicius did this at greater length than was essential because, as he tells us, a particular ancient work had become so rare.

Aristotle, like Plato, gave comparatively few direct quotations, and his main value is as a summarizer and critic of earlier thinkers. Apart from Plato, Aristotle, and Simplicius, the following notable sources of *verbatim* extracts may be singled out for special mention:

(i) Plutarch, the Academic philosopher, historian and essayist of the second century A.D., in his extensive *Moral Essays* made hundreds of quotations (often expanded, interpolated or partly reworded by himself) from the Presocratic thinkers.

(ii) Sextus 'Empiricus', the Sceptic philosopher and physician of the late second century A.D., expounded the theories of Aenesidemus, who lived some two centuries earlier and himself relied to a great extent on Hellenistic sources. Sextus quotes many early passages bearing on cognition and the reliability of the senses.

(iii) Clement of Alexandria, the learned head of the Catechetical school, lived in the second half of the second century A.D. and the early years of the third. A convert to Christianity, Clement nevertheless maintained his interest in Greek literature of all kinds, and used a wide knowledge and a remarkable memory to point his comparisons between paganism and Christianity with frequent quotations from the Greek poets and philosophers (chiefly in his *Protrepticus* and the eight books of *Stromateis* or *Miscellanies*).

(iv) Hippolytus, a theologian in Rome in the third century A.D., wrote a *Refutation of all Heresies* in nine books, which attacked Christian heresies by claiming them to be revivals of pagan philosophy. For example, the Noetian heresy was a revival of Heraclitus' theory of the coincidence of opposites – a contention which Hippolytus attempted to substantiate by the quotation of no less than seventeen sayings of Heraclitus, many of them otherwise unknown.

(v) Diogenes Laertius compiled, probably in the third century A.D., a trivial but from our point of view important *Lives of Famous Philosophers* in ten books. In his biographical and doxographical notices, derived mainly from Hellenistic sources, he included occasional short quotations.

(vi) John Stobaeus, the fifth-century A.D. anthologist, assembled in his *Anthologium* educative extracts from the whole range of Greek literature, but with special emphasis on ethical sayings. Many Presocratic fragments (notably of Democritus) are preserved by him, often in a somewhat impure form. Stobaeus' main sources were the handbooks and compendia which proliferated in the Alexandrian period.

In addition to the main sources noted above, quotations from the Presocratics occur sporadically elsewhere: in the Epicurean Philodemus; in Stoics like Marcus Aurelius and eclectics like Maximus of Tyre; in Christian writers other than Clement and Hippolytus, for example in Origen; occasionally in Aetius (see B, 4, *b*; direct quotations in Aetius are rare); in technical authors like Galen the doctor, Strabo the geographer and Athenaeus the anthologist of food and drink; and, not least important, in Neoplatonic writers from Numenius, Plotinus, Porphyry and Iamblichus (the last two of whom wrote on Pythagoras) down to Proclus and, of course, the invaluable Simplicius.

To conclude these notes on the sources of direct quotations, it must be emphasized that the author of a direct quotation need not have seen the original work, since summaries, anthologies and compendia of every kind, known as early as Hippias (p. 96 n. 2) and produced in large numbers in the three centuries following the foundation of Alexandria, were regarded as an adequate substitute for most prose originals of a technical nature.

B. Testimonia

(1) PLATO is the earliest commentator on the Presocratics (though there were occasional references in Euripides and Aristophanes). His comments, however, are for the most part only casual ones, inspired, like many of his quotations, by irony or amusement. Thus his references to Heraclitus, Parmenides and Empedocles are more often than not light-hearted *obiter dicta*, and one-sided or exaggerated ones at that, rather than sober and objective historical judgements. Provided this is recognized, Plato has much of value to tell us. One passage, *Phaedo* 96ff., gives a useful but brief survey of fifth-century physical preoccupations.

(2) ARISTOTLE gave more serious attention to his philosophical predecessors than Plato had done, and prefaced some of his treatises with formal surveys of their opinions, notably in *Metaphysics* A. However, his judgements are often distorted by his view of earlier philosophy as a stumbling progress towards the truth that Aristotle himself revealed in his physical doctrines, especially those concerning causation. There are also, of course, many acute and valuable criticisms, and a store of factual information.

(3) THEOPHRASTUS undertook the history of previous philosophy, from Thales to Plato, as part of his contribution to the encyclopaedic activity organized by his master Aristotle – just as Eudemus undertook the history of theology, astronomy and mathematics and Menon that of medicine. According to Diogenes Laertius' list of his works, Theophrastus wrote sixteen (or eighteen) books of *Physical Opinions* (or *Opinions of the Physicists*; the Greek genitive is Φυσικῶν δοξῶν); these were later epitomized in two volumes. Only the last book, *On sensation*, is extant in its greater part; but important extracts from the first book, *On material principles*, were copied down by Simplicius in his commentary on Aristotle's *Physics*. (Some of these extracts Simplicius derived from lost commentaries by the important Peripatetic commentator Alexander of Aphrodisias.) In this first book Theophrastus treated the different thinkers in roughly chronological order, adding their city, patronymic, and sometimes date or mutual relationship. In the remaining books the order was chronological only within the main logical divisions. In addition to the general history Theophrastus wrote special works on Anaximenes,

3

Empedocles, Anaxagoras, Archelaus, and (in several volumes) Democritus. These have unfortunately perished; presumably Theophrastus went to greater pains to consult the original sources for these thinkers. From the available evidence, however, his judgements even on them were often derived directly from Aristotle, without much attempt to apply a new and objective criticism.

(4) THE DOXOGRAPHICAL TRADITION. (a) *Its general nature.* Theophrastus' great work became the standard authority for the ancient world on Presocratic philosophy, and is the source of most subsequent collections of 'opinions' (δόξαι, ἀρέσκοντα or *placita*). These collections took different forms. (i) In close reproductions of Theophrastus' arrangement each major topic was considered in a separate section, the different thinkers being treated successively within each section. This was the method of Aetius and his source, the '*Vetusta Placita*' (see p. 5). (ii) Biographical doxographers considered all the opinions of each philosopher together, in company with details of his life – supplied, to a large extent, by the febrile imaginations of Hellenistic biographers and historians like Hermippus of Smyrna, Hieronymus of Rhodes and Neanthes of Cyzicus. The result is exemplified in the biographical medley of Diogenes Laertius. (iii) Another type of doxographical work is seen in the Διαδοχαί, or accounts of philosophical successions. Its originator was the Peripatetic Sotion of Alexandria, who around 200 B.C. wrote a survey of previous philosophers arranged by schools. The known thinkers were related to each other in a descending line of master and pupil (here Sotion was extending and formalizing a process begun by Theophrastus); in addition, the Ionian school was clearly distinguished from the Italian. Many of the patristic doxographical summaries (notably those in Eusebius, Irenaeus, Arnobius, Theodoretus – who, however, also made direct use of Aetius – and St Augustine) were based on the brief accounts in the Succession-writers. (iv) The chronographer Apollodorus of Alexandria composed, in the middle of the second century B.C., a metrical account of the dates and opinions of the philosophers. This rested partly on Sotion's division into schools and masters, partly on the chronology of Eratosthenes, who had sensibly assigned dates to artists, philosophers and writers as well as to political events. Apollodorus filled in the gaps left by Eratosthenes, on very arbitrary principles: a philosopher's *acme* or period of chief activity was assumed to be at the age of forty, and was made to coincide with the nearest of a number of major chronological epochs, for example the capture of Sardis in 546/5 B.C. or the foundation of Thurii in 444/3. Further,

a supposed pupil was always made forty years younger than his supposed master.

(b) *Aetius and the 'Vetusta Placita'*. Two extant doxographical summaries, closely resembling each other, were independently derived from a lost original – the collection of *Opinions* made by Aetius, an otherwise unknown compilator, probably of the second century A.D., whose name is known from a reference in Theodoretus. These extant summaries are the *Epitome of Physical Opinions*, in five books, which falsely claims to be by Plutarch; and the *Physical Extracts* which appear in book I (for the most part) of Stobaeus' *Anthologium*. (From the former, which was widely read, are derived notices in pseudo-Galen, Athenagoras, Achilles and Cyril.) Diels in his great *Doxographi Graeci* arranged these two sources in parallel columns as the *Placita* of Aetius. This forms our most extensive, if not always our most accurate, doxographical authority.

Aetius' work was based, not directly on Theophrastus' history, but upon an intermediate summary of it produced, probably, in the Posidonian school in the first century B.C. This lost work was named by Diels the *Vetusta Placita*. In it Stoic, Epicurean and Peripatetic opinions were added to those recorded by Theophrastus, and much that was derived from Theophrastus was subjected to Stoic reformulation. Aetius himself added further Stoic and Epicurean opinions, as well as a few definitions and introductory comments. A direct use of the *Vetusta Placita* was made by Varro (in Censorinus' *de die natali*), and is seen also in the brief doxography in Cicero, *Academica priora* II, 37, 118.

(c) *Other important doxographical sources*. (i) *Hippolytus*. The first book of his *Refutation of all Heresies*, the so-called *Philosophoumena* once attributed to Origen, is a biographical doxography containing separate accounts of the main philosophers. The sections on Thales, Pythagoras, Empedocles, Heraclitus, the Eleatics and the Atomists come from a trifling biographical summary and are of small value, unlike those on Anaximander, Anaximenes, Anaxagoras, Archelaus and Xenophanes, which come from a fuller and much more valuable biographical source. At many points the comments of the second group are more detailed, and less inaccurate, than the corresponding ones in Aetius. (ii) *The pseudo-Plutarchean Stromateis*. These short 'Miscellanies' (which must be distinguished from the *Epitome*, from Aetius, also ascribed to Plutarch) are preserved by Eusebius; they come from a source similar to that of the second group in Hippolytus. They differ in that they concentrate on the subject-matter of the earlier books in Theophrastus, those that dealt with the material

5

principle, cosmogony, and the heavenly bodies; and they contain much verbiage and pretentious interpretation. However, some important details are preserved which do not occur elsewhere. (iii) *Diogenes Laertius*. Apart from biographical details culled from many sources, some useful chronological data from Apollodorus, and deplorable epigrams from the pen of Diogenes himself, the opinions of each thinker are usually set out in two distinct doxographical notes: the first (what Diogenes called the κεφαλαιώδης or summary account) from a worthless biographical source like that used by Hippolytus in the first group, and the second (the ἐπὶ μέρους or detailed account) from a fuller and more reliable epitome like that used by Hippolytus for his second group.

(5) CONCLUSION. It must be remembered that many writers who were independent of the direct Theophrastean tradition are known to have devoted special works to the early philosophers. For example the fourth-century B.C. Academic, Heraclides of Pontus, wrote four books on Heraclitus, and so did the Stoic Cleanthes; while Aristotle's pupil Aristoxenus wrote biographies which included one of Pythagoras. Allowance must be made, therefore, for the possibility of isolated non-Theophrastean judgements appearing in later eclectic sources like Plutarch or Clement; though most such judgements that we can recognize show signs, nevertheless, of Aristotelian, or of Stoic, Epicurean, or Sceptic, influence. Theophrastus remains the main source of information, and his work is known to us through the doxographers, through the quotations by Simplicius, and through the extant *de sensu*. From these it is evident that Theophrastus was strongly influenced by Aristotle – who, as has been stated, did not aim, as Theophrastus should have done, at extreme historical objectivity. Theophrastus was no more successful than is to be expected in understanding the motives of an earlier period and a different world of thought; a further defect was that, once having extracted a general pattern of explanations, particularly for cosmological events, he tended to impose it, perhaps too boldly, in cases where he lacked full evidence – cases which seem to have been not infrequent. Thus it is legitimate to feel complete confidence in our understanding of a Presocratic thinker only when the Aristotelian or Theophrastean interpretation, even if it can be accurately reconstructed, is confirmed by relevant and well-authenticated extracts from the philosopher himself.

CHAPTER I

The Forerunners of Philosophical Cosmogony

In this long preliminary chapter certain ideas are examined which are not truly 'philosophical'; they are mythic rather than rational in kind, but may nevertheless appear as significant preludes to the sort of attempt to explain the world that began with Thales.

We are not concerned here with pure mythology, but with concepts which, although expressed in the language and through the persons of myth, are the result of a more direct, empirical, non-symbolical way of thinking. These quasi-rationalistic views of the world are most frequently concerned with its earliest history, starting from its actual birth or creation, and overlap the attempt (made most notably by Hesiod in the *Theogony*) to systematize the manifold deities of legend by deriving them from a common ancestor or pair of ancestors at the beginning of the world. Yet the active investigation of the world's ancestry, whether mainly mythical as in Hesiod or mainly rational as in the Milesian philosophers, must have been carried on only by the few. The general structure of the present world, the common environment of experience, was of wider interest; and here a common, naïve, extroverted but nevertheless partly mythical outlook seems to have been widely accepted. It appears from time to time in Homer and is briefly described in §1. In §§2 and 3 two concepts are examined which were later credited with cosmogonical importance by the Greeks themselves, those of Okeanos and of Nyx (Night). §§4, 5 and 6 are concerned with four special accounts, all of primarily non-philosophical character but all treating of cosmological topics: first the various cosmogonical ideas associated with Orpheus, then the Hesiodic *Theogony*, then the intriguing but fragmentary views of Alcman and (admittedly at rather disproportionate length) Pherecydes of Syros. Finally in §7 comes a brief consideration of what was needed for the transition to a more fully rational approach.

On some points reference will be made to the comparative mythology of earlier near-eastern cultures, especially Babylonian, Egyptian and Hittite. There are strong similarities between some of the Greek cosmogonical stories and the theogonical myths of the great river-civilizations and their neighbours; these similarities help to explain some details of Greek accounts down to and including Thales. Translations of the main non-Greek texts are most conveniently to be found in *Ancient Near Eastern Texts relating to the Old Testament*, ed. J. B. Pritchard (Princeton, 3rd ed. 1969), which will be referred to as Pritchard, *ANET*. Useful summaries, all in the Pelican series, are H. Frankfort and others, *Before Philosophy* (Harmondsworth, 1949) originally published as *The Intellectual Adventure of Ancient Man* (Chicago University Press, 1946), O. R. Gurney, *The Hittites* (Harmondsworth, rev. ed. 1961) and G. S. Kirk, *The Nature of Greek Myths* (Harmondsworth, 1974), ch. xi.

Little is said in this chapter about the development of the concept of the soul. The Homeric idea of the *psyche* or breath-soul as an insubstantial image of the body, giving it life and surviving it in a wretched, bloodless existence in Hades, is too familiar to need description here. E. R. Dodds' *The Greeks and the Irrational* (Berkeley, 1951) and chapter v of Jaeger's *Theology of the Early Greek Philosophers* (Oxford, 1947) give a good account of the popular, pre-philosophical idea of the soul. Pythagoras was possibly the first Greek explicitly to treat the soul as something of moral importance, and Heraclitus first clearly indicated that knowledge of it was relevant to knowledge of the structure of the cosmos. Yet the idea that the substance of the soul was related to *aither*, or to the substance of the stars, seems from fifth-century B.C. poetical contexts to have existed for some time already as part of the complex body of popular beliefs, alongside the distinct Homeric concept of a breath-soul. These antecedents will be summarized in the chapters on Thales, Anaximenes and Heraclitus.

The main object of the earliest deliberate efforts to explain the world remained the description of its *growth* from a simple, and therefore fully comprehensible, beginning. Matters concerned with human life seemed to belong to a different type of enquiry – to the poetical tradition, in fact, in which the old inherited assumptions, though sometimes inconsistent, were still regarded as valid. Moreover the world's original state, and the method by which it diversified itself, were often imagined anthropomorphically, in terms of a parent or pair of parents. This genealogical attitude persisted even after the eventual abandonment by the Milesian philosophers of the traditional mythological framework, discussed in §7. It is part of Heraclitus' originality that he rejected such an approach altogether.

1. The naïve view of the world

A popular conception of the nature of the world, which can be traced mainly in scattered references in Homer, is roughly as follows. The sky is a solid hemisphere like a bowl (*Il.* xvii, 425 χάλκεον οὐρανόν, cf. Pindar *Nem.* 6, 3–4; οὐρανὸν ἐς πολύχαλκον at *Il.* v, 504, *Od.* iii, 2; σιδήρεον οὐρανόν at *Od.* xv, 329 and xvii, 565. Solidity as well as brightness is presumably conveyed by these metallic epithets). It covers the round flat earth. The lower part of the gap between earth and sky, up to and including the clouds, contains ἀήρ or mist; the upper part (sometimes called the οὐρανός itself) is αἰθήρ, *aither*, the shining upper air, which is sometimes conceived as fiery. At *Il.* xiv, 288 (ἐλάτη) δι' ἠέρος αἰθέρ' ἵκανεν, 'the fir-tree reached through the *aer* to the *aither*'. Below its surface, the earth stretches far downwards, and has its roots in or above Tartarus:

1 Homer *Il.* viii, 13 (Zeus speaks)
 ἤ μιν ἑλὼν ῥίψω ἐς Τάρταρον ἠερόεντα
 τῆλε μάλ', ἧχι βάθιστον ὑπὸ χθονός ἐστι βέρεθρον,
 ἔνθα σιδήρειαί τε πύλαι καὶ χάλκεος οὐδός,
 τόσσον ἔνερθ' Ἀίδεω ὅσον οὐρανός ἐστ' ἀπὸ γαίης.

2 Hesiod *Theogony* 726 (Τάρταρον)
 τὸν πέρι χάλκεον ἕρκος ἐλήλαται· ἀμφὶ δέ μιν νὺξ
 τριστοιχεὶ κέχυται περὶ δειρήν· αὐτὰρ ὕπερθεν
 γῆς ῥίζαι πεφύασι καὶ ἀτρυγέτοιο θαλάσσης.

 1 Or seizing him I will hurl him into misty Tartaros, very far, where is the deepest gulf below earth; there are iron gates and brazen threshold, as far beneath Hades as sky is from earth.
 2 Around it [Tartaros] a brazen fence is drawn; and all about it Night in three rows is poured, around the throat; and above are the roots of earth and unharvested sea.

The circuit of Tartarus is thus 'brazen' (and so firm, unyielding) like the sky; the symmetry is reflected also in the equal distance between sky and earth's surface, and earth's surface and its foundations – for 'Hades' in the last line of 1 seems to be an illogical variant upon an original 'earth', as in *Theogony* 720 τόσσον ἔνερθ' ὑπὸ γῆς ὅσον οὐρανός ἐστ' ἀπὸ γαίης ('as far below, under earth, as sky is distant from it'). There was a certain vagueness about the relationship of Hades, Erebos, and Tartarus, although Tartarus was certainly the lowest part of the underworld. The symmetry between underworld and overworld was not complete; the shape of Tartarus was not normally conceived as hemispherical, and that of the sky is often complicated by the idea of Mount Olympus merging with it as abode of the gods. A variant conception made the earth stretch downwards indefinitely:

3 Xenophanes fr. 28 (= **180**)

γαίης μὲν τόδε πεῖρας ἄνω παρὰ ποσσὶν ὁρᾶται
ἠέρι προσπλάζον, τὸ κάτω δ' ἐς ἄπειρον ἱκνεῖται.

(Cf. Strabo I, p. 12 Cas.)

3 Of earth this is the upper limit which we see by our feet, in contact with air; but its underneath continues indefinitely.

This is a later formulation, but again a popular rather than an intellectual one.

Round the edge of the earth-disc, according to the unsophisticated view, flowed the vast river Okeanos. This concept was of considerable importance in pre-scientific Greek thought, and is discussed in the section which now follows.

2. Okeanos

(i) *As the river surrounding the earth, and source of all waters*

4 Homer *Il.* xviii, 607 (Hephaistos)

ἐν δὲ τίθει ποταμοῖο μέγα σθένος Ὠκεανοῖο
ἄντυγα πὰρ πυμάτην σάκεος πύκα ποιητοῖο.

5 Herodotus IV, 8   τὸν δὲ Ὠκεανὸν λόγῳ μὲν λέγουσι (*sc.* Ἕλληνες)
ἀπὸ ἡλίου ἀνατολέων ἀρξάμενον γῆν περὶ πᾶσαν ῥέειν, ἔργῳ δὲ
οὐκ ἀποδεικνῦσι. (Cf. also *id.* II, 21; II, 23.)

6 Homer *Il.* xxi, 194 (Zeus)

τῷ οὐδὲ κρείων Ἀχελώιος ἰσοφαρίζει
οὐδὲ βαθυρρείταο μέγα σθένος Ὠκεανοῖο,
ἐξ οὗ περ πάντες ποταμοὶ καὶ πᾶσα θάλασσα
καὶ πᾶσαι κρῆναι καὶ φρείατα μακρὰ νάουσιν.

4 He put on it the great might of river Okeanos, along the well-made shield's outer rim.
5 They [the Greeks] affirm in words that Okeanos, beginning from the sun's risings, flows round the whole earth, but they give no effective demonstration of this.
6 Him not even Lord Acheloos equals, nor the great might of deep-flowing Okeanos, from whom, indeed, all rivers and all sea and all springs and deep wells flow.

That Okeanos surrounds the circular surface of the earth, though not explicitly stated in the Homeric poems, is suggested in 4 (where the shield made for Achilles is obviously thought of as round), in 8, and by some of the epithets applied to Okeanos – especially ἀψόρροος, 'back-flowing' (which probably means 'flowing back into itself'). Passages in Euripides and others as well as in Herodotus (5) show that the idea of a circular surrounding Okeanos was widely accepted; though occasionally in Homer, especially in the *Odyssey*, a looser usage, as the broad outer sea, had already begun to appear. 4 describes Okeanos as a river, and this too was a commonly accepted view; references are frequent to the streams, ῥοαί, of Okeanos. As such, it was presumably composed of fresh water, and 6 describes it as the source of all waters, whether fresh or salt, which are enclosed within its orbit, on or under the earth. The idea that salt water is simply fresh water somehow flavoured by the earth was commonly held in the scientific period.

The earth-encircling river differs from other elements of the popular world-picture in that it is not so obviously based on experience. The sky looks hemispherical and, to some eyes, impenetrable; it is called 'brazen', therefore, and treated as ice-like or solid even by Anaximenes and Empedocles. The earth appears to be flat, and the horizon to be circular. Yet experience cannot so easily suggest that the ultimate horizon is bounded by a fresh-water river. Voyagers may have brought back reports of vast seas beyond the Mediterranean, but these would be salt. Springs bubbling up from the earth may suggest underground rivers, but these need not entail a surrounding river. The possibility must be considered, then, that this particular conception originated in the great river-civilizations of Egypt and Mesopotamia, and was somehow introduced into Greece and given a specific Hellenic form. It will be seen on pp. 92f. that Thales' idea of the earth floating on water was probably so borrowed; and the coincidences in detail between Greek versions of certain myths, and Babylonian or Hittite versions, prove that conceptions not native either to the Aegean area, or to the proximate culture-centres of the Greek-speaking peoples before their entry into Greece, had embedded themselves in Greek thought even by the time of Hesiod and probably much earlier. Such coincidences are briefly discussed on pp. 43–6. The isolated Homeric references to Okeanos as origin of all things will also appear (pp. 16f.) as a probable allusion to non-Greek mythological ideas. In Babylonian accounts, and in some Egyptian versions, the earth was regarded as drying out, or thrusting itself up, in the midst of the primeval waters.[1] The development of such an idea is not surprising in Mesopotamia, where the land had indeed been formed from the marshlands between the two rivers; nor in Egypt, where the fertile land emerged each year as the Nile floods receded. The earth that emerges from an indefinite expanse of primeval water will still be surrounded by water. This does seem to provide a plausible, though not a certain, motive for the formation of the Greek concept of Okeanos.[2] In this popular development of the primeval-water motif the earth is regarded as being solidly rooted, once it has emerged, and the indefinite waste of water (which seems always to have been conceived as having an upper limit, a surface) is contracted into a vast but not necessarily illimitable river.[3]

[1] Cf. the Babylonian creation-epic, which originated probably in the second millennium B.C.: tablet I, 1–6 (Pritchard, *ANET*, 6of.), 'When on high the heaven had not been named, Firm ground below had not been called by name, Naught but primordial Apsu, their begetter, (And) Mummu-Tiamat, she who bore them all, Their waters commingling as a single body; No reed-hut had been matted, no marshland had appeared...' (Trans. E. A. Speiser. Apsu and Tiamat were the male and female principles of primeval water. Sometimes, but perhaps not here, they represent fish and salt water respectively.) For Egypt cf. e.g. the twenty-fourth-century B.C. text from Heliopolis, *ANET*, p. 3: 'O Atum-Kheprer, thou wast on high on the (primeval) hill...' (The primeval hillock was the first patch of land to rise above the boundless waters; it was located in many different cult-centres, and is symbolized by the pyramid.) Also another version, from the Book of the Dead (in this form, latter part of second millennium): 'I am Atum when I was alone in Nun; I am Re in his (first) appearances, when he began to rule that which he had made.' (Trans. J. A. Wilson. Atum was the creator-god worshipped at Heliopolis and equated with the sun-god Re. Nun is the primeval expanse of waters.)

[2] In origin Ὠκεανός was perhaps a non-personal descriptive term, conceivably related to Akkadian 'uginna', meaning 'ring', or Sanskrit 'a-çáyāna-ḥ', meaning 'that which surrounds'. Its development as a mythological figure, as sometimes in Homer and Hesiod, must have been comparatively late. See also M. L. West, *Hesiod, Theogony* (Oxford, 1966), p. 201.

[3] Okeanos has a further bank in the (probably late) underworld-episode in the *Odyssey* (xxiv, 11) and in Hesiod, where 'beyond Okeanos' (*Theog.* 215, 274, 294) is 'the region no man knows' (M. L. West).

The encircling river was presupposed in the myth that the sun, after crossing the sky with his horses and chariot, sails in a golden bowl round the stream of Okeanos and so arrives back in the east just before dawn:

7   Mimnermus fr. 10 Diehl

Ἠέλιος μὲν γὰρ πόνον ἔλλαχεν ἤματα πάντα,
οὐδέ κοτ' ἄμπαυσις γίγνεται οὐδεμία
ἵπποισίν τε καὶ αὐτῷ, ἐπεὶ ῥοδοδάκτυλος Ἠώς
Ὠκεανὸν προλιποῦσ' οὐρανὸν εἰσαναβῇ·

τὸν μὲν γὰρ διὰ κῦμα φέρει πολυήρατος εὐνὴ
κοίλη Ἡφαίστου χερσὶν ἐληλαμένη
χρυσοῦ τιμήεντος, ὑπόπτερος, ἄκρον ἐφ' ὕδωρ
εὕδονθ' ἁρπαλέως χώρου ἀφ' Ἑσπερίδων
γαῖαν ἐς Αἰθιόπων, ἵνα δὴ θοὸν ἅρμα καὶ ἵπποι
ἑστᾶσ', ὄφρ' Ἠὼς ἠριγένεια μόλῃ·
ἔνθ' ἐπεβή⟨σεθ' ἑ⟩ῶν ὀχέων Ὑπερίονος υἱός.

7 Helios gained a portion of toil for all his days, nor is there ever any rest for his horses and himself, when rosy-fingered Dawn, leaving Okeanos, mounts the sky; for him does his lovely bed bear across the wave, hollow and fashioned by the hands of Hephaestus out of precious gold, and winged; swiftly does it bear him sleeping over the surface of the water, from the dwelling of the Hesperides to the land of the Aithiopes, where his swift chariot and his horses stand till early-born Dawn shall come; there does the son of Hyperion mount his car.

This detail (on which see also Stesichorus fr. 8, 1–4 Page) is not mentioned in Homer.[1] In Egypt the sun was conceived as travelling from west to east in a ship, across the subterranean waters. This may or may not have been the origin of the Greek account; but the choice of a cup or bowl may be based upon the round shape of the sun itself, and suggests a more empirical and not wholly mythopoeic approach. In Heraclitus (227) the sun itself is described as a hollow bowl filled with fire, and there may have been a popular account of this kind which gave way to the more graphic conception of the sun as a charioteer.

[1] The sun rises *from* Okeanos (e.g. *Il.* VII, 422), but there is no suggestion of a vessel of any kind. The refinement of the sun sailing round Okeanos could be post-Homeric. At *Od.* x, 191 the sun goes *under* the earth, but this probably just means 'sets'. The stars in Homer *bathe* in Okeanos (e.g. *Il.* v, 6; XVIII, 489); they can hardly all have boats, and might be conceived as going through Okeanos and passing under the earth, though such details need not have been visualized.

(ii) *Okeanos as the source or origin of all things*

8 Homer *Il.* XIV, 200 (repeated at XIV, 301. Hera speaks)
εἶμι γὰρ ὀψομένη πολυφόρβου πείρατα γαίης,
Ὠκεανόν τε θεῶν γένεσιν καὶ μητέρα Τηθύν...

9 Homer *Il.* XIV, 244 (Hypnos speaks)
ἄλλον μέν κεν ἔγωγε θεῶν αἰειγενετάων
ῥεῖα κατευνήσαιμι, καὶ ἂν ποταμοῖο ῥέεθρα
Ὠκεανοῦ, ὅς περ γένεσις πάντεσσι τέτυκται·

Ζηνὸς δ' οὐκ ἂν ἔγωγε Κρονίονος ἆσσον ἱκοίμην
οὐδὲ κατευνήσαιμ', ὅτε μὴ αὐτός γε κελεύοι.

8 For I am going to see the limits of fertile earth, Okeanos begetter of gods and mother Tethys...

9 Another of the everlasting gods would I easily send to sleep, even the streams of river Okeanos who is the begetter of all; but Zeus son of Kronos would I not approach, nor send to sleep, except that he himself so bid me.

The preceding section outlined the usual account of Okeanos in Homer. In the present passages the description of Okeanos as origin of the gods (8) and of all things (9) is unique and unexpected, going far beyond what was implied by 6. It is notable that outside the particular episode in which these two passages occur, the Διὸς ἀπάτη or Deception of Zeus by Hera (*Il.* xiv, 153–360 and xv, *init.*), there is almost nothing in Homer that can reasonably be construed as specifically cosmogonical or cosmological in content; that is, as going beyond the accepted outline of what has been termed the popular world-picture. Even in this episode there is not very much.[1] Indeed, there is little which might not be explained without introducing cosmological interpretations, if a slight oddity of expression is allowed. That might apply even to Okeanos: 8 and 9 need imply little more than that the river of Okeanos is the source of all fresh water (as in 6); water is necessary for life, therefore life must have originated, directly or indirectly, from Okeanos. This would not explain his parenthood of the gods in 8, but that could be a poetical extension. It would also involve limiting the application of πάντεσσι in 9 to living creatures and plant-life, but again the same kind of poetic looseness might be presupposed. It must be admitted, however, that the references, if so understood, would be pointlessly abbreviated and give a somewhat bizarre effect.

[1] Namely 14 (Night); *Il.* xv, 189–93 (division of the world between Zeus, Poseidon, Hades); *Il.* xiv, 203f., 274 (= xv, 225), 279 (the only Homeric references to Kronos, the Titans and Tartaros except for two important passages in bk. viii, *Il.* viii, 13ff. and 478ff.); *Il.* xiv, 271; xv, 37f. (two of the four references in Homer to Styx as oath of the gods). The last two cases might be regarded as intrusions with Hesiodic affinities, though they are not derived from the Hesiodic poems that we know.

To Plato and Aristotle, at least, 8 and 9 certainly seemed to have some kind of cosmological relevance:

10 Plato *Theaetetus* 152E ...Ὅμηρος, ⟨ὃς⟩ εἰπὼν ''Ωκεανόν τε θεῶν γένεσιν καὶ μητέρα Τηθύν' πάντα εἴρηκεν ἔκγονα ῥοῆς τε καὶ κινήσεως. (Cf. also 12.)

11   Aristotle *Met.* A3, 983b27 (following **85**) εἰσὶ δέ τινες οἳ καὶ τοὺς παμπαλαίους καὶ πολὺ πρὸ τῆς νῦν γενέσεως καὶ πρώτους θεολογήσαντας οὕτως οἴονται (*sc.* ὥσπερ Θαλῆς) περὶ τῆς φύσεως ὑπολαβεῖν· Ὠκεανόν τε γὰρ καὶ Τηθὺν ἐποίησαν τῆς γενέσεως πατέρας καὶ τὸν ὅρκον τῶν θεῶν ὕδωρ, τὴν καλουμένην ὑπ' αὐτῶν Στύγα τῶν ποιητῶν· τιμιώτατον μὲν γὰρ τὸ πρεσβύτατον, ὅρκος δὲ τὸ τιμιώτατόν ἐστιν. (Cf. also **15**.)

10   ...Homer, who by saying 'Okeanos begetter of gods and mother Tethys' declared all things to be offspring of flux and motion.
11   There are some who think that the very ancient and indeed first speculators about the gods, long before the present age, made the same supposition about nature (*sc.* as Thales); for they wrote that Okeanos and Tethys were the parents of coming-to-be, and the oath of the gods water – that which by the poets themselves is called Styx; for what is oldest is most honourable, and the most honourable thing is used as an oath.

Plato in **10** and elsewhere is obviously not entirely serious in his treatment of Homer as forerunner of the flux-idea assigned to Heraclitus, so we cannot be sure of the precise value he attached to the Homeric Okeanos-passage. Aristotle obviously took it seriously, and later antiquity was persuaded through him to accept Okeanos and Tethys as representative of an early cosmogonical theory, since Eudemus adduced the same passage (obviously following Aristotle in **11**) in the Peripatetic history of theology.[1]

[1] As we know from the disagreement of Damascius, the Neoplatonist writer, in the last sentence of **16**. Cf. Philodemus in **17** and Athenagoras 18, p. 20 Schwartz (DK 1 B 13); Plutarch *de Is. et Osir.* 34, 364D even assumed that Homer, like Thales, must have got the idea from Egypt.

It has often been assumed that there is another and earlier class of testimony for the cosmogonical importance of Okeanos, namely early Orphic poetry:

12   Plato *Cratylus* 402B   ...ὥσπερ αὖ Ὅμηρος 'Ὠκεανόν τε θεῶν γένεσίν' φησιν 'καὶ μητέρα Τηθύν'· οἶμαι δὲ καὶ Ἡσίοδος. λέγει δέ που καὶ Ὀρφεὺς ὅτι
            Ὠκεανὸς πρῶτος καλλίρροος ἦρξε γάμοιο,
            ὅς ῥα κασιγνήτην ὁμομήτορα Τηθὺν ὄπυιεν.

13   Plato *Timaeus* 40D–E   ...πειστέον δὲ τοῖς εἰρηκόσιν ἔμπροσθεν, ἐκγόνοις μὲν θεῶν οὖσιν, ὡς ἔφασαν, σαφῶς δέ που τούς γε αὐτῶν προγόνους εἰδόσιν·...Γῆς τε καὶ Οὐρανοῦ παῖδες Ὠκεανός τε καὶ

Τηθὺς ἐγενέσθην, τούτων δὲ Φόρκυς Κρόνος τε καὶ ʽΡέα καὶ ὅσοι μετὰ τούτων...

12 ...as Homer, again, says 'Okeanos begetter of gods and mother Tethys'; and I think Hesiod too. Orpheus, too, says somewhere that 'Fair-streamed Okeanos first began the marriages, who wed Tethys, his sister by the same mother'.

13 ...we must believe those who formerly gave utterance, those who were, as they said, offspring of the gods, and must, I suppose, have truly known their own ancestors:...Okeanos and Tethys were born as children of Ge [earth] and Ouranos [sky], and their children were Phorkys, Kronos, Rhea and their companions...

But the Orphic verses of 12, though established by Plato's time, are not necessarily so early in origin even as the sixth century B.C. (but see pp. 29ff. below for new evidence of relatively early 'Orphic' beliefs). In any case, the view they express does not necessarily differ greatly from that of the Hesiodic *Theogony*, as Plato may have perceived. There, Okeanos, Tethys and the other Titans are born to Gaia and Ouranos at a comparatively late stage from the point of view of cosmogonical production, but it is in their generation that the regular reproduction, by bisexual means, of fully personal figures (as opposed to world-constituents like Tartaros or Pontos) begins. 13, in which 'offspring of the gods' shows that Plato is describing an Orphic view, indicates that according to one Orphic account Okeanos and Tethys were the parents of Titans (including the theogonically vital pair Kronos and Rhea), and not their coevals as in the *Theogony*. That is probably another reason for πρῶτος in the Orphic verses of 12; Okeanos and Tethys are the first fully anthropomorphized couple, prior even to Kronos and Rhea. Hesiod had assigned less importance to Okeanos than might have been expected, especially in view of the well-known Homeric passages 8 and 9; so the Orphic versions presumably emended the Hesiodic account to the extent of putting Okeanos and Tethys one generation earlier than the Titans.

The evidence does not show that there existed in Greece at a comparatively early date a systematic doctrine of the cosmogonical priority of Okeanos. Hesiod gives no indication of it, and later suppositions seem to be based on two unusual Homeric passages, which are left as the only direct evidence for any such cosmogonical theory. They might have meant no more than that water is essential for life, though this would be rather oddly expressed. It was seen in (i) that the idea of an encircling river Okeanos may well have been adapted from Egyptian or Babylonian beliefs. It was part of those beliefs, too, that the world *originated* from primeval water (see n. 1 on p. 12); the isolated Homeric passages could, then, be a reference to that basic near-eastern assumption. The concept of the encircling river had, of course, become assimilated in Greece at a far earlier date.

3. Night

(i) *In Homer*

14 Homer *Il.* xiv, 258 (Hypnos speaks)

> ...καί κέ μ' ἄιστον ἀπ' αἰθέρος ἔμβαλε πόντῳ (*sc.* Ζεύς)
> εἰ μὴ Νὺξ δμήτειρα θεῶν ἐσάωσε καὶ ἀνδρῶν·
> τὴν ἱκόμην φεύγων, ὁ δὲ παύσατο χωόμενός περ·
> ἄζετο γὰρ μὴ Νυκτὶ θοῇ ἀποθύμια ἔρδοι.

14 ...and he [Zeus] would have cast me from the aither into the sea, out of sight, had not Night, subduer of gods and men, saved me; to her did I come in flight, and Zeus ceased, angry though he was; for he was in awe of doing what would be displeasing to swift Night.

This is the only place in the Homeric poems where Night is fully personified. Again, as with the two special Okeanos passages, it occurs in the episode of the Deceit of Zeus; and again there is an unusual implication of special power or priority among the gods. Zeus' respect for Night here is certainly strange, and quite unparalleled in Homer and Hesiod. In view of later interpretations it might suggest that the poet of this episode knew some story about Nyx as a cosmogonical figure. But the reference is an isolated one, and might be no more than a poetical development of the idea implicit in the phrase Νὺξ δμήτειρα θεῶν, 'Night subduer of gods': even gods are overcome by sleep, hence even the virtually all-powerful Zeus hesitates to offend Night, the mother of sleep, lest she should subdue him on some unsuitable occasion.

(ii) *An archaic cosmogonical concept according to Aristotle*

15 Aristotle *Met.* N4, 1091b4 ...οἱ δὲ ποιηταὶ οἱ ἀρχαῖοι ταύτῃ ὁμοίως, ᾗ βασιλεύειν καὶ ἄρχειν φασὶν οὐ τοὺς πρώτους οἷον Νύκτα καὶ Οὐρανὸν ἢ Χάος ἢ 'Ωκεανόν, ἀλλὰ τὸν Δία. (Cf. *Met.* Λ6, 1071b27 οἱ θεολόγοι οἱ ἐκ Νυκτὸς γεννῶντες: also *ibid.* 1072a8.)

15 ...the ancient poets similarly, inasmuch as they say that not the first figures have rule and kingship (Night and Ouranos or

Chaos or Okeanos, for example), but Zeus. (Cf. ...those writers about the gods who generate from Night.)

Aristotle thus accepted that there were poets and writers about the gods who put Night 'first', or who generated from Night. He may have had the Homeric passage, **14**, in mind; but this alone would hardly motivate his inclusion of Night, and it seems probable that he was thinking partly of 'Orphic' verses (on which see **30**, (2) and pp. 32ff.) but also of the post-Hesiodic cosmogonies, compiled mainly in the sixth and fifth centuries, to be described under (iii). In these, Night, which was produced at a very early stage (though not the first) in the Hesiodic cosmogonical account (**31**), and was classed with Gaia, Okeanos and Ouranos in other more casual references in the *Theogony* (20 and 106f.), is elevated to the first stage of all, either by herself or jointly with other figures, Air or Tartaros. It is natural that both Day and Night should come into being as soon as Sky and Earth have separated, to occupy the gap between the two.

(iii) *In cosmogonies assigned to Orpheus, Musaeus and Epimenides*

16 Damascius *de principiis* 124 (DK 1 B 12) ἡ δὲ παρὰ τῷ Περι-πατητικῷ Εὐδήμῳ ἀναγεγραμμένη ὡς τοῦ Ὀρφέως οὖσα θεολογία πᾶν τὸ νοητὸν ἐσιώπησεν...ἀπὸ δὲ τῆς Νυκτὸς ἐποιήσατο τὴν ἀρχήν, ἀφ᾽ ἧς καὶ Ὅμηρος, εἰ καὶ μὴ συνεχῆ πεποίηται τὴν γενεα-λογίαν, ἵστησιν· οὐ γὰρ ἀποδεκτέον Εὐδήμου λέγοντος ὅτι ἀπὸ Ὠκεανοῦ καὶ Τηθύος ἄρχεται...

17 Philodemus *de pietate* 47a (DK 3 B 5) ἐν δὲ τοῖς εἰς Ἐπιμενίδην (*sc.* ἀναφερομένοις ἔπεσιν) ἐξ Ἀέρος καὶ Νυκτὸς τὰ πάντα συστῆναι, ⟨ὥσπερ καὶ⟩ Ὅμηρος ⟨ἀποφαί⟩νετ᾽ Ὠκεανὸν ἐκ Τηθύος τοὺς θεοὺς γεννᾶν... (Cf. also **27**.)

18 Philodemus *de pietate* 137, 5 ἐν μέν τισιν ἐκ Νυκτὸς καὶ Ταρτάρου λέγεται τὰ πάντα, ἐν δέ τισιν ἐξ Ἅιδου καὶ Αἰθέρος· ὁ δὲ τὴν Τιτανομαχίαν γράψας ἐξ Αἰθέρος φησίν, Ἀκουσίλαος δὲ ἐκ Χάους πρῶτου τἄλλα· ἐν δὲ τοῖς ἀναφερομένοις εἰς Μουσαῖον γέγραπται Τάρταρον πρῶτον ⟨καὶ Ν⟩ύκτα.

16 The theology ascribed to Orpheus in Eudemus the Peripatetic kept silence about the whole intelligible realm...but he made the origin from Night, from whom Homer too (even though he does not describe the succession of generations as continuous) establishes the beginning of things; for we must not accept it when Eudemus says that Homer begins from Okeanos and Tethys...

17 In the verses ascribed to Epimenides all things are composed from Air and Night; as Homer, also, declared that Okeanos begets the gods from Tethys...

18 In some sources all things are said to come from Night and Tartaros, and in some from Hades and Aither; the author of the *Titanomachy* says they came from Aither, and Acusilaus says that the other things come from Chaos, which was the first; while in the verses ascribed to Musaeus it is written that Tartaros and Night were first.

Orphic cosmogonies will be discussed in §4; meanwhile **16** shows that Eudemus did not explain the Orphic priority of Night as being dependent on the Homeric passage, **14**.[1] This was because he considered that Homer clearly assigned cosmological priority to Okeanos and Tethys (**8**, **9**). **17** and **18** confirm that there were poetical accounts, composed probably in the late seventh or the sixth century B.C. (and including, perhaps, 'Orphic' poetry, cf. **30**, (2)), which made Night (in association with Aer or Tartaros, both conveying the idea of darkness) the origin of the world. But with the exception of Ἀήρ in 'Epimenides',[2] the cosmic figures involved are all to be found in the Hesiodic cosmogony proper, **31**; and even Ἀήρ, implying mist and darkness rather than the transparent stuff we call 'Air', is an element of the Hesiodic description although it does not achieve personification – thus in the second stage of production, before Night, comes *misty* Tartaros, Τάρταρά τ' ἠερόεντα (but see p. 35 n. 1). When we see from Damascius' reference to 'Epimenides' in **27** that Night and Ἀήρ *produce* Tartaros, it begins to look as though these people were working strictly within the limits of the Hesiodic formulation – at least down to the production of an egg (pp. 26–9). That is equally the case with Musaeus[3] and Acusilaus[4] according to **18**.

[1] The importance of Night for Orphics is confirmed by **30**, the Derveni papyrus. Much later she was described in the Orphic Rhapsodies (see p. 23 n. 1) as a figure of great importance, the near-equal and successor of Phanes-Protogonos: **19** Proclus in Plato *Crat.* 396B (Kern fr. 101) (Φάνης) σκῆπτρον δ' ἀριδείκετον εἶο χέρεσσιν / θῆκε θεᾶς Νυκτός, ⟨ἵν' ἔχῃ⟩ βασιληίδα τιμήν. *([Phanes] placed his famous sceptre in the hands of goddess Night, so that she might have the prerogative of rulership.)*

[2] The hexameter cosmogony and theogony ascribed to Epimenides was probably not by him (as Philodemus evidently suspected), but may nevertheless have originated in the sixth century B.C. Damascius, too, stated that Aer and Night were Epimenides' first principles, and gave Eudemus as his source for this (**27**). Philodemus, therefore, who must also have relied on Eudemus' standard history of theology, provides in **17** an earlier confirmation of Damascius' reliability.

[3] The name of Musaeus, mythical disciple of Orpheus and eponymous author

of oracle-literature, tended to become attached to any kind of other-worldly verses – including, evidently, a theogonical poem like that assigned to Epimenides. The late sixth century B.C. is a plausible *terminus ante quem* for such a poem and ascription; compare the case of Onomacritus, who according to Herodotus VII, 6 (DK 2 B 20*a*) was banished from Athens by Hipparchus when, having been entrusted with the collection and arrangement of Musaeus' oracles, he was found to have inserted a spurious one.

[4] Acusilaus of Argos (late sixth or early fifth century B.C.) was a genealogist who might well have given a summary and of course unoriginal account of the first ancestors; although some of the material assigned to him was later suspected. According to Damascius (DK 9 B 1) he made a limited rearrangement of the Hesiodic figures which came after Chaos; but he is almost entirely irrelevant to the history of Presocratic thought, and scarcely deserves the space accorded him in DK.

A fresh consideration may be introduced here. After the episode of the defeat of the Titans in the *Theogony* comes a series of passages (734–819) of which some at least are additions to the 'original' text; they are short variant descriptions apparently designed to improve on the integral references to the underworld. If this is so, they belong to the later part of the seventh century B.C. at the earliest, while the early sixth century seems a likelier period for their composition. Thus in **2**, which is certainly by Hesiod, Night surrounds the 'throat' of Tartaros, and above are the roots of the earth – in itself probably a genuinely primitive conception. But in **34** (q.v., with discussion on pp. 40f.) this conception is further developed, and the sources and limits of all things are located in the great windy gap which is probably a later specification of Chaos in line 116 (**31**); the halls of dark night are said to be in or around this χάσμα. It is easy to see that this trend of thought could lead to the elevation of Night to be representative of the original, inchoate state of things. In the original cosmogonical account (**31**) Night comes at an early and important stage; the tendency to rearrange the Hesiodic figures is already indicated for the sixth century (probably); Homer provided one piece of cryptic encouragement for a further elevation of Night; and added elaborations of the Hesiodic picture of the underworld tended to reinterpret Tartaros and Night as local forms of an originative Χάος. The new Orphic evidence (pp. 31f.) provides some support for Aristotle's judgement in **15**, but even so there seems little indication so far that the idea of an absolute priority of Night occurred early enough, or in a sufficiently independent form, to have had much effect on quasi-scientific cosmogonical thought.

4. Orphic cosmogonies

Several variations in cosmogony were ascribed to 'Ορφικοί, 'Orphics'. These have been described as people who, uniting elements from the cult of Apollo Καθάρσιος, purifier, on the one hand and from Thracian reincarnation beliefs on the other, thought that the soul could survive if it were kept pure, and elaborated a partly individual mythology, wth Dionysus as a central figure, to illustrate this theory. The Thracian Orpheus, with his sexual purity, his musical gifts and his power of prophecy after death represented the combination of the two elements; such Orphic beliefs were recorded in sacred accounts, ἱεροὶ λόγοι. Now this description would certainly be true, say, of the third century B.C.; but there has been much controversy about how early there appeared a distinct class of people with well-defined and individual beliefs of this kind. One view, well represented by W. K. C. Guthrie in chapter XI of *The Greeks and their Gods* (London, 1950) is that the Orphic doctrine was already set out in sacred books in the sixth century B.C. A completely different view had been advanced by Wilamowitz and, most clearly, by I. M. Linforth in *The Arts of Orpheus* (Berkeley, 1941); he analysed all the then extant texts mentioning Orpheus and Orphics and showed that, at any rate until 300 B.C., the description 'Orphic' was applied to all sorts of ideas connected with practically every kind of rite (τελετή). There were writings attributed to Orpheus, as indeed to Musaeus and Epimenides (see pp. 18f.), as early as the sixth century B.C.; Herodotus knew of Orphics and Pythagoreans sharing a taboo in the fifth; Orphic oracle- and dispensation-mongers were familiar to Plato, and 'so-called Orphic accounts' to Aristotle. But the corpus of individual sectarian literature (of which descriptions of Hades, accounts of theogony and cosmogony, hymns, etc., are known to us) could not for the most part – so Linforth argued – be traced back earlier than the Hellenistic period, and in its present form mostly belongs to the Roman period.

It may be, as Linforth held, that there was no exclusively Orphic body of belief in the archaic age. However, Orpheus was then beginning to be treated as the patron saint of rites and ritual ways of life – and death; and his name, like that of his legendary disciple Musaeus, became attached to theogonical literature of this period. Beliefs about reincarnation were becoming current in the Greek world, particularly on its fringes, and some adherents of these beliefs were calling themselves 'Ορφικοί, as well as Bacchants, by the fifth century. The formation of an exclusive sect with a definite body of relevant sacred literature was beginning even then, as pp. 29ff. will

21

confirm; other elements are almost certainly later in origin, and often show awareness of the details of oriental cult and iconography.[1] Some of these will be considered next.

[1] Most conspicuously, Time, Χρόνος, as a primary cosmogonical figure may derive from the Iranian hypostatization *Zvran Akarana* (unending time). But this Iranian concept finds its earliest testimony in a late fourth-century B.C. Greek reference by Eudemus as reported in Damascius, and there is no reason to think that it was formulated as early as the Greek archaic period. 'Time' is a sophisticated cosmogonical concept in Plato's *Timaeus*; it was also personified, probably as an etymology of Kronos, by Pherecydes of Syros as early as the sixth century, though probably not with a profound abstract significance (see n. 1 on p. 28 and n. 1 on p. 57). Its oriental derivation in the Orphic accounts is indicated by its concrete shape as a multi-headed winged snake. Such multipartite monsters, as distinct from simpler fantasies like centaurs, are orientalizing in character, mainly Semitic in origin, and begin to appear in Greek art around 700 B.C. They were, of course, extremely popular as decoration during the seventh and the first quarter of the sixth centuries. (Minoan art, too, had had its monsters, mainly dog-headed deities and other relatively simple theriomorphic creations.) That the winged-snake form of Time is much later in its Greek appearances than the orientalizing period in art is chiefly suggested by the identification of an *abstraction* with such a form. This shows an acquaintance with rather complex eastern (especially Assyrian or Babylonian) modes of thought – something very different from the mere borrowing of a pictorial motif, or even the assimilation of a fully concrete myth-form. Such extravagances of the imagination evoked little sympathy in the Greek mind before the Hellenistic period.

NEOPLATONIC ACCOUNTS OF ORPHIC COSMOGONIES

The later Neoplatonists (fourth to sixth centuries A.D.), and in particular Damascius, with their long schematic allegorizations of earlier mythological accounts, are the most prolific source for Orphic versions of the formation of the world. These writers are more reliable than appears at first sight, since much of their information was derived from summaries of Eudemus' great Peripatetic history of theology. In some cases fragments of late Orphic poetry can be adduced to confirm details of the Neoplatonic descriptions, which are tiresomely diffuse (and are therefore schematized in (ii) and (iii) below) and are expressed in the peculiar terminology of that school. Four accounts of a cosmogony specifically named as Orphic are extant.

(i) *Derivation from Night*

Damascius in **16** (q.v.) stated that according to Eudemus 'the theology ascribed to Orpheus...made the origin of things from Night'. According to the Rhapsodies,[1] Night was the daughter of

Phanes (see n. 1 on p. 19 and n. 3 on p. 24), himself descended from Chronos. She was given prophetic powers by Phanes, succeeded him as ruler, and seems somehow to have given birth for a second time to Gaia and Ouranos.[2] The secondary and repetitive nature of this production of sky and earth, and the obvious intention to make Phanes the ultimate creator of the world, suggest that Night's cosmogonical priority (as distinct from her undoubted position as a venerable figure among the gods) is here mainly the result of the derivative and syncretistic character of the Orphic theogony.

[1] The so-called Orphic Rhapsodies (ἱεροὶ λόγοι ἐν ῥαψῳδίαις κ̄δ̄ according to the Suda s.v. 'Ορφεύς), of which many fragments survive (Kern, frr. 59–235), mostly through quotation in Neoplatonic works, are a late compilation of hexameter verses of varying date of composition. Most are post-Hellenistic and many much later. Yet the Derveni papyrus (30) shows that some derive from the fifth or even the sixth century B.C. Nevertheless no other author before the full Christian period seems to have heard of most of them, and it seems highly probable that their elaboration into an Orphic *Iliad* was not taken in hand until the third or fourth century A.D. Genuinely archaic beliefs might, of course, be embedded in some of these verses, late as they are in compilation.

[2] 20 Orph. Rhaps. fr. 109 Kern (from Hermias) (Νύξ) ἡ δὲ πάλιν Γαῖάν τε καὶ Οὐρανὸν εὐρὺν ἔτικτε / δεῖξέν τ' ἐξ ἀφανῶν φανεροὺς οἵ τ' εἰσὶ γενέθλην. *(And she [Night], again, bore Gaia and broad Ouranos, and revealed them as manifest, from being unseen, and who they are by birth.)* But Phanes had already created Olympus, sun, moon and earth (frr. 89, 96, 91–3, 94 Kern, from the Rhapsodies), and sky is also presupposed.

(ii) '*The usual Orphic theology*' *in the Rhapsodies*

21 Damascius *de principiis* 123 (DK 1 B 12) ἐν μὲν τοίνυν ταῖς φερομέναις ταύταις 'Ραψῳδίαις 'Ορφικαῖς ἡ θεολογία ἥδε τίς ἐστιν ἡ περὶ τὸ νοητόν, ἣν καὶ οἱ φιλόσοφοι διερμηνεύουσιν, ἀντὶ μὲν τῆς μιᾶς τῶν ὅλων ἀρχῆς τὸν Χρόνον τιθέντες... (the full description, for which see DK, is lengthy and expressed in difficult Neoplatonic terms. The substance of it is here given schematically:

$$\text{Χρόνος} \underset{\text{Χάος}}{\overset{\text{Αἰθήρ}}{\Big\langle}}\Bigg\}^1 \to \text{ᾠόν}^2 \text{ [or ἀργὴς χιτών,} \to \text{Φάνης}^3$$
$$\text{or νεφέλη]} \quad [\sim \text{Μῆτις,}$$
$$\text{'Ηρικεπαῖος])}$$

...τοιαύτη μὲν ἡ συνήθης 'Ορφικὴ θεολογία.

21 In these Orphic Rhapsodies, then, as they are known, this is the theology concerned with the intelligible; which the philosophers, too, expound, putting Chronos in place of the one origin of all...

(Chronos ⟵ Aither / Chaos) ^{1} → egg^2 [or shining tunic, → Phanes^3 or cloud] [∼ Metis, Erikepaios])

...Such is the usual Orphic theology.

^{1} Cf. **22** Orph. Rhaps. fr. 66 Kern (from Proclus) Αἰθέρα μὲν Χρόνος οὗτος ἀγήραος ἀφθιτόμητις / γείνατο, καὶ μέγα χάσμα πελώριον ἔνθα καὶ ἔνθα. (*This Chronos, unageing and of imperishable counsel, produced Aither, and a great, mighty gulf here and there.*) Syrianus (fr. 107 Kern) also gave Aither and Chaos as the second stage, but after 'one and the good' as first. The μέγα χάσμα is taken directly from Hesiod *Theogony* 740 (**34**).

^{2} Cf. **23** Orph. Rhaps. fr. 70 Kern (from Damascius) ἔπειτα δ' ἔτευξε μέγας Χρόνος αἰθέρι δίῳ / ὠεὸν ἀργύφιον. (*Then great Chronos made in divine aither a silvery egg.*) On the egg see pp. 26–9 below.

^{3} Phanes, connected by the Orphics with φαίνειν etc., is an exclusive Orphic development, of a comparatively late date, of the Hesiodic cosmogonical Eros (**31**); also perhaps of the phallus swallowed by Zeus according to **30**, (6) and (7). Winged, bisexual and self-fertilizing, bright and aitherial, he gives birth to the first generation of gods and is the ultimate creator of the cosmos.

(iii) *The version of Hieronymus and Hellanicus*

24 Damascius *de principiis* 123 *bis* (DK 1 B 13) ἡ δὲ κατὰ τὸν Ἱερώνυμον φερομένη καὶ Ἑλλάνικον (*sc.* Ὀρφικὴ θεολογία),^{1} εἴπερ μὴ καὶ ὁ αὐτός ἐστι, οὕτως ἔχει· ὕδωρ ἦν, φησίν, ἐξ ἀρχῆς καὶ ὕλη, ἐξ ἧς ἐπάγη ἡ γῆ... See DK for full description, of which a summary is given here:

ὕδωρ / ὕλη → γῆ } Χρόνος ἀγήραος → { Αἰθήρ / Χάος / Ἔρεβος }^{2} → ᾠόν → θεὸς ἀσώματος (a winged, multi-headed, bisexual snake; also called Heracles, and accompanied by Ἀνάγκη and Ἀδράστεια) (having wings and animal heads)

24 The Orphic Theology which is said to be according to Hieronymus and Hellanicus (if indeed he is not the same man) is as follows: water existed from the beginning, he says, and matter, from which earth was solidified...

Water / Matter → Earth } Unageing Chronos/ Heracles (with Necessity and Adrasteia) → { Aither / Chaos / Erebos } → Egg → an incorporeal god

¹ These authors cannot be identified with certainty. Damascius evidently suspected that they might be the same person, but more probably, for example, one was the epitomizer of the other. Hieronymus may be the author of Phoenician antiquities mentioned at Josephus *Ant.* I, 94; a winged symbol for El-Kronos comes in 'Sanchuniathon', Eusebius *P.E.* I, 10, 36 (see p. 41 n.). Hellanicus may have been the father (2nd–1st cent. B.C.) of one Sandon, probably of Tarsus, an Orphic writer mentioned in the Suda; this is much more likely than that he was the fifth-century B.C. Lesbian logographer.

² ἐν τούτοις ὁ Χρόνος ᾠὸν ἐγέννησεν, says Damascius – i.e. in Aither, Chaos and Erebos. It is not explicitly stated that the 'incorporeal god' comes out of the egg, but he obviously does so; compare 25, and see next note for ἀσώματος.

(iv) *Athenagoras' variant of* (iii)

25 Athenagoras *pro Christianis* 18, p. 20 Schwartz (DK 1 B 13) ...ἦν γὰρ ὕδωρ ἀρχὴ κατ' αὐτὸν (*sc.* 'Ορφέα) τοῖς ὅλοις, ἀπὸ δὲ τοῦ ὕδατος ἰλὺς κατέστη, ἐκ δὲ ἑκατέρων ἐγεννήθη ζῷον, δράκων προσπεφυκυῖαν ἔχων κεφαλὴν λέοντος, διὰ μέσου δὲ αὐτῶν θεοῦ πρόσωπον, ὄνομα 'Ηρακλῆς καὶ Χρόνος. (So far this is almost identical with the version of Hieronymus and Hellanicus.) οὗτος ὁ 'Ηρακλῆς ἐγέννησεν ὑπερμέγεθες ᾠόν, ὃ συμπληρούμενον ὑπὸ βίας τοῦ γεγεννηκότος ἐκ παρατριβῆς εἰς δύο ἐρράγη. τὸ μὲν οὖν κατὰ κορυφὴν αὐτοῦ Οὐρανὸς εἶναι ἐτελέσθη, τὸ δὲ κάτω ἐνεχθὲν Γῆ· προῆλθε δὲ καὶ θεός τις δισώματος.¹ Οὐρανὸς δὲ Γῆ μιχθεὶς γεννᾷ θηλείας μὲν Κλωθὼ Λάχεσιν Ἄτροπον... (a theogony of the Hesiodic type follows).

> ¹ γη διὰ σώματος MS; em. Lobeck, accep. Diels, Kranz; τρίτος ἤδη ἀσώματος Th. Gomperz. – In any case Phanes is meant. δισώματος and ἀσώματος are easily confused, and we cannot be certain that instances of the latter in the text of 24 are necessarily correct. δισώματος implies 'bisexual' (which Phanes was); 'incorporeal', of a being described as having more than its quota of bodily attributes, and those of a very peculiar sort, is perhaps odd even in a Neoplatonist.

25 ...for water was the origin for the totality of things, according to him [Orpheus], and from water slime was established, and from both of them was generated a living creature, a snake with a lion's head growing on to it, and in the middle of them the face of a god, Heracles and Chronos by name. This Heracles generated a huge egg, which being completely filled by the force of its begetter burst into two through friction. So its top part ended up as Ouranos, and the underneath part as Ge; and a certain double-bodied god also came forth. And Ouranos having mingled with Ge begets, as female offspring, Clotho, Lachesis and Atropos...

Of these four types of Orphic-denominated cosmogony, (i) mentions a first stage, Night, that does not occur in the others. Night's importance in the Orphic pantheon probably depended, directly or indirectly, on modifications to the Hesiodic *schema* of cosmogony and theogony (see §5). Eudemus seems to have known Orphic accounts similar to the earlier versions associated with Epimenides and Musaeus, and the Derveni papyrus (**30**, (2)) confirms that Night was there given a specific cosmogonical function as a secondary parent of Ouranos and Gaia. (ii) is termed the usual Orphic account presumably because it more or less corresponded with the broad picture given in the late Rhapsodies. (iii) is an elaboration of (ii). It cannot, as it stands, be pre-Hellenistic; its fantastic concrete description of the abstract Chronos is a sign of late origin or at least of late remodelling. (iv) is quoted by a second-century Christian apologist of Neoplatonic leanings; it gives one significant detail, the splitting of the egg to form sky and earth, which is completely absent from the later Neoplatonic accounts. (iii) and (iv) have a first stage, slime in one form or another, which is no doubt an eclectic philosophical–physical intrusion. It might conceivably be taken directly from Ionian systems like that of Anaximander, but is more likely to have come from derivative Stoic cosmogony.

THE EGG IN EARLIER GREEK SOURCES, NOT SPECIFICALLY ORPHIC

26 Aristophanes *Birds* 693 (the chorus of birds speak)
Χάος ἦν καὶ Νὺξ Ἔρεβός τε μέλαν πρῶτον καὶ Τάρταρος εὐρύς,
Γῆ δ' οὐδ' Ἀὴρ οὐδ' Οὐρανὸς ἦν· Ἐρέβους δ' ἐν ἀπείροσι κόλποις
τίκτει πρώτιστον ὑπηνέμιον Νὺξ ἡ μελανόπτερος ᾠόν,
ἐξ οὗ περιτελλομέναις ὥραις ἔβλαστεν Ἔρως ὁ ποθεινός,
στίλβων νῶτον πτερύγοιν χρυσαῖν, εἰκὼς ἀνεμώκεσι δίναις.   697
οὗτος δὲ Χάει πτερόεντι μιγεὶς νυχίῳ κατὰ Τάρταρον εὐρὺν
ἐνεόττευσεν γένος ἡμέτερον, καὶ πρῶτον ἀνήγαγεν ἐς φῶς.
πρότερον δ' οὐκ ἦν γένος ἀθανάτων πρὶν Ἔρως ξυνέμειξεν ἅπαντα·
ξυμμιγνυμένων δ' ἑτέρων ἑτέροις γένετ' Οὐρανὸς Ὠκεανός τε
καὶ Γῆ πάντων τε θεῶν μακάρων γένος ἄφθιτον. ὧδε μέν ἐσμεν
πολὺ πρεσβύτατοι πάντων μακάρων.

26 First of all was Chaos and Night and black Erebos and wide Tartaros, and neither Ge nor Aer nor Ouranos existed; in the boundless bosoms of Erebos black-winged Night begets, first, a wind-egg, from which in the fulfilment of the seasons ardent Eros burgeoned forth, his back gleaming with golden wings, like as he was to the whirling winds. Eros, mingling with winged, gloomy

Chaos in broad Tartaros, hatched out our race and first brought it into the light. There was no race of immortals before Eros mingled all things together; but as one mingled with another Ouranos came into being, and Okeanos and Ge and the unfading race of all the blessed gods. Thus we are by far the oldest of all the blessed ones.

27 Damascius *de principiis* 124 (DK 3 B 5; from Eudemus) τὸν δὲ Ἐπιμενίδην δύο πρώτας ἀρχὰς ὑποθέσθαι Ἀέρα καὶ Νύκτα...ἐξ ὧν γεννηθῆναι Τάρταρον...ἐξ ὧν δύο Τιτᾶνας¹...ὧν μιχθέντων ἀλλήλοις ᾠὸν γενέσθαι...ἐξ οὗ πάλιν ἄλλην γενεὰν προελθεῖν.

¹ The manuscript has δύο τινάς, but Kroll's emendation to δύο Τιτᾶνας (accepted by Kranz in DK) is indicated by the etymology implied in the Neoplatonist parenthesis that follows the disputed word, τὴν νοητὴν μεσότητα οὕτω καλέσαντα, διότι ἐπ᾽ ἄμφω ᾽διατείνει᾽ τό τε ἄκρον καὶ τὸ πέρας. The other omissions in the text as printed above are Neoplatonic paraphrases which throw no light on the interpretation.

27 Epimenides posited two first principles, Air and Night...from which Tartaros was produced...from all of which two Titans were produced...from whose mutual mingling an egg came into being...from which, again, other offspring came forth.

26 was written in 414 B.C. or shortly before. The only thing we can say with certainty about the content of **27** is that it is pre-Eudemian; but in view of the proliferation of mythological accounts in hexameters, concerned with genealogy and therefore liable to begin with a theogony, probably towards the end of the sixth century B.C., it might be tentatively dated between then and the middle of the fifth century (on Epimenides see **17** and n. 2 on p. 19). Thus an egg as an element in cosmogony, which is a typical feature of later Orphic accounts as recorded in the Neoplatonic tradition, is mentioned certainly near the end of the fifth century and probably before that. Were these earlier accounts specifically Orphic in character?

The manner of production of the egg does not differ significantly in the earlier and in the later, definitely Orphic accounts. In the latter, Chronos in a late and bizarre form begets the egg in Aither or in Aither–Chaos–Erebos (**23**, **24**). In **26** *Night* produces the egg in Erebos; in **27** it is begotten by two Titans – presumably Kronos (cf. **52**?) and Rhea – who are themselves the product of Air–Night and Tartaros. There is no mention of Chronos, of course, but Pherecydes of Syros (pp. 57–60) had already associated Kronos with Chronos, and there may be a connexion here with the later accounts; see also **52** and discussion.¹ There is a distinct similarity between what is produced from the egg in the birds' account and in the later Orphic versions; golden-winged Eros is an obvious prototype of the Orphic Phanes.[2] Yet most of Aristophanes' bird-cosmogony is indubitably derived from the Hesiodic *Theogony*, with appropriate modifications. Chaos, Night, Erebos and Tartaros are involved in the first stages of both accounts; only Earth is postponed in Aristophanes, to be produced (in some ways more logically) simultaneously with Sky. The egg is a 'wind-egg' partly to make it more bird-like, partly because of the traditional windiness of Tartaros (**34**). So Night, Chaos and Eros are all winged, because this is meant to be a birds' cosmogony. It is a parody of a traditional type of cosmogony; yet the original of a parody must be recognizable, and while the Hesiodic elements are clear enough the egg is non-Hesiodic. Eminently suited to bird-generation as it is, the device is unlikely to have been just invented by Aristophanes for that reason. It must have been familiar as a means for producing, not necessarily a cosmogonical figure, but at least an important deity like Eros.[3]

[1] The Kronos–Chronos identification was also made in Orphic circles, cf. e.g. Proclus in Plato *Crat.* 396B (Kern fr. 68). This does not imply that Pherecydes was an Orphic or took his ideas from early Orphic sources (though the Suda reports, probably on account of these similarities, that he 'collected Orpheus' writings'); rather that the later Orphic eclectics used him for source-material just as they used Hesiod and other early mythological writings. In any case the assimilation of the two names was an obvious move.

[2] The language of the Rhapsodic account is indeed strongly reminiscent of Aristophanes; compare χρυσείαις πτερύγεσσι φορεύμενος ἔνθα καὶ ἔνθα (*sc.* Φάνης), 'Phanes...borne here and there by golden wings' (fr. 78 Kern), with line 697 of **26**. ἔνθα καὶ ἔνθα in the Orphic verse, as in **22**, recalls Hesiod *Theogony* 742 (**34**), part of the description of windy Tartarus; Hesiod is indeed the chief linguistic and formal model for the Rhapsodies.

[3] Possibly the birth of Helen from an egg is significant here; connected with a tree-cult perhaps of Mycenean origin (M. Nilsson, *Gesch. d. griech. Religion* I[3] (Munich, 1967), 22 and 211), she is a ward and representative of Aphrodite–Eros in Homer.

One reason for doubting an early Orphic use of the egg-motif may be that, if there were any such early use, one would expect later applications to be consistent with an earlier tradition, which in a sacred-book sect would tend to be regarded as sacrosanct. Yet three quite different later uses are known. First, the egg simply produces Phanes (**21, 24**). Secondly, in **25** the upper part of the egg forms the sky, the lower part the earth; the equivalent of Phanes emerges too, and sky and earth then mate as in Hesiod or the popular tradition. Thirdly, certain Orphics used the arrangement of shell and skin (and presumably also of white and yolk) as an analogue for the arrangement of sky (outer heaven) and aither:

28 Achilles *Isag.* 4 (DK I B 12, Kern fr. 70) τὴν δὲ τάξιν ἣν δεδώκαμεν τῷ σφαιρώματι οἱ Ὀρφικοὶ λέγουσι παραπλησίαν εἶναι τῇ ἐν τοῖς ᾠοῖς· ὃν γὰρ ἔχει λόγον τὸ λέπυρον ἐν τῷ ᾠῷ, τοῦτον ἐν τῷ παντὶ ὁ οὐρανός, καὶ ὡς ἐξήρτηται τοῦ οὐρανοῦ κυκλοτερῶς ὁ αἰθήρ, οὕτως τοῦ λεπύρου ὁ ὑμήν.

28 The arrangement which we have assigned to the celestial sphere the Orphics say is similar to that in eggs: for the relation which the shell has in the egg, the outer heaven has in the universe, and as the aither depends in a circle from the outer heaven, so does the membrane from the shell.

RECENT DISCOVERIES AND PROVISIONAL CONCLUSIONS

Conclusions that might be formed from the evidence presented so far have been given something of a new dimension by recent discoveries. First, the well-known series of gold plates carrying instructions for the dead and found in graves in Magna Graecia and Crete has now been extended by an important new example from Hipponion (modern Vibo Valentia) in southern Italy, inscribed as early as *c.* 400 B.C. After the usual instructions to the dead person – a woman in this case – not to drink from the spring by the white cypress but from the water flowing out of the lake of Memory further on (on which see G. Zuntz, *Persephone* (Oxford, 1971) 355ff.), the text continues as follows:

29 Gold plate from Hipponion (after G. Pugliese Carratelli, *Parola del Passato* 29 (1974), 108–26 and 31 (1976), 458–66), 10–16:

εἶπον· ὑὸς Γαίας καὶ Ὀρανῶ ἀστερόεντος.   10
δίψαι δ' ἐμὶ αὖος καὶ ἀπόλλυμαι· ἀλὰ δότ' ὄ[κα
ψυχρὸν ὕδωρ προρέον τὲς Μνεμοσύνες ἀπὸ λίμ[ν]α[ς].
καὶ δέ τοι ἐλεῦσ(ιν) ⟨ο⟩ὶ ὑπὸ Χθονίοι Βασιλῆι,
καὶ δέ τοι δόσοσι πιὲν τᾶς Μναμοσύνας ἀπ[ὸ] λίμνας.
καὶ δὲ καὶ συχνὸν hοδὸν ἔρχεα⟨ι⟩, ἄν τε καὶ ἄλλοι   15
μύσται καὶ βάχχοι hιερὰν στείχοσι κλ⟨ε⟩εινοί.

29 Say: '[I am] the son of Earth and starry Sky. I am parched with thirst and am dying; so quickly give me cold water flowing forth from the lake of Memory.' And the Kings of under the earth will pity you, and they will give you to drink from the lake of Memory. And it is a thronged road you are setting out on, a holy one along which other famous initiates and bacchants are proceeding.

In the concluding verse the typical eschatology of the gold-plate believers is credited, for the first time in the surviving evidence, to 'bacchic initiates' – that is, to followers of Dionysus with secret religious beliefs. Bacchic funerary practices were equated with Orphic ones by Herodotus, II, 81, who added significantly that they were really Pythagorean and Egyptian. G. Zuntz (*op. cit.*) had argued that the gold tablets are specifically Pythagorean, but the connexion with Dionysus here suggests an Orphic association, rather. Herodotus' scepticism implies that there were no clear-cut sectarian divisions, but it is perhaps significant that Dionysus was to become the central figure of the special Orphic myth of the creation of men out of the ashes of the Titans who had killed and eaten the child-god. Moreover there is fresh evidence on this point, also, for in 1951 bone tablets were found in the central sanctuary in Olbia in the Crimea, an ancient Milesian colony; on one of them was scratched, probably in the fifth century B.C., the name 'Orphikoi' and also an abbreviation of 'Dionysus', whose name also occurs on several of the other tablets; see also p. 208 n. 1 and for further discussion the valuable article by M. L. West in *ZPE* 45 (1982) 17–29. It was in Olbia, too, according to Herodotus IV, 78–80, that a king Skyles had become an initiate into the ecstatic cult of Dionysus the Bacchant.

The claim that the soul of the dead person is instructed to make in **29**, 10, 'I am the son of Earth and starry Sky', is puzzling in itself, but presupposes a link between the dead person and the early gods. Such a link would be supplied by the (possibly later) myth of Dionysus and the Titans; but a relatively early Orphic interest in the succession of the first nature-gods is now revealed by a remarkable papyrus roll discovered at Derveni near Thessalonica in 1962. Half-burnt over a grave around 330 B.C., the roll contained an allegorical commentary by someone versed in Anaxagoras and Diogenes of Apollonia on a theogony attributed several times to Orpheus. The commentary contains no hint of Platonic or Aristotelian influence, and Walter Burkert (e.g. in *Griechische Religion der archaischen und klassischen Epoche* (Stuttgart, 1977), 473) suggests 'scarcely later than 400 B.C.' as probable date of composition. That would put the Orphic theogony itself – it was composed in hexameters, several of which are quoted – into the fifth century B.C., conceivably even into the sixth. A few of the quoted verses are identical or nearly so with bits of the late compilation, the so-called Orphic Rhapsodies, on which see n. 1 on p. 23. That does not alter the fact that much of the Rhapsodies is Hellenistic or Graeco-Roman, but it shows that the beginnings of beliefs that can be termed specifically Orphic, and were recorded in sacred verses, were much earlier than Wilamowitz or Linforth would have allowed.

A full publication of the papyrus has been delayed for many years, but is now being prepared by Professors Tsantsanoglou and Parassoglou of the University of Thessalonica. Until its appearance any discussion must be provisional; but Professor R. Merkelbach has now published his version of the text in an appendix (pp. 1–12) to *ZPE* 47 (1982), and it is from there that the following particularly relevant extracts from the Orphic poem are drawn. Their application and supplementation are sometimes partially determined by their context in the (extremely wild) ancient commentary, which is not quoted here.

30 Selected verses quoted from 'Orpheus' by the Derveni commentator (numbers in parentheses are purely for reference in this book; the roman and arabic figures that follow refer to columns, and lines in each column, respectively):

(1) x, 5   (Κρόνος) ὃς μέγ' ἔρεξεν (τὸν Οὐρανόν) (cf. x, 7–8)

(2) x, 6   Οὐρανὸς Εὐφρονίδης, ὃς πρώτιστος βασίλευσεν

(3) xi, 6   ἐκ τοῦ δὴ Κρόνος [α]ὖτις, ἔπειτα δὲ μητίετα Ζεύς

(4) vii, 1   ἐξ ἀ[δύτοι]ο...χρῆσαι (*sc.* τὴν Νύκτα)

     vii, 10   [ἡ δὲ] ἔχρησεν ἅπαντα τά οἱ θέ[μις . . . .]αι

(5) ix, 1   Ζεὺς μὲν ἐπεὶ δὴ πατρὸς ἑοῦ πάρα [θέ]σφατ' ἀκούσα[ς]

(6) ix, 4   αἰδοῖον κα[τ]έπινεν, ὃς αἰθέρα ἔκθορε πρῶτος

(7) xii, 3–6   πρωτογόνου βασιλέως αἰδοίου, τοῦ δ' ἄρα πάντες
ἀθάνατοι προσέφυν μάκαρες θεοὶ ἠδὲ θέαιναι
καὶ ποταμοὶ καὶ κρῆναι ἐπήρατοι ἄλλα τε πάντα
[ὅ]σσα τότ' ἦν γεγαῶτ', αὐτὸς δ' ἄρα μοῦνος ἔγεντο.

(8) xix, 3–6   Ὠκεανός...ἔμησατο...σθένος μέγα...εὐρὺ ῥέοντα,
? *sc.* μήσατο δ' Ὠκεανοῖο μέγα σθένος εὐρὺ ῥέοντος
(*restit.* Burkert, *alii*)

(9) xx, 3   (σελήνη, *cf.* xx, 10) ἣ πολλοῖς φαίνει μερόπεσσι ἐπ' ἀπείρονα γαῖαν

(10) xxii, 9–10   μητρὸς ἐν φιλότητι...θέλοντα μιχθῆναι, *cf.* xxii, 1–2 μη[τρ]ὸς...ἑᾶς, ? *sc.* μητρὸς ἑᾶς ἐθέλων μιχθή-μεναι ἐν φιλότητι (*restit.* Burkert, *alii*)

30 (1)   [Kronos] who did a great deed [to Ouranos]

     (2)   Ouranos son of Euphronē [Night], who reigned first

(3)   after him Kronos next, and then counsellor Zeus

(4)   that [Night] prophesied from her inner sanctuary...and she prophesied everything that was lawful for...

(5)   Zeus, having heard the oracles from his father

(6)   swallowed down the phallus [of him] who first leapt up to the upper air

(7)   of the phallus of the first-born king; and from him [it?] grew all the immortal blessed gods and goddesses, and rivers and lovely springs and everything else that was then in being; but he came into being alone

(8)   he devised the great might of Okeanos with broad streams

(9)   [moon] who shines for many mortals over the boundless earth

(10)   wishing to mingle in love with his mother

As might be expected, much of the Orphic theogony revealed by the commentator's quotations closely resembles the Hesiodic theogony, to be considered in §5; it is the departures from it that are interesting and possibly significant. The first king in heaven is Ouranos, Sky; but he is son of Night (2) (i.e. in **30**), who therefore occupies the same position as Hesiod's initial Chaos (**31**, 1) – and bears out Aristotle's information in **15**. Kronos now gains the kingship with a 'great (or dreadful) deed' (1), presumably by castrating Ouranos as in Hesiod (**39**). Next king is Zeus (3), who apparently receives oracles both from Kronos himself (5) and from Night in her sanctuary (4). He is not swallowed by Kronos as in Hesiod (p. 46), rather he himself swallows a phallus (6), indeed the one severed from Ouranos by Kronos (7, 1). As a result of that act he brings everything into being out of himself – gods and goddesses, rivers, springs, everything (7, 2–4), including no doubt Pontos and (8) Okeanos (as in a closely similar passage of the Rhapsodies, fr. 167 Kern) as well as the moon (9). Finally he commits incest with his mother (10) – Rhea, who is probably also identified, here as in the Rhapsodies, with Demeter; the offspring in that case (as Burkert suggests) would be Persephone, with whom he may have then coupled to produce the chthonic form of Dionysus.

Some elements of the much later Rhapsodic account are present in all this, but others are excluded – notably the winged god Phanes (see n. 3 on p. 24). But Phanes was swallowed by Zeus in the depths of Night according to the Rhapsodies (fr. 167 Kern), and so it looks as though a later bowdlerizing taste replaced the phallus by Phanes. Where does the phallus come from? Obviously, like most other details of the Succession-myth (pp. 44f.), from near-eastern sources. In the Hurrian-Hittite Kumarbi myth, described on p. 46, it is Kumarbi that cuts off the sky-god's phallus; he swallows it, becomes pregnant with the weather-god, and has a painful delivery. This seems to have been too strong meat for Hesiod or his closer sources; the act of castration survives (see **39** below), but the phallus is then simply thrown into the sea; any swallowing is by Kronos (equivalent in other respects to Kumarbi) *of his children* – a somewhat tamer conception, also a probable theme of folktale. It begins to appear as though 'Orpheus' preserved the original oriental account whereby a god becomes pregnant by swallowing the severed phallus; however, it is not the castrator himself that does so, nor is this the means whereby he is displaced by the weather-god. Rather the weather-god (Zeus) swallows the phallus, which seems to have been preserved as a symbol or instrument of generation in order to give birth to the whole universe in a second and final act of creation – just as Phanes will do, indeed, in the later Rhapsodic account.

The relevance of Orphic beliefs to Presocratic philosophy is still, even in the light of the new evidence, fairly slight. Fresh support is given to the priority of Night, perhaps related to the Hesiodic idea of initial Chaos, as also to a wide variety of cosmogonical and theogonical elaborations of Hesiod in the fifth and even perhaps the sixth century B.C. Orphic departures from Hesiod are not numerous judging by the Derveni papyrus, but are significant in that they seem to restore and to develop motifs from the near-eastern Succession-myth which Hesiod himself had toned down, especially over Zeus' pregnancy and subsequent birth of the whole of nature. That makes it more likely that Pherecydes of Syros (§6B), and perhaps certain sixth-century Presocratics too, were indebted to Asiatic sources for otherwise unattested ideas. Apart from that, the main originality of the Derveni theogony may have lain in the conception of the single creator-god, combining the demiurgical powers of Babylonian Marduk (see p. 43) with the sexual-generation theme of the Hesiodic *Theogony*. But it is in the new aspect of the gold-tablet material that the greatest interest may ultimately lie; for that does much to confirm that there were people in the fifth century B.C., at least, who related cosmogonic speculation to concern with the fate of the soul after death. That is something the initiates at Eleusis do not seem to have done, and it does much to account for the productive and comprehensive world-view of Heraclitus in particular.

5. The Hesiodic cosmogony, and the separation of earth and sky

There is an obvious sense in which Hesiod should have been directly considered before this, since his *Theogony* and *Works and Days* were both composed probably in the early seventh century B.C., and many of the themes developed by 'Orphics' and others, and already discussed, are clearly influenced here and there by his treatment. Yet they belong to a tradition of popular, non-analytic ideas about the world and its development that found occasional expression in Homer (see §§1–3). Hesiod, on the other hand, although he worked only a generation or so later than the composer (or composers) of the *Iliad* and *Odyssey*, represents an apparently quite new attempt to systematize the ancient myths. He too deals with the relations of gods and goddesses to each other and to more primitive powers, but with the evident intention not only of reducing age-old mythical material to some kind of order but also of demonstrating the ultimate sources of Zeus' authority and grandeur. It is the cosmogonical developments described in the *Theogony*, which led up to that, that are singled out for special attention in the pages which follow; but *Works and Days*, with its emphasis on Zeus' eventual rule of the world in accordance with Order or Justice (*Dikē*), was also a probable if less obvious influence on Presocratic ideas – especially, through Heraclitus, on the concept of an underlying arrangement of the cosmos, on which see further §7 below.

31   Hesiod *Theogony* 116

 Ἤ τοι μὲν πρώτιστα Χάος γένετ᾽, αὐτὰρ ἔπειτα   116
 Γαῖ᾽ εὐρύστερνος, πάντων ἔδος ἀσφαλὲς αἰεί,   117
 Τάρταρά τ᾽ ἠερόεντα μυχῷ χθονὸς εὐρυοδείης,[1]   119
 ἠδ᾽ Ἔρος, ὃς κάλλιστος ἐν ἀθανάτοισι θεοῖσι,   120
 λυσιμελής, πάντων δὲ θεῶν πάντων τ᾽ ἀνθρώπων
 δάμναται ἐν στήθεσσι νόον καὶ ἐπίφρονα βουλήν.
 ἐκ Χάεος δ᾽ Ἔρεβός τε μέλαινά τε Νὺξ ἐγένοντο·
 Νυκτὸς δ᾽ αὖτ᾽ Αἰθήρ τε καὶ Ἡμέρη ἐξεγένοντο,
 οὓς τέκε κυσαμένη Ἐρέβει φιλότητι μιγεῖσα.   125
 Γαῖα δέ τοι πρῶτον μὲν ἐγείνατο ἶσον ἑαυτῇ
 Οὐρανὸν ἀστερόενθ᾽, ἵνα μιν περὶ πάντα καλύπτοι,
 ὄφρ᾽ εἴη μακάρεσσι θεοῖς ἔδος ἀσφαλὲς αἰεί.
 γείνατο δ᾽ Οὔρεα μακρά, θεῶν χαρίεντας ἐναύλους
 Νυμφέων, αἳ ναίουσιν ἀν᾽ οὔρεα βησσήεντα.   130
 ἡ δὲ καὶ ἀτρύγετον πέλαγος τέκεν, οἴδματι θυῖον,

Πόντον, ἄτερ φιλότητος ἐφιμέρου· αὐτὰρ ἔπειτα
Οὐρανῷ εὐνηθεῖσα τέκ' Ὠκεανὸν βαθυδίνην,
Κοῖόν τε Κρῖόν θ' Ὑπερίονά τ' Ἰαπετόν τε...²

31 Verily first of all did Chaos come into being, and then broad-bosomed Gaia [earth], a firm seat of all things for ever, and misty Tartaros in a recess of broad-wayed earth, and Eros, who is fairest among immortal gods, looser of limbs, and subdues in their breasts the mind and thoughtful counsel of all gods and all men. Out of Chaos, Erebos and black Night came into being; and from Night, again, came Aither and Day, whom she conceived and bore after mingling in love with Erebos. And Earth first of all brought forth starry Ouranos [sky], equal to herself, to cover her completely round about, to be a firm seat for the blessed gods for ever. Then she brought forth tall Mountains, lovely haunts of the divine Nymphs who dwell in the woody mountains. She also gave birth to the unharvested sea, seething with its swell, Pontos, without delightful love; and then having lain with Ouranos she bore deep-eddying Okeanos, and Koios and Krios and Hyperion and Iapetos...

¹ Line 118, ἀθανάτων οἳ ἔχουσι κάρη νιφόεντος Ὀλύμπου, is organic and quite inappropriate here, and has been omitted. It occurs in the medieval MSS, but is absent from quotations by Plato (*Symp.* 178b) and ps.-Aristotle (*M.X.G.* 1, 975a11), as well as by Sextus Empiricus and Stobaeus. Line 119 was also omitted in these quotations (as, apparently, in the copy used by Zeno of Citium: *SVF* I, 104–5), and a scholiast remarks ἀθετεῖται ('it is marked as spurious'); yet it is quoted in its correct place by Chalcidius (*in Tim.* 122), who omitted 118. Plato's continuation of 117 by 120 is not necessarily significant; he was solely interested in Eros, and quoted what was relevant to Eros and no more. The scholiast's doubt, and post-Platonic omissions, may have originated in Plato's omission; or the line may have been felt to be incongruous, having been added at the time when the variant descriptions of Hades accrued (p. 20).
² The list of Titans is completed in the lines that follow; Gaia's subsequent offspring are patently non-cosmological. At 154ff. comes the story of the mutilation of Kronos (**39**). At 211ff. there is a reversion to the production of personified abstractions, e.g. by Night and Strife, but they have no cosmological significance.

The author of the *Theogony* decided to trace back the ancestry of the gods to the beginning of the world, and **31** is his account of the earliest stages, in which the production of cosmic constituents like Ouranos (sky) gradually leads to the generation of vague but fully anthropomorphic mythical persons like the Titans. This poetical cosmogony, composed presumably early in the seventh century B.C., was not, however, *invented* by Hesiod; its occasional irrationality and reduplication of stages indicate that it is a synthesis of at least two earlier variant accounts. For example, Erebos (which may be of Hittite etymology), although there is some vagueness about it in Homer, must be locally related to the whole complex Gaia–Hades–Tartaros (Ἐρέβεσφιν ὑπὸ χθονός at *Theogony* 669); yet it is produced a stage later than Gaia and Tartaros. It might be explained as a local differentiation, as Mountains and Sea (Pontos) are produced as local differentiations from Earth; but in that case it should naturally originate from Tartaros or Gaia and not from Chaos. It is grouped with Night, no doubt, because it shares a major characteristic (darkness), as Aither is grouped with Day. Generation is of opposites (e.g. of Aither and Day by Erebos – whose neuter gender does not inhibit parental activities – and Night), or of similars (Erebos and Night from Chaos, see p. 41), or of local differentiations. Some births, however, cannot be explained on any of these principles – notably that of Ouranos from Gaia. Again, there is inconsistency over the method of production. Eros is produced at the first stage of differentiation, presumably to provide an anthropomorphic, sexual explanation of subsequent differentiation. It is not, however, consistently used. Gaia produces Pontos 'without love' at 132; Night mates with Erebos at 125 but produces again 'without sleeping with anyone' at 213; Chaos at 123, and Gaia again at 126, produce independently though Love is already in existence. Immediately after producing Pontos independently at 132, Gaia produces the more fully personalized Okeanos by mating with her son and consort Ouranos.[1]

[1] In view of his cosmological importance as the surrounding river (§2) one would expect Okeanos to occur earlier, rather than later, than Pontos, which can properly be regarded as a detail of the earth. The production of Okeanos by Gaia and Ouranos may have a rationalistic motive, since the surrounding stream forms the point of contact between earth and the enclosing bowl of sky.

'First of all Chaos came-to-be': the primacy of Chaos is remarkable, and a careful enquiry must be made into what Hesiod is likely to have meant by Χάος here. Three interpretations may be rejected immediately: (i) Aristotle (*Phys.* Δ1, 208b29) took it to mean 'place'. But interest in this and related spatial concepts probably began with the Eleatics, much later than the *Theogony*, and finds its first major expression in Plato's *Timaeus*. (ii) The Stoics followed Zeno of Citium (e.g. *SVF* I, 103), who perhaps took the idea from Pherecydes of Syros (DK 7 B 1a), in deriving χάος from χέεσθαι and therefore interpreting it as what is poured, i.e. water. (iii) The common modern sense of chaos as disorder can be seen e.g. in Lucian *Amores* 32, where Hesiod's χάος is interpreted as disordered, shapeless matter. This, again, may be Stoic in origin.

The noun is derived from √χα, meaning 'gape, gap, yawn', as in χαίνειν, χάσκειν, etc. Of the certain uses of the word before 400 B.C., one group simply refers to the cosmogonic Χάος of this passage (so Acusilaus in **18**, Aristophanes *Birds* 693, *Clouds* 627); the other group has the special meaning 'air', in the sense of the region between sky and earth, the region in which birds fly (so Bacchylides 5, 27, Euripides fr. 448 (Nauck²), Aristophanes *Clouds* 424, *Birds* 1218). One may suspect that Bacchylides' poetical and perhaps original use of the highly individual phrase ἐν ἀτρύτῳ χάει (as that in which the eagle flies – the free air, as opposed to earth or sea) was consciously imitated by Euripides and Aristophanes, either lyrically (*Birds* 1218) or as a convenient though not necessarily serious interpretation to be placed on the cosmogonical *chaos* of Hesiod. The evidence, then, does not point to an extensive use of χάος as the space between sky and earth, though such a use was certainly known. Here we must consider another instance of the word in the *Theogony* itself:

32 Hesiod *Theogony* 695 (Zeus hurls thunderbolts at the Titans)

ἔζεε δὲ χθὼν πᾶσα καὶ Ὠκεανοῖο ῥέεθρα
πόντος τ' ἀτρύγετος· τοὺς δ' ἄμφεπε θερμὸς ἀϋτμὴ
Τιτῆνας χθονίους, φλὸξ δ' αἰθέρα δῖαν ἵκανεν
ἄσπετος, ὄσσε δ' ἄμερδε καὶ ἰφθίμων περ ἐόντων
αὐγὴ μαρμαίρουσα κεραυνοῦ τε στεροπῆς τε.
καῦμα δὲ θεσπέσιον κατέχεν Χάος· εἴσατο δ' ἄντα   700
ὀφθαλμοῖσι ἰδεῖν ἠδ' οὔασι ὄσσαν ἀκοῦσαι
αὔτως ὡς εἰ Γαῖα καὶ Οὐρανὸς εὐρὺς ὕπερθε
πίλνατο· τοῖος γάρ κε μέγας ὑπὸ δοῦπος ὀρώρει...

32 The whole earth boiled, and the streams of Okeanos, and the unharvested sea; and them, the earth-born Titans, did a warm blast surround, and flame unquenchable reached the holy aither, and the darting gleam of thunderbolt and lightning blinded the eyes even of strong men. A marvellous burning took hold of Chaos; and it was the same to behold with the eyes or to hear the noise with the ears as if earth and broad heaven above drew together; for just such a great din would have risen up...

There has been dispute about which region of the world is represented by Χάος in line 700. Either (*a*) it represents the whole or part of the underworld – there is a parallel for this usage at *Theogony* 814 (**35**), perhaps one of the added variants (see pp. 20 and 40); or (*b*) it represents the region between earth and aither. But (*a*) would be difficult: why should the *heat* penetrate to the underworld (the concussion of missiles does so at 681ff., but that is natural and effective)? The Titans are not in the underworld, but on Mount Othrys (632); we have been told that the flash reaches the upper air, and it is relevant to add that the heat, also, filled the whole intermediate region. The following lines imagine earth and sky as clashing together – again, the emphasis is certainly not on the underworld. An objective judge would surely conclude that Χάος at line 700 describes the region between earth and sky.

In view of the basic meaning of χάος (as a gap, i.e. a bounded interval, not 'void' or anything like that),[1] and of one certain fifth-century usage as the region between sky and earth, and of another use of the word in the *Theogony* in which the meaning is probably the same, serious attention must be paid to an interpretation propounded most notably by Cornford (e.g. *Principium Sapientiae* (Cambridge, 1952) 194f.), that Χάος γένετ' in the first line of **31** implies that *the gap between earth and sky came into being*; that is, that the first stage of cosmogony was the separation of earth and sky. This would not be consistent with one existing and indubitable feature of the cosmogony, the postponement of the birth of Ouranos until a second stage, at lines 126f. (Production from Chaos, lines 123ff., and from Gaia, 126ff., may take place simultaneously.) Apart from this peculiarity, the other conditions fit the proposed interpretation; earth, with its appendage Tartaros, appears directly the gap is made; so does Eros, which in its most concrete form as rain/semen exists between sky and earth according to poetical references.[2] It seems not improbable that in the Hesiodic scheme the explicit description of the formation of Ouranos has been delayed through the confused use of two separate accounts (a confusion which can be paralleled from other details of the scheme), and that it is implied in line 116 at the very first stage of cosmogony. The separation of sky and earth is certainly reduplicated in the *Theogony*, in a fully mythopoeic form, in the story of the mutilation of Kronos (**39**); though reduplication of accounts of a different logical character (quasi-rationalistic and mythical) is easier to accept than reduplication on the same, quasi-rationalistic level.

[1] A comparison has often been drawn between χάος and *ginnunga-gap* in the Nordic cosmogony. This *gap* (which, however, preceded the creation of the giant from whom earth and sky were made) has been taken to imply simply an indefinite empty space: but it is important to observe that in Snorri's schematization it is conceived as being terminated by the realm of ice (*Niflheim*) to the north and that of fire (*Muspellsheim*) to the south. This certainly does not

invalidate the supposition that χάος implies primarily a region of vast size, but secondarily and implicitly its boundaries.

² Not in Homer or Hesiod; most notably in **33** Aeschylus fr. 44, 1–5 (from the *Danaids*)

> ἐρᾷ μὲν ἁγνὸς οὐρανὸς τρῶσαι χθόνα,
> ἔρως δὲ γαῖαν λαμβάνει γάμου τυχεῖν.
> ὄμβρος δ' ἀπ' εὐνατῆρος οὐρανοῦ πεσὼν
> ἔκυσε γαῖαν· ἡ δὲ τίκτεται βροτοῖς
> μήλων τε βοσκὰς καὶ βίον Δημήτριον.

(*Holy sky passionately longs to penetrate the earth, and desire takes hold of earth to achieve this union. Rain from her bedfellow sky falls and impregnates earth, and she brings forth for mortals pasturage for flocks and Demeter's livelihood.*) This idea of the rain actually fertilizing the earth may be of great antiquity.

Cornford's interpretation may be helped by the verb used to describe the first stage of cosmogony: not ἦν but γένετ', perhaps implying that Χάος was not the eternal precondition of a differentiated world, but a modification of that precondition. (It is out of the question that Hesiod or his source was thinking of the originative substance as coming into being out of nothing.) The idea that earth and sky were originally one mass may have been so common (see pp. 42–4) that Hesiod could take it for granted, and begin his account of world-formation at the first stage of differentiation. This would be, undoubtedly, a cryptic and laconic procedure; and it seems probable that something more complicated was meant by Χάος γένετ' than, simply, 'sky and earth separated' – though I am inclined to accept that this was originally implicit in the phrase. The nature of the gap between sky and earth after their first separation may well have been somehow specified in the popular traditions on which Hesiod was presumably drawing. There was, conceivably, an attempt to imagine what would be the appearance of things when there was simply dark sky, and earth, and the gap between. Here we must turn for assistance to two of the elaborations (see p. 20) on the Hesiodic description of the underworld.

34 Hesiod *Theogony* 736

> ἔνθα δὲ γῆς δνοφερῆς καὶ Ταρτάρου ἠερόεντος
> πόντου τ' ἀτρυγέτοιο καὶ οὐρανοῦ ἀστερόεντος
> ἑξείης πάντων πηγαὶ καὶ πείρατ' ἔασιν
> ἀργαλέ' εὐρώεντα, τά τε στυγέουσι θεοί περ,
> χάσμα μέγ', οὐδέ κε πάντα τελεσφόρον εἰς ἐνιαυτὸν   740
> οὖδας ἵκοιτ', εἰ πρῶτα πυλέων ἔντοσθε γένοιτο.
> ἀλλά κεν ἔνθα καὶ ἔνθα φέροι πρὸ θύελλα θυέλλης
> ἀργαλέη· δεινὸν δὲ καὶ ἀθανάτοισι θεοῖσι
> τοῦτο τέρας· Νυκτὸς δ' ἐρεβεννῆς οἰκία δεινὰ
> ἕστηκεν νεφέλης κεκαλυμμένα κυανέῃσιν.   745

35 Hesiod *Theogony* 811 (following a repetition of lines 736–9, *vide* **34**)

ἔνθα δὲ μαρμάρεαί τε πύλαι καὶ χάλκεος οὐδὸς
ἀστεμφής, ῥίζῃσι διηνεκέεσσιν ἀρηρώς,
αὐτοφυής· πρόσθεν δὲ θεῶν ἔκτοσθεν ἁπάντων
Τιτῆνες ναίουσι, πέρην Χάεος ζοφεροῖο.

34 There of murky earth and misty Tartaros and unharvested sea and starry sky, of all of them, are the springs in a row and the grievous, dank limits which even the gods detest; a great gulf, nor would one reach the floor for the whole length of a fulfilling year, if one were once within the gates. But hither and thither storm on grievous storm would carry one on; dreadful is this portent even for immortal gods; and the dreadful halls of gloomy Night stand covered with blue-black clouds.
35 There are gleaming gates, and brazen threshold unshaken, fixed with continuous roots, self-grown; and in front, far from all the gods, dwell the Titans, across murky Chaos.

Of these, **34** is evidently an attempt to improve 726–8 (**2**), where Tartaros (perhaps its upper part) is said to be surrounded by Night, and above it are the roots of earth and sea. In πείρατ' there is a more exact reversion to the apparent source of **2**, i.e. *Il.* VIII, 478–9, τὰ νείατα πείραθ'...γαίης καὶ πόντοιο; while πηγαί are introduced as being especially appropriate to the sea. 740ff. are a special and peculiar development of 720ff. **35**, on the other hand, which follows a repetition of the first four lines of **34**, begins with a slightly altered line (*Il.* VIII, 15) from the Homeric description of Tartaros (**1**), then continues with the 'roots' of **2**, quite vague this time, and ends with the χάσμα μέγ' of 740 repeated as Χάεος. Both passages contain inconsistencies compatible with their being somewhat superficial expansions; for example the alteration of the reasonable idea that the roots of earth are above Tartaros to the idea that the 'sources and boundaries' of earth, sea, sky *and Tartaros* are in Tartaros (**34**). What is interesting is the further description of Tartaros as a χάσμα μέγ', a great gulf or chasm (cf. Euripides *Phoen.* 1605), full of storms and containing the halls of Night. In **35** this gulf is described as 'gloomy Chaos' (we need not concern ourselves with its peculiar geography, except to note that Chaos is not absolutely unbounded). This must contain a reference to the initial Χάος of line 116 (**31**), and it seems reasonable to suppose that the author or authors of these expansions understood the initial Χάος to be dark and windy, like Tartaros. This interpretation gains some support from the fact that in the original cosmogonical account Erebos and Night (both, presumably, gloomy) are produced from Chaos.

The evidence seems to point to the following conclusion. For Hesiod's source, at all events, the first stage in the formation of a differentiated world was the production of a vast gap between sky and earth. By Hesiod the emphasis is placed on the nature of the gap itself, not on the act of separation which produced it. The gap is conceived as dark and windy – because aither and sun had not yet come into being, and night and storms go together. The same kind of description is applied, quite naturally, to the lightless gulfs of Tartaros; and sometimes Tartaros is considered in terms of, or actually as part of, the original gap.[1]

[1] G. Vlastos (*Gnomon* 27 (1955), 74–5) finds **34** significant for the origin of Hesiod's cosmogonical Χάος, and even suggests that it was from here that Anaximander got the idea of τὸ ἄπειρον. U. Hölscher, too (*Hermes* 81 (1953), 391–401), has completely rejected the Cornford interpretation, and takes Χάος to be a dark and boundless waste. He supports this by the assumption that a cosmogony, attributed to Sanchuniathon (a Phoenician said to have lived before the Trojan war) by Philo of Byblus *ap.* Eusebium *P.E.* 1, 10, is really of great antiquity, much older than Hesiod. According to the summary in Eusebius the first state of things was gloomy, boundless air and wind (χάος θολερόν, ἐρεβῶδες is one of its descriptions). When this 'passionately desired its own ἀρχαί' (whatever that may mean) there was intermixture. *Mot* (some kind of slime) was produced, and became the sowing of creation. Now it is true that the discoveries at Ras Shamra and elsewhere have shown (*a*) that some motifs in Greek mythology originated long before Homer and Hesiod, and outside Greece; (*b*) that Phoenicia had its own versions of myths about the early history of the gods, in the second millennium B.C., and was a meeting-place of cultures. It is also true that in the theogony attributed to Sanchuniathon, after the cosmogonical summary, there is one detail (a deity, Eliun, in the generation before Ouranos) which does not correspond with Hesiod and does correspond with the cognate Hittite account of the second millennium (see pp. 45f.). But this may be a detail of the genuine and ancient local cosmogonical tradition, which could be incorporated at any date: it does not prove that every part of the whole farrago assigned to Sanchuniathon (Hermes Trismegistus and all) has any claim to incorporate ancient material. In particular, it does not even begin to suggest that the cosmogonical account is anything but what it appears to be, i.e. a Hellenistic eclectic pastiche of Hesiod and later cosmogonical sources (there is a possible mention of an egg). To use it as a means of interpreting Χάος in the *Theogony*, and of showing that the idea of an originative windy darkness was already established for Hesiod to assimilate, must be considered interesting rather than scientific.

41

THE SEPARATION OF EARTH AND SKY IN GREEK LITERATURE

36   Euripides fr. 484 (from *Melanippe the Wise*)
        κοὐκ ἐμὸς ὁ μῦθος ἀλλ' ἐμῆς μητρὸς πάρα,
        ὡς οὐρανός τε γαῖά τ' ἦν μορφὴ μία·
        ἐπεὶ δ' ἐχωρίσθησαν ἀλλήλων δίχα
        τίκτουσι πάντα κἀνέδωκαν εἰς φάος,
        δένδρη, πετεινά, θῆρας, οὕς θ' ἅλμη τρέφει,
        γένος τε θνητῶν.

37   Diodorus I, 7, I (DK68 B 5, I) κατὰ γὰρ τὴν ἐξ ἀρχῆς τῶν
        ὅλων σύστασιν μίαν ἔχειν ἰδέαν οὐρανόν τε καὶ γῆν, μεμειγμένης
        αὐτῶν τῆς φύσεως· μετὰ δὲ ταῦτα διαστάντων τῶν σωμάτων ἀπ'
        ἀλλήλων τὸν μὲν κόσμον περιλαβεῖν ἅπασαν τὴν ὁρωμένην ἐν αὐτῷ
        σύνταξιν...[1]

38   Apollonius Rhodius I, 496
        ἤειδεν δ' ὡς γαῖα καὶ οὐρανὸς ἠδὲ θάλασσα
        τὸ πρὶν ἐπ' ἀλλήλοισι μιῇ συναρηρότα μορφῇ
        νείκεος ἐξ ὀλοοῖο διέκριθεν ἀμφὶς ἕκαστα·
        ἠδ' ὡς ἔμπεδον αἰὲν ἐν αἰθέρι τέκμαρ ἔχουσιν
        ἄστρα σεληναίη τε καὶ ἠελίοιο κέλευθοι...[2]

36   And the tale is not mine but from my mother, how sky and
earth were one form; and when they had been separated apart
from each other they bring forth all things. and gave them up into
the light: trees, birds, beasts, the creatures nourished by the salt
sea, and the race of mortals.

37   For by the original composition of the universe sky and earth
had one form, their natures being mingled; after this their bodies
parted from each other, and the world took on the whole
arrangement that we see in it...

38   He sang how earth and sky and sea, being formerly connected
with each other in one form, through destructive strife separated
apart each from the other; and how stars, moon and the sun's paths
have forever in the aither a firm boundary...

[1] The cosmogony and anthropogony in this first book of Diodorus (who, shortly
after this passage, quoted 36) were ascribed by Diels to Democritus. There is no
mention of atoms, as Cornford noted; but some details of later stages may
nevertheless come from the Μικρὸς διάκοσμος (p. 405 and n.). The development
of society is similar to that described by Protagoras in the Platonic dialogue. The
whole account is eclectic, but its main features are of fifth-century origin and
predominantly Ionian character; as such it may well embody traditional
cosmogonical ideas.

[2] Orpheus is the singer. The cosmogony has nothing in common with special 'Orphic' accounts (§4); Apollonius would naturally put into Orpheus' mouth the most primitive-sounding version that he knew.

It has been suggested above that the implied, although not emphasized, first stage of the Hesiodic cosmogony was the separation of sky and earth. That this idea was familiar enough in Greece is shown by 36–8. Only 36, admittedly, is even as early as the fifth century; but it is particularly important as explicitly describing the separation of sky and earth as being passed on from mother to child, i.e. as a popular and traditional account. No scientific parallel is known; though the idea may have been merged with specialized Ionian theories as in 37 and its continuation.

SEPARATION IN NON-GREEK SOURCES

The splitting of earth from sky is a cosmogonical mechanism that was widely used, long before the earliest known Greek cosmogonical ideas, in the mythological accounts of the great near-eastern cultures. (It is in fact common to many different cultures: cf., most notably, the Maori myth of the separation of Rangi (sky) and Papa (earth) by their constricted offspring, a close parallel to 39.) Thus a gloss from the end of the first millennium B.C. on the Egyptian Book of the Dead explains that 'Re began to appear as a king, as one who was before the liftings of Shu had taken place, when he was on the hill which is in Hermopolis' (ANET, 4). Shu is the air-god which is sputtered out by Re and lifts the sky-goddess, Nut, from the earth-god, Keb. In the Hurrian-Hittite 'Song of Ullikummi' (ANET, 125; Gurney, The Hittites, 190–4) Upelluri, a counterpart of Atlas, says: 'When heaven and earth were built upon me I knew nothing of it, and when they came and cut heaven and earth asunder with a cleaver I knew nothing of it.' In the Babylonian Creation-epic (IV, 137ff.; ANET, 67) Marduk splits the body of the primeval water-goddess Tiamat and makes one half of it into sky (containing the celestial waters) and the other half into Apsu, the deep, and Esharra, the 'great abode' or firmament of earth. This is the first stage in the composition of the world as we know it, though a secondary stage in the far older history of the Babylonian pantheon. In another, later Semitic version, Genesis i, the primeval waters are similarly divided: 'And God said, Let there be a firmament in the midst of the waters, and let it divide the waters from the waters. And God made the firmament, and divided the waters which were under the firmament from the waters which were above the firmament; and it was so. And God called the firmament Heaven.' (Gen. i, 6–8.)[1]

[1] The opening words of the first chapter of Genesis, 'In the beginning God created the heaven and the earth. And the earth was without form, and void', are a confusing anticipation of what is to follow. The initial state is boundless, dark water; the first stage of differentiation is the separation of the waters into those of the sky and those of the earth. The anticipation in the initial summary provides a parallel for the reduplication involved in the Hesiodic cosmogony (p. 38).

The separation of sky and earth was implied, therefore, in various non-Greek mythological accounts older than Hesiod. It will be seen in the next section that Hesiod's description of the earliest generations of gods is a version of a basic near-eastern myth, which is also reproduced in an extant Hurrian-Hittite form. There is nothing surprising, therefore, in the separation-motif appearing in Hesiod – whether implicitly in the quasi-rationalistic Χάος γένετ' of the formal cosmogony, or more explicitly, but in fully mythopoeic guise, in the mutilation-story now to be considered.

THE MUTILATION-MYTH IN THE THEOGONY

39   Hesiod *Theogony* 154

όσσοι γὰρ Γαίης τε καὶ Οὐρανοῦ ἐξεγένοντο,
δεινότατοι παίδων, σφετέρῳ δ' ἤχθοντο τοκῆι
ἐξ ἀρχῆς· καὶ τῶν μὲν ὅπως τις πρῶτα γένοιτο
πάντας ἀποκρύπτασκε, καὶ εἰς φάος οὐκ ἀνίεσκε,
Γαίης ἐν κευθμῶνι, κακῷ δ' ἐπετέρπετο ἔργῳ
Οὐρανός· ἡ δ' ἐντὸς στοναχίζετο Γαῖα πελώρη
στεινομένη· δολίην δὲ κακήν τ' ἐφράσσατο τέχνην.   160
...εἷσε δέ μιν (*sc.* Κρόνον) κρύψασα λόχῳ· ἐνέθηκε δὲ χερσὶν
ἅρπην καρχαρόδοντα, δόλον δ' ὑπεθήκατο πάντα.   175
ἦλθε δὲ Νύκτ' ἐπάγων μέγας Οὐρανός, ἀμφὶ δὲ Γαίη
ἱμείρων φιλότητος ἐπέσχετο καί ῥ' ἐτανύσθη
πάντη· ὁ δ' ἐκ λοχεοῖο πάις ὠρέξατο χειρὶ
σκαιῇ, δεξιτερῇ δὲ πελώριον ἔλλαβεν ἅρπην
μακρήν, καρχαρόδοντα, φίλου δ' ἀπὸ μήδεα πατρὸς   180
ἐσσυμένως ἤμησε, πάλιν δ' ἔρριψε φέρεσθαι
ἐξοπίσω...

(The drops of blood fertilize Gaia and generate Furies, Giants and Melian nymphs; the severed parts fall into the sea, and from the foam Aphrodite is born.)

39 All who came forth from Gaia and Ouranos, the most dire of children, from the beginning were hated by their own begetter; and just as soon as any of them came into being he hid them all away and did not let them into the light, in the inward places of Gaia; and Ouranos rejoiced over the evil deed. And she, prodigious Gaia, groaned within, for she was crowded out; and she contrived a crafty, evil device...she sent him [Kronos] into a hidden place of ambush, placed in his hands a jagged-toothed sickle, and enjoined on him the whole deceit. Great Ouranos came bringing Night with him, and over Gaia, desiring love, he stretched himself, and spread all over her; and he, his son, from his place of ambush stretched out with his left hand, and with his right he grasped the monstrous sickle, long and jagged-toothed, and swiftly sheared off the genitals of his dear father, and flung them behind him to be carried away...

The details of the present version suggest that Ouranos *did* separate from Gaia, in the daytime at least: but why in this case could not Gaia emit her offspring during his absence? It is probable that in other versions of the story Ouranos covered Gaia continuously (as Rangi covers Papa in the Maori myth), so that in a manner of speaking 'sky and earth were one form'. There can be little doubt that this crude sexual account envisages, on another and less sophisticated plane, the same cosmogonical event that is implied first by Χάος γένετ' and second by Γαῖα...ἐγείνατο ἶσον ἑαυτῇ Οὐρανόν in the deliberate cosmogony of **31**.[1]

[1] The most obvious parallel for the repetition in mythopoeic form of an event that has already been accounted for in a quasi-rationalistic and much more sophisticated summary is seen in Genesis: the abstract Elohim of the first chapter is replaced by the fully anthropomorphic and much cruder Jahweh of the second, and the vague 'God created man in his own image' of chapter i is repeated in a far more graphic and more primitive form in the second chapter, where Jahweh creates man out of dust and breathes life into his nostrils. (For man formed from clay cf. e.g. the Old Babylonian text *ANET*, 99 col. *b*, as well as the Greek Prometheus-myth.)

That some of the contents of the *Theogony* are of non-Greek origin and of a date far earlier than Hesiod's immediate predecessors is most strikingly shown by the parallelism between the Hesiodic account of the succession of oldest gods and the Hittite Kumarbi-tablet, of Hurrian origin and in its extant form dating from around the middle of the second millennium B.C.[1] In the Hittite version the first king in heaven is Alalu, who is driven out by the sky-god Anu; Anu is deposed by the father of the developed gods, Kumarbi (equivalent to Kronos 'father of the gods'). As Anu tries to escape into the sky Kumarbi bites off, and swallows, his member. On being told that he has become impregnated with the storm-god and two other 'terrible gods', Kumarbi spits out the member, which impregnates the earth with the two other gods; Kumarbi cannot, however, rid himself of the storm-god, and eventually gives birth to him. With the help of Anu, it is evident, the storm-god (to whom the Greek equivalent is obviously the thunder-and-lightning god Zeus) deposes Kumarbi and becomes king in heaven. The similarities to the Greek myth are obvious: the succession sky-god, father of gods, storm-god is common to each; so is the emasculation of the sky-god by Kumarbi/Kronos, and the impregnation of earth by the rejected member. There are, of course, significant differences too: the Hittite version (like other near-eastern accounts) has a god, Alalu, before the sky-god; what *Kronos* swallows is a stone (by mistake for the storm-god, *Theog.* 468ff., and after swallowing all his other children); and it is Rhea, not he, that bears the storm-god Zeus. It is thought that in the broken part of the Hittite tablet there may have been some reference to Kumarbi eating a stone, but this is uncertain. It should be noted that in Hesiod, also, the sky-god (with Gaia) helps the storm-god to survive. The Hittite version carries no implication that the emasculation of the sky-god was concerned with the separation of sky from earth; indeed, no earth-goddess is involved. This is an important difference, but it suggests, not that the Greek separation-motive had no second-millennium archetype, but that the Greek version incorporates variants which do not happen to be found in the Hittite account. The Greek version was not derived specifically from the Hittite, of course; there was a widely diffused common account, with many local variants, of which the Hittite tablet gives one version and Hesiod another – a version, moreover, which had suffered the vicissitudes of transmission to a younger and very different culture.

[1] For the Kumarbi tablet see *ANET*, 120–1; Gurney, *The Hittites*, 190–2; R. D. Barnett, *JHS* 65 (1945), 100f.; H. G. Güterbock, *Kumarbi* (Zürich, 1946), 100ff.; G. S. Kirk, *Myth, its Meaning and Functions in Ancient and Other Cultures* (Berkeley and Cambridge, 1970), 214–19. The 'Song of Ullikummi' (see p. 43) records, on separate tablets, the further doings of Kumarbi while he is king in heaven; that sky and earth had been separated is plainly implied there.

6. 'Mixed' theogonies

(A) ALCMAN

The Spartan lyricist Alcman was active around 600 B.C., and it was a great surprise when the publication of Oxyrhynchus Papyrus no. 2390 in 1957 revealed that one of his poems had contained a kind of theogonical cosmogony ('in this song Alcman concerns himself with nature' as the commentator put it, fr. 3, col. i, 26), perhaps arising out of an invocation of the Muses as children of Earth. Of the poem itself we have the merest glimpses; the papyrus (of the second century A.D.) preserves parts of a prose commentary, crudely Aristotelian in character, on the poem, which was evidently quite puzzling and had attracted several other attempts at interpretation (col. i, 27f.). The central part of the commentary is as follows in 40; but it is important to note that it also contained lemmata, that is, short phrases from Alcman on which the comment was hung, and that ἐκ δε τῶ π[early in col. ii (line 3), followed by the explanation πόρον ἀπὸ τῆς πορ.[in line 6, shows by the dialect form τῶ for τοῦ that Alcman himself undoubtedly did use the term πόρος – with which τέκμωρ, a poetical form in any case, is firmly associated. Other lemmata (which follow 40) are πρέσγ[υς and then ἁμάρ τε καὶ σελάνα καὶ τρίτον σκότος, that is, 'venerable' and 'day and moon and, third, darkness'.

40 Alcman fr. 3 (Page), col. ii, 7–20

> ὡς γὰρ ἤρξατο ἡ ὕλη κατασκευα[σθῆναι
> ἐγένετο πόρος τις οἱονεὶ ἀρχή· λ[έγει
> οὖν ὁ Ἀλκμὰν τὴν ὕλην πάν[των τετα-
> ραγμένην καὶ ἀπόητον· εἶτα [γενέ-   10
> σθαι τινά φησιν τὸν κατασκευά[ζοντα
> πάντα, εἶτα γενέσθαι [πό]ρον, τοῦ [δὲ πό-
> ρου παρελθόντος ἐπακολουθῆ[σαι] τέ-
> κμωρ· καὶ ἔστιν ὁ μὲν πόρος οἷον ἀρχή, τὸ δὲ τέ-
> κμωρ οἱονεὶ τέλος. τῆς Θέτιδος γενο-   15
> μένης ἀρχὴ καὶ τέ[λ]ο[ς ταῦτ]α πάντων ἐ-
> γένε[τ]ο, καὶ τὰ μὲν πάντα [ὁμο]ίαν ἔχει
> τὴν φύσιν τῆι τοῦ χαλκοῦ ὕληι, ἡ δὲ
> Θέτις τ[ῆι] τοῦ τεχνίτου, ὁ δὲ πόρος καὶ τὸ τέ-
> κμωρ τῆι ἀρχῆι καὶ τῶι τέλει...   20

40 For when matter began to be arranged there came into being a kind of way [or passage, *poros*], as it were a beginning [or origin,

archē]. So Alcman says that the matter of all things was disturbed and unmade; then someone [masculine] came into being who was arranging everything, then a way [*poros*] came into being, and when the way had passed by, a limit [or goal, *tekmōr*] followed on. And the way is like a beginning [or origin], whereas the limit is like an end [or limit, *telos*]. When Thetis had come into being these became beginning and end of all things, and the totality of things has a similar nature to that of the bronze material, Thetis to that of the craftsman, and the way and the limit to that of the beginning and the end...

The commentator assimilates Alcman to Aristotle's discussion of the four 'causes' – that is, preconditions or aspects of physical existence – in *Physics* B. There is indeed an obvious resemblance between Thetis (especially if we accept that her name might have been associated with the root meaning of τιθέναι, θέσθαι, i.e. to place or set in place) and the efficient cause or craftsman, as also of Poros and the formal cause, and Tekmōr and the final cause; but Alcman was certainly thinking in less abstract and perhaps less analytical terms than that. Quite what his line of thought was has been matter for much recent speculation, none of it really compelling: *tekmōr* (the vacillation over whether or not to print a capital letter is deliberate) is the *sign* that shows the *way* or *poros* (so Burkert); *poros* represents *paths* in the primeval sea, *tekmōr signs* of direction through it (West) – or the stars (Vernant); Poros is 'apportionment' (cf. πέπρωται < *πόρω) to balance Aisa in Alcman fr. 1, 13 (on which see further p. 49) (Page). Thetis is of course a sea-goddess, which accounts for West's attractive conjecture; but her name, with the possible derivation noted above, together with an ancient cult of her in Sparta itself, may be more germane. For Poros and Tekmōr we must hesitate between more concrete and more abstract meanings, with a natural inclination to the former: between physical path or track, and the way or means of passage or progress; and between visible sign, mark or limit, and end or culmination (both of these being Homeric). And the degree of abstraction or the reverse must correspond for the two different terms; thus 'limit' in a more concrete sense might conceivably be Okeanos (cf. §2), especially if Thetis has her sea-goddess connotation among others; but it is not easy to see what the 'path' might then be.

The lemma about *skotos*, darkness, conceivably suggests an affinity with Night (§3). The commentator (24f.) set darkness at the stage at which matter was still 'unseparated', which means that 'and, third' (in relation to day and moon) has to be given a logical and not a chronological sense. He continued by saying that 'there came into being by the agency of [...] way and limit and darkness', in which the lacuna presumably contained the name of Thetis. Darkness here may represent the primeval state, akin to Hesiod's Chaos (§5), despite the commentator's implication at this point that it is not prior to *poros* and *tekmōr*.

Difficulties are compounded by the probability that in the fragmentary verses 13f. of Alcman's fr. 1 (Page), the 'Partheneion', Poros was linked with Aisa as 'eldest of the gods'. The commentator on v. 14 there (Page, *Lyrica Graeca Selecta* (Oxford, 1968) p. 6) makes the remarkable suggestion that Poros is the same as Hesiod's Chaos, although the context itself, defective though it is, would seem to require man's destiny or portion as the general sense of both Aisa and Poros – which is why Page suggested a connection with the root of πέπρωται etc. for the latter, rather than the more obvious περάω etc. It seems not improbable, however, that the link with Hesiodic Chaos is derived by the Partheneion-commentator from our cosmogonical fragment; and it may give a clue to the sense of Poros there, whatever its role in the Partheneion. Yet *poros*, *qua* passage or way, cannot be *identical* with Chaos in the sense of dark, unformed matter (or anything like that); it must succeed or impinge upon it, as the commentator in **40**, 8–12 implies. The mention of Hesiod is interesting nevertheless, and may suggest, what we might otherwise be inclined to suspect, that Alcman like other dabblers in cosmogonical matters was always aware of the Hesiodic account in the background.

Yet Poros and Tekmōr, no less than Thetis, are definitely non-Hesiodic (and are not apparently orientalizing either). They tantalize us – but what might they have implied for the Presocratics? No important or specific influence at any rate; but they demonstrate that cosmogonical speculation *was* in the air around Thales' time, not only in Ionia but also amid the very different cultural environment of mainland Greece – of Sparta, indeed, which Anaximander seems to have visited a generation later (pp. 103–5). Moreover that kind of cosmogonical imagination was not simply concerned with the elaboration or minor rearrangement of traditional Hesiodic concepts (as 'Epimenides' had been, see §3 (iii)), but extended to novel metaphorical applications of broad general ideas like those included in the range of meanings that can be assigned to *tekmōr* – with which one might be tempted to connect Anaximander's more prosaic obverse, τὸ ἄπειρον or the Indefinite.

(B) PHERECYDES OF SYROS

This Pherecydes was a mythographer and theogonist, and must be distinguished from the fifth-century Athenian genealogist of the same name, also from a later and less important Lerian.[1] According to Aristotle he was not entirely mythological in his approach:

41   Aristotle *Met.* N4, 1091b8   ...ἐπεὶ οἵ γε μεμειγμένοι αὐτῶν (*sc.* τῶν θεολόγων) [καὶ] τῷ μὴ μυθικῶς ἅπαντα λέγειν, οἷον Φερεκύδης καὶ ἕτεροί τινες, τὸ γεννῆσαν πρῶτον ἄριστον τιθέασι, καὶ οἱ Μάγοι.

41   ...since the 'mixed' theologians, those who do not say everything in mythical form, such as Pherecydes and certain of the others, and also the Magi, make the first generator the *best* thing.

[1] F. Jacoby, *Mnemosyne* 13 (3rd series), 1947, 13ff., finally discredited Wilamowitz's theory that 'Pherecydes' was a generic name attached to all early Ionian prose writing not specifically ascribed, as 'Hippocrates' became attached to all medical literature.

DATE

Pherecydes was active in the sixth century B.C., perhaps around the middle of it. Ancient authorities diverge: according to one tradition he was roughly contemporary with the Lydian king Alyattes (*c.* 605–560 B.C.) and the Seven Sages (conventionally dated around Thales' eclipse, 585/4, or the archonship of Damasias, 582/1); according to another, dependent on Apollodorus, his *acme* was in the 59th Olympiad, 544–541 B.C., and he was a contemporary of Cyrus.[1] The Apollodoran dating thus makes him a generation younger than Thales and a younger contemporary of Anaximander. It accords with the later Pythagorean tradition which made Pythagoras bury Pherecydes (p. 52), though this event was itself probably fictitious. None of these chronological traditions looks particularly historical, and we know that such synchronisms were assigned by the Hellenistic chronographers largely on *a priori* grounds. Yet interest in Pherecydes was certainly alive in the fourth century B.C. (a crucial era for the transmission of information about the archaic period), and the broad limits of dating, i.e. in the sixth century, are unlikely to be wrong.

[1] The early dating is seen e.g. in the Suda (DK 7A2) and in Diog. L. 1, 42 (DK 9A1, after Hermippus). The later dating appears e.g. in Diog. L. 1, 118 (after Aristoxenus) and 1, 121 (after Apollodorus) – see DK 7A1; also in Cicero *Tusc.* 1, 16, 38 (DK 7A5), Pliny *N.H.* VII, 205, Eusebius *Chron.* (DK 7A1a).

PHERECYDES' BOOK

42 Diogenes Laertius I, 119 σώζεται δὲ τοῦ Συρίου τό τε βιβλίον ὃ συνέγραψεν οὗ ἡ ἀρχή· Ζὰς μὲν καὶ Χρόνος ἦσαν ἀεὶ καὶ Χθονίη... (for continuation see **49**).

43 Suda s.v. Pherecydes ἔστι δὲ ἅπαντα ἃ συνέγραψε ταῦτα· Ἑπτάμυχος ἤτοι Θεοκρασία ἢ Θεογονία. (ἔστι δὲ Θεολογία ἐν βιβλίοις ῑ ἔχουσα θεῶν γένεσιν καὶ διαδοχάς.)

44 Diogenes Laertius I, 116 τοῦτόν φησι Θεόπομπος πρῶτον περὶ φύσεως καὶ θεῶν γράψαι. Cf. Suda s.v. Pherecydes πρῶτον δὲ συγγραφὴν ἐξενεγκεῖν πεζῷ λόγῳ τινὲς ἱστοροῦσιν.

> **42** There is preserved of the man of Syros the book which he wrote of which the beginning is: 'Zas and Chronos always existed and Chthonie...'
> **43** Everything he wrote is as follows: Seven Recesses or Divine Mingling or Theogony. (And there is a Theology in ten books containing the birth and successions of the gods.)
> **44** This man is said by Theopompus to have been the first to write on nature and the gods. – Some relate that he was the first to bring out a book in prose.

According to **42** Pherecydes' book (or what was taken for it) survived in Diogenes' time, the third century A.D. The opening words might be known well enough from the entry in Callimachus' catalogue of the Alexandrian library (the patronymic, omitted here, was given shortly before as Βάβυος, 'son of Babys'). That the book survived the burning of the Library in 47 B.C. may be confirmed by a longer quotation, **50**; though this and other fragments could have survived through the medium of handbooks or anthologies. The title is given in **43**. Ἑπτάμυχος, '(of) seven recesses', seems to be the book's true title; variants descriptive of the contents are added, as often, but are probably of later origin.[1] The 'ten-volume theology' is probably a confusion with a ten-volume work on Attic history (itself beginning, no doubt, from gods and heroes) ascribed to the Athenian Pherecydes in the lines that follow in the Suda. The precise reference of the cryptic and unusual title '(of) seven recesses' is very obscure: see pp. 58f. **44** exemplifies the widespread tradition that this was the earliest prose book. What Theopompus (fourth century B.C.) must actually have said is that Pherecydes first wrote about the gods *in prose*, as opposed to e.g. Hesiod. Prose annals were presumably recorded before Pherecydes, but he and Anaximander (whose book may have been roughly contemporary, and might possibly be assigned to 547/6 B.C., pp. 101f.) might well have been the first substantial prose writers to have survived.

¹ Some incline to accept '*five* recesses' from **50** as the title, with Diels followed by Jaeger and others, on the strength of Damascius' statement there that the divine products of Chronos' seed, when disposed in five recesses, were called πεντέμυχος.

HIS LIFE AND LEGEND

(i) *The connexion with Pythagoras*

Many miracles were attributed to Pherecydes, e.g. predictions of an earthquake, a shipwreck, the capture of Messene. These were variously located: in Sparta, near Ephesus, in Samos, in Syros, and so on. The difficulty is that the same miracles were also attributed to Pythagoras. Apollonius the paradoxographer, not certainly using Aristotle, said that 'Pythagoras afterwards indulged in the miracle-working, τερατοποιΐα, of Pherecydes' (DK 14, 7); and it was certainly accepted in the Peripatetic circle that when Pherecydes fell ill of louse-disease in Delos his disciple Pythagoras came and cared for him until his death (Diog. L. I, 118, Diodorus x, 3, 4; DK 7 A 1 and 4). So Aristoxenus asserted, and Dicaearchus too according to Porphyry *Life of Pythagoras* 56. Porphyry also related (as quoted by Eusebius, DK 7 A 6) that according to the fourth-century B.C. writer Andron of Ephesus the miracles belonged properly to Pythagoras; but that Theopompus plagiarized the miracle-stories from Andron and, to disguise his theft, assigned them instead to Pherecydes and slightly altered the localities involved. Andron was far from critical, however, since he invented another Pherecydes of Syros, an astronomer (Diog. L. I, 119, DK 7 A 1); and Porphyry's explanation of the divergence is unconvincing. The confusion and disagreement which patently existed in the fourth century show that reliable details of the life of Pherecydes were lacking. If Pherecydes had been a sage of the type naturally to attract miracle-stories (as Pythagoras was), the connexion between two similar contemporaries would have been invented whether it existed or not; but apart from the feats otherwise attributed to Pythagoras, Pherecydes seems to have had little of the shaman or magician about him. It has been suggested that the whole tissue of legend might have arisen from a well-known fifth-century B.C. comment:

45   Ion of Chios *ap.* Diogenem Laertium I, 120   Ἴων δ' ὁ Χῖός φησι περὶ αὐτοῦ (*sc.* Φερεκύδου)·

ὡς ὁ μὲν ἠνορέῃ τε κεκασμένος ἠδὲ καὶ αἰδοῖ
καὶ φθίμενος ψυχῇ τερπνὸν ἔχει βίοτον,
εἴπερ Πυθαγόρης ἐτύμως σοφός, ὃς περὶ πάντων
ἀνθρώπων γνώμας εἶδε καὶ ἐξέμαθεν.

45   Ion of Chios says about him [Pherecydes]: 'Thus did he excel in manhood and honour, and now that he is dead he has a delightful existence for his soul – if Pythagoras was truly wise, who above all others knew and learned thoroughly the opinions of men.'

As H. Gomperz maintained (*Wiener St.* 47 (1929), 14 n. 3), this probably means no more than 'If Pythagoras is right about the survival of the soul, then Pherecydes' soul should be enjoying a blessed existence'. It might have been misinterpreted, even in antiquity, to imply a friendship between the two men, and have encouraged the transference to Pherecydes of stories about Pythagoras. Elaborate biographical accounts were invented on the slightest pretext, especially in the third and second centuries B.C. (see e.g. p. 182); even so one hesitates to suppose that the fourth-century controversy can have been founded on evidence so slight as Ion's little encomium. Yet none of the evidence on this point looks at all convincing, and it is as well to preserve a high degree of scepticism about the relationship between the two men.

(ii) *Alleged access to Phoenician secret books*

46   Suda s.v. Pherecydes   διδαχθῆναι δὲ ὑπ' αὐτοῦ Πυθαγόραν λόγος, αὐτὸν δὲ οὐκ ἐσχηκέναι καθηγητήν, ἀλλ' ἑαυτὸν ἀσκῆσαι κτησάμενον τὰ Φοινίκων ἀπόκρυφα βιβλία. (See also 60.)

46   There is a story that Pythagoras was taught by him; but that he himself had no instructor, but trained himself after obtaining the secret books of the Phoenicians.

The assertion that Pherecydes was self-taught probably means no more than that no teacher could conveniently be supplied for him when his complete biography came to be written. That he used Phoenician secret books (an unlikely story) is another piece of speculation of the type beloved by the biographical compilers. Yet it must have had some foundation, and may be based on apparently oriental motifs in his thought; he was later connected with Zoroastrianism (n. 2 on pp. 65f.), and the battle of Kronos and Ophioneus, like that of Zeus and Typhoeus in Hesiod, had important Phoenician affinities (p. 68).

(iii) *The solstice-marker*

47 Diogenes Laertius I, 119 σώзεται δὲ τοῦ Συρίου τό τε βιβλίον ...(cf. 49)...σώзεται δὲ καὶ ἡλιοτρόπιον ἐν Σύρῳ τῇ νήσῳ.

48 Homer *Od.* xv, 403–4, with scholia

νῆσός τις Συρίη κικλήσκεται, εἴ που ἀκούεις,
'Ορτυγίης καθύπερθεν, ὅθι τροπαὶ ἠελίοιο.

ὅθι τροπαὶ ἠελίοιο] ἔνθα φασὶν εἶναι ἡλίου σπήλαιον, δι' οὗ σημαιοῦνται τὰς τοῦ ἡλίου τροπάς (QV). οἷον ὡς πρὸς τὰς τροπὰς ἡλίου, ὅ ἐστιν ἐπὶ τὰ δυτικὰ μέρη ὑπεράνωθεν τῆς Δήλου (BHQ). – οὕτως 'Αρίσταρχος καὶ 'Ηρωδιανός (H).

47 There is preserved of the man of Syros the book...[cf. 49] ...and there is preserved also a solstice-marker in the island of Syros.

48 'There is an island called Syrie – perhaps you have heard of it – above Ortygie, where are the turnings of the sun.'

Where are the turnings of the sun] They say there is a cave of the sun there, through which they mark the sun's turnings (QV). As it were toward the turnings of the sun, which is in the westward direction, above Delos (BHQ). – So Aristarchus and Herodian (H).

The implication in **47** that a solstice-marker preserved in Syros in Diogenes' time had belonged to, or been used by, Pherecydes must be approached with caution. (A solstice-marker is a device to mark the point at which the sun 'turns' on the ecliptic, at midsummer or midwinter.) There seems to be some connexion with a cryptic couplet in Homer, **48**. The scholia show that two alternative interpretations of this couplet were known in Alexandria: either (*a*) ὅθι τροπαὶ ἠελίοιο describes Syrie (rather than Ortygie), and means that there was there a bearing-marker in the form of a cave; or (*b*) the meaning is that Syrie lies 'above', i.e. north of, Ortygie, and also west of it, where the sun 'turns' in the sense of setting.[1] Both (*a*) and (*b*) improbably assume that Ortygie represents Delos, and Sȳrie Sȳros (which lies some twenty miles slightly north of west from Delos).[2] Now whatever the intended meaning of the Homeric phrase,[3] there evidently was a sun-cave reported from Syros in the Alexandrian period, and this is presumably the form of marker that Diogenes referred to three or four centuries later. We hear of another type of natural solstice-marker from Itanos in Crete in the fourth century B.C., and such things must have been relatively common for calendar purposes. The sun-cave in Syros cannot, it seems, have been the original motive of the Homeric reference, but it was nevertheless seized upon at a later date (and certainly, one would think, later than Pherecydes) in an attempt to explain the description in the *Odyssey*. Whatever its antecedents, it would as a matter of course have become associated with the island's most notable inhabitant, Pherecydes. Although there is no other evidence that he was a practical scientist, many other sixth-century sages, especially the Milesians, were known to have had applied as well as theoretical interests; and it would be almost inevitable for an Alexandrian scholar, for instance, auto-matically to provide a historical association between the only two apparently scientific products of Syros – Pherecydes and the solstice-marker. Reluctant as one is, therefore, to disconnect such a pleasing device from such an intriguing man, extreme scepticism again seems desirable.

[1] This sense of τροπαί is absolutely unparalleled and highly improbable, especially since τροπαί ἠελίοιο are mentioned three times in the Hesiodic *Works and Days*, always meaning solstice. But (*a*), as well as (*b*), is virtually impossible; for even though τροπαί ἠελίοιο can, and indeed does, mean 'solstice' or 'solstices', it cannot conceivably in any kind of Greek mean a device (whether a cave or anything else) for *marking* or *observing* solstices.

[2] There were other actual Ortygias as well as Delos (to which the name is only applied in contexts which could have been affected by learned speculation on **48**): notably the island forming part of Syracuse, and a precinct near Ephesus. Ὀρτυγίη means 'of the quail' (ὄρτυξ), and might be applied to any locality at which quails habitually rested in their migrations between Egypt and the north. One difficulty in identifying Ortygie with Delos is that the two places are distinguished in the Homeric Hymn to Apollo (16); another is that Συρίη has a short upsilon and Σῦρος a long one. The connexion of Syrie with Syracuse is also philologically improbable. H. L. Lorimer *(Homer and the Monuments* (London, 1950), 8off.) argued for Συρίη referring to Sȳria (which, she maintained, might have been naïvely taken for an island), and for τροπαί meaning 'sunrise', i.e. the east. But it seems impossible that Syria should be termed an island; and the Phoenicians would hardly have been conceived as spending a whole year trading with a place so near their own country (cf. *Od.* xv, 455).

[3] ὅθι τροπαί ἠελίοιο could describe either Syrie or Ortygie. Here another observation of Miss Lorimer's is of great importance: the only other place in Homer where Ortygie is mentioned is *Od.* v, 123, where Orion, having been carried off by Eos, is slain in Ortygie by Artemis. The implication is that Ortygie was the dwelling-place of Eos, the dawn, and therefore that it lies in the east. Miss Lorimer thought that solstices could not carry a directional meaning. But, since solstices would normally be observed at sunrise and in summer, and so in the north-east-by-east direction, that is what the phrase might suggest. Thus the intention may be to indicate the general direction of this probably mythical

Ortygie. In fact the dwelling-place of Eos was often conceived as being *Aia*, commonly identified with Colchis; and Colchis does lie roughly north-east-by-east from the centre of the Ionian coastline.

THE CONTENTS OF HIS BOOK

(i) *The primeval deities; initial creation by Chronos; the recesses*

49 Diogenes Laertius I, 119 σῴζεται δὲ τοῦ Συρίου τό τε βιβλίον ὃ συνέγραψεν οὗ ἡ ἀρχή· (Fr. 1) Ζὰς μὲν καὶ Χρόνος ἦσαν ἀεὶ καὶ Χθονίη· Χθονίη δὲ ὄνομα ἐγένετο Γῆ, ἐπειδὴ αὐτῇ Ζὰς γῆν γέρας διδοῖ.

50 Damascius *de principiis* 124 *bis* Φερεκύδης δὲ ὁ Σύριος Ζάντα μὲν εἶναι ἀεὶ καὶ Χρόνον καὶ Χθονίαν τὰς τρεῖς πρώτας ἀρχάς...τὸν δὲ Χρόνον ποιῆσαι ἐκ τοῦ γόνου ἑαυτοῦ πῦρ καὶ πνεῦμα καὶ ὕδωρ...ἐξ ὧν ἐν πέντε μυχοῖς διηρημένων πολλὴν ἄλλην γενεὰν συστῆναι θεῶν, τὴν πεντέμυχον καλουμένην, ταὐτὸν δὲ ἴσως εἰπεῖν πεντέκοσμον.

49 There is preserved of the man of Syros the book which he wrote of which the beginning is: 'Zas and Chronos always existed and Chthonie; and Chthonie got the name of Ge, since Zas gave her Ge as a present [*or* prerogative].'
50 Pherecydes of Syros said that Zas always existed, and Chronos and Chthonie, as the three first principles...and Chronos made out of his own seed fire and wind [*or* breath] and water...from which, when they were disposed in five recesses, were composed numerous other offspring of gods, what is called 'of the five recesses', which is perhaps the same as saying 'of five worlds'.

Zas and Chronos and Chthonie 'always existed': this resolves the difficulty of creation *ex nihilo*. An analogous declaration is seen, some two generations later, in Heraclitus' world-order, which no god or man made, but always was, and is, and shall be (**217**); and a little later still in Epicharmus fr. 1 (DK 23 B 1 – probably genuine), where the case is explicitly argued. But already in the sixth century B.C. the divinity assigned to Anaximander's ἄπειρον and Anaximenes' air probably implies that these, too, had always existed. It is surprising to find this concept stated so explicitly, of plural beings and in a theogonical context, at this relatively early date. Yet the gods who always existed are probably conceived as original forms (by etymology) of conventional figures from the traditional theogony; and one of them is 'Time', which might naturally be felt, without any deep abstract reflexion, to have been unborn. Thus Pherecydes was not trying to solve a logical difficulty about creation so much as to substitute a new first stage, dependent on etymology and particularly on a new understanding of Kronos the father of the gods, for the imprecise, if more rationalistic, 'Chaos came into being' of Hesiod.

The names are unusual. Ζάς (accusative Ζάντα) is obviously an etymological form of Ζεύς, and is perhaps intended to stress the element 3α- (an intensive prefix), as in 3άθεος, 3αής. Χθονίη, from χθών, is presumably intended to represent Earth in a primitive role, perhaps as the abode of chthonic daimons, and at all events with stress on its under-parts. As for Χρόνος, it has been argued, notably by Wilamowitz, that the true reading must be Κρόνος: Kronos played an important part in Pherecydes' theogony according to one extant fragment, 57, and 'Time' is a sophisticated cosmogonical concept for the sixth century B.C. But Χρόνος, which is widely supported in the sources, is almost certainly correct; the other two figures are etymologizing variants of well-known theogonical figures, and we naturally anticipate a similar case with the third. The substitution of Χρόνος for Κρόνος is just what we should expect here.[1] It appears likely that by the later stages of the theogony the primeval trio assumed their familiar form as Zeus, Kronos and Hera.[2] That Pherecydes was addicted to etymologies emerges clearly from our scanty evidence; thus, in addition to the idiosyncratic derivations of names already discussed, Χάος was perhaps connected by him (as later by the Stoics) with χέεσθαι (p. 60 n.), and so interpreted as water; Rhea was called 'Ρή (DK 7 B 9), and perhaps connected with ῥεῖν etc.; Okeanos was called Ogenos (53); the gods called a table θυωρός, 'watcher over offerings' (DK 7 B 12).

---

[1] Wilamowitz roundly declared that 'Time', as a cosmogonical god in the sixth century, was impossible. Certainly the abstraction implied in the χρόνου δίκη (Solon, see 111), or τὴν τοῦ χρόνου τάξιν (Anaximander, see 110), is less start-ling in its implications, as are the Χρόνος ὁ πάντων πατήρ of Pindar Ol. 2, 17 and the hypostatized Time of tragedy; though the two last instances provide some parallel. The Iranian cosmogonical Time, Zvran Akarana, was introduced as a refinement of Mazdaism and cannot be assumed earlier than the fourth cen-tury B.C. (n. on p. 22), though the possibility of oriental influence in this respect cannot be entirely discounted. The Chronos of the late Orphic cosmogonies was presented in a Hellenistic shape, and cannot be taken as any kind of parallel or precedent for the sixth century B.C. The connexion of Kronos with Chronos was certainly made by later Orphics (cf. e.g. Kern Orph. Frag. fr. 68), but according to Plutarch (de Is. et Osir. 32) this was a common Greek identification; we cannot say whether or not Pherecydes was the originator.

[2] Chthonie gets the name of Ge, Earth, at a subsequent stage, presumably when Zas presents her with the cloth embroidered with earth in 53. But at that point she apparently takes over the control and guardianship of marriages; this was

57

Hera's prerogative (as Γαμηλία) according to the general view, and in so far as Chthonie-Ge is the wife of Zas-Zeus she is also thought of as becoming Hera. Hera was probably not an earth-goddess in origin, but there are other isolated cases where she replaces Gaia; for example, she appears to be the mother of Typhaon in the Homeric Hymn to Apollo, 351f., also in Stesichorus (*Et. Magn.* 772. 50); cf. **52**, and Virgil *Aen.* IV, 166.

Damascius in **50** is following Eudemus. Chronos makes fire, wind and water out of his own seed,[1] and this is implied to take place at an early stage. The episode cannot be entirely invented, though it would not be surprising if some details were distorted. One is reminded of Egyptian cosmogonical accounts in which the first world-constituents are produced by the onanism of a primeval god, notably that of Atum-Re mentioned in the Memphis theology (*ANET*, 5); and also of the mutilation of Ouranos *by Kronos* in **39**, where certain mythological figures are begotten by Ouranos' member and the blood from it. The idea that the human seed is creative, and therefore that a primary deity's seed is cosmogonically creative, is neither surprising nor illogical. What is surprising here, however, is the things which are thus created: they smack of fifth-century four-element theory, earth being omitted because already accounted for in the very name of Chthonie-Ge. πνεῦμα looks suspiciously anachronistic, even though Anaximenes emphasized its importance at roughly this period (pp. 144ff.). These substances cannot have formed the raw material of later cosmic arrangement, for according to **50** what they produce is not a world but deities of some kind. In fact, we would suggest that the seed producing fire, wind (πνεῦμα) and water is probably a later rationalizing interpretation, perhaps Stoic in origin but based on the Aristotelian concept (itself to some extent indebted to Diogenes of Apollonia, cf. **616** *fin.*) that the human σπέρμα, seed, contains σύμφυτον πνεῦμα, innate breath, which is also described as being 'hot' and aitherial (cf. e.g. *de gen. animalium* B3, 736b33ff.). In accounts of early Stoic physiology, too, the seed is described as πνεῦμα μεθ' ὑγροῦ ('breath with moisture', Arius Didymus on Zeno) and is associated with πνεῦμα ἔνθερμον, 'warm breath'. It therefore seems probable that the three unexpected products of Chronos' seed – fire, wind and water – are an intrusive later interpretation of the nature of the seed itself, and that originally it was Chronos' semen that was placed in the recesses. As for these, the seven in the title as given in the Suda might be obtained by adding to the five recesses connected with Chronos in **50** the two other pre-existing deities Zas and Chthonie, the latter of which, certainly, had a local and indeed a recess-like connotation.

Alternatively all seven recesses could have been part of Chthonie; it is notable that the Babylonian world of the dead was conceived as having seven regions,[2] and in the myth of the Descent of Ishtar, Ishtar has to pass through seven gates (*ANET*, 107f.).[3]

[1] Or possibily, if Kern's αὐτοῦ for MS ἑαυτοῦ is right, out of Zas'. But there is no essential conflict with **41**, where τὸ γεννῆσαν πρῶτον must be Zas-Zeus; for it is Zas who first creates the parts of the world (**53**), while Chronos produces theogonical, not cosmogonical, constituents.

[2] In the first eleven chapters of the Hippocratic treatise Περὶ ἑβδομάδων the world is divided into seven parts to correspond with the seven parts of the human body. Some scholars date this fragmentary and unattractive work in the sixth century B.C. There seem to be no strong grounds for such an early date, and stylistically a fourth-century B.C. origin is more probable.

[3] Compare the doors and gates that Porphyry found in Pherecydes: **51** Porphyrius *de antro nymph.* 31 ...τοῦ Συρίου Φερεκύδου μυχοὺς καὶ βόθρους καὶ ἄντρα καὶ θύρας καὶ πύλας λέγοντος καὶ διὰ τούτων αἰνιττομένου τὰς τῶν ψυχῶν γενέσεις καὶ ἀπογενέσεις (...*when Pherecydes, the man of Syros, talks of recesses and pits and caves and doors and gates, and through these speaks in riddles of the becomings and deceases of souls*). The recesses, pits and caves suggest that something more elaborate than mere depressions in the earth was in question.

A possible clue to the production by Chronos from his own seed appears in the following:

52 Σb *in* Homeri *Il.* II, 783   φασὶ τὴν Γῆν ἀγανακτοῦσαν ἐπὶ τῷ φόνῳ τῶν Γιγάντων διαβαλεῖν Δία τῇ Ἥρᾳ· τὴν δὲ πρὸς Κρόνον ἀπελθοῦσαν ἐξειπεῖν· τὸν δὲ δοῦναι αὐτῇ δύο ᾠά, τῷ ἰδίῳ χρίσαντα θορῷ καὶ κελεύσαντα κατὰ γῆς ἀποθέσθαι, ἀφ' ὧν ἀναδοθήσεται δαίμων ὁ ἀποστήσων Δία τῆς ἀρχῆς. ἡ δέ, ὡς εἶχεν ὀργῆς, ἔθετο αὐτὰ ὑπὸ τὸ Ἄριμον τῆς Κιλικίας. ἀναδοθέντος δὲ τοῦ Τυφῶνος Ἥρα διαλλαγεῖσα Διὶ τὸ πᾶν ἐκφαίνει· ὁ δὲ κεραυνώσας Αἴτνην τὸ ὄρος ὠνόμασεν.

52 They say that Ge in annoyance at the slaughter of the Giants slandered Zeus to Hera, and that Hera went off and told Kronos about this. He gave her two eggs, smearing them with his own semen, and telling her to store them underground: from them, he said, a daimon would be produced who would displace Zeus from power. And she in her anger put them under Arimon in Cilicia. But when Typhon had been produced, Hera had become reconciled to Zeus, and revealed everything; and Zeus blasted Typhon and named the mountain Aetna.

The exegetical class of older Homeric scholia retains much learned material from the Hellenistic era (so H. Erbse, *Scholia Graeca in Homeri Iliadem* I (Berlin, 1969), xii). This particular comment adds a Homeric element (Arimon) to those seen in fifth-century poetry (Pindar *Pyth.* 1, 16ff., Aeschylus *Pr.* 351ff.). Orphic influence is also possible, although the eggs are placed not in the windy wastes of Aither or Erebos (as in the Rhapsodic account) but in Gaia. That Kronos not Chronos is named is not necessarily important (see p. 57). The notable thing is that Kronos impregnates two eggs (why two?) *with his own seed*, and that the eggs have to be placed *underground*, κατὰ γῆς, possibly in a recess of some kind – here, under a mountain. From the eggs, when fertilized by the seed, comes Typhon/Typhoeus, an analogue of Pherecydes' Ophioneus (pp. 66ff.). There does seem to be a striking parallel with the cryptic mention of Chronos' seed in **50**; if so, it provides some confirmation of the speculation that some kind of theogonical figure or figures ('numerous other divine offspring') came directly from Chronos' seed.[1] It makes a faint possibility, too, that generation from an egg (but not of cosmological constituents) occurred in Pherecydes (see pp. 26–9) – though this device became so popular in Hellenistic and later accounts that it might well have been imposed on a simpler story.

[1] Porphyry (cf. DK 7 B 7) mentioned people who took what he called τὴν ἐκροήν, in Pherecydes, to refer to semen; though they applied the same interpretation to Hesiod's Styx and Plato's Ameles. H. Gomperz (*Wiener St.* 47 (1929), 19 n. 10) suggested that Chronos produced a generation of primeval deities from the ἐκροή, just as his later form Kronos did from Rhea; this would in fact fit in with the suggestion made above, that fire, wind and water are an intrusive gloss. The connexion of Rhea, called 'Ρῆ by Pherecydes (DK 7 B 9), with ἐκροή seems quite possible. A further but more remote possibility is that Chronos' semen became primeval water. We are told in one source (Achilles *Isag.* 3, DK 7 B 1 a) that Pherecydes, like Thales, declared the element to be water, which he called χάος (presumably deriving it from χέεσθαι, if the whole thing is not Stoic accommodation). The Suda, too, says that 'he imitated the opinion of Thales' (DK 7 A 2); though Sextus, on the other hand, said that his principle was earth (DK 7 A 10). Great penetration is not to be sought in these interpretations, but it does seem probable that Pherecydes understood Hesiod's Chaos in a special sense, perhaps because of a specious etymology. The surviving fragments show that there was no question of water coming first; but the special interpretation of Chaos may have been connected with Chronos' seed at a relatively early stage of cosmic development.

(ii) *The wedding of Zas and Chthonie and the embroidering of the cloth*

53 Grenfell and Hunt *Greek Papyri* Ser. II, no. 11, p. 23 (3rd cent. A.D.) (DK 7 B 2) αὐ⟩τῷ ποιοῦσιν τὰ οἰκία πολλά τε καὶ μεγάλα. ἐπεὶ δὲ ταῦτα ἐξετέλεσαν πάντα καὶ χρήματα καὶ θεράποντας καὶ θεραπαίνας καὶ τἆλλα ὅσα δεῖ πάντα, ἐπεὶ δὴ πάντα ἑτοῖμα γίγνεται τὸν γάμον ποιεῦσιν. κἀπειδὴ τρίτη ἡμέρη γίγνεται τῷ γάμῳ, τότε

Ζὰς ποιεῖ φᾶρος μέγα τε καὶ καλὸν καὶ ἐν αὐτῷ ⟨ποικίλλει Γῆν⟩ καὶ
'Ωγη⟨νὸν καὶ τὰ 'Ω⟩γηνοῦ ⟨δώματα *** [col. 2] βουλόμενος⟩ γὰρ
σέο τοὺς γάμους εἶναι τούτῳ σε τι⟨μῶ⟩. σὺ δέ μοι χαῖρε καὶ σύνισθι.
ταῦτά φασιν ἀνακαλυπτήρια πρῶτον γενέσθαι· ἐκ τούτου δὲ ὁ νόμος
ἐγένετο καὶ θεοῖσι καὶ ἀνθ⟨ρώποι⟩σιν. ἡ δέ μι⟨ν ἀμείβε⟩ται δεξα-
μ⟨ένη εὐ τὸ⟩ φᾶ⟨ρος...⟩[1]

[1] The attribution to Pherecydes, and the supplements of ⟨ποικίλλει...⟩ to
⟨δώματα⟩, are confirmed by Clement of Alexandria *Strom.* VI, 9, 4, Φ. ὁ Σύριος
λέγει· Ζὰς ποιεῖ φᾶρος...'Ωγηνοῦ δώματα. Other supplements by Blass, Weil,
Diels; text as in DK, except for alterations to the slightly erroneous record there
of gaps in the papyrus.

53 His halls they make for him, many and vast. And when they
had accomplished all these, and the furniture and manservants
and maidservants and everything else necessary, when everything
was ready, they hold the wedding. And on the third day of the
wedding Zas makes a great and fair cloth and on it he decorates
Ge and Ogenos and the halls of Ogenos*** 'for wishing [*or some
such word*] marriages to be yours, I honour you with this. Hail to
you, and be my consort.' And this they say was the first Anacalypteria: from this the custom arose both for gods and for men.
And she replies, receiving from him the cloth....

The marriage is between Zas and Chthonie, as is confirmed by **56**.
Zas' declaration 'desiring [*or some such word*] marriages to belong
to you' suggests strongly that Chthonie is here partially equated with
Hera, the goddess of marriage (n. 2 on pp. 57f.) The preparations
are of a fairly-tale quality, and are carried out by unspecified agents.
On the third day of the wedding festivities[1] Zas makes a great cloth,
decorating it with Ge (earth) and Ōgēnos (evidently Pherecydes'
name for Okeanos).[2] He presents it to Chthonie; the gift of this
representation of Ge seems to be what was referred to in **49**, where
Chthonie took the name Ge 'since Zas gave her earth as a gift [*or
prerogative*]'. With the cloth he also gives her Ogenos, which may
be regarded as a part of the earth's surface in the broad sense but
is not a prerogative of Chthonie in the way that Ge is. Chthonie
initially represents the solid structure of earth rather than its
variegated surface, Ge and Ogenos. Now the main question is
whether the weaving or embroidering of earth and Okeanos is an
allegory of an actual creation-act. It seems probable that it is;
otherwise, what is the point of Zas undertaking this odd and
unmasculine task – one very different, for example, from Hephaestus' decoration of the shield of Achilles in *Iliad* book XVIII? Not simply

to symbolize the gift of Ge, or as a mythological precedent for the Anacalypteria, the Unveiling of the bride; there is this aetiological element in the story, as is explicitly stated, but the gift need not have been of this bizarre kind if it had no more significance than that of an Unveiling-gift.[3] A more positive indication is provided in the following:

54 Proclus *in Tim.* II, p. 54 Diehl ὁ Φερεκύδης ἔλεγεν εἰς Ἔρωτα μεταβεβλῆσθαι τὸν Δία μέλλοντα δημιουργεῖν, ὅτι δὴ τὸν κόσμον ἐκ τῶν ἐναντίων συνιστὰς εἰς ὁμολογίαν καὶ φιλίαν ἤγαγε καὶ ταυτότητα πᾶσιν ἐνέσπειρε καὶ ἕνωσιν τὴν δι' ὅλων διήκουσαν.

54 Pherecydes used to say that Zeus had changed into Eros when about to create, for the reason that, having composed the world from the opposites, he led it into agreement and peace and sowed sameness in all things, and unity that interpenetrates the universe.

The whole of this from ὅτι δή onwards is palpably Stoic interpretation with a slight Neoplatonic colouring, and tells us nothing about Pherecydes. The first statement, however, that Zeus turned into Eros when about to create, must be based on something in Pherecydes. It suggests first that Zas did undertake some kind of cosmogonical creation, and secondly that he did so as Eros, or at least in some erotic situation. This might appear to mean no more than the liaisons and births of the *Theogony*; but that some particular description was envisaged is shown also by **56**, in which a specific Eros exists between Zas and Chthonie.[4] This tells us clearly that Zas' creation is concerned with an erotic situation between himself and Chthonie; the wedding itself may, therefore, be meant, and since we hear nothing of any offspring of cosmogonical relevance, while the depiction of earth and Okeanos (whether surrounding river, or sea in general) is the prelude to the consummation of the marriage and could well represent a cosmogonical act, we may provisionally accept that such is the case – especially after consideration of **55** below.

[1] Wedding ceremonies took three days in all, the final unveiling accompanied by gifts, and the consummation, taking place on the third; so Hesychius s.v., who put the ἀνακαλυπτήρια on the third day, though all other ancient authorities (none of them early) imply that the whole ceremony took only one day.

[2] Ogēnos (Ogĕnos in Lycophron and Stephanus of Byzantium) is an odd variant of Ὠκεανός, on which see p. 12 n. 2. Pherecydes' use of it is another indication of his preference for archaizing or etymological forms.

[3] A πέπλος was given to Harmonia by Cadmus at their wedding (Apollodorus III, 4, 2), but we are not told that it was decorated in any particular way, and

Cadmus did not make it. Nor does there seem to be more than an adventitious connexion with the ἱερὸς γάμος at Plataea (cf. L. R. Farnell, *The Cults of the Greek States* 1 (Oxford, 1896), 244), in which a statue carved from an oak-tree was dressed as a bride to represent Hera.
[4] Cf. the golden-winged Eros who is imagined as groomsman at the wedding of Zeus and Hera in the hymeneal song in Aristophanes, *Birds* 1737ff.

(iii) *The winged oak and the cloth*

55 Isidorus (the Gnostic, 1st–2nd cent. A.D.) *ap.* Clement. Al. *Strom.* vi, 53, 5 (DK 7 B 2) ...ἵνα μάθωσι τί ἐστιν ἡ ὑπόπτερος δρῦς καὶ τὸ ἐπ' αὐτῇ πεποικιλμένον φᾶρος, πάντα ὅσα Φερεκύδης ἀλληγορήσας ἐθεολόγησεν, λαβὼν ἀπὸ τῆς τοῦ Χὰμ προφητείας τὴν ὑπόθεσιν.

56 Maximus Tyrius iv, 4, p. 45, 5 Hobein ἀλλὰ καὶ τοῦ Συρίου τὴν ποίησιν σκόπει καὶ τὸν Ζῆνα καὶ τὴν Χθονίην καὶ τὸν ἐν τούτοις Ἔρωτα, καὶ τὴν Ὀφιονέως γένεσιν καὶ τὴν θεῶν μάχην καὶ τὸ δένδρον καὶ τὸν πέπλον.

55 ...that they may learn what is the winged oak and the decorated cloth upon it, all that Pherecydes said in allegory about the gods, taking his idea from the prophecy of Ham.
56 But consider also the work of the man of Syros, and Zas and Chthonie and the Eros between them, and the birth of Ophioneus and the battle of gods and the tree and the robe.

We learn in **55** that the embroidered cloth (i.e. that given by Zas to Chthonie in **53**) was somehow on a winged oak; this must also be what 'the tree and the robe' refer to in **56**. One modern suggestion (by H. Gomperz, *Wiener St.* 47 (1929), 22) is that the oak represents the frame of the loom on which Zas made the cloth. This involves taking ὑπόπτερος to mean simply 'swift', with total suppression of the concrete wing-image; there is no parallel for such a use with a concrete subject. More serious, a loom could hardly be called an *oak-tree*, simply, even in a fantastic context. According to another interpretation (Diels, *SB Ber.* 1897, 147f.) the oak resembles the mast on which Athene's *peplos* was carried in the Panathenaic procession. It is true that **56** uses the word πέπλος, and 'winged' might be explained as describing the cross-piece on which the robe was hung; but there is really no reason whatever for thinking of the Panathenaia, and to refer to the mast as an oak would be distinctly odd.[1] Both Diels and K. von Fritz (author of the article on Pherecydes in Pauly-Wissowa) believed that an allegorical version of *Anaximander* is also in question: the earth is shaped like a tree-trunk because it is cylindrical as in Anaximander (see **122**); it is described as a tree because Anaximander said that a sphere of flame fitted round air and earth like the bark round a tree (**121**); the earth is winged because it floats free in space (**123**); the embroidering of its surface is reminiscent of Anaximander's map (pp. 104f.); and the treatment of Okeanos as an integral part of the earth's surface is a new development found also in Anaximander. But none of these arguments is valid, let alone cogent: the shape of the earth cannot be represented by the shape of the trunk alone, which is not the only or even the most conspicuous part of an oak-tree; Anaximander's bark round a tree is a *simile*; 'winged', if it is to be given an abstract connotation at all, would tend to mean 'swift-moving' rather than 'floating'; Anaximander's map had no known connexion with his cosmology; and the tendency to integrate Okeanos with the inner seas is occasionally detectable even in Homer. Other alleged borrowings from Anaximander (Time, and γόνος ~ γόνιμον) are no more convincingly in favour of an interpretation which von Fritz was over-optimistic in calling 'practically certain'.

[1] Diels, followed by e.g. Jaeger, Mondolfo and von Fritz, was impressed by the whole context (DK 7 B 5) of **59** below, where Origen reports that Celsus interpreted certain rites and mythological incidents as symbolizing the subjection of matter by god. Two passages in Homer, then Pherecydes' description of Tartaros (**59**), and finally the Panathenaic *peplos* are so interpreted; the last is said to show 'that a motherless and immaculate deity prevails over the boastful Earthborn', and it did, of course, traditionally represent the victory of Athena over Enceladus in the battle of gods and giants. The interpretation is quoted as a separate instance, parallel to the Pherecydes extract because adduced as another illustration of the same thesis; but there is nothing to suggest that Pherecydes should be interpreted *in terms of* the Panathenaia.

The following interpretation is proposed as more probable than any of those described above. The oak represents the solidly fixed substructure and foundations of the earth (the 'frame' of the earth, Zeller suggested). Its trunk and branches are the support and roots of the earth. That the earth has roots is part of the popular world-picture (pp. 9f.), and a tree's branches, in winter, appear as large inverted roots. That the roots of earth *and* sea were sometimes conceived as being above Tartarus, and that Tartarus itself could be imagined as a narrower pit beneath, is clearly shown by the important description at *Theogony* 726ff., already quoted as **2**: 'Around Tartarus a brazen fence is drawn; and all about it Night in three rows is poured, around the throat; and above are the roots of earth and unharvested sea.' The throat or neck that is Tartarus (or a part of it) corresponds with the trunk of the oak-tree, the roots which are above it correspond with the branches.[1] The oak is 'winged' partly, at least, because of the spreading, wing-like appearance of these same branches. On them Zas has laid the cloth embroidered with Earth and Ogenos; these represent the earth's surface, flat or slightly convex, rather, as indeed it appears to be. We cannot say whether Ogenos is conceived as a surrounding river or as the sea. The oak is specified because it is associated more than any other tree with Zeus (cf. the prophetic oaks in his shrine at Dodona, *Od.* xiv, 328), and because of its notable strength and the great spread of its branches. Thus according to the interpretation offered here Zas must have chosen, or magically grown, a broad oak as the foundation of the earth; or (following a suggestion by T. B. L. Webster) he summoned an oak from afar which magically flies to him, using its branches as wings. Zas then weaves a cloth, decorating it with earth and Okeanos, and lays the embroidered cloth on the outspread branches of the oak to form the earth's surface.[2]

[1] **59** mentions Tartaros below the earth, which suggests that Pherecydes broadly accepted the popular world-picture, not the rationalized construction of Anaximander. The kind of world-tree postulated above must be distinguished from e.g. the Scandinavian world-tree *Yggdrasil*, whose branches form *the heavens*, not the support for the earth's surface; though the roots of the tree are regarded as supporting the earth.

[2] A clue to the meaning of the winged oak and the cloth is apparently given by Isidorus' comment in **55** that Pherecydes 'took the supposition from the prophecy of Ham'. Unfortunately, little can be determined about this work. Harnack suggested that Ham in this context is a name for Zoroaster (Bidez and Cumont, *Les Mages hellénisés* II (Paris, 1938), 62 n.); this identification was occasionally made, cf. *op. cit.* I, 43; II, 49–50. Zoroaster was well established as a sage by the early Hellenistic period, and Aristoxenus had stated that Pythagoras visited Zoroaster in Babylon (Hippolytus *Ref.* I, 2, 12; DK 14, 11). Of the vast mass of pseudo-Zoroastrian literature produced in the Hellenistic epoch, there was a work *On Nature* in four books, and special accounts of the magical properties of stones and plants, as well as descriptions of Hades. The book on nature seems to have contained nothing of cosmogonical interest, but, like the rest, to have dealt with astrology, minerals and so on. A second wave of Zoroastrian literature was produced in the first two centuries A.D. by various Gnostic sects – in the Clementine apocrypha, by the Sethians, by the disciples of Prodicus. More of genuine Zoroastrianism (dualism of good and evil, importance of fire) was to be found in these works than in the earlier group. It is a question to which group Isidorus was referring; though the facts that Isidorus' father Basilides inclined to Iranian dualism, and that the Ham–Zoroaster identification is probably first found in a Gnostic source, suggest that it was the later one. On the other hand Isidorus is less likely to have been taken in by a product of his own age. But in neither group can we detect anything which might have been regarded as a significant precedent for the winged oak or the embroidered cloth; we cannot even assume that Isidorus was struck by the oriental character of Pherecydes'

allegory, since much of the Greek Zoroastrian literature was not oriental in origin or colouring. One cannot be certain that Pherecydes' allegory had not itself been absorbed into some pseudo-Zoroastrian source, and so misled Isidorus.

(iv) The fight between Kronos and Ophioneus

57 Celsus *ap.* Origen. *c. Celsum* VI, 42 (DK 7 B 4) Φερεκύδην δὲ πολλῷ ἀρχαιότερον γενόμενον Ἡρακλείτου μυθοποιεῖν στρατείαν στρατείᾳ παραταττομένην καὶ τῆς μὲν ἡγεμόνα Κρόνον ⟨ἀπο⟩διδόναι, τῆς ἑτέρας δ' Ὀφιονέα, προκλήσεις τε καὶ ἁμίλλας αὐτῶν ἱστορεῖν, συνθήκας τε αὐτοῖς γίγνεσθαι ἵν' ὁπότεροι αὐτῶν εἰς τὸν Ὠγηνὸν ἐμπέσωσι, τούτους μὲν εἶναι νενικημένους, τοὺς δ' ἐξώσαντας καὶ νικήσαντας, τούτους ἔχειν τὸν οὐρανόν.

58 Apollonius Rhodius I, 503 (following **38**)
(Ὀρφεύς) ἤειδεν δ' ὡς πρῶτον Ὀφίων Εὐρυνόμη τε
    Ὠκεανὶς νιφόεντος ἔχον κράτος Οὐλύμποιο·
    ὥς τε βίη καὶ χερσὶν ὁ μὲν Κρόνῳ εἴκαθε τιμῆς,
    ἡ δὲ Ῥέη, ἔπεσον δ' ἐνὶ κύμασιν Ὠκεανοῖο·
    οἱ δὲ τέως μακάρεσσι θεοῖς Τιτῆσιν ἄνασσον,
    ὄφρα Ζεὺς ἔτι κοῦρος ἔτι φρεσὶ νήπια εἰδὼς
    Δικταῖον ναίεσκεν ὑπὸ σπέος...

59 Celsus *ap.* Origen. *c. Celsum* VI, 42 (DK 7 B 5) ταῦτα δὲ τὰ Ὁμήρου ἔπη οὕτω νοηθέντα τὸν Φερεκύδην φησὶν (*sc.* Κέλσος) εἰρηκέναι τὸ (fr. 5) Κείνης δὲ τῆς μοίρας ἔνερθέν ἐστιν ἡ Ταρταρίη μοῖρα· φυλάσσουσι δ' αὐτὴν θυγατέρες Βορέου Ἅρπυιαί τε καὶ Θύελλα· ἔνθα Ζεὺς ἐκβάλλει θεῶν ὅταν τις ἐξυβρίσῃ.

57 Pherecydes, who lived much earlier than Heraclitus, made the myth that army was drawn up against army, and he gave Kronos as leader of one, Ophioneus of the other, and recounted their challenges and struggles, and that they made an agreement that whichever of them fell into Ogenos, these were the vanquished, while those who thrust them out and were victorious were to possess the sky.

58 He [Orpheus] sang how first of all Ophion and Eurynome, daughter of Okeanos, held sway over snowy Olympus; and how by strength of hands the former yielded his lordship to Kronos, the latter to Rhea, and they fell in the waves of Okeanos; and the other two meantime held sway over the blessed gods, the Titans, while Zeus, still a boy and still having childish thoughts in his heart, dwelt by the Dictaean cave...

59 [Celsus] says that with this interpretation of these Homeric lines in mind Pherecydes has said: 'Below that portion is the portion of Tartaros; the daughters of Boreas, the Harpies, and Storm, guard it; there Zeus expels whosoever of the gods behaves insolently.'

Pherecydes evidently described in some detail an encounter between Kronos (probably derived from the primeval deity Chronos: see p. 57) and Ophioneus, the preliminaries of which appear in 57. This must form part, at least, of 'the battle of gods' in Maximus' summary (56). Ophioneus is obviously connected with ὄφις, snake, and is a snake-like monster of the type of Typhoeus in the Hesiodic *Theogony* (line 825, Typhoeus had a hundred snake-heads). The battle with Kronos is otherwise known from rare Hellenistic references, of which the description in 58 is the most important. There, Ophion (as he is there called) has a consort, the Oceanic Eurynome, while Kronos is helped by Rhea. There are enough divergences to suggest that Apollonius is not merely copying Pherecydes,[1] and it seems that there was an old story, not mentioned in Hesiod, which formed part of the manifold lost mythology of Kronos and related his encounter with a monster. In Pherecydes the victor is to have possession of the sky (and so become, or remain, supreme god); according to Apollonius in 58 (supported by a scholion on Aristophanes *Clouds* 247) Ophion and Eurynome had already ruled on Olympus and were trying to repel a challenge. There may be a reference here to the concept of Okeanos and Tethys as the first gods (8, 9); Eurynome was a daughter of Okeanos,[2] and with Ophion may represent a second generation replacing, somehow, that of Ouranos and Gaia. Yet in Pherecydes there is nothing to suggest that Ophioneus had ever ruled the sky; Maximus in 56 mentions 'the birth of Ophioneus and the battle of gods', which may suggest that Ophioneus was, like Typhoeus in Hesiod, an unsuccessful challenger for power; and Tertullian (*de corona* 7, DK 7B4) asserted that according to Pherecydes Kronos was the first king of the gods. Further, Pherecydes cannot have accepted the usual view, seen in Apollonius, that Zeus was a child in Crete during part of the reign of Kronos. The primeval Zas probably turned into Zeus (*Zeus* not *Zas* occurs in 59; though this could be due to carelessness in the transmission), just as Chronos probably turned into Kronos, and this would scarcely be by the medium of a birth. In Pherecydes, as in the common version, Kronos-Chronos must have eventually been deposed by Zas, to be despatched below the earth (as in Homer, *Il.* xiv, 203f., and Hesiod). Unfortunately 59, which locates the 'portion' of Tartaros below, presumably, that of Gaia (rather than of Hades in the sense of *Il.* viii, 16), does not mention

Kronos; it seems to come from a description of the assignment of parts of the cosmos to different deities, which followed Zeus' final subjection of his adversaries in Homer and Hesiod also.

[1] Nor need we believe that Apollonius was reproducing an ancient Orphic account. There is a great deal in this cosmogony and theogony as sung by Orpheus in the *Argonautica* that is not Orphic (see also **38** and n. 2 on p. 43).

[2] Also at *Il.* xviii, 398ff.; *Theog.* 358. At *Theog.* 295ff. another Oceanid, Callirhoe, produced the snake-woman Echidna, who mated with Typhaon.

The battle of Kronos against Ophion has obvious correspondences with that of Zeus against Typhoeus in the *Theogony*. The cosmic fight with a snake-god is not, of course, exclusive to Greece, but is found all over the Near East long before Hesiod, in both Semitic and Indo-European contexts. Compare the fight of Marduk with the serpent-aided Tiamat in the Babylonian creation-myth (*ANET*, 62ff.); the victory of the storm-god over the dragon Illuyanka in the Hurrian-Hittite story of that name (*ANET*, 125f.; Gurney, *The Hittites*, 181ff.); and the nightly overcoming of the dragon Apophis by the Egyptian sun-god Re in his journey under the earth (*ANET*, 6–7). The battle between Zeus and Typhoeus-Typhon (who was equated with the Egyptian Seth) was in later accounts, though not in Hesiod, located in Cilicia, especially on Mount Casius near the proto-Phoenician Minoan *entrepôt* of Ras-Shamra/Ugarit. It clearly coincided with a local version of the sky-god and snake-monster motif, and this correspondence may have been the chief motive for the assertion that Pherecydes borrowed from the Phoenicians:

60 Philo Byblius *ap.* Eusebium *P.E.* 1, 10, 50 παρὰ Φοινίκων δὲ καὶ Φερεκύδης λαβὼν τὰς ἀφορμὰς ἐθεολόγησε περὶ τοῦ παρ' αὐτῷ λεγομένου Ὀφιονέως θεοῦ καὶ τῶν Ὀφιονιδῶν.[1]

[1] It is a question whether the Ὀφιονίδαι are literally 'the children of Ophioneus', or simply his army or supporters, cf. **57**. If the former, one may compare the monsters born to Typhaon by Echidna at *Theogony* 306ff. – though these are not involved in the Typhoeus episode.

60 From the Phoenicians Pherecydes, too, took his impulse, when he wrote about him whom he called the god Ophioneus, and the children of Ophioneus.

The earlier parallel of the Hesiodic Typhoeus makes it unnecessary to suppose that Pherecydes was borrowing directly from an oriental source, and one may wonder whether the reference in the Suda (**46**) to his access to Phoenician secret books was based on anything more than the Ophioneus–Typhon comparison.

THE ORDER OF EVENTS IN PHERECYDES' BOOK

The evidence reviewed in the preceding pages presents us with a number of phases described by Pherecydes: (a) the three pre-existing deities; (b) the making by Chronos out of his own seed of things disposed in five recesses, which produce other generations of gods; (c) the making of the cloth by Zas, the depiction on it of Earth and Ogenos, the wedding of Zas and Chthonie, and the presentation of the cloth, followed (?) by the spreading of it over the winged oak; (d) the battle between Kronos and Ophioneus; (e) the assignment of portions to different deities, perhaps implied in **59**.

Several incidents must have taken place about which we possess no information; for example, Chronos-Kronos was presumably supplanted by Zas-Zeus, as in the common account, but Pherecydes' views here are unknown. Another problem is the birth of Ophioneus mentioned in Maximus' summary, **56**: who were the parents? It seems unlikely that Zas and Chthonie were (although all mythological weddings have offspring, and we do not know the offspring of this particular one), since it must be assumed that the battle of Kronos and Ophioneus, the reward of which is possession of the sky, takes place either during or as a prelude to the rule of Chronos-Kronos, which seems to have preceded the wedding of Zas and Chthonie and the assumed creation of earth and Okeanos. But a difficulty arises here. In the fight between Ophioneus and Kronos the loser is to be he who falls into Ogenos; but according to the creation-allegory interpretation Ogenos is made at the wedding of Zas and Chthonie, which should therefore precede and not follow the Ophioneus-fight. This difficulty applies to all reconstructions that make the weaving of the cloth a creation-allegory; for Chronos' mastery of the sky is suggested by all the other evidence (especially **50** and the analogy of the Homeric–Hesiodic account) to have preceded the period of Zas' activity. Either, therefore, Pherecydes was inconsistent in pre-supposing Ogenos before it had been formally created; or Ogenos existed *before* it was woven into or embroidered on the cloth; or Ogenos is not an original element in Celsus' account of the Kronos–Ophioneus fight. The last of these hypotheses is not impossible. A somewhat different version of this encounter is known from the Hellenistic period, and is best seen in **58**. There Ophion and his bride Eurynome, the daughter of Okeanos, ruled the sky, but were forcibly displaced by Kronos and Rhea and *fell into the waves of Okeanos*. Falling into Okeanos makes sense for an *Oceanid* and her consort; but in Pherecydes there seems to be no place for a female consort of any kind, let alone an Oceanid. It is possible, therefore, that Celsus or his source transferred into the Pherecydes version a detail from a rather different Hellenistic version, and adapted it to the known Pherecydean terminology.

Yet if Zas and Chthonie cannot *jointly* have produced Ophioneus after their wedding, it remains true that the earth-goddess Chthonie-Ge is the obvious parent for a snake (whose home is traditionally in the earth), just as Gaia is normally the mother of the snakish Typhoeus. A liaison between Zas and Chthonie *before* their marriage (as suggested by *Il.* xiv, 296) would fit the order of **56**: the passion of Zas and Chthonie, the birth of Ophioneus, the battle of gods, the tree and the robe (and, therefore, the marriage). But there is no strong reason for assuming that Maximus set down these themes in the exact order in which they occurred in Pherecydes' book; and the dramatic force of the description of the wedding, which has obvious literary pretensions, would undoubtedly be weakened if Zas and Chthonie had been living together for ages beforehand. It seems more probable that if Ophioneus was the child of Chthonie the father, if any, was other than Zas. Here Chronos springs to mind. His seed was placed in 'recesses', presumably in the earth, according to **50**; and there was a story, known only from **52** and not connected there with Pherecydes, that Kronos impregnated two eggs with his seed, gave the eggs to Hera to place underground, and so produced the snakish Typhoeus (to whom Ophioneus is similar). If this is the case, Chronos with Chthonie would produce Ophioneus and, perhaps, other monsters; Ophioneus would attack Chronos (already perhaps called Kronos) and be defeated; Zas in his turn would attack and overthrow Kronos, and would marry Chthonie, now to be called Ge and in some ways to become equivalent to Hera; in so doing he would create earth and sea as we know them (the existence of sky being somehow presupposed, perhaps implicit in Zas himself). How Zas subjected Kronos we do not know; it might be thought that Ophioneus was acting as his agent, but in view of **58** it *must* be assumed that Ophioneus was defeated and that Kronos was deposed by some other means. In this case the order of events might be: three pre-existing deities; Chronos rules the sky, plants his seed in Chthonie; birth of Ophioneus (with other chthonic creatures); Ophioneus challenges Kronos, but fails; Kronos somehow subjected by Zas; marriage of Zas and Chthonie-Ge-Hera, and creation of our world; apportionment of spheres, Zeus' enemies in Tartaros. But it must be emphasized that most of this is very speculative indeed.[1]

[1] Plato probably had Pherecydes in mind in **61** *Sophist* 242C–D   μῦθόν τινα ἕκαστος φαίνεταί μοι διηγεῖσθαι παισὶν ὡς οὖσιν ἡμῖν, ὁ μὲν ὡς τρία τὰ ὄντα, πολεμεῖ δὲ ἀλλήλοις ἐνίοτε αὐτῶν ἄττα πῃ, τοτὲ δὲ καὶ φίλα γιγνόμενα γάμους τε καὶ τόκους καὶ τροφὰς τῶν ἐκγόνων παρέχεται... (*Each seems to me to tell us a kind of story, as though we were children, one saying that existing things are three, and that certain of them in some way fight with each other at times, and at times they become good friends and provide marriages and births and nurturings of their offspring...*)

CONCLUSION

In spite of all uncertainties, Pherecydes is not a negligible figure in the history of Greek cosmogonical speculation. As Aristotle wrote in **41**, his approach is not purely mythical. The assertion that three deities always existed implies a rational amendment of the traditional genealogical pattern; yet the method of creation pursued by Chronos is as crudely anthropomorphic as anything in Hesiod, to whom he is obviously indebted for the broad outline of the succession-myth. The allegory of the decorated cloth, if correctly interpreted, is genuinely mythic, and that shows that Pherecydes accepted the naïve but not unempirical view of the structure of the world outlined in §1. His interest in etymology and consequent handling of the first gods is the first clear manifestation of a way of thinking conspicuous in Aeschylus and Heraclitus, and it evidently still impressed Orphic eclectics of three and more centuries later. Pherecydes was an individualist both in his handling of the traditional stories of the gods and in his use of uncommon motifs. There is little indication of any very direct near-eastern influence, except conceivably in the seven recesses; but oriental motifs are none the less relatively dense. Moreover there is one general respect in which his narrative is closer to oriental accounts than to Greek ones. It is evident that in his book many incidents concerning the three pre-existing deities were related before the cosmogony proper (that is, the formation of earth and Ogenos) was reached. This may be compared with the Babylonian creation-myth, for example, where the splitting of Tiamat to form sky and earth comes only at the end of a long saga of the gods; and contrasted with the Hesiodic *Theogony*, where the cosmic constituents are produced almost immediately and as prelude to the history of the gods. But this may be simply because Hesiod, and not Pherecydes and the Babylonian cosmogony, is quasi-rationalistic.

7. Toward philosophy

The ideas considered so far, whatever their occasional stirrings of scientific interest, have been bound up with the whole background of gods and myths, and the shape and development of the world are seen primarily in their terms. Much of the progress toward something approaching philosophy is made by transcending that kind of world-view and reaching after a more direct, less symbolic and less anthropomorphic one. Defining the twists and turns of that progress has been a favourite occupation of modern scholars, but the matter is less straightforward than is often assumed.

One of the cruder guesses is that what was principally required was the abandonment of personification, so that the interplay of sky and earth (for example) need no longer be seen in terms of a sexual relation between Ouranos and Gaia; cosmic components could be directly identified, much as Empedocles' 'roots' were, and organizing principles could be expressed as forces of separation and aggregation, for example, rather than as Ares and Aphrodite or even War and Harmony. In fact the Presocratics were slow to reject entirely these useful and malleable symbols – they had, of course, to disappear eventually, at least before anything resembling logic could appear – and often contented themselves, like Heraclitus, with reinterpreting their functions and values. Even the very idea of personification had not been wholly anti-rational. The division of the world between a plurality of deities and daimons with different properties and powers was in itself a valuable act of classification; what was ultimately retarding was the *institutionalizing* of a mode of interpretation that men are apt to overplay even at their most rational, namely by seeing the world in human terms as animate or even purposive. In particular, the genetic model of nature differentiating itself out of primordial 'parents' proved hard to abandon; but Heraclitus, for one, succeeded, in part at least by confronting that particular mythico-religious model (exemplified most plainly in Hesiod's *Theogony*) with another and even more powerful one, exemplified in *Works and Days*, of Zeus eternally ruling the developed world with the assistance of Justice.

It is important not to exaggerate the sheer irrationality of the world-view that the Presocratic tradition came to build upon and eventually overthrow. That it had strong elements of un-reason, here and there, is of course incontrovertible; but at the same time ancient Greece in Homer's age (the latter part of the eighth century B.C.), or even in the period he purported to describe (say the thirteenth

72

century B.C.), was in no real sense a primitive place. Both the administrative structure of the latter and the literary perception and organization of the former are strong evidence of both logical and psychological refinement. The Homeric conception of Odysseus, for instance, is of a man capable, in most ways at least, of philosophy – distinguished not so much by 'cunning' as by the power of analysing complex circumstances and making rational choices as a result. We see this when he debates the detailed alternatives open to him, and their multiple possibilities of consequence, as he swims despondently off the rocky coast of Scheria in *Odyssey* book v. His relation to gods and goddesses, even to Athena, is almost incidental to most of his decisions and behaviour; he is a rational man with a strong sense of what properly counts in human existence.

In a rather different way Hesiod, too, though ostensibly a purveyor of a mythical and therefore ultimately irrational picture of the world, was exercising a useful kind of reasonableness in grading and synthesizing tales from different regions and with different emphases. But he did much more than that – more, too, than gathering together the interesting cosmogonical themes of §5. For the plan of compiling a systematic cosmogony and theogony on the one hand, followed by an examination of the rule of order (or its perversion) in the developed world on the other, is one that presupposes a comprehensive view of the world (its organization and principle of operation as well as man's part within it) which is un-philosophical only because of the symbolic language of myths in which it is expressed and, admittedly, to some extent conceived. It is for that reason that scholars have from time to time been tempted to treat Hesiod as the first Presocratic philosopher; but between him and Anaximander, for instance, there is an enormous gulf whose nature it is important to glimpse even if we cannot fully understand it.

For the transition from myths to philosophy, from *muthos* to *logos* as it is sometimes put, is far more radical than that involved in a simple process of de-personifying or de-mythologizing, understood either as a rejection of allegory or as a kind of decoding; or even than what might be involved (if the idea is not complete nonsense) in an almost mystical mutation of ways of thinking, of intellectual process itself. Rather it entails, and is the product of, a change that is political, social and religious rather than sheerly intellectual, away from the closed traditional society (which in its archetypal form is an oral society in which the telling of tales is an important instrument of stability and analysis) and toward an open society in which the values of the past become relatively unimportant and radically fresh

73

opinions can be formed both of the community itself and of its expanding environment.

It is that kind of change that took place in Greece between the ninth and the sixth centuries B.C. – a change complicated, to be sure, by the exceptional persistence of non-literacy there. The growth of the *polis*, the independent city-state, out of earlier aristocratic structures, together with the development of foreign contacts and a monetary system, transformed the Hesiodic view of society and made the old divine and heroic archetypes seem obsolete and, except when they were directly protected by religious cult, irrelevant. Much, no doubt, of the rational undertone of the Homeric tradition, as well as the classificatory craft of Hesiod, survived; but in the speculative and cosmopolitan societies of Ionia, not least in Miletus itself, they took on a sharper form and were applied, without too much distraction from myths and religion, to a broader and more objective model of the world.

THE IONIAN THINKERS

It was in Ionia that the first really rational attempts to describe the nature of the world took place. There, material prosperity and special opportunities for contact with other cultures – with Sardis, for example, by land, and with the Pontus and Egypt by sea – were allied, for a time at least, with a strong cultural and literary tradition dating from the age of Homer. Within the space of a century Miletus produced Thales, Anaximander, and Anaximenes, each dominated by the assumption of a single primary material, the isolation of which was the most important step in any systematic account of reality. This attitude was clearly a development of the genetic or genealogical approach to nature exemplified by the Hesiodic *Theogony* and described in chapter I. After the great Milesians, however, the attitude was moderated or abandoned. Xenophanes is here treated among the Ionians (chapter v), but in fact he does not fit into any general category. Born and brought up in Colophon, and strongly aware of Ionian ideas (more so, apparently, than Pythagoras), he moved to western Greece and was only incidentally interested in the details of cosmogony and cosmology. In Ephesus, meanwhile, the individualistic Heraclitus outstepped the limits of material monism, and, while retaining the idea of a basic (though not a cosmogonic) substance, discovered the most significant unity of things in their structure or arrangement. Here there is a parallel with Pythagorean theories in the west of the Greek world. Pythagoras and (a little after him) Parmenides were influential thinkers, and for a time the western schools were all-important; but the Ionian materialistic monism reasserted itself, to a certain extent, in the compromises of some of the post-Parmenidean systems.

CHAPTER II

Thales of Miletus

DATE

Traditionally the earliest Greek physicist, or enquirer into the nature of things as a whole (**85**), Thales predicted an eclipse which took place in 585 B.C. (**74**). He was presumably not active, therefore, much earlier than the beginning of the sixth century.[1]

[1] The eclipse took place in Ol. 48, 4 (585/4) according to Pliny, *N.H.* II, 53 (DK 11 A 5), who presumably followed Apollodorus; and a year or more later according to the Eusebian scheme (DK 11 A 5). Modern calculations put it on 28 May 585 B.C., i.e. in Ol. 48, 3. Tannery's view that the eclipse predicted by Thales was that of 610 is now rejected. Apollodorus according to Diogenes Laertius I, 37–8 (DK 11 A 1) put Thales' birth in Ol. 35, 1 (640), his death in Ol. 58 (548–545) at the age of seventy-eight. There is a fault in the mathematics here: probably Ol. 35, 1 is a mistake, by the common confusion of Ϛ and ϑ, for Ol. 39, 1 (624). Apollodorus, then, characteristically placed Thales' death around the epoch-year of the capture of Sardis, his *acme* at the time of the eclipse, and his birth the conventional forty years earlier. This accords approximately with a different and slightly earlier dating authority: Demetrius of Phaleron, according to Diog. L. I, 22 (DK 11 A 1), placed the canonization of the Seven Sages (of whom Thales was a universally accepted member) in the archonship of Damasias at Athens, i.e. 582/1 B.C., the epoch-year of the first restored Pythian festival.

NATIONALITY

62 Diogenes Laertius I, 22 (DK 11 A 1 *init.*)   ἦν τοίνυν ὁ Θαλῆς, ὡς μὲν Ἡρόδοτος καὶ Δοῦρις καὶ Δημόκριτός φασι, πατρὸς μὲν Ἐξαμύου μητρὸς δὲ Κλεοβουλίνης, ἐκ τῶν Θηλιδῶν, οἵ εἰσι Φοίνικες, εὐγενέστατοι τῶν ἀπὸ Κάδμου καὶ Ἀγήνορος...ἐπολιτογραφήθη δὲ (*sc.* Ἀγήνωρ) ἐν Μιλήτῳ ὅτε ἦλθε σὺν Νείλεῳ ἐκπεσόντι Φοινίκης. ὡς δ' οἱ πλείους φασίν, ἰθαγενὴς Μιλήσιος ἦν (*sc.* Θαλῆς) καὶ γένους λαμπροῦ.

63 Herodotus I, 170 (from **65**)   ...Θαλέω ἀνδρὸς Μιλησίου...τὸ ἀνέκαθεν γένος ἐόντος Φοίνικος...

62 Now Thales, as Herodotus and Douris and Democritus say, was the son of Examyes as father and Cleobuline as mother, from

the descendants of Theleus, who are Phoenicians, nobles from the line of Cadmus and Agenor...and he [Agenor] was enrolled as a citizen in Miletus when he came with Neileos, when the latter was exiled from Phoenicia. But most people say that Thales was a true Milesian by descent, and of high family.
63 ...of Thales, a man of Miletus...being a Phoenician by ultimate descent...

The story of Thales' Phoenician ancestry, barely mentioned by Herodotus in 63 (though 62 makes it appear as though he had said more; the references in Douris and Democritus are otherwise unknown), was later much elaborated, partly, no doubt, to support the common theory of the eastern origins of Greek science. If Thales drew the attention of the Milesians to the navigational value of the Little Bear, used earlier by Phoenician sailors (see 78), this would add to the force of Herodotus' comment. The probability is that Thales was as Greek as most Milesians.[1]

[1] Cf. 64 Herodotus I, 146 ...Μινύαι Ὀρχομένιοί σφι (sc. the Ionian colonists) ἀναμεμείχαται καὶ Καδμεῖοι καὶ Δρύοπες... (...Minyans from Orchomenus are mixed with them [the Ionian colonists], and Cadmeians and Dryopes...). Thus Thales' 'Phoenician' ancestors were probably Cadmeians from Boeotia and not full-blooded Semites. His father, Examyes, seems to have had a Carian name. Herodotus went on to say that even the ostensibly purest Ionian families were mixed by intermarriage with Carian women.

PRACTICAL ACTIVITIES

65 Herodotus I, 170 χρηστὴ δὲ καὶ πρὶν ἢ διαφθαρῆναι Ἰωνίην Θαλέω ἀνδρὸς Μιλησίου ἐγένετο (sc. ἡ γνώμη), τὸ ἀνέκαθεν γένος ἐόντος Φοίνικος, ὃς ἐκέλευε ἓν βουλευτήριον Ἴωνας ἐκτῆσθαι, τὸ δὲ εἶναι ἐν Τέῳ (Τέων γὰρ μέσον εἶναι Ἰωνίης), τὰς δὲ ἄλλας πόλιας οἰκεομένας μηδὲν ἧσσον νομίζεσθαι κατά περ εἰ δῆμοι εἶεν.

66 Herodotus I, 75 ὡς δὲ ἀπίκετο ἐπὶ τὸν Ἅλυν ποταμὸν ὁ Κροῖσος, τὸ ἐνθεῦτεν, ὡς μὲν ἐγὼ λέγω, κατὰ τὰς ἐούσας γεφύρας διεβίβασε τὸν στρατόν, ὡς δὲ ὁ πολλὸς λόγος Ἑλλήνων, Θαλῆς οἱ ὁ Μιλήσιος διεβίβασε. ἀπορέοντος γὰρ Κροίσου ὅκως οἱ διαβήσεται τὸν ποταμὸν ὁ στρατός (οὐ γὰρ δὴ εἶναί κω τοῦτον τὸν χρόνον τὰς γεφύρας ταύτας) λέγεται παρεόντα τὸν Θαλῆν ἐν τῷ στρατοπέδῳ ποιῆσαι αὐτῷ τὸν ποταμὸν ἐξ ἀριστερῆς χειρὸς ῥέοντα τοῦ στρατοῦ καὶ ἐκ δεξιῆς ῥέειν, ποιῆσαι δὲ ὧδε· ἄνωθεν τοῦ στρατοπέδου ἀρξάμενον διώρυχα βαθέαν ὀρύσσειν ἄγοντα μηνοειδέα, ὅκως ἂν τὸ στρατόπεδον ἱδρυμένον κατὰ νώτου λάβοι, ταύτῃ κατὰ τὴν διώρυχα ἐκτραπόμενος

ἐκ τῶν ἀρχαίων ῥεέθρων, καὶ αὖτις παραμειβόμενος τὸ στρατόπεδον ἐς τὰ ἀρχαῖα ἐσβάλλοι, ὥστε ἐπείτε καὶ ἐσχίσθη τάχιστα ὁ ποταμὸς ἀμφοτέρῃ διαβατὸς ἐγένετο.

65 Useful also was the opinion, before the destruction of Ionia, of Thales, a man of Miletus, being a Phoenician by ultimate descent, who advised the Ionians to have a single deliberative chamber, saying that it should be in Teos, for this was in the middle of Ionia; the other cities should continue to be inhabited but should be regarded as if they were demes.

66 When he came to the Halys river, Croesus then, as I say, put his army across by the existing bridges; but, according to the common account of the Greeks, Thales the Milesian transferred the army for him. For it is said that Croesus was at a loss how his army should cross the river, since these bridges did not yet exist at this period; and that Thales, who was present in the army, made the river, which flowed on the left hand of the army, flow on the right hand also. He did so in this way: beginning upstream of the army he dug a deep channel, giving it a crescent shape, so that it should flow round the back of where the army was encamped, being diverted in this way from its old course by the channel, and passing the camp should flow into its old course once more. The result was that as soon as the river was divided it became fordable in both its parts.

Herodotus provides important evidence for Thales' activities as statesman and engineer (also as astronomer, 74). Such versatility seems to have been typical of the Milesian thinkers, whom it is tempting to consider too exclusively as theoretical physicists. Thales, especially, became a symbol for ingenuity of a mathematical and geometrical kind: ἄνθρωπος Θαλῆς ('the man's a Thales'), says a character in Aristophanes (Birds 1009) of Meton the town-planner; and Plato (Rep. 600A) coupled him with Anacharsis. Herodotus, it is true, did not believe the story in 66 about Thales diverting the river Halys, but he did not deny that this is the sort of thing Thales might have done. There probably were crossings over the Halys, but Croesus' army might not have found them; Herodotus was rightly cautious, although the grounds of his suspicion were not certainly correct. He went on to mention a variant account by which the river was totally diverted into a new bed; the story, therefore, may have been widespread. The circumstantial and restrained nature of the version of 66 suggests that it contained a kernel of truth.[1]

[1] For a far more sceptical account of Thales' ideas one can refer to D. R. Dicks, CQ N.S. 9 (1959), 294–309.

TRADITION OF A VISIT TO EGYPT

67   Aetius I, 3, 1   Θαλῆς...φιλοσοφήσας δὲ ἐν Αἰγύπτῳ ἦλθεν εἰς Μίλητον πρεσβύτερος.

68   Proclus in Euclidem p. 65 Friedl. (from Eudemus) (DK 11A11) Θαλῆς δὲ πρῶτον εἰς Αἴγυπτον ἐλθὼν μετήγαγεν εἰς τὴν Ἑλλάδα τὴν θεωρίαν ταύτην (sc. τὴν γεωμετρίαν)...

67   Thales...having practised philosophy in Egypt came to Miletus when he was older.
68   Thales, having first come to Egypt, transferred this study [geometry] to Greece...

It was the custom to credit the sixth-century sages (notably, for example, Solon) with visits to Egypt, the traditional fountain-head of Greek science. Thales as the earliest known Greek geometer had a special reason for being associated with the home of land-measurement.[1] The implication of 67 that he spent a considerable time there is unique and not persuasive. That he did visit Egypt, however, is possible enough; several of his achievements are quite plausibly located there (e.g. 79; see also p. 88), and Miletus' relations with its colony Naucratis were so close as to make a visit by any prominent citizen, trader or not, perfectly feasible.

[1] Cf. 69 Herodotus II, 109   δοκέει δέ μοι ἐνθεῦτεν γεωμετρίη εὑρεθεῖσα εἰς τὴν Ἑλλάδα ἐπανελθεῖν. (It seems to me that geometry was discovered from this source [sc. re-measurement of holdings after the Nile flood] and so came to Greece.)

Further, Thales appears in Aetius as the holder of a theory about the flooding of the Nile which is one of three already recorded by Herodotus:

70   Herodotus II, 20 (there are two particularly improbable theories about the cause of the flood)   τῶν ἡ ἑτέρη μὲν λέγει τοὺς ἐτησίας ἀνέμους εἶναι αἰτίους πληθύειν τὸν ποταμόν, κωλύοντας ἐς θάλασσαν ἐκρέειν τὸν Νεῖλον.

71   Aetius IV, 1, 1   Θαλῆς τοὺς ἐτησίας ἀνέμους οἴεται πνέοντας τῇ Αἰγύπτῳ ἀντιπροσώπους ἐπαίρειν τοῦ Νείλου τὸν ὄγκον διὰ τὸ τὰς ἐκροὰς αὐτοῦ τῇ παροιδήσει τοῦ ἀντιπαρήκοντος πελάγους ἀνακόπτεσθαι.

70   Of these, one theory says that the Etesian winds are the cause of the river flooding, by preventing the Nile from running out into the sea.
71   Thales thinks that the Etesian winds, blowing straight on to

Egypt, raise up the mass of the Nile's water through cutting off its outflow by the swelling of the sea coming against it.

Aetius probably depends on a lost Peripatetic treatise, of which traces have survived in other sources (Diels, *Doxographi Graeci* 226f.): therefore his information may be reliable and not, as is nevertheless possible, a purely speculative ascription. If Thales did advance this theory then he may have seen the Nile himself; though it should be remembered that he could easily have got the relevant information (that the Etesian winds blow in Egypt too), and even the idea, from Milesian traders.

ANECDOTES ABOUT THALES AS THE TYPICAL PHILOSOPHER

72   Plato *Theaetetus* 174A   ...ὥσπερ καὶ Θαλῆν ἀστρονομοῦντα, ὦ Θεόδωρε, καὶ ἄνω βλέποντα, πεσόντα εἰς φρέαρ, Θρᾷττά τις ἐμμελὴς καὶ χαρίεσσα θεραπαινὶς ἀποσκῶψαι λέγεται, ὡς τὰ μὲν ἐν οὐρανῷ προθυμοῖτο εἰδέναι, τὰ δ' ὄπισθεν αὐτοῦ καὶ παρὰ πόδας λανθάνοι αὐτόν.

73   Aristotle *Politics* A11, 1259a9   ὀνειδιζόντων γὰρ αὐτῷ διὰ τὴν πενίαν ὡς ἀνωφελοῦς τῆς φιλοσοφίας οὔσης, κατανοήσαντά φασιν αὐτὸν ἐλαιῶν φορὰν ἐσομένην ἐκ τῆς ἀστρολογίας, ἔτι χειμῶνος ὄντος, εὐπορήσαντα χρημάτων ὀλίγων ἀρραβῶνας διαδοῦναι τῶν ἐλαιουργείων τῶν τ' ἐν Μιλήτῳ καὶ Χίῳ πάντων, ὀλίγου μισθωσά-μενον ἅτ' οὐδενὸς ἐπιβάλλοντος. ἐπειδὴ δ' ὁ καιρὸς ἧκε, πολλῶν ζητουμένων ἅμα καὶ ἐξαίφνης, ἐκμισθοῦντα ὃν τρόπον ἠβούλετο πολλὰ χρήματα συλλέξαντα ἐπιδεῖξαι ὅτι ῥᾴδιόν ἐστι πλουτεῖν τοῖς φιλοσόφοις ἂν βούλωνται, ἀλλ' οὐ τοῦτ' ἐστὶ περὶ ὃ σπουδάζουσιν. (Cf. also Diog. L. I, 26 (DK 11 A 1), from Hieronymus of Rhodes, and Cicero *Div.* I, 49, 111.)

72   ...just as, Theodorus, a witty and attractive Thracian servant-girl is said to have mocked Thales for falling into a well while he was observing the stars and gazing upwards; declaring that he was eager to know the things in the sky, but that what was behind him and just by his feet escaped his notice.

73   For when they reproached him because of his poverty, as though philosophy were no use, it is said that, having observed through his study of the heavenly bodies that there would be a large olive-crop, he raised a little capital while it was still winter, and paid deposits on all the olive presses in Miletus and Chios, hiring them cheaply because no one bid against him. When the

appropriate time came there was a sudden rush of requests for the presses; he then hired them out on his own terms and so made a large profit, thus demonstrating that it is easy for philosophers to be rich, if they wish, but that it is not in this that they are interested.

Neither of these stories is likely to be strictly historical, even though they originated in the fourth century B.C. at the latest, before the great period of fictitious biography in the third and second centuries. They well demonstrate how at a comparatively early date Thales had become accepted as the typical philosopher; though **72**, one of the oldest versions of the absent-minded professor theme, would have had more point if applied to someone not so notoriously practical in his interests as Thales. The detail of the witty slave-girl is added to make the whole situation more piquant; possibly it is a vestige of a separate and mildly malicious joke at the philosopher's expense. Plato liked making fun of the Presocratics, a truth frequently overlooked in the interpretation of certain less obvious passages.

THE PREDICTION OF THE ECLIPSE, AND OTHER ASTRONOMICAL ACTIVITIES

74 Herodotus I, 74 διαφέρουσι δέ σφι (*sc.* τοῖσι Λυδοῖσι καὶ τοῖσι Μήδοισι) ἐπ᾽ ἴσης τὸν πόλεμον τῷ ἕκτῳ ἔτει συμβολῆς γενομένης συνήνεικε ὥστε τῆς μάχης συνεστεώσης τὴν ἡμέρην ἐξαπίνης νύκτα γενέσθαι. τὴν δὲ μεταλλαγὴν ταύτην τῆς ἡμέρης Θαλῆς ὁ Μιλήσιος τοῖσι Ἴωσι προηγόρευσε ἔσεσθαι, οὖρον προθέμενος ἐνιαυτὸν τοῦτον ἐν τῷ δὴ καὶ ἐγένετο ἡ μεταβολή.

75 Diogenes Laertius I, 23 δοκεῖ δὲ κατά τινας πρῶτος ἀστρο-λογῆσαι καὶ ἡλιακὰς ἐκλείψεις καὶ τροπὰς προειπεῖν, ὥς φησιν Εὔδημος ἐν τῇ περὶ τῶν ἀστρολογουμένων ἱστορίᾳ· ὅθεν αὐτὸν καὶ Ξενοφάνης καὶ Ἡρόδοτος θαυμάζει. μαρτυρεῖ δ᾽ αὐτῷ καὶ Ἡράκλειτος καὶ Δημόκριτος.

76 Dercyllides *ap.* Theon. Smyrn. p. 198, 14 Hiller Εὔδημος ἱστορεῖ ἐν ταῖς ᾿Αστρολογίαις ὅτι Οἰνοπίδης εὗρε πρῶτος τὴν τοῦ ζῳδιακοῦ λόξωσιν [Diels; διάζωσιν ms] καὶ τὴν τοῦ μεγάλου ἐνιαυτοῦ περίστασιν, Θαλῆς δὲ ἡλίου ἔκλειψιν καὶ τὴν κατὰ τὰς τροπὰς αὐτοῦ περίοδον, ὡς οὐκ ἴση ἀεὶ συμβαίνει.

74 In the sixth year of the war, which they [Medes and Lydians] had carried on with equal fortunes, an engagement took place in which it turned out that when the battle was in progress the day suddenly became night. This alteration of the day Thales the Milesian foretold to the Ionians, setting as its limit this year in which the change actually occurred.

75 Some think he was the first to study the heavenly bodies and to foretell eclipses of the sun and solstices, as Eudemus says in his history of astronomy; for which reason both Xenophanes and Herodotus express admiration; and both Heraclitus and Democritus bear witness for him.

76 Eudemus relates in the *Astronomy* that Oenopides first discovered the obliquity of the Zodiac and the cycle of the Great Year, and Thales the eclipse of the sun and the variable period of its solstices.

The prediction of the eclipse must have been based on a long series of empirical observations, not upon a scientific theory of the true cause of eclipses. The cause was unknown to Thales' immediate successors in Miletus and therefore, presumably, to him. If the contrary was implied by Eudemus in **76** (it is asserted by Aetius, e.g. II, 24, 1, DK 11 A 17 a), then Eudemus was guilty of drawing a wrong conclusion from the undoubted fact of Thales' prediction. The Babylonian priests had made observations of eclipses of the sun, both partial and total, for religious purposes, at any rate since 721 B.C.; and by the sixth century they had probably established a cycle of solstices (or less plausibly of lunations) within which eclipses might occur at certain points. It is overwhelmingly probable that Thales' feat depended on his access to these Babylonian records; see further Kahn, *Anaximander and the Origins of Greek Cosmology* (New York, 1960), p. 76 n. 2. We know that many cultivated Greeks visited Sardis at this period,[1] and relations with Ionia were naturally particularly close. Some scholars have argued that Thales' information more probably came from Egypt, with which he had other contacts; but there is no evidence that sufficiently detailed observations, over a long enough period, were made and recorded by the Egyptian priests. Even on the Babylonian data it could not be predicted that an eclipse would be visible at a particular point. Priests were despatched to different parts of the Babylonian empire when a possible eclipse was due, and even within this large area the expected phenomenon was sometimes not visible. Further, no precise date could be predicted, only broad limits of time. Thus Thales appears to have said that an eclipse was likely to occur within a certain year.[2] It was pure chance that it happened on the day of the battle and so seemed especially remarkable, and to some degree a matter of luck that it was visible near the Ionian area at all.

[1] 77 Herodotus I, 29 ...ἀπικνέονται ἐς Σάρδις ἀκμαζούσας πλούτῳ ἄλλοι τε οἱ πάντες ἐκ τῆς Ἑλλάδος σοφισταί...καὶ δὴ καὶ Σόλων... (...*there arrived at Sardis in this bloom of its wealth all the sages from Greece...among whom came Solon...*).
[2] Some scholars have felt a whole year to be too large a period, and have tried to restrict the meaning of ἐνιαυτόν in 74 to the summer solstice (by which the year-interval could be gauged); but there is no satisfactory evidence for such a usage.

The information added by Eudemus in 75 and 76, that Thales predicted solstices and noted that their cycle is not always equal (by which is probably meant the slight variations in length of the solar seasons, as divided by solstices and equinoxes), is more straightforward. All that would be needed would be a rather long series of observations with a solstice-marker, a ἡλιοτρόπιον of some kind, such as was connected with Pherecydes (47), to mark the bearings of the sun at its most northerly and southerly points in the year – that is, the summer and winter solstices. Alternatively a *gnomon* or stable vertical rod, by which the length of the sun's shadow could be exactly recorded, would suffice. This was said by Herodotus to be a Babylonian invention (97), and its introduction was credited to Anaximander and not to Thales (94). However, measurement of shadows was certainly involved in the computation of the height of pyramids ascribed to Thales (p. 85), and one cannot be completely confident that the observation of the sun's zenith by similar means was unknown to him. The technique seems obvious to us now, and might be thought to have occurred to anyone who had reached Thales' by no means primitive stage of celestial observation. Diogenes (I, 24, DK 11 A 1) added that Thales discovered the passage of the sun from solstice to solstice, and the relation of the diameter of sun and moon to their orbits. The former phrase is very vague, and might imply no more than the knowledge that the sun moves between the tropics – which Thales obviously possessed. But it perhaps refers to the discovery of the inclination of the Zodiac, which Eudemus in 76 ascribed to Oinopides of Chios over a century later. Diogenes' second piece of information is quite anachronistic, for Thales cannot have thought that the heavenly bodies had orbits, since they did not pass under the earth (which was not made free-swinging until Anaximander); at the most they had semi-orbits, and the ratio of diameter to celestial path would be twice that given.[1]

[1] The determination of this ratio was a recurrent problem in Greek astronomy, which might naturally come to be associated with the earliest known astronomer. The ratio suggested in Diogenes, 1:720, implies a sexagesimal measurement of the circle of the ecliptic such as was adopted by the Babylonians: so A. Wasserstein, *JHS* 75 (1955), 114–16. Cf. Herodotus II, 109 (97), also II, 4.

One further observation is attributed to Thales, again with a possible implication that he may be indebted to foreign sources:

78 Callimachus *Iambus* I, 52, fr. 191 Pfeiffer (DK 11 A 3 *a*)

...ἦν γὰρ ἡ νίκη
Θάλητος, ὅς τ᾽ ἦν ἄλλα δεξιὸς γνώμην
καὶ τῆς Ἀμάξης ἐλέγετο σταθμήσασθαι
τοὺς ἀστερίσκους, ἧ πλέουσι Φοίνικες.

78 ...for the victory belonged to Thales, who was clever in judgement, not least because he was said to have measured out the little stars of the Wain, by which the Phoenicians sail.

This is part of the apocryphal story of the cup (in some versions, tripod) which had to be presented to the wisest man living: Thales was the first, and in some versions also the final, choice, but he modestly sent it on to Bias, and he to others of the Seven Sages. The 'little stars of the Wain' are the Little Bear (cf. Aratus *Phaen.* 39, with scholion); this constellation, because its revolution is smaller, provides a more accurate fixed point than the Great Bear or Wain as a whole (as opposed to the Pole star itself). σταθμᾶσθαι strictly means 'to measure', but sometimes, more vaguely, 'to mark out, define' (Σ on Pindar *Ol.* 10, 53). The probable meaning is that Thales defined the Little Bear, and drew the attention of Milesian sailors to its navigational usefulness. Diogenes Laertius, I, 23, interpreted the lines of Callimachus as meaning simply that Thales 'discovered' the Little Bear. Ionian sailors may previously have neglected it, since for all except long open-sea crossings the more conspicuous Great Bear was adequate.

Thus the ἀστρολογία, the study of heavenly bodies, mentioned as characteristic of Thales by Plato (**72**) and Aristotle (**73**),[1] seems to have comprised these activities: the lucky prediction of an eclipse, probably with the aid of Babylonian tables; the measurement of solstices and their variations, possibly undertaken in part for calendar-making purposes; and the study of star-groups, perhaps mainly as a navigational aid.

[1] Cf. also **75**, where nothing is otherwise known of the references to Thales by Xenophanes, Heraclitus and Democritus.

MATHEMATICAL DISCOVERIES

79 Diogenes Laertius I, 27 ὁ δὲ Ἱερώνυμος καὶ ἐκμετρῆσαί φησιν αὐτὸν τὰς πυραμίδας ἐκ τῆς σκιᾶς, παρατηρήσαντα ὅτε ἡμῖν ἰσομεγέθης ἐστίν.

80 Proclus *in Euclidem* p. 352 Friedl. (DK I I A 20) Εὔδημος δὲ ἐν ταῖς Γεωμετρικαῖς ἱστορίαις εἰς Θαλῆν τοῦτο ἀνάγει τὸ θεώρημα (*sc.* that triangles having one side and its adjacent angles equal are themselves equal)· τὴν γὰρ τῶν ἐν θαλάττῃ πλοίων ἀπόστασιν δι' οὗ τρόπου φασὶν αὐτὸν δεικνύναι τούτῳ προσχρῆσθαί φησιν ἀναγκαῖον.

79 Hieronymus says that he [Thales] actually measured the pyramids by their shadow, having observed the time when our own shadow is equal to our height.

80 Eudemus in the *History of Geometry* refers this theorem to Thales; for the method by which they say he demonstrated the distance of ships out at sea must, he says, have entailed the use of this theorem.

In 79 Hieronymus of Rhodes attributes to Thales the simplest possible method of measuring the height of a pyramid. Thales might conceivably have learned this from the Egyptians; or it is not impossible that the pyramids were merely local colour, to fit the tradition of a visit to Egypt. Pliny (*N.H.* xxxvi, 82, DK I I A 21) gave the same account, but a more complex variant appears in Plutarch, *Sept. sap. conv.* 2, 147A (DK I I A 21), that the height of a pyramid is related to the length of its shadow exactly as the height of any mensurable vertical object is related to the length of *its* shadow at the same time of day. It is probable, though not certain, that Hieronymus is here dependent on his near-contemporary Eudemus (whose book on the history of geometry and mathematics, as opposed to his history of astronomy, Diogenes himself does not appear to have used for Thales); if so, there is a probability that Thales used the simpler method. On the other hand, the more complex one is based on an argument from similar triangles analogous to that ascribed to him by Eudemus in 80, as a means of measuring the distance of ships out at sea. Provided the height of the observer above sea-level were known, this calculation could be made with the aid of a primitive theodolite, two sticks (one as a sight-line, the other as an approximate level-line) pivoting on a nail. It is to be observed that Eudemus credited Thales with a knowledge of similar triangles only on the *a priori* ground that he could not otherwise have performed this kind of calculation. Yet a man may make an empirical use of a rudimentary angle-measurer without forming an explicit theory about the principles involved, and certainly without stating those principles as a geometer.[1] Three other theorems attributed to Thales by Proclus following Eudemus, in the same commentary as 80 (DK I I A I I) – circle bisected by diameter; angles at base of isosceles triangle are

85

equal; vertically opposed angles are equal – are, again, probably just the neatest abstract solutions of particular practical problems associated with Thales. All this is very much a matter for conjecture: my own guess would be that Thales did gain a reputation with his contemporaries for carrying out various far from straightforward empirical feats of mensuration, without necessarily stating the geometry that lay behind them. This is perhaps confirmed by the fact that Thales' Milesian successors seem to have paid little attention to mathematical theory.

[1] Burnet, *EGP*, 45f., observed that a knowledge of the Egyptian *seqt* ratio (a trigonometrical approximation) could have produced a solution of both problems. In view of the possibility of Thales' acquaintance with Egypt, and his analogous use (it is assumed) of an empirical Babylonian formula, this explanation can by no means be excluded. – Pamphila's report in Diog. L. I, 24 that Thales inscribed a right-angled triangle in a circle 'and sacrificed an ox' is entertaining, if not convincing (cf. pp. 334f. below).

WRITINGS

81 Simplicius *in Phys.* p. 23, 29 Diels Θαλῆς δὲ πρῶτος παραδέδοται τὴν περὶ φύσεως ἱστορίαν τοῖς Ἕλλησιν ἐκφῆναι, πολλῶν μὲν καὶ ἄλλων προγεγονότων, ὡς καὶ Θεοφράστῳ δοκεῖ, αὐτὸς δὲ πολὺ διενεγκὼν ἐκείνων ὡς ἀποκρύψαι πάντας τοὺς πρὸ αὐτοῦ. λέγεται δὲ ἐν γραφαῖς μηδὲν καταλιπεῖν πλὴν τῆς καλουμένης Ναυτικῆς ἀστρολογίας.

82 Diogenes Laertius I, 23 καὶ κατά τινας μὲν σύγγραμμα κατέλιπεν οὐδέν· ἡ γὰρ εἰς αὐτὸν ἀναφερομένη Ναυτικὴ ἀστρολογία Φώκου λέγεται εἶναι τοῦ Σαμίου. Καλλίμαχος δ' αὐτὸν οἶδεν εὑρετὴν τῆς ἄρκτου τῆς μικρᾶς λέγων ἐν τοῖς Ἰάμβοις οὕτως... [**78**, ll. 3–4], κατά τινας δὲ μόνα δύο συνέγραψε Περὶ τροπῆς καὶ Ἰσημερίας, τὰ ἄλλ' ἀκατάληπτα εἶναι δοκιμάσας.

83 Suda s.v. (from Hesychius) (DK I I A 2) ...ἔγραψε περὶ μετεώρων ἐν ἔπεσι, περὶ ἰσημερίας, καὶ ἄλλα πολλά.

81 Thales is traditionally the first to have revealed the investigation of nature to the Greeks; he had many predecessors, as also Theophrastus thinks, but so far surpassed them as to blot out all who came before him. He is said to have left nothing in the form of writings except the so-called 'Nautical Star-guide'.

82 And according to some he left no book behind; for the 'Nautical Star-guide' ascribed to him is said to be by Phokos the Samian. Callimachus knew him as the discoverer of the Little Bear, and wrote as follows in his *Iambs*...[78, lines 3–4]; while according to some he wrote only two works, *On the Solstice* and *On the Equinox*, considering the rest to be incomprehensible.

83 ...he wrote on celestial matters in epic verse, on the equinox, and much else.

These passages show that there was profound doubt in antiquity about Thales' written works. It is plain, at all events, that there was no work by him in the Alexandrian library, except the dubious 'Nautical Star-guide' (cf. also 96). Aristotle appears not to have seen any book by him, at least on cosmological matters; he was extremely cautious in ascribing opinions to him, using the expressions 'deriving the supposition perhaps from...', 'the account which they say Thales gave' (85, 84), and 'from what they relate' (89). Aristotle was not necessarily conscientious in using original sources; Theophrastus, as a professed historian of earlier philosophy, should have been conscientious (though he was not always so, in fact), but he evidently had little to add to Aristotle about Thales (except for the minor amendment implied by the conjecture in 81 that Thales *did* have predecessors). Eudemus made some positive assertions about Thales as geometer and astronomer (75, 76, 80), but we have seen on 80 that these were sometimes very speculative; they were perhaps partly based on the quasi-legendary biographical tradition, and do not imply that Eudemus had seen written works by Thales.

Diogenes' doubt in 82 about the 'Nautical Star-guide' was shared by Plutarch, *de Pyth. or.* 18, 402E (DK11B1), who added that the work in question was in verse; we may thus conjecture that this was the verse work described by Hesychius in 83 as περὶ μετεώρων. Lobon of Argos (a disreputable stichometrist of the second century B.C.), according to Diog. L. 1, 34, said that Thales wrote 200 hexameters. Only mild suspicion is expressed in 81, where any uncertainty implied by καλουμένης is perhaps restricted to the nature of the title. But this last sentence almost certainly contains Simplicius' own judgement and not that of Theophrastus, the paraphrase of whom seems to end before λέγεται. Diogenes' information in 82, that the work was also ascribed to one Phokos of Samos, almost settles the matter; any astronomical work of archaic appearance might naturally be credited to Thales, but works actually by Thales would not be alternatively ascribed to men of comparative obscurity. It is possible that the 'Nautical Star-guide' was a genuine sixth-century work similar to the hexameter Ἀστρολογία of Cleostratus of Tenedos (DK ch. 6) or the so-called Hesiodic Ἀστρονομίη (DK ch. 4): so Diels and others have assumed. It is also possible that it was a Hellenistic forgery. Diogenes in **82** is a little worried by Callimachus' mention in **78** of a particular nautical star-aid ascribed to Thales; but this need not have been described by Thales in writing. However, there is nothing inherently improbable in Thales having recorded such aids to navigation, a plausible enough activity for a practical sage in a maritime centre: but it was probably not in the 'Nautical Star-guide' known to the Hellenistic world that he did so. The other works mentioned in **82**, on the solstice and the equinox (only the latter in **83**), are unlikely, from their similar contents, to have been separate books. Simplicius in **81**, and those recorded in **82** who thought that Thales left no book, evidently did not accept this work as genuine. Thales studied the solstices according to Eudemus in **75** and **76**, and it would be on the ground of this known interest that such a work would be ascribed to him. Once again, however, it must be remembered that observations of solstices and of star-risings and -settings were widely made in the archaic period, and also set down in verse, partly in the attempt to establish a satisfactory calendar: see Cleostratus fr. 4 (DK6B4) and the Hesiodic *Astronomy* (DK4B1–5). Observations about the Hyades and the setting of the Pleiades were also attributed to Thales (scholion on Aratus 172, Pliny *N.H.* xviii, 213; DK 11 B 2, 11 A 18); the latter observation, incidentally, was accurate for the latitude of Egypt, not that of Greece.

The evidence does not allow a certain conclusion, but the probability is that Thales did not write a book; though the ancient holders of this view might have been misled by the absence of a genuine work from the Alexandrian library, and also by the apophthegmatic nature of the wisdom assigned to the Seven Sages in general.

COSMOLOGY

(i) *The earth floats on water, which is in some way the source of all things*

84 Aristotle *de caelo* B13, 294a28 οἱ δ᾽ ἐφ᾽ ὕδατος κεῖσθαι (*sc.* φασὶ τὴν γῆν). τοῦτον γὰρ ἀρχαιότατον παρειλήφαμεν τὸν λόγον, ὃν φασιν εἰπεῖν Θαλῆν τὸν Μιλήσιον, ὡς διὰ τὸ πλωτὴν εἶναι μένουσαν ὥσπερ ξύλον ἤ τι τοιοῦτον ἕτερον (καὶ γὰρ τούτων ἐπ᾽ ἀέρος μὲν οὐθὲν πέφυκε μένειν, ἀλλ᾽ ἐφ᾽ ὕδατος), ὥσπερ οὐ τὸν αὐτὸν λόγον ὄντα περὶ τῆς γῆς καὶ τοῦ ὕδατος τοῦ ὀχοῦντος τὴν γῆν.

85 Aristotle *Met.* A3, 983b6 τῶν δὴ πρῶτον φιλοσοφησάντων οἱ πλεῖστοι τὰς ἐν ὕλης εἴδει μόνας ᾠήθησαν ἀρχὰς εἶναι πάντων· ἐξ οὗ

γὰρ ἔστιν ἅπαντα τὰ ὄντα, καὶ ἐξ οὗ γίγνεται πρώτου καὶ εἰς ὃ
φθείρεται τελευταῖον, τῆς μὲν οὐσίας ὑπομενούσης τοῖς δὲ πάθεσι
μεταβαλλούσης, τοῦτο στοιχεῖον καὶ ταύτην ἀρχήν φασιν εἶναι τῶν
ὄντων, καὶ διὰ τοῦτο οὔτε γίγνεσθαι οὐδὲν οἴονται οὔτ' ἀπόλλυσθαι,
ὡς τῆς τοιαύτης φύσεως ἀεὶ σωζομένης...δεῖ γὰρ εἶναί τινα φύσιν ἢ
μίαν ἢ πλείους μιᾶς ἐξ ὧν γίγνεται τἆλλα σωζομένης ἐκείνης. τὸ μέντοι
πλῆθος καὶ τὸ εἶδος τῆς τοιαύτης ἀρχῆς οὐ τὸ αὐτὸ πάντες λέγουσιν,
ἀλλὰ Θαλῆς μὲν ὁ τῆς τοιαύτης ἀρχηγὸς φιλοσοφίας ὕδωρ εἶναί φησιν
(διὸ καὶ τὴν γῆν ἐφ' ὕδατος ἀπεφαίνετο εἶναι), λαβὼν ἴσως τὴν
ὑπόληψιν ταύτην ἐκ τοῦ πάντων ὁρᾶν τὴν τροφὴν ὑγρὰν οὖσαν καὶ
αὐτὸ τὸ θερμὸν ἐκ τούτου γιγνόμενον καὶ τούτῳ ζῶν (τὸ δ' ἐξ οὗ
γίγνεται, τοῦτ' ἐστὶν ἀρχὴ πάντων), διά τε δὴ τοῦτο τὴν ὑπόληψιν
λαβὼν ταύτην καὶ διὰ τὸ πάντων τὰ σπέρματα τὴν φύσιν ὑγρὰν
ἔχειν· τὸ δ' ὕδωρ ἀρχὴ τῆς φύσεως ἐστὶ τοῖς ὑγροῖς.

84 Others say that the earth rests on water. For this is the most
ancient account we have received, which they say was given by
Thales the Milesian, that it stays in place through floating like a
log or some other such thing (for none of these rests by nature on
air, but on water) – as though the same argument did not apply
to the water supporting the earth as to the earth itself.

85 Most of the first philosophers thought that principles in the
form of matter were the only principles of all things; for the
original source of all existing things, that from which a thing first
comes-into-being and into which it is finally destroyed, the
substance persisting but changing in its qualities, this they declare
is the element and first principle of existing things, and for this
reason they consider that there is no absolute coming-to-be or
passing away, on the ground that such a nature is always
preserved...for there must be some natural substance, either one
or more than one, from which the other things come-into-being,
while it is preserved. Over the number, however, and the form of
this kind of principle they do not all agree; but Thales, the founder
of this type of philosophy, says that it is water (and therefore
declared that the earth is on water), perhaps taking this supposition
from seeing the nurture of all things to be moist, and the warm
itself coming-to-be from this and living by this (that from which
they come-to-be being the principle of all things) – taking the
supposition both from this and from the seeds of all things having
a moist nature, water being the natural principle of moist things.

Our knowledge of Thales' cosmology depends virtually completely
on these two passages, with the cryptic addition of **89–91**. Apart from

Aristotle's own criticism and conjecture, they assign two propositions to Thales: (i) the earth floats on water (like a piece of wood or something of the sort); (2) the 'principle' of all things is water (in Aristotle's sense of ἀρχή as explained in the first half of **85**, i.e. the original constituent material of things, which persists as a substratum and into which they will perish). (1) was professedly known to Aristotle only indirectly, on the information of others; further, it is impossible to tell whether the supporting argument (solid things do not rest on air, but they do on water, therefore the earth floats on water) was also derived from the reports of Thales, or whether it was entirely supplied by Aristotle. His final objection, that Thales has solved nothing because he would still have to find something to support the water that supports the earth, shows how little Aristotle understood the probable nature of Thales' way of thinking; Thales would almost certainly still accept the popular conception of the underparts of earth stretching down so far that the problem almost disappeared, as in Homer (**1**) and long after Thales in Xenophanes (**3**). The probable direct origin of Thales' idea of the earth floating on water was from non-Greek mythological accounts (pp. 92f.); the device might have attracted him in part because it provided support for the earth, but it is by no means certain that Thales felt this to be a serious problem, and most improbable in any case that he worked out the theory for himself as a conscious answer to that problem. As for proposition (2), Aristotle evidently knew nothing beyond what he wrote, since the reasons given for Thales' choice of water are professedly conjectural (λαβὼν ἴσως...). The first half of **85** is quoted to show the kind of analysis and terminology which Aristotle (and following him Theophrastus[1] and thus the subsequent doxographical tradition) applied to the early physicists or natural philosophers, the φυσικοί – those who, according to Aristotle, posited solely, or primarily, the first (material) of his four causes. His application of a single rigid analysis to his predecessors, while justly and usefully emphasizing certain resemblances between them, is also a source of confusion. Thus Thales' 'principle' (in Aristotle's sense) and Heraclitus' 'principle' (fire according to Aristotle) were clearly, for Thales and for Heraclitus themselves, very different kinds of thing. In fact, all we know about Thales' views on water (apart from that the earth floats on it) is that, in a hearsay and probably much abbreviated and somewhat distorted form, they appeared to the not over-discriminating Aristotle to fit his own idea of a material ἀρχή. Yet it is possible, contrary to Aristotle's automatic assumption, that Thales declared earth to *come from* water (i.e. to be solidified out of it in some way) without therefore thinking that the earth and its contents *are* somehow water, that they have any continuing relation to it (beyond the fact that the earth floats on water) except perhaps that of a man to his remote ancestors. See further pp. 93f.

[1] Theophrastus' abbreviated account of Thales' material principle is given by Simplicius, *in Phys.* p. 23, 21 Diels (= Theophrastus *Phys. op.* fr. 1), DK 11 A 13. It is a close parallel of Aristotle in 85, using in many parts the same phraseology. It adds one more conjectural reason for Thales' choice of water, that corpses dry up (τὰ νεκρούμενα ξηραίνεται): this perhaps came from Hippon (see next n.), who is probably credited with a similar argument in Anon. Lond. xi, 22 (DK 38 A 11), i.e. in a Peripatetic source. The addition occurs also in Aetius.

The reasons conjectured by Aristotle in 85 for the importance attached by Thales to water as a constituent of things are mainly physiological.[1] From the analogy of his immediate successors we might have expected Thales to have adduced meteorological reasons, more conspicuously, in support of the cosmic importance of water.[2] Yet we must beware of exaggerated generalizations like that implied in Burnet's view that sixth-century thinkers were almost exclusively interested in meteorological (in the strict sense, including astronomical) phenomena. It is undoubtedly true that the *scientific* study of medicine began in the fifth century B.C., and that analogies between the world and details of human structure become much commoner then. Yet chapter 1 has shown the strongly genealogical colouring of much pre-philosophical Greek speculation, and also the importance of the analogy of physiological reproduction. In the case of Thales there are reasons for thinking that his explanation of the world was influenced not only by this variegated traditional background of earlier Greek quasi-mythological cosmogonical versions, but also by a specific cosmological idea derived directly, perhaps, from further east.

[1] It seems more probable than not that Aristotle took them from Hippon of Samos (or of Rhegium, Croton, or Metapontum), who in the second half of the fifth century B.C. revived and modified the idea of water as constituent material of things. Hippon, whose intellect Aristotle did not admire, evidently had strong physiological interests. Cf. in particular 86 Aristotle *de an.* A2, 405b1 τῶν δὲ φορτικωτέρων καὶ ὕδωρ τινὲς ἀπεφήναντο (*sc.* τὴν ψυχήν), καθάπερ Ἵππων· πεισθῆναι δ᾽ ἐοίκασιν ἐκ τῆς γονῆς, ὅτι πάντων ὑγρά· καὶ γὰρ ἐλέγχει τοὺς αἷμα φάσκοντας τὴν ψυχήν, ὅτι ἡ γονὴ οὐχ αἷμα. (*Of the cruder thinkers some actually declared it [*sc. the soul*] to be water, like Hippon; they seem to have been persuaded by the seed of all things being moist. In fact he refutes those who say that the soul is blood; because the seed is not blood.*) Note that there is a good deal of conjecture in this, too. Against the assumption that Aristotle's conjectured reasons for Thales' choice of water were derived from Hippon is that the additional reason given in

Theophrastus (see previous note) probably did come from Hippon, and might therefore have been expected to be included by Aristotle.

2 As in **87** Heraclitus Homericus *Quaest. Hom.* 22   ἡ γὰρ ὑγρὰ φύσις, εὐμαρῶς εἰς ἕκαστα μεταπλαττομένη, πρὸς τὸ ποικίλον εἴωθε μορφοῦσθαι· τό τε γὰρ ἐξατμιζόμενον αὐτῆς ἀεροῦται, καὶ τὸ λεπτότατον ἀπὸ ἀέρος αἰθὴρ ἀνάπτεται, συνιζάνον τε τὸ ὕδωρ καὶ μεταβαλλόμενον εἰς ἰλὺν ἀπογαιοῦται· διὸ δὴ τῆς τετράδος τῶν στοιχείων ὥσπερ αἰτιώτατον ὁ Θαλῆς ἀπεφήνατο στοιχεῖον εἶναι τὸ ὕδωρ. *(For moist natural substance, since it is easily formed into each different thing, is accustomed to undergo very various changes: that part of it which is exhaled is made into air, and the finest part is kindled from air into aither, while when water is compacted and changes into slime it becomes earth. Therefore Thales declared that water, of the four elements, was the most active, as it were, as a cause.)* These reasons certainly stem from a Stoic source – there is much Stoic phraseology – and may well be entirely conjectural. According to Theophrastus, evidently, Thales used water and its products to explain earthquakes (**88**: this depends on the special conception that the earth *rests on* water), also winds and movements of stars (Hippolytus *Ref.* i, 1); but these would scarcely provide the reason for Thales adopting the theory in the first place.

The near-eastern origin of part of Thales' cosmology is indicated by his conception that the earth floats or rests on water. In Egypt the earth was commonly conceived as a flat, rimmed dish resting upon water, which also filled the sky; the sun sailed each day across the sky in a boat, and also sailed under the earth each night (not round it, as in the Greek legend, e.g. **7**). In the Babylonian creation-epic Apsu and Tiamat represent the primeval waters, and Apsu remains as the waters under the earth after Marduk has split the body of Tiamat to form sky (with its waters) and earth. In the story of Eridu (seventh century B.C. in its youngest extant version), in the beginning 'all land was sea'; then Marduk built a raft on the surface of the water, and on the raft a reed-hut which became the earth. An analogous view is implied in the Psalms (where also Leviathan is an analogue of Tiamat), where Jahweh 'stretched out the earth above the waters' (136, 6), 'founded it upon the seas, and established it upon the floods' (24, 2). Similarly Tehom is 'the deep that lieth under' (Gen. xlix. 25), 'the deep that coucheth beneath' (Deut. xxxiii. 13).[1] Against this profusion of parallel material from the east and south-east for the waters under the earth, there is no comparable Greek evidence apart from Thales. The naïve Greek conception of a river Okeanos *surrounding* the earth (ch. 1 §2) is not strictly comparable (for it is clear that there is no Okeanos under the earth), although it was probably a much earlier development, in a different direction, of the widely-diffused near-eastern generic concept of the earth rising in the midst of the primeval waters – a concept almost certainly not native to the Greek-speaking peoples, whose home before the migrations into the Greek peninsula lay far from the sea. Similarly, although the isolated references in *Iliad* book xiv (**8** and **9**) to Okeanos as origin of all things were also probably based upon the same near-eastern concept, from a slightly different aspect, they contain no implication of the special idea that the earth floats on water, and so are unlikely to have been the origin of Thales' assertion of this idea. For any more general contention that the earth came from, or is maintained by, water, Thales would no doubt be encouraged and gratified to have the apparently native Homeric precedents. Thus Thales' view that the earth floats on water seems to have been most probably based upon direct contact with near-eastern mythological cosmology. We have already seen that he had associations both with Babylonia and with Egypt. The idea that the earth actually floats upon water was more clearly and more widely held in the latter of these countries; and the conjecture might be hazarded that Thales was indebted to Egypt for this element of his world-picture.[2]

[1] These instances are cited by U. Hölscher in his convincing discussion of Thales, *Hermes* 81 (1953), 385–91. Some of the material is treated in ch. 1, especially pp. 11ff. For the idea of Nun, the Egyptian primeval ocean, supporting the earth, see also the remarks of J. A. Wilson, *Before Philosophy* 59ff., and H. Frankfort, *Ancient Egyptian Religion* (N.Y., 1948), 114.

[2] Thales evidently used the floating-earth idea to explain earthquakes: **88** Seneca *Qu. nat.* III, 14 (presumably from Theophrastus, through a Posidonian source): ait enim (*sc.* Thales) terrarum orbem aqua sustineri et vehi more navigii mobilitateque eius fluctuare tunc cum dicitur tremere. (*For he [Thales] said that the world is held up by water and rides like a ship, and when it is said to 'quake' it is actually rocking because of the water's movement.*)

The cosmological scope of the idea is, however, limited; and it seems reasonable to conclude from Aristotle's information in **85** that Thales also thought that the world *originated* from water, since this is implicit in the near-eastern mythologies and is stated in the Homeric Okeanos-passages which are thought to be based on those mythologies. Thales may have rationalized the idea from a Greek mythological form like the Homeric one; he may also have been directly influenced (as he seems to have been for the special detail that the earth floats on water) by foreign, perhaps Egyptian versions. Even more uncertainty attaches to a problem that has already been foreshadowed: are we justified in inferring from the Peripatetic identification of Thales' water as 'material principle' that he believed the visible, developed world to *be* water in some way? This is the normal interpretation of Thales; but it is important to realize that it rests ultimately on the Aristotelian formulation, and that Aristotle, knowing little about Thales, and that indirectly, would surely have found the mere information that the world originated from water sufficient justification for saying that water was Thales' material principle or ἀρχή, with the implication that water is a persistent substrate. It must be emphasized once more that no such development was necessary, and that it was not implicit in the near-eastern concepts which were ultimately Thales' archetype. Thales might have held that the world originated from an indefinite expanse[1] of primeval water, on which it still floats and which is still responsible for certain natural phenomena, without also believing that earth, rocks, trees or men are in any way *made of* water or a form of water. There would be a remote ancestral connexion, no more. On the other hand Thales *could* have made the entirely new inference that water is the continuing, hidden constituent of all things. Certainly his near successor Anaximenes believed that all things were made of air (but he had thought of a way in which this could be so: air takes on different forms when compressed or rarefied), and it is invariably assumed that he was extending and refining a line of thought initiated by Thales. It would be imprudent entirely to reject this assumption, which goes back to Theophrastus and Aristotle. The physiological reasons instanced by Aristotle, that all living things depend on water for nourishment, that the sperm is moist, and so on, although conjectural, are of a kind that might well have struck Thales. With other indications (e.g. the Homeric statement that the surrounding Okeanos is the source of all springs and rivers, **6**) they could have led him to the conclusion that water, as well as being the cosmogonical source, is also involved in the very essence of the developed world. On the other hand one must remain aware of the possibility that Aristotle was simply making his own kind of inference, in the absence of other information, from Thales' belief that the world originated from water and that water still plays a major part in the cosmos by supporting the earth.

[1] Thales would have accepted Simplicius' judgement (*in Phys.* 458, 23, DK 11 A 13) that water was, for him, ἄπειρον; though for Thales this would mean 'limitless', i.e. of indefinite extent, and not 'infinite', and be a natural assumption rather than a consciously propounded theory. Simplicius was more seriously misleading in asserting (*in Phys.* 180, 14) that Thales, like Anaximenes, generated by means of the condensation and rarefaction of his material principle. This is a purely schematic judgement based on an over-rigid dichotomy in Aristotle (**104**). Theophrastus only found the device explicitly used in Anaximenes; see **142**.

Two things, then, have emerged from the present discussion: (i) 'all things are water' is not necessarily a reliable summary of Thales'

THALES

cosmological views; and (ii) even if we do accept Aristotle's account (with some allowance, in any event, for his inevitably altered viewpoint), we have little idea of *how* things were felt to be essentially related to water.

(ii) *Even apparently inanimate things can be 'alive'; the world is full of gods*

89 Aristotle *de an.* A2, 405a19 ἔοικε δὲ καὶ Θαλῆς, ἐξ ὧν ἀπομνημονεύουσι, κινητικόν τι τὴν ψυχὴν ὑπολαβεῖν, εἴπερ τὴν λίθον ἔφη ψυχὴν ἔχειν ὅτι τὸν σίδηρον κινεῖ.

90 Diogenes Laertius I, 24 Ἀριστοτέλης δὲ καὶ Ἱππίας φασὶν αὐτὸν καὶ τοῖς ἀψύχοις μεταδιδόναι ψυχῆς, τεκμαιρόμενον ἐκ τῆς λίθου τῆς μαγνήτιδος καὶ τοῦ ἠλέκτρου.

91 Aristotle *de an.* A5, 411a7 καὶ ἐν τῷ ὅλῳ δέ τινες αὐτὴν (*sc.* τὴν ψυχὴν) μεμεῖχθαί φασιν, ὅθεν ἴσως καὶ Θαλῆς ᾠήθη πάντα πλήρη θεῶν εἶναι.

89 Thales, too, seems, from what they relate, to have supposed that the soul was something kinetic, if he said that the [Magnesian] stone possesses soul because it moves iron.
90 Aristotle and Hippias say that he gave a share of soul even to inanimate [*lit.* soulless] objects, using Magnesian stone and amber as indications.
91 And some say that it [soul] is intermingled in the universe, for which reason, perhaps, Thales also thought that all things are full of gods.

The two passages from Aristotle's *de anima* allow us to conjecture, but no more, about Thales' vision of the whole world as somehow alive and animated. Aristotle himself was reporting second-hand evidence, and his statements are jejune and cautious (although in **89** εἴπερ need not, and probably does not, express doubt, while ἴσως in **91** qualifies ὅθεν and not the assertion that follows). The concluding words of **91**, 'all things are full of gods', occur also in Plato, in a probably conscious but unattributed quotation.[1] **90** cites the sophist and polymath Hippias as an earlier source than Aristotle for Thales' attribution of motive power to Magnesian (magnetic) stone, to which is added amber, which becomes magnetic when rubbed. Presumably the addition is from Hippias, who may well have been Aristotle's source here.[2]

[1] **92** Plato *Laws* 10, 899B ἔσθ' ὅστις ταῦτα ὁμολογῶν ὑπομενεῖ μὴ θεῶν εἶναι πλήρη πάντα; (*Is there anyone who will accept this and maintain that all things are not full of gods?*) The context deals with souls being called gods; it is quite in Plato's

95

style to introduce, rather laboriously, a familiar phrase to enlighten an unfamiliar argument of his own, without naming the author. His use of the words in question is important, in any case, because it shows that they are not simply an Aristotelian summary. They could (in direct speech) be a genuine quotation from Thales; they have a totally different appearance from the banal apophthegms hopefully assigned to Thales in Demetrius of Phaleron's collection (*ap.* Stob. III, 1, 172, DK 10, 3). Aristotle repeated them, with the substitution of ψυχῆς for θεῶν and without attribution, at *Generation of Animals* Γ11, 762a21.

[2] Snell, in *Philologus* 96 (1944), 170–82, showed that Hippias was quite possibly the source of Aristotle's other remarks on Thales, including the comparison with older ideas on Okeanos etc. (11, cf. 12). The fragment of Hippias quoted by Clement, DK 86 b 6, shows that he made a collection of key passages on similar topics from Homer, Hesiod, Orphic writings, and Greek and other prose-sources. He was therefore the earliest systematic doxographer.

All that Aristotle seems to have known in **89** was that Thales thought that magnetic stone possesses soul because it is able to move iron; but the further inference, that for Thales the soul was something motive, is clearly legitimate. Soul, whether it was associated with breath, blood, or spinal fluid, was universally regarded as the source of consciousness and life. A man is alive, he can move his limbs and so move other things; if he faints, it means that his soul has withdrawn or become incapacitated; if he dies, it has become permanently so, and the 'soul' that goes squeaking down to Hades in Homer is a mere shadow, because it is dissociated from the body and can no longer produce life and movement. It is a common primitive tendency to regard rivers, trees and so on as somehow animated or inhabited by spirits: this is partly, though not wholly, because they seem to possess the faculty of self-movement and change, they differ from mere stocks and stones. Thales' attitude was not primitive, of course, but there is a connexion with that entirely unphilosophical animism. It should be noted, however, that his examples are of a different order; magnetic stone looks as unalive as could be, and cannot move or change itself, only a certain kind of external object. Thus Thales appears to have made explicit, in an extreme form, a way of thinking that permeated Greek mythology but whose ultimate origins were almost prearticulate. Now it is possible that our second piece of specific information, **91**, is a generalization based on this very conclusion that certain kinds of apparently inanimate object are alive, possess soul, because they have a limited power of movement. 'All things are full of gods':[1] the chief distinguishing marks of the gods are that they are immortal, they enjoy perpetual life, and that their power (their life-force, as it were) is unlimited, it extends both over the animate and over the inanimate world. Thus the assertion may well imply (since even apparently dead things like stone may possess soul of a kind) that the world as a whole manifests a power of change and motion which is certainly not even predominantly human, and must, both because of its permanence and because of its extent and variation, be regarded as divine, as due to the inherence of some form of immortal ψυχή.[2]

[1] Or of daimons, according to the paraphrase in Aetius after Theophrastus: **93** Aetius I, 7, 11 Θαλῆς νοῦν τοῦ κόσμου τὸν θεόν, τὸ δὲ πᾶν ἔμψυχον ἅμα καὶ δαιμόνων πλῆρες· διήκειν δὲ καὶ διὰ τοῦ στοιχειώδους ὑγροῦ δύναμιν θείαν κινητικὴν αὐτοῦ. *(Thales said that the mind of the world is god, and that the sum of things is besouled, and full of daimons; right through the elemental moisture there penetrates a divine power that moves it.)* The juxtaposition of the two statements from Aristotle is not significant. The last sentence is Stoic in form and content; the first clause (Θαλῆς...θεόν), too, is entirely anachronistic, and probably due to Stoic reinterpretation. It was repeated by Cicero, *de natura deorum* I, 10, 25, who added that god, as mind, made the world out of water. A considerable number of recognizably fictitious opinions, like this one, were attributed to Thales by puzzled or unscrupulous doxographers and biographers. Compare, perhaps, the 30,000 daimons of Hesiod *Works and Days* 252ff.

[2] The claim by Choerilus of Iasus (3rd–2nd cent. B.C.) and others, recorded in Diog. L. I, 24 (DK11A1), that according to Thales the soul was immortal, obviously arose as an illegitimate conclusion from this kind of argument, and is again due to Stoic perversion (primarily) of the type of **93**. Thales could have distinguished clearly between the human ψυχή and the divine life-force in the world as a whole, at the same time as implicitly recognizing their underlying connexion.

The precise nature of Thales' belief that all things are full of gods is obviously not determinable. Even along the line of interpretation suggested above there is one notable uncertainty: did Thales make the bold induction, from the observation about Magnesian stone and amber, that *all* apparently inanimate things really possess soul to some degree? Or was Burnet right in maintaining (*EGP* 50) that 'to say the magnet and amber are alive is to imply, if anything, that other things are not'? In itself the fragmentary observation implies nothing either way. Nor does the assertion that all things are full of gods, even if it is closely connected with the observation about magnetic stone, necessarily imply that the universal induction was made; for just as one can say in English 'this book is full of absurdities' without meaning that every single thing in it is absurd, so πλήρης in Greek could mean 'containing a great number of', as well as 'absolutely filled out by'. *A priori*, it perhaps seems more probable that Thales meant that all things in sum (rather than each single thing) were interpenetrated by some kind of life-principle; although there would be many kinds of matter from which this life-principle, with its kinetic power, might be absent. The point was that the range of soul, or of life, was much greater than it appeared to be. Thales was giving an explicit and individual statement of a broad presupposition common to all the early physicists, that the world was somehow alive, that it underwent spontaneous change, and (what irritated Aristotle) that there was therefore no need to give any special account of natural change. This presupposition is still sometimes called 'hylozoism'; but this name implies too strongly that it is something uniform, determinable, and conscious. In fact the term applies to at least three possible and distinct attitudes of mind: (a) the assumption (conscious or not) that all things absolutely are in some way alive; (b) the belief that the world is interpenetrated by life, that many of its parts which appear inanimate are in fact animate; (c) the tendency to treat the world as a whole, whatever its detailed constitution, as a single living organism. (a) is an extreme, but in view of the universalizing tendency of Greek thought not an impossible, form of the general presupposition; in a way it might be said to be exemplified by Xenophanes. Thales' belief, it has been suggested, approaches close to (b). (c) is implicit in the old genealogical view of the world's history described in chapter I, which still persisted to some extent under the new rationalized form of philosophical cosmogony. Aristotle is seen at his most perspicuous in **116**, where, perhaps with Thales especially in mind, he shows himself aware of the possibility of this kind of attitude.[1]

---

[1] The spears in the *Iliad* (XI, 574 etc.) which are 'eager to devour flesh', and other similar cases, are sometimes cited as an indication that the animistic view was an old one. Animism is, of course, as old as man himself, and it arises out of the failure to objectify one's experience of the outside world, a technique which requires some practice. The Homeric expressions are better described as a literary conceit, like the pathetic fallacy – a deliberate rejection of the technique.

CONCLUSION

Thales was chiefly known for his prowess as a practical astronomer, geometer, and sage in general. His prediction of the eclipse was probably made feasible by his use of Babylonian records, perhaps obtained at Sardis; he also probably visited Egypt. His theory that the earth floats on water seems to have been derived from near-eastern cosmogonical myths, perhaps directly; water as the origin of things was also a part of these myths, but had been mentioned in a Greek context long before Thales. His development of this concept may in itself have seemed to Aristotle sufficient warrant for saying that Thales held water to be the ἀρχή, in its Peripatetic sense of a persisting substrate. Yet Thales could indeed have felt that since water is essential for the maintenance of plant and animal life – we do not know what meteorological arguments he used – it remains still as the basic constituent of things. Although these ideas were strongly affected, directly or indirectly, by mythological precedents, Thales evidently abandoned mythic formulations; this alone justifies the claim that he was the first philosopher, naïve though his thought still was. Further, he noticed that even certain kinds of stone could have a limited power of movement and therefore, he thought, of life-giving soul; the world as a whole, consequently, was somehow permeated (though probably not completely) by a life-force which might naturally, because of its extent and its persistence, be called divine. Whether he associated this life-force with water, the origin and perhaps the essential constituent of the world, we are not told.

CHAPTER III

Anaximander of Miletus

DATE, BOOK, AND SCIENTIFIC ACTIVITIES

94 Diogenes Laertius II, 1–2 (DK 12 A 1) Ἀναξίμανδρος Πραξιάδου Μιλήσιος· οὗτος ἔφασκεν ἀρχὴν καὶ στοιχεῖον τὸ ἄπειρον, οὐ διορίζων ἀέρα ἢ ὕδωρ ἢ ἄλλο τι... εὗρεν δὲ καὶ γνώμονα πρῶτος καὶ ἔστησεν ἐπὶ τῶν σκιοθήρων ἐν Λακεδαίμονι, καθά φησι Φαβωρῖνος ἐν Παντοδαπῇ ἱστορίᾳ, τροπάς τε καὶ ἰσημερίας σημαίνοντα, καὶ ὡροσκοπεῖα κατεσκεύασε. καὶ γῆς καὶ θαλάσσης περίμετρον πρῶτος ἔγραψεν, ἀλλὰ καὶ σφαῖραν κατεσκεύασε. τῶν δὲ ἀρεσκόντων αὐτῷ πεποίηται κεφαλαιώδη τὴν ἔκθεσιν, ᾗ που περιέτυχεν καὶ Ἀπολλόδωρος ὁ Ἀθηναῖος· ὃς καί φησιν αὐτὸν ἐν τοῖς Χρονικοῖς τῷ δευτέρῳ ἔτει τῆς πεντηκοστῆς ὀγδόης ὀλυμπιάδος (547/6 B.C.) ἐτῶν εἶναι ἑξήκοντα τεττάρων καὶ μετ' ὀλίγον τελευτῆσαι (ἀκμάσαντά πη μάλιστα κατὰ Πολυκράτη τὸν Σάμου τύραννον).

95 Suda s.v. Ἀναξίμανδρος Πραξιάδου Μιλήσιος φιλόσοφος συγγενὴς καὶ μαθητὴς καὶ διάδοχος Θάλητος. πρῶτος δὲ ἰσημερίαν εὗρε καὶ τροπὰς καὶ ὡρολογεῖα, καὶ τὴν γῆν ἐν μεσαιτάτῳ κεῖσθαι. γνώμονά τε εἰσήγαγε καὶ ὅλως γεωμετρίας ὑποτύπωσιν ἔδειξεν. ἔγραψε Περὶ φύσεως, Γῆς περίοδον καὶ Περὶ τῶν ἀπλανῶν καὶ Σφαῖραν καὶ ἄλλα τινά.

94 Anaximander son of Praxiades, of Miletus: he said that the principle and element is the Indefinite, not distinguishing air or water or anything else...he was the first to discover a *gnomon*, and he set one up on the Sundials(?) in Sparta, according to Favorinus in his *Universal History*, to mark solstices and equinoxes; and he also constructed hour-indicators. He was the first to draw an outline of earth and sea, but also constructed a [celestial] globe. Of his opinions he made a summary exposition, which I suppose Apollodorus the Athenian, also, encountered. Apollodorus says in his *Chronicles* that Anaximander was sixty-four years old in the second year of the fifty-eighth Olympiad [547/6 B.C.], and that he died shortly afterwards (having been near his prime approximately during the time of Polycrates, tyrant of Samos).

movement of sun
" " winter.

95 Anaximander son of Praxiades, of Miletus, philosopher, was a kinsman, pupil and successor of Thales. He first discovered the equinox and solstices and hour-indicators, and that the earth lies in the centre. He introduced the *gnomon* and in general made known an outline of geometry. He wrote *On Nature, Circuit of the Earth* and *On the Fixed Stars* and a *Celestial Globe* and some other works.

(i) *Date*

If Thales earned the title of the first Greek philosopher mainly because of his abandonment of mythological formulations, Anaximander is the first of whom we have concrete evidence that he made a comprehensive and detailed attempt to explain all aspects of the world of man's experience. He was younger than Thales, but probably not by much. Burnet (*EGP* 51) inferred from the latter part of **94** that the chronographer Apollodorus found definite evidence, perhaps in a summary version of his book, that Anaximander was sixty-four in 547/6 B.C.; and that his death 'soon afterwards' was placed by Apollodorus in the next year, the epoch-year of the capture of Sardis. (The last clause of **94** is presumably a mistake: Polycrates did not come to power until *c.* 540 B.C. and died *c.* 522.) If this is so, then Thales and Anaximander died in the same Olympiad, and Anaximander was only fourteen years younger than Thales (n. on p. 76).[1] Anaximander was called the 'successor and pupil' of Thales by Theophrastus (**101** A), also his kinsman, companion, acquaintance or fellow-citizen in the later doxographical tradition. In most cases this kind of statement need only imply that the one was thought to come from the same city as, and to be somewhat younger than, the other.[2] If there were fixed dates both for Thales (the prediction of the eclipse in 585/4) and for Anaximander (for the information that he was sixty-four in 547/6 was presumably available also to Theophrastus), the *a priori* basis for Theophrastus' conjecture would be a reasonable one.

[1] That Thales and Anaximander are not separated by the conventional Apollodoran 40-year interval (see next note) is in favour of 547/6 being a non-arbitrary date. It is true that, if Anaximander could be made the master of Pythagoras, then his birth should be eighty years earlier than the latter's *floruit* (which Apollodorus placed in 532/1), and he would be very close to 64 (in fact 65) in 547/6. According to the evidence of Hippolytus (*Ref.* 1, 6, 7, DK 12A11) even Apollodorus was wrong by one year, since Hippolytus gives the birth-year as Ol. 42, 3 (610/9 B.C.) instead of Ol. 42, 2. What is significant, however, is that Anaximander's age was known for a particular year which was not his *floruit* and not necessarily that of his death, although it was close to his death. Further, no

connexion of Pythagoras with Anaximander is known in the great majority of our sources (only in Porphyry *Life of Pythagoras* 2, after Apollonius, presumably of Tyana, and in Apuleius *Florida* 15, 20). Nevertheless, the possibility cannot be entirely excluded that Apollodorus' dating of Anaximander was arbitrarily hinged to his Polycrates–Pythagoras system. This might help to account for the last clause of **94**.

[2] The arrangement of the early philosophers into 'schools', and into masters and pupils within these schools, was initiated by Theophrastus and systematically applied in the *Successions* of Sotion, *c.* 200 B.C. Apollodorus used the latter work, and normally assumed a 40-year interval in age between master and pupil.

(ii) *Anaximander's book*

The book-titles ascribed to Anaximander in **95**, presumably from Hesychius, should be regarded with reserve. It was the custom with Alexandrian writers to supply titles, in the absence of definite evidence, to suit an early thinker's known interests. 'On nature' was a standard comprehensive title which tended to be assigned to all those whom Aristotle called φυσικοί, that is, to almost all the Presocratics.[1] That Anaximander certainly wrote a book of some kind is shown both by Theophrastus' incontrovertible quotation in **101A**, and possibly by Diogenes' information in **94** that there was a 'summary exposition', which he took to be by the philosopher himself. What Diogenes knew of may have been a later summary (produced either by a pupil or, more probably, in the fourth century B.C. or later); or it may have been the original work, whose short, perhaps discontinuous, and apophthegmatic nature was not what was normally expected of a philosophical book.[2] It is not clear whether it was from this source that Apollodorus determined the year in which Anaximander was sixty-four; it seemed probable to Diogenes, though that age is considerably greater than the average for authorship.[3] Theophrastus had access to at least one original sentence, but seems to have lacked full information about Anaximander's originative substance. The possibility cannot be ignored that he, too, used a summary or handbook, partly at least in the form of a collection of excerpts, and one which concentrated on cosmology, anthropology and so on rather than on the nature of the parent-material. On the other hand, Anaximander himself might have offered little information on the originative substance.

[1] Cf. **96** Themistius *Or.* 26 p. 383 Dindorf (Ἀναξίμανδρος) ἐθάρρησε πρῶτος ὧν ἴσμεν Ἑλλήνων λόγον ἐξενεγκεῖν περὶ φύσεως συγγεγραμμένον. (*[Anaximander] was the first of the Greeks whom we know who ventured to produce a written account on nature.*) Thales was thought not to have written a book, at any rate one of a general cosmological kind: see pp. 87f. One of the objections to Περὶ φύσεως as a genuine sixth-century book-title is that φύσις is probably not used in the

collective sense, 'Nature', before about the middle of the fifth century (cf. Kirk, *Heraclitus, the Cosmic Fragments* (Cambridge, 1954), 227ff.). Gorgias' sardonic title Περὶ φύσεως ἢ περὶ τοῦ μὴ ὄντος implies that Περὶ φύσεως was common *in his time*, but no more than that. On the other hand, the addition of a word like χρημάτων or ἁπάντων to φύσεως would make the usage possible. The fact remains that Περὶ φύσεως was indiscriminately applied to any work of a vaguely physical nature: cf. e.g. pp. 166f. for Xenophanes' poetry; also Kahn, *Anaximander and the Origins of Greek Cosmology* (New York, 1960) p. 6 n. 2.

² For Pherecydes' roughly contemporary book see p. 51. – We do not know how many words a papyrus roll is likely to have held in the sixth century B.C. The letters were probably large (papyrus should have been relatively cheap in Miletus, from Naucratis), and the total product quite short. See p. 356 and n. 2 for Anaxagoras' book.

³ The elder Pliny (*N.H.* II, 31, DK 12A5) stated that Anaximander discovered the obliquity of the Zodiac in this same Olympiad, the fifty-eighth; but the ascription of this discovery is probably false (p. 104 n.), and Pliny perhaps merely misapplied Apollodorus' dating.

(iii) *Scientific activities: (a) the gnomon*

Anaximander did not *discover* the gnomon, as **94** claims (the gnomon is a set-square or any vertical rod whose shadow indicates the sun's direction and height): compare

97 Herodotus II, 109 πόλον μὲν γὰρ καὶ γνώμονα καὶ τὰ δυώδεκα μέρεα τῆς ἡμέρης παρὰ Βαβυλωνίων ἔμαθον οἱ Ἕλληνες.

97 The Greeks learned from the Babylonians of the celestial sphere and the *gnomon* and the twelve parts of the day.

95 may be correct, nevertheless, in suggesting that Anaximander *introduced* the gnomon into Greece. We cannot be sure, however, that Thales did not use some form of the instrument (p. 83), and it is possible that Anaximander gained the credit by accident, or because his use of the gnomon was more sophisticated. No special discoveries involving its use were assigned to him which were not also assigned to Thales; but he may have gained notoriety by the incident referred to by Favorinus in **94**. The statement that Anaximander set up a gnomon in Sparta ἐπὶ τῶν σκιοθήρων is mysterious. A σκιόθηρον (or σκιοθήρης) was a sun-dial, but the prepositional phrase cannot mean anything like 'for a sun-dial' or 'for the benefit of the sun-dials', and perhaps there was a prominence in Sparta later known as 'the sun-dials', from the gnomon or gnomons that existed there; ἐπί, then, would be local. ὡροσκοπεῖα in **94** and ὡρολογεῖα in **95** imply that the ground near the gnomon was calibrated so as to give the time of day, as well as the position of the sun on the ecliptic and so the season of the year. For another association of Anaximander with Sparta see n. on p. 105.[1]

¹ Pliny *N.H.* II, 187 (DK 13 A 14 a), held that it was Anaximenes who first demonstrated in Sparta the 'horologium quod appellant sciothericon', and who discovered the use of the gnomon. This is probably a mistake by Pliny, who tended to confound his facts in writing about early astronomy. He attributed the discovery of the obliquity of the Zodiac to Anaximander (p. 103), but Eudemus in 76 probably assigned this to Oenopides. The full comprehension of the ecliptic doubtless belonged to the fifth century; that the sun moves from north to south and back was known much earlier – and certainly, for example, by Thales.

(iii) *Scientific activities:* (b) *the map*

98 Agathemerus I, I   Ἀναξίμανδρος ὁ Μιλήσιος ἀκουστὴς Θαλέω πρῶτος ἐτόλμησε τὴν οἰκουμένην ἐν πίνακι γράψαι· μεθ᾽ ὃν Ἑκαταῖος ὁ Μιλήσιος ἀνὴρ πολυπλανὴς διηκρίβωσεν, ὥστε θαυμασθῆναι τὸ πρᾶγμα.

99 Strabo I, p. 7 Casaubon   ...τοὺς πρώτους μεθ᾽ Ὅμηρον δύο φησὶν Ἐρατοσθένης, Ἀναξίμανδρόν τε Θαλοῦ γεγονότα γνώριμον καὶ πολίτην καὶ Ἑκαταῖον τὸν Μιλήσιον. τὸν μὲν οὖν ἐκδοῦναι πρῶτον γεωγραφικὸν πίνακα, τὸν δὲ Ἑκαταῖον καταλιπεῖν γράμμα πιστούμενον ἐκείνου εἶναι ἐκ τῆς ἄλλης αὐτοῦ γραφῆς.

98 Anaximander the Milesian, a disciple of Thales, first dared to draw the inhabited world on a tablet; after him Hecataeus the Milesian, a much-travelled man, made the map more accurate, so that it became a source of wonder.

99 ...Eratosthenes says that the first to follow Homer were two, Anaximander, who was an acquaintance and fellow-citizen of Thales, and Hecataeus the Milesian. The former was the first to publish a geographical map, while Hecataeus left behind a drawing believed to be his from the rest of his writings.

These passages are obviously based on the same one statement by Eratosthenes, as is Diogenes' remark in **94** that 'Anaximander first drew an outline of land and sea'. Diogenes' addition, 'but he also constructed a sphere' (that is, a map of the heaven), is unsubstantiated and, in the light of Anaximander's theory of the heavenly bodies (pp. 134ff.), improbable. The general nature of his map can probably be inferred from the following passage:

100 Herodotus IV, 36   γελῶ δὲ ὁρῶν γῆς περιόδους γράψαντας πολλοὺς ἤδη καὶ οὐδένα νόον ἐχόντως ἐξηγησάμενον· οἳ Ὠκεανόν τε ῥέοντα γράφουσι πέριξ τὴν γῆν, ἐοῦσαν κυκλοτερέα ὡς ἀπὸ τόρνου, καὶ τὴν Ἀσίην τῇ Εὐρώπῃ ποιεύντων ἴσην.

100 I smile when I see that many have drawn circuits of the earth, up to now, and none of them has explained the matter sensibly; they draw Okeanos running around the earth, which is drawn as though with a compass, and make Asia equal to Europe.

It is a reasonable assumption that the (probably Ionian) maps referred to here resembled that of Anaximander as improved by his fellow-citizen Hecataeus; and therefore that Anaximander produced a circular plan in which the known regions of the world formed roughly equal segments; see further Kahn, *op. cit.*, 81–4. His empirical knowledge of geography was presumably based in part on seafarers' reports, which in Miletus, as a commercial centre and founder of colonies, would be both accessible and varied. The philosopher himself was said to have led a colonizing expedition to Apollonia (the city on the Black Sea, presumably), cf. Aelian *V.H.* III, 17 (DK 12A3). Otherwise his only known foreign contacts are with Sparta.[1]

[1] Apart from the sun-indicator story in **94**, Cicero related (*de divinat.* I, 50, 112, DK 12A5*a*) that Anaximander warned the Spartans to move into the fields when an earthquake was imminent. One is reminded of miraculous predictions assigned to Pherecydes and Pythagoras (pp. 52f.); but as a citizen of Miletus, in the earthquake belt, Anaximander would have had special experience. The modern Thessalians, for example, know that an earthquake is imminent when the storks become agitated. At all events Anaximander seems to have visited Sparta, otherwise two separate anecdotes about him would hardly be located there.

THE NATURE OF ANAXIMANDER'S ORIGINATIVE SUBSTANCE, τὸ ἄπειρον (THE INDEFINITE)

Part of Theophrastus' account of Anaximander's originative material is preserved by Simplicius. It is disputed whether Simplicius derived this and similar doxographical extracts direct from a version of Theophrastus, or by the medium of Alexander's lost commentary on the *Physics*; some extracts certainly came from this source. A more important question is whether Simplicius, or Alexander, was using the full edition of Theophrastus, or the two-volume summary, or an even shorter compendious account. The long surviving fragment on sensation, also in Simplicius, is on a very much larger scale than the extremely cursory extracts on the material principle, which suggests that they were derived from different versions of Theophrastus; the latter probably do not come from the complete edition. Hippolytus and the author of the pseudo-Plutarchean *Stromateis* also have doxographical summaries of Anaximander; they follow Theophrastus less closely than does Simplicius (whose text in **101**A 'can be treated as largely identical with that of Theophrastus' according to Kahn, *op. cit.*, 33), but provide confirmation and expansion at certain points. They also cover a greater range of subjects, some of which (e.g. zoogony, astronomy) are dealt with at greater length than the question of the ἀρχή. Simplicius' extract is printed in the left-hand column of **101**, with the corresponding parts of the two subsidiary versions alongside. Briefer and less accurate versions of this doxography appear in **94** and in Aetius (1, 3, 3, DK 12A14). It should be remembered that the passages in **101** are versions of *Theophrastus*' view of Anaximander; it will be seen that, so far as the material principle was concerned, he differed little from Aristotle, from whom some of his phraseology is directly derived. He quoted one original sentence (bold type in **101**A; see pp. 117ff.); this need not imply that he had seen the whole of Anaximander's book, as is almost invariably assumed. If he did see the whole, either it was very obscure about the originative stuff or he was untypically obtuse.

101 Versions of Theophrastus' account of Anaximander's originative substance:

A. Simplicius *in Phys.* 24, 13; DK 12A9

B. Hippolytus *Ref.* 1, 6, 1–2; DK 12A11

C. Ps.-Plutarch *Strom.* 2; DK 12A10

τῶν δὲ ἓν καὶ κινούμενον καὶ ἄπειρον λεγόντων Ἀναξίμανδρος μὲν Πραξιάδου Μιλήσιος Θαλοῦ γενόμενος διάδοχος καὶ μαθητής
ἀρχήν τε καὶ στοιχεῖον εἴρηκε τῶν ὄντων τὸ ἄπειρον,

πρῶτος τοῦτο τοὔνομα κομίσας τῆς ἀρχῆς.

Θαλοῦ τοίνυν Ἀναξίμανδρος γίνεται ἀκροατής. Ἀ. Πραξιάδου Μιλήσιος· ...

οὗτος μὲν ἀρχὴν καὶ στοιχεῖον εἴρηκε τῶν ὄντων τὸ ἄπειρον,

πρῶτος ⟨τοῦτο⟩ τοὔνομα καλέσας τῆς ἀρχῆς. (πρὸς δὲ τούτῳ κίνησιν ἀΐδιον εἶναι, ἐν ᾗ συμβαίνει γίνεσθαι τοὺς οὐρανούς.)

...Ἀναξίμανδρον Θάλητος ἕταιρον γενόμενον

τὸ ἄπειρον φάναι τὴν πᾶσαν αἰτίαν ἔχειν τῆς τοῦ παντὸς γενέσεώς τε καὶ φθορᾶς,

λέγει δ᾽ αὐτὴν μήτε ὕδωρ μήτε ἄλλο τι τῶν καλουμένων εἶναι στοιχείων, ἀλλ᾽ ἑτέραν τινὰ φύσιν ἄπειρον,
ἐξ ἧς ἅπαντας γίνεσθαι τοὺς οὐρανοὺς καὶ τοὺς ἐν αὐτοῖς κόσμους.

...οὗτος ἀρχὴν ἔφη τῶν ὄντων φύσιν τινὰ τοῦ ἀπείρου,

ἐξ ἧς γίνεσθαι τοὺς οὐρανοὺς καὶ τὸν ἐν αὐτοῖς κόσμον.

ἐξ οὗ δή φησι τούς τε οὐρανοὺς ἀποκεκρίσθαι καὶ καθόλου τοὺς ἅπαντας ἀπείρους ὄντας κόσμους.

ταύτην δ'
ἀΐδιον εἶναι καὶ ἀγήρω, ἣν
καὶ πάντας περιέχειν τοὺς
κόσμους.

ἐξ ὧν δὲ ἡ γένεσίς
ἐστι τοῖς οὖσι, καὶ τὴν
φθορὰν εἰς ταῦτα γίνεσθαι
κατὰ τὸ χρεών·

λέγει δὲ χρόνον
ὡς ὡρισμένης τῆς γενέσ-
εως καὶ τῆς οὐσίας καὶ
τῆς φθορᾶς.

ἀπεφήνατο δὲ
τὴν φθορὰν γίνεσθαι καὶ
πολὺ πρότερον τὴν
γένεσιν ἐξ ἀπείρου αἰῶνος
ἀνακυκλουμένων πάντων
αὐτῶν.

**διδόναι γὰρ αὐτὰ
δίκην καὶ τίσιν αλλήλοις
τῆς ἀδικίας κατὰ τὴν
τοῦ χρόνου τάξιν,** ποιητικωτέροις οὕτως ὀνόμασιν
αὐτὰ λέγων.
(What follows is Simpl.,
not Theophrastus.)

(λέγει δὲ χρόνον...)

A

Of those who say that it is
one, moving, and infinite,
Anaximander, son of
Praxiades, a Milesian,
the successor and pupil of
Thales,
——said that the prin-
ciple and element of existing things was the *apeiron*
[indefinite, *or* infinite],

being the first to introduce
this name of the material
principle.

He says that
it is neither water nor
any other of the so-called
elements, but some other
apeiron nature,
from
which come into being all
the heavens and the worlds
in them.

B

Now Anaximander was
the disciple of Thales.
Anaximander, son of
Praxiades, of Miletus:...

he said that
the principle and element
of existing things was the
apeiron,

being the first to use this
name of the material
principle.
(In addition to
this he said that motion
was eternal, in which it
results that the heavens
come into being.)
...he said
that the material principle
of existing things was some
nature coming under the
heading of the *apeiron,*
from which come into
being the heavens and the
world in them.

C

...Anaximander, who
was the companion of
Thales,

said that the
apeiron contained the
whole cause of the coming-
to-be and destruction of
the world,

from which he says
that the heavens are separated off, and in general all
the worlds, being *apeirous*
[innumerable].

107

And the source of coming-to-be for existing things is that into which destruction, too, happens 'according to necessity;

This nature is eternal and unageing, and it also surrounds all the worlds.

He talks of Time as though coming-to-be and existence and destruction were limited.

He declared that destruction, and much earlier coming-to-be, happen from infinite ages, since they are all occurring in cycles.

for they pay penalty and retribution to each other for their injustice according to the assessment of Time',
as he describes it in these rather poetical terms.

(He talks of Time...)

(i) Did Anaximander call the originative substance ἀρχή?

Most modern critics (including Kahn, *op. cit.*, 29–32) think that Theophrastus named Anaximander as the first to have used ἀρχή (literally 'beginning' or 'source') as a special term for the originative substance. They infer this from πρῶτος τοῦτο τοὔνομα κομίσας τῆς ἀρχῆς in **101**A, its equivalent in **101**B, and one further context in Simplicius (*in Phys.* 150, 23) where Anaximander is described as πρῶτος αὐτὸς ἀρχὴν ὀνομάσας τὸ ὑποκείμενον. Burnet, however (*EGP* 54 n. 2), maintained that what Theophrastus said was simply that Anaximander was the first to call the material principle (ἀρχή in its normal Peripatetic sense) by the name τὸ ἄπειρον, without further qualification. This, indeed, is the most obvious sense of the extract from Theophrastus, **101**A, while in **101**B τοῦτο has presumably dropped out by haplography before τοὔνομα. The other passage of Simplicius is more difficult: its most obvious meaning is 'being the first to call the substratum of the opposites ἀρχή', but Burnet explained it as meaning 'being the first to name the substratum of the opposites as the material cause' (that is, because according to Aristotle the opposites in Anaximander were specifically produced from the originative stuff). Burnet's interpretation, while admittedly not the most apparent meaning of the clause in isolation, is certainly more relevant to the trend of Simplicius' argument. Further (a point ignored by Kahn in his discussion), Theophrastus had used the word ἀρχή in his remarks on Thales as already reported by Simplicius (*in Phys.* 23, 23, DK 11 A 13), with no special note that Thales himself did not actually use this word – a note that would perhaps have been natural if Theophrastus had gone on to assert that Anaximander was its originator. It is possible, of course, that Simplicius misunderstood Theophrastus' comment about ἀρχή and ἄπειρον. The whole question is of limited importance; it still seems probable, however, that no technical use of ἀρχή by Anaximander was implied *by Theophrastus* – the use he referred to was of τὸ ἄπειρον.

(ii) *What did Anaximander mean by* τὸ ἄπειρον?

102 Aristotle *Phys.* Γ4, 203a16 οἱ δὲ περὶ φύσεως πάντες ὑποτιθέασιν ἑτέραν τινὰ φύσιν τῷ ἀπείρῳ τῶν λεγομένων στοιχείων, οἷον ὕδωρ ἢ ἀέρα ἢ τὸ μεταξὺ τούτων.

> **102** All the physicists make the infinite a property of some other nature belonging to the so-called elements, such as water or air or that which is intermediate between these.

First, it is advisable to isolate the Peripatetic, and so also the doxographical, interpretation of τὸ ἄπειρον. Aristotle, curiously enough, mentioned Anaximander by name only four times, but made several probable references to his primary substance (e.g. **109** *fin.*). There is little doubt that he took ἄπειρον in Anaximander, and in the monists in general, to mean primarily 'spatially infinite'. This is suggested in **102**. In **108**, part of his discussion of the concept of infinity, Aristotle attributes some specific quality, presumably that of the intermediate in the case of Anaximander (pp. 111ff.), to the material principles of all the φυσικοί who recognize the infinite. Theophrastus seems to have felt that Anaximander had given his primary substance a name which described its spatial property, but which said nothing except by implication (that it was not identified with any of the later 'elements') about its qualitative properties. Thus in **101**A line 2, and in other such classifications, ἄπειρον means 'infinite'; it is 'neither water nor any other of the so-called elements, but some other infinite nature from which come all the heavens...' (Anaximander's heavens being infinite in number for Theophrastus).[1]

[1] The words ἑτέραν τινὰ φύσιν ἄπειρον seem to echo Aristotle's radically different ἑτέραν τινὰ φύσιν τῷ ἀπείρῳ in **102**, especially since the wider contexts of the two phrases have much in common. This superficial similarity of phraseology suggests that Theophrastus had made himself familiar with his master's discussion of infinity in the *Physics* before he set about summarizing the theories of Anaximander.

It is, however, uncertain that Anaximander himself intended τὸ ἄπειρον to mean precisely 'the spatially infinite'. We may legitimately doubt whether the concept of infinity was apprehended before questions of continuous extension and continuous divisibility were raised by Melissus and Zeno. ἄπειρον means 'without boundary, limit, definition'; this indefiniteness is spatial in early usages, as in the ἀπείρονα πόντον of Homer (Anaximander's ἄπειρον is presumably from ἄπειρος, of which ἀπείρων is a more poetical equivalent), and as in Xenophanes (3), who said that the earth went down ἐς ἄπειρον, indefinitely, i.e. beyond the imagination or the concern of men. Now Anaximander certainly assumed the original stuff to have been indefinitely huge in extent; but he perhaps gave formal expression to this idea by saying that this stuff 'surrounded all things' (108), and might not have felt this characteristic (which must have been assumed as a matter of course by Thales, see n. on p. 94) to be sufficiently remarkable to be applied as sole description, that is as 'the spatially indefinite'. We might expect any such single description to refer first to the *kind* of substance, not to its commonly assumed vastness of extent. Thus Cornford and others argued that τὸ ἄπειρον meant 'that which is internally unbounded, without internal distinctions', i.e. that which is indistinct, indefinite in kind. There is no need to stress *internal* divisions,[1] but the general point seems not improbable: for Anaximander the original world-forming stuff was indefinite, it resembled no one kind of matter in the developed world. Yet no parallel early use of ἄπειρος in a certainly non-spatial sense can be cited, and this is in favour of retaining the interpretation 'spatially indefinite'. In any case the lack of positive identification was conspicuously implied. Either τὸ ἄπειρον meant 'the spatially indefinite', and was implied to be indefinite in kind because it was not formally identified as fire, air, water or earth (to use Theophrastus' terms of 101 A); or Anaximander intended it to mean primarily 'that which is indefinite in kind', but naturally assumed it also to be of unlimited extent and duration – properties which, when expressed, would be expressed in terms of all-inclusiveness and divine immortality.[2]

---

[1] Nor is it easy to accept the suggestion of Diels and Cornford that the ἄπειρον was conceived as circular or spherical, cf. ἄπειρον ἀμφίβληστρον at Aeschylus *Ag.* 1382, ἄπειρος of a ring in Aristophanes and Aristotle, etc. It is impossible to prove that any particular application of the word that was feasible in the archaic period was entirely absent from Anaximander's mind; but the intention seems to have been to deny any fixed determination. See further Kahn, *op. cit.*, 231ff.

[2] Cherniss, *Aristotle's Criticism of Presocratic Philosophy* (Baltimore, 1935), 377f., maintained that Anaximander meant ἄπειρον ⟨τὸ πλῆθος⟩, i.e. 'with an

indeterminate number of internal divisions'. But in this case ἄπειρον would have to be expressly qualified by a word implying number, as in Anaxagoras frr. 1 and 2 (467, 488).

(iii) *The Indefinite as an intermediate substance in Aristotle*

103 Aristotle *de gen. et corr.* B5, 332a19 ...οὐκ ἔστιν ἓν τούτων (*sc.* πυρός, ἀέρος, ὕδατος, γῆς) ἐξ οὗ τὰ πάντα· οὐ μὴν οὐδ' ἄλλο τί γε παρὰ ταῦτα, οἷον μέσον τι ἀέρος καὶ ὕδατος ἢ ἀέρος καὶ πυρός, ἀέρος μὲν παχύτερον καὶ πυρός, τῶν δὲ λεπτότερον· ἔσται γὰρ ἀὴρ καὶ πῦρ ἐκεῖνο μετ' ἐναντιότητος· ἀλλὰ στέρησις τὸ ἕτερον τῶν ἐναντίων· ὥστ' οὐκ ἐνδέχεται μονοῦσθαι ἐκεῖνο οὐδέποτε, ὥσπερ φασί τινες τὸ ἄπειρον καὶ τὸ περιέχον.

104 Aristotle *Phys.* A4, 187a12 ὡς δ' οἱ φυσικοὶ λέγουσι, δύο τρόποι εἰσίν. οἱ μὲν γὰρ ἓν ποιήσαντες τὸ σῶμα τὸ ὑποκείμενον, ἢ τῶν τριῶν τι ἢ ἄλλο ὅ ἐστι πυρὸς μὲν πυκνότερον ἀέρος δὲ λεπτότερον, τἆλλα γεννῶσι πυκνότητι καὶ μανότητι πολλὰ ποιοῦντες ...οἱ δ' ἐκ τοῦ ἑνὸς ἐνούσας τὰς ἐναντιότητας ἐκκρίνεσθαι, ὥσπερ Ἀναξίμανδρός φησι καὶ ὅσοι δ' ἓν καὶ πολλά φασιν εἶναι, ὥσπερ Ἐμπεδοκλῆς καὶ Ἀναξαγόρας· ἐκ τοῦ μίγματος γὰρ καὶ οὗτοι ἐκκρίνουσι τἆλλα.

> **103** ...There is no *one* of these things [fire, air, water, earth] from which come all things; and certainly nothing else beside these, such as something half-way between air and water, or air and fire, being thicker than air and fire and finer than the others: for that will be air and fire, simply, together with contrariety; but one of the two opposites is a privation – so that it is impossible for the intermediate ever to exist in isolation, as some say the infinite [*apeiron*] and the surrounding does.
>
> **104** Two types of explanation are given by the physicists. Those who have made the subsisting body *one*, either one of the three or something else which is thicker than fire and finer than air, generate the rest by condensation and rarefaction, making it into many...But the others say that the opposites are separated out from the One, being present in it, as Anaximander says and all who say there are one and many, like Empedocles and Anaxagoras; for these, too, separate out the rest from the mixture.

Aristotle, when listing various monistic theories of the φυσικοί, on a number of occasions speaks of a substance *between* the elements – normally between fire and air or between air and water.[1] In three or four of these passages it looks as though Anaximander is meant as the proponent of an intermediate substance, not because he is directly named but because the substance is implied to have been called simply τὸ ἄπειρον. In **103** the people who said that 'the ἄπειρον and the surrounding' existed on its own, in isolation from the elements, appear from the terminology (cf. **108**) to be Anaximander and followers; see also **109**, where the intermediate between water and air is said to 'surround all the heavens, being boundless'. Now Aristotle in **102** declared that all the φυσικοί who envisaged it gave some specific description of the infinite (τὸ ἄπειρον); we may ask what description Anaximander was deemed by Aristotle, when he wrote those words, to have given, if not as an intermediate – which is, indeed, actually mentioned in that passage as a typical description. Were it not for one passage, namely **104**, there would be no difficulty in accepting that Aristotle had Anaximander in mind in most, at any rate, of his references to an intermediate material principle. One of Aristotle's most acute ancient commentators, Alexander of Aphrodisias, did in fact accept this; so, usually, did Simplicius. Yet in **104**, on the only possible interpretation, Aristotle placed the intermediate substance and Anaximander in opposed groups.[2] Various unenlightening guesses have been made about the historical author of the intermediate-substance theory; but a careful study of all Aristotle's references indicates that Anaximander was, after all, in his mind – although Anaximander in fact held no such theory. Aristotle evidently felt that Anaximander's (for Aristotle) 'infinite' ἀρχή must have had *some* expressible relationship to the so-called elements; and there are some passages (e.g. **105**) in which he wrote simply of τὸ παρὰ τὰ στοιχεῖα, 'that which is beside the elements', not identifiable with any one of them, and not of τὸ μεταξύ or τὸ μέσον. By this formulation one possibility was that it was intermediate between two elements; another, that it was a mixture of them all. In **104** Aristotle seems to take the latter view; but he elsewhere considered the former possibility, and had arrived at the theoretical hypothesis of an intermediate (a hypothesis which he himself, of course, regarded as untenable: cf. **103**) as a by-product of his reflections on Anaximander. That he had no explicit historical example in mind, however, is shown by his variation of the elements between which the intermediate came. Usually when he mentioned an intermediate in lists of possible primary substances he had Anaximander in mind, though he also tended to add the intermediate indiscriminately to any such list for the sake of exhaustivity. It is so added in **104**, where, as the result of a different type of critique, he applies the mixture-interpretation to Anaximander by name; see also pp. 113f.; Kahn, *op. cit.*, 44–6; Hussey, *The Presocratics* (London, 1972),

p. 71; Kirk, 'Some problems in Anaximander', *CQ* N.s. 5 (1955), 24ff.; M. Whitby, *Mnemosyne* 35 (1982), 225–47.

[1] Apart from **102, 103, 104, 109**, cf. *Met.* A7, 988a30; 989a14; *Phys.* A6, 189b1; *de gen. et corr.* B1, 328b35.

[2] It might be argued that τὸ ἕν, the One, is common to both groups, therefore that Anaximander might occur in each. But the contrast is really between those who retain the One as a substratum, and those who (like Anaximander) do not.

(iv) *Why 'the Indefinite' and not a specific originative substance?*

105 Aristotle *Phys.* Γ5, 204b22   ἀλλὰ μὴν οὐδὲ ἕν καὶ ἁπλοῦν εἶναι ἐνδέχεται τὸ ἄπειρον σῶμα, οὔτε ὡς λέγουσί τινες τὸ παρὰ τὰ στοιχεῖα, ἐξ οὗ ταῦτα γεννῶσιν, οὔθ' ἁπλῶς. εἰσὶ γάρ τινες οἳ τοῦτο ποιοῦσι τὸ ἄπειρον, ἀλλ' οὐκ ἀέρα ἢ ὕδωρ, ὡς μὴ τἆλλα φθείρηται ὑπὸ τοῦ ἀπείρου αὐτῶν· ἔχουσι γὰρ πρὸς ἄλληλα ἐναντίωσιν, οἷον ὁ μὲν ἀὴρ ψυχρός, τὸ δ' ὕδωρ ὑγρόν, τὸ δὲ πῦρ θερμόν· ὧν εἰ ἦν ἓν ἄπειρον ἔφθαρτο ἂν ἤδη τἆλλα. νῦν δ' ἕτερον εἶναί φασι ἐξ οὗ ταῦτα.

106 Aristotle *Phys.* Γ4, 203b15   τοῦ δ' εἶναί τι ἄπειρον ἡ πίστις ἐκ πέντε μάλιστ' ἂν συμβαίνοι σκοποῦσιν...ἔτι τῷ οὕτως ἂν μόνως μὴ ὑπολείπειν γένεσιν καὶ φθοράν, εἰ ἄπειρον εἴη ὅθεν ἀφαιρεῖται τὸ γιγνόμενον.

> **105** But yet, nor can the infinite body be one and simple, whether it be, as some say, that which is beside the elements, from which they generate the elements, or whether it be expressed simply. For there are some people who make what is beside the elements the infinite, and not air or water, so that the rest be not destroyed by their infinite substance; for the elements are opposed to each other (for example, air is cold, water moist, and fire hot), and if one of those were infinite the rest would already have been destroyed. But, as it is, they say that the infinite is different from these, and that they come into being from it.
>
> **106** Belief in infinity would result, for those who consider the matter, for the most part from five factors...further, because only so would generation and destruction not fail, if there were an infinite source from which that which is coming-to-be is derived.

These passages present two possible motives for the idea of the Indefinite as primary substance. The reason in **105** – that the infinite primary substance, if identified with a specific world-constituent, would swamp the other world-constituents and never allow them to develop – is assigned to those who posited an ἄπειρον substance 'beside the elements', i.e. not identical with any of them. When Aristotle used this formulation he usually, though not necessarily invariably, had Anaximander in mind (§ (iii)), and Simplicius in his comment on the passage (*in Phys.* 479, 33) ascribed this reason to Anaximander. On the other hand the totally different reason suggested in 106 – that an infinite source-material ensures that coming-to-be within the world shall not fail for want of material – is given as Anaximander's by Aetius (1, 3, 3, DK 12 A 4) and by Simplicius elsewhere (*de caelo* 615, 15, DK 12 A 17). Aetius' attribution suggests that Theophrastus applied the motive of 106 to Anaximander; but we cannot be sure that he did not apply that of 105 also, and in either case he was probably working from what Aristotle had said.

Most modern critics have accepted 106 as giving Anaximander's true motive, and many have rejected 105 as not (in spite of appearances) applying to Anaximander. Thus Cherniss called the argument in 105 'the peculiarly Aristotelian argument of the necessary equilibrium of contrary forces'. It is true that it is expressed, naturally enough, in an Aristotelian form. But Anaximander had postulated a comprehensive balance between opposed substances (see 110 with discussion), and might well have reasoned in some such way as this: 'Thales said that all things originated from water; but water (which we see in the form of rain, sea and rivers) is opposed to fire (the sun, the fiery aither, volcanoes etc.), and these things are mutually destructive. How then can fire have become such a prominent part of our world, if it were from the beginning constantly opposed by the whole indefinitely-extended mass of its very opposite? How, indeed, can it have appeared at all, for a single moment? The warring constituents of our world, then, must have developed from a substance different from any of them – something indefinite or indeterminable.' (Aristotle's interpretation of ἄπειρον as 'infinite' does not affect this issue.)

As for 106, Aristotle himself pointed out its fallacy:

107 Aristotle *Phys.* Γ8, 208a8 οὔτε γάρ, ἵνα ἡ γένεσις μὴ ἐπιλείπη, ἀναγκαῖον ἐνεργείᾳ ἄπειρον εἶναι σῶμα αἰσθητόν· ἐνδέχεται γὰρ τὴν θατέρου φθορὰν θατέρου εἶναι γένεσιν, πεπερασμένου ὄντος τοῦ παντός.

107 Nor, in order that generation may not fail, is it necessary for perceptible body to be *actually* infinite: for it is possible for the destruction of one thing to be the generation of the other, the sum of things being limited.

But this was precisely Anaximander's view of physical change – that there is no wastage: opposed substances make retribution *to each other* for their encroachments (pp. 119ff.). Provided the balance is maintained, all change in the developed world takes place between the same original quantity of separate, opposed substances. (It may be noted that **105** gives a reason for positing a *qualitatively* indefinite primary substance, **106** for a *spatially* indefinite, or infinite, substance; cf. pp. 109f.)

(v) *The Indefinite is all-enfolding and all-controlling*(?), *divine and immortal*

108 Aristotle *Phys.* Γ4, 203b7 ...τοῦ δὲ ἀπείρου οὐκ ἔστιν ἀρχή ...ἀλλ᾽ αὕτη τῶν ἄλλων εἶναι δοκεῖ, καὶ περιέχειν ἅπαντα καὶ πάντα κυβερνᾶν, ὥς φασιν ὅσοι μὴ ποιοῦσι παρὰ τὸ ἄπειρον ἄλλας αἰτίας οἷον νοῦν ἢ φιλίαν· καὶ τοῦτ᾽ εἶναι τὸ θεῖον· ἀθάνατον γὰρ καὶ ἀνώλεθρον, ὥσπερ φησὶν ὁ Ἀναξίμανδρος καὶ οἱ πλεῖστοι τῶν φυσιολόγων.

109 Aristotle *de caelo* Γ5, 303b10 ἔνιοι γὰρ ἓν μόνον ὑποτίθενται, καὶ τοῦτο οἱ μὲν ὕδωρ, οἱ δ᾽ ἀέρα, οἱ δὲ πῦρ, οἱ δ᾽ ὕδατος μὲν λεπτότερον ἀέρος δὲ πυκνότερον· ὃ περιέχειν φασὶ πάντας τοὺς οὐρανοὺς ἄπειρον ὄν.

> **108** ...of the infinite there is no beginning...but this seems to be the beginning of the other things, and to enfold all things and steer all, as all those say who do not postulate other causes, such as mind or love, above and beyond the infinite. And this is the divine; for it is immortal and indestructible, as Anaximander says and most of the physical speculators.
>
> **109** For some posit one substance only, and this some posit as water, some as air, some as fire, some as finer than water and thicker than air; which they say surrounds all the heavens, being infinite.

The assertion in **108** that the primary substance 'enfolds all and steers all' is assigned to those who according to Aristotle imagined an infinite primary stuff but no separate cause of motion – certainly, therefore, to the Milesians, Heraclitus, and Diogenes of Apollonia. 'Steers all' obviously reproduces Presocratic terminology, and the whole phrase 'enfolds all things and steers all' may form a single rhythmical unit. Anaximander, who is mentioned below in connexion with another phrase describing the same subject, and who is probably referred to in **109** in connexion with περιέχειν, could have been its author.[1]

---

[1] περιέχει is presumably genuine in Anaximenes fr. 2 (**160**), even if some of its context is reworded; Anaxagoras (who is not in question in the Aristotelian passage) certainly used τὸ περιέχον in fr. 2 (**488**). κυβερνᾶν, of the steering of

cosmic constituents or events, occurs in Heraclitus fr. 41 (**227**), Parmenides fr. 12, 3 (**306**), Diogenes of Apollonia fr. 5 (**603**). The two words could, of course, have been combined by Aristotle from different sources.

It is not easy, however, to see what manner of control could be exercised on all things by Anaximander's Indefinite. The Greek does not necessarily mean that the steering is due to the enfolding – both properties independently are natural ones for something conceived as divine – but it probably implies it. Again, the metaphor of steering does not necessarily entail a conscious and intelligent agent, for the steering of a ship can be regarded as a purely mechanical process, with reference to changes of direction imposed by the steering mechanism and not to the intentions of the navigator. Yet if the Indefinite was envisaged as somehow divine (**108** *ad fin.*), this favours the assumption of purposeful action. Possible methods of control are the following: (1) by means of surrounding or enfolding: either (*a*) by preventing the further expansion of the differentiated world ('all things'), or (*b*) by making good the waste involved in change in the world; (2) by being immanent in all things, or some things, and providing either (*a*) motive power or life-force, or (*b*) a principle or rule or law of change; (3) by having initiated the world in such a way as to provide a continuing rule or law of change. (1, *b*) was implied in **106**, but it was argued on pp. 114f. that this is unlikely to be valid for Anaximander; the same argument applies to (1, *a*). (2, *a*) would perhaps apply to Thales; (2, *b*), rather than (3), to Heraclitus (pp. 187–8, 199). (2), as well as (1), seems unlikely for Anaximander, for the Indefinite clearly cannot have been imagined as *immanent* in the developed world, even in the way that Thales' world was somehow interpenetrated with a divine life-substance; the Indefinite was probably so named because it was not identical with anything in nature. (3), however, could apply to Anaximander: it is feasible that the control exercised on all things was through the law of retribution between opposites, a law (or manner of behaviour) which was initiated when the first opposed substances appeared within the Indefinite and which still governs all change in the world. Nevertheless, it remains true that Aristotle *could* have had in mind someone other than Anaximander – Heraclitus, perhaps, or Diogenes of Apollonia – in the first part of **108**, and particularly, perhaps, in the phrase 'steers all things'.

The ascription of the idea of περιέχειν to the monists is repeated in **109**; here again the infinite material suggests Anaximander, though it surrounds not 'all things' but 'all the heavens'. This statement seems to have been taken up by Theophrastus (**101**), who evidently thought that it implied separate first heavens, each enclosing a separate world: see pp. 122ff. for the idea of innumerable worlds. But Aristotle's phrase could be due to his using οὐρανοί in a special sense, as the spheres of the sun, moon and stars (cf. *de caelo* A9, 278b9); he might naturally apply his own analysis of the cosmos (based on the Eudoxan–Callippean scheme) to Anaximander, with his separate circles for the heavenly bodies (pp. 134ff.), and intend nothing more than one complex world.

In the latter part of **108** we are told that the enfolding stuff 'is the divine; for it is immortal and indestructible, as Anaximander says and most of the physicists'. It is legitimate to suppose that the words 'immortal and indestructible' were intended to belong to Anaximander himself, though others said something similar. According to Theophrastus as reported in **101** B, however, the phrase was ἀίδιον καὶ ἀγήρω. There is a Homeric formula used of gods or their appurtenances, 'immortal and free from old age': so at *Od.* v, 218 (to Calypso), ἡ μὲν γὰρ βροτός ἐστι, σὺ δ' ἀθάνατος καὶ ἀγήρως (cf. also *Il.* II, 447). Short epic formulas often found their way into archaic prose, and it seems likely that this, rather than the somewhat repetitive equivalent in Aristotle, was the original form.[1] At all events Anaximander seems to have applied to the Indefinite the chief attributes of the Homeric gods, immortality and boundless power (connected in his case with boundless extent); it seems not improbable that he actually called it 'divine', and in this he was typical of the Presocratic thinkers in general.

[1] Especially since the two words are applied to the structure of the natural world, in a description of philosophical contemplation, by Euripides (fr. 910 Nauck²): 'observing the unageing structure of immortal Nature', ἀθανάτου καθορῶν φύσεως κόσμον ἀγήρω.

(vi) *The Indefinite is not in eternal motion, nor is it a mixture*

(These further points concerning the Indefinite are discussed under 'Cosmogony', pp. 126ff.)

THE EXTANT FRAGMENT OF ANAXIMANDER

110 Simplicius *in Phys.* 24, 17 (repeated from **101** A) ...ἑτέραν τινὰ φύσιν ἄπειρον, ἐξ ἧς ἅπαντας γίνεσθαι τοὺς οὐρανοὺς καὶ τοὺς ἐν αὐτοῖς κόσμους. ἐξ ὧν δὲ ἡ γένεσίς ἐστι τοῖς οὖσι, καὶ τὴν φθορὰν εἰς ταῦτα γίνεσθαι 'κατὰ τὸ χρεών· διδόναι γὰρ αὐτὰ δίκην καὶ τίσιν ἀλλήλοις τῆς ἀδικίας κατὰ τὴν τοῦ χρόνου τάξιν', ποιητικωτέροις οὕτως ὀνόμασιν αὐτὰ λέγων.

110 ...some other *apeiron* nature, from which come into being all the heavens and the worlds in them. And the source of coming-to-be for existing things is that into which destruction, too, happens, 'according to necessity; for they pay penalty and retribution to each other for their injustice according to the assessment of Time', as he describes it in these rather poetical terms.

(i) *Extent*

Simplicius is undoubtedly quoting from a version of Theophrastus' history of earlier philosophy, and from the section on the material principle, περὶ ἀρχῆς. The concluding clause, a judgement on Anaximander's style, shows that what immediately precedes is a direct quotation. Thus κατὰ τὴν τοῦ χρόνου τάξιν, which many have held to be a Theophrastean paraphrase of κατὰ τὸ χρεών, should provisionally be accepted as original.[1] διδόναι – ἀδικίας is certainly original, and well exemplifies the poetical style noted by Theophrastus. κατὰ τὸ χρεών, too, should probably be accepted as by Anaximander: χρεών retained a marked poetical colouring (except in the special usage χρεών ἐστι) until the expression τὸ χρεών became popular in the Hellenistic period as a circumlocution for death. It is the most plausible restoration in Heraclitus fr. 80, κατ' ἔριν καὶ χρεών (for χρεώμενα), to give a similar phrase to the one under discussion. The preceding words, ἐξ ὧν – εἰς ταῦτα γίνεσθαι, have been much disputed. The use of the abstracts γένεσις and φθορά, well established in Peripatetic but not (from the other extant evidence) in Presocratic vocabulary, suggests that these belong to Theophrastus. The sentiment, too, looks Peripatetic: it is a close restatement of one of Aristotle's basic dogmas about the primary substance of the physical monists, 'all things are destroyed into that from which they came-to-be' (*Phys.* Γ5, 204b33; cf. also **85** l. 3). Theophrastus was given to quoting single words or phrases; thus he could have quoted the concluding phrase of a sentence, the rest of which he had paraphrased, in order to emphasize the connexion with the following sentence which he quotes in full. See further under §(v).

[1] Theophrastus certainly used similar phraseology himself, notably τάξιν τινὰ καὶ χρόνον ὡρισμένον (of Heraclitus). But this is very different from the bold personification of τὴν τοῦ χρόνου τάξιν, on which see also §(iv).

(ii) *The meaning of the main assertion*

The context shows that Theophrastus regarded the quotation as appropriate to the view he had just attributed to Anaximander, that 'all the heavens and the worlds in them' came from the Indefinite. ἐξ ὧν... (the plural is presumably generic) adds that, since they came from the Indefinite, they will also return to it 'of necessity; for they pay penalty and retribution to each other...' It appears from the version of ps.-Plutarch, **101**C, that by 'the heavens and the worlds in them' Theophrastus was referring to ἄπειροι κόσμοι, innumerable worlds. But there is a very strong objection to understanding the words quoted from Anaximander to refer to innumerable worlds coming-to-be from, and being destroyed into, the Indefinite. ἀλλήλοις shows that retribution is made *mutually* between the parties who are the subject of the sentence. Can we really believe that the divine Indefinite commits *injustice* on its own products, and has to pay them recompense? This, surely, is intolerable; but if so, then Theophrastus (whatever he meant by the 'heavens' and 'worlds') mistook the proper application of Anaximander's dictum.[1] It has long been observed that the things which commit injustice on each other must be equals, different but correlative; and that these are most likely to be the opposed substances which make up the differentiated world.[2]

[1] Kahn, *op. cit.*, 34f., considers the mistake to belong just to ps.-Plutarch, not to Theophrastus; but his suggestion (p. 50) that κόσμος in the latter might refer to some lower 'arrangement', of earth or atmosphere, is hardly convincing.

[2] G. Vlastos, *CP* 42 (1947), 171f., following Cherniss, tried to show how the ultimate balance between opposites could be reconciled with the reabsorption of the world into the Indefinite: when this happens, he said, the opposites finally settle up accounts with each other (not with the Indefinite). But if the principle of justice applies in the present world, it is not easy to see how such a drastic change, affecting all its constituents, as the return of the world to the Indefinite could ever come about.

(iii) *The opposites*

It will be seen later (**118, 121**) that the production of something that could be described as 'opposites' was an essential stage of cosmogony for Anaximander; it is therefore reasonable to assume that they played an important part in the developed world. The interplay of opposites is basic in Heraclitus, who seems to have deliberately corrected Anaximander by his paradox 'strife is *justice*' (fr. 80, **211**). Anaximander is the first in whom the concept of opposed natural substances (which recurs in Heraclitus, Parmenides, Empedocles, Anaxagoras, and in the Pythagoreans certainly as early as Alcmaeon) clearly appears. Doubtless he was influenced by observation of the main seasonal changes, in which heat and drought in summer seem to be pitted against cold and rain in winter. The constant interchange between opposed substances is explained by Anaximander in a legalistic metaphor derived from human society; the prevalence of one substance at the expense of its contrary is 'injustice', and a reaction takes place through the infliction of punishment by the restoration of equality – of more than equality, since the wrong-doer is deprived of part of his original substance, too. This is given to the victim in addition to what was his own, and in turn leads (it might be inferred) to κόρος, surfeit, on the part of the former victim, who now commits injustice on the former aggressor. Thus both the continuity and the stability of natural change were motivated, for Anaximander, by means of this anthropomorphic metaphor. The main opposites in cosmogony were the hot substance and the cold substance – flame or fire and mist or air. These, with which are associated dryness and moisture, are also the main cosmological opposites, most notably involved in the large-scale changes in the natural world. They were probably isolated by Heraclitus (fr. 126) before ever they were elevated to the form of standard irreducible elements by Empedocles. Caution must be shown, to be sure, about the opposites in Anaximander: it is possible, for example, that the Peripatetics substituted their own more abstract formulations, the hot and the cold and so on, for more concrete expressions used by Anaximander himself. For him, the world may have been made up of substances which, while they each possessed individual tendencies contrary to those of some of the others, need not have been formally described as opposites, that is, for example, as the hard and the soft; but simply as fire, wind, iron, water, man, woman and so on.

(iv) 'The assessment of Time'

The concluding phrase of the quotation, 'according to the assessment of Time', elaborates the injustice-metaphor. What kind of assessment does Time make? The word τάξις suggests the ordaining of punishment by a judge or, more aptly, the assessment of tribute as in the Athenian tribute-lists. In these cases what is ordained or assessed is the *amount* of the punishment or payment; this can hardly be the primary purpose of *Time*'s assessment. Time must presumably control the time-limit for payment; the amount would be fixed, as total restitution plus a proportionate *amende*. The idea of a time-limit is appropriate: the injustice of summer has to be made good within the roughly equal period of winter, that of night during the period of day, and so on. No uniform period can be meant; Time makes the assessment to meet the particular case. That the additional idea of inevitability is implicit in the remarkable personification of Time here may be indicated by the strikingly similar 'trial conducted by Time' in Solon, roughly a generation before Anaximander:

111   Solon fr. 24 Diehl, lines 1–7

ἐγὼ δὲ τῶν μὲν οὕνεκα ξυνήγαγον
δῆμον, τί τούτων πρὶν τυχεῖν ἐπαυσάμην;
συμμαρτυροίη ταῦτ' ἂν ἐν δίκῃ Χρόνου
μήτηρ μεγίστη δαιμόνων Ὀλυμπίων
ἄριστα, Γῆ μέλαινα, τῆς ἐγώ ποτε
ὅρους ἀνεῖλον πολλαχῇ πεπηγότας·
πρόσθεν δὲ δουλεύουσα, νῦν ἐλευθέρα.

111   Why did I cease before I gained the objects for whose sake I brought together the people? The great mother of the Olympian deities would be my best supporting witness for this in the court of Time – black Earth, whose boundary-stones, fixed in many places, I once removed; formerly was she enslaved, now is she free.

Here Earth justifies Solon's claim because *with the lapse of time* she has become free; that is what Time's trial signifies. No pre-determined time-limit is intended here. Elsewhere in Solon, too, it is the inevitability of retribution that is stressed again and again; so in Anaximander, we may infer, injustice must *inevitably* be punished, sooner or later in time – but here the periods, since they are those of the great seasonal changes, as well as other less important ones, must be supervised and assessed appropriately to each case.

(v) *The original of Theophrastus' paraphrase*

It has been suggested on pp. 118f. that (literally) 'from what things coming-to-be is for the things that are, destruction, too, takes place into these' may be a paraphrase by Theophrastus of something in Anaximander which Theophrastus thought could be recast in terms of the common Aristotelian formula. If that statement in Anaximander immediately preceded Anaximander's dictum about the retribution of opposites (as the transitional phrase κατὰ τὸ χρεών may suggest), then it too was presumably concerned with the behaviour of opposites in the developed world. One sentiment, I suggest, which Anaximander might have expressed in this context, and which could have deceived Theophrastus in the way indicated, was that *opposing substances pay recompense each to its own opposite and to no other*; for example the hot substance to the cold, and not to the heavy or the hard. This is a necessary hypothesis for Anaximander's theory of cosmic stability, obvious to us but not so obvious then, since Heraclitus also had to emphasize it for his own special purposes. The axiom may have been stated in terms so general, and possibly in a context so incomplete, that Theophrastus was able to mistake its proper reference.

INNUMERABLE WORLDS

(i) *Successive rather than coexistent*

Plural worlds of some kind were attributed to Anaximander by Theophrastus: '...some other substance of infinite spatial extent, from which come into being all the heavens and the worlds in them' (**101A**). The fragment, about things paying to each other the penalty for injustice, was adduced as somehow relevant to this process; in this Theophrastus seems to have been mistaken (p. 118f.). In the doxographical versions of Theophrastus we learn that these plural worlds were ἄπειροι, i.e. infinite or innumerable. There has been much controversy as to whether these innumerable worlds were successive in time (so that our world will eventually pass away, to be succeeded by another, and so on), or coexistent. Zeller supported the former interpretation, Burnet the latter; Cornford demonstrated the fallacy of many of Burnet's arguments and reinstated the Zellerian interpretation in general favour (see *CQ* 28 (1934), 1ff., and *Principium Sapientiae*, 177ff.).

(ii) *But are even successive worlds plausible in Anaximander?*

I have elsewhere suggested (*CQ* N.s. 5 (1955), 28ff.) that Anaximander may in reality have believed in *no* type of innumerable worlds; and this suggestion (which receives support from Kahn, *op. cit.*, 46–53) is further argued here.

If coexistent worlds might be suggested to some people (though not, as it happens, to Anaximander, who saw them as apertures in rings of fire, pp. 135ff.) by the heavenly bodies, there is nothing whatever in 'the appearance of nature' to suggest *successive* worlds – successive separate worlds, that is (for such are clearly meant by both Theophrastus or his successors and his modern followers), as distinct from successive changes in the state of the one continuing world. These last are envisaged in the mythical catastrophes by fire and flood described in Plato's *Timaeus*, 22c–e, or in Deucalion's flood, and were to some extent suggested by natural phenomena; cf. pp. 139f. But there was no reason to assume that the whole world was going to be destroyed, or that if destroyed it would be succeeded by another. It would be contrary both to the whole mythical background of Greek thought and to the dictates of common sense to believe in a cycle of separate worlds; and their appearance in Anaximander would be most surprising. But to anyone already familiar with Empedocles' radical changes of the σφαῖρος (pp. 295ff.) and with the atomist theory of Leucippus and Democritus, of innumerable worlds coming-to-be and passing away throughout infinite space (pp. 416ff.), and already perhaps prone to misinterpret Heraclitus as having postulated a succession of worlds (p. 200n.), the oddity would not be conspicuous. Given a specific motive Theophrastus or his reproducers might, therefore, have made a false and anachronistic attribution. Such a motive, it is suggested, was provided by the atomists' arguments for innumerable worlds, as succinctly and influentially restated by Aristotle in the following passage.

(iii) *Atomist arguments applied by Theophrastus to Anaximander?*

112 Aristotle *Phys.* Γ4, 203b23 ...διὰ γὰρ τὸ ἐν τῇ νοήσει μὴ ὑπολείπειν καὶ ὁ ἀριθμὸς δοκεῖ ἄπειρος εἶναι καὶ τὰ μαθηματικὰ μεγέθη καὶ τὸ ἔξω τοῦ οὐρανοῦ· ἀπείρου δ' ὄντος τοῦ ἔξω, καὶ σῶμα ἄπειρον εἶναι δοκεῖ καὶ κόσμοι· τί γὰρ μᾶλλον τοῦ κενοῦ ἐνταῦθα ἢ ἐνταῦθα:

> 112 ...through not giving out in our thought, number seems to be infinite, and also mathematical magnitudes and what lies outside the heaven. But if what lies outside is infinite, body also seems to be infinite, and worlds too: for why should they exist more in one part of the void than in another?

This passage gives the fifth and most important motive, according to Aristotle, for the development of a concept of infinity. The argument that if what is outside the heaven is infinite then body is infinite, and that if body is infinite then worlds are infinite, is derived from the atomists, of whom Aristotle was undoubtedly thinking here. But the infinite worlds are necessitated by the hypothesis of infinite body, whether or not this is in turn argued (as by the atomists) from infinite void. On this reasoning Theophrastus might have been impelled to assume that the first and most notable believer in infinite body (as he thought τὸ ἄπειρον to imply) – namely Anaximander – also posited infinite worlds. These would behave like the atomists' in that they would be coexistent and also successive – that is, coming-to-be and passing away continually. The assumption that all innumerable worlds are of this kind appears to be made by Aristotle in the latter part of 116. If we find evidence that Theophrastus treated Anaximander's worlds as *both* coexistent *and* successive, this will suggest strongly that he was applying atomistic reasoning to Anaximander.

(iv) *The doxographical evidence may suggest that Theophrastus applied atomist-type worlds to Anaximander*

If one turns to the doxographical sources for further elucidation of Theophrastus' views, the evidence is found to be confused and to some extent corrupt. Thus one of our twin sources for Aetius (ps.-Plutarch; cf. Aetius II, 1, 3, DK 12A17) assigns innumerable worlds only to the atomists, while the other (Stobaeus) assigns them in addition to Anaximander, Anaximenes, Archelaus, Xenophanes(!), and Diogenes of Apollonia. Neither version can correctly represent Theophrastus; but both could have arisen from a generalization of the atomistic arguments. There was a further confusion in Aetius (I, 7, 12, DK 12A17) between the innumerable-world hypothesis and the common opinion that the stars were gods. These confusions (which are seen also in Cicero) are unlikely to have been caused by a simple statement in Theophrastus that Anaximander postulated successive worlds. Two important witnesses had quite definite views:

113 Simplicius *in Phys.* 1121, 5   οἱ μὲν γὰρ ἀπείρους τῷ πλήθει τοὺς κόσμους ὑποθέμενοι, ὡς οἱ περὶ Ἀναξίμανδρον καὶ Λεύκιππον καὶ Δημόκριτον καὶ ὕστερον οἱ περὶ Ἐπίκουρον, γινομένους αὐτοὺς καὶ φθειρομένους ὑπέθεντο ἐπ' ἄπειρον, ἄλλων μὲν ἀεὶ γινομένων ἄλλων δὲ φθειρομένων, καὶ τὴν κίνησιν ἀίδιον ἔλεγον....

113   For those who supposed the worlds to be infinite in number, like the associates of Anaximander and Leucippus and Democritus and afterwards those of Epicurus, supposed them to be coming-to-be and passing away for an infinite time, with some of them always coming-to-be and others passing away; and they said that motion was eternal....

This comment on **112** is probably Simplicius' own, and does not directly reproduce Theophrastus. Simplicius might, however, be expected to be influenced by the Theophrastean interpretation; and indeed the same interpretation appears in a source earlier than Simplicius, and one which is dependent on the Theophrastean tradition through a different channel (there is a confusion with Anaxagoras in the first part):

114 Augustinus *de civ. dei* VIII, 2   non enim ex una re sicut Thales ex umore, sed ex suis propriis principiis quasque res nasci putavit (*sc.* Anaximander). quae rerum principia singularum esse credidit infinita, et innumerabiles mundos gignere et quaecumque in eis oriuntur; eosque mundos modo dissolvi modo iterum gigni existimavit, quanta quisque aetate sua manere potuerit.

114 For he [Anaximander] thought that things were born not from one substance, as Thales thought from water, but each from its own particular principles. These principles of individual things he believed to be infinite, and to give birth to innumerable worlds and whatsoever arises in them; and those worlds, he thought, are now dissolved, now born again, according to the age to which each is able to survive.

Worlds coming-to-be and passing away throughout space (or the Indefinite) are surely intended here; 'quanta...potuerit' suggests an irregularity which is foreign to the idea of a sequence of single worlds, but which is essential to the atomistic conception.[1]

[1] A passage in Cicero (*de natura deorum* I, 10, 25, DK 12A17) which ascribes to Anaximander worlds rising and setting 'longis intervallis' might point in the same direction, though certainty is impossible because of the ambiguity of 'intervallis' (spatial or temporal?).

Thus two sources independent of each other, the one indirectly and the other directly influenced by the tradition from Theophrastus, assigned atomistic worlds to Anaximander. Further, such an ascription by Theophrastus himself, of worlds both coexistent and successive, would provide a reason for the confusion between the two in some parts of the doxographical tradition on Anaximander.

(v) *Further considerations against and for the hypothesis*

Two difficulties in this interpretation must be mentioned.

(*a*) It is possible from **109** that Aristotle meant to attribute plural worlds to the monistic physicists in general; the infinite primary substance, they said, 'surrounds all the heavens (οὐρανούς)'. To meet this, it was proposed on p. 117 that Aristotle was using οὐρανοί in his special sense of 'celestial spheres'; he meant 'everything enclosed by the first heaven' and (perhaps because of the analogy of Anaximander's circles) expressed this concept in language appropriate to his own cosmology. Certainly in **108** the infinite primary substance is said to enclose simply 'all things', and there is no suggestion elsewhere in Aristotle of innumerable separate worlds before the atomists.

(*b*) If Theophrastus thought that anyone who posited infinite material should also posit innumerable worlds like the atomists, why did Simplicius write in **147** (the continuation of **113**) that *Anaximenes*, whose primary substance was described as infinite by Theophrastus and Simplicius, believed in successive *single* worlds? The distinction from Anaximander is puzzling on any interpretation. But Heraclitus and Diogenes are mentioned as sharing the belief; Simplicius certainly ascribed successive worlds to Heraclitus, and he may have thought that Anaximenes should be classed with him, as a believer in a specific primary substance, rather than with Anaximander and the atomists, whose ἀρχή was undifferentiated. There is also a possibility that Anaximenes does not belong here at all: see n. on p. 151. Nevertheless these two pieces of evidence, puzzling as they are, cannot be regarded as neutralized. On the other side there were three special characteristics of Anaximander's cosmology which might well have encouraged an innumerable-world interpretation: (1) the theory that the earth was surrounded by a number – perhaps an indefinite number – of rings of the celestial bodies (pp. 134ff.); (2) the theory that the earth was drying up, which was probably part of a wider theory of cycles of change on the earth's surface – a succession of κόσμοι in the sense of local arrangements (pp. 138ff.); (3) the potential ambiguity of the fragment known to Theophrastus. This fragment seems properly to have described the interaction of substances within the world, but Theophrastus misapplied it to interaction between the world and the Indefinite. Thus (1) might help to suggest coexistent worlds, (2) and (3) successive ones. Theophrastus may have applied atomistic arguments and imposed upon Anaximander worlds that were both.

COSMOGONY

(i) *'Eternal motion' and vortex: are they relevant to Anaximander?*

115 Hippolytus *Ref.* 1, 6, 2 (from **101**B) ...κίνησιν ἀίδιον εἶναι, ἐν ᾗ συμβαίνει γίνεσθαι τοὺς οὐρανούς.

116 Aristotle *Phys.* Θ1, 250b11 πότερον γέγονέ ποτε κίνησις...ἢ οὔτ᾽ ἐγένετο οὔτε φθείρεται ἀλλ᾽ ἀεὶ ἦν καὶ ἀεὶ ἔσται, καὶ τοῦτ᾽ ἀθάνατον καὶ ἄπαυστον ὑπάρχει τοῖς οὖσιν, οἷον ζωή τις οὖσα τοῖς φύσει συνεστῶσι πᾶσιν;...ἀλλ᾽ ὅσοι μὲν ἀπείρους τε κόσμους εἶναί φασι, καὶ τοὺς μὲν γίγνεσθαι τοὺς δὲ φθείρεσθαι τῶν κόσμων, ἀεί φασιν εἶναι κίνησιν...ὅσοι δ᾽ ἕνα, ⟨ἢ ἀεὶ⟩ ἢ μὴ ἀεί, καὶ περὶ τῆς κινήσεως ὑποτίθενται κατὰ λόγον.[1]

117 Aristotle *de caelo* B13, 295a7 ἀλλὰ μὴν εἴ γε ἔστι κίνησίς τις κατὰ φύσιν, οὐκ ἂν ἡ βίαιος εἴη φορὰ μόνον οὐδ᾽ ἠρέμησις· ὥστ᾽ εἰ βίᾳ νῦν ἡ γῆ μένει, καὶ συνῆλθεν ἐπὶ τὸ μέσον φερομένη διὰ τὴν δίνησιν. ταύτην γὰρ τὴν αἰτίαν πάντες λέγουσιν ἐκ τῶν ἐν τοῖς ὑγροῖς καὶ περὶ τὸν ἀέρα συμβαινόντων· ἐν τούτοις γὰρ ἀεὶ φέρεται τὰ μείζω καὶ τὰ βαρύτερα πρὸς τὸ μέσον τῆς δίνης. διὸ δὴ τὴν γῆν πάντες ὅσοι τὸν οὐρανὸν γεννῶσιν ἐπὶ τὸ μέσον συνελθεῖν φασίν.

115 ...motion was eternal, in which it results that the heavens come into being.

116 Did motion come into being at some time...or did it neither come-to-be nor is it destroyed, but did it always exist and will it go on for ever, and is it immortal and unceasing for existing things, being like a kind of life for all natural objects?...But all who say that there are infinite worlds, and that some of them are coming-to-be and others passing away, say that motion always exists...while all who say that there is one world, whether eternal or not, make an analogous supposition about motion.

117 Yet if indeed there is some kind of natural motion, there would not be enforced motion only, or enforced rest; so that if the earth now stays in place by force, it also came together to the centre by being carried there because of the vortex. (For this is the cause that everyone gives, through what happens in water and in air; for in these the larger and heavier objects are always carried toward the centre of the vortex.) Therefore all who generate the heaven say that the earth came together to the centre.

¹ ⟨ἤ ἀεί⟩ (Ross) is supported by the comments of both Themistius and Simplicius. The sense is that those who postulate one eternal world also postulate eternal motion; those who postulate one non-eternal world do not. Note that successive single worlds (which would require eternal motion) are not included in this analysis.

Theophrastus evidently stated that the Indefinite was characterized by an eternal motion, which was somehow responsible for the innumerable worlds. He likewise attributed eternal motion to Anaximenes, presumably because, like Anaximander, Anaximenes did not specify anything that could obviously act as a cause of change. Aristotle frequently rebuked the monists for this very fault; but **116** shows that he could on occasion understand their ways of thinking better than his pupil Theophrastus. There he considers an ungenerated motion which is 'deathless', which inheres in things as a kind of life. He was thinking of Thales, perhaps (p. 98); but the phrase 'immortal and unceasing' reminds one of the phraseology which he attributed to Anaximander, among others, in **108**; he probably realized, then, that for Anaximander change in the cosmos was bound up with the divinity, the power of life and movement, of the Indefinite. What Theophrastus had in mind as Anaximander's 'eternal motion' was probably some more explicit, mechanical kind of motion like that of the atomists, who are mentioned indirectly in the latter part of **116**; we have seen (pp. 124f.) that Theophrastus may well have grouped Anaximander with the atomists over the question of innumerable worlds. Some modern scholars (e.g. Burnet) have held that Anaximander postulated a confused agitation like the winnowing motion in Plato's *Timaeus*; others (e.g. Tannery) have assigned a circular motion to the Indefinite. Both are equally unlikely. It is highly improbable that Anaximander himself ever isolated this question of motion; the Indefinite was divine, and naturally possessed the power to move what and where it willed. To define its properties further would defeat Anaximander's purpose.

One often reads of a vortex or vortices in Anaximander. There is in fact no evidence for this apart from Aristotle in **117**, a highly involved piece of *a priori* reasoning. But in any case Anaximander was presumably not in Aristotle's mind when he wrote this passage; for shortly afterwards (**123**) he is distinguished from the majority of the physicists on the ground that his earth remained at the centre by equilibrium and not by conventional kinds of 'force'. This distinction and the subsequent discussion come as an appendix to the discussion of vortex-action, which is no longer under consideration; thus it may be accepted that Aristotle was talking loosely in saying in **117** that 'all who generate the heaven say that the earth came together to the centre', if this implies more than accretion. Vortices are not associated in our doxographical sources with anyone before Empedocles, though Aristotle's generalization in **117** would surely have led Theophrastus to mention earlier occurrences, had he been able to find them. It is, nevertheless, just possible that what was separated off from the Indefinite in the first stage of Anaximander's cosmogony was a vortex, see p. 132; what is quite out of the question is either that the whole Indefinite was in vortex-motion, or that the diurnal movement of the heavenly bodies is due to this cause (which would not suit the earth's equilibrium in **123**). The tendency of heavy bodies to the centre is assumed in most early cosmogonies. This may have been due in part, as implied in **117**, to the observation of vortex-action in everyday experience; but in part it simply reflected the obvious arrangement of the components of the visible cosmos.

(ii) *How did the opposites come from the Indefinite?*

118 Aristotle *Phys.* A4, 187a20 (from **104**) οἱ δ᾽ ἐκ τοῦ ἑνὸς ἐν-ούσας τὰς ἐναντιότητας ἐκκρίνεσθαι, ὥσπερ Ἀναξίμανδρός φησι καὶ ὅσοι δ᾽ ἓν καὶ πολλά φασιν εἶναι, ὥσπερ Ἐμπεδοκλῆς καὶ Ἀναξα-γόρας· ἐκ τοῦ μίγματος γὰρ καὶ οὗτοι ἐκκρίνουσι τἄλλα.

119 Simplicius *in Phys.* 24, 21 (continuing **101**A) δῆλον δὲ ὅτι τὴν εἰς ἄλληλα μεταβολὴν τῶν τεττάρων στοιχείων οὗτος θεασάμενος οὐκ ἠξίωσεν ἕν τι τούτων ὑποκείμενον ποιῆσαι, ἀλλά τι ἄλλο παρὰ ταῦτα· οὗτος δὲ οὐκ ἀλλοιουμένου τοῦ στοιχείου τὴν γένεσιν ποιεῖ, ἀλλ' ἀποκρινομένων τῶν ἐναντίων διὰ τῆς ἀιδίου κινήσεως.

118 But the others say that the opposites are separated out from the One, being present in it, as Anaximander says and all who say there are one and many, like Empedocles and Anaxagoras; for these, too, separate out the rest from the mixture.

119 It is clear that he [Anaximander], seeing the changing of the four elements into each other, thought it right to make none of these the substratum, but something else beside these; and he produces coming-to-be not through the alteration of the element, but by the separation off of the opposites through the eternal motion.

It is almost certain from the first sentence of **119** that Simplicius is no longer quoting Theophrastus, but giving his own paraphrase of what he has just quoted. In the second sentence he partly depends on the analysis by Aristotle in **104**. There are two notable differences between his comment and the Aristotelian original: (*a*) the opposites are separated *out* (ἐκκρίνεσθαι) in Aristotle, separated *off* (ἀποκρινομένων) in Simplicius; (*b*) Simplicius, but not Aristotle, said that the separation was due to the eternal motion. Now it has been argued by U. Hölscher (*Hermes* 81 (1953), 258ff.) that Simplicius in the second sentence of **119** (as at *in Phys.* 150, 22) is simply and solely enlarging on Aristotle, and reproduces no Theophrastean interpretation whatever; this passage, therefore, is not good evidence for Anaximander unless Aristotle is reliable in **118**. But, the argument continues, Aristotle was prone to read his own simple bodies, and two pairs of basic opposites, into everything, and he perverted Anaximander by substituting separating *out* for separating *off* from the Indefinite, thus making this into a mixture of opposites. Theophrastus attributed separating *off* to Anaximander, but of the innumerable worlds and not of opposites (ἀποκεκρίσθαι in **101**c); and this, according to Hölscher, was the proper application of the word. Against this ingenious theory the following points may be made. The mention of the eternal motion by Simplicius is Theophrastean and not Aristotelian in source (see **115**); so, apparently, is his use of the verb for separating *off*. Therefore, while it is agreed that he was not here quoting Theophrastus, he probably did have Theophrastus' assessment of Anaximander in mind. Further, Hölscher has not succeeded in convincingly destroying a most damaging piece of evidence, passage **121**. This continuation of ps.-Plutarch's doxography in 101C states that 'the productive from the eternal of hot and cold was separated off at the beginning of this world', and continues with details of the cosmogony. This, though garbled, represents Theophrastus, and shows that Theophrastus accepted separation off from the Indefinite, and opposites, as involved in Anaximander's cosmogony. Since the extant fragment (110) suggests that the world is still composed of opposites, it seems legitimate to accept from both Theophrastus and Aristotle that opposites were involved in cosmogony.

Nevertheless, we may accept the warning about ἐκκρίνεσθαι in Aristotle; it seems quite likely that this is a distortion of ἀποκρίνεσθαι. And according to 121 what was separated off was not opposite substances (flame and mist) but something that produced them. This might have been a kind of seed, it might have been a vortex; there was perhaps a confusion in the tradition (see p. 132). At all events we have no right to assume with Aristotle that the opposites were *in* (ἐνούσας) the Indefinite, and were separated *out* of it; still less may we define the Indefinite as a mixture, as Aristotle perhaps did.[1] The Indefinite was not clearly defined and analysed by Anaximander; but this does not mean, of course, that he might not have been making it behave, in respect of its products, in some way like a compound – either a mechanical mixture or a fusion.[2] If the opposites arose directly from the Indefinite by being separated off, as Simplicius states in 119, then the Indefinite was being unconsciously treated as unhomogeneous; for separation off cannot simply imply the isolation of one part of the Indefinite, that part which becomes the world; it implies this *and* some change in the isolated part. If this change was not the appearance of opposites, but of something productive of them, then one might infer that the Indefinite was the kind of thing that contained, for example, sperms or embryos; but that still does not mean that Anaximander thought of it as being of a specific character.

[1] Cf. 120 Aristotle *Met.* Λι, 1069b20 ...καὶ τοῦτ' ἐστὶ τὸ 'Αναξαγόρου ἓν (βέλτιον γὰρ ἢ ὁμοῦ πάντα) καὶ 'Εμπεδοκλέους τὸ μίγμα καὶ 'Αναξιμάνδρου, καὶ ὡς Δημόκριτός φησιν (...*and this is the One of Axaxagoras (for this is a better description than 'all things together') and the mixture of Empedocles and of Anaximander, and what Democritus describes).* If 118 is doubtful, this passage certainly seems to attribute a mixture to Anaximander; although G. Calogero suggests 'Αναξιμάνδρου ⟨τὸ ἄπειρον⟩.

[2] As suggested by Cornford and by Vlastos (*CP* 42 (1947), 170–2). Theophrastus is quoted by Simplicius (492) as saying that the mixture of all things in Anaxagoras could be regarded as 'one substance indefinite both in kind and in size', and that he would resemble Anaximander – but whether in the idea of *mixture* is not clear.

(iii) *The actual formation of the cosmos*

121 Ps.-Plutarch *Strom.* 2 (continuing **101**c and **122**a; DK 12 a 10)
φησὶ δὲ τὸ ἐκ τοῦ ἀιδίου γόνιμον θερμοῦ τε καὶ ψυχροῦ κατὰ τὴν
γένεσιν τοῦδε τοῦ κόσμου ἀποκριθῆναι καί τινα ἐκ τούτου φλογὸς
σφαῖραν περιφυῆναι τῷ περὶ τὴν γῆν ἀέρι ὡς τῷ δένδρῳ φλοιόν·
ἧστινος ἀπορραγείσης καὶ εἴς τινας ἀποκλεισθείσης κύκλους ὑπο-
στῆναι τὸν ἥλιον καὶ τὴν σελήνην καὶ τοὺς ἀστέρας. (Continues at
134.)

> **121** He says that that which is productive from the eternal of hot
> and cold was separated off at the coming-to-be of this world, and
> that a kind of sphere of flame from this was formed round the
> air surrounding the earth, like bark round a tree. When this was
> broken off and shut off in certain circles, the sun and the moon
> and the stars were formed.

This passage (supplemented, for the heavenly bodies, by Hippolytus
in **125**) is virtually our only authority for Theophrastus' report of the
details of the cosmogonical process in Anaximander. The *Stromateis*
are usually less accurate than either Simplicius or Hippolytus in
reproducing Theophrastus (cf. **101**); but it cannot be doubted that
the present passage is based on him, and the citation of the bark-simile,
which looks as though it is derived from Anaximander himself,
suggests that in places, at least, the passage follows Theophrastus
fairly closely.

The phrase ἐκ τοῦ ἀιδίου, 'from the eternal', perhaps means 'from
the Indefinite', which was described as immortal.[1] 'The productive
from the eternal of hot and cold...was separated off' is still difficult.
γόνιμος (productive) was a favourite Peripatetic word, which usually
retained some flavour, if only a slight one, of biological generation.
In the fifth century, on the other hand, γόνιμος only occurs twice,
in Euripides and Aristophanes – the latter use being a weakened
metaphor – except for a special medical-technical use (of critical
periods in disease; the biological meaning is almost suppressed) in
the Hippocratic *Visits*. It seems unlikely, therefore, that it is an
Anaximandrean term; and in view of occurrences of the word,
especially in Plutarch, as a dead metaphor with no biological
implications we cannot be sure that it was here intended to represent
generation of a biological kind, however remotely. This must be
emphasized because of the popularity of Cornford's suggestion that
this stage in Anaximander corresponds with the production of a
cosmogonical egg in 'Orphic' accounts (on which see pp. 23–9). It

would not be surprising to find that Anaximander resorted to the old mythological medium of sexual generation to account for the most difficult stage in world-formation – the production of heterogeneous plurality out of a single source, and that, here, an Indefinite one. One would not, however, expect a crude and explicit device like the egg; and the evidence is not certainly in favour of any such sexual device, however metaphorical. A completely different suggestion was made by Vlastos (*CP* 42 (1947), 171 n. 140), that τὸ γόνιμον was not a thing so much as a process. A vortex, for instance, might well account for the appearance of opposites; for the phraseology we may compare Democritus fr. 167, δῖνον ἀπὸ τοῦ παντὸς ἀποκριθῆναι ('a vortex was separated off from the whole').² Yet, apart from the considerations raised under § (i) above, why did Theophrastus not simply use the word δῖνος or δίνη to describe a process completely familiar to him, and one which would further have emphasized the resemblance of Anaximander and Anaxagoras (n. 2 on p. 130)? If he had used the word, we should not have this vague circumlocution in ps.-Plutarch. It is at least a possibility that Theophrastus himself was in doubt about this first stage, perhaps through lack of full information, and used a vague expression to cover himself; but he would not have *invented* an intermediary between the Indefinite and the opposites (which could have been more easily produced, as in **118**, directly), and judgement must be reserved on its character.

¹ Another possibility is that the whole phrase means 'that which was capable from all time of producing...' In this case we should expect ἐξ ἀιδίου, without the article. But the insertion of ἐκ τοῦ ἀιδίου between τὸ and γόνιμον, on the other interpretation, is almost as strange. In any case, the tortuosity of expression is not immediately due to Anaximander, and the obscure meaning is not greatly affected either way. On Anaximander's possible vagueness, see the neat analysis by J. Barnes, *The Presocratic Philosophers* (London, 1979) 1, 43.
² That 'separating off' can be applied to the products of a vortex, as well as to the vortex itself, is demonstrated by Anaxagoras fr. 9 *init.*, οὕτω τούτων περιχωρούντων τε καὶ ἀποκρινομένων ὑπὸ βίης τε καὶ ταχυτῆτος... ('these things thus revolving and being separated off by force and speed...').

The nature of the hot (substance) and cold (substance) thus cryptically produced appears from what follows in ps.-Plutarch: they are flame and air-mist (the inner part of which is assumed to have condensed into earth). The ball of flame fits closely round the air, as closely as bark grows round a tree; this can be the point of the simile, which does not necessarily suggest that the flame is annular (though the eventual shape of the earth is cylindrical, see **122**). So far, then, something has been isolated in the Indefinite which produces flame and air-mist; earth condenses at the core, flame fits closely round the air. Now the ball of flame bursts, breaks up into circles which are enclosed by mist which has also expanded (cf. 125), and forms the heavenly bodies. From 132 we learn that the moist earth is dried by the sun, the remnants of the moisture being sea.[1]

[1] It is possible that 121 contains other signs of biological–embryological language, apart from the dubious γόνιμον. H. C. Baldry (CQ 26 (1932), 27ff.) pointed out that ἀπόκρισις was used in embryological treatises to describe the separation of the seed from the parent; φλοιός could be used of a caul, and was perhaps used in a similar sense by Anaximander – see 133; ἀπορρήγνυσθαι is sometimes used of a new growth detaching itself from the parent body (which it can hardly mean here, contra Heidel and Baldry). But none of these words has an exclusively embryological sense; they are common terms (except φλοιός, which most frequently means 'bark') which would naturally be applied to both embryology and cosmogony.

COSMOLOGY: THE PRESENT STRUCTURE OF THE WORLD

(i) The earth

122 (A) Ps.-Plutarch Strom. 2

ὑπάρχειν δέ φησι τῷ μὲν σχήματι τὴν γῆν κυλινδροειδῆ, ἔχειν δὲ τόσουτον βάθος ὅσον ἂν εἴη τρίτον πρὸς τὸ πλάτος.

(B) Hippolytus Ref. 1, 6, 3

τὸ δὲ σχῆμα αὐτῆς (sc. τῆς γῆς) γυρόν, στρογγύλον, κίονος λίθῳ παραπλήσιον.[1] τῶν δὲ ἐπιπέδων ᾧ μὲν ἐπιβεβήκαμεν, ὃ δὲ ἀντίθετον ὑπάρχει.

[1] ὑγρόν, χίονι MSS; κίονι Aetius III, 10, 2 (DK 12A25). γυρόν (Roeper) is plausible for the impossible ὑγρόν; originally meaning 'curved' (e.g. of a hook, or of hunched shoulders), it came to mean also 'round'. στρογγύλον, then, may be an interpolated gloss. I have emended χίονι to κίονος, exempli gratia; perhaps we should read κίονι λιθίνῳ (cf. Diels, Doxographi Graeci, 218); in any case the sense is not in doubt. (Kahn, op. cit., 55f., is unconvincing.)

123 Aristotle de caelo B 13, 295b10 εἰσὶ δέ τινες οἳ διὰ τὴν ὁμοιότητά φασιν αὐτὴν (sc. τὴν γῆν) μένειν, ὥσπερ τῶν ἀρχαίων Ἀναξίμανδρος. μᾶλλον μὲν γὰρ οὐθὲν ἄνω ἢ κάτω ἢ εἰς τὰ πλάγια φέρεσθαι προσήκει τὸ ἐπὶ τοῦ μέσου ἱδρυμένον καὶ ὁμοίως πρὸς τὰ ἔσχατα ἔχον· ἅμα δ' ἀδύνατον εἰς τἀναντία ποιεῖσθαι τὴν κίνησιν, ὥστ' ἐξ ἀνάγκης μένειν.

124 Hippolytus Ref. 1, 6, 3 (preceding 122B) τὴν δὲ γῆν εἶναι μετέωρον ὑπὸ μηδενὸς κρατουμένην, μένουσαν δὲ διὰ τὴν ὁμοίαν πάντων ἀπόστασιν.

122 (A) He says that the earth is cylindrical in shape, and that its depth is a third of its width. (B) Its shape is curved, round,

similar to the drum of a column; of its flat surfaces we walk on one, and the other is on the opposite side.

123 There are some who say, like Anaximander among the ancients, that it [the earth] stays still because of its equilibrium. For it behoves that which is established at the centre, and is equally related to the extremes, not to be borne one whit more either up or down or to the sides; and it is impossible for it to move simultaneously in opposite directions, so that it stays fixed by necessity.
124 The earth is on high, held up by nothing, but remaining on account of its similar distance from all things.

The earth is shaped like a column-drum; men live on its upper surface. There is no question of the meaning being (as Kahn thinks) that the earth's surface is concave – or convex for that matter. The term γυρός refers to its round section, in accordance with the traditional view (see p. 11 above on Okeanos); cf. LSJ s.v. γῦρος. Nor does the mention of an undersurface in 122B imply that it, too, was inhabited (*contra* Kahn, 56 and 84f.). It is three times as wide as it is deep – a ratio which is analogous to the distances of the heavenly bodies (pp. 135f.). Its evident stability is explained in a new way which represents a radical advance on Thales' idea that it *floated* on water (an idea revived and modified by Anaximenes, p. 153). What the earth is at the centre of, presumably, is the rings of the heavenly bodies, of which the sun's is the largest (125). Anaximander was not talking of the world as a whole, or saying that *it* was at the centre of the Indefinite, though he would doubtless have accepted this if the idea were put to him. At all events he completely broke away from the popular idea that the earth must be supported by something concrete, that it must have 'roots'; his theory of equilibrium was a brilliant leap into the realms of the mathematical and the *a priori* – one which he would not have been tempted to take, it might be suggested, if vortex-action had been applied in his cosmogony and was at hand, as it were, to explain the stability of the earth. On the broader implications of Anaximander's theory see further Kahn, *op. cit.*, 76–81.

(ii) *The heavenly bodies*

125 Hippolytus *Ref.* 1, 6, 4–5   τὰ δὲ ἄστρα γίνεσθαι κύκλον πυρός ἀποκριθέντα τοῦ κατὰ τὸν κόσμον πυρός, περιληφθέντα δ' ὑπὸ ἀέρος (cf. 121). ἐκπνοὰς δ' ὑπάρξαι, πόρους τινὰς αὐλώδεις, καθ' οὓς φαίνεται τὰ ἄστρα· διὸ καὶ ἐπιφρασσομένων τῶν ἐκπνοῶν τὰς ἐκλείψεις γίνεσθαι. τὴν δὲ σελήνην ποτὲ μὲν πληρουμένην φαίνεσθαι ποτὲ δὲ μειουμένην παρὰ τὴν τῶν πόρων ἐπίφραξιν ἢ ἄνοιξιν.

εἶναι δὲ τὸν κύκλον τοῦ ἡλίου ἑπτακαιεικοσαπλασίονα ⟨τῆς γῆς, ὀκτωκαιδεκαπλασίονα δὲ τὸν⟩ τῆς σελήνης, καὶ ἀνωτάτω μὲν εἶναι τὸν ἥλιον, κατωτάτω δὲ τοὺς τῶν ἀπλανῶν ἀστέρων κύκλους.

126 Aetius II, 20, 1 Ἀναξίμανδρος (*sc.* τὸν ἥλιόν φησι) κύκλον εἶναι ὀκτωκαιεικοσαπλασίονα τῆς γῆς, ἁρματείῳ τροχῷ παραπλήσιον, τὴν ἁψῖδα ἔχοντα κοίλην, πλήρη πυρός, κατά τι μέρος ἐκφαίνουσαν διὰ στομίου τὸ πῦρ ὥσπερ διὰ πρηστῆρος αὐλοῦ. (Cf. Aetius II, 25, 1, DK 12 A 22, for the moon.)

127 Aetius II, 21, 1 Ἀναξίμανδρος (*sc.* φησὶ) τὸν μὲν ἥλιον ἴσον εἶναι τῇ γῇ, τὸν δὲ κύκλον ἀφ' οὗ τὴν ἐκπνοὴν ἔχει καὶ ὑφ' οὗ περιφέρεται ἑπτακαιεικοσαπλασίω τῆς γῆς.

128 Aetius II, 16, 5 Ἀναξίμανδρος ὑπὸ τῶν κύκλων καὶ τῶν σφαιρῶν ἐφ' ὧν ἕκαστος βέβηκε φέρεσθαι (*sc.* τοὺς ἀστέρας φησίν).

125 The heavenly bodies come into being as a circle of fire separated off from the fire in the world, and enclosed by air. There are breathing-holes, certain pipe-like passages, at which the heavenly bodies show themselves; accordingly eclipses occur when the breathing-holes are blocked up. The moon is seen now waxing, now waning according to the blocking or opening of the channels. The circle of the sun is 27 times the size of ⟨the earth, that of⟩ the moon ⟨18 times⟩; the sun is highest, and the circles of the fixed stars are lowest.
126 Anaximander [says the sun] is a circle 28 times the size of the earth, like a chariot wheel, with its felloe hollow and full of fire, and showing the fire at a certain point through an aperture as though through the nozzle of a bellows.
127 Anaximander [says] that the sun is equal to the earth, but that the circle from which it has its breathing-hole and by which it is carried round is 27 times the size of the earth.
128 Anaximander [says that the heavenly bodies] are carried by the circles and spheres on which each one goes.

The sun and moon are each an aperture in separate solid rings like the felloes of cartwheels. These rings consist of fire surrounded by air (regarded as concealing mist), and out of the single aperture in each of them fire emerges like air from the nozzle of a bellows; the similes of the cartwheels and the bellows perhaps derive from Anaximander himself. Eclipses, and phases of the moon, are due to a total or partial blocking of the aperture; typically, no motive is given for this blockage. The aperture of the sun is the same size as the surface (presumably) of the earth (**127**) – a remarkable view contradicted by

Heraclitus in fr. 3; the diameter of its wheel is twenty-seven times as great as this (twenty-eight times in **126**).[1] The moon-wheel is nineteen earth-diameters (or eighteen, presumably) across; the obvious lacuna in **125** has been filled after Aetius II, 25, 1, which gives the corresponding information to **126** for the moon, only adding that the circles of sun and moon lie obliquely. The star-wheels (on which see below), although we are not told so, were presumably of nine (or ten) earth-diameters, being nearest to the earth (**125** *fin.*). Thus Anaximander gave the structure of the world a mathematical basis, developing the assumption (seen already in Homer and Hesiod, cf. **1** with comment) that it is orderly – even then in a crudely quantifiable way – and determinable. His proportionate distances may have influenced Pythagoras.

[1] This larger figure ($28x$) cannot represent the distance from the outer, as opposed to the inner, edges of the celestial circle if diameters are meant; for 2, not 1, should then be added to the multiple, to give $29x$. If the radius and not the diameter were intended the figures given would hold: but 'the circle of the sun is twenty-seven times that of the earth' (**125**, **126**) – the earth whose 'breadth' is specified in **122** – implies clearly enough that the diameter is really meant. In that case the larger figure might represent the diameter from outer edge to outer edge, the smaller one that from points half-way between the outer and inner edges of the actual felloe of air – assuming, what seems reasonable, that the felloe is one earth-diameter thick.

The stars present certain difficulties. (*a*) **125** *fin.* mentions the fixed stars as closest to the earth. Possibly, as Diels thought, there is another lacuna here and the planets were mentioned too. That the fixed stars and the planets were at the same distance from the earth is perhaps implied by Aetius II, 15, 6 (DK 12 A 18), and is suggested by the series of proportionate distances: 1 (diameter of earth)–x–18 (moon-ring)–27 (sun-ring). Here x, the missing distance, must be that of the stars and planets: it must be 9, to fit into the series, and there is no vacant number to allow a different distance for stars and planets. (*b*) **128** mentions both circles and spheres of the stars (while **125** has a circle of stars at the beginning, circles at the end). The two are incompatible; possibly a sphere for the fixed stars, rings for the planets were meant. But this is inconsistent with the argument that fixed stars and planets must be at the same distance from the earth; there would not be room for both a sphere and rings. Indeed a sphere, although the simplest explanation of the fixed stars, is impossible: the cosmogonical account (**121**) showed that a ball of flame broke up, or broke away from the mist round the earth, and was then shut into circles (obviously of air-mist) which composed sun, moon and stars. There is no possibility, let alone any mention, of part of the sphere of flame remaining as a sphere after it had broken away. Thus it must be assumed that each star, including the planets, has its own wheel; these wheels are equal in diameter and are inclined on countless different planes. They do not obscure the sun and moon (cf. e.g. Homer *Il.* xx, 444ff.; xxi, 549). If their centre is the same as the centre of the earth, the circumpolar stars (which do not set) are unexplained – as they would be even by a sphere; and yet if their centres were at different distances up and down the earth's axis, which could account for some stars not setting, they would be likely to infringe the equilibrium described in 123 and 124. Probably Anaximander did not think of these difficulties. The movement of the sun on the ecliptic, the declination of the moon, and the wanderings of the planets were probably explained as due to wind (see 132); the east-to-west movements were due to rotation of the wheels (cf. φέρεσθαι in 128) in the planes of their circumferences.

It is plain that much of Anaximander's astronomy is speculative and aprioristic – which is not to say that it is mystical or poetical exactly (see Kahn, *op. cit.*, 94f.). Rather, the symmetry of the universe that was already assumed in Homer and Hesiod is developed further, made more precise, and more closely related to 'commonsense' observation of a somewhat incomplete and casual kind.

(iii) *Meteorological phenomena*

129 Hippolytus *Ref.* 1, 6, 7 ἀνέμους δὲ γίνεσθαι τῶν λεπτοτάτων ἀτμῶν τοῦ ἀέρος ἀποκρινομένων καὶ ὅταν ἀθροισθῶσι κινουμένων, ὑετοὺς δὲ ἐκ τῆς ἀτμίδος τῆς ἐκ τῶν ὑφ᾽ ἥλιον ἀναδιδομένης· ἀστραπὰς δὲ ὅταν ἄνεμος ἐκπίπτων διιστᾷ τὰς νεφέλας.[1]

[1] ἐκ τῆς ἀτμίδος – ἀναδιδομένης Cedrenus; the MSS give an obviously corrupt reading (DK 1 p.84n.) which implies if anything that the exhalation is from the earth. A dual exhalation was imposed also on Heraclitus (p. 202 n. 1); it was probably a refinement by Aristotle. Cedrenus (11th cent. A.D.) is sometimes correct: e.g. his ἐκπίπτων in 129 is shown by 130 to be correct against MSS ἐμπίπτων.

130 Aetius III, 3, 1–2 (περὶ βροντῶν ἀστραπῶν κεραυνῶν πρηστήρων τε καὶ τυφώνων.) Ἀναξίμανδρος ἐκ τοῦ πνεύματος ταυτὶ πάντα συμβαίνειν· ὅταν γὰρ περιληφθὲν νέφει παχεῖ βιασάμενον ἐκπέσῃ τῇ λεπτομερείᾳ καὶ κουφότητι, τότε ἡ μὲν ῥῆξις τὸν ψόφον, ἡ δὲ διαστολὴ παρὰ τὴν μελανίαν τοῦ νέφους τὸν διαυγασμὸν ἀποτελεῖ.

131 Seneca *Qu. nat.* II, 18 Anaximandrus omnia ad spiritum rettulit: tonitrua, inquit, sunt nubis ictae sonus...(see DK 12A23).

129 Winds occur when the finest vapours of the air are separated off and when they are set in motion by congregation; rain occurs from the exhalation that issues upwards from the things beneath the sun, and lightning whenever wind breaks out and cleaves the clouds.

130 (On thunder, lightning, thunderbolts, whirlwinds and typhoons.) Anaximander says that all these things occur as a result of wind: for whenever it is shut up in a thick cloud and then bursts out forcibly, through its fineness and lightness, then the bursting makes the noise, while the rift against the blackness of the cloud makes the flash.

131 Anaximander referred everything to wind: thunder, he said, is the noise of smitten cloud...

These passages suggest that Anaximander shared in, and perhaps to a large degree originated, a more or less standard Ionian way of accounting for meteorological (in our sense) events. The chief elements of this scheme are wind, the evaporation from the sea, and the condensed masses of vapour which form the clouds. All testimonies on the subject are, of course, based on Theophrastus, whom we may suspect of not always resisting the temptation to supply 'appropriate' explanations, where none existed, of certain natural phenomena which he thought interested all Presocratics. The explanation of wind in 129 (cf. also Aetius III, 7, 1, DK 12 A 24) is very involved; note that it is somehow due to 'separation off' of the finest part of air. Rain is caused by the condensation (presumably) of moist vapours evaporated by the sun; wind causes most other phenomena (130, 131), including, probably, the movements north and south of sun and moon. 132, with 133, is ambiguous on this point – it could be the exhalation (as Kahn thinks, *op. cit.*, p. 66) rather than the winds themselves, that cause these movements, although 131 suggests that the latter is what Aristotle meant. The emphasis on wind, a product of air, might in any case suggest a degree of conflation with Anaximenes; he gave the same explanation of lightning as Anaximander but in an appendix to 130 is distinguished as having cited a special parallel (oars flash in water; see 158). On this and § (iv) see further Kahn's interesting discussion, *op. cit.*, 98–109. On p. 102 he stresses the parallel between the meteorological fire of lightning, emanating from wind, and that of the celestial rings.

(iv) *The earth is drying up*

132 Aristotle *Meteor.* B1, 353b6 εἶναι γάρ τὸ πρῶτον ὑγρὸν ἅπαντα τὸν περὶ τὴν γῆν τόπον, ὑπὸ δὲ τοῦ ἡλίου ξηραινόμενον τὸ

μὲν διατμίσαν πνεύματα καὶ τροπὰς ἡλίου καὶ σελήνης φασὶ ποιεῖν, τὸ δὲ λειφθὲν θάλατταν εἶναι· διὸ καὶ ἐλάττω γίνεσθαι ξηραινομένην οἴονται καὶ τέλος ἔσεσθαί ποτε πᾶσαν ξηράν...Alexander *in Meteor.* p. 67, 11 (DK 12 A 27) ...ταύτης τῆς δόξης ἐγένετο, ὡς ἱστορεῖ Θεόφραστος, ᾽Αναξίμανδρός τε καὶ Διογένης.

132 For first of all the whole area round the earth is moist, but being dried by the sun the part that is exhaled makes winds and turnings of the sun and moon, they say, while that which is left is sea; therefore they think that the sea is actually becoming less through being dried up, and that some time it will end up by all being dry ...of this opinion, as Theophrastus relates, were Anaximander and Diogenes.

It is helpful to have Theophrastus' attribution reported by Alexander (and confirmed by Aetius III, 16, 1), although it must be noted that the only name mentioned by *Aristotle* in connexion with the drying up of the sea is that of Democritus (*Meteor.* B3, 356b10, DK68A100). Aristotle had previously mentioned (*Meteor.* A14, 352a17) that those who believed the sea to be drying up were influenced by local examples of this process (which, we may note, was conspicuous around sixth-century Miletus); he himself rebuked them for their false inference, and pointed out that in other places the sea was gaining; also, there were long-term periods of comparative drought and flood which Aristotle called the 'great summer' and 'great winter' in a 'great year'.[1]

[1] Here Aristotle may be aiming particularly at Democritus, who thought that the sea was drying up *and that the world would come to an end.* Anaximander need not have thought this any more than Xenophanes did; in fact Aristotle might have been rebuking Democritus in terms of the earlier cyclical theory. – There may well be a special reference to Anaximander in Aristotle's words (*Meteor.* B2, 355a22) 'those who say...that when the world around the earth was heated by the sun, air came into being and the whole heaven *expanded*...' (cf. **121**).

It is clear that if Anaximander thought that the sea would dry up once and for all this would be a serious betrayal of the principle enunciated in the extant fragment (**110**), that things are punished for their injustice; for land would have encroached on sea without suffering retribution. Further, although only the sea is mentioned, it is reasonable to conclude that, since rain was explained as due to the condensation of evaporation (**129**), the drying up of the sea would lead to the drying up of the whole earth. But could our whole interpretation of the fragment as an assertion of cosmic stability be wrong; could the drying up of the earth be the prelude to reabsorption into the Indefinite? This it could not be, since if the earth were destroyed by drought that would implicitly qualify the Indefinite itself as dry and fiery, thus contradicting its very nature; and, in addition, the arguments from the form of the fragment still stand. The principle of the fragment could, however, be preserved if the diminution of the sea were only one part of a cyclical process: when the sea is dry a 'great winter' (to use Aristotle's term, which may well be derived from earlier theories) begins, and eventually the other extreme is reached when all the earth is overrun by sea and turns, perhaps, into slime.

That this is what Anaximander thought is made more probable by the fact that Xenophanes, another Ionian of a generation just after Anaximander's, postulated cycles of the earth drying out and turning into slime: see pp. 176–8. Xenophanes was impressed by fossils of plant and animal life embedded in rocks far from the present sea, and deduced that the earth was once mud. But he argued, not that the sea will dry up even more, but that everything will turn back into mud; men will be destroyed, but then the cycle will continue, the land will dry out, and men will be produced anew. For Anaximander, too, men were born ultimately from mud (**133, 135**). The parallelism is not complete, but it is extremely close: Xenophanes may have been correcting or modifying Anaximander. Anaximander, too, was familiar with the great legendary periods of fire and flood, in the ages of Phaethon and Deucalion; impressed by the recession of the sea from the Ionian coastline he might well have applied such periods to the whole history of the earth.

ZOOGONY AND ANTHROPOGONY

133 Aetius v, 19, 4 Ἀναξίμανδρος ἐν ὑγρῷ γεννηθῆναι τὰ πρῶτα ζῷα φλοιοῖς περιεχόμενα ἀκανθώδεσι, προβαινούσης δὲ τῆς ἡλικίας ἀποβαίνειν ἐπὶ τὸ ξηρότερον καὶ περιρρηγνυμένου τοῦ φλοιοῦ ἐπ' ὀλίγον χρόνον μεταβιῶναι.

134 Ps.-Plutarch *Strom.* 2 ἔτι φησὶν ὅτι κατ' ἀρχὰς ἐξ ἀλλοειδῶν ζῴων ὁ ἄνθρωπος ἐγεννήθη, ἐκ τοῦ τὰ μὲν ἄλλα δι' ἑαυτῶν ταχὺ νέμεσθαι, μόνον δὲ τὸν ἄνθρωπον πολυχρονίου δεῖσθαι τιθηνήσεως· διὸ καὶ κατ' ἀρχὰς οὐκ ἄν ποτε τοιοῦτον ὄντα διασωθῆναι.

135 Censorinus *de die nat.* 4, 7 Anaximander Milesius videri sibi ex aqua terraque calefactis exortos esse sive pisces seu piscibus simillima animalia; in his homines concrevisse fetusque ad pubertatem intus retentos; tunc demum ruptis illis viros mulieresque qui iam se alere possent processisse.

136 Hippolytus *Ref.* 1, 6, 6 τὰ δὲ ζῷα γίνεσθαι ⟨ἐξ ὑγροῦ⟩ ἐξατμιζομένου [Diels, -όμενα MSS] ὑπὸ τοῦ ἡλίου. τὸν δὲ ἄνθρωπον ἑτέρῳ ζῴῳ γεγονέναι, τουτέστι ἰχθύι, παραπλήσιον κατ' ἀρχάς.

137 Plutarch *Symp.* VIII, 730E (DK 12 A 30) διὸ καὶ σέβονται (*sc.* Σύροι) τὸν ἰχθῦν ὡς ὁμογενῆ καὶ σύντροφον, ἐπιεικέστερον Ἀναξιμάνδρου φιλοσοφοῦντες· οὐ γὰρ ἐν τοῖς αὐτοῖς ἐκεῖνος ἰχθῦς καὶ ἀνθρώπους, ἀλλ' ἐν ἰχθύσιν ἐγγενέσθαι τὸ πρῶτον ἀνθρώπους ἀποφαίνεται καὶ τραφέντας, ὥσπερ οἱ γαλεοί,[1] καὶ γενομένους ἱκανοὺς ἑαυτοῖς βοηθεῖν ἐκβῆναι τηνικαῦτα καὶ γῆς λαβέσθαι.

[1] Emperius' γαλεοί for the impossible MSS παλαιοί is a brilliant emendation based on another passage in Plutarch, *de soll. an.* 33, 982A, where the shark is said to produce an egg, then to nurture the young inside itself until it is bigger; Aristotle had noted this at *Hist. animalium* Z10, 565b1. But 'like sharks' may well be a parenthetical remark by Plutarch (note the case: nominative not accusative), who knew about them indirectly from Aristotle; he would naturally quote them as an illustration of Anaximander's idea.

133 Anaximander said that the first living creatures were born in moisture, enclosed in thorny barks; and that as their age increased they came forth on to the drier part and, when the bark had broken off, they lived a different kind of life for a short time. **134** Further he says that in the beginning man was born from creatures of a different kind; because other creatures are soon self-supporting, but man alone needs prolonged nursing. For this reason he would not have survived if this had been his original form. **135** Anaximander of Miletus conceived that there arose from heated water and earth either fish or creatures very like fish; in these man grew, in the form of embryos retained within until puberty; then at last the fish-like creatures burst and men and women who were already able to nourish themselves stepped forth. **136** Living creatures came into being from moisture evaporated by the sun. Man was originally similar to another creature – that is, to a fish. **137** Therefore they [the Syrians] actually revere the fish as being of similar race and nurturing. In this they philosophize more suitably than Anaximander; for he declares, not that fishes and men came into being in the same parents, but that originally men came into being inside fishes, and that having been nurtured there – like sharks – and having become adequate to look after themselves, they then came forth and took to the land.

This is virtually all the information we have about Anaximander's evidently brilliant conjectures on the origins of animal and human life. The first living creatures are generated from slime (elsewhere called ἰλύς) by the heat of the sun: this became a standard account, and even Aristotle accepted spontaneous generation in such cases. The observation behind the theory was perhaps that of mud-flies and sand-worms which abound in the hot sand at the edge of the sea. Yet the first creatures were not of that kind, but were surrounded by prickly barks – like sea-urchins, Cornford suggested. Aetius (**133**) seems to preserve special information about these first creatures, which presumably were prior to the fish-like creatures in which men were reared. The use of φλοιός here reminds one of the bark-simile in the cosmogonical account (**121**); both ball of flame and prickly shell broke away from round the core (here περι- not ἀπορρήγνυσθαι).

The meaning of the concluding words of **133** is disputed; but μετα- in new late-Greek compounds usually implies change rather than succession, and the sense is probably that the creatures, emerged from their husks, lived a different life (i.e. on land) for a short time longer. Possibly Anaximander had some conception of the difficulties of adaptation to environment.[1] This would be no more startling than his intelligent observation that man (with nine months' gestation and many years' helplessness) could not have survived in primitive conditions without protection of some kind. This consideration led to the conjecture that man was reared in a kind of fish – presumably because the earth was originally moist, and the first creatures were of the sea.

[1] Kahn, *op. cit.*, 69, may be right in saying that a short life was the consequence of their difficult mode of birth.

Anaximander's is the first attempt of which we know to explain the origin of man, as well as of the world, rationally. Moreover the general principles of the development of birth are similar (see **121** in particular): moisture is contained in a bark-like covering, and heat somehow causes an expansion or explosion of the husk and the release of a completed form within. Not all Anaximander's successors concerned themselves with man's history (they were more interested in his present condition), and none surpassed him in the thoughtful ingenuity of his theories. Incomplete as our sources are, they show that his account of nature, though among the earliest, was one of the broadest in scope and most imaginative of all.

CHAPTER IV

Anaximenes of Miletus

HIS DATE, LIFE AND BOOK

138 Diogenes Laertius ΙΙ, 3 Ἀναξιμένης Εὐρυστράτου Μιλήσιος ἤκουσεν Ἀναξιμάνδρου, ἔνιοι δὲ καὶ Παρμενίδου φασὶν ἀκοῦσαι αὐτόν. οὗτος ἀρχὴν ἀέρα εἶπε καὶ τὸ ἄπειρον. κινεῖσθαι δὲ τὰ ἄστρα οὐχ ὑπὸ γῆν ἀλλὰ περὶ γῆν. κέχρηταί τε λέξει Ἰάδι ἁπλῇ καὶ ἀπερίττῳ. καὶ γεγένηται μέν, καθά φησιν Ἀπολλόδωρος, περὶ τὴν Σάρδεων ἅλωσιν, ἐτελεύτησε δὲ τῇ ἑξηκοστῇ τρίτῃ ὀλυμπιάδι (528–525 Β.C.).

138 Anaximenes son of Eurystratus, of Miletus, was a pupil of Anaximander; some say he was also a pupil of Parmenides. He said that the material principle was air and the infinite; and that the stars move, not under the earth, but round it. He used simple and economical Ionic speech. He was active, according to what Apollodorus says, around the time of the capture of Sardis, and died in the 63rd Olympiad.

It may be doubted whether the chronographical tradition knew more about Anaximenes' date than the statement of Theophrastus (**140**) that he was an associate of Anaximander. The Succession-writers would establish him in the next philosophical generation to Anaximander, and Eratosthenes, followed by Apollodorus, would choose a suitable epoch-year for his *acme*, i.e. the age of forty. The obvious epoch-year was that of the capture of Sardis by Cyrus, 546/5 Β.C. (= Ol. 58, 3; Hippolytus *Ref.* I, 7, 9, DK 13 A 7, gave Ol. 58, 1, complicated in the Suda, 13 A 2). This puts his birth around the *acme* of Thales, his death around the commonly-chosen age of sixty, and makes him twenty-four years younger than Anaximander. This is all quite hypothetical; but we may accept what seems likely from his thought, that he was younger than Anaximander; while his active life can scarcely have continued far into the fifth century (Miletus was destroyed in 494 Β.C.).[1]

[1] The MSS of Diogenes in **138** reverse the position of περὶ τὴν Σάρδεων ἅλωσιν and τῇ ἑξηκοστῇ τρίτῃ ὀλυμπιάδι. Diels emended (as printed here). G. B.

Kerferd points out (*Mus. Helvet.* 11 (1954), 117ff.) that if the capture of Sardis were that of 498 B.C., and γεγένηται meant (as it certainly can, and perhaps should) 'was born' rather than 'flourished', then the MS text could be correct *if* Anaximenes died at the age of 30 or less. But it is unlikely that Apollodorus would have ignored Theophrastus' connexion of Anaximenes with Anaximander (who according to Apollodorus was dead by 528); or that he would have used two separate captures of Sardis as epochs (he certainly uses that of 546/5). Further, Hippolytus (DK 13 A 7) supports a *floruit* at or near 546/5.

About Anaximenes' life and practical activities we know practically nothing (cf. n. on p. 104). From the stylistic judgement in **138**, however, it is clear that he wrote a book, a part of which at least must have been known to Theophrastus, from whom the criticism presumably emanates. The 'simple and unsuperfluous' Ionic may be contrasted with the 'rather poetical terminology' of Anaximander (**110**).

AIR IN ANAXIMENES

(i) *Air is the originative substance and basic form of matter; it changes by condensation and rarefaction*

139 Aristotle *Met.* A3, 984a5 Ἀναξιμένης δὲ ἀέρα καὶ Διογένης πρότερον ὕδατος καὶ μάλιστ' ἀρχὴν τιθέασι τῶν ἁπλῶν σωμάτων.

140 Theophrastus *ap.* Simplicium *in Phys.* 24, 26 Ἀναξιμένης δὲ Εὐρυστράτου Μιλήσιος, ἑταῖρος γεγονὼς Ἀναξιμάνδρου, μίαν μὲν καὶ αὐτὸς τὴν ὑποκειμένην φύσιν καὶ ἄπειρόν φησιν ὥσπερ ἐκεῖνος, οὐκ ἀόριστον δὲ ὥσπερ ἐκεῖνος ἀλλὰ ὡρισμένην, ἀέρα λέγων αὐτήν· διαφέρειν δὲ μανότητι καὶ πυκνότητι κατὰ τὰς οὐσίας. καὶ ἀραιούμενον μὲν πῦρ γίνεσθαι, πυκνούμενον δὲ ἄνεμον, εἶτα νέφος, ἔτι δὲ μᾶλλον ὕδωρ, εἶτα γῆν, εἶτα λίθους, τὰ δὲ ἄλλα ἐκ τούτων. κίνησιν δὲ καὶ οὗτος ἀίδιον ποιεῖ, δι' ἣν καὶ τὴν μεταβολὴν γίνεσθαι.

141 Hippolytus *Ref.* 1, 7, 1 Ἀναξιμένης...ἀέρα ἄπειρον ἔφη τὴν ἀρχὴν εἶναι, ἐξ οὗ τὰ γινόμενα καὶ τὰ γεγονότα καὶ τὰ ἐσόμενα καὶ θεοὺς καὶ θεῖα γίνεσθαι, τὰ δὲ λοιπὰ ἐκ τῶν τούτου ἀπογόνων. (2) τὸ δὲ εἶδος τοῦ ἀέρος τοιοῦτον· ὅταν μὲν ὁμαλώτατος ᾖ, ὄψει ἄδηλον, δηλοῦσθαι δὲ τῷ ψυχρῷ καὶ τῷ θερμῷ καὶ τῷ νοτερῷ καὶ τῷ κινουμένῳ. κινεῖσθαι δὲ ἀεί· οὐ γὰρ μεταβάλλειν ὅσα μεταβάλλει, εἰ μὴ κινοῖτο. (3) πυκνούμενον γὰρ καὶ ἀραιούμενον διάφορον φαίνεσθαι· ὅταν γὰρ εἰς τὸ ἀραιότερον διαχυθῇ, πῦρ γίνεσθαι, ἀνέμους δὲ πάλιν εἶναι ἀέρα πυκνούμενον, ἐξ ἀέρος ⟨δὲ⟩ νέφος ἀποτελεῖσθαι κατὰ τὴν πίλησιν, ἔτι δὲ μᾶλλον ὕδωρ, ἐπὶ πλεῖον πυκνωθέντα γῆν καὶ εἰς τὸ μάλιστα πυκνότατον λίθους. ὥστε τὰ κυριώτατα τῆς γενέσεως ἐναντία εἶναι, θερμόν τε καὶ ψυχρόν.

139 Anaximenes and Diogenes make air, rather than water, the material principle above the other simple bodies.

140 Anaximenes son of Eurystratus, of Miletus, a companion of Anaximander, also says, like him, that the underlying nature is one and infinite, but not undefined as Anaximander said but definite, for he identifies it as air; and it differs in its substantial nature by rarity and density. Being made finer it becomes fire, being made thicker it becomes wind, then cloud, then (when thickened still more) water, then earth, then stones; and the rest come into being from these. He, too, makes motion eternal, and says that change, also, comes about through it.

141 Anaximenes...said that infinite air was the principle, from which the things that are becoming, and that are, and that shall be, and gods and things divine, all come into being, and the rest from its products. The form of air is of this kind: whenever it is most equable it is invisible to sight, but is revealed by the cold and the hot and the damp and by movement. It is always in motion; for things that change do not change unless there be movement. Through becoming denser or finer it has different appearances; for when it is dissolved into what is finer it becomes fire, while winds, again, are air that is becoming condensed, and cloud is produced from air by felting. When it is condensed still more, water is produced; with a further degree of condensation earth is produced, and when condensed as far as possible, stones. The result is that the most influential components of generation are opposites, hot and cold.

139, together with **150** and **159**, is all that Aristotle had to say about Anaximenes by name, and our tradition depends on Theophrastus, who according to Diogenes Laertius v, 42 wrote a special monograph on him (see pp. 3f.). A short version of Theophrastus' account of the material principle is preserved by Simplicius in **140**. In the present case Hippolytus' version is longer than Simplicius', but inspection of **141** shows that this is mainly due to wordy expansion and additional (sometimes non-Theophrastean) interpretation. However, the expression πίλησις (πιλεῖσθαι), 'felting', for the condensation of air, is found also in ps.-Plutarch's summary (**148**) and probably comes from Theophrastus; it was a common fourth-century term and need not have been used in this form by Anaximenes himself, contrary to what Diels and others say.

For Anaximenes the originative stuff was explicitly the basic form of material in the differentiated world, since he had thought of a way in which it could become other components of the world, like sea or earth, without losing its own nature. It was simply condensed or rarefied – that is, it altered its appearance according to how much there was of it in a particular place. This met the objection which Anaximander may well have felt against Thales' water (**105** and pp. 113f.), and which encouraged him to postulate an indefinite originative material. Anaximenes' air, too, was indefinitely vast in extent – it surrounded all things (**108** and **160**), and was thus described as ἄπειρον, infinite, by Theophrastus. It is questionable exactly what he meant by air. ἀήρ in Homer and sometimes in later Ionic prose meant 'mist', something visible and obscuring; and Anaximander's cosmogony included a damp mist, part of which congealed to form a slimy kind of earth (pp. 132, 142). Anaximenes probably said (**160**) that all things were surrounded by πνεῦμα καὶ ἀήρ, 'wind (or breath) and air', and that the soul is related to this air; which suggests that for him ἀήρ was not mist but, as Hippolytus in **141** assumed, the invisible atmospheric air. This is confirmed by the fact that he evidently described winds as a slightly condensed form of air (**140, 141**).

Now atmospheric air was certainly not included as a world-component by Heraclitus (e.g. **218**), and its substantiality – that is, corporeality – needed to be emphasized by Anaxagoras (**470**). It looks, then, as though Anaximenes simply assumed that some part, at least, of the atmospheric air was substantial, and indeed the basic form of substance; although he did not offer any notable demonstration of its substantiality and so convince his immediate successors. This assumption would be a very remarkable one; though it must be remembered that πνεῦμα in the sense of breath was certainly regarded as existing, and yet it was invisible. It was not, however, totally insensible; its presence was revealed by tangible properties – in Hippolytus' terms by 'the cold and the hot and the moist and the moving'. Atmospheric air, on occasions, makes itself known by none of these things.

The main forms assumed by air as a result of condensation and rarefaction were outlined by Theophrastus. They are obvious enough, and were clearly based on observation of natural processes – rain coming from clouds, water apparently condensing into earth, evaporation, and so on. Such changes were accepted by all the Presocratics; it was only Anaximenes that explained them solely in terms of the density of a single material.[1] It may be asked why *air* was specified as the normal or basic form of matter; from the point of view of natural change within the world, water, equally, might be basic, with air as a rarefied variant. In view of **160** (pp. 158ff.), where cosmic air is compared with the πνεῦμα or breath which is traditionally conceived as the breath-soul or life-giving ψυχή, it seems that Anaximenes regarded air as the breath of the world, and so as its ever-living, and therefore divine, source; see also p. 161. Moreover air might have seemed to possess some of the *indefinite* qualities of Anaximander's originative stuff (not being naturally characterized by any particular opposite); in addition it had the advantage of occupying a large region of the developed world. Anaximenes seems at first sight to have abandoned the principle of general opposition in the world (it was shortly to be revived in a more Anaximandrean form, though with some modification, by Heraclitus), and so to have lost even the metaphorical motives, of injustice and retribution, for natural change. Yet one pair of opposites, the rare and the dense, took on a new and special significance, and it could legitimately be argued that all changes are due to the reaction of these two: see further p. 149. In addition, no doubt, Anaximenes shared Thales' assumption that matter was somehow alive, which would be confirmed by the constant mobility of air – especially if this was only accepted as being air when it was perceptible. Theophrastus, as usual, reduced these assumptions to the formula of 'eternal motion', adding that all change would depend on this motion.

[1] Cf. **142** Simplicius *in Phys.* 149, 32 ἐπὶ γὰρ τούτου (*sc.* ᾿Αναξιμένου) μόνου Θεόφραστος ἐν τῇ ῾Ιστορίᾳ τὴν μάνωσιν εἴρηκε καὶ πύκνωσιν, δῆλον δὲ ὡς καὶ οἱ ἄλλοι τῇ μανότητι καὶ πυκνότητι ἐχρῶντο. *(For in the case of him [Anaximenes] alone did Theophrastus in the* History *speak of rarefaction and condensation, but it is plain that the others, also, used rarity and density.)* There is no difficulty here (and no need for drastic expedients like the supposition that μόνου means πρώτου): 'the others' (e.g. Hippasus and Heraclitus in DK 22 A 5) were loosely described by Theophrastus as using condensation, but only Anaximenes explicitly used the rare and the dense as an essential part of his theory. Simplicius then slightly misunderstood Theophrastus' comment on Anaximenes.

It appears that according to Theophrastus ('the other things, from these' in **140** *fin.*, also in a vague and inaccurate paraphrase in **141** *init.*; cf. Cicero *Acad. pr.* II, 37, 118, DK 13 A 9) Anaximenes did not think that every kind of natural substance could be explained as a direct form of air, but that there were certain basic forms (fire, air, wind, cloud, water, earth, stone) of which other kinds were compounds. If true, this is important, since it makes Anaximenes the pioneer of the idea that there are elements from which other objects are compounded – an idea first formally worked out by Empedocles. Yet it seems questionable whether this interpretation is justified.

There is no other evidence that anyone before Empedocles tried to give a detailed account of any but the main cosmic substances; having invented a device to explain diversity, it would be more in the Milesian character for Anaximenes to have adhered to it; and Theophrastus was prone to add just such generalizing summaries, often slightly misleading, to a specific list.[1] Yet the difficulty of air turning into rocks or myrtle-bushes might indeed have struck Anaximenes, and suggested the advantages of mixture as an additional mechanism (see Guthrie, *HGP* I, 122f.). In any event, J. Barnes has a point when he rejects the idea of Anaximenes as a 'Presocratic Boyle' and of his physics as 'fundamentally quantitative' (*op. cit.*, I, 45f.).

[1] A more certainly false interpretation is that which makes Anaximenes the forerunner of atomism. He cannot have conceived of matter as continuous, it is argued; therefore, since there can be more or less of it in the same space, it must have been composed of particles which can be more or less heavily concentrated. But it seems unlikely that anyone before Heraclitus bothered about the formal constitution of matter, or about precisely what was involved in condensation, which could be simply an objective description of certain observed processes.

(ii) *Hot and cold are due to rarefaction and condensation*

143 Plutarch *de prim. frig.* 7, 947F (DK13B1) ...ἢ καθάπερ Ἀναξιμένης ὁ παλαιὸς ᾤετο, μήτε τὸ ψυχρὸν ἐν οὐσίᾳ μήτε τὸ θερμὸν ἀπολείπωμεν, ἀλλὰ πάθη κοινὰ τῆς ὕλης ἐπιγιγνόμενα ταῖς μεταβολαῖς· τὸ γὰρ συστελλόμενον αὐτῆς καὶ πυκνούμενον ψυχρὸν εἶναί φησι, τὸ δ' ἀραιὸν καὶ τὸ 'χαλαρόν' (οὕτω πως ὀνομάσας καὶ τῷ ῥήματι) θερμόν. ὅθεν οὐκ ἀπεικότως λέγεσθαι τὸ καὶ θερμὰ τὸν ἄνθρωπον ἐκ τοῦ στόματος καὶ ψυχρὰ μεθιέναι· ψύχεται γὰρ ἡ πνοὴ πιεσθεῖσα καὶ πυκνωθεῖσα τοῖς χείλεσιν, ἀνειμένου δὲ τοῦ στόματος ἐκπίπτουσα γίγνεται θερμὸν ὑπὸ μανότητος. τοῦτο μὲν οὖν ἀγνόημα ποιεῖται τοῦ ἀνδρὸς ὁ Ἀριστοτέλης... (Cf. *Problemata* 34, 7, 964a10.)

143 ...or as Anaximenes thought of old, let us leave neither the cold nor the hot as belonging to substance, but as common dispositions of matter that supervene on changes; for he says that matter which is compressed and condensed is cold, while that which is fine and 'relaxed' (using this very word) is hot. Therefore, he said, the dictum is not an unreasonable one, that man releases both warmth and cold from his mouth: for the breath is chilled by being compressed and condensed with the lips, but when the mouth is loosened the breath escapes and becomes warm through its rarity. This theory Aristotle claims to be due to the man's [*sc.* Anaximenes'] ignorance...

Plutarch seems to have had access to a genuine citation from Anaximenes: the word χαλαρός, 'slack', if no more, is definitely said to be his, and there is no reason to doubt it. Conceivably Plutarch depends on a lost passage of Aristotle; the passage from the Aristotelian *Problems* discusses the phenomenon in the manner suggested in the continuation of **143**, but without naming Anaximenes. The example of breath was evidently cited by Anaximenes as showing that rarefaction and condensation of air can produce, not merely obvious variations like those of hardness and softness, thickness and thinness, but a variation of the hot and the cold which seems to have little directly to do with density. On this evidence alone one would expect the instance to be part of an argument that condensation and rarefaction can produce quite unexpected alterations, and so could be responsible for every kind of diversity.

Hippolytus in **141**, however, suggests that hot and cold play a vital part in coming-to-be; in other words Anaximenes still attributed special importance to the chief cosmogonical substances in Anaximander, the hot stuff and the cold stuff. There is no mention of this in Simplicius' extract from Theophrastus (**140**), but Hippolytus or his immediate source is unlikely to be entirely responsible for it. It is, however, difficult to see how these opposed substances could be basic in Anaximenes' scheme of things, and it seems highly probable that Theophrastus, seeing that some prominence was given to hot and cold in Anaximenes, suggested that they were for him, as they were for Aristotle and for Theophrastus himself, one of the essential elements of γένεσις. (The Peripatetic simple bodies were composed of prime matter informed by either hot or cold and either wet or dry.) This interpretation is anachronistic, and leaves us free to accept the natural one suggested by Plutarch himself, expressed though it still is in Peripatetic terms. But can even Anaximenes have thought that temperature varied directly with density? There is such a thing, for example, as hot stone or cold air. This difficulty might not have occurred to him, since in general it is true that the ascending scale of density represents also a descending scale of temperature, from fire down to stones; air itself normally not striking one (at any rate in the Mediterranean) as consistently either hot or cold. Alternatively, the instance of breath compressed by the lips might seem to illustrate that density *can* affect temperature, without implying that it always does so to the same degree.[1]

---

[1] The instance of the breath is one of the first recorded Greek uses of a detailed observation to support a physical theory. Note, however, (i) that it is not strictly an 'experiment', i.e. the deliberate production of a chain of events the unknown

conclusion of which will either confirm or deny a prior hypothesis; (ii) that because of lack of control and of thoroughness the conclusion drawn from the observation is the exact opposite of the truth; (iii) that the word λέγεσθαι may suggest that the observation was a common one, not made for the first time by Anaximenes.

(iii) *Air is divine*

144 Cicero *de natura deorum* I, 10, 26   post Anaximenes aera deum statuit eumque gigni esseque immensum et infinitum et semper in motu, quasi aut aer sine ulla forma deus esse possit...aut non omne quod ortum sit mortalitas consequatur.

145 Aetius I, 7, 13 Ἀναξιμένης τὸν ἀέρα (*sc.* θεὸν εἶναί φησι)· δεῖ δ' ὑπακούειν ἐπὶ τῶν οὕτως λεγομένων τὰς ἐνδιηκούσας τοῖς στοιχείοις ἢ τοῖς σώμασι δυνάμεις.

146 Augustinus *de civ. dei* VIII, 2   iste (*sc.* Anaximander) Anaximenen discipulum et successorem reliquit, qui omnes rerum causas aeri infinito dedit, nec deos negavit aut tacuit; non tamen ab ipsis aerem factum, sed ipsos ex aere ortos credidit.

> **144** Afterwards, Anaximenes determined that air is a god, and that it comes into being, and is measureless and infinite and always in motion; as though either formless air could be a god...or mortality did not attend upon everything that has come into being.
> **145** Anaximenes [says that] the air [is god]: one must understand, in the case of such descriptions, the powers which interpenetrate the elements or bodies.
> **146** He [Anaximander] left Anaximenes as his disciple and successor, who attributed all the causes of things to infinite air, and did not deny that there were gods, or pass them over in silence; yet he believed not that air was made by them, but that they arose from air.

The first and third of these passages assert that according to Anaximenes a god or gods came into being from the primal air; Hippolytus also, in the first sentence of **141**, wrote that 'gods and things divine' arose from air. Theophrastus, therefore, probably said more than that Anaximenes' primal air itself was divine (cf. Aristotle's assertion in **108** that Anaximander and most of the physicists considered their originative stuff to be divine). It is probable, then, that Anaximenes himself said something about gods; it may be reasonably inferred that this was to the effect that such gods as there were in the world were themselves derived from the all-encompassing air, which was truly divine. If so, Anaximenes might be a precursor of Xenophanes and Heraclitus in their criticisms of the deities of conventional religion; though there is no evidence that Anaximenes went so far as actually to deny their existence, any more than Heraclitus did. That air itself was divine is implied both by Aristotle's generalization and by Aetius in **145**, who gives a Stoicizing description of the kind of divinity involved as 'powers permeating elements or bodies', i.e. a motive and organizing capacity that inheres in varying degrees in the constituents of the world.[1]

[1] It has sometimes been maintained (e.g. by Burnet, *EGP*, 78) that Anaximenes' gods are innumerable worlds. This is because according to Aetius I, 7, 12 and Cicero *de natura deorum* I, 10, 25 *Anaximander's* innumerable worlds were called gods (DK 12 A 17). These statements seem to have arisen from a confusion of the innumerable worlds with the stars; and Cicero cannot possibly have had the same kind of evidence for Anaximenes, since in the very next sentence, **144**, he only mentions *one* god as coming into being (and confusedly describes it as infinite, i.e. as primal air). There are in fact only two doxographical indications that Anaximenes postulated innumerable worlds: Aetius II, 1, 3 (Stob. only; see p. 124) and **147** Simplicius *in Phys.* 1121, 12 γενητὸν δὲ καὶ φθαρτὸν τὸν ἕνα κόσμον ποιοῦσιν ὅσοι ἀεὶ μέν φασιν εἶναι κόσμον, οὐ μὴν τὸν αὐτὸν ἀεί, ἀλλὰ ἄλλοτε ἄλλον γινόμενον κατά τινας χρόνων περιόδους, ὡς ᾿Αναξιμένης τε καὶ ῾Ηράκλειτος καὶ Διογένης καὶ ὕστερον οἱ ἀπὸ τῆς Στοᾶς. (*All those make the one world born and destructible who say that there is always a world, yet it is not always the same but becoming different at different times according to certain periods of time, as Anaximenes and Heraclitus and Diogenes said, and later the Stoics.*) Here Simplicius appears to assign *successive* worlds to Anaximenes. One possible reason for this is given on p. 126; but Simplicius' passage is very closely based on Aristotle *de caelo* A 10, 279 b 12 (DK 22 A 10), in which Empedocles, not Anaximenes, precedes Heraclitus; and the possibility of contamination cannot be excluded. There is far less reason to assign innumerable worlds to Anaximenes than to Anaximander, from the state of the doxographical evidence; though something was probably said on the subject by Theophrastus, on the grounds that Anaximenes, too, postulated what Theophrastus considered to be an infinite originative stuff (see pp. 123ff.).

COSMOGONY

148 Ps.-Plutarch *Strom.* 3 (cf. DK 13 A 6) ...γεννᾶσθαί τε πάντα κατά τινα πύκνωσιν τούτου (*sc.* ἀέρος) καὶ πάλιν ἀραίωσιν. τήν γε μὴν κίνησιν ἐξ αἰῶνος ὑπάρχειν· πιλουμένου δὲ τοῦ ἀέρος πρώτην γεγενῆσθαι λέγει τὴν γῆν πλατεῖαν μάλα· διὸ καὶ κατὰ λόγον αὐτὴν ἐποχεῖσθαι τῷ ἀέρι· καὶ τὸν ἥλιον καὶ τὴν σελήνην καὶ τὰ λοιπὰ ἄστρα τὴν ἀρχὴν τῆς γενέσεως ἐκ γῆς ἔχειν. ἀποφαίνεται γοῦν τὸν ἥλιον γῆν, διὰ δὲ τὴν ὀξεῖαν κίνησιν καὶ μάλ᾿ ἱκανῶς θερμότητα λαβεῖν [Zeller; θερμοτάτην κίνησιν λαβεῖν codd. plurimi].

149 Hippolytus *Ref.* 1, 7, 5 γεγονέναι δὲ τὰ ἄστρα ἐκ γῆς διὰ τὸ τὴν ἰκμάδα ἐκ ταύτης ἀνίστασθαι, ἧς ἀραιουμένης τὸ πῦρ γίνεσθαι, ἐκ δὲ τοῦ πυρὸς μετεωριζομένου τοὺς ἀστέρας συνίστασθαι.

148 ...and all things are produced by a kind of condensation, and again rarefaction, of this [*sc.* air]. Motion, indeed, exists from everlasting; he says that when the air felts, there first of all comes into being the earth, quite flat – therefore it accordingly rides on the air; and sun and moon and the remaining heavenly bodies have their source of generation from earth. At least, he declares the sun to be earth, but that through the rapid motion it obtains heat in great sufficiency.

149 The heavenly bodies have come into being from earth through the exhalation arising from it; when the exhalation is rarefied fire comes into being, and from fire raised on high the stars are composed.

Anaximenes presumably gave an account of the development of the world from undifferentiated air; as with Anaximander, only ps.-Plutarch summarizes the subject in general, and he does little more than apply the obvious changes of air (outlined by Theophrastus with reference to continuing natural processes, cf. the present tense of γίνεσθαι in **140**) to what could be an *a priori* cosmogonical pattern. Only in the case of the formation of the heavenly bodies is there detailed information; here Hippolytus in **149** is almost certainly right as against the last sentence of **148**, which seems to impose on Anaximenes ideas from Xenophanes (ignition through motion) and Anaxagoras (the same, and sun made of earth; cf. pp. 155f. for a similar confusion with Empedocles). The heavenly bodies (ἄστρα) certainly originate from the earth, but only in that moist vapour is exhaled or evaporated from (the moist parts of) earth; this is further rarefied and so becomes fire, of which the heavenly bodies are composed. The formation of the earth had occurred by the condensation of a part of the indefinitely-extended primal air. No reason is even suggested for this initial condensation, except possibly the 'eternal motion'; as with Anaximander, this was Theophrastus' way of expressing the capacity of the divine originative stuff to initiate change and motion where it willed.[1]

[1] As with Anaximander, there is no ground for positing a vortex in Anaximenes except Aristotle's generalization in **117**; in Anaximenes' case there is not even the mysterious 'producer of the hot and the cold' to be accounted for. Yet Anaximenes was not implicitly excepted from the generalization, as Anaximander may have been (p. 128). However, Aristotle had reason a few lines earlier, **150**,

to class Anaximenes with Anaxagoras and Democritus (they all assumed that the earth remains stable because of its breadth); the two others certainly postulated a vortex, and so Aristotle might have been content to class Anaximenes with them in this respect too – if he was not simply being careless in his use of 'all', πάντες, in **117**. Of course, as Zeller pointed out, vortex-action would produce the variations of pressure required for a cosmos; though Anaximenes did not in fact explain the heavenly bodies by direct rarefaction of the extremities.

COSMOLOGY

(i) *The earth is flat and rides on air*

150 Aristotle *de caelo* B13, 294b13 (DK 13 A 20) Ἀναξιμένης δὲ καὶ Ἀναξαγόρας καὶ Δημόκριτος τὸ πλάτος αἴτιον εἶναί φασι τοῦ μένειν αὐτήν (*sc.* τὴν γῆν)· οὐ γὰρ τέμνειν ἀλλ' ἐπιπωματίζειν τὸν ἀέρα τὸν κάτωθεν, ὅπερ φαίνεται τὰ πλάτος ἔχοντα τῶν σωμάτων ποιεῖν· ταῦτα γὰρ καὶ πρὸς τοὺς ἀνέμους ἔχει δυσκινήτως διὰ τὴν ἀντέρεισιν.

150 Anaximenes and Anaxagoras and Democritus say that its [the earth's] flatness is responsible for it staying still: for it does not cut the air beneath but covers it like a lid, which flat bodies evidently do; for they are hard to move even for the winds, on account of their resistance.

Anaximenes seems to have consolidated the conception of the earth as broad, flat and shallow in depth – 'table-like' according to Aetius III, 10, 3 (DK 13 A 20) – and as being supported by air. This idea was closely followed by Anaxagoras and the atomists (**502** *init.* and p. 419), who in details of cosmology conservatively selected from the earlier Ionian tradition. That the earth was supported by air was obviously an adaptation, encouraged no doubt by the observation of leaves floating in the air, of Thales' idea that the earth floated on water. Aristotle in the continuation of **150** was wrong in suggesting that support is provided because the air underneath is trapped and cannot withdraw; for Anaximenes the surrounding air was unbounded in any way, and was doubtless unthinkingly supposed to support the earth because of its indefinite depth – and because leaves do float on air. Theophrastus, judging from **148**, **151**, and Aetius III, 15, 8 (DK 13 A 20), wrote that according to Anaximenes the earth *rides*, ἐποχεῖσθαι, on air; the verb occurs in Homer and could well have been used by Anaximenes. Aristotle's 'covers the air below like a lid' is probably his own expression, an improvement perhaps on Plato's reference (*Phaedo* 99 B) to an unnamed physicist – Anaximenes or Anaxagoras or the atomists or all of them – who 'puts air underneath as a support for the earth, which is like a broad kneading-trough'.

(ii) *The heavenly bodies*

151 Hippolytus *Ref.* I, 7, 4 τὴν δὲ γῆν πλατεῖαν εἶναι ἐπ' ἀέρος ὀχουμένην, ὁμοίως δὲ καὶ ἥλιον καὶ σελήνην καὶ τὰ ἄλλα ἄστρα πάντα πύρινα ὄντα ἐποχεῖσθαι τῷ ἀέρι διὰ πλάτος.

152 Aetius II, 13, 10 Ἀναξιμένης πυρίνην μὲν τὴν φύσιν τῶν ἄστρων, περιέχειν δέ τινα καὶ γεώδη σώματα συμπεριφερόμενα τούτοις ἀόρατα.

153 Aetius II, 23, 1 Ἀναξιμένης ὑπὸ πεπυκνωμένου ἀέρος καὶ ἀντιτύπου ἐξωθούμενα τὰ ἄστρα τὰς τροπὰς ποιεῖσθαι.

154 Aetius II, 14, 3–4 Ἀναξιμένης ἥλων δίκην καταπεπηγέναι τὰ ἄστρα τῷ κρυσταλλοειδεῖ· ἔνιοι δὲ πέταλα εἶναι πύρινα ὥσπερ ζωγραφήματα.

155 Aetius II, 22, 1 Ἀναξιμένης πλατὺν ὡς πέταλον τὸν ἥλιον.

156 Hippolytus *Ref.* I, 7, 6 οὐ κινεῖσθαι δὲ ὑπὸ γῆν τὰ ἄστρα λέγει, καθὼς ἕτεροι ὑπειλήφασιν, ἀλλὰ περὶ γῆν, ὡσπερεὶ περὶ τὴν ἡμετέραν κεφαλὴν στρέφεται τὸ πιλίον. κρύπτεσθαί τε τὸν ἥλιον οὐχ ὑπὸ γῆν γενόμενον ἀλλ' ὑπὸ τῶν τῆς γῆς ὑψηλοτέρων μερῶν σκεπόμενον καὶ διὰ τὴν πλείονα ἡμῶν αὐτοῦ γενομένην ἀπόστασιν.

157 Aristotle *Meteor.* B1, 354a28 πολλοὺς πεισθῆναι τῶν ἀρχαίων μετεωρολόγων τὸν ἥλιον μὴ φέρεσθαι ὑπὸ γῆν ἀλλὰ περὶ τὴν γῆν καὶ τὸν τόπον τοῦτον, ἀφανίζεσθαι δὲ καὶ ποιεῖν νύκτα διὰ τὸ ὑψηλὴν εἶναι πρὸς ἄρκτον τὴν γῆν.

151 The earth is flat, being borne upon air, and similarly sun, moon and the other heavenly bodies, which are all fiery, ride upon the air through their flatness.

152 Anaximenes says that the nature of the heavenly bodies is fiery, and that they have among them certain earthy bodies that are carried round with them, being invisible.

153 Anaximenes says that the heavenly bodies make their turnings through being pushed out by condensed and opposing air.

154 Anaximenes says that the stars are implanted like nails in the 'ice-like'; but some say they are fiery leaves like paintings.

155 Anaximenes says the sun is flat like a leaf.

156 He says that the heavenly bodies do not move under the earth, as others have supposed, but round it, just as if a felt cap turns round our head; and that the sun is hidden not by being under the earth, but through being covered by the higher parts of the earth and through its increased distance from us.

157 Many of the old astronomers were convinced that the sun is not carried under the earth, but round the earth and this region; and that it is obscured, and makes night, through the earth being high towards the north.

That the heavenly bodies were created by the rarefaction into fire of vapour from the earth was asserted in **149**. Like the earth, they ride on air (**151**); though since they are made of fire, as **151** and **152** confirm, and since fire is more diffuse than air, there is a difficulty which Anaximenes may not have seen in making them rest on air in the same way as the denser earth does. That the movements of the sun on the ecliptic, of the moon in declination, and perhaps of the planets, are caused by winds (which are slightly condensed air, cf. **140**) is suggested by **153**; Aristotle had referred at *Meteor.* B1, 353b5 and B2, 355a21 (**609**) to old writers who had explained the first two of these three celestial motions in just this way. **154** creates a difficulty, however, in stating that the ἄστρα (which can mean all the heavenly bodies, or the fixed stars and the planets, or just the fixed stars) are attached like studs to the ice-like outer heaven (which according to **156** would be hemispherical), and not floating free. This could only apply to the fixed stars; but we hear nothing more about the 'ice-like', and indeed the concept of a solid outer heaven is foreign to the little that is known of Anaximenes' cosmogony and to the other details of cosmology. The same term was applied three times by Aetius to Empedocles' heaven (which would be spherical), and at II, 13, 11 he said that Empedocles' fixed stars were bound to the 'ice-like', while the planets were free. It appears that this concept may have been mistakenly transferred to Anaximenes. The second part of **154** is introduced as an opinion held by 'some people'; but since Anaximenes certainly held the heavenly bodies to be fiery, and since **155** compares the sun to a leaf, it looks as though he is the author of the opinion that they were fiery leaves, and as if the text is astray. What the comparison to paintings implies is quite uncertain. If Anaximenes *is* meant, the ἄστρα in question could be the heavenly bodies in general, or (if the first part is accepted) they could be the planets, which would be distinguished, as by Empedocles, from the fixed stars on the 'ice-like'. Presumably this last term refers to the apparent transparency of the sky; it represents an improvement, from the empirical point of view, on the Homeric solid metal bowl (p. 9).

155

Such an improvement would not be uncharacteristic of Anaximenes; but the attribution of this view to him remains very doubtful.[1]

[1] W. K. C. Guthrie (*HGP* I, 136f.) ingeniously suggested that the simile might be a physiological one, since in Galen's time, at least, ἧλος could be used for a spot or lump growing on the pupil of the eye, while the cornea itself was sometimes described as 'the ice-like membrane'. This membrane was regarded as viscous, not as solid; which removes one difficulty of the attribution to Anaximenes. Yet the confident statement (*op. cit.*, p. 137) that Anaximenes 'regarded the world as a living and breathing creature' surely goes too far.

The inaccuracy of doxographical attributions, particularly in Aetius, is probably demonstrated by the second part of **152**. It is usually assumed that Anaximenes postulated these invisible celestial bodies in order to explain eclipses; but according to Hippolytus I, 8, 6 (DK 59 A 42) Anaxagoras, too, believed in them. Yet Anaxagoras knew the true cause of eclipses, therefore he cannot have postulated the invisible bodies for this purpose. The previous sentence in Aetius explains all: Diogenes of Apollonia invented these bodies to explain meteorites like the famous one which fell at Aegospotami in 467 B.C. (**608**). Anaxagoras, too, had probably been persuaded by this notable event to account for meteorites; but Anaximenes had no such good reason, and the theory was probably projected on to him from his assumed follower Diogenes. In any case the theory concerned meteorites and not eclipses.[1]

[1] Eudemus(?) in the sequel to **76** (DK 13 A 16) assigns to Anaximenes the discovery that the moon shines by reflected light. This is incompatible with the belief that the moon is fiery, and is probably due to another backward projection, this time of a belief common to Parmenides (DK 28 A 42), Empedocles (**370**), and Anaxagoras (**500**).

. The heavenly bodies do not pass under the earth, but (as in the pre-philosophical world-picture, where the sun, at least, floats round river Okeanos to the north: see pp. 12f.) they move round it, like a cap revolving round our head as Hippolytus adds in **156**. This image is scarcely likely to have been invented by anyone except Anaximenes. The cap in question is a close-fitting, roughly hemispherical felt cap; conceivably it supports the dubious implication of **154** that the heaven can be regarded as a definite (though perhaps a viscous) hemisphere, carrying the fixed stars. As has been remarked, this is merely a refinement of the naïve view of the sky as a metal bowl. The second part of **156** adds that the sun is hidden (that is, in its passage from the west back again to the east) 'by the higher parts of the earth' (also by its greater distance; this may be a doxographical addition). If the sun does not go under the earth, some explanation has to be given of why it is not visible at night. But do the 'higher parts' refer to high mountains in the north – the mythical Rhipaean mountains, that is – or to the actual tilting of the flat earth on its horizontal axis? The latter explanation was certainly ascribed to Anaxagoras, Leucippus, and Diogenes, who were strongly influenced by Anaximenes in cosmological matters. This tilting would explain how the stars could set, supposing that they are somehow fixed in the heaven: they rotate on the hemisphere (whose pole is the Wain) and pass below the upper, northern edge of the earth but not below its mean horizontal axis. Yet attractive as this interpretation is, it is made very doubtful by **157**; here Aristotle refers to the theory of 'higher parts' (again, in ambiguous terms) as being held by many of the old astronomers. But his context, which is concerned with showing that the greatest rivers flow from the greatest mountains, in the north, makes it quite clear that he understands 'the earth being high to the north' to refer to its northern mountain ranges. It must be assumed that Aristotle was thinking in part of Anaximenes, details of whose cosmological views were known to him (cf. **150**, **159**); Anaxagoras and Leucippus, then, either made an advance on Anaximenes here or were themselves misinterpreted later. A serious difficulty in the tilted-earth hypothesis is that the earth would not thus float on air, but would slip downwards as leaves do; this applies also to Leucippus' earth. The cap-image must illustrate the hemispherical shape of the sky, not its obliquity; it is difficult, indeed, to see why the cap should be imagined as being tilted on the head. Thus Anaximenes appears to have accepted the broad structure of the naïve world-picture, but to have purged it of its more obviously mythological details like the sun's golden bowl (which presumably helped to conceal its light during the voyage north).

(iii) *Meteorological phenomena*

158 Aetius III, 3, 2 Ἀναξιμένης ταὐτὰ τούτῳ (*sc.* Ἀναξιμάνδρῳ), προστιθεὶς τὸ ἐπὶ τῆς θαλάσσης, ἥτις σχιζομένη ταῖς κώπαις παραστίλβει. III, 4, 1 Ἀναξιμένης νέφη μὲν γίνεσθαι παχυνθέντος ἐπὶ πλεῖον τοῦ ἀέρος, μᾶλλον δ' ἐπισυναχθέντος ἐκθλίβεσθαι τοὺς ὄμβρους, χάλαζαν δὲ ἐπειδὰν τὸ καταφερόμενον ὕδωρ παγῇ, χιόνα δ' ὅταν συμπεριληφθῇ τι τῷ ὑγρῷ πνευματικόν.

159 Aristotle *Meteor.* Β7, 365b6 Ἀναξιμένης δέ φησι βρεχομένην τὴν γῆν καὶ ξηραινομένην ῥήγνυσθαι καὶ ὑπὸ τούτων τῶν ἀπορρηγνυμένων κολωνῶν ἐμπιπτόντων σείεσθαι· διὸ καὶ γίνεσθαι τοὺς σεισμοὺς ἔν τε τοῖς αὐχμοῖς καὶ πάλιν ἐν ταῖς ὑπερομβρίαις· ἔν τε γὰρ τοῖς αὐχμοῖς, ὥσπερ εἴρηται, ξηραινομένην ῥήγνυσθαι καὶ ὑπὸ τῶν ὑδάτων ὑπερυγραινομένην διαπίπτειν.

158 Anaximenes said the same as he [Anaximander], adding what happens in the case of sea, which flashes when cleft by oars. – Anaximenes said that clouds occur when the air is further thickened; when it is compressed further, rain is squeezed out, and hail occurs when the descending water coalesces, snow when some windy portion is included together with the moisture.

159 Anaximenes says that the earth, through being drenched and dried off, breaks asunder, and is shaken by the peaks that are thus broken off and fall in. Therefore earthquakes happen in periods both of drought and again of excessive rains; for in droughts, as has been said, it dries up and cracks, and being made over-moist by the waters it crumbles apart.

Anaximenes is said to have given the same explanation of thunder and lightning, in terms of wind, as Anaximander; see **130** and comment. The oar-image may be original. Clouds, rain, hail and snow are mainly due to the condensation of air, as one would expect; this was indicated by Theophrastus in **140**, and Aetius (also Hippolytus, *Ref.* 1, 7, 7–8, DK 13 A 7) adds further details. Winds, too, are slightly condensed air (**140**), and according to Hippolytus the rainbow was due to the reflexion of different sun-beams by air. Aristotle in **159** gives a relatively full account of Anaximenes' explanation of earthquakes, and it is notable that air plays no part in this whatever.

THE COMPARISON BETWEEN COSMIC AIR AND THE BREATH-SOUL

160 Aetius I, 3, 4 Ἀναξιμένης Εὐρυστράτου Μιλήσιος ἀρχὴν τῶν ὄντων ἀέρα ἀπεφήνατο· ἐκ γὰρ τούτου πάντα γίγνεσθαι καὶ εἰς αὐτὸν πάλιν ἀναλύεσθαι. οἶον ἡ ψυχή, φησίν, ἡ ἡμετέρα ἀὴρ οὖσα συγκρατεῖ ἡμᾶς, καὶ ὅλον τὸν κόσμον πνεῦμα καὶ ἀὴρ περιέχει· λέγεται δὲ συνωνύμως ἀὴρ καὶ πνεῦμα. ἁμαρτάνει δὲ καὶ οὗτος ἐξ ἁπλοῦ καὶ μονοειδοῦς ἀέρος καὶ πνεύματος δοκῶν συνεστάναι τὰ ζῷα... (For continuation see DK 13 B 2.)

160 Anaximenes son of Eurystratus, of Miletus, declared that air is the principle of existing things; for from it all things come-to-be and into it they are again dissolved. As our soul, he says, being air holds us together and controls us, so does wind [*or* breath] and air enclose the whole world. (Air and wind are synonymous here.) He, too, is in error in thinking that living creatures consist of simple and homogeneous air and wind...

The underlined words here are often accepted as a direct quotation from Anaximenes. There must, however, have been some alteration and some rewording; for the sentence is not in Ionic (cf. **138**), and it contains one word, συγκρατεῖ, which could not possibly have been used by Anaximenes, and another, κόσμον, which is unlikely to have been used by him in precisely this sense.[1] That the sentence does, however, represent some kind of reproduction of a statement by Anaximenes is shown by Aetius' comment that 'air' and 'wind [or breath]' have the same meaning here, and also by the fact that the comparison with the soul complicates the simple Aristotelian criticism which Aetius is reproducing, that Anaximenes did not specify a moving cause. On the other hand the use of φησί, 'he says', does not guarantee a direct quotation in this kind of writing. περιέχει, of air enfolding all things, is quite likely to be Anaximenean, cf. **108**; while the concept of the soul as breath (one suspects that πνεῦμα, not ἀήρ, originally stood in the first clause) is certainly an archaic one – compare the Homeric distinction between the life-soul, which normally seems to be identified with the breath, and the sensory and intellectual soul normally called θυμός. τὸν κόσμον could have replaced e.g. simply ἅπαντα, 'all things'. The degree of rewording, then, is probably not very great; unfortunately we cannot determine whether, or how far, it affected the exact point and degree of comparison.

[1] συγκρατεῖν is otherwise first used in Plutarch (twice), then in second-century A.D. medical writers and Diog. L. (of restraining the breath etc.); also in the *Geoponica* and the Christian fathers. It is an unnatural compound which could only have occurred in the Κοινή; it is really a compendium for συνέχειν καὶ κρατεῖν. This is illustrated in Plutarch *Phocion* 12, συνεκράτει τὸ μαχιμώτατον τῆς δυνάμεως: he kept control of his troops by keeping them together (on a hill-top). κόσμος originally means 'order', and it is probably not established in the meaning 'world-order' until the middle of the fifth century B.C. It must have been used in *descriptions* of the order apparent in nature much before then, and probably by early Pythagoreans; Pythagoras himself is credited with using κόσμος = οὐρανός, but this is perhaps an over-simplification (Diog. L. vIII, 48). Heraclitus' κόσμον τόνδε (**217**) is probably transitional to the later and widely accepted usage, which appears unequivocally for the first time in Empedocles fr. 134, 5 (**397**). For a full discussion of κόσμος see Kahn, *op. cit.*, 219–39; and see n. 1 on p. 161 below for the possibility of (later) influence from Diogenes of Apollonia.

As it stands the comparison is not very clear: 'Breath and air enclose (surround) the whole world in the way that our soul, being breath, holds us (i.e. our bodies) together and controls us.' The similarity in the two cases cannot just be that of the subject, air, without further implication; it would be pointless to say, for example, 'just as air dries moisture, so does it fill balloons'. Four possibilities, out of many, may be mentioned: (i) συγκρατεῖ in Aetius has replaced a simple notion like συνέχει, and the meaning is 'air holds us together, from inside, and the world together, from outside, ⟨and therefore man and the world are more alike than at first appears⟩, *or* ⟨and therefore air is operative in the most diverse kinds of object⟩'. (ii) περιέχει carries with it the implication of καὶ κυβερνᾷ, cf. **108**. The meaning would then be 'as our soul holds the body together and so controls it, so the originative substance (which is basically the same stuff as soul) holds the world together and so controls *it*'. (iii) 'The soul, which is breath, holds together and controls man; therefore what holds together and controls the world must also be breath or air, because the world is like a large-scale man or animal.' (iv) 'The life-principle and motive force of man is, traditionally, πνεῦμα or the breath-soul; ⟨πνεῦμα is seen in the outside world, as wind;⟩ therefore the life-principle of the outside world is πνεῦμα; ⟨therefore wind, breath, or air is the life and substance of all things⟩.'

Now it has been seen that the form συγκρατεῖ is impossible for Anaximenes, but the question also arises whether even a verb like συνέχει could, for him, have described the relation of the soul to the body. The fact is that the idea of the soul *holding together* the body has no other parallel in a Presocratic source, or indeed in any Greek source before Aristotle. The concept involved is admittedly not a complex one; for when the life-soul departs, the body, or most of it, obviously disintegrates, it is no longer held together. Nevertheless the absence of parallels, together with the knowledge that Anaximenes' terminology has certainly been tampered with at this point, makes it unwise to accept the sense even of συνέχει here. This damages (ii), but not (i) and (iii); their main arguments can be restated with the substitution of 'possess', for example, in place of 'hold together (and control)'; for Anaximenes could certainly have held that the soul *possesses*, ἔχει, the body, meaning that it permeates the whole of it (cf. e.g. Heraclitus fr. 67a); and possibly, even, that it controls it. (iv) avoids emphasizing συγκρατεῖ, and depends in part on the fact that Anaximenes' is the first extant use of the word πνεῦμα, which became common (both for breath and for gust of wind) with the tragedians; its possible dual application *could* have led Anaximenes to the parallelism of man and the world. Indeed all three remaining interpretations, (iv) and the revised forms of (i) and (iii), express this parallelism in one form or another; it is the essence of the statement to be interpreted.

Beyond that, to the particular form of the inference that must have been based upon it, we can hardly hope to penetrate with certainty. Yet the fully developed and clear-cut use of the inference from the known microcosm, man, to the unknown macrocosm, the world as a whole, does not otherwise appear until the latter part of the fifth century, under the influence, it is thought, of the new interest in theoretical medicine at that time; it is perhaps unlikely to occur in such a plain form as (iii) so early as Anaximenes. It is possible, moreover, that he did not argue so logically as even (i) or (iv) suggest; rather that a conjecture about the world was *illustrated* by reference to man and the soul, just as a dogma about the cause of lightning was illustrated by the example of the oar-blade, or that about the heavenly bodies by that of the cap on the head. This would be more plausible as the first stage in the development of the man–world argument, and accords with Anaximenes' known use of imagery.

All this is necessarily very conjectural. It remains uncertain to what extent Anaximenes was tending to treat the world itself as alive, as a kind of huge animal organism; it has been noticed that, although he introduced a thoroughly rational description of change, Anaximenes in some respects clung to the framework of the popular, non-philosophical world-construction, and so might retain more of the old anthropomorphic attitude than at first sight seems probable. However, his perception that air is the cosmic equivalent of the life-soul in man goes far beyond that attitude; it must, in fact, have been an important motive for his choice of air as the originative substance.[1] The mention of soul is important in itself; apart from **89** it is the first Presocratic psychological statement to survive – though the actual structure of the soul envisaged, as breath, belonged to an age-old popular tradition. Another conception of the soul, as made of the fiery aither which also fills the outer sky, was accepted from another channel of the popular tradition by Heraclitus, who was also to develop the assumption, probably implicit in Anaximenes, that man and the outside world are made of the same material and behave according to similar rules.

[1] It is perhaps odd that Aristotle did not name Anaximenes at *de an.* A2, 405a21, where 'Diogenes and some others' are named as holding the view that the soul is air; Aristotle is arguing that the Presocratics made the soul out of their ἀρχή. Plato, *Phaedo* 96B (what we think with is air), was probably referring to Diogenes (cf. pp. 444f.), who held that soul was *warm* air, thus perhaps conjoining the view of soul as aither or fire. There is no reason to think with Vlastos (*AJP* 76

(1955) 364 and n. 56) that Diogenes was here exclusively indebted to Anaximenes; nor is it probable (as Karin Alt argued, *Hermes* 101 (1973), 129ff.) that Aetius in **160** has confused Anaximenes with Diogenes, at least in the οἶον ἡ ψυχή... statement. That is very different, in tone and sophistication, from e.g. **602**, even if Aetius' further comment (...δοκῶν συνεστάναι τὰ 3ῷα) could apply to Diogenes.

CONCLUSION

Anaximenes is the last of the great Milesian thinkers. He was obviousiy indebted to Anaximander, but also probably to Thales, to whose concept of the originative stuff as an actual component of the world he was enabled to return by his great idea of condensation and rarefaction – an observable means of change by which quantity controls kind. This idea was probably accepted by Heraclitus and submerged in a system of a rather different nature; for after the Milesians the old cosmogonical approach, according to which the most important object was to name a single kind of material from which the whole differentiated world could have grown, was both enlarged and moderated. New problems, of theology and of unity in the arrangement, rather than the material, of things, exercised Anaximenes' successors Xenophanes and Heraclitus – although they too (even though the former migrated) were Ionians. Still more basic departures from the Milesian tradition were made in the west. But when the fifth-century thinkers of the east and the mainland (Anaxagoras, Diogenes, Leucippus and Democritus) had recovered from the western elenchus of the Eleatics, it was to the Milesians, and particularly to Anaximenes, that they chiefly turned for details of cosmology; not so much because of the great intuition of a kind of cosmic breath-soul, as because those details had been in part adapted from, and were still protected by, the popular, non-scientific tradition.

CHAPTER V

Xenophanes of Colophon

DATE AND LIFE

161 Diogenes Laertius ix, 18 (DK 21 A 1) Ξενοφάνης Δεξίου ἤ, ὡς Ἀπολλόδωρος, Ὀρθομένους Κολοφώνιος...οὗτος ἐκπεσὼν τῆς πατρίδος ἐν Ζάγκλη τῆς Σικελίας διέτριβε καὶ ἐν Κατάνη....γέγραφε δὲ ἐν ἔπεσι καὶ ἐλεγείας καὶ ἰάμβους καθ' Ἡσιόδου καὶ Ὁμήρου, ἐπικόπτων αὐτῶν τὰ περὶ θεῶν εἰρημένα. ἀλλὰ καὶ αὐτὸς ἐρραψῴδει τὰ ἑαυτοῦ. ἀντιδοξάσαι τε λέγεται Θαλῇ καὶ Πυθαγόρᾳ, καθάψασθαι δὲ καὶ Ἐπιμενίδου. μακροβιώτατός τε γέγονεν, ὥς που καὶ αὐτός φησιν·

> (Fr. 8) ἤδη δ' ἑπτά τ' ἔασι καὶ ἑξήκοντ' ἐνιαυτοὶ
> βληστρίζοντες ἐμὴν φροντίδ' ἀν' Ἑλλάδα γῆν·
> ἐκ γενετῆς δὲ τότ' ἦσαν ἐείκοσι πέντε τε πρὸς τοῖς,
> εἴπερ ἐγὼ περὶ τῶνδ' οἶδα λέγειν ἐτύμως.

...(20) καὶ ἤκμαζε κατὰ τὴν ἑξηκοστὴν ὀλυμπιάδα.

162 Clement *Strom.* I, 64, 2 τῆς δὲ Ἐλεατικῆς ἀγωγῆς Ξενοφάνης ὁ Κολοφώνιος κατάρχει, ὅν φησι Τίμαιος κατὰ Ἱέρωνα τὸν Σικελίας δυνάστην καὶ Ἐπίχαρμον τὸν ποιητὴν γεγονέναι, Ἀπολλόδωρος δὲ κατὰ τὴν τεσσαρακοστὴν ὀλυμπιάδα γενόμενον παρατετακέναι ἄχρι Δαρείου τε καὶ Κύρου χρόνων.

161 Xenophanes son of Dexios or, according to Apollodorus, of Orthomenes, of Colophon...he, being expelled from his native land, passed his time in Zancle in Sicily and in Catana...He wrote in epic metre, also elegiacs and iambics, against Hesiod and Homer, reproving them for what they said about the gods. But he himself also recited his own original poems. He is said to have held contrary opinions to Thales and Pythagoras, and to have rebuked Epimenides too. He had an extremely long life, as he himself somewhere says: 'Already there are seven and sixty years tossing my thought up and down the land of Greece; and from my birth there were another twenty-five to add to these, if I know how to speak truly about these things.'...And he was at his prime in the 6oth Olympiad.

162 Of the Eleatic school Xenophanes the Colophonian is the pioneer, who Timaeus says lived in the time of Hieron, tyrant of Sicily, and the poet Epicharmus, while Apollodorus says that he was born in the 40th Olympiad and lasted until the times of Darius and Cyrus.

Xenophanes, as opposed to the Milesians, wrote in verse; and a number of fragments of his work have survived. If we assume that he left Colophon in Ionia about the time of its capture by the Medes in 546/5 B.C. (he certainly knew it before this time, since in fr. 3, DK 21 B 3, he referred to the corruption of the Colophonians by Lydian luxury), then from his own words in **161** he would have been born around 570 B.C., twenty-five years earlier. Even if this assumption is made, his great age – at least 92 from his words in **161** – makes it impossible to assign his extant poetry to any narrow period. He referred to Pythagoras (**260**) and Simonides (DK 21 B 21), as well as to Thales and Epimenides – no more is known than the bare fact of his reference to the last three – and was himself referred to by Heraclitus (**190**); and Parmenides was later supposed to be his pupil. All this is possible enough if he lived from c. 570 to c. 475 B.C. The statement of Timaeus (the fourth-/third-century B.C. historian of Sicily) in **162** is compatible with this assumption, since Hiero reigned from 478 to 467 B.C. and Epicharmus was at Syracuse during this time. Apollodorus is perhaps wrongly reported in **162**: Ol. 40 (620–617 B.C.) is improbably early for Xenophanes' birth, and 'until the times of Darius and Cyrus' is curious, since Cyrus died in 529 and Darius gained power in 521. Yet there is no absolutely positive evidence that Xenophanes died later than e.g. 525, when Pythagoras had not been long in Italy. However, Diogenes in **161**, after mentioning Apollodorus, put Xenophanes' *floruit* in Ol. 60 (540–537 B.C.); this seems to be the true Apollodoran dating, based on the epoch-year of the foundation of Elea (on which Xenophanes was said to have written a poem) in 540.

The details of Xenophanes' life are even more uncertain. Born and brought up in Ionia, and obviously acquainted with the trends of Ionian thought, he was compelled to leave when a young man, and from then on lived a wandering life, chiefly perhaps in Sicily; his connexion with Elea may have been a later invention (see pp. 165f.). He was a poet and sage, a singer of his own songs rather than those of others: he was certainly not, as some have mistakenly assumed from **161**, a Homeric rhapsode. In the longest of his extant elegies (fr. 1, an interesting poem with no immediate philosophical relevance) he has authority enough to outline the rules of behaviour for the symposium that is to follow; he seems therefore to have been honourably received in aristocratic households.

THE ASSOCIATION OF XENOPHANES WITH ELEA

163 Plato *Sophist* 242D (DK 21 A 29) τὸ δὲ παρ' ἡμῖν Ἐλεατικὸν ἔθνος, ἀπὸ Ξενοφάνους τε καὶ ἔτι πρόσθεν ἀρξάμενον, ὡς ἑνὸς ὄντος τῶν πάντων καλουμένων οὕτω διεξέρχεται τοῖς μύθοις.

164 Aristotle *Met.* A5, 986b18 Παρμενίδης μὲν γὰρ ἔοικε τοῦ κατὰ τὸν λόγον ἑνὸς ἅπτεσθαι, Μέλισσος δὲ τοῦ κατὰ τὴν ὕλην· διὸ καὶ ὁ μὲν πεπερασμένον, ὁ δ' ἄπειρόν φησιν εἶναι αὐτό· Ξενοφάνης δὲ πρῶτος τούτων ἑνίσας (ὁ γὰρ Παρμενίδης τούτου λέγεται γενέσθαι μαθητής) οὐθὲν διεσαφήνισεν... (For continuation see **174**.)

> **163** Our Eleatic tribe, beginning from Xenophanes and even before, explains in its myths that what we call all things are actually one.
> **164** For Parmenides seems to fasten on that which is one in definition, Melissus on that which is one in material; therefore the former says that it is limited, the latter that it is unlimited. But Xenophanes, the first of these to postulate a unity (for Parmenides is said to have been his pupil), made nothing clear

It is commonly assumed in the doxographers that Xenophanes spent a part at least of his life in Elea, and that he was the founder of the Eleatic school of philosophy. This is exemplified in **162**. That he was Parmenides' master stems from Aristotle in **164**, and was categorically asserted by Theophrastus according to Simplicius (**165**). Yet Aristotle's judgement possibly arises from Plato's remark in **163**. This remark was not necessarily intended as a serious historical judgement (one may compare the statements in the *Theaetetus* (152D–E, 160D) that Homer and Epicharmus were the founders of the Heraclitean tradition), as is confirmed by the addition of the words καὶ ἔτι πρόσθεν, 'and even before'. The connexion between Xenophanes and Parmenides obviously depends on the superficial similarity between the motionless one deity of the former and the motionless sphere of Being in the latter – though it will be seen that Parmenides' theoretical construction was reached in a quite different way from Xenophanes', a way which is in fact incompatible. The extreme example of the treatment of Xenophanes as an Eleatic is seen in the pseudo-Aristotelian *de Melisso Xenophane Gorgia* (DK 21 A 28), a treatise written probably about the time of Christ in which Xenophanes' god is explained in fully Eleatic terms, and the inference is drawn from Aristotle's judgement in **164** that it was neither limited as in Parmenides nor unlimited as in Melissus. Unfortunately Simplicius, who had not encountered this part of Xenophanes' poetry (*de caelo* 522, 7, DK21A47), relied on this treatise and quoted far less than usual from Theophrastus. Other evidence connecting Xenophanes with Elea is slight: he is said by Diogenes Laertius (IX, 20, DK21A1) to have written 2,000 lines on the foundation of Colophon and the colonization of Elea, but this probably comes from the stichometrist and forger Lobon of Argos and is unreliable; while Aristotle (*Rhet.* B23, 1400b5, DK21A13) told an anecdote of some advice of his to the Eleans – but this was a 'floating' anecdote also connected with Heraclitus and others. It is not improbable that Xenophanes visited Elea; that was perhaps the extent of his connexion with it. He was not in any way typical of the new western trend in philosophy initiated by Pythagoras; nor was he typically Ionian, but since his ideas were a direct reaction from Ionian theories and from the originally Ionian Homer he is placed in this book with the Ionians, and not in his probable chronological place after Pythagoras – like him an emigrant from eastern to western Greece.

HIS POEMS

Some of Xenophanes' extant fragments are in elegiac metre, some are hexameters; while **167** consists of an iambic trimeter followed by a hexameter. This accords with Diogenes' mention of these three metres in **161**. Some at any rate of his poems were called Σίλλοι, 'squints' or satires, and the third-century B.C. 'sillographer' Timon of Phlius is said by Sextus (DK21A35) to have dedicated his own Σίλλοι to Xenophanes, about whom he certainly wrote; see also DK21A20–23. According to three late sources, Stobaeus (from an allegorizing author), the Geneva scholiast on the *Iliad*, and Pollux (DK21A36, 21B30, 21B39), there was a physical work by Xenophanes called Περὶ φύσεως, *On Nature*. The value of this title has already been discussed (p. 102 and pp. 102–3 n. 1), and it is only to be expected that at least some later references to physical opinions in Xenophanes should occur in this form. It is notable that Aetius, who also quoted the passages cited in the first two cases above, said nothing about a Περὶ φύσεως (DK21A36 and 46). That Xenophanes wrote a formal work on physical matters is highly improbable. Theophrastus, we may observe, said that Xenophanes' monistic conception was not 'physical' in the normal sense.[1] Xenophanes was not, like Anaximenes or Heraclitus, primarily engaged in giving a comprehensive explanation of the natural world. He was particularly interested, without doubt, in theology, and many of his remarks on physical topics are connected with that; others may have been ironical rejections of previous theories, and others again would naturally reflect the interest which many educated Greeks must have felt in natural problems at this time. Such remarks, together with comments on particular poets and thinkers (e.g. **166**; cf. also DK 21 A 22), could have been expressed in separate poems in a variety of metres – though the extant theological and physical fragments are nearly all in hexameters. There may have been a separate collection of convivial songs in elegiacs.

[1] Cf. **165** Simplicius *in Phys.* 22, 26   μίαν δὲ τὴν ἀρχὴν ἤτοι ἓν τὸ ὂν καὶ πᾶν (καὶ οὔτε πεπερασμένον οὔτε ἄπειρον οὔτε κινούμενον οὔτε ἠρεμοῦν) Ξενοφάνην τὸν Κολοφώνιον τὸν Παρμενίδου διδάσκαλον ὑποτίθεσθαί φησιν ὁ Θεόφραστος, ὁμολογῶν ἑτέρας εἶναι μᾶλλον ἢ τῆς περὶ φύσεως ἱστορίας τὴν μνήμην τῆς τούτου δόξης. (*Theophrastus says that Xenophanes the Colophonian, the teacher of Parmenides, supposed the principle to be single, or that the whole of existence was one (and neither limited nor unlimited, neither in motion nor at rest); and Theophrastus agrees that the record of Xenophanes' opinion belongs to another study rather than that of natural philosophy.*) Theophrastus is here misled by Aristotle in **174** into thinking that Xenophanes' one god is definitely non-physical, and is the whole of existence like the Parmenidean Being. But he can hardly have thought this if there was a poem which in any way resembled the works of the Milesians.

HIS IMPORTANCE

Widely different views have been held on the intellectual importance of Xenophanes. Thus Jaeger (*Theology*, 52) writes of his 'enormous influence on later religious development', while Burnet (*EGP*, 129) maintained that 'he would have smiled if he had known that one day he was to be regarded as a theologian'. Burnet's depreciation is certainly much exaggerated. Yet it is plain that Xenophanes differed considerably from the Milesians or Heraclitus or Parmenides. He was a poet with thoughtful interests, especially about religion and the gods, which led him to react against the archetype of poets and the mainstay of contemporary education, Homer. His attacks on Homeric theology must have had a deep influence both on ordinary men who heard his poems and on other thinkers; Heraclitus' attack on blood-purification and images (**241**), for example, was presumably influenced by him. His positive description of deity conceivably lay behind Aeschylus' description of divine power in the *Supplices* (**173**).

The assessment of the true relative merits of poets and athletes (fr. 2) was developed by Euripides in the *Autolycus* (fr. 282 Nauck², DK21C2); this is a less specialized instance of Xenophanes' rational intellectualism. Nor is it safe to exaggerate his non-scientific character on the grounds of his theological interest; the study of gods was not divorced from that of nature, and the deduction from fossils (pp. 177f.), whether or not it reflects original observation, shows careful and by no means implausible argument from observed fact to general hypothesis – a procedure notoriously rare among the Presocratics. Some of his other physical statements are unutterably bizarre, but we cannot tell how serious they were meant to be. He was a critic, primarily, with an original and often idiosyncratic approach; not a specialist but a true σοφιστής or sage, prepared to turn his intelligence upon almost any problem (though as it happens we know of no political pronouncements) – which is why Heraclitus attacked him in **190**. His opinions on almost all subjects deserve careful attention.

THEOLOGY

(i) *Attacks on (a) the immorality, (b) the anthropomorphic nature, of the gods of the conventional religion*

166 Fr. 11, Sextus *adv. math.* IX, 193
πάντα θεοῖς ἀνέθηκαν Ὅμηρός θ᾽ Ἡσίοδός τε
ὅσσα παρ᾽ ἀνθρώποισιν ὀνείδεα καὶ ψόγος ἐστίν,
κλέπτειν μοιχεύειν τε καὶ ἀλλήλους ἀπατεύειν.

167 Fr. 14, Clement *Strom.* v, 109, 2
ἀλλ᾽ οἱ βροτοὶ δοκέουσι γεννᾶσθαι θεούς,
τὴν σφετέρην δ᾽ ἐσθῆτα ἔχειν φωνήν τε δέμας τε.

168 Fr. 16, Clement *Strom.* VII, 22, 1
Αἰθίοπές τε ⟨θεοὺς σφετέρους⟩ σιμοὺς μέλανάς τε
Θρῆκές τε γλαυκοὺς καὶ πυρρούς ⟨φασι πέλεσθαι⟩.

169 Fr. 15, Clement *Strom.* v, 109, 3
ἀλλ᾽ εἰ χεῖρας ἔχον βόες ⟨ἵπποι τ᾽⟩ ἠὲ λέοντες,
ἢ γράψαι χείρεσσι καὶ ἔργα τελεῖν ἅπερ ἄνδρες,
ἵπποι μέν θ᾽ ἵπποισι βόες δέ τε βουσὶν ὁμοίας
καί ⟨κε⟩ θεῶν ἰδέας ἔγραφον καὶ σώματ᾽ ἐποίουν
τοιαῦθ᾽ οἷόν περ καὐτοὶ δέμας εἶχον ⟨ἕκαστοι⟩.[1]

166 Homer and Hesiod have attributed to the gods everything that is a shame and reproach among men, stealing and committing adultery and deceiving each other.

167 But mortals consider that the gods are born, and that they have clothes and speech and bodies like their own.

168 The Ethiopians say that their gods are snub-nosed and black, the Thracians that theirs have light blue eyes and red hair.

169 But if cattle and horses or lions had hands, or were able to draw with their hands and do the works that men can do, horses would draw the forms of the gods like horses, and cattle like cattle, and they would make their bodies such as they each had themselves.

[1] **168** is convincingly reconstructed by Diels from an unmetrical quotation in Clement. The supplements in **169** are respectively by Diels, Sylburg and Herwerden; the text as in DK. Line 1 of **167** is an iambic trimeter.

Xenophanes' criticisms are clear enough: first, the gods of Homer and Hesiod are often immoral – this is patently true; second, and more fundamental, there is no good reason for thinking that the gods are anthropomorphic at all. Xenophanes brilliantly perceives, first that different races credit the gods with their own particular characteristics (this is an early example of the new anthropological approach which is seen in Herodotus and culminated in the *physis/nomos* distinction); second, as a *reductio ad absurdum*, that animals would also do the same. The conclusion is that such assessments are subjective and without value, and that the established picture in Homer ('according to whom all have learned', fr. 10) of gods as men and women must be abandoned.

(ii) *Constructive theology: there is a single non-anthropomorphic deity*

170 Fr. 23, Clement *Strom.* v, 109, 1
εἷς θεός, ἔν τε θεοῖσι καὶ ἀνθρώποισι μέγιστος,
οὔτι δέμας θνητοῖσιν ὁμοίιος οὐδὲ νόημα.

171 Fr. 26 + 25, Simplicius *in Phys.* 23, 11 + 23, 20
αἰεὶ δ' ἐν ταὐτῷ μίμνει κινούμενος οὐδέν
οὐδὲ μετέρχεσθαί μιν ἐπιπρέπει ἄλλοτε ἄλλῃ,
ἀλλ' ἀπάνευθε πόνοιο νόου φρενὶ πάντα κραδαίνει.

172 Fr. 24, Sextus *adv. math.* IX, 144
οὖλος ὁρᾷ, οὖλος δὲ νοεῖ, οὖλος δέ τ' ἀκούει.[1]

[1] Diog. L. IX, 19 (DK 21 A 1) implies that the words οὐ μέντοι ἀναπνεῖ, 'but does not breathe', formed part of the quotation. This is probably a later version by someone interested in Pythagorean cosmology.

170 One god, greatest among gods and men, in no way similar to mortals either in body or in thought.

171 Always he remains in the same place, moving not at all; nor

is it fitting for him to go to different places at different times, but without toil he shakes all things by the thought of his mind.
172 All of him sees, all thinks, and all hears.

'Greatest among gods and men' in **170** should not be taken literally; men are mentioned by a 'polar' usage, as in Heraclitus fr. 30 (**217**), where this world-order was made by 'none of gods or men'. This is probably just an emphatic device, rather than (as Barnes claims, *The Presocratic Philosophers* I, 89–92) part of an argument that a hierarchy of gods is logically impossible. In fact Xenophanes wrote of 'gods' in other places also, e.g. in **188**; partly, no doubt, this was a concession, perhaps not a fully conscious one, to popular religious terminology. It seems very doubtful whether Xenophanes would have recognized other, minor deities as being in any way related to the 'one god', except as dim human projections of it. The one god is unlike men in body and thought – it has, therefore (and also in view of **172**), a body; but it is motionless,[1] for the interesting reason that it is 'not fitting' for it to move around. Xenophanes thus appears to accept the well-established Greek criterion of *seemliness*.[2] Not only is it unfitting for the god to move, but movement is actually unnecessary, for the god 'shakes all things by the active will proceeding from his insight' (**171**, line 3).[3] This insight is related to seeing and hearing, but like them is accomplished not by special organs but by the god's whole unmoving body. This remarkable description was reached, probably, by taking the very antithesis of the characteristics of a Homeric god. That thought or intelligence can affect things outside the thinker, without the agency of limbs, is a development – but a very bold one – of the Homeric idea that a god can accomplish his end merely by implanting, for example, Infatuation (Ἄτη) in a mortal. That it seemed a plausible idea is shown by its acceptance and expansion by Aeschylus.[4]

[1] It was probably because of its motionless unity that Xenophanes' god was identified with Parmenides' Being, and later absorbed some of its properties. As early as Timon of Phlius it is called 'equal in every way' (ἴσον ἀπάντῃ, cf. μεσσόθεν ἰσοπαλὲς πάντῃ in Parmenides, **299**), and so becomes credited with spherical shape. Xenophanes may have described it as 'all alike' (ὁμοίην in Timon fr. 59, DK 21 A 35), since this is implicit in the whole of it functioning in a particular way as in **172**; its sphericity goes beyond the fragments and is perhaps debatable.
[2] J. Barnes, *op. cit.* I, 85f., interestingly maintains that 'seemliness' is logical: 'it is not logically possible...that divinities locomote'.
[3] This translation is based on K. von Fritz, *CP* 40 (1945), 230, who has a good discussion of the sense of νόος and φρήν. The phrase νόου φρενί looks more curious than it is; it is obviously based on νόει φρεσί and νοέω φρεσί at *Iliad* IX, 600 and

xxii, 235 respectively. Further, κραδαίνει can only mean 'shakes', which suggests that Xenophanes had in mind *Il.* 1, 530, where Zeus shakes great Olympus with a nod of his head. These are other indications that Xenophanes' god is more Homeric (in a negative direction) than it seems.

[4] **173** Aeschylus *Supplices* 96–103 (Ζεύς) / ἰάπτει δ' ἐλπίδων / ἀφ' ὑψιπύργων πανώλεις / βροτούς, βίαν δ' οὔτιν' ἐξοπλίζει. / πᾶν ἄπονον δαιμονίων. / ἥμενος ὃν φρόνημά πως / αὐτόθεν ἐξέπραξεν ἔμ-/πας ἑδράνων ἀφ' ἁγνῶν. (*[Zeus] hurls mortals in destruction from their high-towered expectations, but puts forth no force: everything of gods is without toil. Sitting, he nevertheless at once accomplishes his thought, somehow, from his holy resting-place.*) In some ways this reminds one of Solon; we cannot be quite sure that Xenophanes' view of deity was as original as it now seems to be.

(iii) *Is the one god coextensive with the world?*

174 Aristotle *Met.* A5, 986b21 (for what precedes see **164**) ...Ξενοφάνης δὲ πρῶτος τούτων ἑνίσας (ὁ γὰρ Παρμενίδης τούτου λέγεται γενέσθαι μαθητής) οὐθὲν διεσαφήνισεν, οὐδὲ τῆς φύσεως τούτων οὐδετέρας (*sc.* formal or material unity) ἔοικε θιγεῖν, ἀλλ' εἰς τὸν ὅλον οὐρανὸν ἀποβλέψας τὸ ἓν εἶναί φησι τὸν θεόν.

174 ... but Xenophanes, the first of these to postulate a unity (for Parmenides is said to have been his pupil), made nothing clear, nor does he seem to have touched the nature of either of these [*sc.* Parmenides' formal unity or Melissus' material unity]; but with his eye on the whole heaven he says that the One is god.

Xenophanes arrived at the concept of one god by reaction from Homeric anthropomorphic polytheism; Parmenides arrived at the sphere of Being by logical inference from a purely existential axiom. The processes are absolutely different, and, as has already been emphasized, Parmenides is unlikely to have been a pupil of Xenophanes, even though he might have noted the older poet's view with some interest. Aristotle obviously could not understand what Xenophanes meant by his one motionless god, but complained that he 'made nothing clear' and went on to dismiss both him and Melissus as being 'rather too uncouth' (μικρὸν ἀγροικότεροι). This puzzlement of Aristotle's suggests that Xenophanes did not produce a discursive elaboration of his theological views, which might not, indeed, have gone very far beyond the extant fragments on the subject. Aristotle's implication that the one god was neither immaterial (as he thought Parmenides' One to be) nor material like Melissus' One (cf. **164**) was due to the presence of both corporeal and apparently non-corporeal elements in Xenophanes' description – the body, δέμας, on the one hand (**170**), and the shaking of all things by intellect on the other (**171**). It is significant here that Aristotle did not adduce Anaxagoras' Nous (which was the ultimate source of movement and the finest kind of body, and which permeated some but not all things) in illustration of Xenophanes' deity. Instead he made the cryptic remark that Xenophanes 'with his eye on the whole world said that the One was god' ' (for οὐρανός can hardly mean 'first heaven' here). This clearly implies that god is identical with the world, which is what Theophrastus seems to have assumed (**165**). But Aristotle must be wrong here: how could the god be motionless if it is identical with a world which is itself implied to move (**171**)? It is probable, indeed, that although Xenophanes' god is not a direct development from the cosmogonical tradition, yet it is to some extent based upon the Milesian idea of a divine substance which, in the case of Thales and Anaximenes, was regarded as somehow permeating objects in the world and giving them life and movement. Yet Xenophanes cannot have precisely worked out the local relationship of the god on the one hand and the manifold world (which he cannot have intended to reject) on the other. Aristotle, by treating him as a primitive Eleatic, misled the whole ancient tradition on this point. The conclusion seems to be that Xenophanes' god was conceived as the negation of Homeric divine properties, and was not precisely located – any more than the old Homeric gods were thought by Xenophanes' contemporaries to be necessarily located on Olympus. It had a body of sorts because totally incorporeal existence was inconceivable, but that body, apart from its perceptual-intellectual activity, was of secondary importance, and so perhaps was its location.

PHYSICAL IDEAS

(i) *The heavenly bodies*

175 Hippolytus *Ref.* I, 14, 3   τὸν δὲ ἥλιον ἐκ μικρῶν πυριδίων ἀθροιζομένων γίνεσθαι καθ' ἑκάστην ἡμέραν, τὴν δὲ γῆν ἄπειρον εἶναι καὶ μήτε ὑπ' ἀέρος μήτε ὑπὸ τοῦ οὐρανοῦ περιέχεσθαι. καὶ ἀπείρους ἡλίους εἶναι καὶ σελήνας, τὰ δὲ πάντα εἶναι ἐκ γῆς.

176 Ps.-Plutarch *Strom.* 4 (DK 21 A 32)   τὸν δὲ ἥλιόν φησι καὶ τὰ ἄστρα ἐκ τῶν νεφῶν γίνεσθαι.

177 Aetius II, 20, 3   Ξενοφάνης ἐκ νεφῶν πεπυρωμένων εἶναι τὸν ἥλιον. Θεόφραστος ἐν τοῖς Φυσικοῖς γέγραφεν ἐκ πυριδίων μὲν τῶν συναθροιζομένων ἐκ τῆς ὑγρᾶς ἀναθυμιάσεως, συναθροιζόντων δὲ τὸν ἥλιον.

178   Fr. 32, Σ bT *in Iliadem* XI, 27

ἥν τ' Ἶριν καλέουσι, νέφος καὶ τοῦτο πέφυκε,
πορφύρεον καὶ φοινίκεον καὶ χλωρὸν ἰδέσθαι.

179   Aetius II, 24, 9   Ξενοφάνης πολλοὺς εἶναι ἡλίους καὶ σελήνας
κατὰ κλίματα τῆς γῆς καὶ ἀποτομὰς καὶ ζώνας, κατὰ δέ τινα καιρὸν
ἐκπίπτειν τὸν δίσκον εἴς τινα ἀποτομὴν τῆς γῆς οὐκ οἰκουμένην ὑφ'
ἡμῶν καὶ οὕτως ὥσπερ κενεμβατοῦντα ἔκλειψιν ὑποφαίνειν· ὁ δ'
αὐτὸς τὸν ἥλιον εἰς ἄπειρον μὲν προϊέναι, δοκεῖν δὲ κυκλεῖσθαι διὰ τὴν
ἀπόστασιν.

175   The sun comes into being each day from little pieces of fire
that are collected, and the earth is infinite and enclosed neither
by air nor by the heaven. There are innumerable suns and moons,
and all things are made of earth.

176   He says that the sun and the stars come from clouds.

177   Xenophanes says that the sun is made of ignited clouds.
Theophrastus in the *Physical Philosophers* wrote that it is made of
little pieces of fire collected together from the moist exhalation, and
themselves collecting together the sun.

178   What they call Iris [rainbow], this too is cloud, purple and
red and yellow to behold.

179   Xenophanes said there are many suns and moons according
to regions, sections and zones of the earth, and that at a certain
time the disc is banished into some section of the earth not
inhabited by us, and so treading on nothing, as it were, produces
the phenomenon of an eclipse. The same man says that the sun
goes onwards *ad infinitum*, but seems to move in a circle because
of the distance.

There is a divergence in the doxographical accounts of the constitution
of the heavenly bodies: were they a *concentration of fiery particles* as the
sun is said to be in **175**, the second part of **177**, and ps.-Plutarch a
few sentences before **176**; or *ignited clouds* as is said of sun and stars
in **176**, of the sun in **177**, and of the stars, which are said to rekindle
at night like embers, in Aetius II, 13, 14, DK 21 A 38? Theophrastus
is named in **177** as supporting the former view, but the latter also,
which is widely represented in the doxographers, must somehow stem
from him. It seems possible that the idea of the sun, at least, as a
concentration of fire, which arose from the exhalation from the sea,
is in part due to a conflation of Xenophanes with Heraclitus, who
probably thought that the bowls of the heavenly bodies were filled
with fire nourished in their courses by the exhalation (**224**). Heraclitus

also thought that the sun was new every day, which accords with Xenophanes in **175**. But Heraclitus was certainly influenced in other respects by Xenophanes, and the similarity here might be so caused. Yet are the two theories as different as they appear to be at first sight? It is conceivable that the concentrations of fire *resemble* fiery clouds, and that some such statement in Theophrastus became dissected in the epitomes. Alternatively, the sun alone, because of its special brightness, might be a 'concentration' of fire, the other heavenly bodies being merely ignited clouds. That Xenophanes explained the rainbow as a cloud (a development, perhaps, of Anaximenes, cf. p. 158) is demonstrated by **178**; according to Aetius II, 18, 1 (DK 21 A 39) what we term St Elmo's fire was due to little clouds ignited by motion, and perhaps this explains the καί in **178** line 1. It is not safe to deduce from this particle that some heavenly bodies were clouds; though it seems possible that this was in fact Xenophanes' view. It is notable that this (as opposed to some of his other ideas) is an entirely reasonable physical theory, which proves that Xenophanes cannot be classified solely as a theologian; though it is possible enough that his motive for giving physical explanations of the heavenly bodies was to disprove the popular conception of them as gods. This is certainly implied by the phrase 'what men call Iris' in **178**.

Hippolytus' statement in **175** that there are 'innumerable suns and moons' seems to refer to the rekindling of the sun (and presumably also of the moon) each day; but in **179** a completely different and much more bizarre explanation is given. There are many suns and moons in different regions, zones or segments of the earth; eclipses of the sun are caused by our sun as it were treading on nothing and being forced into another segment not inhabited by 'us'. The concluding sentence of **179**, however, accords with the view of **175** that the sun is new every day. There is certainly a confusion here by Aetius or his source. It seems probable that the plurality of suns and moons is simply due to their being renewed each day; that Xenophanes explained eclipses as caused by the sun withdrawing to another region of the earth; and that the two ideas became confused. That the sun continues westward indefinitely looks like a deliberately naïve statement of the anti-scientific viewpoint (Heraclitus perhaps reacted in a similar way to excessive dogmatism about astronomy, cf. fr. 3). It is possible that the segments of the earth were regarded as hollow depressions, as in Plato's *Phaedo* myth; this might seem to account for the sun's apparent rising and setting, though not its disappearance at eclipses. Whatever is the true explanation, it is clear that Xenophanes permitted himself a certain degree of fantasy here (and possibly, judging by the expression 'treading on nothing', of humour). Perhaps there was some kind of irony, too; at any rate the explanation of eclipses must be plainly distinguished from his more empirical, if not necessarily original, views on the actual constitution of the heavenly bodies.[1]

[1] The same combination of a bizarre original statement by Xenophanes and misunderstanding by the doxographers probably accounts for Aetius' mention (II, 24, 4, DK 21 A 41) of a month-long, and a continuous, eclipse.

(ii) *The earth's roots*

180　Fr. 28, Achilles *Isag.* 4, p. 34, 11 Maass
　　　γαίης μὲν τόδε πεῖρας ἄνω παρὰ ποσσὶν ὁρᾶται
　　　ἠέρι προσπλάζον, τὸ κάτω δ' ἐς ἄπειρον ἱκνεῖται.[1]

[1] ἠέρι Diels, αἰθέρι Karsten, καὶ ῥεῖ MSS. Both suggested emendations are possible, but the former is in every respect preferable: -ει was written for -ι by a common misspelling, and then καὶ was substituted for what appeared to be an impossible disjunctive ἠὲ.

180　Of earth this is the upper limit which we see by our feet, in contact with air; but its underneath continues indefinitely.

Xenophanes seems to be reacting against the Homeric and Hesiodic descriptions of Tartarus (the underparts of the earth in some sense) as being as far below earth as sky is above it (*Il.* VIII, 116, **1**; *Theog.* 720). That picture is in any case not altogether clear, and at *Theog.* 727f., **2**, earth's 'roots' are said to be above Tartarus; but in any event the distances involved are huge, indefinitely large in fact. Yet Xenophanes' intention may not have been to amend or controvert Homer and Hesiod on this particular matter (as he had done over theology, cf. on **166** above), as to take issue, perhaps in the sceptical spirit of **186** below, with Milesian dogmatism on such points (cf. e.g. **84** (Thales), **122** (Anaximander), **150** (Anaximenes)). He was rebuked for his pains by Aristotle (*de caelo* B13, 294a21, DK 21 A 47), for idleness in not seeking a proper explanation!

(iii) *Water, or sea, and earth*

181　Fr. 29, Simplicius *in Phys.* 189, 1
　　　γῆ καὶ ὕδωρ πάντ' ἐσθ' ὅσα γίνοντ' ἠδὲ φύονται.

182　Fr. 33, Sextus *adv. math.* x, 34
　　　πάντες γὰρ γαίης τε καὶ ὕδατος ἐκγενόμεσθα.

183 Fr. 30, Σ Genav. *in Iliadem* XXI, 196

πηγὴ δ᾽ ἐστὶ θάλασσ᾽ ὕδατος, πηγὴ δ᾽ ἀνέμοιο·
οὔτε γὰρ ἐν νέφεσιν ⟨γίνοιτό κε ἲς ἀνέμοιο
ἐκπνείοντος⟩ ἔσωθεν ἄνευ πόντου μεγάλοιο
οὔτε ῥοαὶ ποταμῶν οὔτ᾽ αἰ⟨θέρος⟩ ὄμβριον ὕδωρ,
ἀλλὰ μέγας πόντος γενέτωρ νεφέων ἀνέμων τε
καὶ ποταμῶν.

181 All things that come-to-be and grow are earth and water.
182 For we all came forth from earth and water.
183 Sea is the source of water, and source of wind; for neither
⟨would there be the force of wind blowing forth from⟩ inside clouds
without the great ocean, nor river-streams nor the showery water
from the upper air: but the great ocean is begetter of clouds and
winds and rivers.

The idea that everything, men included, is composed of and
originates from water and earth is a naïve popular one: flesh and bone
may be compared with earth and stone, blood with water. Compare
our burial service, 'earth to earth, ashes to ashes, dust to dust'; and
Iliad VII, 99, 'but may you all become earth and water'. Further, the
surface of the earth, that which lies by our feet (**180**), is obviously
broadly composed of earth and sea. Xenophanes takes this simple
apprehension and develops it into a rudimentary physical theory in
183 (where the main supplement is by Diels): sea, which is the most
extensive form of water, is noted as the source of all rivers as in Homer
(see **6**), but also of rain and of clouds (which Anaximander had
assumed to be condensations of the exhalation from the sea) and of
the winds which appear to issue from clouds. This importance
attached to the sea gains significance from the observation and
deduction to be described in the next section, that the earth's surface
in its present form must have developed from sea.

(iv) *The earth's surface becomes sea once again*

184 Hippolytus *Ref.* I, 14, 5   ὁ δὲ Ξενοφάνης μίξιν τῆς γῆς πρὸς
τὴν θάλασσαν γίνεσθαι δοκεῖ καὶ τῷ χρόνῳ ὑπὸ τοῦ ὑγροῦ λύεσθαι,
φάσκων τοιαύτας ἔχειν ἀποδείξεις, ὅτι ἐν μέσῃ γῇ καὶ ὄρεσιν εὑρίσκονται κόγχαι, καὶ ἐν Συρακούσαις δὲ ἐν ταῖς λατομίαις λέγει εὑρῆσθαι
τύπον ἰχθύος καὶ φυκῶν [Gomperz; φωκῶν MSS], ἐν δὲ Πάρῳ τύπον
δάφνης ἐν τῷ βάθει τοῦ λίθου, ἐν δὲ Μελίτῃ πλάκας συμπάντων τῶν
θαλασσίων. (6) ταῦτα δέ φησι γενέσθαι ὅτε πάντα ἐπηλώθησαν
πάλαι, τὸν δὲ τύπον ἐν τῷ πηλῷ ξηρανθῆναι. ἀναιρεῖσθαι δὲ τοὺς
ἀνθρώπους πάντας ὅταν ἡ γῆ κατενεχθεῖσα εἰς τὴν θάλασσαν πηλὸς

γένηται, εἶτα πάλιν ἄρχεσθαι τῆς γενέσεως, καὶ ταύτην πᾶσι τοῖς κόσμοις γίνεσθαι καταβολήν [H. Lloyd-Jones; καταβάλλειν MSS, μεταβολήν Diels, DK].

185 Fr. 37, Herodian π. μον. λέξ. 30, 30
καὶ μὲν ἑνὶ σπεάτεσσί τεοις καταλείβεται ὕδωρ.

184 Xenophanes thinks that a mixture of the earth with the sea is going on, and that in time the earth is dissolved by the moist. He says that he has demonstrations of the following kind: shells are found inland and in the mountains, and in the quarries in Syracuse he says that an impression of a fish and of seaweed has been found, while an impression of a bay-leaf was found in Paros in the depth of the rock, and in Malta flat shapes of all marine objects. These, he says, were produced when everything was long ago covered with mud, and the impression was dried in the mud. All mankind is destroyed whenever the earth is carried down into the sea and becomes mud; then there is another beginning of coming-to-be, and this foundation happens for all the worlds.
185 And in some caves water drips down.

The deduction based upon fossils is a remarkable and impressive one. The enumeration of different occurrences is in itself unusually scientific; the assertion ascribed to Xenophanes in the Aristotelian *Mirabilia* (DK 21 A 48), that Stromboli tended to erupt in the seventeenth year, shows a similar method. Not that the poet himself need have observed fossils in all three places – fossil-impressions might naturally arouse popular curiosity, and so become known; though it is notable that two of the three places were in Xenophanes' Sicilian orbit. (Paros has been doubted on geological grounds; but its north-eastern part is neither marble nor schist, and could have contained fossils. The Director of the Institute for Geology, Athens, confirms that plant fossils have been found there.) We cannot be sure that the observations were first made in Xenophanes' lifetime; they might also have been available to Anaximander. However, Xenophanes may have been the first to draw attention to the real significance of fossils. The conjecture that the earth's surface had once been mud or slime was again not new; this was a Milesian theory possibly originating with Thales and certainly held by Anaximander, who believed that life started from mud. The fossils, however, seemed to be positive proof. It has been seen (pp. 139f.) that Alexander attributed to Anaximander (as well as to Diogenes) the belief that the sea is diminishing and will eventually dry up. In Anaximander, however, there is no positive information that the process is a cyclical one. Hippolytus in **184** *ad fin.* definitely ascribes a cyclical theory to Xenophanes: the earth must once have been mud because plants once existed in what is now rock, fishes in what is now dry land, and men are destroyed when it turns back to mud; then they are produced anew, and this happens for all the arrangements of the earth's surface. Thus Xenophanes accepted that living creatures come from mud, after Anaximander; but while Anaximander seems to have seen their destruction as arising from extreme drought, for Xenophanes it was due to flood; it has already been suggested that myths of great catastrophes, notably the flood of Deucalion and Pyrrha and the earth-scorching of Phaethon, may have provided a precedent for this kind of theory. This divergence between the two thinkers was connected with divergent interpretations of the present trend of change in the earth's surface: for Anaximander it was drying up, for Xenophanes it was already turning back into sea or mud. This might have been a conscious correction on the part of the latter; for it may not be coincidence that the sea was receding round Miletus, but in Sicily was supposed to have engulfed the land-bridge which became the Messina strait.

The cyclical transformations between earth and sea – neither of which, however, can have been completely eliminated – were clearly related to the assertions in **181** and **182** that things come from earth and sea; while the products of sea in **183** showed that sea is surprisingly potent. **185**, fragmentary as it is, may be intended to illustrate the passage between the two basic materials; Diels and others have thought of stalactitic caves, i.e. of water turning to earth (rock not being clearly differentiated), while Deichgräber (*Rh. M.* 87 (1938), 16) considered that both this and the reverse process might be meant; certainly, damp caves can appear to produce moisture from earth. This, like much else, remains uncertain (for example, at what stage is the drying-up of the sea reversed?). The clear exposition of a cyclical theory supported by concrete evidence is indisputable, and once again shows that Xenophanes must be seriously reckoned with.[1]

---

[1] The way in which such a cyclical theory could encourage the doxographers in an innumerable-world interpretation is demonstrated by the ambiguous use of κόσμοις in **184** (there properly 'world-arrangements', i.e. of the earth's surface, but appearing to mean 'separate worlds').

THE LIMITATIONS OF HUMAN KNOWLEDGE

186 Fr. 34, Sextus *adv. math.* VII, 49 and 110, cf. Plutarch *Aud. poet.*
2, 17E

καὶ τὸ μὲν οὖν σαφὲς οὔτις ἀνὴρ ἴδεν οὐδέ τις ἔσται
εἰδὼς ἀμφὶ θεῶν τε καὶ ἄσσα λέγω περὶ πάντων·
εἰ γὰρ καὶ τὰ μάλιστα τύχοι τετελεσμένον εἰπών,
αὐτὸς ὅμως οὐκ οἶδε· δόκος δ' ἐπὶ πᾶσι τέτυκται.

187 Fr. 35, Plutarch *Symp.* IX, 7, 746B

ταῦτα δεδοξάσθω μὲν ἐοικότα τοῖς ἐτύμοισι...

188 Fr. 18, Stobaeus *Anth.* I, 8, 2

οὔτοι ἀπ' ἀρχῆς πάντα θεοὶ θνητοῖσ' ὑπέδειξαν,
ἀλλὰ χρόνῳ ζητοῦντες ἐφευρίσκουσιν ἄμεινον.

189 Fr. 38, Herodian π. μον. λέξ. 41, 5

εἰ μὴ χλωρὸν ἔφυσε θεὸς μέλι, πολλὸν ἔφασκον
γλύσσονα σῦκα πέλεσθαι.

186 No man knows, or ever will know, the truth about the gods
and about everything I speak of; for even if one chanced to say
the complete truth, yet oneself knows it not; but seeming is
wrought over all things [*or* fancy is wrought in the case of all men].
187 Let these things be opined as resembling the truth.
188 Yet the gods have not revealed all things to men from the
beginning; but by seeking men find out better in time.
189 If god had not made yellow honey, men would consider figs
far sweeter.

It has been suggested by K. Deichgräber (*Rh. M.* 87 (1938), 23ff.)
that Xenophanes in his utterances on the shortcomings of human
knowledge is developing a common poetical contrast between the
comparative ignorance of the poet and the all-knowledge of the Muse
whom he calls on to assist him: cf. e.g. Homer *Il.* II, 485f., Pindar
Paean 6, 51ff. Yet this contrast is merely a special form of that between
the capacity of the gods in general and the limitations of men, which
is restated, after Xenophanes, by Heraclitus in fr. 78 (**205**) and by
Alcmaeon in fr. 1 (**439**). In Xenophanes himself it is implicit, too,
in the assertion of **170** that the one god is unlike men either in body
or in thought. Parmenides, when he came to propose dogmatic views
which could not be corroborated from human experience, gave them
the form of a divine revelation. Yet there is no indication that
Xenophanes claimed anything like a revelation; **188** suggests that

arduous investigation is rewarded, and the probability is that he, like Heraclitus, felt himself to be in a special state of insight for this reason. Deichgräber also thought that **186** was intended as the prooemium of the physical doctrine, not of the constructive theology; but it seems most unlikely that the plural of ἀμφὶ θεῶν should be taken literally to mean 'about the gods of conventional religion'; the phrase means simply 'about theology'. The assumption of two distinct poems is, it has been suggested, a dubious one; and this is confirmed by the linking of 'theology' and 'what I say about all things'. The constructive description of the one god must ultimately have come within the scope of **186**; it was the antithesis of the mistaken Homeric concept, but, though it might be 'like the truth' in the words of **187**, it could not be taken as absolutely certain. Even Xenophanes' special position as one who had given much attention to the subject could not ensure that. However, Xenophanes did not suggest that one could not be certain that a belief was *wrong*; and his destructive criticism of the Homeric gods, based as it was on a demonstrated subjectivity, might be accepted as true.

189 shows that Xenophanes thought about problems of relationship, which were to be especially significant for Heraclitus (pp. 188f.). For Xenophanes the observation about honey (which may have been proverbial) presumably confirmed his beliefs about the limitation of knowledge – again the contrast between god, or gods, and men is conspicuously present. Once again Xenophanes was developing an idea already implicit in popular literature and giving it a special philosophical significance. After the dogmatism of the Milesians (and also of Pythagoras, mocked by Xenophanes in **260** for his extravagant theory of metempsychosis) an appeal to caution was salutary, and from this time on there was certainly more verbal reference to the broadest aspects of epistemology. But Xenophanes' revival of the traditional doctrine of human limitations, this time in a partly philosophical context, did little else that is noticeable to curb the naturally over-dogmatic tendency of Greek philosophy in its first buoyant stages.[1]

[1] See also J. Barnes, *op. cit.* I, ch. VIII, for a fuller and more exuberant discussion of Xenophanean 'scepticism' – although much of what he suggests is possible rather than probable.

CHAPTER VI

Heraclitus of Ephesus

DATE AND LIFE

190 Diogenes Laertius IX, I (DK 22 A I) Ἡράκλειτος Βλόσωνος ἤ, ὥς τινες, Ἡράκωντος Ἐφέσιος. οὗτος ἤκμαζε μὲν κατὰ τὴν ἐνάτην καὶ ἑξηκοστὴν ὀλυμπιάδα. μεγαλόφρων δὲ γέγονε παρ' ὁντιναοῦν καὶ ὑπερόπτης, ὡς καὶ ἐκ τοῦ συγγράμματος αὐτοῦ δῆλον, ἐν ᾧ φησι· (Fr. 40) Πολυμαθίη νόον ἔχειν οὐ διδάσκει· Ἡσίοδον γὰρ ἂν ἐδίδαξε καὶ Πυθαγόρην αὖτίς τε Ξενοφάνεά τε καὶ Ἑκαταῖον... (3)...καὶ τέλος μισανθρωπήσας καὶ ἐκπατήσας ἐν τοῖς ὄρεσι διῃτᾶτο, πόας σιτούμενος καὶ βοτάνας. καὶ μέντοι καὶ διὰ τοῦτο περιτραπεὶς εἰς ὕδερον κατῆλθεν εἰς ἄστυ καὶ τῶν ἰατρῶν αἰνιγματωδῶς ἐπυνθάνετο εἰ δύναιντο ἐξ ἐπομβρίας αὐχμὸν ποιῆσαι· τῶν δὲ μὴ συνιέντων αὐτὸν εἰς βούστασιν κατορύξας τῇ τῶν βολίτων ἀλέᾳ ἤλπισεν ἐξατμισθήσεσθαι. οὐδὲν δὲ ἀνύων οὐδ' οὕτως ἐτελεύτα βιοὺς ἔτη ἑξήκοντα.

190 Heraclitus son of Bloson (or, according to some, of Herakon) of Ephesus. This man was at his prime in the 69th Olympiad. He grew up to be exceptionally haughty and supercilious, as is clear also from his book, in which he says: 'Learning of many things does not teach intelligence; if so it would have taught Hesiod and Pythagoras, and again Xenophanes and Hecataeus.'...Finally he became a misanthrope, withdrew from the world, and lived in the mountains feeding on grasses and plants. However, having fallen in this way into a dropsy he came down to town and asked the doctors in a riddle if they could make a drought out of rainy weather. When they did not understand he buried himself in a cow-stall, expecting that the dropsy would be evaporated off by the heat of the manure; but even so he failed to effect anything, and ended his life at the age of sixty.

The information that Heraclitus was at his *acme*, i.e. aged forty, in Ol. 69 (504–501 B.C.) was doubtless taken from the chronographer Apollodorus: Heraclitus' middle age is placed about forty years after Anaximenes' assumed *acme* and Xenophanes' departure from Colophon. There is no need seriously to doubt Apollodorus' dating here, since, as Diogenes tells us, Heraclitus mentioned Pythagoras and Hecataeus as well as Xenophanes;[1] and he was perhaps indirectly referred to by Parmenides (**293**; also fr. 8, 55ff., **302**). Attempts have nevertheless been made to place Heraclitus' philosophical activity later than the Apollodoran dating would reasonably suggest, after 478 B.C. (and even, most improbably, after Parmenides); but they have not won acceptance, and rest on implausible hypotheses such as that no trace of self-government, suggested by the information of fr. 121 that the Ephesians had exiled Heraclitus' friend Hermodorus, would be possible in Ephesus until after its liberation from Persia around 478. Heraclitus might have lived longer than Apollodorus' sixty years (at which age Anaximenes also, and Empedocles according to Aristotle, were said to die); but we may nevertheless provisionally accept that he was in his middle years at the end of the sixth century and that his main philosophical activity had ended by about 480.

[1] The past tense in fr. 40 (quoted in **190**), 'would have taught', need not mean that all those mentioned were dead (Xenophanes at any rate lived until after 478), but it implies that they were all widely known at the time of writing. Another fragment, 129 (**256**; it may be to some extent reworded but is not spurious, see p. 217 n. 1), implies that Pythagoras was already dead. He is said to have 'flourished' in 532/1 B.C. (p. 224), and perhaps died between 510 and 505. The Suda places Hecataeus' birth as late as 520–516 B.C. According to the succession-writer Sotion (Diog. L. IX, 5, DK 22A 1), some claimed Heraclitus as Xenophanes' pupil. Other factors apart, that is hardly suggested by the critical tone of fr. 40.

The rest of **190** is quoted as a sample of the kind of biographical fiction that proliferated round the name of Heraclitus. We are also told by Diogenes that he refused to make laws for the Ephesians but preferred playing with children in the temple of Artemis. Most of these stories are based on well-known sayings of Heraclitus; many were intended to make him look ridiculous, and were invented with malicious intent by Hellenistic pedants who resented his superior tone. For example, extreme misanthropy is deduced from his criticisms of the majority of men (e.g. **194**), vegetarianism from a mention of blood-pollution in **241**, the fatal dropsy from his assertion 'it is death for souls to become water' in **229**. He was known as an obscure propounder of riddles, and this is made out to have cost him his life: the doctors, whom he appeared to criticize in fr. 58 (p. 189), do nothing to save him. He is said to have buried himself in dung because he had said in fr. 96 that corpses are more worthless than dung; 'being exhaled' refers to his theory of exhalations from the sea (pp. 201f. and n.). The only details about Heraclitus' life which it might be safe to accept as true are that he spent it in Ephesus, that he came of an old aristocratic family,[1] and that he was on bad terms with his fellow-citizens.

[1] Cf. **191** Diog. L. IX, 6 σημεῖον δ' αὐτοῦ τῆς μεγαλοφροσύνης 'Αντισθένης φησὶν ἐν Διαδοχαῖς· ἐκχωρῆσαι γὰρ τἀδελφῷ τῆς βασιλείας. *(Antisthenes in his Successions quotes as a sign of his [Heraclitus'] arrogance that he resigned the hereditary 'kingship' to his brother.)* There is no apparent reason why this information should be fictitious. Strabo, 14, p. 633 Cas. (DK 22 A 2), said that the descendants of Androclus founder of Ephesus were still called 'kings', and had certain privileges like that of front seats at the games.

'THE OBSCURE'

Timon of Phlius, the third-century B.C. satirist, called Heraclitus αἰνικτής, 'riddler' (Diog. L. IX, 6). This legitimate criticism of his style later gave rise to the almost invariable epithet σκοτεινός, *obscurus* in Latin (Cicero *de finibus* II, 5, 15, etc.). Another common description in the Roman period was 'the weeping philosopher'. This latter judgement is entirely trivial, being founded partly on humorous references to the idea that all things flow like rivers (cf. e.g. Plato *Crat.* 440c, believers in flux are like people with catarrh), and partly on Theophrastus' well-known attribution to Heraclitus of μελαγχολία (Diog. L. IX, 6), by which, however, he meant 'impulsiveness' (see Aristotle's description at *Eth. Nic.* H8, 1150b25) and not 'melancholy' in its later and its modern sense.

HERACLITUS' BOOK

192 Diogenes Laetius IX, 5 τὸ δὲ φερόμενον αὐτοῦ βιβλίον ἐστὶ μὲν ἀπὸ τοῦ συνέχοντος Περὶ φύσεως, διῄρηται δὲ εἰς τρεῖς λόγους, εἴς τε τὸν περὶ τοῦ παντὸς καὶ πολιτικὸν καὶ θεολογικόν. (6) ἀνέθηκε δ' αὐτὸ εἰς τὸ τῆς 'Αρτέμιδος ἱερόν, ὡς μέν τινες, ἐπιτηδεύσας ἀσαφέστερον γράψαι ὅπως οἱ δυνάμενοι προσίοιεν αὐτῷ καὶ μὴ ἐκ τοῦ δημώδους εὐκαταφρόνητον ᾖ...τοσαύτην δὲ δόξαν ἔσχε τὸ σύγγραμμα ὡς καὶ αἱρετιστὰς ἀπ' αὐτοῦ γενέσθαι τοὺς κληθέντας 'Ηρακλειτείους.

192 The book said to be his is called 'On Nature', from its chief content, and is divided into three discourses: On the Universe, Politics, Theology. He dedicated it and placed it in the temple of Artemis, as some say, having purposely written it rather obscurely so that only those of rank and influence should have access to it, and it should not be easily despised by the populace... The work had so great a reputation that from it arose disciples, those called Heracliteans.

Ancient biographers and historians of philosophy assumed that all the Presocratics wrote one or more books (though there was doubt over Thales, see pp. 86ff.). They certainly assumed that Heraclitus wrote one, and Diogenes tells us that its title was 'On Nature'. This title was regularly assigned to works by those whom Aristotle and the Peripatetics called 'natural philosophers', and cannot be regarded as necessarily authentic in all cases; see pp. 102–3 n. 1. The division into three sections is unlikely to have been original, and suggests that Diogenes or his source was thinking of an edition or collection of sayings, probably made in Alexandria, which followed a Stoic analysis of the parts of philosophy. Diels maintained that Heraclitus wrote no consecutive book, but merely gave repeated utterance to a series of carefully-formulated opinions or γνῶμαι. This view has found few supporters, but perhaps has an element of truth. The surviving fragments have very much the appearance of oral pronouncements put into a concise and striking, and therefore easily memorable, form; they do not resemble extracts from a continuous written work. The obstacle to this view is fr. 1 (**194**), a structurally complicated sentence which looks very like a written introduction to a book. Possibly when Heraclitus achieved fame as a sage a collection of his most famous utterances was made, for which a special prologue was composed. In any event the fragments we possess (and not all those in DK are fully authentic) were for the most part obviously framed as oral apophthegms rather than as parts of a discursive treatise; this was in keeping with Heraclitus' oracular intentions (see p. 210).[1] It also accords with his views on divine knowledge (**205** and **206**) and on the inability of most men to respond to the true nature of things, even when helped by a logos or account (revelation) such as Heraclitus' own. The suggestion in **192** that the 'Heracliteans', also mentioned by Plato and Aristotle, were devotees of the book is almost certainly guesswork; its importance lies in its implication that there was no 'school' of direct followers at Ephesus.[2] No follower of note is known until Cratylus, an older contemporary (probably) of Plato, who developed a debased form of Heracliteanism by exaggerating, and combining together, the Ephesian's belief in the inevitability of change and his belief (quite a common one in his time) in the significance of names.

[1] For an interesting discussion of this whole topic from a slightly different point of view, see Kahn, *The Art and Thought of Heraclitus* (Cambridge, 1979), 3–9.

[2] In spite of **193** Plato *Theaetetus* 179D πολλοῦ καὶ δεῖ φαύλη εἶναι (*sc.* ἡ μάχη), ἀλλὰ περὶ μὲν τὴν 'Ιωνίαν καὶ ἐπιδίδωσι πάμπολυ. οἱ γὰρ τοῦ 'Ηρακλείτου ἑταῖροι χορηγοῦσι τούτου τοῦ λόγου μάλα ἐρρωμένως. (Cf. *ibid.* 179E, ... αὐτοῖς μὲν τοῖς περὶ τὴν "Εφεσον.) (*[The battle] is far from being a slight one, but in the region of Ionia it is even greatly increasing. For the companions of Heraclitus minister to this argument with might and main. (Cf. ...to those around Ephesus.)*) This whole passage is intentionally humorous, as indeed are most of Plato's remarks about Heraclitus, and the local references need not be intended literally; anyone using what Plato would consider to be a Heraclitean type of argument might be ironically associated with Ephesus. Plato's most extreme Heraclitean acquaintance, at any rate, namely Cratylus, was neither an Ephesian nor even from Ionia.

SPECIAL DIFFICULTIES OF INTERPRETATION

As has been seen, Heraclitus was renowned in antiquity for his obscurity. His pronouncements were undeniably often cryptic, probably intentionally so, and little serious attempt seems to have been made by Plato and Aristotle to penetrate his real meaning. Theophrastus, on whom the later doxographical tradition depends, unfortunately based his interpretation on Aristotle's. He does not appear to have had access to a complete book by Heraclitus, or even (to judge, for example, from the omission of all but the barest reference to Heraclitus in his *de sensu*) to a fully representative collection of separate utterances; in fact he complained that Heraclitus' pronouncements were either unfinished or inconsistent. The Stoics further distorted the account by adopting Heraclitus as their ancient authority on physical matters. In some respects they produced an accurate development of his ideas, for example in their ideal of ὁμολογουμένως ζῆν, living in accord with Nature (cf. e.g. **195**); in others, however, they radically readapted his views to meet special requirements of their own – for example in their attribution to him of the idea of *ecpyrosis*, the periodical consumption of the whole world by fire. Our sources subsequent to the founder of Stoicism, Zeno of Citium, accepted this particular interpretation of Heraclitus, which can be reconciled with some of the extant sayings and may have been encouraged by Theophrastus, but is incompatible with others and at variance with the basic Heraclitean concept of measure in natural change; see further pp. 194ff. and n. on p. 200.

As for Plato and Aristotle, there is little *verbatim* quotation of Heraclitus in either, nor were they really interested in the accurate *objective* assessment of early predecessors. Plato occasionally mentions him, mainly in a humorous or ironical way and with emphasis on a view freely attributed to him in the dialogues, that 'all things are in flux' – πάντα ῥεῖ or πάντα χωρεῖ. According to Aristotle at *Met.* A6, 987a32, Plato was influenced in youth by the emphasis laid by Cratylus on this kind of view. But all Presocratic thinkers were struck by the dominance of change in the world of our experience. Heraclitus was obviously no exception, indeed he probably expressed the universality of change more clearly and more dramatically than his predecessors; but for him it was the complementary idea of the *measure* inhering in change, the stability that persists through it and controls it, that was of vital importance. Plato may have been genuinely misled, especially by fifth-century sophistic exaggerations, in his distortion of Heraclitus' emphasis here; and Aristotle accepted the Platonic flux-interpretation and carried it still further. Other references to Heraclitus in Aristotle attack him for denying the law of contradiction in his assertions that opposites are 'the same'. Again, this is a misinterpretation by Aristotle, who applied his own tight logical standards anachronistically; by 'the same' Heraclitus evidently meant not 'identical' so much as 'not essentially distinct'.

In view of these defects in the authors of the ancient assessment it is safer to attempt the reconstitution of Heraclitus' thought, in the first instance, on the basis of the extant genuine fragments. Even so one cannot hope for more than a very limited understanding, partly because Heraclitus, as Aristotle found, did not use the categories of formal logic, and tended to describe the same thing (or roughly the same thing) now as a god, now as a form of matter, now as a rule of behaviour or principle which was nevertheless a physical constituent of things. He was, indeed, more of a metaphysician than his Ionian predecessors, less concerned with the mechanics of development and change than with the unifying reality that underlay them.

HERACLITUS' THOUGHT

(1) *Men should try to comprehend the underlying coherence of things: it is expressed in the Logos, the formula or element of arrangement common to all things*

194 Fr. 1, Sextus *adv. math.* VII, 132 τοῦ δὲ λόγου τοῦδ' ἐόντος ἀεὶ ἀξύνετοι γίνονται ἄνθρωποι καὶ πρόσθεν ἢ ἀκοῦσαι καὶ ἀκούσαντες τὸ πρῶτον· γινομένων γὰρ πάντων κατὰ τὸν λόγον τόνδε ἀπείροισιν ἐοίκασι, πειρώμενοι καὶ ἐπέων καὶ ἔργων τοιούτων ὁκοίων ἐγὼ διηγεῦμαι κατὰ φύσιν διαιρέων ἕκαστον καὶ φράζων ὅκως ἔχει· τοὺς δὲ ἄλλους ἀνθρώπους λανθάνει ὁκόσα ἐγερθέντες ποιοῦσιν ὅκωσπερ ὁκόσα εὕδοντες ἐπιλανθάνονται.

195 Fr. 2, Sextus *adv. math.* VII, 133   διὸ δεῖ ἕπεσθαι τῷ ⟨ξυνῷ⟩· τοῦ λόγου δ' ἐόντος ξυνοῦ ζώουσιν οἱ πολλοὶ ὡς ἰδίαν ἔχοντες φρόνησιν.[1]

[1] διὸ δεῖ ἕπεσθαι τῷ κοινῷ· ξυνὸς γὰρ ὁ κοινός· τοῦ...MSS. ξυνός and κοινός are different words for the same idea, the former being the normal epic and Ionic form and that used by Heraclitus. The later form was evidently given in a gloss, and then this gloss replaced the original word, though the appended explanation remained.

196 Fr. 50, Hippolytus *Ref.* IX, 9, 1   οὐκ ἐμοῦ ἀλλὰ τοῦ λόγου ἀκούσαντας ὁμολογεῖν σοφόν ἐστιν ἓν πάντα εἶναι.

194 Of the Logos which is as I describe it men always prove to be uncomprehending, both before they have heard it and when once they have heard it. For although all things happen according to this Logos men are like people of no experience, even when they experience such words and deeds as I explain, when I distinguish each thing according to its constitution and declare how it is; but the rest of men fail to notice what they do after they wake up just as they forget what they do when asleep.

195 Therefore it is necessary to follow the common; but although the Logos is common the many live as though they had a private understanding.

196 Listening not to me but to the Logos it is wise to agree that all things are one.

These assertions make it plain that Heraclitus regarded himself as having access to, and trying vainly to propagate, an all-important truth about the constitution of the world of which men are a part. The great majority fail to recognize this truth,[1] which is 'common' – that is, both valid for all things and accessible to all men, if only they use their observation and their understanding[2] and do not fabricate a private and deceptive intelligence. What they should recognize is the *Logos*, which is perhaps to be interpreted as the unifying formula or proportionate method of arrangement of things, what might almost be termed their structural plan both individual and in sum. The technical sense of λόγος in Heraclitus is probably related to the general meaning 'measure', 'reckoning' or 'proportion'; it cannot be simply Heraclitus' own 'account' that is in question (otherwise the distinction in **196** between ἐμοῦ and τοῦ λόγου is meaningless), although the Logos was revealed in that account and in a manner of speaking coincides with it. The effect of arrangement according to a common plan or measure is that all things, although apparently plural and totally discrete, are really united in a coherent complex

(**196**) of which men themselves are a part, and the comprehension of which is therefore logically necessary for the adequate enactment of their own lives. Yet 'formula', 'proportionate arrangement' and so on are misleadingly abstract as translations of this technical sense of λόγος. Logos was probably conceived by Heraclitus at times as an actual component of things, and in many respects it is co-extensive with the primary cosmic constituent, fire (see p. 199).

[1] Men are attacked for this failure in many other extant fragments: see frr. 17, 19, 28, 34, 56, 72. But nothing substantial is added there to the content of **194**, **195**, **196**. Analogous rebukes are also hurled at individuals – Homer, Hesiod, Xenophanes, Hecataeus, Archilochus and Pythagoras; see e.g. **190** and **255**, where the ground of criticism is that such men (of whom Pythagoras comes in for special attack elsewhere, cf. e.g. **256**) pursued the wrong kind of knowledge, πολυμαθίη or the mere collection of disparate and unrelated facts.

[2] Cf. **197** Fr. 55, Hippolytus *Ref.* ix, 9, 5   ὅσων ὄψις ἀκοὴ μάθησις, ταῦτα ἐγὼ προτιμέω. *(The things of which there is seeing and hearing and perception, these do I prefer.)* But observation must be checked by understanding, νοῦς or φρόνησις: this is shown not only by **250** but also by **198** fr. 107, Sextus *adv. math.* vii, 126   κακοὶ μάρτυρες ἀνθρώποισιν ὀφθαλμοὶ καὶ ὦτα βαρβάρους ψυχὰς ἐχόντων. *(Evil witnesses are eyes and ears for men, if they have souls that do not understand their language.)* Here 'barbarian souls' are those that cannot understand the language of, cannot correctly interpret, the senses, but are misled by superficial appearances. An analogous distinction between mere sensation and the intelligent interpretation of sense-data was later made by Democritus (pp. 412–13).

(2) *Different kinds of instance of the essential unity of opposites*

199   Fr. 61, Hippolytus *Ref.* ix, 10, 5   θάλασσα ὕδωρ καθαρώτατον καὶ μιαρώτατον, ἰχθύσι μὲν πότιμον καὶ σωτήριον, ἀνθρώποις δὲ ἄποτον καὶ ὀλέθριον.

200   Fr. 60, Hippolytus *Ref.* ix, 10, 4   ὁδὸς ἄνω κάτω μία καὶ ὡυτή.

201   Fr. 111, Stobaeus *Anth.* iii, 1, 177   νοῦσος ὑγιείην ἐποίησεν ἡδὺ καὶ ἀγαθόν, λιμὸς κόρον, κάματος ἀνάπαυσιν.

202   Fr. 88, ps.-Plutarch *Cons. ad Apoll.* 10, 106E   ταὐτό τ' ἔνι ζῶν καὶ τεθνηκὸς καὶ τὸ ἐγρηγορὸς καὶ τὸ καθεῦδον καὶ νέον καὶ γηραιόν· τάδε γὰρ μεταπεσόντα ἐκεῖνά ἐστι κἀκεῖνα [πάλιν] μεταπεσόντα ταῦτα.

199   Sea is the most pure and the most polluted water; for fishes it is drinkable and salutary, but for men it is undrinkable and deleterious.
200   The path up and down is one and the same.
201   Disease makes health pleasant and good, hunger satiety, weariness rest.

202   And as the same thing there exists in us living and dead and the waking and the sleeping and young and old; for these things having changed round are those, and those having changed round are these.

These fragments exemplify four different kinds of connexion between evident opposites:

(i) In **199** the same thing produces opposite effects upon different classes of critic; so also fr. 13 (pigs like mud ⟨but men do not⟩) and fr. 9 (donkeys prefer rubbish to gold, ⟨men gold to rubbish⟩).

(ii) In **200** different aspects of the same thing may justify opposite descriptions;[1] so also fr. 58 (cutting and burning ⟨which are normally bad⟩ call for a fee when done by a surgeon) and fr. 59 (the act of writing combines straight, in the whole line, and crooked, in the shape of each letter).

(iii) In **201** good and desirable things like health or rest are seen to be possible only if we recognize their opposites, sickness or weariness; so probably fr. 23 (there would be no right without wrong).

(iv) In **202** certain opposites are said to be essentially connected (literally, to be 'the same', a pregnant expression) because they succeed, and are succeeded by, each other and nothing else. So in fr. 126 the hot substance and the cold form what we might call a hot–cold continuum, a single entity (i.e. temperature). So also fr. 57: night and day, which Hesiod had made parent and child, are, and must always have been, essentially connected and interdependent.

These four kinds of connexion between opposites can be further reduced to two main headings: (*a*) i–iii, opposites which inhere in, or are simultaneously produced by, a single subject; (*b*) iv, opposites which are connected through being different stages in a single invariable process.

[1] This seems the most probable interpretation of 'the road up and down'. Theophrastus and a few of his followers applied the phrase to the interchanges between world-masses in the cosmic process, and most modern scholars have done the same. But the same words 'one and the same' are used of evident opposites in the formally similar fr. 59; and Hippolytus, a reliable source of *verbatim* quotations from Heraclitus who seems to have used a good handbook in which the philosopher's sayings were grouped by subject, certainly took 'the road up and down' as another illustration of the unity of opposites and not as a cosmological metaphor, to which indeed it is not completely appropriate. We should think of an actual road or path, which is called 'the road up' by those who live at the bottom, 'the road down' by those at the top. Vlastos, *AJP* 76 (1955), 349 n. 26, objects to this interpretation on the grounds of its 'banality'; but fr. 59, for example, on writing, undoubtedly has precisely the same quality.

Reflections such as these (cf. also frr. 103, 48, 126, 99), on objects conventionally treated as entirely separate from and opposed to each other, evidently persuaded Heraclitus that there is *never* any real absolute division of opposite from opposite. (For a more straightforward restatement of this view by Anaxagoras see p. 371.)

(3) *Each pair of opposites thus forms both a unity and a plurality. Different pairs are also found to be inter-connected*

203 Fr. 10, [Aristotle] *de mundo* 5, 396b20 συλλάψιες ὅλα καὶ οὐχ ὅλα, συμφερόμενον διαφερόμενον, συνᾷδον διᾷδον· ἐκ πάντων ἓν καὶ ἐξ ἑνὸς πάντα.[1]

[1] συλλάψιες is textually slightly preferable to συνάψιες, which would mean 'things in contact'. A more important question is whether the word is subject or predicate. Snell showed it to be the former, contrary to the common view; neither 'wholes' and 'not wholes' nor 'in tune' and 'out of tune' are typical pairs of Heraclitean opposites, nor indeed do they fall under the classes outlined on p. 189.

204 Fr. 67, Hippolytus *Ref.* IX, 10, 8 ὁ θεὸς ἡμέρη εὐφρόνη, χειμὼν θέρος, πόλεμος εἰρήνη, κόρος λιμός [τἀναντία ἅπαντα, οὗτος ὁ νοῦς]· ἀλλοιοῦται δὲ ὅκωσπερ ⟨πῦρ⟩ ὁπόταν συμμιγῇ θυώμασιν ὀνομάζεται καθ' ἡδονὴν ἑκάστου. [πῦρ suppl. Diels.]

203 Things taken together are wholes and not wholes, something which is being brought together and brought apart, which is in tune and out of tune; out of all things there comes a unity, and out of a unity all things.
204 God is day night, winter summer, war peace, satiety hunger [all the opposites, this is the meaning]; he undergoes alteration in the way that fire, when it is mixed with spices, is named according to the scent of each of them.

In 203 'things taken together' must be, primarily, opposites: what one takes together with night, for example, is day. (Here we may note that Heraclitus expresses what we should call 'quality' in terms of simple extremes, which he can then classify as opposites; so that all change can thus be regarded as that between opposites.) Such 'things taken together' are truly described in one sense as 'wholes', that is, forming one continuum, in another sense as 'not wholes', that is, as single components. Applying these alternative analyses to the conglomeration of 'things taken together', we can see that 'from all things a unity is formed', and also that from this unity (ἐξ ἑνός) there can be separated the superficial, discrete, plural aspect of things (πάντα).

204 asserts a relationship between god and a number of pairs of opposites, each pair separately connected by automatic succession; these, as the glossator saw, probably stand for all pairs of opposites however connected. The relationship in question is a loose predicative one; and Heraclitus, perhaps enlarging on Xenophanes, seems to have regarded 'god' as in some probably undefined way immanent in things, or as the sum total of things.[1] One recalls the Milesian view that the originative material, which may still be represented in the world, is divine. Heraclitus, although not so explicitly corporealistic in his conception of divinity, was little more conventionally religious than the Milesians in that he did not associate 'god' with the need for cult and worship (although he did not utterly reject all cult, see pp. 209f.). The particular point of **204** is that every opposite can be expressed in terms of god: because peace is divine it does not follow that war is not equally divine, is not equally permeated by the directive and unifying constituent which is on occasions equated with the whole ordered cosmos (pp. 187f., 199). God cannot here be essentially different from Logos; and the Logos is, among other things, the constituent of things which makes them opposed, and which ensures that change between opposites will be proportional and balanced overall. God, then, is said to be the common connecting element in all extremes, just as fire is the common element of different vapours (because these were conceived as a compound of fire with different kinds of incense). Change from one to another brings about a total change of name, which is misleading, because only a superficial component has altered and the most important constituent remains. This difficult saying implies that, while each separate pair of contraries forms a single continuum, the several continua, also, are connected with each other, though in a different manner. Thus the total plurality of things forms a single, coherent, determinable complex – what Heraclitus called 'unity'.

[1] The superiority of god to man, and of the divine synthetic view of things to the human chaotic view, is heavily stressed by Heraclitus; e.g. **205** Fr. 78, Origen *c. Celsum* VI, 12 ἦθος γὰρ ἀνθρώπειον μὲν οὐκ ἔχει γνώμας, θεῖον δὲ ἔχει. (*Human disposition does not have true judgement, but divine disposition does.*) See also frr. 79, 82–3, and compare the Hebrew concept: 'As the heavens are higher than the earth, so are my ways higher than your ways, and my thoughts than your thoughts', Isaiah lv. 8f. One saying specifically asserts that for god the separateness implied by opposites does not exist: **206** Fr. 102, Porphyrius *in Iliadem* IV, 4 τῷ μὲν θεῷ καλὰ πάντα καὶ ἀγαθὰ καὶ δίκαια, ἄνθρωποι δὲ ἃ μὲν ἄδικα ὑπειλήφασιν ἃ δὲ δίκαια. (*To god all things are beautiful and good and just, but men have supposed some things to be unjust, others just.*)

(4) *The unity of things lies beneath the surface; it depends upon a balanced reaction between opposites*

207 Fr. 54, Hippolytus *Ref.* ιχ, 9, 5 ἁρμονίη ἀφανὴς φανερῆς κρείττων.

208 Fr. 123, Themistius *Or.* 5, p. 69 D.   φύσις κρύπτεσθαι φιλεῖ.

209 Fr. 51, Hippolytus *Ref.* ιχ, 9, ι   οὐ ξυνιᾶσιν ὅκως διαφερόμενον ἑωυτῷ ξυμφέρεται· παλίντονος ἁρμονίη ὅκωσπερ τόξου καὶ λύρης.[1]

[1] Hippolytus, the fullest source here, and usually a reliable one, has ὁμολογέειν (for ὁμολογέει) and παλίντροπος. ξυμφέρεται is a probable restoration from Plato's version, *Symp.* 187A, and avoids a difficult use of ὁμολογεῖν – a verb which could easily have been repeated accidentally, since Hippolytus used it twice in the infinitive just before he quoted the fragment. παλίντονος has as much support as παλίντροπος in the versions (of the second part only) by Plutarch and Porphyry, and is preferred because it gives a fully intelligible sense. G. Vlastos, *AJP* 76 (1955), 348ff., defends παλίντροπος, noting that Diog. L. ιχ, 7, a summary and often imprecise version of Theophrastus, has the phrase διὰ τῆς ἐναντιοτροπῆς ἡρμόσθαι. This certainly appears at first sight to be based upon παλίντροπος ἁρμονίη; yet the ἐναντιοτροπή (which would have to be ἐναντιοτροπία if derived from an adjectival form -τροπος) probably refers to the τροπαί of **218**, combined (as they certainly were by Theophrastus, cf. the fuller account of him in Diog. L. ιχ, 8) with the 'way up and down' interpreted as change between opposites. The παλίντροπος κέλευθος in Parmenides fr. 6 (**293**) is, of course, perfectly intelligible, and does not necessarily contain a reference to Heraclitus (cf. pp. 247f.), or at any rate to this fragment. For further discussion of the correct reading see Guthrie, *HGP* 1, n. 3 on pp. 439f.

207 An unapparent connexion is stronger than an apparent one.
208 The real constitution is accustomed to hide itself.
209 They do not apprehend how being at variance it agrees with itself [*lit.* how being brought apart it is brought together with itself]: there is a back-stretched connexion, as in the bow and the lyre.

What is stated in **207** is a general rule; comparison with **208** (where φύσις probably means not 'Nature' but 'a thing's true constitution'), and also with **209**, suggests that the rule is intended to apply to the working of the world as a whole, as a sum of constituent parts whose connexion is not apparent at first sight. The unseen connexion of opposites is in fact stronger than other, more obvious types of connexion.[1] **209**, one of Heraclitus' most familiar sayings, contains a characteristic looseness in predication: the subject of ξυμφέρεται is probably not ⟨τὸ⟩ διαφερόμενον, i.e. another example of a specific opposite, but a generalizing διαφερόμενόν ⟨τι⟩, where 'anything being carried apart' means something like 'any discrete pair of opposites'. Thus the sense given is similar to that implicit in συμφερόμενον διαφερόμενον in **203**: any pair, or sum of pairs, can be regarded either (*a*) as heterogeneous and analysable in terms of separate poles or extremes, or (*b*) as tending together with itself to form a unity. Now comes an important addition: there is (*sc.* in it, i.e. it exemplifies) a connexion or means of joining (the literal sense of ἁρμονίη) through opposite tensions,[2] which ensures this coherence – just as the tension in the string of bow or lyre, being exactly balanced by the outward tension exerted by the arms of the instrument, produces a coherent, unified, stable and efficient complex. We may infer that if the balance between opposites were *not* maintained, for example if 'the hot' (i.e. the sum of hot substances) began seriously to outweigh the cold, or night day, then the unity and coherence of the world would cease, just as, if the tension in the bow-string exceeds the tension in the arms, the whole complex is destroyed.

[1] A number of fragments imply that it needs both faith and persistence to find the underlying truth. So e.g. **210** Fr. 18, Clement *Strom.* II, 17, 4   ἐὰν μὴ ἔλπηται ἀνέλπιστον οὐκ ἐξευρήσει, ἀνεξερεύνητον ἐὸν καὶ ἄπορον. *(If one does not expect the unexpected one will not find it out, since it is not to be searched out, and is difficult to compass.)* See also **244**, and frr. 22, 86; compare Xenophanes fr. 18 (**188**).

[2] παλίντονος = 'counter-stretched', i.e. tending equally in opposite directions. A tension in one direction automatically produces an equivalent tension in the other; if not, the system collapses

(5) *The total balance in the cosmos can only be maintained if change in one direction eventually leads to change in the other, that is, if there is unending 'strife' between opposites.*

211   Fr. 80, Origen *c. Celsum* VI, 42   εἰδέναι χρὴ τὸν πόλεμον ἐόντα ξυνόν, καὶ δίκην ἔριν, καὶ γινόμενα πάντα κατ' ἔριν καὶ χρεών.[1]

[1] χρεών Diels, χρεώμενα MS. The emendation is not certain, but is hard to improve; the three extra letters may be connected with the omission of three letters just before, where the unique Vatican MS has εἰ δέ for the obvious original εἰδέναι.

212   Fr. 53, Hippolytus *Ref.* IX, 9, 4   πόλεμος πάντων μὲν πατήρ ἐστι, πάντων δὲ βασιλεύς, καὶ τοὺς μὲν θεοὺς ἔδειξε τοὺς δὲ ἀνθρώπους, τοὺς μὲν δούλους ἐποίησε τοὺς δὲ ἐλευθέρους.

211   It is necessary to know that war is common and right is strife and that all things happen by strife and necessity.
212   War is the father of all and king of all, and some he shows as gods, others as men; some he makes slaves, others free.

Strife or war is Heraclitus' favourite metaphor for the dominance of change in the world. It is obviously related to the reaction between opposites; most kinds of change (except for e.g. growth, which is the accretion of like to like), it may be inferred, could be resolved into change between opposites. At all events, change from one extreme to the other might seem to be the most radical possible. The 'war' which underlies all events is 'common' in **211** in a special sense (Homer had used the term, but to mean 'impartial'): it is universal, and is responsible for different and indeed opposed conditions of men – even for their fate after death, for death in battle (**212**) could make some into 'gods', cf. **237** and **239**. It is also called δίκη, the 'indicated way' (from the same root as δείκνυμι), or the normal rule of behaviour. This must be a deliberate amendment of Anaximander's dictum (**110**) that things pay retribution to each other for the *injustice* of their alternate encroachments in the processes of natural change. Heraclitus points out that if strife – that is, the action and reaction between opposed substances – were to cease, then the victor in every contest of extremes would establish a permanent domination, and the world as such would be destroyed.[1] Yet just as in a battle there are temporary local stoppages, or deadlocks produced by the exact balance of opposing forces, so Heraclitus must have allowed that temporary stability is to be found here and there in the cosmic battlefield, so long as it is only temporary and is balanced by a corresponding state elsewhere. This would not diminish the validity of the domination of strife (which, as for Anaximander, provides a metaphorical motive for change), but it allows the principle to be applied to the world of our actual experience, in which all things must eventually change but some things are for the time being obviously stable.

[1] Cf. **213** Aristotle *Eth. Eudem.* H1, 1235a25 καὶ Ἡράκλειτος ἐπιτιμᾷ τῷ ποιήσαντι 'Ὡς ἔρις ἔκ τε θεῶν καὶ ἀνθρώπων ἀπόλοιτο (= *Il.* 18, 107)· οὐ γὰρ ἂν εἶναι ἁρμονίαν μὴ ὄντος ὀξέος καὶ βαρέος οὐδὲ τὰ ζῷα ἄνευ θήλεος καὶ ἄρρενος ἐναντίων ὄντων. (*Heraclitus rebukes the author of the line 'Would that strife might be destroyed from among gods and men': for there would be no musical scale unless high and low existed, nor living creatures without female and male, which are opposites.*) Here ἁρμονία has its special sense of 'musical scale'.

(6) *The river-image illustrates the kind of unity that depends on the preservation of measure and balance in change*

214 Fr. 12, Arius Didymus *ap.* Eusebium *P.E.* xv, 20, +fr. 91, Plutarch *de E* 18, 392B ποταμοῖσι τοῖσιν αὐτοῖσιν ἐμβαίνουσιν ἕτερα καὶ ἕτερα ὕδατα ἐπιρρεῖ (= fr. 12).[1]...σκίδνησι καὶ...συνάγει...συνίσταται καὶ ἀπολείπει...πρόσεισι καὶ ἄπεισι (= fr. 91).

214 Upon those that step into the same rivers different and different waters flow...They scatter and...gather...come together and flow away...approach and depart.

[1] The words καὶ ψυχαὶ δὲ ἀπὸ τῶν ὑγρῶν ἀναθυμιῶνται, which follow ὕδατα ἐπιρρεῖ in Arius, are counted as part of fr. 12 by most editors; but they are almost certainly part of an attempt by Cleanthes to find an exhalation of soul in Heraclitus as in Zeno; see Kirk, *Heraclitus, the Cosmic Fragments*, 367ff. The pairs of verbs which form fr. 91 occur in Plutarch immediately after a summary by him (in Platonic terms) of the main river-statement; see further p. 197.

According to the Platonic interpretation, accepted and expanded by Aristotle, Theophrastus and the doxographers, this river-image was cited by Heraclitus to emphasize the absolute continuity of change in every single thing: everything is in perpetual flux like a river. So **215** Plato *Cratylus* 402A λέγει που Ἡράκλειτος ὅτι πάντα χωρεῖ καὶ οὐδὲν μένει, καὶ ποταμοῦ ῥοῇ ἀπεικάζων τὰ ὄντα λέγει ὡς δὶς ἐς τὸν αὐτὸν ποταμὸν οὐκ ἂν ἐμβαίης. *(Heraclitus somewhere says that all things are in process and nothing stays still, and likening existing things to the stream of a river he says that you would not step twice into the same river.)* It is to this interpretation that Aristotle refers in **216** Aristotle *Phys.* Θ3, 253b9 καί φασί τινες κινεῖσθαι τῶν ὄντων οὐ τὰ μὲν τὰ δ' οὔ, ἀλλὰ πάντα καὶ ἀεί, ἀλλὰ λανθάνειν τοῦτο τὴν ἡμετέραν αἴσθησιν. *(And some say not that some existing things are moving, and not others, but that all things are in motion all the time, but that this escapes our perception.)* Aristotle here makes explicit what is implicit in Plato, that many things (those that appear to be stable) must be undergoing *invisible* or unnoticed changes. Can Heraclitus really have thought that a rock or a bronze cauldron, for example, was invariably undergoing invisible changes of material? Perhaps so; but nothing in the extant fragments suggested that he did, and his clearly-expressed reliance on the senses, provided they be interpreted intelligently, may suggest that he did not.[1] Before Parmenides and his apparent proof that the senses were completely fallacious – a proof that was clearly a shock to his contemporaries – gross departures from common sense should, we believe, only be accepted when the evidence for them is quite strong. In the present case it is conceivable that Plato was misled by post-Heraclitean exaggerations and distortions of Heraclitus' emphasis on eventual change; in particular, perhaps, by Cratylus, who is said by Aristotle to have influenced Plato as a young man (*Met.* A6, 987a32).

[1] See **197, 198**. It is true that Melissus in fr. 8 (**537**) drew attention to the appearance that some 'stable' things do change: iron is worn away by the finger, and so on. This observation occurs in a context which perhaps has verbal

references to Heraclitus (e.g. τό τε θερμὸν ψυχρὸν γίνεσθαι καὶ τὸ ψυχρὸν θερμόν, cf. fr. 126). Yet there is no reason to think that Melissus meant that change must in this case be *continuous*, even though it can be *invisible*. Every time the finger rubs, it rubs off an invisible portion of iron; yet when it does not rub, what reason is there to think that the iron is still changing? Melissus' point is rather that appearances show that everything, even the apparently stable, is *subject to change*. This is precisely what Heraclitus must have thought; he may or may not have mentioned infra-visible changes, but in any case would only accept them when they were deducible – and continuous change is not deducible in many apparently stable objects. Melissus' argument, of course, was that the senses must be fallacious; for between Heraclitus and himself had come Parmenides. With Empedoclean effluences (pp. 309f.) the situation changes again.

Most scholars, however, do not accept this view, because they feel that Plato must be right – partly because of his importance, partly because of his date (which is relatively early compared with that of Arius Didymus, the source of fr. 12), partly because Aristotle believed him, and partly because Cratylus' amendment ('you could not step into the same river *even once*', Aristotle *Met* Γ5, 1010a13) seems to depend on the Platonic form of what Heraclitus said, or something like it. But Plato can often be seen making Socrates distort his predecessors for his own, or Plato's own, reasons; and Cratylus' amendment does not necessarily depend on the Platonic version, but could easily be rephrased as a comment on that of Arius. Perhaps, then, one should admit the general development of ideas about perception and change into the calculation, and also the implication of Heraclitus' other fragments. But there is also the question of the apparently Heraclitean diction of fr. 12, with its Ionic dative plurals and its archaic 'different and different waters'. Guthrie (like Vlastos in *AJP* 76, 1955, 338ff.) objects that it is less pithy and paradoxical, and therefore less Heraclitean, than the Platonic version, but in sum we feel that fr. 12 has every appearance of belonging to Heraclitus, being in natural and unforced Ionic and having the characteristic rhythm of archaic prose; while the latter looks Platonic, and could more easily be a reformulation of fr. 12 than vice versa.

The matter is hard to be certain about; one interpretation is presented here quite forcefully, the other is argued in e.g. Guthrie, *HGP* I, 449–54. Further reflection on the underlying implications of the alternative versions may strengthen the case advanced here. The Platonic formulation implies that the river is never the same in successive moments (and so Cratylus was really right), and is accompanied by a categorical statement that everything in nature resembles the river in that respect – οὐδὲν μένει, 'nothing stays still'. The Arius formulation, that of fr. 12, is less drastic; there is such a thing as the same river, but it is also different, in a way. This draws a contrast between 'same' and 'different' in a specific instance, and therefore belongs with the list of Heraclitus' concrete examples of the coincidence of opposites. But if its intention is more than that (as Plato at least implies), then the meaning is not that every single object must be like a river, but rather that a complex whole, like the world, might remain 'the same' while its constituent parts are for ever changing – which would have a reassuring similarity to Heraclitus' physical views discussed in §7 below. Seen in this light, the addition to fr. 12 (in **214**) of the verbs which compose fr. 91 (which the context, and their own nature, seem to indicate as describing the flow of water, with special attention to the regularity of its replacement) brings out what is implicit in fr. 12: that the *unity* of the river as a whole is dependent upon the *regularity* (also suggested by the repetition ἕτερα καὶ ἕτερα) of the flux of its constituent waters. The river, then, may provide an image of the balance of constituents in the world. Obviously, a rock or a mountain or a table is temporarily static, and will remain so, perhaps, for a long time; what matters for Heraclitus' theory of balanced reaction and strife is that *eventually* it should change and so help to maintain the process of world-constituents. Meanwhile the stability of a mountain, for example, is balanced by a corresponding stability elsewhere of corresponding masses of sea, and of fire or aither (the mountain being mostly earth); on which see the next section.

(7) *The world is an ever-living fire, parts of which are always extinguished to form the two other main world-masses, sea and earth. Changes between fire, sea and earth balance each other; pure, or aitherial, fire has a directive capacity*

217   Fr. 30, Clement *Strom.* v, 104, 1   κόσμον τόνδε [τὸν αὐτὸν ἁπάντων]¹ οὔτε τις θεῶν οὔτε ἀνθρώπων ἐποίησεν, ἀλλ᾽ ἦν ἀεὶ καὶ ἔστιν καὶ ἔσται· πῦρ ἀείζωον, ἁπτόμενον μέτρα καὶ ἀποσβεννύμενον μέτρα.

218   Fr. 31, Clement *Strom.* v, 104, 3   πυρὸς τροπαί· πρῶτον θάλασσα, θαλάσσης δὲ τὸ μὲν ἥμισυ γῆ τὸ δὲ ἥμισυ πρηστήρ...⟨γῆ⟩ θάλασσα διαχέεται, καὶ μετρέεται εἰς τὸν αὐτὸν λόγον ὁκοῖος πρόσθεν ἦν ἢ γενέσθαι γῆ.

219   Fr. 90, Plutarch *de E.* 8, 388D   πυρός τε ἀνταμοιβὴ τὰ πάντα καὶ πῦρ ἁπάντων ὅκωσπερ χρυσοῦ χρήματα καὶ χρημάτων χρυσός.

220   Fr. 64, Hippolytus *Ref.* ix, 10, 6   τὰ δὲ πάντα οἰακίζει κεραυνός.

217 This world-order [the same of all] did none of gods or men make, but it always was and is and shall be: an everliving fire, kindling in measures and going out in measures.

218 Fire's turnings: first sea, and of sea the half is earth, the half 'burner' [*i.e.* lightning or fire]...⟨earth⟩ is dispersed as sea, and is measured so as to form the same proportion as existed before it became earth.

219 All things are an equal exchange for fire and fire for all things, as goods are for gold and gold for goods.

220 Thunderbolt steers all things.

[1] Vlastos, *AJP* 76 (1955), 344ff., argues that 'the same of all' is original, and contrasts the real physical world of common experience with the deceptive private imaginings of men who do not follow the Logos (cf. **195** etc.). This would be possible enough if (what does not seem particularly probable) fr. 30 followed directly upon a reference to men's delusions; but neither Plutarch nor Simplicius, who also quote the first part of the fragment, gives the debated phrase. More important, Vlastos does not mention that Clement in the context of the quotation is following some Stoic source in endeavouring to explain away this fragment's inconsistency with the Stoic *ecpyrosis*-interpretation (on which see further p. 200n.), by arguing that 'this world-order' in Heraclitus is the all-inclusive, eternal system, τὸν ἐξ ἁπάσης τῆς οὐσίας ἰδίως ποιὸν κόσμον as Clement had just said, and not this particular world. Thus the interpolation is very strongly motivated; see further Kirk, *Heraclitus, the Cosmic Fragments*, 307ff.

Fire is the archetypal form of matter. The world-order as a whole can be described as a fire of which measures are being extinguished, corresponding measures being rekindled; not all of it is burning at the same time. It always has been, and always will be, in this condition (**217**). Cosmogony in the Milesian sense is therefore not to be found in Heraclitus. Fire cannot be an originative stuff in the way that water or air was for Thales or Anaximenes, and according to Aristotle and his followers it is no longer indefinite or infinite (cf. Theophrastus *ap.* Simpl. *in Phys.* 24, 1, DK 22 A 5); it is nevertheless the continuing source of the natural processes in **218**. Regarded as *a part* of the cosmos, fire is on a par with sea (presumably representing water in general, as in Xenophanes) and earth, as one of the three obvious world-masses. The pure cosmic fire was probably identified by Heraclitus with αἰθήρ (aither), the brilliant fiery stuff which fills the shining sky and surrounds the world; this aither was widely regarded both as divine and as a place of souls.[1] The idea that the soul may be fire or aither, not breath as Anaximenes had thought, must have helped to determine the choice of fire as the controlling form of matter (cf. p. 161). **220** shows that Heraclitus' fire – the purest and brightest sort, that is, as of the aitherial and divine thunderbolt –

has a directive capacity. In part this reflects the divinity assigned to aither in the popular conception; more important, perhaps, is the fact that all fire (even the lower, mundane sort), by the regularity with which it absorbs fuel and emits smoke, while maintaining a kind of stability between them, patently embodies the rule of measure in change which inheres in the world process, and of which the Logos is an expression (pp. 187f.). Thus it is naturally conceived as the very constituent of things which actively determines their structure and behaviour – which ensures not only the opposition of opposites, but also their unity through 'strife'.

[1] Cf. e.g. **221** Aristotle *de caelo* B1, 284a11   τὸν δ' οὐρανὸν καὶ τὸν ἄνω τόπον οἱ μὲν ἀρχαῖοι τοῖς θεοῖς ἀπένειμαν ὡς ὄντα μόνον ἀθάνατον... (*The ancients assigned to the gods the heaven and the upper region as being the only immortal place...*) **222** *Inscriptiones Graecae*[2] 1, 945, 6 (Athens, 5th cent. B.C.)   αἰθὴρ μὲν ψυχὰς ὑπεδέξατο, σῶμ[ατα δὲ χθών]. (*Aither received their souls, earth their bodies.*) **223** [Hippocrates] *de carnibus* 2   δοκέει δέ μοι ὁ καλέομεν θερμὸν ἀθάνατόν τε εἶναι καὶ νοέειν πάντα καὶ ὁρῆν καὶ ἀκούειν καὶ εἰδέναι πάντα, ἐόντα τε καὶ ἐσόμενα. τοῦτο οὖν τὸ πλεῖστον, ὅτε ἐταράχθη ἅπαντα, ἐξεχώρησεν εἰς τὴν ἀνωτάτω περιφορήν, καὶ αὐτό μοι δοκέει αἰθέρα τοῖς παλαιοῖς εἰρῆσθαι. (*What we call 'hot' seems to me to be immortal and to apprehend all things and to see and hear and know all things, both present and future. This, then, the most of all, when all things became confused, went out to the furthermost revolution, and seems to me to have been what was called aither by the men of old.*) Cf. also Euripides fr. 839, 9ff., fr. 941 (Nauck[2]), *Helen* 1014ff.; Aristophanes *Peace* 832f. None of these passages, of course, is as early as Heraclitus, and **223** clearly shows the influence of Anaxagoras and Diogenes of Apollonia. But the belief is described as ancient in **221** and **223** and is so widely represented in fifth-century poetry that it must have been well established and widely known by then. It is comparable with the belief in the divinity of the sun, which must be of great antiquity.

The cosmos consists, broadly, of the masses of earth (interpenetrated with secondary fire, as in volcanoes) and sea, surrounded by the bright integument of fire or aither. This fire, we may conjecture on the basis of **218**, was regarded by Heraclitus as the motive point of the cosmological processes: from its region appears to come rain, which ultimately nourishes the sea, and it is itself replenished (for fire 'consumes' moisture) by the moist evaporation ascending from the sea. Sea, as Xenophanes had shown, turns into earth, and earth at other times and places merges into water. Thus sea and earth are what cosmic or aitherial fire 'turns to' (**218**).[1] Changes between the three world-masses are going on simultaneously in such a way that the total of each always remains the same. If a quantity of earth dissolves into sea, an equivalent quantity of sea in other parts is condensing into earth, and so with changes between sea and 'burner' (fire); this seems to be the sense of **218**. The λόγος or proportion remains the same – again it is the measure and regularity of change, this time of large-scale cosmological change, that is stressed. The only surprising thing about this cosmology is its apparent avoidance of analysis into opposites and of the relation of opposites to fire–sea–earth. The probable explanation is that the opposites are invoked in the logical examination of change, but that in the consideration of large-scale changes a more empirical description can be retained, particularly as the Logos is closely related to fire. The connexion between the two types of analysis is the underlying concept of measure and proportion, but fire in itself (as Guthrie observes, *HGP* I, 457) is an extreme, not a potential mediator like the Milesians' water, Indefinite or air.

[1] Or 'is exchanged for' in the phrase of **219**. Note that **217** and **219** both tend to invalidate the Stoic ascription to Heraclitus of a periodic ἐκπύρωσις or consumption of the world by fire (which is supported, however, by Kahn, *The Art and Thought of Heraclitus*, 134ff.). The world-order *is and shall be* an ever-living fire kindling and going out in measures (simultaneously, that is); and in the trade-image of goods and gold the situation could not arise that all the goods (the manifold world) are simultaneously absorbed into gold (fire), so that there is all gold and no goods. Theophrastus, after referring to this image, added 'He makes an order and a definite time of the change of the world according to some destined necessity' (Simpl. *in Phys.* 24, 4ff., DK 22 A 5), possibly in relation to Aristotle's remark *(de caelo* A 10, 279b14, DK 22 A 10) that Empedocles and Heraclitus made the world fluctuate between its present condition and destruction. But Aristotle may have been thinking of a great-year cycle of 10,800 years apparently mentioned by Heraclitus (DK 22 A 13); this may have applied to a cycle of favoured souls, or more probably to the time taken for a single portion of fire to pass through all its stages, and in either case could have been misleading if presented incompletely. Plato (*Sophist* 242D, DK 22 A 10) clearly distinguished between Heraclitus' *simultaneous* unity and plurality of the cosmos and Empedocles' separate *periods* of Love and Strife. At the same time, they are mentioned together as both alike believing in the unity and plurality of the cosmos; and Aristotle's coupling of the two might conceivably have been motivated by the Platonic comparison, the important distinction between them being overlooked. See also Guthrie, *HGP* I, 455f. and 458, with further references, and D. Wiggins, 'Heraclitus' conceptions of flux, etc.', in *Language and Logos*, ed. Schofield and Nussbaum (Cambridge, 1982), 1ff.

(8) *Astronomy. The heavenly bodies are bowls of fire, nourished by exhalations from the sea; astronomical events, too, have their measures*

224 Diogenes Laertius ix, 9–10 (DK 22 A 1) τὸ δὲ περιέχον ὁποῖόν ἐστιν οὐ δηλοῖ· εἶναι μέντοι ἐν αὐτῷ σκάφας ἐπεστραμμένας κατὰ κοῖλον πρὸς ἡμᾶς, ἐν αἷς ἀθροιζομένας τὰς λαμπρὰς ἀναθυμιάσεις ἀποτελεῖν φλόγας, ἃς εἶναι τὰ ἄστρα. (10) λαμπροτάτην δὲ εἶναι τὴν τοῦ ἡλίου φλόγα καὶ θερμοτάτην.... ἐκλείπειν τε ἥλιον καὶ σελήνην ἄνω στρεφομένων τῶν σκαφῶν· τούς τε κατὰ μῆνα τῆς σελήνης σχηματισμοὺς γίνεσθαι στρεφομένης ἐν αὐτῇ κατὰ μικρὸν τῆς σκάφης.

225   Fr. 6, Aristotle *Meteor.* B2, 355a13   ὁ ἥλιος...νέος ἐφ' ἡμέρη ἐστίν.

226   Fr. 94, Plutarch *de exil.* 11, 604A   Ἥλιος οὐχ ὑπερβήσεται μέτρα· εἰ δὲ μή, Ἐρινύες μιν Δίκης ἐπίκουροι ἐξευρήσουσιν.

224   He does not reveal the nature of the surrounding; it contains, however, bowls turned with their hollow side towards us, in which the bright exhalations are collected and form flames, which are the heavenly bodies. Brightest and hottest is the flame of the sun.... And sun and moon are eclipsed when the bowls turn upwards; and the monthly phases of the moon occur as its bowl is gradually turned.
225   The sun...is new each day.
226   Sun will not overstep his measures; otherwise the Erinyes, ministers of Justice, will find him out.

No extant fragment clearly reveals Heraclitus' ideas on the nature of the heavenly bodies; but Theophrastus evidently gave a moderately detailed if subjective account of his views, the non-Peripatetic parts of which might be moderately accurate – although Heraclitus was probably not so concerned with exact astronomical details as the Milesians had been. Diogenes preserves the fullest version of this account, of which 224 is a part; for the rest (the stars are further from the earth than the sun, the moon nearer) see DK 22 A 1. The heavenly bodies are solid bowls filled with fire. This fire is maintained by moist exhalations or evaporations from the sea, which are somehow collected in them and burned as fuel.[1] This is presumably the way in which water changes into fire in the balanced interaction between world-masses described in 218. The idea that, since moisture is evaporated by fire, fire is physically nourished by it is a naïve and popular one. Similarly the solid celestial bowls are probably a quasi-scientific elaboration of the popular myth that the sun each night sails from west to east *in a golden bowl* round the northern stream of Okeanos (see 7). Eclipses and phases of the moon were explained by the turning away of the bowls; but no true cause (as opposed to a mere mechanism) was given, and Diogenes (IX, 11, DK22A1), presumably still following Theophrastus, stated that Heraclitus said nothing about the constitution of the bowls; indeed he seems to have been content with adaptations of popular accounts so long as his general theory of cosmological change was preserved. 225 is consonant with Theophrastus' account of the celestial bowls; the sun is 'new' every day in the sense that its fire is replenished each night with entirely fresh exhalations. Naturally, this replenishment and consumption form a regular cycle, though one which could admit slight variations. The principle of measure in natural change is illustrated also in 226, where the sun is restrained by Dike, the personification of normality and therefore regularity, from exceeding its measures – for example from coming too close to the earth or shining beyond its proper time.

[1] Theophrastus and his followers usually attributed *two* exhalations, a moist and a dry one, to Heraclitus. This is most probably a misunderstanding based upon Aristotle's own dual-exhalation explanation of meteorological (as opposed, in his case, to astronomical) events. Aristotle seems to have elaborated the theory out of Heraclitus' ideas on the importance of the exhalation from the sea and other terrestrial waters; but it appears from passages in his *Meteorologia* that Aristotle considered the dry exhalation from the earth to be his own discovery (Kirk, *Heraclitus, the Cosmic Fragments*, 273ff.). Yet, because it is kindled, he can treat Heraclitus' exhalation as fiery; see p. 204 n. 1. The explanation of night and day (as well as winter and summer) as due to the alternating prevalence of the dark and bright exhalations, ascribed to Heraclitus in Diogenes' Theophrastean account, is unlikely; Heraclitus knew as well as anyone that day is due to the sun, and declared in fr. 99 that 'if there were no sun, it would be night'.

(9) *Wisdom consists in understanding the way the world works*

227 Fr. 41, Diogenes Laertius IX, 1 ἓν τὸ σοφόν· ἐπίστασθαι γνώμην, ὅκη κυβερνᾶται πάντα διὰ πάντων.[1]

[1] ὁτέη κυβερνῆσαι P¹B, ὅτ' ἐγκυβερνῆσαι F; ὁτέη ἐκυβέρνησε Diels, DK, ὁπῆ κυβερνᾶται Gigon, Walzer, ὁτέη κυβερνᾶται Vlastos, ὅκη κυβερνᾶται scripsi. The feminine form ὁτέη is not, in fact, found; ὅκη is one obvious source of corruption. This involves taking γνώμην as internal accusative with ἐπίστασθαι, after Heidel: 'to be acquainted with true judgement how all things are steered through all'. This would be a development of Solon fr. 16 Diehl: γνωμοσύνης δ' ἀφανὲς χαλεπώτατόν ἐστι νοῆσαι / μέτρον, ὃ δὴ πάντων πείρατα μοῦνον ἔχει ('Most hard is it to apprehend the unapparent measure of judgement, which alone holds the limits of all things'). On the other hand the Stoics took γνώμην in Heraclitus' saying as direct object of ἐπίστασθαι (cf. Cleanthes *Hymn to Zeus* 34f.), as representing their own familiar idea of divine Reason; that they should place this interpretation on the dictum is not surprising, in any case. But that *Heraclitus* should have used γνώμη by itself, with no definite article and no possessor expressed, to stand for Fire or Logos (cf. 220), has seemed improbable to some. Each of the two alternative interpretations has its difficulties, but the resulting sense in each case is not very different: wisdom consists in understanding how the world works – which in any event involves understanding the divine Logos.

228 Fr. 32, Clement *Strom.* V, 115, 1 ἓν τὸ σοφὸν μοῦνον λέγεσθαι οὐκ ἐθέλει καὶ ἐθέλει Ζηνὸς ὄνομα.

227 The wise is one thing, to be acquainted with true judgement, how all things are steered through all.
228 One thing, the only truly wise, does not and does consent to be called by the name of Zeus.

227 gives the real motive of Heraclitus' philosophy: not mere curiosity about nature (although this was doubtless present too) but the belief that man's very life is indissociably bound up with his whole surroundings. Wisdom – and therefore, it might be inferred, satisfactory living – consists in understanding the Logos, the analogous structure or common element of arrangement in things, embodying the μέτρον or measure which ensures that change does not produce disconnected, chaotic plurality. Absolute understanding here can only be achieved by god (**228**; cf. also **206**), who in some respects, therefore (but not of course in anthropomorphism and in the demand for cult), resembles the Zeus of the conventional religion. God, with his synoptic view, is thus 'the only thing that is (completely) wise'. Fire (**220**) and the Logos itself (**196**) are to a large degree co-extensive with, or different aspects of, this completely wise thing.

It remains to describe Heraclitus' views about men – their soul, institutions and ideas. But for Heraclitus this subject was in no way separate from the study of the outside world; the same materials and the same laws are found in each sphere. **227** clearly depends upon this assumption, which was implicit also in **194** (fr. 1).

(10) *The soul is composed of fire; it comes from, and turns into, moisture, total absorption by which is death for it. The soul-fire is related to the world-fire.*

229 Fr. 36, Clement *Strom.* vi, 17, 2 ψυχῆσιν θάνατος ὕδωρ γενέσθαι, ὕδατι δὲ θάνατος γῆν γενέσθαι· ἐκ γῆς δὲ ὕδωρ γίνεται, ἐξ ὕδατος δὲ ψυχή.

230 Fr. 118, Stobaeus *Anth.* iii, 5, 8 αὔη ψυχὴ σοφωτάτη καὶ ἀρίστη.

231 Fr. 117, Stobaeus *Anth.* iii, 5, 7 ἀνὴρ ὁκόταν μεθυσθῇ ἄγεται ὑπὸ παιδὸς ἀνήβου, σφαλλόμενος, οὐκ ἐπαΐων ὅκη βαίνει, ὑγρὴν τὴν ψυχὴν ἔχων.

232 Fr. 45, Diogenes Laertius ix, 7 ψυχῆς πείρατα ἰὼν οὐκ ἂν ἐξεύροιο, πᾶσαν ἐπιπορευόμενος ὁδόν· οὕτω βαθὺν λόγον ἔχει.

229 For souls it is death to become water, for water it is death to become earth; from earth water comes-to-be, and from water, soul.

230 A dry soul is wisest and best.

231 A man when he is drunk is led by an unfledged boy, stumbling and not knowing where he goes, having his soul moist.

232 You would not find out the boundaries of soul, even by travelling along every path: so deep a measure does it have.

Anaximenes had probably drawn cosmological conclusions from the nature of the soul, which, following the Homeric view, he envisaged as breath. Heraclitus abandoned this idea in favour of another popular conception of the soul, that it was made of fiery aither. On this foundation he built up a rationalistic psychological theory, in which for the first time (unless Pythagoras himself went further in this direction than we suspect) the structure of the soul is related not only to that of the body, but also to that of the world as a whole.

The soul in its true and effective state is made of fire; in **229** it replaces fire in a list of what might otherwise be taken for the main interactions of the world-masses (cf. **218**). The implication is not only that soul is fiery, but also that it plays some part in the great cycle of natural change. It comes into being from moisture (and, if it is analogous to cosmic fire, is maintained, at least in part, by some kind of moisture – see p. 201), and is destroyed when it turns entirely into water.[1] The efficient soul is dry (**230**), that is, fiery. A soul that is moistened, for example by excessive drinking as in **231** (which well illustrates the still naïve character of Heraclitus' psychology), is diminished in capacity and makes its owner behave childishly, without either wits or physical strength. Thus intellect is explicitly placed in the soul. The soul, which can move to all parts of the body at need,[2] has limits that cannot be reached (**232**); probably the thought here is not so much of the problem of self-consciousness as of the soul being a representative portion of the cosmic fire – which, compared with the individual, is obviously of vast extent. Thus it could be conceived as an adulterated fragment of the surrounding cosmic fire,[3] and so as the possessor in some degree of that fire's directive power (**218**). All this, as has been indicated, is a development of what may be reasonably taken as a popular conception of the nature of aither (n. 1 on p. 199); but a simpler and more empirical indication of the fiery nature of soul was at hand, since it must have been commonly observed that warmth is associated with the living body and that the dead, soulless body is cold (so Vlastos, *op. cit.* 364f.).

[1] A Stoic reformulation of **229**, in which air is characteristically added to the three genuinely Heraclitean world-masses (to produce the four 'elements' of post-Empedoclean speculation), gives 'the death of fire is the birth of air', etc.; this appears as fr. 76 in DK, but is totally misleading for Heraclitus. He appears to have ignored air as a major cosmic constituent, despite Anaximenes; though the exhalation from the sea, by which sea turns to fire, might have been termed ἀήρ. Aristotle (*de an.* A2, 405a24, DK 22 A 15) wrote that Heraclitus made soul the same as the material principle, namely 'the exhalation from which he compounds the other things'. Aristotle himself accepted two kinds of exhalation, one being fiery, so that the 'exhalation' here represents fire; see also the first n. 1 on p. 202.

[2] According to the scholiast on Chalcidius (fr. 67a in DK) Heraclitus compared the soul to a spider which rushes to any part of its web which is damaged. The soul is described as 'firme et proportionaliter iuncta' to the body; the idea of proportion is appropriate to Heraclitus. Cf. on Anaximenes, pp. 158ff.

[3] So Macrobius S. Scip. 14, 19 (DK22A15), 'Heraclitus said that the soul is a spark of the essential substance of the stars' (scintillam stellaris essentiae) – the stars being no doubt conceived as concentrations of aither.

(11) *Waking, sleeping and death are related to the degree of fieriness in the soul. In sleep the soul is partly cut off from the world-fire, and so decreases in activity*

233 Fr. 26, Clement *Strom*. IV, 141, 2 ἄνθρωπος ἐν εὐφρόνῃ φάος ἅπτεται ἑαυτῷ [ἀποθανὼν] ἀποσβεσθεὶς ὄψεις, ζῶν δὲ ἅπτεται τεθνεῶτος εὕδων [ἀποσβεσθεὶς ὄψεις], ἐγρηγορὼς ἅπτεται εὕδοντος. (Text as in DK, after Wilamowitz.)

234 Sextus *adv. math*. VII, 129 (DK22A16) τοῦτον οὖν τὸν θεῖον λόγον καθ᾽ Ἡράκλειτον δι᾽ ἀναπνοῆς σπάσαντες νοεροὶ γινόμεθα, καὶ ἐν μὲν ὕπνοις ληθαῖοι, κατὰ δὲ ἔγερσιν πάλιν ἔμφρονες· ἐν γὰρ τοῖς ὕπνοις μυσάντων τῶν αἰσθητικῶν πόρων χωρίζεται τῆς πρὸς τὸ περιέχον συμφυΐας ὁ ἐν ἡμῖν νοῦς, μόνης τῆς κατὰ ἀναπνοὴν προσφύσεως σῳζομένης οἱονεί τινος ῥίζης, χωρισθεὶς τε ἀποβάλλει ἣν πρότερον εἶχε μνημονικὴν δύναμιν. (130) ἐν δὲ ἐγρηγόρσει πάλιν διὰ τῶν αἰσθητικῶν πόρων ὥσπερ διά τινων θυρίδων προκύψας καὶ τῷ περιέχοντι συμβαλὼν λογικὴν ἐνδύεται δύναμιν...

233 A man in the night kindles a light for himself when his vision is extinguished; living he is in contact with the dead, when asleep, and with the sleeper, when awake.

234 According to Heraclitus we become intelligent by drawing in this divine reason [*logos*] through breathing, and forgetful when asleep, but we regain our senses when we wake up again. For in sleep, when the channels of perception are shut, our mind is sundered from its kinship with the surrounding, and breathing is the only point of attachment to be preserved, like a kind of root; being sundered, our mind casts off its former power of memory. But in the waking state it again peeps out through the channels of perception as though through a kind of window, and meeting with the surrounding it puts on its power of reason...

The light kindled at night in 233 must be what a man sees in dreaming, when the actual darkness seems to be illuminated; we are also told that 'sleepers are workers' (fr. 75) and that 'what we see when asleep is sleep' (fr. 21). Naturally this light is deceptive: see the last sentence of fr. 1 (194). It is an individual, private illumination which supplants the real illumination of the Logos which is common to all (**195**). In sleep a man is 'in contact with' death (there is a typical Heraclitean word-play in **233** between the two senses of ἅπτεσθαι, 'kindle' and 'touch'); his soul-fire is burning low, is almost extinguished, and in most respects he resembles a dead man. Sleep, then, is a medial state between waking life, and death.

Sextus' information in **234** is obviously important, but must be treated with caution; he naturally imposed Sceptic epistemological interpretations upon Heraclitus, for whom his sources were, in addition, Stoic-influenced. Yet he goes on to make clearly accurate quotations of the long fr. 1 and of fr. 2 (**194** and **195**). It is to be expected from **229** that the soul-fire has some kind of physical affinity, and therefore connexion, with the cosmic fire outside. Sextus tells us that in the waking state the connexion is provided by a direct contact through the senses with the eternal fire – with the 'surrounding', in his own terminology, by which it may be inferred that the surrounding aither is meant; or rather the Logos-element in things, which may be envisaged as a direct offshoot of the pure aitherial fire. Sight is presumably of particular importance among the senses, since it receives and absorbs the fiery impressions of light. In sleep the only possible contact is provided by breathing; it may be wondered whether this draws in fire so much as moisture (though cf. n. 3 on p. 208), since 'souls come from water' (**229**) and should draw nourishment from moisture. According to Aetius IV, 3, 12, DK 22 A 15 (where there is some Stoic influence), souls are nourished by both external and internal exhalations; the internal exhalations, if they exist, would be from blood and other bodily liquids, the external ones would be those absorbed by breathing, and likewise moist. Unfortunately the extant fragments are no help here.[1] It is possible that in sleep the moist nourishment of the soul-fire, no longer balanced by the direct fiery accretions received in waking through the senses, subdues the soul and brings it into a death-like state. It may be noted that the intelligent condition consequent upon the apprehension of the Logos (see fr. 1, **194**) would mean in psychological terms that the active, fiery part of the soul has made contact with the fiery Logos-constituent of the objective situation, and has been increased by it.[2]

[1] Sextus went on to compare the resuscitation of the soul-fire by restored contact with the universal Logos (here expressed in Stoic–Sceptic terms) with the way in which embers glow again when brought near to a live fire. This image, already perhaps used by Xenophanes (p. 174), may well have been reused by Heraclitus. Conceivably the word ἀγχιβασίη, 'going near to', which Heraclitus used (fr. 122) according to the Suda, belonged to the same image.

² Chalcidius, probably after Posidonius, ascribed to Heraclitus a view quite different from Sextus', according to which the soul only has contact with the cosmic reason when free in sleep from the interruption of the senses (*in Tim.* ch. 251, DK 22 A 20). The 'cosmic reason' is Stoic, and the rest mainly Platonic, though compare Pindar fr. 131 b.

(12) *Virtuous souls do not become water on the death of the body, but survive to join, eventually, the cosmic fire*

235 Fr. 25, Clement *Strom.* IV, 49, 3   μόροι γὰρ μέζονες μέζονας μοίρας λαγχάνουσι καθ᾽ Ἡράκλειτον.

236 Fr. 63, Hippolytus *Ref.* IX, 10, 6   †ἔνθα δ᾽ ἐόντι† ἐπανίστασθαι καὶ φύλακας γίνεσθαι ἐγερτὶ ζώντων καὶ νεκρῶν.

237 (Fr. 136), Σ Bodl. ad Epictetum, p. lxxxiii Schenkl
ψυχαὶ ἀρηίφατοι καθαρώτεραι ἢ ἐνὶ νούσοις.

235 For better deaths gain better portions according to Heraclitus.
236 †To him [*or* it], being there,† they rise up and become guardians, wakefully, of living and dead.
237 Souls slain in war are purer than those [that perish] in diseases.

The 'better portions' which are won in **235** must belong to the soul alone, since after death the body is 'more fit to be cast out than dung' (fr. 96). Therefore not all souls can equally undergo the 'death' (**229**) of becoming water, that is, of ceasing to be soul, which is essentially fiery. **236** (whose first words are probably corrupt) seems to suggest that certain souls survive death and become daimons; this is manifestly developed from a famous passage in Hesiod.[1] The key to Heraclitus' belief here may be provided by **237**, which is clearly not a *verbatim* quotation but a verse summary of perhaps considerably later date than Heraclitus himself (although we know from Diog. L. IX, 16, DK 22 A 1, that Scythinus made a metrical version of Heraclitus in the late fourth or third century B.C.). It probably owes something to fr. 24, 'Gods and men honour those slain in battle', but the comparison with those who die from illness is new, and is unlikely to have been simply invented after Heraclitus. How can the souls of those dying in battle be 'purer' than the souls of those dying from disease? The answer may be that the latter are moistened and inefficient, and their possessors are in a semi-conscious and sleep-like condition. Those slain in battle, on the contrary, are cut off at their most active, when their souls are fiery from virtuous and courageous activity.[2] At the moment of death the enfeebled souls of the sick lose their last residue of fieriness and become completely watery, so that they cease to exist as souls; while the souls of those slain in battle (almost instantaneously, for the most part) are predominantly fiery. It seems plausible, then, that the latter avoid the soul-death of becoming water.[3] They leave the body and, we may guess, are reunited with the aitherial fire. Before this happens they probably remain for a time as disembodied daimons after the Hesiodic pattern. But there can be no idea of individual survival apart from this, or indeed of perpetual survival as aitherial fire; for measures of that fire are constantly being drawn into the cosmological process, and undergo the changes of **218** (see n. on p. 200 for a possible soul-period of some kind). Thus Heraclitus does not appear to be indebted here to Pythagoras.

[1] **238** Hesiod *Works and Days* 121ff. (of the golden race) αὐτὰρ ἐπεὶ δὴ τοῦτο γένος κατὰ γαῖ᾽ ἐκάλυψε / τοὶ μὲν δαίμονές εἰσι Διὸς μεγάλου διὰ βουλὰς / ἐσθλοί, ἐπιχθόνιοι φύλακες θνητῶν ἀνθρώπων. *(But when the earth hid this race, they are noble daimons through the counsels of great Zeus, guardians on earth of mortal man.)* See also *ibid.* 252ff. Another saying of Heraclitus preserved by Hippolytus is very obscure; it evidently has some connexion with the doctrine of opposites, but also suggests the deification of some souls (cf. **213**): **239** Fr. 62, Hippolytus *Ref.* IX, 10, 6 ἀθάνατοι θνητοί, θνητοὶ ἀθάνατοι, ζῶντες τὸν ἐκείνων θάνατον τὸν δὲ ἐκείνων βίον τεθνεῶτες. *(Immortal mortals, mortal immortals [or mortal immortals, immortal mortals; or immortals are mortal, mortals are immortal; or immortals are mortals, mortals are immortals, etc.], living their death and dying their life.)* It is interesting that one of the bone tablets from Olbia, of the fifth century B.C. (see p. 30), had scratched on it 'Dio(nysos)', 'Orphikoi' and βίος θάνατος βίος. Heraclitus, therefore, may be giving a special interpretation of an alternation between life and death that was broadly accepted in exotic mystery-cults of Bacchic or Orphic flavour.

[2] Though it has been ingeniously suggested by W. J. Verdenius that another saying implies that θυμός, anger or emotion, entails a fiery expenditure or *decrease* of the soul-fire (compare 'flashing eyes', 'breathing fire', etc. in our own idiom): **240** Fr. 85, Plutarch *Coriol.* 22 θυμῷ μάχεσθαι χαλεπόν· ὃ γὰρ ἂν θέλῃ ψυχῆς ὠνεῖται. *(It is hard to fight with anger; for what it wants it buys at the price of soul.)* It is difficult to control anger because the soul-fire (which presumably does the controlling) has been diminished *by* anger. This is probably correct; but in virtuous anger or emotion (as in the heroic conception of battle) this loss might be more than made up by an increase of fire.

[3] Fr. 98 describes souls as 'using smell in Hades': this, too, suggests that some souls, at least, exist after the death of the body. 'Hades' should not be taken too literally. The point of this cryptic saying is perhaps that those souls which survive death are surrounded by dry matter (in other words, fire); for it was a common view that the sense of smell operates on objects drier than the smelling organ ([Hippocrates] *de carnibus* 16; Aristotle *de sensu* 5, 444a22). It is possible, however, that the fragment is quite naïve in implication: simply that soul according to one popular view is breath, that smell is inhaled with the breath, and therefore that smell is the sense used by the soul when the other organs have perished with the body. If that is so the saying could be ironic, or an attack on the idea of the breath-soul.

(13) *The uses of conventional religion are foolish and illogical, although on occasion they accidently point to the truth*

241 Fr. 5, Aristocritus *Theosophia* 68 καθαίρονται δ' ἄλλως ⟨αἷμα⟩ αἵματι μιαινόμενοι οἷον εἴ τις εἰς πηλὸν ἐμβὰς πηλῷ ἀπονίζοιτο. μαίνεσθαι δ' ἂν δοκοίη, εἴ τις αὐτὸν ἀνθρώπων ἐπιφράσαιτο οὕτω ποιέοντα, καὶ τοῖς ἀγάλμασι δὲ τουτέοισιν εὔχονται, ὁκοῖον εἴ τις δόμοισι λεσχηνεύοιτο, οὔ τι γινώσκων θεοὺς οὐδ' ἥρωας οἵτινές εἰσι. [⟨αἷμα⟩ D. S. Robertson.]

242 Fr. 14, Clement *Protrepticus* 22 τὰ νομιζόμενα κατ' ἀνθρώπους μυστήρια ἀνιερωστὶ μυεῦνται.

243 Fr. 15, Clement *Protrepticus* 34 εἰ μὴ γὰρ Διονύσῳ πομπὴν ἐποιοῦντο καὶ ὕμνεον ᾆσμα αἰδοίοισιν, ἀναιδέστατα εἴργαστ' ἄν· ωὑτὸς δὲ Ἀίδης καὶ Διόνυσος, ὅτεῳ μαίνονται καὶ ληναΐζουσιν.

244 Fr. 93, Plutarch *de Pyth. or.* 21, 404E ὁ ἄναξ οὗ τὸ μαντεῖόν ἐστι τὸ ἐν Δελφοῖς οὔτε λέγει οὔτε κρύπτει ἀλλὰ σημαίνει.

241 They vainly purify themselves of blood-guilt by defiling themselves with blood, as though one who had stepped into mud were to wash with mud; he would seem to be mad, if any of men noticed him doing this. Further, they pray to these statues, as if one were to carry on a conversation with houses, not recognizing the true nature of gods or demi-gods.

242 The secret rites practised among men are celebrated in an unholy manner.

243 For if it were not to Dionysus that they made the procession and sung the hymn to the shameful parts, the deed would be most shameless; but Hades and Dionysus, for whom they rave and celebrate Lenaean rites, are the same.

244 The lord whose oracle is in Delphi neither speaks out nor conceals, but gives a sign.

Heraclitus followed Xenophanes in ridiculing the anthropomorphism and idolatry of the contemporary Olympian religion. Yet the last words of **241** (and also, e.g., **204** and **236**) show that he did not reject the idea of divinity altogether, or even some conventional descriptions of it. **242** implies that mysteries would not be utterly worthless if they were correctly celebrated. **243** suggests how this is so: such rituals can possess (and sometimes accidentally do so) a positive value, because they guide men indirectly to the apprehension of the Logos. The precise grounds on which Hades and Dionysus are here identified are not known, but presumably the former represents death, the latter exuberant life; and it is the implied identification of these especially significant opposites (cf. **202, 239**) that prevents the cult from being utterly shameful.[1] The method adopted by Apollo in his Delphic pronouncements is praised in **244**, because a *sign* may accord better than a misleadingly explicit *statement* with the nature of the underlying truth, that of the Logos (cf. **207-9**). Probably Heraclitus intended by this kind of parallel to justify his own oracular and obscure style.[2]

[1] A possible reference to Orphic/Dionysiac rites was suggested in n. 1 on p. 208; another of the Olbia tablets, again with an abbreviation of 'Dionysos', contains the words 'war peace truth falsehood', once more with a Heraclitean ring about them.

[2] Cf. **245** Fr. 92, Plutarch *de Pyth. or.* 6, 397A Σίβυλλα δὲ μαινομένῳ στόματι καθ' Ἡράκλειτον ἀγέλαστα καὶ ἀκαλλώπιστα καὶ ἀμύριστα φθεγγομένη χιλίων ἐτῶν ἐξικνεῖται τῇ φωνῇ διὰ τὸν θεόν. *(The Sibyl with raving mouth, according to Heraclitus, uttering things mirthless, unadorned and unperfumed, reaches over a thousand years with her voice through the god.)* It is impossible to determine precisely how much of this is a *verbatim* quotation; H. Fränkel, for example, thinks that only down to στόματι is. I would conjecture that down to φθεγγομένη (with the possible exception of καὶ ἀκαλλώπιστα καὶ ἀμύριστα) is probably by Heraclitus, the rest is a loose paraphrase by Plutarch. The saying looks like a justification of the unadorned oracular method of exegesis; but precise interpretation is impossible. Heraclitus himself certainly combined the terseness of the gnomic style with the obscurity of the related oracular style; his underlying meaning was sometimes reinforced by word-plays (e.g. ξὺν νόῳ–ξυνῷ in **250**) and etymological periphrases. A similar use is seen in Aeschylus, whose choral style, especially in the *Oresteia*, has some affinities with Heraclitus.

(14) *Ethical and political advice; self-knowledge, common sense and moderation are ideals which for Heraclitus had a special grounding in his account of the world as a whole*

246 Fr. 101, Plutarch *adv. Colotem* 20, 1118C ἐδιζησάμην ἐμεωυτόν.

247 Fr. 119, Stobaeus *Anth.* IV, 40, 23 ἦθος ἀνθρώπῳ δαίμων.

248 Fr. 43, Diogenes Laertius IX, 2 ὕβριν χρὴ σβεννύναι μᾶλλον ἢ πυρκαϊήν.

249 Fr. 44, Diogenes Laertius IX, 2 μάχεσθαι χρὴ τὸν δῆμον ὑπὲρ τοῦ νόμου ὅκωσπερ τείχεος.

250 Fr. 114, Stobaeus *Anth.* III, 1, 179 ξὺν νόῳ λέγοντας ἰσχυρίζεσθαι χρὴ τῷ ξυνῷ πάντων, ὅκωσπερ νόμῳ πόλις καὶ πολὺ ἰσχυροτέρως· τρέφονται γὰρ πάντες οἱ ἀνθρώπειοι νόμοι ὑπὸ ἑνὸς τοῦ θείου· κρατεῖ γὰρ τοσοῦτον ὁκόσον ἐθέλει καὶ ἐξαρκεῖ πᾶσι καὶ περιγίνεται.

246 I searched out myself.

247 Man's character is his daimon.

248 Insolence is more to be extinguished than a conflagration.

249 The people must fight on behalf of the law as though for the city wall.

250 Those who speak with sense must rely on what is common to all, as a city must rely on its law, and with much greater reliance. For all the laws of men are nourished by one law, the divine law; for it has as much power as it wishes and is sufficient for all and is still left over.

Heraclitus' ethical advice is gnomic in form, and for the most part similar in general content to that of his predecessors and contemporaries; sometimes it is expressed more graphically and often more savagely.[1] It stresses the importance of moderation, which itself depends upon a correct assessment of one's capacities. But this kind of advice (with which one naturally compares the Delphic maxims 'Know thyself' and 'Nothing too much') has a deeper significance in Heraclitus because of its grounding (not explicitly stated but clearly implied in **194** etc.) in his physical theories, and because of his belief that only by understanding the central pattern of things can a man become wise and fully effective; see **194, 196, 227, 234**. That is the real moral of Heraclitus' philosophy, in which ethics is for the first time formally interwoven with physics.

[1] Heraclitus was undoubtedly of a strongly critical temperament, and his abuse can hardly have made him popular with his unfortunate fellow-citizens: cf. e.g. **251** Fr. 29, Clement *Strom.* v, 59, 5 αἱρεῦνται γὰρ ἓν ἀντὶ ἁπάντων οἱ ἄριστοι, κλέος ἀέναον θνητῶν· οἱ δὲ πολλοὶ κεκόρηνται ὅκωσπερ κτήνεα. (*The best choose one thing in place of all else, 'everlasting' glory among mortals; but the majority are glutted like cattle.*) His political ideas seem to have been anti-democratic, though perhaps from empirical rather than ideological motives: 'One man is as ten thousand for me, if he is best', he said (fr. 49), and abused the Ephesians for exiling his friend Hermodorus on the ground of his exceptional ability (fr. 121). Himself of noble birth, he refused his traditional privileges (**191**).

Thus 'searching out oneself' in **246** leads, it may be inferred, to the discovery that the soul ranges outside oneself (see **232, 234**). **247** is a denial of the view, common in Homer, that the individual often cannot be held responsible for what he does. δαίμων here means simply a man's personal destiny; it is determined by his own character, over which he has some control, and not by external and often capricious powers acting perhaps through a 'genius' allotted to each individual by chance or Fate. Helen traditionally blamed Aphrodite for her own weakness, but for Heraclitus (as indeed for

Solon, who had already reacted against the moral helplessness of the heroic mentality) there was a real point in intelligent and prudent behaviour. **248** has no special overtones; it shows how conventional the practical side of Heraclitus' ethics often was, and also that he did not always think of human behaviour in terms of the *fiery* nature of the soul (for ὕβρις should involve a moistening of the soul, not its conflagration). By contrast, the insistence on respect for law in **249**, though again expressed in conventional terms, takes on a far deeper significance, and is given a profound justification, in the light of **250** (which should be compared with **194**, **195** and **196**). Human laws are nourished by the divine universal law; they accord with the Logos, the formulaic constituent of the cosmos. 'Nourished' is mainly, but not completely, metaphorical; the contact between human laws and the Logos is indirect, though not without material basis, since good laws are the product of wise men with fiery souls (**230**) who thereby understood, as Heraclitus himself does, the proper relation of men with the world.

CONCLUSION

In spite of much obscurity and uncertainty of interpretation, it does appear that Heraclitus' thought possessed a comprehensive unity which (conceivably because of the lack of information about Anaximander) seems completely new. Practically all aspects of the world are explained systematically, in relation to a central discovery – that natural changes of all kinds are regular and balanced, and that the cause of this balance is fire, the common constituent of things that was also termed their Logos. Human behaviour, as much as changes in the external world, is governed by the same Logos; the soul is made of fire, part of which (like part of the whole world-order) is extinguished. Understanding of the Logos, of the true constitution of things, is necessary if our souls are not to be excessively moistened and rendered ineffective by private folly. Heraclitus' relation of the soul to the world was more credible than that of Pythagoras, since it was more rational; it pointed a direction which was not, on the whole, followed until the atomists and, later, Aristotle. In the intervals a new tendency, towards the rejection of nature, flourished with the Eleatics, Socrates and Plato.

PHILOSOPHY IN THE WEST

The first two philosophers known to have taught in the Greek cities of South Italy were two emigrants from Ionia, Xenophanes and Pythagoras, who flourished towards the end of the sixth century B.C. But the philosophies which developed in South Italy were from the outset very different in motive and character from those of the Milesians. Whereas the Milesians were impelled by intellectual curiosity and dissatisfaction with the old mythological accounts to attempt a systematic physical explanation of physical phenomena, the impulse underlying Pythagoreanism was a religious one, and the Eleatics Parmenides and Zeno propounded metaphysical paradoxes which cut at the roots of belief in the very existence of the natural world. The only major thinker in the west to continue the Ionian tradition of enquiry into nature in anything like the Ionian spirit was the Sicilian philosopher Empedocles. Yet he was deeply influenced both by Pythagoreanism and by Parmenides' thought; and his system is marked by metaphysical and religious preoccupations, as well as by a bold (not to say bizarre) imagination which is utterly individual.

It is tempting to conjecture that these differences between western Greek and Ionian philosophy are connected with, or even functions of, differences in the social and political conditions of life in these distant parts of the Greek world. Certainly South Italy and Sicily were the home of mystery cults concerned with death and with worship of the gods of the underworld, whereas we hear little of this sort of religious activity in the cities of the Ionian seaboard. And it has been suggested that the cities of the west were inherently less stable, and the commitment of their citizens to the characteristic political values of the Greek *polis* less firmly rooted, than elsewhere in Greece (certainly warfare between Italian and Sicilian states seems to have been unusually bitter, leading to the deportation of whole populations and the razing of their homes to the ground: the destruction of Sybaris in 510 B.C. was the most celebrated of these atrocities). Whatever truth there may be in these speculations, it was in South Italy, not Ionia, that the two most distinctive elements in the modern conception of philosophy were born. Pythagoras is the archetype of the philosopher considered as the sage who teaches men the meaning of life and death, and Parmenides the founder of philosophy understood not as a first-order enquiry into the nature of things (that is now the province of the natural sciences), but as a second-order study of what it means to say that something exists or is in motion or is a plurality. It is significant that from the first these two preoccupations were associated with two very different types of mind, yet remained characteristic of one and the same calling, philosophy.

CHAPTER VII

Pythagoras of Samos

THE EVIDENCE

252 Plato *Republic* 600A–B (DK 14, 10) Ἀλλὰ δὴ εἰ μὴ δημοσίᾳ, ἰδίᾳ τισὶν ἡγεμὼν παιδείας αὐτὸς ζῶν λέγεται Ὅμηρος γενέσθαι, οἳ ἐκεῖνον ἠγάπων ἐπὶ συνουσίᾳ καὶ τοῖς ὑστέροις ὁδόν τινα παρέδοσαν βίου Ὁμηρικήν, ὥσπερ Πυθαγόρας αὐτός τε διαφερόντως ἐπὶ τούτῳ ἠγαπήθη, καὶ οἱ ὕστεροι ἔτι καὶ νῦν Πυθαγόρειον τρόπον ἐπονομάζοντες τοῦ βίου διαφανεῖς πῃ δοκοῦσιν εἶναι ἐν τοῖς ἄλλοις;

253 Plato *Republic* 530D (DK 47 B 1) Κινδυνεύει, ἔφην, ὡς πρὸς ἀστρονομίαν ὄμματα πέπηγεν, ὡς πρὸς ἐναρμόνιον φορὰν ὦτα παγῆναι, καὶ αὗται ἀλλήλων ἀδελφαί τινες αἱ ἐπιστῆμαι εἶναι, ὡς οἵ τε Πυθαγόρειοί φασι καὶ ἡμεῖς, ὦ Γλαύκων, συγχωροῦμεν.

252 Well, if he has no reputation for public services, do we hear that Homer was in his lifetime the personal guide and educator to any private individuals? Are there any who loved him for his company and handed down to later generations a Homeric way of life? Such was Pythagoras, who was himself especially loved on this account, and his followers have a distinctive reputation for a way of life they call Pythagorean to this day.

253 It transpires, I said, that as the eyes are made for astronomy, so the ears are made for harmony, and these are sister sciences, as the Pythagoreans say and we, Glaucon, agree.

252 and 253, Plato's only references to Pythagoras or the Pythagoreans by name, show us the two faces of Pythagoreanism – the religious and ethical and the philosophical and scientific. How were these two aspects of Pythagorean teaching related? Did both originate in Pythagoras' own thought? These questions will dominate our discussion here and in chapter XI, as they have dominated study of Pythagoreanism for a century or more: witness such titles as F. M. Cornford's 'Mysticism and science in the Pythagorean tradition' and Walter Burkert's *Weisheit und Wissenschaft* (this masterpiece of post-war classical scholarship is now available in a good translation timidly entitled *Lore and Science in Ancient Pythagoreanism* (Cambridge, Mass., 1972)). Controversy has dragged on because the evidence is peculiarly unsatisfactory. For that Plato is largely if indirectly to blame.

It is notorious that Plato's own metaphysics is deeply imbued with ideas we recognize (even if he did not avow) to be Pythagorean. The *Phaedo*, for example, eloquently recreates an authentically Pythagorean blend of eschatological teaching about the fate of the soul with ethical and religious prescription, and sets it in the Pythagorean context of a philosophical discussion between friends. (Burnet felicitously suggested that 'the *Phaedo* is dedicated, as it were, to the Pythagorean community at Phleious', *EGP*, 83 n. 1.) But just because Plato is reworking Pythagorean materials, the historian of Presocratic philosophy has to be cautious in using the *Phaedo* as evidence even of early fourth-century Pythagoreanism, let alone Pythagoras' own philosophy. At the same time, it would be wrong and in any case impossible not to let the *Phaedo* and other dialogues influence our picture of early Pythagoreanism.

As Plato colours our understanding of Pythagoras, so he affected or infected a vast amount of what was written and thought about him in antiquity. Particularly influential was Plato's espousal of numerological ideas in the *Timaeus*, the *Philebus*, and the famous but obscure 'unwritten doctrines' (for which see e.g. W. D. Ross, *Plato's Theory of Ideas* (Oxford, 1951), chs. IX–XVI). These ideas set a fashion within the Academy for metaphysics in a 'Pythagorean' style. It was cultivated more single-mindedly by his pupils than by Plato himself, to judge from the pseudo-Platonic *Epinomis* and from what we know of the writings of Speusippus and Xenocrates. They had no interest in distinguishing their own Platonizing developments of Pythagorean principles from the doctrine of Pythagoras himself. Their distinctive brand of Platonism probably never lacked sympathizers, and was revived from the first century B.C. onwards by such 'neo-Pythagorean' authors as Moderatus and Numenius. It is what most authors of the Christian era offer as the authentic metaphysical teaching of the Pythagoreans or indeed of Pythagoras himself (e.g. Sextus *adv. math.* x, 248–309). Only Aristotle presented substantial resistance to the Platonists' interpretation of Pythagoreanism in their own image. He was intent on showing what a primitive and confused mode of thinking Pythagoreanism represents and how different it really is from the Platonism which exploits it. We shall draw heavily on his full and comparatively objective accounts of fifth-century Pythagorean metaphysics and cosmology in ch. XI. In the present chapter we shall use the fragments of his monographs on the Pythagoreans for their information about Pythagoras himself and very early Pythagorean doctrines and traditions.

Pythagoras wrote nothing.[1] Hence a void was created which was to become filled by a huge body of literature, much of it worthless as historical evidence of Pythagoras' own teachings. It included accounts of Pythagorean physics, ethics and political theory as well as metaphysics; biographies of Pythagoras; and several dozen treatises (many still extant) whose authorship was ascribed to early Pythagoreans – although all of them (excepting some fragments of Philolaus and Archytas) are nowadays judged to be pseudonymous fictions of later origin.[2] Of this enormous mass of material only the three major *Lives* by Diogenes Laertius, Porphyry and Iamblichus will concern us here. They are scissors-and-paste compilations of the Christian era. But they contain, together with some extremely credulous matter, extracts or epitomes of authors of the period 350–250 B.C. who had access to fairly early traditions about Pythagoras and the Pythagoreans: notably, Aristoxenus, Dicaearchus and Timaeus (who is also quoted in historical writers).

[1] **254** Josephus *contra Apionem* I, 163 (DK 14, 18) αὐτοῦ (*sc.* Πυθαγόρου) μὲν οὖν οὐδὲν ὁμολογεῖται σύγγραμμα, πολλοὶ δὲ τὰ περὶ αὐτὸν ἱστορήκασι, καὶ τούτων ἐπισημότατός ἐστιν ῞Ερμιππος. (*There is no book generally agreed to be the work of Pythagoras, but many have recorded his story, and of these the most notable is Hermippus.*) This sceptical view about Pythagoras as author was accepted e.g. by Plutarch (*Alex. fort.* 328A) and Posidonius (Galen, *Plac. Hipp. et Plat.* 459 M), but rejected in Diogenes Laertius (VIII, 6): texts in DK 14, 18–19.

[2] An extensive collection of pseudonymous Pythagorean literature has been published by H. Thesleff, *The Pythagorean Texts of the Hellenistic Period* (Åbo, 1965).

EARLY REFERENCES TO PYTHAGORAS

In view of the state of the evidence, it is particularly fortunate that there survive a good number of references to Pythagoras and his followers in authors of the fifth century. These references yield a picture composed of three main elements.

(i) *Dubious reputation as a sage*

255 Heraclitus fr. 40, Diogenes Laertius IX, 1 πολυμαθίη νόον ἔχειν οὐ διδάσκει· ῾Ησίοδον γὰρ ἂν ἐδίδαξε καὶ Πυθαγόρην αὖτίς τε Ξενοφάνεά τε καὶ ῾Εκαταῖον.

216

256 Heraclitus fr. 129, Diogenes Laertius VIII, 6 Πυθαγόρης Μνησάρχου ἱστορίην ἤσκησεν ἀνθρώπων μάλιστα πάντων καὶ ἐκλεξάμενος ταῦτα ἐποιήσατο ἑαυτοῦ σοφίην, πολυμαθίην, κακοτεχνίην.[1]

257 Herodotus IV, 95 (DK 14, 2) ὡς δὲ ἐγὼ πυνθάνομαι τῶν τὸν Ἑλλήσποντον καὶ Πόντον οἰκεόντων Ἑλλήνων, τὸν Σάλμοξιν τοῦτον ἐόντα ἄνθρωπον δουλεῦσαι ἐν Σάμῳ, δουλεῦσαι δὲ Πυθαγόρη τῷ Μνησάρχου·...ἄτε δὲ κακοβίων τε ἐόντων τῶν Θρηίκων καὶ ὑπαφρονεστέρων, τὸν Σάλμοξιν τοῦτον ἐπιστάμενον δίαιτάν τε Ἰάδα καὶ ἤθεα βαθύτερα ἢ κατὰ Θρήικας, οἷα Ἕλλησί τε ὁμιλήσαντα καὶ Ἑλλήνων οὐ τῷ ἀσθενεστάτῳ σοφιστῇ Πυθαγόρη, κατασκευάσασθαι ἀνδρεῶνα, ἐς τὸν πανδοκεύοντα τῶν ἀστῶν τοὺς πρώτους καὶ εὐωχέοντα ἀναδιδάσκειν ὡς οὔτε αὐτὸς οὔτε οἱ συμπόται αὐτοῦ οὔτε οἱ ἐκ τούτων αἰεὶ γινόμενοι ἀποθανέονται, ἀλλ᾽ ἥξουσι ἐς χῶρον τοῦτον ἵνα αἰεὶ περιεόντες ἕξουσι τὰ πάντα ἀγαθά.

258 Ion fr. 4, Diogenes Laertius I, 120 Ἴων δ᾽ ὁ Χῖός φησι περὶ αὐτοῦ (*sc.* Φερεκύδου)

ὡς ὁ μὲν ἠνορέῃ τε κεκασμένος ἠδὲ καὶ αἰδοῖ
καὶ φθίμενος ψυχῇ τερπνὸν ἔχει βίοτον,
εἴπερ Πυθαγόρης ἐτύμως σοφός, ⟨ὃς⟩ περὶ πάντων
ἀνθρώπων γνώμας εἶδε καὶ ἐξέμαθεν.[2] (= **45**)

---

[1] In place of our emendation ταῦτα the MSS have ταύτας τὰς συγγραφάς, 'these writings'. But it is hard to conceive of a preceding reference to specific books; the phrase sounds un-Heraclitean and spoils the rhythm of the sentence; and it is doubtful whether ἐκλεξάμενος can mean 'make a selection of/from', as it is usually construed upon the MSS reading. Probably the words derive from a reader anxious to find evidence of Pythagoras' work as an author. Read ταῦτα as 'these qualities', looking forward to σοφίην κτλ.

[2] For the emendation of the MSS ἐτύμως ὁ σόφος see F. H. Sandbach, *PCPS* N.S. 5 (1958–9), 36.

255 The learning of many things does not teach understanding; if it did, it would have taught Hesiod and Pythagoras, and again Xenophanes and Hecataeus.

256 Pythagoras, son of Mnesarchus, practised enquiry beyond all other men and selecting these made them his own – wisdom, the learning of many things, artful knavery.

257 As I have heard from the Greeks who live on the Hellespont and the Black Sea, this Salmoxis was a man, who was a slave in Samos, the slave in fact of Pythagoras son of Mnesarchus...The Thracians lived a miserable life and were not very intelligent, whereas this Salmoxis knew the Ionian way of life and minds deeper than the Thracians', since he had associated with Greeks and among Greeks with Pythagoras, not the weakest of their wise men. So he built a hall in which he received and entertained the leading citizens, and taught them that neither he nor his guests nor any of their descendants would die, but that they would go to a place where they would survive for ever and possess every good thing.

258 Ion of Chios says about him [Pherecydes]: 'Thus did he excel in manhood and honour, and now that he is dead has a delightful existence for his soul – if indeed Pythagoras was truly wise, who above all others knew and learned the opinions of men.'

In **256** Pythagoras is ironically described as an exemplary exponent of the voracious and critical practice of enquiry characteristic of Ionian intellectuals and not despised by Heraclitus (cf. fr. 35: 'Men who love wisdom (φιλοσόφους) must be enquirers into many things.'). His enquiry consisted simply in selecting and idiosyncratically exploiting skills he found in others. The third and crowning member of the triad, artful knavery, further undermines the credit of the first two: his wisdom was bogus, his polymathy without understanding (**255**). Does **256** suggest that Pythagoras passed himself off as a practitioner of ἱστορίη, enquiry, or was at any rate popularly regarded in that light? Or did he perhaps claim to be a 'lover of wisdom' (cf. again Heraclitus fr. 35)?

Ion, who wrote in the middle of the fifth century, echoes in **258** Heraclitus' words in **256**. He seems more disposed to believe Pythagoras a true sage and to accept the doctrine of the afterlife he ascribes to him. Herodotus, too, alludes to the question of whether Pythagoras was a charlatan both by his ambiguous choice of words in **257** ('not the weakest of their wise men') and by virtue of the context of the passage (which portrays Salmoxis as a rogue).

Quite different is the fervour of Empedocles:

259 Empedocles fr. 129, Porphyrius *Life of Pythagoras* 30   τούτοις καὶ Ἐμπεδοκλῆς μαρτυρεῖ λέγων περὶ αὐτοῦ (*sc.* Πυθαγόρου)

> ἦν δέ τις ἐν κείνοισιν ἀνὴρ περιώσια εἰδώς
> παντοίων τε μάλιστα σοφῶν ⟨τ'⟩ ἐπιήρανος ἔργων
> ὃς δὴ μήκιστον πραπίδων ἐκτήσατο πλοῦτον·
> ὁππότε γὰρ πάσησιν ὀρέξαιτο πραπίδεσσιν,
> ῥεῖά γε τῶν ὄντων πάντων λεύσσεσκεν ἕκαστον
> καί τε δέκ' ἀνθρώπων καί τ' εἴκοσιν αἰώνεσσιν.[1]

---

[1] Lines 2 and 3 are transposed from the MSS order: see G. Zuntz, *Persephone*, 208.

259   Empedocles too bears witness to this, writing of him: 'And there was among them a man of surpassing knowledge, master especially of all kinds of wise works, who had acquired the utmost wealth of understanding: for whenever he reached out with all his understanding, easily he saw each of all the things that are, in ten and even twenty generations of men.'

Like Heraclitus, Empedocles gives the impression both that there was no topic on which Pythagoras would not have something to say and that his methods were not exclusively rational or scientific. 'All kinds of wise works' suggests that he was a man of practical skills and sagacity as much as a theorist. We shall see this theme differently developed in the Pythagoras miracle literature and in the evidence of his activities at Croton.

(ii)   *Teaching on reincarnation*

260   Xenophanes fr. 7, Diogenes Laertius VIII, 36   περὶ δὲ τοῦ ἄλλοτ᾽ ἄλλον γεγενῆσθαι Ξενοφάνης ἐν ἐλεγείᾳ προσμαρτυρεῖ, ἧς ἀρχή,

νῦν αὖτ᾽ ἄλλον ἔπειμι λόγον, δείξω δὲ κέλευθον.
ὃ δὲ περὶ αὐτοῦ (*sc.* Πυθαγόρου) φησιν οὕτως ἔχει·
καί ποτέ μιν στυφελιζομένου σκύλακος παριόντα
φασὶν ἐποικτῖραι καὶ τόδε φάσθαι ἔπος·
Παῦσαι μηδὲ ῥάπιζ᾽, ἐπεὶ ἦ φίλου ἀνέρος ἐστὶν
ψυχή, τὴν ἔγνων φθεγξαμένης ἀΐων.

261   Herodotus II, 123   πρῶτοι δὲ καὶ τόνδε τὸν λόγον Αἰγύπτιοί εἰσιν οἱ εἰπόντες ὡς ἀνθρώπου ψυχὴ ἀθάνατός ἐστι, τοῦ σώματος δὲ καταφθίνοντος ἐς ἄλλο ζῷον αἰεὶ γινόμενον ἐσδύεται, ἐπεὰν δὲ πάντα περιέλθῃ τὰ χερσαῖα καὶ τὰ θαλάσσια καὶ τὰ πετεινὰ αὖτις ἐς ἀνθρώπου σῶμα γινόμενον ἐσδύνειν, τὴν περιήλυσιν δὲ αὐτῇ γίνεσθαι ἐν τρισχιλίοισι ἔτεσι. τούτῳ τῷ λόγῳ εἰσὶ οἳ Ἑλλήνων ἐχρήσαντο, οἱ μὲν πρότερον οἱ δὲ ὕστερον, ὡς ἰδίῳ ἑωυτῶν ἐόντι· τῶν ἐγὼ εἰδὼς τὰ οὐνόματα οὐ γράφω.

260   On the subject of reincarnation Xenophanes bears witness in an elegy which begins: 'Now I will turn to another tale and show the way.' What he says about Pythagoras runs thus: 'Once they say that he was passing by when a puppy was being whipped, and he took pity and said: "Stop, do not beat it; for it is the soul of a friend that I recognized when I heard it giving tongue."'

261   Moreover, the Egyptians are the first to have maintained the doctrine that the soul of man is immortal, and that, when the body perishes, it enters into another animal that is being born at the time, and when it has been the complete round of the creatures of the dry land and of the sea and of the air it enters again into the body of a man at birth; and its cycle is completed in 3,000 years. There are some Greeks who have adopted this doctrine, some in former times, and some in later, as if it were their own invention; their names I know but refrain from writing down.

Neither of these texts names Pythagoras, but each probably refers to him, although Herodotus may have Empedocles in mind too (cf. **401**). Xenophanes' remark is a jest, but as Barnes remarks 'the jest has no point if its butt was not a transmigrationist' (*The Presocratic Philosophers* I, 104). Herodotus gives the Egyptians credit for the doctrine. But while belief in reincarnation may have been a foreign import into Greece (e.g. from India or Central Asia or Southern Russia), metempsychosis, unlike metamorphosis into animal forms, is not attested in Egyptian documents or art: Herodotus frequently posits Egyptian origins for thoroughly Greek ideas and practices.

260 and **261**, together with **258**, makes it likely that it was Pythagoras himself who expressed the doctrine of reincarnation in terms of ψυχή, soul. Plato's *Phaedo* shows what an elastic expression 'ψυχή' can be, meaning sometimes 'principle of life', sometimes 'mind', sometimes 'self'. Pythagoras clearly refers to the essential self, the person, while also exploiting the sense 'life-principle'. Ion in **258** (cf. **257**) suggests that Pythagoras envisaged a blessed fate for some human souls after death. How this idea was related to the notion of a cycle of transmigrations, and whether a Day of Judgement was also posited, are questions best considered in the light of further indirect evidence for Pythagorean teaching (see pp. 237f. below).

(iii) *Association with Orphic cults and writings*

262 Clement *Strom.* I, 131 (DK 36 B 2; 15) Ἴων δὲ ὁ Χῖος ἐν τοῖς Τριαγμοῖς καὶ Πυθαγόραν εἰς Ὀρφέα ἀνενεγκεῖν τινα ἱστορεῖ. Ἐπιγένης δὲ ἐν τοῖς περὶ τῆς εἰς Ὀρφέα ⟨ἀναφερομένης⟩ ποιήσεως Κέρκωπος εἶναι λέγει τοῦ Πυθαγορείου τὴν εἰς Ἅιδου κατάβασιν καὶ τὸν ἱερὸν λόγον, τὸν δὲ πέπλον καὶ τὰ φυσικὰ Βροντίνου.

263 Herodotus II, 81 (DK 14, 1) οὐ μέντοι ἔς γε τὰ ἱρὰ ἐσφέρεται εἰρίνεα οὐδὲ συγκαταθάπτεταί σφι· οὐ γὰρ ὅσιον. ὁμολογέει[1] δὲ ταῦτα τοῖσι Ὀρφικοῖσι καλεομένοισι καὶ Βακχικοῖσι, ἐοῦσι δὲ Αἰγυπτίοισι καὶ Πυθαγορείοισι. οὐδὲ γὰρ τούτων τῶν ὀργίων μετέχοντα ὅσιόν ἐστι ἐν εἰρινέοισι εἵμασι ταφθῆναι. ἔστι δὲ περὶ αὐτῶν ἱρὸς λόγος λεγόμενος.

[1] On the text of the second sentence see Burkert, *Lore*, 127–8.

262 Ion of Chios in the *Treblings* relates that Pythagoras too attributed certain writings to Orpheus. But Epigenes in his work on the poetry ascribed to Orpheus says that the *Descent into Hades* and the *Sacred Account* are the work of Cercops the Pythagorean, and the *Robe* and the *Physics* the work of Brontinus.

263 But woollen articles are never taken into temples, nor are they buried with them; that is unholy. These practices are in agreement with those that are called Orphic and Bacchic, but are in reality Egyptian and Pythagorean. For it is not holy for one who partakes in these rites to be buried in woollen clothes. There is a sacred account which is told about the matter.

There were a number of Orphic 'books' in existence in the fifth and fourth centuries B.C. (cf. Euripides *Hipp.* 953–4, Aristophanes *Frogs* 1030–2, Plato *Rep.* 364E). Our limited knowledge of these poems is presented in ch. 1 §4 above. No doubt they were ascribed to Orpheus in order to exploit the reputation of a poet who was believed to have lived before Homer. Pythagorean authorship is not much more likely, but from **262** we may infer that their contents must have had some affinity with Pythagorean teaching.[1]

263 shows that in matters of cult, too, there must have been considerable similarity between Pythagorean practice and that described as Orphic. Just what counted as 'Orphic' ritual is obscure, but we can safely say that the name of Orpheus was associated, from at least the fifth century on, with the institution of various rites (τελεταί), which included initiation into mysteries depicting the terrors of Hades, and whose object was to procure a happy state for initiates before and after death. Herodotus is presumably claiming that it was not Orpheus but Pythagoras, borrowing from Egyptian cult, who instituted such rites.

There were no doubt differences between Orphics and Pythagoreans. For example, it was on books that the Orphics rested the authority of their teaching, whereas Pythagoreans eschewed the written word. The Pythagoreans undoubtedly formed a sect (or sects), whereas the expression 'Orphics' seems usually to designate individual practitioners of techniques of purification. Nor are Orphics and Pythagoreans in general identified or closely associated with each other in the fifth- and fourth-century evidence. It is probably best to think of distinct religious movements which borrowed ideas and practices extensively from each other.

We can make some guesses about what these borrowings were. The Orphics taught that the body is a sort of prison in which the soul is preserved (σώʒεται: hence σῶμα) until it has paid its penalty (Plato

Crat. 400B–C). They claimed that by ritual means they could purify and release men and cities from their misdeeds (Plato *Rep.* 363C–E). And they neither ate nor sacrificed animals, teaching men to abstain from bloodshed (Euripides *Hipp.* 952, Aristophanes *Frogs* 1032, Plato *Laws* 782C). All these ideas and practices echo and find echoes in early Pythagoreanism. Again, the Orphic poems included elaborate cosmogonies, composed in part by exploitation of Hesiodic materials, and couched in mythical form (see pp. 21–33). Again, some of the Pythagorean *acusmata* betray signs of mythological speculation of this sort.[2]

[1] From Diog. L. VIII, 8 (ἔνια ποιήσαντα ἀνενεγκεῖν εἰς Ὀρφέα) it seems likely that what Ion meant was that poems actually written by Pythagoras himself were circulated by him under Orpheus' name. Epigenes (probably fourth century B.C.), certain that Pythagoras wrote nothing, presumably cast about for associates of the great man as suitable substitutes.

[2] For further discussion of the subject of this section: W. Burkert, 'Craft versus sect: the problem of Orphics and Pythagoreans', in *Jewish and Christian Self-definition*, ed. B. E. Meyer and E. P. Sanders, III (London, 1982), 1–22.

HISTORICAL CONTEXT OF PYTHAGORAS' LIFE AND WORK

It is time to set this sketch of Pythagoras and his teaching in a historical framework based on later evidence.

(i) *Aristoxenus on the life of Pythagoras*

264 Aristoxenus fr. 11A Wehrli, Diogenes Laertius VIII, 1 (DK 14, 8) ...Πυθαγόρας Μνησάρχου δακτυλιογλύφου, ὥς φησιν Ἕρμιππος Σάμιος, ἢ ὡς Ἀριστόξενος Τυρρηνὸς ἀπὸ μιᾶς τῶν νήσων, ἃς ἔσχον Ἀθηναῖοι Τυρρηνοὺς ἐκβαλόντες.

265 Aristoxenus fr. 14, Diogenes Laertius I, 118 (DK 14, 8) Ἀριστόξενος δ᾽ ἐν τῷ περὶ Πυθαγόρου καὶ τῶν γνωρίμων αὐτοῦ φησι νοσήσαντα αὐτὸν (*sc.* Φερεκύδην) ὑπὸ Πυθαγόρου ταφῆναι ἐν Δήλῳ.

266 Aristoxenus fr. 16, Porphyrius *Life of Pythagoras* 9 (DK 14, 8) γεγονότα δ᾽ ἐτῶν τεσσαράκοντα, φησὶν ὁ Ἀριστόξενος, καὶ ὁρῶντα τὴν τοῦ Πολυκράτους τυραννίδα συντονωτέραν οὖσαν ὥστε καλῶς ἔχειν ἐλευθέρῳ ἀνδρὶ τὴν ἐπιστατείαν τε καὶ δεσποτείαν [μὴ] ὑπομένειν, οὕτως δὴ τὴν εἰς Ἰταλίαν ἄπαρσιν ποιήσασθαι.

267 Aristoxenus fr. 18, Iamblichus *Vita Pythagorae* 248–9 (DK 14, 16) Κύλων, ἀνὴρ Κροτωνιάτης, γένει μὲν καὶ δόξῃ καὶ πλούτῳ πρωτεύων τῶν πολιτῶν, ἄλλως δὲ χαλεπός τις καὶ βίαιος καὶ θορυβώδης καὶ τυραννικὸς τὸ ἦθος, πᾶσαν προθυμίαν παρασχόμενος πρὸς τὸ κοινωνῆσαι τοῦ Πυθαγορείου βίου καὶ προσελθὼν πρὸς αὐτὸν τὸν Πυθαγόραν ἤδη πρεσβύτην ὄντα, ἀπεδοκιμάσθη διὰ τὰς προειρημένας αἰτίας. γενομένου δὲ τούτου πόλεμον ἰσχυρὸν ἤρατο καὶ αὐτὸς καὶ οἱ φίλοι αὐτοῦ πρὸς αὐτόν τε τὸν Πυθαγόραν καὶ τοὺς ἑταίρους, καὶ οὕτω σφοδρά τις ἐγένετο καὶ ἄκρατος ἡ φιλοτιμία αὐτοῦ τε τοῦ Κύλωνος καὶ τῶν μετ' ἐκείνου τεταγμένων, ὥστε διατεῖναι μέχρι τῶν τελευταίων Πυθαγορείων. ὁ μὲν οὖν Πυθαγόρας διὰ ταύτην τὴν αἰτίαν ἀπῆλθεν εἰς τὸ Μεταπόντιον, κἀκεῖ λέγεται καταστρέψαι τὸν βίον.

264 ... Pythagoras, son of Mnesarchus the gem-engraver, and a Samian (as Hermippus says) or (as Aristoxenus says) a Tyrrhenian from one of the islands which the Athenians held after expelling the Tyrrhenians.

265 But Aristoxenus in his work on *Pythagoras and his Associates* says that Pherecydes became ill and was buried by Pythagoras on Delos.

266 Aristoxenus says that at the age of forty, seeing that the tyranny of Polycrates was too intense for it to be becoming for a free man to endure such domination and despotism, he made his departure for Italy for that reason.

267 Cylon, who came from one of the old families of Croton, was its leading citizen by virtue of his birth, his reputation and his wealth; but otherwise he was a difficult man, violent, turbulent, and tyrannical in disposition. He evinced all eagerness to share in the Pythagorean way of life and approached Pythagoras himself, who was already an old man, but he was rejected as unfit on the grounds just mentioned. When that happened he and his friends declared a vigorous war on Pythagoras himself and his associates, and so excessive and intemperate became the rivalry of Cylon himself and those who ranged themselves with him that it continued until the time of the last Pythagoreans. For this reason Pythagoras went away to Metapontum, and there he is said to have died.

Aristoxenus, a pupil of Aristotle and expert on musical theory, came from Tarentum, a city in which the Pythagoreans survived more tenaciously than anywhere else in South Italy, and where Plato's Pythagorean friend Archytas was the leading political figure for many years during the first half of the fourth century (Diog. L. VIII, 79). Aristoxenus himself knew many of the 'last generation' of Pythagoreans – i.e. of those who traced a direct line of succession to the disbanded Italian communities of the fifth century (Diog. L. VIII, 46 (= **421**); Iambl. *V.P.* 251). We may presume that he drew on oral tradition preserved by them, as well as on the reminiscences of his father Spintharos (Iambl. *V.P.* 197).

His evidence in **264–7** is impossible to verify or falsify. His merit is to include in relatively restrained and credible form most of the points in Pythagoras' biography which other writers treat more elaborately. We have already commented on Pythagoras' supposed relationship with Pherecydes (pp. 52ff.). More trustworthy is his connexion with Samos and emigration during Polycrates' tyranny, which probably lasted from some point between 540 and 532 to *c.* 522. (Greater chronological precision about Pythagoras' biography is impossible: ancient guesses contradict each other, and are complicated by a detailed and implausible chronology for his alleged travels in the East, e.g. Iambl. *V.P.* 11–19.) Croton was a natural destination, as the most celebrated city in South Italy, distinguished for its run of Olympic victories. Perhaps Pythagoras knew Polycrates' physician Democedes, a member of the famous Crotoniate 'school' of doctors (Herodotus III, 125, 131–2). There is no doubt that during Pythagoras' lifetime his followers won great political influence there, and considerable unpopularity, too, although this is minimized by Aristoxenus, keen to portray Pythagoras as enemy of tyranny. Aristoxenus also attests the extension of Pythagorean influence or control to other South Italian cities in the period 500–450 (when Croton, to judge from the evidence of coinage, was indeed the dominant state in the area) and its eventual overthrow (*c.* 450; cf. Polybius II, 39, with Walbank *ad loc.*). He is clearly particularly well informed about the fate of the two survivors of the catastrophe, Archippus and Lysis:

268 Aristoxenus fr. 18 (continued), Iamblichus *Vita Pythagorae* 249–51 (DK14, 16) οἱ δὲ Κυλώνειοι λεγόμενοι διετέλουν πρὸς Πυθαγορείους στασιάζοντες καὶ πᾶσαν ἐνδεικνύμενοι δυσμένειαν. ἀλλ' ὅμως ἐπεκράτει μέχρι τινὸς ἡ τῶν Πυθαγορείων καλοκαγαθία καὶ ἡ τῶν πόλεων αὐτῶν βούλησις, ὥστε ὑπ' ἐκείνων οἰκονομεῖσθαι βούλεσθαι τὰ περὶ τὰς πολιτείας. τέλος δὲ εἰς τοσοῦτον ἐπεβούλευσαν τοῖς ἀνδράσιν, ὥστε ἐν τῇ Μίλωνος οἰκίᾳ ἐν Κρότωνι συνεδρευόντων τῶν Πυθαγορείων καὶ βουλευομένων περὶ πολιτικῶν πραγμάτων ὑφάψαντες τὴν οἰκίαν κατέκαυσαν τοὺς ἄνδρας πλὴν δυεῖν, Ἀρχίππου τε καὶ Λύσιδος. οὗτοι δὲ νεώτατοι ὄντες καὶ εὐρωστότατοι διεξεπαίσαντο ἔξω πως. γενομένου δὲ τούτου καὶ λόγον οὐδένα ποιησαμένων τῶν πόλεων περὶ τοῦ συμβάντος πάθους ἐπαύσαντο τῆς ἐπιμελείας οἱ Πυθαγόρειοι...

...τῶν δὲ δύο τῶν περισωθέντων, ἀμφοτέρων Ταραντίνων
ὄντων, ὁ μὲν Ἄρχιππος ἀνεχώρησεν εἰς Τάραντα, ὁ δὲ Λῦσις μισήσας
τὴν ὀλιγωρίαν ἀπῆρεν εἰς τὴν Ἑλλάδα καὶ ἐν Ἀχαίᾳ διέτριβε τῇ
Πελοποννησιακῇ, ἔπειτα εἰς Θήβας μετῳκίσατο σπουδῆς τινος γενομένης, οὗπερ ἐγένετο Ἐπαμεινώνδας ἀκροατὴς καὶ πατέρα τὸν Λῦσιν
ἐκάλεσεν. ὧδε καὶ τὸν βίον κατέστρεψεν. οἱ δὲ λοιποὶ τῶν Πυθαγορείων
ἀθροισθέντες εἰς τὸ Ῥήγιον ἐκεῖ διέτριβον μετ' ἀλλήλων. προϊόντος
δὲ τοῦ χρόνου καὶ τῶν πολιτευμάτων ἐπὶ τὸ χεῖρον προβαινόντων
ἀπέστησαν τῆς Ἰταλίας πλὴν Ἀρχύτου τοῦ Ταραντίνου.[1]

[1] For the text of the last two sentences (which involves a transposition of the MS
text) see K. von Fritz, *Pythagorean Politics in Southern Italy* (New York, 1940), 13,
103–4.

268 The Cylonians (as they were known) continued to intrigue
against the Pythagoreans and to show them every kind of enmity.
Nonetheless for a time the noble character of the Pythagoreans
prevailed, together with the desire of the cities themselves to have
their affairs administered by them. But eventually the Cylonians
carried their plots against them to such an extreme that, when the
Pythagoreans were holding a council in Milo's house at Croton
and deliberating on political matters, they set fire to the house and
burned all of them to death except for two, Archippus and Lysis.
Being the youngest and strongest of them, these two somehow
managed to break out. When this happened and the cities took
no account of the calamity which had occurred, the Pythagoreans
abandoned their involvement in politics... Of the two (both
Tarentines) who survived, Archippus returned to Tarentum, but
Lysis left for Greece because of his disgust about the cities'
indifference, and spent some time in Achaea in the Peloponnese,
but then moved to Thebes where some interest in him had
developed. There Epaminondas became his pupil and called him
'father'. There too he died. The rest of the Pythagoreans collected
in Rhegium and spent some time with each other there. But as time
went on and the political situation deteriorated they left Italy,
except for Archytas of Tarentum.

(ii) *Pythagoras' activities at Croton*

269 Iustinus *ap.* Pomp. Trog. *Hist. Phil. Epit.* xx, 4, 1–2 and 5–8
Post haec Crotoniensibus nulla virtutis exercitatio, nulla armorum
cura fuit. oderant enim quae infeliciter sumpserant, mutassentque
vitam luxuria, ni Pythagoras philosophus fuisset...quibus omnibus
instructus Crotonam venit populumque in luxuriam lapsum auc-
toritate sua ad usum frugalitatis revocavit. laudabat cotidie virtutem

et vitia luxuriae casumque civitatium ea peste perditarum enumerabat tantumque studium ad frugalitatem multitudinis provocavit, ut aliquos ex his luxuriatos incredibile videretur. matronarum quoque separatam a viris doctrinam et puerorum a parentibus frequenter habuit.

270 Dicaearchus fr. 33 Wehrli, Porphyrius *Life of Pythagoras* 18 (DK 14, 8*a*) ἐπεὶ δὲ τῆς Ἰταλίας ἐπέβη καὶ ἐν Κρότωνι ἐγένετο, φησὶν ὁ Δικαίαρχος, ὡς ἀνδρὸς ἀφικομένου πολυπλάνου τε καὶ περιττοῦ καὶ κατὰ τὴν ἰδίαν φύσιν ὑπὸ τῆς τύχης εὖ κεχορηγημένου, τήν τε γὰρ ἰδέαν εἶναι ἐλευθέριον καὶ μέγαν χάριν τε πλείστην καὶ κόσμον ἐπί τε τῆς φωνῆς καὶ τοῦ ἤθους καὶ ἐπὶ τῶν ἄλλων ἁπάντων ἔχειν, οὕτως διαθεῖναι τὴν Κροτωνιατῶν πόλιν, ὥστ' ἐπεὶ τὸ τῶν γερόντων ἀρχεῖον ἐψυχαγώγησεν πολλὰ καὶ καλὰ διαλεχθείς, τοῖς νέοις πάλιν ἡβητικὰς ἐποιήσατο παραινέσεις ὑπὸ τῶν ἀρχόντων κελευσθείς, μετὰ δὲ ταῦτα τοῖς παισὶν ἐκ τῶν διδασκαλείων ἀθρόοις συνελθοῦσιν, εἶτα ταῖς γυναιξί, ⟨ἐπεὶ⟩ καὶ γυναικῶν σύλλογος αὐτῷ κατεσκευάσθη.

269 After this [*sc.* the battle of Sagras] the Crotonians abandoned training in the manly virtues and practice of arms. They began to hate what they had undertaken with such ill success, and would have given themselves over to self-indulgence, if it had not been for Pythagoras the philosopher... Equipped with all this experience [*sc.* the wisdom of the East and the laws of Crete and Sparta], he came to Croton; and finding the people fallen into luxurious ways recalled them by his authority to the pursuit of simplicity. He praised virtue day by day; and recounted the evils of self-indulgence and the fate of cities ruined by that disease. He engendered in the common people such enthusiasm for simplicity of life that it seemed impossible to believe that some of them had indulged in luxury. He often taught married women apart from their husbands and boys apart from their parents. (*Tr. after J. S. Morrison*)

270 Dicaearchus says that when he set foot in Italy and arrived in Croton, he was received as a man of remarkable powers and experience after his many travels, and as someone well supplied by fortune with regard to his personal characteristics. For his manner was grand and liberal, and in his voice, his character and everything else about him there was grace and harmony in abundance. Consequently he was able so to organize the city of Croton that, when he had persuaded the governing council of elders by many noble discourses, at the behest of the government he then delivered to the young men appropriate exhortations, and

after that he addressed the boys, collected together from their schools, and then the women, since he had called a meeting of women too.

269 (derived from Timaeus, third-century historian of Sicily) and **270** (from Dicaearchus, another pupil of Aristotle) sound more like extracts from the *Life of St Pythagoras* than sober history. But they may contain kernels of truth. One plausible interpretation infers that 'Pythagoras, arriving at the height of his powers and reputation as a *sophos*, was immediately required to present his credentials to the Crotoniate equivalent of the Athenian Areopagus. He was then invited, like Epimenides at Athens, to do what he could to restore the city's morale [weak, according to Iustinus, after unexpected defeat in battle]' (J. S. Morrison, *CQ* N.s. 6 (1956), 144–5). It is hard to know what to make of the addresses Pythagoras is alleged to have given subsequently to the young men, the boys, and the women. Perhaps the story 'may...reflect an archaic, club-like organisation of society' (Burkert, *Lore*, 115). There can at any rate be little doubt that a society or *hetaireia* of young men came to form about Pythagoras:

271 Timaeus fr. 13a Jacoby, Schol. *in* Plat. *Phaedr.* 279C φησὶ γοῦν ὁ Τίμαιος ἐν τῇ θ οὕτω· 'προσιόντων δ' οὖν αὐτῷ τῶν νεωτέρων καὶ βουλομένων συνδιατρίβειν, οὐκ εὐθὺς συνεχώρησεν, ἀλλ' ἔφη δεῖν καὶ τὰς οὐσίας κοινὰς εἶναι τῶν ἐντυγχανόντων.' εἶτα μετὰ πολλὰ φησί· 'καὶ δι' ἐκείνους πρῶτον ῥηθῆναι κατὰ τὴν Ἰταλίαν ὅτι "κοινὰ τὰ τῶν φίλων".'

272 Iustinus *ap.* Pomp. Trog. *Hist. Phil. Epit.* xx, 4, 14 Sed CCC ex iuvenibus cum sodalicii iure sacramento quodam nexi separatam a ceteris civibus vitam exercerent, quasi coetum clandestinae coniurationis haberent, civitatem in se converterunt.

271 At any rate, Timaeus says in book VIII: 'So when the younger men came to him wanting to associate with him, he did not immediately agree, but said that they must also hold their property in common with whoever else might be admitted to membership.' Then after much intervening matter he says: 'And it was because of them that it was first said in Italy: "What belongs to friends is common property."'

272 Three hundred of the young men, bound to each other by oath like a brotherhood, lived segregated from the rest of the citizens, as if to form a secret band of conspirators, and brought the city [*sc.* Croton] under their control.

Polybius' reference to συνέδρια, 'club-houses', in several Italian cities (II, 39, 1) suggests that it was by means similar to those described in 272 that the Pythagoreans acquired power elsewhere. The existence of *hetaireiai* as religious bodies committed to a particular and exclusive way of life helps to account for such diverse phenomena as the form and substance of the *acusmata*, the secrecy adherents were reputed to maintain, and the evidence of distinctive Pythagorean ritual. And the slogan κοινὰ τὰ τῶν φίλων ('What belongs to friends is common property') finds an echo in the anecdotes about Pythagorean friendship told by Aristoxenus and others (Iambl. *V.P.* 233–7 = fr. 31 Wehrli; cf. e.g. *V.P.* 127, 239).

MIRACLE STORIES

273 Aristotle fr. 191 Rose, Aelian *V.H.* II, 26 (DK 14, 7) Ἀριστοτέλης λέγει ὑπὸ τῶν Κροτωνιατῶν τὸν Πυθαγόραν Ἀπόλλωνα Ὑπερβόρειον προσαγορεύεσθαι. κἀκεῖνα δὲ προσεπιλέγει ὁ τοῦ Νικομάχου ὅτι τῆς αὐτῆς ἡμέρας ποτὲ καὶ κατὰ τὴν αὐτὴν ὥραν καὶ ἐν Μεταποντίῳ ὤφθη ὑπὸ πολλῶν καὶ ἐν Κρότωνι. ⟨καὶ ἐν Ὀλυμπίᾳ δὲ ἐν⟩ τῷ ἀγῶνι ἐξανιστάμενος ἐν θεάτρῳ καὶ τῶν μηρῶν ὁ Πυθαγόρας παρέφηνε τὸν ἕτερον χρυσοῦν. λέγει δὲ ὁ αὐτὸς καὶ ὅτι ὑπὸ τοῦ Κόσα τοῦ ποταμοῦ διαβαίνων προσερρήθη· καὶ πολλούς φησιν ἀκηκοέναι τὴν πρόσρησιν ταύτην.[1]

274 Aristotle fr. 191, Apollonius *Hist. Mir.* 6 (DK 14, 7) πάλιν δ' ἐν Καυλωνίᾳ, ὥς φησιν Ἀριστοτέλης, ⟨προυσήμηνε τὴν λευκὴν ἄρκτον. καὶ ὁ αὐτὸς Ἀριστοτέλης⟩ γράφων περὶ αὐτοῦ πολλὰ μὲν καὶ ἄλλα λέγει καὶ 'τὸν ἐν Τυρρηνίᾳ, φησίν, δάκνοντα θανάσιμον ὄφιν αὐτὸς δάκνων ἀπέκτεινεν'. καὶ τὴν γινομένην δὲ στάσιν τοῖς Πυθαγορείοις προειπεῖν. διὸ καὶ εἰς Μεταπόντιον ἀπῆρεν ὑπὸ μηδενὸς θεωρηθείς.[2]

[1] For the supplement see *V.H.* IV, 17.
[2] Supplement by Diels, on the strength of comparison with Iambl. *V.P.* 142.

273 Aristotle says that Pythagoras was called by the people of Croton the Hýperborean Apollo. The son of Nicomachus [*i.e.* Aristotle] adds that Pythagoras was once seen by many people, on the same day and at the same hour, both at Metapontum and at Croton; and at Olympia, during the games, he got up in the theatre and showed that one of his thighs was golden. The same writer says that while crossing the Cosas he was hailed by the river, and that many people heard him so hailed. (*Tr. W. D. Ross*)

274 Again in Caulonia, according to Aristotle, he prophesied the advent of a white she-bear; and Aristotle also, in addition to much other information about him, says that in Tuscany he killed a deadly biting serpent by biting it himself. He also says that Pythagoras foretold to the Pythagoreans the coming political strife; by reason of which he departed to Metapontum unobserved by anyone. (*Tr. W. D. Ross*)

Pythagoras' success was clearly not that of a mere magician or occultist, appealing only to the feeble-minded and insecure. But **273–4** suggest that he did claim and perhaps possessed uncommon psychic powers. Certainly from antiquity on he has been compared with various shadowy figures of the late Archaic age, such as Aristeas, Abaris and Epimenides, of whom a number of uncanny spiritual feats were believed, including prophecies, displays of power over evil, fastings, and mysterious disappearances and reappearances. His name probably became entangled at Metapontum with that of the exotic traveller Aristeas, who is connected by Herodotus with the introduction of the cult of the Hyperborean Apollo to that city (Herodotus IV, 15; cf. Burkert, *Lore*, 147ff.). On the strength of this sort of evidence Pythagoras has sometimes been called a shaman. But it is doubtful how far a historical case can be made for an influence upon Archaic Greece from Central Asian shamanistic cultures, or to what extent an institution central to the life of politically primitive nomadic peoples could in any case illuminate the activities of a Greek sage in the more complex society of a rich and powerful city state.[1]

[1] The shamanistic interpretation is advanced by E. R. Dodds, *The Greeks and the Irrational* (Berkeley, 1951), ch. v; it could perhaps be further developed by use of the theoretical work of I. M. Lewis, *Ecstatic Religion* (Harmondsworth, 1971).

'ACUSMATA'

Various late authors preserve collections of maxims which they represent as parts of Pythagorean teaching. They were evidently transmitted by word of mouth, as the name *acusmata* ('things heard') indicates. The Pythagorean initiate was presumably required to commit them to memory, as containing a catechism of doctrine and practice. Their alternative description as *sumbola*, 'passwords' or 'tokens', suggests that they were believed to assure him of recognition of his new status by his fellows and by the gods, of this world and the next. Much of the material in our collections is plainly of considerable but indeterminate antiquity: the *acusmata* were already the subject of learned interpretation by the fourth century, e.g. by an Anaximander of Miletus known to Xenophon (cf. Suda s.v. = DK 58 c 6; Xenophon *Symp.* 3, 6). We may therefore have some confidence but no certainty in including a few of these texts in a chapter devoted to the life and thought of Pythagoras himself.

(i) *Rules of abstinence*

275 Aristotle fr. 195, Diogenes Laertius VIII, 34–5 (DK 58 c 3) φησὶ δ' Ἀριστοτέλης ἐν τῷ περὶ τῶν Πυθαγορείων παραγγέλλειν αὐτὸν ἀπέχεσθαι τῶν κυάμων ἤτοι ὅτι αἰδοίοις εἰσὶν ὅμοιοι ἢ ὅτι Ἅιδου πύλαις (ἀγόνατον γὰρ μόνον)· ἢ ὅτι φθείρει ἢ ὅτι τῇ τοῦ ὅλου φύσει ὅμοιον· ἢ ὅτι ὀλιγαρχικόν· κληροῦνται γοῦν αὐτοῖς. τὰ δὲ πεσόντα μὴ ἀναιρεῖσθαι, ὑπὲρ τοῦ ἐθίζεσθαι μὴ ἀκολάστως ἐσθίειν ἢ ὅτι ἐπὶ τελευτῇ τινος· καὶ Ἀριστοφάνης δὲ τῶν ἡρώων φησὶν εἶναι τὰ πίπτοντα, λέγων ἐν τοῖς Ἥρωσι

> μηδὲ γεύεσθ' ἅττ' ἂν ἐντὸς τῆς τραπέζης καταπέσῃ.

ἀλεκτρυόνος μὴ ἅπτεσθαι λευκοῦ, ὅτι ἱερὸς τοῦ Μηνὸς καὶ ἱκέτης· τὸ δ' ἦν τῶν ἀγαθῶν· τῷ τε Μηνὶ ἱερός· σημαίνει γὰρ τὰς ὥρας, καὶ τὸ μὲν λευκὸν τῆς τἀγαθοῦ φύσεως, τὸ δὲ μέλαν τοῦ κακοῦ. τῶν ἰχθύων μὴ ἅπτεσθαι, ὅσοι ἱεροί· μὴ γὰρ δεῖν τὰ αὐτὰ τετάχθαι θεοῖς καὶ ἀνθρώποις, ὥσπερ οὐδ' ἐλευθέροις καὶ δούλοις. (35) ἄρτον μὴ καταγνύειν, ὅτι ἐπὶ ἕνα [sc. ἄρτον] οἱ πάλαι τῶν φίλων ἐφοίτων, καθάπερ ἔτι καὶ νῦν οἱ βάρβαροι· μηδὲ διαιρεῖν, ὃς συνάγει αὐτούς· οἱ δὲ πρὸς τὴν ἐν Ἅιδου κρίσιν, οἱ δ' εἰς πόλεμον δειλίαν ποιεῖν· οἱ δέ, ἐπεὶ ἀπὸ τούτου ἄρχεται τὸ ὅλον.

275 Aristotle says, in his work *On the Pythagoreans*, that Pythagoras enjoined abstention from beans either because they are like the privy parts, or because they are like the gates of Hades (for this is the only plant that has no joints), or because they are destructive, or because they are like the nature of the universe, or because they are oligarchical (being used in the choice of rulers by lot). Things that fall from the table they were told not to pick up – to accustom them to eating with moderation, or because such things marked the death of someone. And Aristophanes, too, says that the things that fall belong to the heroes, when in his *Heroes* he urges: 'Do not taste what falls inside the table.' They must not touch a white cock, because this animal is sacred to the Month and is a suppliant, and supplication is a good thing. The cock was sacred to the Month because it announces the hours; also, white is of the nature of the good, black of the nature of the bad. They were not to touch any fish that was sacred, since it was not right that the same dishes should be served to gods and to men, any more than they should to freemen and to slaves. They must not break the loaf (because in old times friends met over a single loaf, as barbarians do to this day), nor must they divide the loaf which brings them together. Others explain the rule by reference to the judgement in Hades; others say that dividing the loaf would produce cowardice in war; others explain that it is from the loaf that the universe starts. (*Tr. W. D. Ross*)

Some of these rules (concerning beans, cocks, fish) resemble ritual precautions that were enjoined upon initiates of various Greek mystery cults as they prepared for participation in the rite. In the other cases (crumbs, loaves) Aristotle is doubtless right to compare popular beliefs and barbarian practices. In general, it seems significant that the explanations he offers are so many and diverse: probably the Pythagoreans were themselves clearer on what prohibitions they must obey than on their rationale. In particular, it is noteworthy that the rules of **275** do not enjoin the complete vegetarianism which is a natural corollary of the doctrine of transmigration (cf. Diog. L. VIII, 19 (Aristotle fr. 194), which shows that only specific parts of the body were prohibited). There is in fact no fifth-century evidence for Pythagorean renunciation of animal sacrifice, which was after all the focal point of much of the religion of the Greek *polis*, in whose affairs the Pythagoreans of South Italy played so notable a part. The conflicts in the fourth-century evidence (DK 14, 9; 58E) show that it was to become a very controversial issue within the movement.

(ii) *Other prohibitions*

276 Aristotle fr. 197, Porphyrius *Life of Pythagoras* 42 (DK 58c6) ἦν δὲ καὶ ἄλλο εἶδος τῶν Συμβόλων τοιοῦτον, 'ζυγὸν μὴ ὑπερβαίνειν', τουτέστι μὴ πλεονεκτεῖν, 'μὴ τὸ πῦρ τῇ μαχαίρᾳ σκαλεύειν', ὅπερ ἦν μὴ τὸν ἀνοιδοῦντα καὶ ὀργιζόμενον κινεῖν λόγοις παρατεθηγμένοις, 'στέφανόν τε μὴ τίλλειν', τουτέστι τοὺς νόμους μὴ λυμαίνεσθαι· στέφανοι γὰρ πόλεων οὗτοι. πάλιν δ' αὖ ἕτερα τοιαῦτα 'μὴ καρδίαν ἐσθίειν', οἷον μὴ λυπεῖν ἑαυτὸν ἀνίαις, 'μηδ' ἐπὶ χοίνικος καθέζεσθαι', οἷον μὴ ἀργὸν ζῆν, 'μηδ' ἀποδημοῦντα ἐπιστρέφεσθαι', μὴ ἔχεσθαι τοῦ βίου τούτου ἀποθνήσκοντα.

276 There was also another kind of symbol,[1] illustrated by what follows: 'Step not over a balance', i.e. be not covetous; 'Poke not the fire with a sword', i.e. do not vex with sharp words a man swollen with anger; 'Pluck not the crown', i.e. offend not against the laws, which are the crowns of cities. Or again, 'Eat not heart', i.e. vex not yourself with grief; 'Sit not on the corn ration', i.e. live not in idleness; 'When on a journey, turn not back', i.e. when you are dying, cling not to this life. (*Tr. W. D. Ross*)

¹ *Sc.* besides that illustrated in **281**.

These *acusmata* (the first half of a long list preserved by Porphyry) sound like proverbial wisdom, although they are so selected and interpreted as to point to a more thoroughgoing puritan ethic than most Greeks would have been conscious of accepting. Such proverbs were obviously never meant to be taken literally,[1] but some of the meanings given (e.g. those about the laws and about life and death) reflect distinctively Pythagorean preoccupations: the maxims thus explained may originally have had broader application.

¹ But elsewhere there are recorded *acusmata* which are to all appearances just primitive superstitions, such as 'Spit on the trimmings of your hair and your finger-nails' and 'Putting on your shoes, start with the right foot, washing your feet, with the left' (from Iambl. *Protr.* 21, DK 58 c 6).

(iii) *Number and* harmonia

277 Iamblichus *Vita Pythagorae* 82 (DK 58 c 4)   πάντα δὲ τὰ οὕτως ⟨καλούμενα⟩ ᾿Ακούσματα διήρηται εἰς τρία εἴδη· τὰ μὲν γὰρ αὐτῶν τί ἐστι σημαίνει, τὰ δὲ τί μάλιστα, τὰ δὲ τί δεῖ πράττειν ἢ μὴ πράττειν. τὰ μὲν οὖν τί ἐστι τοιαῦτα, οἷον τί ἐστιν αἱ μακάρων νῆσοι; ἥλιος καὶ σελήνη. τί ἐστι τὸ ἐν Δελφοῖς μαντεῖον; τετρακτύς· ὅπερ ἐστὶν ἡ ἁρμονία, ἐν ᾗ αἱ Σειρῆνες. τὰ δὲ τί μάλιστα, οἷον τί τὸ δικαιότατον; θύειν. τί τὸ σοφώτατον; ἀριθμός, δεύτερον δὲ ὁ τοῖς πράγμασι τὰ ὀνόματα θέμενος. τί σοφώτατον τῶν παρ᾿ ἡμῖν; ἰατρική. τί κάλλιστον; ἁρμονία. τί κράτιστον; γνώμη. τί ἄριστον; εὐδαιμονία. τί δὲ ἀληθέστατον λέγεται; ὅτι πονηροὶ οἱ ἄνθρωποι.

277 All the so-called *acusmata* fall into three divisions: some of them signify what a thing is, some of them what is the most such and such, some of them what one must do or not do. Examples of the 'what is it?' sort are: What are the isles of the blessed? Sun and moon. What is the oracle at Delphi? The *tetractys*: which is the *harmonia* in which the Sirens sing. Examples of the 'what is the most...?' sort are: What is the most just thing? To sacrifice. What is the wisest? Number; but second, the man who assigned names to things. What is the wisest of the things in our power? Medicine. What is the finest? *Harmonia*. What is the most powerful? Knowledge. What is the best? Happiness. What is the truest thing said? That men are wicked.

It is not known who was originally responsible for the threefold classification, although Aristotle is sometimes given the credit by modern scholars. We have already studied examples of Iamblichus' third class (275-6). His examples of the second, old though it is as a form of proverbial wisdom, seem much influenced by later philosophy, both in content and in terminology. More distinctively Pythagorean are the illustrations of the 'what is it?' class, and particularly important the one about the Delphic oracle.[1] The true source of wisdom about things is the *tetractys*, i.e. the first four natural numbers conceived of as connected in various relations. The meaning of the *tetractys*, like that of the oracle, needs interpretation (cf. Heraclitus **244**); and an intimation of its meaning is given: from these four numbers one can construct the harmonic ratios of the fourth, the fifth and the octave (cf. the *acusma* on beauty).[2] The capital importance of these ratios for the early Pythagoreans can be glimpsed in the reference to the Sirens, whose song Plato identifies with the music of the spheres in which the heavenly bodies move (*Rep.* 616B–617E; cf. **449** below). *Harmonia* or 'attunement' had for them a general, indeed cosmic, significance.

---

[1] Pythagoras' teaching may have owed less metaphorical debts to the Delphic Apollo. So **278** Aristoxenus fr. 15 Wehrli, Diogenes Laertius VIII, 8 (DK 14, 3) φησὶ δὲ καὶ Ἀριστόξενος τὰ πλεῖστα τῶν ἠθικῶν δογμάτων λαβεῖν τὸν Πυθαγόραν παρὰ Θεμιστοκλείας τῆς ἐν Δελφοῖς. *(And Aristoxenus says that Pythagoras got most of his ethical doctrines from the Delphic priestess Themistocleia.)* Such doctrines might have found a particularly favourable reception at Croton and Metapontum, cities devoted to the worship of Apollo the 'purifier' (see Burkert, *Lore*, 113–14; cf. also **273**).

[2] See further **279** Sextus *adv. math.* VII, 94–5 καὶ τοῦτο ἐμφαίνοντες οἱ Πυθαγορικοὶ ποτὲ μὲν εἰώθασι λέγειν τὸ 'ἀριθμῷ δέ τε πάντ' ἐπέοικεν', ὁτὲ δὲ τὸν φυσικώτατον ὀμνύναι ὅρκον οὑτωσί, 'οὐ μὰ τὸν ἀμετέρᾳ κεφαλᾷ παραδόντα τετρακτύν, / πηγὴν ἀενάου φύσεως ῥίζωμά τ' ἔχουσαν', τὸν μὲν παραδόντα λέγοντες Πυθαγόραν (τοῦτον γὰρ ἐθεοποίουν), τετρακτὺν δὲ ἀριθμόν τινα, ὃς ἐκ τεσσάρων τῶν πρώτων ἀριθμῶν συγκείμενος τὸν τελειότατον ἀπήρτιζεν, ὥσπερ τὸν δέκα· ἐν γὰρ καὶ δύο καὶ τρία καὶ τέσσαρα δέκα γίνεται. ἔστι τε οὗτος ὁ ἀριθμὸς πρώτη τετρακτύς, πηγὴ δὲ ἀενάου φύσεως λέλεκται παρόσον κατ' αὐτοὺς ὁ σύμπας κόσμος κατὰ ἁρμονίαν διοικεῖται, ἡ δὲ ἁρμονία σύστημά ἐστι τριῶν συμφωνιῶν, τῆς τε διὰ τεσσάρων καὶ τῆς διὰ πέντε καὶ τῆς διὰ πασῶν, τούτων δὲ τῶν τριῶν συμφωνιῶν αἱ ἀναλογίαι ἐν τοῖς προειρημένοις τέτταρσιν ἀριθμοῖς εὑρίσκονται, ἔν τε τῷ ἑνὶ κἂν τῷ δύο κἂν τῷ τρία κἂν τῷ τέσσαρα. *(And by way of indicating this the Pythagoreans are accustomed sometimes to say 'All things are like number', and sometimes to swear this most potent oath: 'Nay, by him that gave to us the tetractys, which contains the fount and root of ever-flowing nature'. By 'him that gave' they mean Pythagoras (for they deified him); and by 'the tetractys' a number which, being composed of the four primary numbers, produces the most perfect number, as for example ten (for one and two and three and four make ten). This number is the first tetractys, and it is called 'fount of ever-flowing nature' inasmuch as the whole universe is arranged according*

to attunement, and the attunement is a system of three concords, the fourth, the fifth and the octave, and of these three concords the proportions are found in the four numbers just mentioned – in one, two, three and four.)

Very likely this teaching about *harmonia* and the numerical ratio derived from Pythagoras himself. Certainly by the time of Plato and Aristotle the application of number theory to music was a central preoccupation of the Pythagoreans; and it is tempting to see Pythagoras as the thinker who stimulated the fascination with the idea of *harmonia* as a principle of order in things which we find in philosophers as diverse as Heraclitus (**207–9**), Empedocles (especially **348–9, 360, 373–4, 388**) and Philolaus (**424, 429**). Explicit testimony that Pythagoras *discovered* that the fundamental musical relations in the octave can be represented by simple numerical ratios is found only in late and untrustworthy authors, who may depend ultimately (but not therefore credibly) on Xenocrates (fr. 9 Heinze, Porphyry *in Ptol.* 30, 2ff.). Aristoxenus associated a physical demonstration of the idea (using bronze discs) not with Pythagoras but with an early fifth-century Pythagorean named Hippasus (fr. 90 Wehrli, Schol. Plato *Phaedr.* 108D = DK 18, 12). The conflict in the evidence on this point is probably connected with an ancient division of opinion among Pythagoreans about the origins of the scientific or theoretical element in their tradition:

280 Iamblichus *Comm. math. sc.* pp. 76, 16–77, 2 Festa δύο δ' ἐστὶ τῆς Ἰταλικῆς φιλοσοφίας εἴδη, καλουμένης δὲ Πυθαγορικῆς. δύο γὰρ ἦν γένη καὶ τῶν μεταχειριζομένων αὐτήν, οἱ μὲν ἀκουσματικοί, οἱ δὲ μαθηματικοί, τούτων δὲ οἱ μὲν ἀκουσματικοὶ ὡμολογοῦντο Πυθαγόρειοι εἶναι ὑπὸ τῶν ἑτέρων, τοὺς δὲ μαθηματικοὺς οὗτοι οὐχ ὡμολόγουν, οὔτε τὴν πραγματείαν αὐτῶν εἶναι Πυθαγόρου, ἀλλὰ Ἱππάσου. τὸν δ' Ἵππασον οἱ μὲν Κροτωνιάτην φασίν, οἱ δὲ Μεταποντῖνον. οἱ δὲ περὶ τὰ μαθήματα τῶν Πυθαγορείων τούτους τε ὁμολογοῦσιν εἶναι Πυθαγορείους, καὶ αὐτοί φασιν ἔτι μᾶλλον, καὶ ἃ λέγουσιν αὐτοὶ ἀληθῆ εἶναι.

280 There are two varieties of the Italian philosophy which is called Pythagorean. For those who practised it were also of two sorts, the *acusmatici* and the *mathematici*. Of these the *acusmatici* were accepted as Pythagoreans by the other party, but they did not allow that the *mathematici* were Pythagoreans, holding that their intellectual pursuits derived not from Pythagoras but from Hippasus. But those of the Pythagoreans who concerned themselves with the sciences agree that the *acusmatici* are Pythagoreans, and claim that they themselves are so in still greater degree, and that what they themselves state is the truth.

There follows an account (purporting to derive from the *mathematici*) of how there was from the very first a distinction among Pythagoras' followers between the older men, active in politics, who adopted Pythagoreanism simply as a way of life (no doubt making the *acusmata* their guide), and the younger men who had more leisure and aptitude for study. We learn that the *mathematici* disowned Hippasus and gave Pythagoras himself the credit for the doctrine denied to him by the *acusmatici*.

The claim that Pythagorean speculation about music and number originated with Hippasus is intrinsically implausible. But it could not have been made if Pythagoras' own name had been as firmly connected with (for example) the discovery of the harmonic ratios as with (for example) belief in reincarnation. The following account seems plausible: (1) The numerical ratios of the three concords mentioned in **279** were already known in Pythagoras' day – probably from observation of the difference in pitch between strings under the same tension whose lengths differ according to the ratios in the *tetractys*. (2) Pythagoras invested the applicability of these ratios to musical intervals with enormous general significance. (3) In consequence an early Pythagorean such as Hippasus might seek to devise new and impressive proofs of their applicability (hence the famous story of the harmonious blacksmith, e.g. Iambl. *V.P.* 115ff., Macrobius *S. Scip.* II, 1, 9ff.; on which see Burkert, *Lore*, 375–7).

The *acusma* on the Delphic oracle contains a mystic promise that the universe exhibits order and rationality. That doctrine is capable both of metaphysical and cosmological and mathematical development by the sophisticated and of childish numerological elaboration by the credulous (not two mutually exclusive classes of men). The presence of both tendencies in later Pythagorean thought is only natural if the doctrine was Pythagoras' own.

(iv) *The fate of the soul*

281 Aristotle fr. 196, Porphyrius *Life of Pythagoras* 41 (DK58c2) ἔλεγε δέ τινα καὶ μυστικῷ τρόπῳ συμβολικῶς, ἃ δὴ ἐπὶ πλέον Ἀριστοτέλης ἀνέγραψεν, οἷον ὅτι τὴν θάλατταν μὲν ἐκάλει εἶναι Κρόνου δάκρυον, τὰς δὲ ἄρκτους Ῥέας χεῖρας, τὴν δὲ Πλειάδα Μουσῶν λύραν, τοὺς δὲ πλανήτας κύνας τῆς Περσεφόνης, τὸν δ' ἐκ χαλκοῦ κρουομένου γινόμενον ἦχον φωνὴν εἶναί τινος τῶν δαιμόνων ἐναπειλημμένην τῷ χαλκῷ.

282 Aristotle fr. 196, Aelian *V.H.* IV, 17 (DK58c2) καὶ τὸν σεισμὸν ἐγενεαλόγει οὐδὲν ἄλλο εἶναι ἢ σύνοδον τῶν τεθνεώτων, ἡ δὲ Ἶρις ἔφασκεν ὡς αὐγὴ τοῦ ἡλίου ἐστὶ καὶ ὁ πολλάκις ἐμπίπτων τοῖς ὡσὶν ἦχος φωνὴ τῶν κρειττόνων.

283 Aristotle *An. Post.* 94b32–4 (DK58c1) εἰ βροντᾷ...εἰ ὡς οἱ Πυθαγόρειοί φασιν, ἀπειλῆς ἕνεκα τοῖς ἐν τῷ Ταρτάρῳ, ὅπως φοβῶνται.

281 Pythagoras said certain things in a mystical and symbolic way, and Aristotle has recorded most of these; e.g. that he called the sea the tear of Kronos, the Bears the hands of Rhea, the Pleiades the lyre of the Muses, the planets the dogs of Persephone; the ringing sound of bronze when struck was, he said, the voice of a divine being (*daimon*) imprisoned in the bronze. (*Tr. W. D. Ross*)

282 The origin of earthquakes was, Pythagoras said, nothing but a concourse of the dead; the rainbow was the gleam of the sun, and the echo that often strikes on our ears was the voice of mightier beings. (*Tr. W. D. Ross*)

283 If it thunders, then – if what the Pythagoreans say is true – this is to threaten those in Tartarus, so that they may be afraid.

By virtue of his scrupulous behaviour (**275–6**) and his superior understanding of the nature of things (cf. **277**), the Pythagorean initiate must have hoped to attain blessedness for his soul after death. **281–3** (together with the *acusma* in **277** on the isles of the blessed), like many of the practical maxims (cf. Iambl. *V.P.* 85), turn his mind to explicit thoughts of death. They constitute a systematic rationalizing interpretation of myth (including some recasting of the nomenclature of the constellations), worked out largely in the service of a distinctive eschatology. Mythical personages and events are construed as features of the natural world about us, yet of a world conceived not really as nature but as a theatre populated by unseen spiritual beings engaged in a drama of life and death. The scheme as a whole is not now fully intelligible, but its focal points are clearly the sun and moon, resting place for the blessed, and the subterranean region of hell (cf. the Eleusinian eschatology of *Hym. Dem.* 480–2). It is also reflected in a famous victory ode written for Theron of Acragas (in Sicily) by Pindar in 476 B.C.:

284 Pindar *Olympians* II, 56–77

θανόντων μὲν ἐν-
θάδ' αὐτίκ' ἀπάλαμνοι φρένες
ποινὰς ἔτεισαν – τὰ δ' ἐν τᾷδε Διὸς ἀρχᾷ
ἀλιτρὰ κατὰ γᾶς δικάζει τις ἐχθρᾷ
λόγον φράσαις ἀνάγκᾳ·
ἴσαις δὲ νύκτεσσιν αἰεί,
ἴσαις δ' ἀμέραις ἅλιον ἔχοντες, ἀπονέστερον

ἐσλοὶ δέκονται βίοτον, οὐ χθόνα τα-
ράσσοντες ἐν χερὸς ἀκμᾷ
οὐδὲ πόντιον ὕδωρ
κεινὰν παρὰ δίαιταν, ἀλλὰ παρὰ μὲν τιμίοις
θεῶν οἵτινες ἔχαιρον εὐορκίαις
ἄδακρυν νέμονται
αἰῶνα, τοὶ δ᾽ ἀπροσόρατον ὀκχέοντι πόνον.
ὅσοι δ᾽ ἐτόλμασαν ἐστρὶς
ἑκατέρωθι μείναντες ἀπὸ πάμπαν ἀδίκων ἔχειν
ψυχάν, ἔτειλαν Διὸς ὁδὸν παρὰ Κρόνου τύρσιν· ἔνθα μακάρων
νᾶσον ὠκεανίδες
αὖραι περιπνέοισιν· ἄνθεμα δὲ χρυσοῦ φλέγει,
τὰ μὲν χερσόθεν ἀπ᾽ ἀγλαῶν δενδρέων,
ὕδωρ δ᾽ ἄλλα φέρβει,
ὅρμοισι τῶν χέρας ἀναπλέκοντι καὶ στεφάνους
βουλαῖς ἐν ὀρθαῖσι ῾Ραδαμάνθυος,
ὃν πατὴρ ἔχει μέγας ἑτοῖμον αὐτῷ πάρεδρον,
πόσις ὁ πάντων ῾Ρέας
ὑπέρτατον ἐχοίσας θρόνον.

284 Those of the dead that are lawless in mind pay the penalty straightway here [*sc.* on earth] – but the sins committed in this realm of Zeus are judged below the earth by one who pronounces sentence with hateful necessity. The good, upon whom the sun shines for evermore, for equal nights and equal days, receive a life of lightened toil, not vexing the soil with the strength of their hand, no, not the water of the sea, thanks to the ways of that place; but in the presence of the honoured gods, all who rejoiced in keeping their oaths share a life that knows no tears, while the others endure labour that none can look upon. And those who, while dwelling in either world, have thrice been courageous in keeping their souls pure from all deeds of wrong, they traverse the highway of Zeus to the tower of Kronos, where the ocean-breezes blow around the Island of the Blest; and flowers of gold are blazing, some on the shore from radiant trees, while others the water fosters; and with chaplets they entwine their hands, and with crowns, according to the righteous councils of Rhadamanthys – for he sits ready with advice beside the great Father, the lord of Rhea with her throne exalted over all.

This poem, like **410** below, was probably written for a patron with distinctively Pythagorean beliefs. Although much must remain obscure about the relationships between judgement and punishment and reincarnation, **284**, taken together with **281-3**, suggests that Pythagoras taught an eschatology according to which: (1) the soul is subject after death to a divine judgement; (2) there follows punishment in the underworld for the wicked (perhaps with hope of eventual release: **410**), but (3) a better fate for the good, who – if they remain free from wickedness in the next world and in a further reincarnation in this – may at last reach the isles of the blessed (cf. Plato *Gorg.* 523A–B).

CONCLUSION

285 Porphyrius *Life of Pythagoras* 19 (DK 14, 8*a*) ἃ μὲν οὖν ἔλεγε τοῖς συνοῦσιν, οὐδὲ εἷς ἔχει φράσαι βεβαίως· καὶ γὰρ οὐδ' ἡ τυχοῦσα ἦν παρ' αὐτοῖς σιωπή. μάλιστα μέντοι γνώριμα παρὰ πᾶσιν ἐγένετο πρῶτον μὲν ὡς ἀθάνατον εἶναί φησι τὴν ψυχήν, εἶτα μεταβάλλουσαν εἰς ἄλλα γένη ζῴων, πρὸς δὲ τούτοις ὅτι κατὰ περιόδους τινὰς τὰ γενόμενά ποτε πάλιν γίνεται, νέον δ' οὐδὲν ἁπλῶς ἔστι καὶ ὅτι πάντα τὰ γινόμενα ἔμψυχα ὁμογενῆ δεῖ νομίζειν. φαίνεται γὰρ εἰς τὴν Ἑλλάδα τὰ δόγματα πρῶτος κομίσαι ταῦτα Πυθαγόρας.

285 What he said to his associates, nobody can say for certain; for silence with them was of no ordinary kind. Nonetheless the following became universally known: first, that he maintains that the soul is immortal; next, that it changes into other kinds of living things; also that events recur in certain cycles, and that nothing is ever absolutely new; and finally, that all living things should be regarded as akin. Pythagoras seems to have been the first to bring these beliefs into Greece.

285 (probably from Dicaearchus) sums up a picture of Pythagoras' teaching which our study of the sources has confirmed, although it leaves out one or two points on which we have laid some stress (notably ideas about number and *harmonia*), and includes some not so far mentioned, such as Pythagorean silence (cf. Aristotle fr. 192, DK 14, 7; Diog. L. VIII, 15) and belief in cyclical recurrence (cf. Eudemus *ap.* Simpl. *in Phys.* 732, 30, DK 58 B 34). Like the other sources it vouchsafes no hint of any reason Pythagoras may have offered for any of his doctrines. Like them it gives little ground for recognizing anything determinately philosophical or scientific in the content of his thought. Pythagoras, we must conclude, was a philosopher only to the extent that he was a sage (cf. p. 213 above). His contribution to Greek thought more broadly considered, however, was original, seductive and durable.

CHAPTER VIII

Parmenides of Elea

DATE AND LIFE

286 Plato *Parmenides* 127A (DK 29 A 11)   ἔφη δὲ δὴ ὁ ᾿Αντιφῶν λέγειν τὸν Πυθόδωρον ὅτι ἀφίκοιντό ποτε εἰς Παναθήναια τὰ μεγάλα Ζήνων τε καὶ Παρμενίδης. τὸν μὲν οὖν Παρμενίδην εὖ μάλα δὴ πρεσβύτην εἶναι, σφόδρα πολιόν, καλὸν δὲ κἀγαθὸν τὴν ὄψιν, περὶ ἔτη μάλιστα πέντε καὶ ἑξήκοντα· Ζήνωνα δὲ ἐγγὺς ἐτῶν τετταράκοντα τότε εἶναι, εὐμήκη δὲ καὶ χαρίεντα ἰδεῖν· καὶ λέγεσθαι αὐτὸν παιδικὰ τοῦ Παρμενίδου γεγονέναι. καταλύειν δὲ αὐτοὺς ἔφη παρὰ τῷ Πυθοδώρῳ ἐκτὸς τείχους ἐν Κεραμεικῷ· οἳ δὴ καὶ ἀφικέσθαι τόν τε Σωκράτη καὶ ἄλλους τινὰς μετ᾿ αὐτοῦ πολλούς, ἐπιθυμοῦντας ἀκοῦσαι τῶν τοῦ Ζήνωνος γραμμάτων – τότε γὰρ αὐτὰ πρῶτον ὑπ᾿ ἐκείνων κομισθῆναι – Σωκράτη δὲ εἶναι τότε σφόδρα νέον.

287 Diogenes Laertius IX, 21–3 (DK 28 A 1)   Ξενοφάνους δὲ διήκουσε Παρμενίδης Πύρητος ᾿Ελεάτης (τοῦτον[1] Θεόφραστος ἐν τῇ ᾿Επιτομῇ ᾿Αναξιμάνδρου φησὶν ἀκοῦσαι). ὅμως δ᾿ οὖν ἀκούσας καὶ Ξενοφάνους οὐκ ἠκολούθησεν αὐτῷ. ἐκοινώνησε δὲ καὶ ᾿Αμεινίᾳ Διοχαίτα τῷ Πυθαγορικῷ, ὡς ἔφη Σωτίων, ἀνδρὶ πένητι μέν, καλῷ δὲ καὶ ἀγαθῷ. ᾧ καὶ μᾶλλον ἠκολούθησε καὶ ἀποθανόντος ἡρῷον ἱδρύσατο γένους τε ὑπάρχων λαμπροῦ καὶ πλούτου, καὶ ὑπ᾿ ᾿Αμεινίου, ἀλλ᾿ οὐχ ὑπὸ Ξενοφάνους εἰς ἡσυχίαν προετράπη... ἤκμαζε δὲ κατὰ τὴν ἐνάτην καὶ ἑξηκοστὴν ὀλυμπιάδα...λέγεται δὲ καὶ νόμους θεῖναι τοῖς πολίταις, ὥς φησι Σπεύσιππος ἐν τῷ Περὶ φιλοσόφων.

286 According to Antiphon's account, Pythodorus said that Parmenides and Zeno once came to Athens for the Great Panathenaea. Parmenides was well advanced in years – about sixty-five – and very grey, but a fine-looking man. Zeno was then nearly forty, and tall and handsome; he was said to have been Parmenides' favourite. They were staying at Pythodorus' house outside the city-wall in the Ceramicus. Thither went Socrates, and several others with him, in the hope of hearing Zeno's treatise; for this was the first time Parmenides and Zeno had brought it to Athens. Socrates was still very young at the time.

287   Parmenides of Elea, son of Pyres, was a pupil of Xenophanes (and he, according to Theophrastus in his *Epitome*, of Anaximander). But though a pupil of Xenophanes, he did not follow him. He associated also, as Sotion recorded, with the Pythagorean Ameinias, son of Diochaitas, a poor but noble man, whom he preferred to follow. When Ameinias died Parmenides, who came of a distinguished family and was rich, built a shrine to him. It was by Ameinias rather than Xenophanes that he was converted to the contemplative life...He flourished in the sixty-ninth Olympiad [*sc.* 500 B.C.]...He is said also to have legislated for the citizens of Elea, as Speusippus records in his work *On the Philosophers*.

¹ Theophrastus' claim must have related to Xenophanes, but Diogenes writes as though Parmenides is in question.

Whether or not Parmenides and Zeno ever visited Athens and met there the young Socrates, Plato need not have been so precise about their respective ages. The fact that he gives these details strongly suggests that he is writing with chronological accuracy. Socrates was just over seventy when he was put to death in 399 B.C., which means that he was born in 470/469. If we assume that the words σφόδρα νέον, 'very young', mean that he was about 20, then the meeting might have taken place in 450 B.C. This places Parmenides' birth in about 515 B.C. and Zeno's in about 490 B.C. It is of course true that the date given by Diogenes, which he probably derived from Apollodorus, does not nearly square with this; but, as Burnet points out (*EGP*, 170), 'the date given by Apollodorus depends solely on that of the foundation of Elea (540 B.C.), which he had adopted as the *floruit* of Xenophanes. Parmenides is born in that year, just as Zeno is born in the year Parmenides "flourished".' Unsatisfactory as a late Platonic dialogue may be as evidence for chronology, it can hardly be doubted that it is more reliable than this.

The other items of information in **287** probably derive from early traditions, which may well be true, particularly Sotion's circumstantial tale. If it was a Pythagorean who converted Parmenides to philosophy, there is little sign that any preoccupation with Pythagorean ideas continued into his mature thought, except perhaps in his description of birth as something 'hateful' (**306**) and in the teaching about the fate of the soul which Simplicius briefly and allusively records in connexion with fr. 13 (*in Phys.* 39, 18). The notion that he was taught by Xenophanes was taken over by Theophrastus from Aristotle, who may in turn have derived it from a remark, perhaps not entirely serious, in Plato's *Sophist* (see **163**, with the discussion on pp. 165ff.). Certainly there are echoes, not merely verbal, of Xenophanes' theology (**170** and **171**) and epistemology (**186–9**) in Parmenides. And Parmenides' decision to write his philosophy in hexameter verse may well have been prompted partly by the example of Xenophanes, who spent the latter part of his long career in Sicily and South Italy.

PARMENIDES' HEXAMETER POEM

Parmenides is credited with a single 'treatise' (Diog. L. 1, 16, DK 28 A 13). Substantial fragments of this work, a hexameter poem, survive, thanks largely to Sextus Empiricus (who preserved the proem) and Simplicius (who transcribed further extracts into his commentaries on Aristotle's *de caelo* and *Physics* 'because of the scarceness of the treatise'). Ancients and moderns alike are agreed upon a low estimation of Parmenides' gifts as a writer. He has little facility in diction, and the struggle to force novel, difficult and highly abstract philosophical ideas into metrical form frequently results in ineradicable obscurity, especially syntactic obscurity. On the other hand, in the less argumentative passages of the poem he achieves a kind of clumsy grandeur.

After the proem, the poem falls into two parts. The first expounds 'the tremorless heart of well-rounded Truth' (**288**, 29). Its argument is radical and powerful. Parmenides claims that in any enquiry there are two and only two logically coherent possibilities, which are exclusive – that the subject of the enquiry exists or that it does not exist. On epistemological grounds he rules out the second alternative as unintelligible. He then turns to abuse of ordinary mortals for showing by their beliefs that they never make the choice between the two ways 'is' and 'is not', but follow *both* without discrimination. In the final section of this first part he explores the one secure path, 'is', and proves in an astonishing deductive *tour de force* that if something exists, it cannot come to be or perish, change or move, nor be subject to any imperfection. Parmenides' arguments and his paradoxical conclusions had an enormous influence on later Greek philosophy; his method and his impact alike have rightly been compared to those of Descartes' *cogito*.

Parmenides' metaphysics and epistemology leave no room for cosmologies such as his Ionian predecessors had constructed nor indeed for any belief at all in the world our senses disclose to us. Nonetheless in the second (and much more scantily preserved) part of the poem he gives an account of 'the opinions of mortals, in which there is no true conviction'. The status and motive of this account are obscure.

THE PROEM

288   Fr. 1 (Sextus *adv. math.* VII, 3 (lines 1–30); Simplicius *de caelo* 557, 25ff. (lines 28–32))

ἵπποι ταί με φέρουσιν ὅσον τ' ἐπὶ θυμὸς ἱκάνοι
πέμπον, ἐπεί μ' ἐς ὁδὸν βῆσαν πολύφημον ἄγουσαι
δαίμονος, ἣ κατὰ πάντ' ἄστη¹ φέρει εἰδότα φῶτα·
τῇ φερόμην· τῇ γάρ με πολύφραστοι φέρον ἵπποι
5   ἅρμα τιταίνουσαι, κοῦραι δ' ὁδὸν ἡγεμόνευον.
ἄξων δ' ἐν χνοίῃσιν ἵει σύριγγος ἀυτὴν
αἰθόμενος (δοιοῖς γὰρ ἐπείγετο δινωτοῖσιν
κύκλοις ἀμφοτέρωθεν), ὅτε σπερχοίατο πέμπειν
Ἡλιάδες κοῦραι, προλιποῦσαι δώματα Νυκτός
10   εἰς φάος, ὠσάμεναι κράτων ἄπο χερσὶ καλύπτρας.
ἔνθα πύλαι Νυκτός τε καὶ Ἤματός εἰσι κελεύθων,
καί σφας ὑπέρθυρον ἀμφὶς ἔχει καὶ λάινος οὐδός·
αὐταὶ δ' αἰθέριαι πλῆνται μεγάλοισι θυρέτροις·
τῶν δὲ Δίκη πολύποινος ἔχει κληῖδας ἀμοιβούς.
15   τὴν δὴ παρφάμεναι κοῦραι μαλακοῖσι λόγοισιν
πεῖσαν ἐπιφραδέως, ὥς σφιν βαλανωτὸν ὀχῆα
ἀπτερέως ὤσειε πυλέων ἄπο· ταὶ δὲ θυρέτρων
χάσμ' ἀχανὲς ποίησαν ἀναπτάμεναι πολυχάλκους
ἄξονας ἐν σύριγξιν ἀμοιβαδὸν εἰλίξασαι
20   γόμφοις καὶ περόνῃσιν ἀρηρότε· τῇ ῥα δι' αὐτέων
ἰθὺς ἔχον κοῦραι κατ' ἀμαξιτὸν ἅρμα καὶ ἵππους.
καί με θεὰ πρόφρων ὑπεδέξατο, χεῖρα δὲ χειρὶ
δεξιτερὴν ἕλεν, ὧδε δ' ἔπος φάτο καί με προσηύδα·
ὦ κοῦρ' ἀθανάτοισι συνάορος ἡνιόχοισιν,
25   ἵπποις ταί σε φέρουσιν ἱκάνων ἡμέτερον δῶ,
χαῖρ', ἐπεὶ οὔτι σε μοῖρα κακὴ προὔπεμπε νέεσθαι
τήνδ' ὁδόν (ἦ γὰρ ἀπ' ἀνθρώπων ἐκτὸς πάτου ἐστίν),
ἀλλὰ θέμις τε δίκη τε. χρεὼ δέ σε πάντα πυθέσθαι
ἠμὲν Ἀληθείης εὐκυκλέος² ἀτρεμὲς ἦτορ
30   ἠδὲ βροτῶν δόξας, ταῖς οὐκ ἔνι πίστις ἀληθής.
ἀλλ' ἔμπης καὶ ταῦτα μαθήσεαι, ὡς τὰ δοκοῦντα
χρῆν δοκίμως εἶναι διὰ παντὸς πάντα περῶντα.³

¹ For the conjectural reading ἄστη see A. H. Coxon, *CQ* N.s. 18 (1968), 69; A. P. D. Mourelatos, *The Route of Parmenides* (New Haven, Conn., 1970), 22 n. 31.

² εὐκυκλέος Simplicius, defended by Diels, *Parmenides Lehrgedicht* (Berlin, 1897),
54–7; εὐπειθέος Sextus (*lectio facilior*) has some contemporary advocates, e.g.
Mourelatos, *Route*, 154–7.
³ περῶντα Simpl. A; περ ὄντα DEF.

288 The mares that carry me as far as my heart ever aspires sped
me on, when they had brought and set me on the far-famed road
of the god, which bears the man who knows over all cities. On that
road was I borne, for that way the wise horses bore me, straining
at the chariot, and maidens led the way. And the axle in the naves
gave out the whistle of a pipe, blazing, for it was pressed hard on
either side by the two well-turned wheels as the daughters of the
Sun made haste to escort me, having left the halls of Night for the
light, and having thrust the veils from their heads with their hands.

There are the gates of the paths of Night and Day, and a lintel
and a stone threshold enclose them. They themselves, high in the
air, are blocked with great doors, and avenging Justice holds the
alternate bolts. Her the maidens beguiled with gentle words and
cunningly persuaded to push back swiftly from the gates the bolted
bar. And the gates created a yawning gap in the door frame when
they flew open, swinging in turn in their sockets the bronze-bound
pivots made fast with dowels and rivets. Straight through them,
on the broad way, did the maidens keep the horses and the chariot.

And the goddess greeted me kindly, and took my right hand in
hers, and addressed me with these words: 'Young man, you who
come to my house in the company of immortal charioteers with
the mares which bear you, greetings. No ill fate has sent you to
travel this road – far indeed does it lie from the steps of men – but
right and justice. It is proper that you should learn all things, both
the unshaken heart of well-rounded truth, and the opinions of
mortals, in which there is no true reliance. But nonetheless you
shall learn these things too, how what is believed would have to
be assuredly, pervading all things throughout.'

Parmenides' chief purpose in these lines is to lay claim to knowledge
of a truth not attained by the ordinary run of mortals. The claim
is dramatically expressed by means of motifs deriving largely from
Homer and Hesiod, in matching diction and metre. It is sometimes
suggested that Parmenides' journey to the goddess recalls the magical
journeys of shamans. But as was observed above (p. 229) the
evidence for a shamanistic tradition in early Greece is doubtful.
Sextus, followed by many modern scholars, took the journey to be
an allegory of enlightenment, a translation from the ignorance of
Night to the knowledge of Light. But Parmenides already begins his

journey in a blaze of light, as befits one who 'knows'. The point of the narration is suggested rather by the obstacle that has to be passed and by the destination, the two things (apart from description of the chariot and its movement) upon which the poet dwells. Parmenides seeks to leave the familiar world of ordinary experience where night and day alternate, an alternation governed – as Anaximander would have agreed (110) – by law or 'justice'. He makes instead for a path of thought ('a highway') which leads to a transcendent comprehension both of changeless truth and of mortal opinion. No less important is his message about the obstacle to achievement of this goal: the barrier to escape from mortal opinion is formidable, but it yields to 'gentle argument'.

The motifs of the gates of Day and Night and of divine revelation, modelled on materials in Hesiod's *Theogony*, are well chosen to convey both the immense gulf which in Parmenides' view separates rational enquiry from common human understanding and the unexpectedness of what his own reason has disclosed to him (cf. for both these points Heraclitus, e.g. **205, 206, 210**). And religious revelation suggests both the high seriousness of philosophy and an appeal to authority – not, however, an authority beyond dispute: 'Judge by reason my strife-encompassed refutation' says the goddess later (**294**).

289 Fr. 5, Proclus *in Parm.* 1, p. 708, 16 Cousin

> ...ξυνὸν δέ μοί ἐστιν
> ὅπποθεν ἄρξωμαι· τόθι γὰρ πάλιν ἵξομαι αὖθις.

289 It is a common point from which I start; for there again and again I shall return.

289 fits neatly after **288** and immediately before **291**, at any rate if its point is that all the proofs of **296–9** take the choice specified in **291** as their common foundation (cf. also **294**).[1]

[1] With **289** may be compared **290** Heraclitus fr. 103, Porphyrius *in Iliadem* xiv, 200 ξυνὸν ἀρχὴ καὶ πέρας ἐπὶ κύκλου. *(In a circle beginning and end are common.)* But despite his talk of 'well-rounded truth' Parmenides need not be implying here that his own thought is circular.

TRUTH

(i) *The choice*

291 Fr. 2, Proclus *in Tim.* 1, 345, 18; Simplicius *in Phys.* 116, 28 (lines 3–8)

εἰ δ' ἄγ' ἐγὼν ἐρέω, κόμισαι δὲ σὺ μῦθον ἀκούσας,
αἵπερ ὁδοὶ μοῦναι διζήσιός εἰσι νοῆσαι·
ἡ μὲν ὅπως ἔστιν τε καὶ ὡς οὐκ ἔστι μὴ εἶναι,
πειθοῦς ἐστι κέλευθος ('Αληθείῃ γὰρ ὀπηδεῖ),
5   ἡ δ' ὡς οὐκ ἔστιν τε καὶ ὡς χρεών ἐστι μὴ εἶναι,
τὴν δή τοι φράζω παναπευθέα ἔμμεν ἀταρπόν·
οὔτε γὰρ ἂν γνοίης τό γε μὴ ἐόν (οὐ γὰρ ἀνυστόν)
οὔτε φράσαις.

291 Come now, and I will tell you (and you must carry my
account away with you when you have heard it) the only ways
of enquiry that are to be thought of. The one, that [it] is and that
it is impossible for [it] not to be, is the path of Persuasion (for she
attends upon Truth); the other, that [it] is not and that it is
needful that [it] not be, that I declare to you is an altogether
indiscernible track: for you could not know what is not – that
cannot be done – nor indicate it.

The goddess begins by specifying the only ways of enquiry which
should be contemplated. They are plainly assumed to be logically
exclusive: if you take the one, you thereby fail to take the other. No
less plainly they are exclusive because they are contradictories (cf.
296, 16: 'the decision on these things lies in this: it is or it is not').[1]
What is the '[it]' which our translation has supplied as grammatical
subject to Parmenides' verb *estin*? Presumably, any subject of enquiry
whatever – in any enquiry you must assume either that your subject
is or that it is not. Interpretation of *estin* itself, here rendered
awkwardly but neutrally as 'is', is more difficult. The two obvious
paraphrases are the existential ('exists') and the predicative ('is
[something or other]'). To try to decide between them we need to
consider the arguments in which *estin* most prominently figures,
particularly the argument against the negative way of enquiry in
lines 5 to 8 of **291**.

Unfortunately consideration of this argument is not decisive.
Certainly it appears impossible to know or point out what does not
exist: nobody can be acquainted with Mr Pickwick or point him out
to anyone else. But a predicative reading of Parmenides' premiss is
also plausible: it seems impossible to know or point out what is not
something or other, i.e. what possesses no attributes and has no
predicates true of it. Clearer is **296**, 5–21, where an analogous
premiss – 'it is not to be said nor thought that it is not', lines 8–9 – is
used to argue against the possibility of coming to be or perishing. The
point Parmenides makes is that if something comes to be, then it must

previously not have been – and at that time it would have been true to say of it 'it is not'; but the premiss forbids saying just that; so there can be no coming into being. Now 'come to be' in this context is plainly to be construed as 'come to exist'. Here, then, 'is not' means 'does not exist'.

At **296**, 10, however, Parmenides goes on immediately to refer to what does not exist (hypothetically, of course) as 'the nothing' (cf. **293**, 2). This suggests that he understands non-existence as *being nothing at all*, i.e. as having no attributes; and so that for him, to exist is in effect *to be something or other*. When later (e.g. **297**, 22–5; **299**, 46–8) he uses the participle *eon*, 'being', it is much easier to construe it as 'reality' or 'the real' than as barely designating existence. And what makes something real is surely that it has some predicate true of it (e.g. 'occupies space'). If this line of interpretation is correct, Parmenides' use of *estin* is simultaneously existential and predicative (as KR held), but not therefore (as KR concluded) confused.

From the unknowableness of what does not exist Parmenides concludes directly that the negative way is 'indiscernible', i.e. that no clear thought is expressed by a negative existential statement. We might put the point thus: 'Take any subject of enquiry you like (e.g. Mr Pickwick). Then the proposition "Mr Pickwick does not exist" fails to express a genuine thought at all. For if it were a genuine thought, it would have to be possible to be acquainted with its subject, Mr Pickwick. But that possibility does not obtain unless Mr Pickwick exists – which is exactly what the proposition denies.' This line of argument, in one guise or another, has exercised a powerful attraction on many philosophers, from Plato to Russell. Its conclusion is paradoxical, but like all good paradoxes it forces us to examine more deeply our grasp of the concepts it employs – notably in this case the relations between meaning, reference and existence.[2]

---

[1] A difficulty: Parmenides further specifies the first way as 'it is impossible for [it] not to be' and the second as 'it is needful that [it] not be', which are not contradictories. A solution: perhaps these further specifications constitute not characterizations of the two ways, but indications of their incompatibility. Line 3 will be saying: the first way is '[it] is'; and it follows necessarily that, if something is, it is not the case that it is not. So *mutatis mutandis* for line 5.

[2] Editors often complete the half-line **291**, 8, with a fragment known only in quite different sources: **292** Fr. 3, Clement *Strom.* VI, 23; Plotinus V, 1, 8 τὸ γὰρ αὐτὸ νοεῖν ἔστιν τε καὶ εἶναι. *(For the same thing is there both to be thought of and to be.)* If thus translated (but some render: 'Thought and being are the same'), it does sound as though it may fit here; **293**, 1 shows that Parmenides explicitly deploys considerations about what can be thought, not just what can be known, in the context of argument against the negative way. But if so it is surprising that neither Proclus nor Simplicius quotes it at the end of **291**. And it is hard to see

what contribution it adds to the reasoning of **291**, 6–8. (If *noein* meant 'know' here, as e.g. C. H. Kahn (*Review of Metaphysics* 22 (1968–9), 700–24) thinks, then perhaps **292** would simply be another way of putting **291**, 7–8. But *noein* is used by Parmenides in parallel with simple verbs of saying (**293**, 1; **296**, 8; cf. *anōnumon*, **296**, 17), and so must be translated 'think'.)

(ii) *Mortal error*

293 Fr. 6, Simplicius *in Phys.* 86, 27–8; 117, 4–13

χρὴ τὸ λέγειν τε νοεῖν τ' ἐὸν ἔμμεναι· ἔστι γὰρ εἶναι,
μηδὲν δ' οὐκ ἔστιν· τά σ' ἐγὼ φράζεσθαι ἄνωγα.
πρώτης γάρ σ' ἀφ' ὁδοῦ ταύτης διζήσιος ⟨εἴργω⟩,
αὐτὰρ ἔπειτ' ἀπὸ τῆς, ἣν δὴ βροτοὶ εἰδότες οὐδὲν
5 πλάττονται, δίκρανοι· ἀμηχανίη γὰρ ἐν αὐτῶν
στήθεσιν ἰθύνει πλακτὸν νόον· οἱ δὲ φοροῦνται
κωφοὶ ὁμῶς τυφλοί τε, τεθηπότες, ἄκριτα φῦλα,
οἷς τὸ πέλειν τε καὶ οὐκ εἶναι ταὐτὸν νενόμισται
κοὐ ταὐτόν, πάντων δὲ παλίντροπός ἐστι κέλευθος.

293 What is there to be said and thought must needs be: for it is there for being, but nothing is not. I bid you ponder that, for this is the first way of enquiry from which I hold you back, but then from that on which mortals wander knowing nothing, two-headed; for helplessness guides the wandering thought in their breasts, and they are carried along, deaf and blind at once, dazed, undiscriminating hordes, who believe that to be and not to be are the same and not the same; and the path taken by them all is backward-turning.

Parmenides' summary of his case against the negative way (lines 1–3), which says in effect that any object of thought must be a real object, confirms despite its obscurity that his rejection of 'is not' is motivated by a concern about what is a possible content for a genuine thought. It is followed by a warning against a second mistaken way, identified as the way of enquiry pursued by mortals. No mention of this third way was made in **291**, and the reason is not far to seek. The goddess was there specifying logically coherent alternatives between which rational enquirers must decide. The third way is simply the path you will find yourself following if, like the generality of mortals, you do not take that decision (**293**, 7) through failure to use your critical powers (**293**, 6–7). You will find yourself saying or implying both that a thing is and that it is not (e.g. by acknowledging change and coming into existence); and so you will wander helplessly from one of the ways distinguished in **291** to the other. Hence your steps will be 'backward-turning', i.e. contradictory. Of course, you will recognize that 'is' and 'is not' are *not* the same. But in failing to decide between them you will treat them as though they were the same.

293 was probably followed, after an interval, by a fragment in which the goddess bids Parmenides to make up his mind (unlike the mortals dismissed in **293**) about her refutation of the second way:

294   Fr. 7, Plato *Sophist* 242A (lines 1–2); Sextus *adv. math.* VII, 114 (lines 2–6)

> οὐ γὰρ μήποτε τοῦτο δαμῇ εἶναι μὴ ἐόντα·
> ἀλλὰ σὺ τῆσδ' ἀφ' ὁδοῦ διζήσιος εἶργε νόημα
> μηδέ σ' ἔθος πολύπειρον ὁδὸν κατὰ τήνδε βιάσθω
> νωμᾶν ἄσκοπον ὄμμα καὶ ἠχήεσσαν ἀκουὴν
> 5   καὶ γλῶσσαν, κρῖναι δὲ λόγῳ πολύδηριν ἔλεγχον
> ἐξ ἐμέθεν ῥηθέντα.

294   For never shall this be forcibly maintained, that things that are not are, but you must hold back your thought from this way of enquiry, nor let habit, born of much experience, force you down this way, by making you use an aimless eye or an ear and a tongue full of meaningless sound: judge by reason the strife-encompassed refutation spoken by me.

(iii) *Signs of truth*

295   Fr. 8, 1–4, Simplicius *in Phys.* 78, 5; 145, 1

> μόνος δ' ἔτι μῦθος ὁδοῖο
> λείπεται ὡς ἔστιν· ταύτῃ δ' ἔπι σήματ' ἔασι
> πολλὰ μάλ', ὡς ἀγένητον ἐὸν καὶ ἀνώλεθρόν ἐστιν,
> οὖλον μουνογενές τε καὶ ἀτρεμὲς ἠδὲ τέλειον.[1]

[1] ἠδ' ἀτέλεστον Simplicius: for the emendation see G. E. L. Owen in *Studies in Presocratic Philosophy* II, ed. R. E. Allen and D. J. Furley (London, 1975), 76–7, who also convincingly rejects KR's reading (taken over from DK): ἔστι γὰρ οὐλομελές τε καὶ ἀτρεμές...(Plutarch).

295   There still remains just one account of a way, that it is. On this way there are very many signs, that being uncreated and imperishable it is, whole and of a single kind and unshaken and perfect.

If we must avoid the way 'is not', our only hope as enquirers lies in pursuit of the way 'is'. At first sight it would appear that if we embrace that alternative, there open for us limitless possibilities of exploration: the requirement that any subject we investigate must exist seems to impose scarcely any restriction on what we might be able to discover about it; and the argument that what is available to be thought of must exist (**293**, 1–2) makes it look as though the range of possible subjects of investigation is enormous, including centaurs and chimaeras as well as rats and restaurants. But in the course of a mere 49 lines Parmenides succeeds in reducing this infinity of possibilities to exactly one. For the 'signs' programmatically listed in **295** in fact constitute further formal requirements which any subject of enquiry must satisfy; and they impose formidable constraints (note the metaphor of chains in **296** and **298** below) on the interpretation of what is compatible with saying of something that it exists. The upshot of Parmenides' subsequent argument for these requirements is a form of monism: it certainly transpires that everything there is must have one and the same character; and it is doubtful whether in fact anything could have that character except reality as a whole.

(iii) (a) *Uncreated and imperishable*

296 Fr. 8, 5–21, Simplicius *in Phys.* 78, 5; 145, 5 (continues **295**)

5   οὐδέ ποτ' ἦν οὐδ' ἔσται, ἐπεὶ νῦν ἐστιν ὁμοῦ πᾶν,
     ἕν, συνεχές· τίνα γὰρ γένναν διζήσεαι αὐτοῦ;
     πῆ πόθεν αὐξηθέν; οὐδ' ἐκ μὴ ἐόντος ἐάσσω
     φάσθαι σ' οὐδὲ νοεῖν· οὐ γὰρ φατὸν οὐδὲ νοητὸν
     ἔστιν ὅπως οὐκ ἔστι. τί δ' ἄν μιν καὶ χρέος ὦρσεν
10   ὕστερον ἢ πρόσθεν, τοῦ μηδενὸς ἀρξάμενον, φῦν;
     οὕτως ἢ πάμπαν πελέναι χρεών ἐστιν ἢ οὐχί.
     οὐδέ ποτ' ἐκ μὴ[1] ἐόντος ἐφήσει πίστιος ἰσχὺς
     γίγνεσθαί τι παρ' αὐτό· τοῦ εἵνεκεν οὔτε γενέσθαι
     οὔτ' ὄλλυσθαι ἀνῆκε Δίκη χαλάσασα πέδησιν,
15   ἀλλ' ἔχει· ἡ δὲ κρίσις περὶ τούτων ἐν τῷδ' ἐστίν·
     ἔστιν ἢ οὐκ ἔστιν· κέκριται δ' οὖν, ὥσπερ ἀνάγκη,
     τὴν μὲν ἐᾶν ἀνόητον ἀνώνυμον (οὐ γὰρ ἀληθὴς
     ἔστιν ὁδός), τὴν δ' ὥστε πέλειν καὶ ἐτήτυμον εἶναι.
     πῶς δ' ἂν ἔπειτα πέλοι τὸ ἐόν; πῶς δ' ἄν κε γένοιτο;
20   εἰ γὰρ ἔγεντ', οὐκ ἔστ', οὐδ' εἴ ποτε μέλλει ἔσεσθαι.
     τὼς γένεσις μὲν ἀπέσβεσται καὶ ἄπυστος ὄλεθρος.

---

[1] Many scholars follow Karsten and Reinhardt in emending μή to τοῦ.

296 It never was nor will be, since it is now, all together, one, continuous. For what birth will you seek for it? How and whence did it grow? I shall not allow you to say nor to think from not being: for it is not to be said nor thought that it is not; and what need would have driven it later rather than earlier, beginning from the nothing, to grow? Thus it must either be completely or not at all. Nor will the force of conviction allow anything besides it to come to be ever from not being. Therefore Justice has never loosed her fetters to allow it to come to be or to perish, but holds it fast. And the decision about these things lies in this: it is or it is not. But it has in fact been decided, as is necessary, to leave the one way unthought and nameless (for it is no true way), but that the other is and is genuine. And how could what is be in the future? How could it come to be? For if it came into being, it is not: nor is it if it is ever going to be in the future. Thus coming to be is extinguished and perishing unheard of.

These lines (as the conclusion, line 21, shows) are designed to prove that what is can neither come to be nor perish.[1] Parmenides is content to marshal explicit arguments only against coming into being, taking it as obvious that a parallel case against perishing could be constructed by parity of reasoning. He advances two principal considerations, corresponding to the dual interrogative: 'How and whence did it grow?' (line 7). He assumes that the only reasonable answer to 'whence?' could be: 'from not existing', which he rejects as already excluded by his argument against 'is not' (lines 7–9). In his treatment of 'how?' he appeals to the Principle of Sufficient Reason. He assumes that anything which comes to be must contain within it some principle of development ('need', χρέος) sufficient to explain its generation. But if something does not exist, how can it contain any such principle?

[1] In lines 5–6 Parmenides appears to go farther than this. The statement 'it never was nor will be, since it is now, all together' seems to claim not merely that what is will not *come to exist*, but that it will not exist *at all* in the future. Probably what Parmenides means to ascribe to what is is existence in an eternal present not subject to temporal distinctions of any sort. It is very unclear how he hoped to ground this conclusion in the arguments of **296**.

(iii) (b) *One and continuous*

297 Fr. 8, 22–5, Simplicius *in Phys.* 144, 29 (continues **296**)

οὐδὲ διαιρετόν ἐστιν, ἐπεὶ πᾶν ἐστιν ὁμοῖον·
οὐδέ τι τῇ μᾶλλον, τό κεν εἴργοι μιν συνέχεσθαι,
οὐδέ τι χειρότερον, πᾶν δ' ἔμπλεόν ἐστιν ἐόντος.
τῷ ξυνεχὲς πᾶν ἐστιν· ἐὸν γὰρ ἐόντι πελάζει.

297 Nor is it divided, since it all exists alike; nor is it more here and less there, which would prevent it from holding together, but

it is all full of being. So it is all continuous: for what is draws near
to what is.

Does Parmenides have in mind spatial or temporal continuity here?
He surely means to show that what is is continuous in any dimension
it occupies; but **296** has probably already denied that it exists in time.
Is the point simply that any subject of enquiry must be characterized
by internal continuity, or is Parmenides more ambitiously claiming
that all reality is one? It is hard to resist the impression that he intends
the stronger thesis, although why he thinks himself entitled to assert
it is unclear (perhaps he would rely, for example, on the identity of
indiscernibles: there is no basis for distinguishing anything that is
from anything else that is). The same ambiguity affects **298** and **299**,
and the same verdict suggests itself.

(iii) (c) *Unchangeable*

298 Fr. 8, 26–31, Simplicius *in Phys.* 145, 27 (continues **297**)

αὐτὰρ ἀκίνητον μεγάλων ἐν πείρασι δεσμῶν
ἔστιν ἄναρχον ἄπαυστον, ἐπεὶ γένεσις καὶ ὄλεθρος
τῆλε μάλ' ἐπλάχθησαν, ἀπῶσε δὲ πίστις ἀληθής.
ταὐτόν τ' ἐν ταὐτῷ τε μένον καθ' ἑαυτό τε κεῖται
30 χοὔτως ἔμπεδον αὖθι μενεῖ· κρατερὴ γὰρ Ἀνάγκη
πείρατος ἐν δεσμοῖσιν ἔχει, τό μιν ἀμφὶς ἐέργει.

298 But changeless within the limits of great bonds it exists
without beginning or ceasing, since coming to be and perishing
have wandered very far away, and true conviction has thrust
them off. Remaining the same and in the same place it lies on its
own and thus fixed it will remain. For strong Necessity holds it
within the bonds of a limit, which keeps it in on every side.

Lines 26–8 suggest the following argument:
    (1) It is impossible for what is to come into being or to perish.
So   (2) it exists unchangeably within the bonds of a limit.
It is then natural to read lines 29–31 as spelling out the content of
(2) more fully. So construed, they indicate a more complex inference
from (1):
    (2a) it is held within the bonds of a limit which keeps it in
       on every side.
So   (2b) it remains the same and in the same place and stays on
       its own.
The notion of *limit* Parmenides is employing here is obscure. It is
easiest to understand it as spatial limit; and then (2b) follows

intelligibly from (2a). But why on this interpretation should (2a) follow from (1)? Perhaps rather 'within limits' is a metaphorical way of talking about *determinacy*. In (2a) Parmenides will then be saying that what is has no potentiality for being different – at any time or in any respect – from what it is at present.

(iii) (d) *Perfect*

299 Fr. 8, 32–49, Simplicius *in Phys.* 146, 5 (continues **298**)

οὔνεκεν[1] οὐκ ἀτελεύτητον τὸ ἐὸν θέμις εἶναι·
ἔστι γὰρ οὐκ ἐπιδευές· [μὴ] ἐὸν δ' ἂν παντὸς ἐδεῖτο.
ταὐτὸν δ' ἔστι νοεῖν τε καὶ οὔνεκεν ἔστι νόημα.

35　ου γὰρ ἄνευ τοῦ ἐόντος, ἐν ᾧ πεφατισμένον ἐστίν,
εὑρήσεις τὸ νοεῖν· οὐδὲν γὰρ ⟨ἢ⟩ ἔστιν ἢ ἔσται
ἄλλο πάρεξ τοῦ ἐόντος, ἐπεὶ τό γε Μοῖρ' ἐπέδησεν
οὖλον ἀκίνητόν τ' ἔμεναι· τῷ πάντ' ὀνόμασται,[2]
ὅσσα βροτοὶ κατέθεντο πεποιθότες εἶναι ἀληθῆ,

40　γίγνεσθαί τε καὶ ὄλλυσθαι, εἶναί τε καὶ οὐχί,
καὶ τόπον ἀλλάσσειν διά τε χρόα φανὸν ἀμείβειν.
αὐτὰρ ἐπεὶ πεῖρας πύματον, τετελεσμένον ἐστί,
πάντοθεν εὐκύκλου σφαίρης ἐναλίγκιον ὄγκῳ,
μεσσόθεν ἰσοπαλὲς πάντη· τὸ γὰρ οὔτε τι μεῖζον

45　οὔτε τι βαιότερον πελέναι χρεόν ἐστι τῇ ἢ τῇ.
οὔτε γὰρ οὐκ ἐὸν ἔστι, τό κεν παύοι μιν ἱκνεῖσθαι
εἰς ὁμόν, οὔτ' ἐὸν ἔστιν ὅπως εἴη κεν ἐόντος
τῇ μᾶλλον τῇ δ' ἧσσον, ἐπεὶ πᾶν ἐστιν ἄσυλον·
οἶ γὰρ πάντοθεν ἶσον, ὁμῶς ἐν πείρασι κύρει.

[1] For οὔνεκεν as 'therefore' cf. τοῦ εἵνεκεν, **296**, 13. 'Because' is the more usual meaning in epic usage, and is preferred by many here.
[2] ὀνόμασται Simplicius (*in Phys.* 87, 1) E; ὄνομα ἔσται DF. Cf. Mourelatos, *Route*, 180–5; M. F. Burnyeat, *Philosophical Review* 91 (1982), 19 n. 32.

299 Therefore it is right that what is should not be imperfect; for it is not deficient – if it were it would be deficient in everything. The same thing is there to be thought and is why there is thought. For you will not find thinking without what is, in all that has been said.[1] For there neither is nor will be anything else besides what is, since Fate fettered it to be whole and changeless. Therefore it has been named all the names which mortals have laid down believing them to be true – coming to be and perishing, being and not being, changing place and altering in bright colour. But since there is a furthest limit, it is perfected, like the bulk of a ball well-rounded on every side, equally balanced in every direction from the centre. For it needs must not be somewhat more or somewhat less here or there. For neither is it non-existent, which would stop it from reaching its like, nor is it existent in such a way that there would be more being here, less there, since it is all inviolate: for being equal to itself on every side, it lies uniformly within its limits.

[1] Or: 'in which thinking is expressed'.

This long and difficult final section of the *Truth* combines a summing-up of the whole first part of the poem with a derivation of the perfection of reality from its determinacy (argued fully in lines 42–9, which are often – as in KR – regarded as presenting a train of thought quite distinct from both lines 32–3 (usually reckoned part of **298**) and lines 34–41). Parmenides first briefly sketches his main argument that what is, if limited or determinate, cannot be deficient, and if not deficient, cannot be imperfect (32–3). Then he takes us right back to his original starting-point: if you have a thought about some object of enquiry, you must be thinking about something that is (34–6). You might suppose you can also think about something besides what already is coming into being. But the argument has shown that what is exists completely and changelessly – it is never in process of coming to be (36–8). So expressions like 'comes to be' and 'changes' employed by mortals can in fact refer (despite their mistaken intentions) only to complete and changeless reality (38–41). Indeed from the fact that what is is limited or determinate, we can infer its perfection (42–4). For its determinacy excludes not just the possibility that it is subject to coming into being and change but any kind of deficiency in its reality (44–9).

Once again we face a puzzling choice between a literal and a metaphorical interpretation of 'limit'. Once again what the argument seems to require is only some form of determinacy (cf. **296**, 14–15). Once again the spatial connotations of the word are hard to forget – indeed they are pressed upon our attention (NB the epithet *pumaton*, '*furthest* limit'). And one can well imagine Parmenides concluding that if reality is both spatially extended and determinate, it must be limited in spatial extension. In the end we must settle for both the literal and the metaphorical reading of the term.

Pursuit of the way 'is' thus leads to a conclusion as astonishing as the result of consideration of 'is not'. Parmenides' final position in **299** is in fact doubly paradoxical. He not only denies the logical coherence of everything we believe about the world, but in making all reality a finite sphere introduces a notion whose own logical coherence must in turn be doubted.[1]

¹ Must there not be real empty space beyond the limits of the sphere if they are to function as limits? This objection might persuade one that Parmenides could not have held reality to be a sphere, were it not that what leads us to think he must have believed that is his apparently uncritical exploitation of the metaphor of limit (i.e. of what we would take to be a metaphor).

MORTAL OPINIONS

(i) *The status of Parmenides' account*

300 Simplicius *in Phys.* 30, 14 (continuation of **299**, cf. *in Phys.* 146, 23) μετελθών δὲ ἀπὸ τῶν νοητῶν ἐπὶ τὰ αἰσθητὰ ὁ Παρμενίδης, ἤτοι ἀπὸ ἀληθείας, ὡς αὐτός φησιν, ἐπὶ δόξαν, ἐν οἷς λέγει
(fr. 8, l. 50) ἐν τῷ σοι παύω πιστὸν λόγον ἠδὲ νόημα
      ἀμφὶς ἀληθείης· δόξας δ' ἀπὸ τοῦδε βροτείας
      μάνθανε κόσμον ἐμῶν ἐπέων ἀπατηλὸν ἀκούων.

300 Parmenides effects the transition from the objects of reason to the objects of sense, or, as he himself puts it, from truth to opinion, when he writes: 'Here I end my trustworthy discourse and thought concerning truth; henceforth learn the beliefs of mortal men, listening to the deceitful ordering of my words.'

The goddess's account will doubtless be unreliable and deceitful principally because it presents beliefs which are themselves utterly confused as though they were in order (cf. **293**). The second half of the poem did not simply describe or analyse current opinions about the cosmos. It contained an elaborate and distinctive theogony and cosmology reminiscent in parts of Hesiod, in parts of Anaximander. Parmenides' object, as we shall see, is to present mortal opinions not as they actually are, but as they might be at best. But that makes the account deceitful in a further sense: in effect it provides a deceptively plausible (although not genuinely convincing) representation of reality.

To understand better the connexion between Parmenides' cosmology and mortal opinions in general, we need to consider the last two lines of **301**:¹

301 Fr. 1, 28–32, Simplicius *de caelo* 557, 25 (from **288**)
        χρεώ δέ σε πάντα πυθέσθαι
  ἠμὲν Ἀληθείης εὐκυκλέος ἀτρεμὲς ἦτορ
30 ἠδὲ βροτῶν δόξας, ταῖς οὐκ ἔνι πίστις ἀληθής.
  ἀλλ' ἔμπης καὶ ταῦτα μαθήσεαι, ὡς τὰ δοκοῦντα
  χρῆν δοκίμως εἶναι διὰ παντὸς πάντα περῶντα.

301 It is proper that you should learn all things, both the unshaken heart of well-rounded truth, and the opinions of mortals, in which there is no true reliance. But nonetheless you shall learn these things too, how what is believed would have to be assuredly, pervading all things throughout.

Lines 31–2 are naturally interpreted as stating the condition upon which the genuine existence of the objects of mortal belief may be secured, viz. that they completely pervade all things. This condition is closely akin to the requirement of the *Truth* that any subject of enquiry exist completely. What Parmenides takes to be false in lines 31–2 is not the goddess's specification of the condition, but her claim that it can be satisfied by objects of mortal belief. It follows that the cosmology of the second part of the poem should be read as a reinterpretation of the world mortals believe in, in terms which explain it (falsely but attractively) as satisfying the pervasiveness condition.

[1] Text, translation and interpretation are vexed: see Mourelatos, *Route*, ch. VIII. The main problem is that lines 31–2 appear to attempt to save the credit of mortal opinions, in flagrant contradiction with the assertion of line 30 that there is no truth in them. The solution is to read the content of the teaching of lines 31–2 as a lie, as indeed it is explicitly presented in **300** (cf. Hesiod *Theog.* 26–7, the model for **301**).

(ii) *Light and night*

302 Fr. 8, 53–61, Simplicius *in Phys.* 38, 28 (continues **300**)

μορφὰς γὰρ κατέθεντο δύο γνώμας ὀνομάζειν,
τῶν μίαν οὐ χρεών ἐστιν – ἐν ᾧ πεπλανημένοι εἰσίν –
55 τἀντία δ᾽ ἐκρίναντο δέμας καὶ σήματ᾽ ἔθεντο
χωρὶς ἀπ᾽ ἀλλήλων, τῇ μὲν φλογὸς αἰθέριον πῦρ,
ἤπιον ὄν, μέγ᾽ ἐλαφρόν, ἑωυτῷ πάντοσε τωὐτόν,
τῷ δ᾽ ἑτέρῳ μὴ τωὐτόν· ἀτὰρ κἀκεῖνο κατ᾽ αὐτὸ
τἀντία νύκτ᾽ ἀδαῆ, πυκινὸν δέμας ἐμβριθές τε.
60 τόν σοι ἐγὼ διάκοσμον ἐοικότα πάντα φατίζω,
ὡς οὐ μή ποτέ τίς σε βροτῶν γνώμῃ παρελάσσῃ.

303 Fr. 9, Simplicius *in Phys.* 180, 8

αὐτὰρ ἐπειδὴ πάντα φάος καὶ νὺξ ὀνόμασται
καὶ τὰ κατὰ σφετέρας δυνάμεις ἐπὶ τοῖσί τε καὶ τοῖς,
πᾶν πλέον ἐστὶν ὁμοῦ φάεος καὶ νυκτὸς ἀφάντου,
ἴσων ἀμφοτέρων, ἐπεὶ οὐδετέρῳ μέτα μηδέν.

302 For they made up their minds to name two forms, of which

they needs must not name so much as one[1] – that is where they
have gone astray – and distinguished them as opposite in appearance and assigned to them signs different one from the other – to
one the aitherial flame of fire, gentle and very light, in every
direction identical with itself, but not with the other; and that
other too is in itself just the opposite, dark night, dense in
appearance and heavy. The whole ordering of these I tell you as
it seems fitting, for so no thought of mortal men shall ever outstrip
you.

303 But because all things have been named light and night, and
things corresponding to their powers have been assigned to this
and that, all is full of light and of obscure night at once, both
equal, since neither has any share of nothing.

[1] Alternatively: (a) 'not name one' (sc. although the other is correct); the culprit
is then identified as *night*, following Aristotle's view (mistaken: see **303**) that
Parmenides 'ranges the hot with what is and the other with what is not' (*Met.*
986b31), or as *not-being* (an over-ingenious suggestion). (b) 'not name only one':
so KR, following Simplicius; but mortals in general *avoid* this error – their
discourse is full of contrary expressions, as **302** obviously recognizes. See further
e.g. A. A. Long in Furley and Allen (eds.), *Studies in Presocratic Philosophy* II, 82–101,
Mourelatos, *Route*, 80–7, D. J. Furley in *Exegesis and Argument*, ed. E. N. Lee *et
al.* (*Phronesis* Supp. Vol. I), 1–15.

302–3 advance the specific hypothesis by which Parmenides seeks to
do the best that can be done to save mortal opinions. He pretends
that they are built upon the foundation of a belief in two basic and
mutually irreducible sensible forms, which are individually ascribed
something like the determinacy required of subjects of enquiry in the
Truth, and which together satisfy the condition of **301**, 31–2 that they
pervade all reality. Other things are treated simply as manifestations
of light or of night (or, presumably, of both), and are characterized
by specific powers associated with one form or the other.

The fiction of an arbitrary decision to introduce the names 'light'
and 'night' has sometimes been implausibly construed as an explanation of how there can be a world of the sort believed in by mortals.
It rather expresses dramatically an epistemological characterization
of their belief. Mortal opinions do not reflect the discovery of
objective truth: the only alternative is to interpret them as products
of conventions elaborated by the human mind. Now it follows that
nothing about the world can explain why mortals should have such
conventions or why they should invest them with the specific content
they give them. Hence the currency of these conventions can only
be represented as due to arbitrary fiat.

Parmenides was evidently quite systematic in his use of light and night in physical explanation, to judge from **305–7** below and from Plutarch's testimony (which also indicates the main topics discussed; cf. fr. 11, Simpl. *de caelo* 559, 20):

304 Plutarch *adv. Colotem* 1114B (DK28B10) ὅς γε καὶ διάκοσμον πεποίηται καὶ στοιχεῖα μιγνὺς τὸ λαμπρὸν καὶ σκοτεινὸν ἐκ τούτων τὰ φαινόμενα πάντα καὶ διὰ τούτων ἀποτελεῖ· καὶ γὰρ περὶ γῆς εἴρηκε πολλὰ καὶ περὶ οὐρανοῦ καὶ ἡλίου καὶ σελήνης καὶ γένεσιν ἀνθρώπων ἀφήγηται· καὶ οὐδὲν ἄρρητον ὡς ἀνὴρ ἀρχαῖος ἐν φυσιολογίᾳ καὶ συνθεὶς γραφὴν ἰδίαν, οὐκ ἀλλοτρίαν διαφορῶν τῶν κυρίων παρῆκεν.

304 Parmenides has actually made an ordering, and by blending as elements the clear and the dark produces out of them and by them all sensible appearances. For he has said much about the earth and about the heavens and sun and moon, and he recounts the coming into being of men; and as befits an ancient natural philosopher, who put together his own book, not pulling apart someone else's, he has left none of the important topics undiscussed.

While Parmenides offers no rational justification for choosing light and night as cosmological principles, he was probably conscious of following Hesiod's *Theogony* 123ff. (**31** above), which was certainly the model for his treatment of the origin of Love (fr. 13; cf. **31**, 116–22) and of War and Discord (Cicero *de natura deorum* 1, 11, 28, DK 28A37; cf. *Theog.* 223–32).

(iii) *Cosmology*

305   Fr. 10, Clement *Strom.* v, 138
εἴσῃ δ' αἰθερίαν τε φύσιν τά τ' ἐν αἰθέρι πάντα
σήματα καὶ καθαρᾶς εὐαγέος ἠελίοιο
λαμπάδος ἔργ' ἀίδηλα καὶ ὁππόθεν ἐξεγένοντο,
ἔργα τε κύκλωπος πεύσῃ περίφοιτα σελήνης
5 καὶ φύσιν, εἰδήσεις δὲ καὶ οὐρανὸν ἀμφὶς ἔχοντα
ἔνθεν ἔφυ τε καὶ ὥς μιν ἄγουσ⟨α⟩ ἐπέδησεν Ἀνάγκη
πείρατ' ἔχειν ἄστρων.

306   Fr. 12, Simplicius *in Phys.* 39, 14 and 31, 13
αἱ γὰρ στεινότεραι (*sc.* στεφάναι) πλῆνται πυρὸς ἀκρήτοιο,
αἱ δ' ἐπὶ ταῖς νυκτός, μετὰ δὲ φλογὸς ἵεται αἶσα·
ἐν δὲ μέσῳ τούτων δαίμων ἣ πάντα κυβερνᾷ·

πάντων γὰρ στυγεροῖο τόκου καὶ μίξιος ἄρχει
5   πέμπουσ' ἄρσενι θῆλυ μιγῆν τό τ' ἐναντίον αὖτις
ἄρσεν θηλυτέρῳ.

307 Aetius ΙΙ, 7, 1 (DK 28 A 37) Παρμενίδης στεφάνας εἶναι περι-
πεπλεγμένας ἐπαλλήλους, τὴν μὲν ἐκ τοῦ ἀραιοῦ, τὴν δὲ ἐκ τοῦ
πυκνοῦ· μικτὰς δὲ ἄλλας ἐκ φωτὸς καὶ σκότους μεταξὺ τούτων. καὶ τὸ
περιέχον δὲ πάσας τείχους δίκην στερεὸν ὑπάρχειν, ὑφ' ᾧ πυρώδης
στεφάνη, καὶ τὸ μεσαίτατον πασῶν στερεόν, περὶ ὃ πάλιν πυρώδης
(sc. στεφάνη). τῶν δὲ συμμιγῶν τὴν μεσαιτάτην ἁπάσαις ⟨ἀρχήν⟩
τε καὶ ⟨αἰτίαν⟩ κινήσεως καὶ γενέσεως ὑπάρχειν, ἥντινα καὶ δαίμονα
κυβερνῆτιν καὶ κληδοῦχον ἐπονομάζει Δίκην τε καὶ Ἀνάγκην. καὶ τῆς
μὲν γῆς ἀπόκρισιν εἶναι τὸν ἀέρα διὰ τὴν βιαιοτέραν αὐτῆς
ἐξατμισθέντα πίλησιν, τοῦ δὲ πυρὸς ἀναπνοὴν τὸν ἥλιον καὶ τὸν
γαλαξίαν κύκλον. συμμιγῆ δ' ἐξ ἀμφοῖν εἶναι τὴν σελήνην, τοῦ τ'
ἀέρος καὶ τοῦ πυρός. περιστάντος δ' ἀνωτάτω πάντων τοῦ αἰθέρος
ὑπ' αὐτῷ τὸ πυρῶδες ὑποταγῆναι τοῦθ' ὅπερ κεκλήκαμεν οὐρανόν,
ὑφ' ᾧ ἤδη τὰ περίγεια.

305 And you shall know the nature of *aither* and all the signs [i.e.
constellations] in it and the destructive works of the pure torch of
the shining sun, and whence they came into being; and you shall
hear of the wandering works of the round-eyed moon and of her
nature; and you shall know too of the surrounding heaven, whence
it grew and how Necessity guiding it fettered it to hold the limits
of the stars.

306 The narrower rings are filled with unmixed fire, those next
to them with night, but into them a share of flame is injected; and
in the midst of them is the goddess who steers all things; for she
governs the hateful birth and mingling of all things, sending female
to mix with male, and again conversely male with female.

307 Parmenides said that there were rings wound one around the
other, one formed of the rare, the other of the dense; and that there
were others between these compounded of light and darkness.
That which surrounds them all like a wall is, he says, by nature
solid; beneath it is a fiery ring; and likewise what lies in the middle
of them all is solid; and around it is again a fiery ring. The
middlemost of the mixed rings is the [primary cause] of movement
and of coming into being for them all, and he calls it the goddess
that steers all, the holder of the keys, Justice and Necessity. The
air, he says, is separated off from the earth, vaporized owing to
the earth's stronger compression; the sun is an exhalation of fire,
and so is the circle of the Milky Way. The moon is compounded

of both air and fire. Aither is outermost, surrounding all; next comes the fiery thing that we call the sky; and last comes the region of the earth.

305 evidently formed part of the introduction to the detailed account of the heavens. It is full of echoes of the *Truth*, e.g. when it speaks of the heaven 'surrounding' (cf. 298, 31), of the 'limits of the stars' (cf. 298, 26, 31; 299, 42, 49), and of how 'Necessity fettered' the heaven (cf. 296, 14; 298, 30–1). Perhaps they are meant to suggest that in attempting to save mortal opinions our descriptions of the world they invent must approximate so far as possible to those used in our account of true reality.

The exiguous surviving evidence of Parmenides' astronomical system is so brief (306) and so obscure (307) that it is impossible with any confidence to reconstruct a coherent account of his extraordinary theory of 'garlands' or rings.[1] The whole construction was built out of the basic forms of light and night, as witness further Parmenides' memorable line about the moon's borrowed light:

308   Fr. 14, Plutarch *adv. Colotem* 1116A
   νυκτιφαὲς περὶ γαῖαν ἀλώμενον ἀλλότριον φῶς

   308   A night-shining, foreign light, wandering around the earth.

The theory seems to have been surprisingly influential. Philolaus (446–7 below) was perhaps following Parmenides when he placed fire both at the extremity of the universe and at its centre, displacing the earth from the position traditionally assigned to it (but Parmenides' idea may have been of a fire *within* the earth). And Plato developed his own version of the scheme, including its presiding deity, in the myth of Er in the *Republic* (617–18). Parmenides for his part probably owed something to Anaximander's rings (125–8), although Hesiod had spoken of 'the shining stars with which the heaven is garlanded' (*Theog.* 282).

---

[1] For some attempts see K. Reinhardt, *Parmenides* (Bonn, 1916) 10–32, H. Fränkel in Furley and Allen (eds.), *Studies in Presocratic Philosophy* II, 22–5, J. S. Morrison, *Journal of Hellenic Studies* 75 (1955), 59–68, U. Hölscher, *Parmenides: Vom Wesen des Seienden* (Frankfurt am Main, 1969), 106–11.

Postulation of a deity as first cause of cosmogonic mixture is supported by appeal to her operation in animal procreation (306, 4–6), which we know was one of the topics of this part of the poem (cf. 304). A single line of Parmenides' embryology is preserved:

309   Fr. 17, Galen *in Epid.* VI, 48
δεξιτεροῖσιν μὲν κούρους, λαιοῖσι δὲ κούρας...

309   On the right boys, on the left girls...

Parmenides' interest in these matters was perhaps stimulated by the Crotoniate medical tradition; his notion of mixture of opposites may be compared with Alcmaeon's theory of health (probably roughly contemporary in date):

310   Aetius v, 30, 1 (DK24B4) Ἀλκμαίων τῆς ὑγιείας εἶναι συνεκτικὴν τὴν 'ἰσονομίαν' τῶν δυνάμεων, ὑγροῦ, ξηροῦ, ψυχροῦ, θερμοῦ, πικροῦ, γλυκέος καὶ τῶν λοιπῶν, τὴν δ' ἐν αὐτοῖς 'μοναρχίαν' νόσου ποιητικήν· φθοροποιὸν γὰρ ἑκατέρου μοναρχίαν. καὶ νόσον συμπίπτειν ὡς μὲν ὑφ' οὗ ὑπερβολῇ θερμότητος ἢ ψυχρότητος, ὡς δὲ ἐξ οὗ διὰ πλῆθος τροφῆς ἢ ἔνδειαν, ὡς δ' ἐν οἷς ἢ ⟨περὶ Diels⟩ αἷμα ἢ μυελόν ἢ ἐγκέφαλον. ἐγγίνεσθαι δὲ τούτοις ποτὲ κἀκ τῶν ἔξωθεν αἰτιῶν, ὑδάτων ποιῶν ἢ χώρας ἢ κόπων ἢ ἀνάγκης ἢ τῶν τούτοις παραπλησίων. τὴν δ' ὑγίειαν τὴν σύμμετρον τῶν ποιῶν κρᾶσιν.

310   Alcmaeon maintains that the bond of health is the 'equal rights' of the powers, moist and dry, cold and hot, bitter and sweet, and the rest, while the 'monarchy' of one of them is the cause of disease; for the monarchy of either is destructive. Illness comes about directly through excess of heat or cold, indirectly through surfeit or deficiency of nourishment; and its centre is either the blood or the marrow or the brain. It sometimes arises in these centres from external causes, moisture of some sort or environment or exhaustion or hardship or similar causes. Health on the other hand is the proportionate admixture of the qualities.

It is unclear whether Parmenides' divine first cause is anything more than a metaphor for the mutual attraction exercised by opposite forms, although there is no room for such a cause in the ontology of **302–3**. What is clear and important in his cosmogony is the general idea that creation is the product not (as the Milesians thought) of separation from an original unity, but of the interaction and harmony of opposite powers. This idea was to be taken up by Empedocles and (in a distinctively Pythagorean form) by Philolaus.

(iv) *Theory of mortal thought*

311   Theophrastus *de sensu* 1ff. (DK28A46)   περὶ δ' αἰσθήσεως αἱ μὲν πολλαὶ καὶ καθόλου δόξαι δύ' εἰσίν· οἱ μὲν γὰρ τῷ ὁμοίῳ ποιοῦσιν, οἱ δὲ τῷ ἐναντίῳ. Παρμενίδης μὲν καὶ Ἐμπεδοκλῆς καὶ Πλάτων τῷ

ὁμοίῳ, οἱ δὲ περὶ Ἀναξαγόραν καὶ Ἡράκλειτον τῷ ἐναντίῳ.... (3)
Παρμενίδης μὲν γὰρ ὅλως οὐδὲν ἀφώρικεν ἀλλὰ μόνον ὅτι δυοῖν ὄντοιν
στοιχείοιν κατὰ τὸ ὑπερβάλλον ἐστὶν ἡ γνῶσις. ἐὰν γὰρ ὑπεραίρῃ
τὸ θερμὸν ἢ τὸ ψυχρόν, ἄλλην γίνεσθαι τὴν διάνοιαν, βελτίω δὲ καὶ
καθαρωτέραν τὴν διὰ τὸ θερμόν· οὐ μὴν ἀλλὰ καὶ ταύτην δεῖσθαί τινος
συμμετρίας·

(Fr. 16) ὡς γὰρ ἑκάστοτ' (φησίν) ἔχει κρᾶσις μελέων πολυπλάγκτων,
  τὼς νόος ἀνθρώποισι παρέστηκεν· τὸ γὰρ αὐτὸ
  ἔστιν ὅπερ φρονέει μελέων φύσις ἀνθρώποισιν
  καὶ πᾶσιν καὶ παντί· τὸ γὰρ πλέον ἐστὶ νόημα.

τὸ γὰρ αἰσθάνεσθαι καὶ τὸ φρονεῖν ὡς ταὐτὸ λέγει· διὸ καὶ τὴν
μνήμην καὶ τὴν λήθην ἀπὸ τούτων γίνεσθαι διὰ τῆς κράσεως·
ἂν δ' ἰσάζωσι τῇ μίξει, πότερον ἔσται φρονεῖν ἢ οὔ, καὶ τίς ἡ διάθεσις,
οὐδὲν ἔτι διώρικεν. ὅτι δὲ καὶ τῷ ἐναντίῳ καθ' αὑτὸ ποιεῖ τὴν
αἴσθησιν, φανερὸν ἐν οἷς φησι τὸν νεκρὸν φωτὸς μὲν καὶ θερμοῦ καὶ
φωνῆς οὐκ αἰσθάνεσθαι διὰ τὴν ἔκλειψιν τοῦ πυρός, ψυχροῦ δὲ καὶ
σιωπῆς καὶ τῶν ἐναντίων αἰσθάνεσθαι. καὶ ὅλως δὲ πᾶν τὸ ὂν ἔχειν
τινὰ γνῶσιν.

311   The majority of general views about sensation are two: some
make it of like by like, others of opposite by opposite. Parmenides,
Empedocles and Plato say it is of like by like, the followers of
Anaxagoras and of Heraclitus of opposite by opposite... Parmen
ides gave no clear definition at all, but said only that there were
two elements and that knowledge depends on the excess of one or
the other. Thought varies according to whether the hot or the cold
prevails, but that which is due to the hot is better and purer; not
but what even that needs a certain balance; for, says he, 'As is
at any moment the mixture of the wandering limbs, so mind is
present to men; for that which thinks is the same thing, namely
the substance of their limbs, in each and all men; for what
preponderates is thought'[1] – for he regards perception and thought
as the same. So too memory and forgetfulness arise from these
causes, on account of the mixture; but he never made clear
whether, if they are equally mixed, there will be thought or not,
or, if so, what its character will be. But that he regards perception
as also due to the opposite as such he makes clear when he says
that a corpse does not perceive light, heat or sound owing to its
deficiency of fire, but that it does perceive their opposites, cold,
silence and so on. And he adds that in general everything that exists
has some measure of knowledge.

[1] Or: 'for the full is thought'. Translation and interpretation of the whole fragment are much disputed. See e.g. Guthrie, *HGP* II, 67–9 for discussion and references to the scholarly literature.

Fr. 16 gains in point if construed as a final dismissive comment on mortal opinion. In *Truth* genuine thought was in a sense identified with the being which is its object. But mortal opinion is mere invention of the human mind, not determined by reality. Mortal thoughts are now reductively 'explained' in terms of the very forms they have invented, as functions of the proportions of light and night in the human body.

CONCLUSION

312   Fr. 19, Simplicius *de caelo* 558, 8
οὕτω τοι κατὰ δόξαν ἔφυ τάδε καί νυν ἔασι
καὶ μετέπειτ' ἀπὸ τοῦδε τελευτήσουσι τραφέντα·
τοῖς δ' ὄνομ' ἄνθρωποι κατέθεντ' ἐπίσημον ἑκάστῳ.

313   Fr. 4, Clement *Strom.* v, 15, 5
λεῦσσε δ' ὅμως ἀπεόντα νόῳ παρεόντα βεβαίως·
οὐ γὰρ ἀποτμήξει τὸ ἐὸν τοῦ ἐόντος ἔχεσθαι
οὔτε σκιδνάμενον πάντῃ πάντως κατὰ κόσμον
οὔτε συνιστάμενον.

312   Thus according to belief these things came to be and now are, and having matured will come to an end after this in the future; and for them men have laid down a name to distinguish each one.

313   But look at things which, though far off, are securely present to the mind; for you will not cut off for yourself what is from holding to what is, neither scattering everywhere in every way in order [*i.e.* cosmic order] nor drawing together.

The goddess may have concluded her account of the content of mortal opinions (rounded off in 312) with the obscure exhortation of 313 to contemplate the truth. Why that elaborate account was included in the poem remains a mystery: the goddess seeks to save the phenomena so far as is possible, but she knows and tells us that the project is impossible. Perhaps Parmenides simply failed to resist the opportunity for versatility afforded by the idea of 'saying many false things resembling the truth and uttering true things when we wish' (Hesiod *Theog.* 27–8).

CHAPTER IX

Zeno of Elea

DATE AND LIFE

The most reliable evidence for Zeno's date is the same passage of Plato's *Parmenides* (**286**) as was used to determine the date of Parmenides. On the basis of that evidence, Zeno seems to have been born about 490–485 B.C. Once again the date given by Apollodorus for Zeno's *floruit*, namely 464–461 (Diog. L. IX, 29 = DK 29A I: text unfortunately lacunose), conflicts with this; but we have already seen that his dating of the Eleatics depends solely on the date of the foundation of Elea. Nonetheless he may fortuitously give us a date only about five years too late for Zeno's book, if it was indeed written (as **314** says) in his youth.

Little is known of Zeno's life. Diogenes Laertius tells us (IX, 28, DK 29A I: a passage apparently intended to contradict the story in **286**) that he loved Elea, 'mean though it was and skilled only in bringing men up to be virtuous, in preference to the arrogance of Athens', which he did not visit, living all his life in his native city. In the one context in which his name repeatedly occurs by itself – the story of his part in a plot against a tyrant and of his courage under torture (see DK 29A I, 2, 6, 7, 8 and 9) – the details vary so much that the facts are impossible to reconstruct.

ZENO'S BOOK

314 Plato *Parmenides* 127D–128A Τὸν οὖν Σωκράτη ἀκούσαντα πάλιν τε κελεῦσαι τὴν πρώτην ὑπόθεσιν τοῦ πρώτου λόγου ἀναγνῶναι, καὶ ἀναγνωσθείσης, Πῶς, φάναι, ὦ Ζήνων, τοῦτο λέγεις; εἰ πολλά ἐστι τὰ ὄντα, ὡς ἄρα δεῖ αὐτὰ ὅμοιά τε εἶναι καὶ ἀνόμοια, τοῦτο δὲ δὴ ἀδύνατον· οὔτε γὰρ τὰ ἀνόμοια ὅμοια οὔτε τὰ ὅμοια ἀνόμοια οἶόν τε εἶναι; οὐχ οὕτω λέγεις;

Οὕτω, φάναι τὸν Ζήνωνα.

Οὐκοῦν εἰ ἀδύνατον τά τε ἀνόμοια ὅμοια εἶναι καὶ τὰ ὅμοια ἀνόμοια, ἀδύνατον δὴ καὶ πολλὰ εἶναι; εἰ γὰρ πολλὰ εἴη, πάσχοι ἂν

τὰ ἀδύνατα. ἆρα τοῦτό ἐστιν ὃ βούλονταί σου οἱ λόγοι, οὐκ ἄλλο
τι ἢ διαμάχεσθαι παρὰ πάντα τὰ λεγόμενα ὡς οὐ πολλά ἐστι; καὶ
τούτου αὐτοῦ οἴει σοι τεκμήριον εἶναι ἕκαστον τῶν λόγων, ὥστε καὶ
ἡγῇ τοσαῦτα τεκμήρια παρέχεσθαι, ὅσουσπερ λόγους γέγραφας, ὡς
οὐκ ἔστι πολλά; οὕτω λέγεις, ἢ ἐγὼ οὐκ ὀρθῶς καταμανθάνω;
    Οὔκ, ἀλλά, φάναι τὸν Ζήνωνα, καλῶς συνῆκας ὅλον τὸ γράμμα ὃ
βούλεται.

314 After Socrates had heard this [sc. Zeno's reading of his book],
he asked him to read again the first hypothesis of the first
argument. When it had been read, he said: 'How is what you say
to be taken, Zeno? If the things that are are many, then you say
they must be both like and unlike, but that this is impossible – for
neither can what is unlike be like, nor what is like unlike? Is not
that what you say?' – 'Yes', said Zeno. – 'So if it is impossible that
what is unlike should be like and what is like unlike, it is also
impossible that there should be many things? For if there were
many things they would be subject to impossibilities. Is this the
purpose of your arguments – precisely to contend, against all that
is commonly said, that there are not many things? And do you
regard each of your arguments as evidence of this very conclusion,
so that in fact you reckon to provide as many proofs as the
arguments you have composed that there are not many things?
Is this what you are saying, or do I not understand you correctly?' –
'No,' said Zeno, 'you have understood the purpose of the whole
treatise beautifully.'

The treatise Plato describes is often taken to be Zeno's only literary
production: a list of titles preserved in the *Suda* (DK 29 A 2) commands
no credence whatever. Opinions differ about its form and plan,
although no one doubts that it was a philosophical puzzle-book of
astonishing ingenuity. It is natural to infer from **314** (see also **315–16**)
that it consisted simply of a collection of arguments, each of which
explicitly attacked the thesis that there are many things by deriving
contradictory consequences from it. But this inference is called into
question by reports of Zenonian arguments which represent them
neither as antinomies nor as directed explicitly against the hypothesis
that there are many things: notably Aristotle's reports of the famous
paradoxes of motion (**317–26** below). The difficulty may be met in
one of three ways. (*a*) The form of the book referred to in **314** was
as stated above. But Zeno wrote at least one other book, which
included the paradoxes of motion, the paradox of the millet seed
(Aristotle *Phys.* 250a19ff., DK 29 A 29), the paradox of place (Aristotle

Phys. 210b22ff., 209a23ff., DK 29 A 24), and doubtless others too. (*b*) Zeno wrote only one book, but our assumptions about its form must be wrong. Perhaps it included arguments whose explicit target was not plurality but motion. Perhaps not all its arguments were antinomies, but other forms of *reductio ad absurdum* were used. Plato either misrepresents the form of the book or else gives not a description of its arguments but an interpretation (conceivably a misinterpretation) of their underlying, although not always explicit, target. (*c*) There was a single Zenonian treatise all of whose arguments were explicit antinomies of plurality. The other paradoxes mentioned in (*a*) originally took that form. For example, the Achilles (**322**) might have been designed to prove that if there are many things, each must be both faster and slower than the others (note the wording in Aristotle's report, which suggests that the picturesque figures of Achilles and the tortoise may not belong to the formulation of the argument which he draws upon).

We do not know what principle of organization Zeno followed in ordering the arguments in his book or books, despite modern attempts to discern an architectonic structure, or at any rate an overall strategy, in their deployment. According to one popular suggestion (adopted in KR), the four paradoxes of motion discussed by Aristotle formed two pairs: one pair (the Stadium and the Achilles) assumed that space and time are infinitely divisible, the other (the Arrow and the Moving Rows) that they consist of indivisible minima; and in each pair one argument produced absurdities in the idea of a body's motion considered just in itself, the other in the idea of its motion considered relative to the motion of another body. A more elaborate and ambitious scheme, taking in **315–16** as well as **318–26**, was published at about the same time by G. E. L. Owen (see *Studies in Presocratic Philosophy* II, 143–65). Such schemes are undoubtedly attractive, but none has any ancient authority, nor have they withstood critical scrutiny very well; in particular, the suggestion that some of the paradoxes of motion assume that space and time are not infinitely divisible has met with fierce opposition (see e.g. D. J. Furley, *Two Studies in the Greek Atomists* (Princeton, 1967), 71–5).

THE EXTANT ANTINOMIES

315 Fr. 3, Simplicius *in Phys.* 140, 28 πάλιν γὰρ δεικνύς, ὅτι εἰ πολλά ἐστι, τὰ αὐτὰ πεπερασμένα ἐστὶ καὶ ἄπειρα, γράφει ταῦτα κατὰ λέξιν ὁ Ζήνων·

'εἰ πολλά ἐστιν, ἀνάγκη τοσαῦτα εἶναι ὅσα ἐστὶ καὶ οὔτε πλείονα αὐτῶν οὔτε ἐλάττονα. εἰ δὲ τοσαῦτά ἐστιν ὅσα ἐστί, πεπερασμένα ἂν εἴη.

'εἰ πολλά ἐστιν, ἄπειρα τὰ ὄντα ἐστίν· ἀεὶ γὰρ ἕτερα μεταξὺ τῶν ὄντων ἐστί, καὶ πάλιν ἐκείνων ἕτερα μεταξύ. καὶ οὕτως ἄπειρα τὰ ὄντα ἐστί.'

315 In proving once again that if there are many things, the same things are limited and unlimited, Zeno's own very words are as follows.

'If there are many things, it is necessary that they are just as many as they are, and neither more nor less than that. But if they are as many as they are, they will be limited.

'If there are many things, the things that are are unlimited; for there are always others between the things that are, and again others between those. And thus the things that are are unlimited.'

315 is the only unquestionably authentic fragment of Zeno which has come down to us intact. The puzzle it proposes is sometimes thought insufficiently puzzling. But each limb of the argument has considerable power to unsettle us. For example, the second probably turns on the thought that any two members of a collection must be separated by something if they are to be two things and not one. To this it may be objected that the principle it states is valid only if applied to densely ordered collections such as sets of points. But Zeno might reasonably feel unmoved by the objection unless we could convince him of alternative conditions of discreteness for three-dimensional objects, and show him why and how they differ from the conditions of discreteness for points. And we will be unable to think out good answers to those questions until we have engaged in just the sort of philosophical reflexion about what makes a thing one and not many which **315** is designed to provoke in us.

316 Frr. 2 and 1, Simplicius *in Phys.* 139, 9 and 140, 34   (a) ἐν δὴ τούτῳ δείκνυσιν, ὅτι οὗ μήτε μέγεθος μήτε πάχος μήτε ὄγκος μηθείς ἐστιν, οὐδ' ἂν εἴη τοῦτο. 'εἰ γὰρ ἄλλῳ ὄντι, φησί, προσγένοιτο, οὐδὲν ἂν μεῖζον ποιήσειεν· μεγέθους γὰρ μηδενὸς ὄντος, προσγενομένου δέ, οὐδὲν οἷόν τε εἰς μέγεθος ἐπιδοῦναι. καὶ οὕτως ἂν ἤδη τὸ προσγινόμενον οὐδὲν εἴη. εἰ δὲ ἀπογινομένου τὸ ἕτερον μηδὲν ἔλαττον ἔστι μηδὲ αὖ προσγινομένου αὐξήσεται, δῆλον ὅτι τὸ προσγενόμενον οὐδὲν ἦν οὐδὲ τὸ ἀπογενόμενον.' καὶ ταῦτα οὐχὶ τὸ ἓν ἀναιρῶν ὁ Ζήνων λέγει, ἀλλ' ὅτι μέγεθος ἔχει ἕκαστον τῶν πολλῶν καὶ ἀπείρων[1] τῷ πρὸ τοῦ

λαμβανομένου ἀεί τι εἶναι διὰ τὴν ἐπ᾽ ἄπειρον τομήν· ὃ δείκνυσι
προδείξας, ὅτι οὐδὲν ἔχει μέγεθος ἐκ τοῦ[2] ἕκαστον τῶν πολλῶν ἑαυτῷ
ταὐτὸν εἶναι καὶ ἕν.

¹ ἀπείρων MSS; ἄπειρον H. Fränkel.
² ἐκ τοῦ transposuit post πολλῶν Fränkel.

(b) τὸ δὲ κατὰ μέγεθος (*sc.* ἄπειρον ἔδειξε) πρότερον κατὰ τὴν αὐτὴν
ἐπιχείρησιν. προδείξας γὰρ ὅτι εἰ μὴ ἔχοι μέγεθος τὸ ὄν, οὐδ᾽ ἂν εἴη,
ἐπάγει 'εἰ δὲ ἔστιν, ἀνάγκη ἕκαστον μέγεθός τι ἔχειν καὶ πάχος καὶ
ἀπέχειν αὐτοῦ τὸ ἕτερον ἀπὸ τοῦ ἑτέρου. καὶ περὶ τοῦ προύχοντος
ὁ αὐτὸς λόγος. καὶ γὰρ ἐκεῖνο ἕξει μέγεθος καὶ προέξει αὐτοῦ τι. ὅμοιον
δὴ τοῦτο ἅπαξ τε εἰπεῖν καὶ ἀεὶ λέγειν· οὐδὲν γὰρ αὐτοῦ τοιοῦτον
ἔσχατον ἔσται οὔτε ἕτερον πρὸς ἕτερον οὐκ ἔσται. οὕτως εἰ πολλά
ἐστιν, ἀνάγκη αὐτὰ μικρά τε εἶναι καὶ μεγάλα· μικρὰ μὲν ὥστε μὴ ἔχειν
μέγεθος, μεγάλα δὲ ὥστε ἄπειρα εἶναι.'

316 (a) In this argument [*sc.* that proving the many both large
and small] he proves that what has neither magnitude nor solidity
nor bulk would not even exist. 'For', he says, 'if it were added to
something else that is, it would make it no larger; for if it were
of no magnitude, but were added, it [*sc.* what it was added to]
could not increase in magnitude. And thus what was added would
in fact be nothing. If when it is taken away the other thing is no
smaller, and again when it is added will not increase, it is clear
that what was added was nothing nor again what was taken away.'
And Zeno says this, not by way of abolishing the One, but because
each of the many infinite things has magnitude, since there is
always something in front of what is taken, because of infinite
division; and this he proves having first proved that it has no
magnitude since each of the many is the same as itself and one.

(b) Unlimitedness in magnitude he proved earlier [*sc.* than **315**]
by the same method of argument. For having first proved [*see* (a)
above] that if what is had no magnitude, it would not even exist,
he goes on: 'But if it is, it is necessary for each to have some
magnitude and thickness, and for the one part of it to be away
from the other. And the same argument holds about the part out
in front; for that too will have magnitude and a part of it will be
out in front. Indeed it is the same thing to say this once and to
go on saying it always; for no such part of it will be last, nor will
there not be one part related to another. – Thus if there are
many things, it is necessary that they are both small and large;
so small as not to have magnitude, so large as to be unlimited.'

Only parts of Zeno's complicated antinomy are quoted by Simplicius, to prove points he happens to be arguing in his commentary on Aristotle's *Physics*. Nonetheless he says enough about its structure for us to be able to reconstruct it with some confidence.

In the first limb of the antinomy Zeno tried to prove that if there are many things, they are so small as to be without any magnitude. Nothing survives of the proof. All we possess is Simplicius' assurance (at the end of **316** (a)) that Zeno inferred the conclusion from the premiss that each member of a plurality must be the same as itself and one – and so (we may guess) cannot have the parts necessary to magnitude (cf. Melissus' argument in **538**). The first extant section of the argument then followed (**316** (a)). It pointed up the un-acceptability of the conclusion of the first limb and prepared the way for the second: if something has no magnitude, then it does not exist at all – which contradicts the original supposition that there *are* many things.

316 (b) preserves the second limb, which starts from the assumption that if there are many things, they must each have magnitude. The Greek of the regress argument which follows is obscure, and it is unclear how Zeno thought he could infer the conclusion that something which has magnitude must have infinite size. Probably he believed the argument entitled him to hold (1) that any magnitude has an infinite number of parts; inferred (2) that the sum of an infinite number of parts of positive magnitude is itself infinite; and so concluded (3) that the magnitude of any member of a plurality is infinite. The conclusion is absurd, as was that of the first limb of the antinomy, which is accordingly not just an antinomy but a dilemma.

'Evidently', says J. Barnes, 'the argument is unsound; and it has found no serious defenders [*sc.* in modern times]. Yet its opponents are in disarray, and there is no agreement on just where the flaws – or the chief flaws – are to be found' (*The Presocratic Philosophers* 1, 244). As with **315**, so yet more emphatically in the present case is it true that a diagnosis requires of one a deep and clear-sighted engagement with the philosophical problems of infinity. Consequently a brief attempt to locate an 'error' on Zeno's part would not constitute a fruitful response to the paradox nor be likely to carry much conviction. But it is perhaps worth noting that (2) is not unrestrictedly true, and is false for infinite series which converge on zero (such as $\frac{1}{2}, \frac{1}{4}, \frac{1}{8}, \ldots$). In **316** (b) Zeno probably has in mind such a series; but his argument could easily be reformulated to generate a series of which (2) is true, e.g. a series which results in parts of equal size. Our critical attention is better directed to (1), and to its claim (which we now express with misleading precision) that if a magnitude is infinitely divisible, it must possess a set of parts which contains infinitely many members.

Zeno's target in **316** is the thesis that there are many things. Yet are not his arguments equally effective against Parmenides' conception of reality? For Parmenides took reality to be both unitary and extended: which makes him apparently vulnerable to each limb of the antinomy. In order to save Parmenides it has been said that Zeno thought infinite divisibility a consequence not of extension only (μέγεθος) but of solidity (πάχος) or bulk (ὄγκος). But his argument plainly and correctly assumes that mere extension is sufficient to generate the regress. It has been claimed that Eleatic monism denies extension to reality. But this seems plainly false. It is hard to resist the conclusion that **316** does indeed undermine Parmenides' *Truth*, and that Zeno was perfectly well aware of this. Perhaps he enjoyed the thought that common sense and Parmenidean metaphysics can be embarrassed by precisely the same dialectical manoeuvres.

THE PARADOXES OF MOTION

317 Aristotle *Phys.* Z9, 239b9 (DK 29 A 25) τέτταρες δ' εἰσὶν οἱ λόγοι περὶ κινήσεως Ζήνωνος οἱ παρέχοντες τὰς δυσκολίας τοῖς λύουσιν.

317 Zeno's arguments about motion, which cause such trouble to those who try to solve the problems that they present, are four in number. (*After Gaye*)

This particular group of paradoxes had evidently already in Aristotle's day achieved the notoriety they still enjoy and become recognized as a distinct set of puzzles, although we do not know whether Zeno himself intended them to be read as such. Our account attempts only to expose the structure of each puzzle and its salient features. For further philosophical exploration the reader is referred to the Selective Bibliography.

(i) *The Stadium*

318 Aristotle *Phys.* Z9, 239b11 (DK 29 A 25: continuing **317**) ...πρῶτος μὲν ὁ περὶ τοῦ μὴ κινεῖσθαι διὰ τὸ πρότερον εἰς τὸ ἥμισυ δεῖν ἀφικέσθαι τὸ φερόμενον ἢ πρὸς τὸ τέλος...

319 Aristotle *Topics* Θ8, 160b7 (DK 29 A 25) πολλοὺς γὰρ λόγους ἔχομεν ἐναντίους ταῖς δόξαις, καθάπερ Ζήνωνος, ὅτι οὐκ ἐνδέχεται κινεῖσθαι οὐδὲ τὸ στάδιον διελθεῖν.

320 Aristotle *Phys.* Z2, 233a21 (DK 29 A 25) διὸ καὶ ὁ Ζήνωνος λόγος ψεῦδος λαμβάνει τὸ μὴ ἐνδέχεσθαι τὰ ἄπειρα διελθεῖν ἢ ἅψασθαι τῶν ἀπείρων καθ' ἕκαστον ἐν πεπερασμένῳ χρόνῳ. διχῶς γὰρ λέγεται καὶ τὸ μῆκος καὶ ὁ χρόνος ἄπειρον, καὶ ὅλως πᾶν τὸ συνεχές, ἤτοι κατὰ διαίρεσιν ἢ τοῖς ἐσχάτοις. τῶν μὲν οὖν κατὰ ποσὸν ἀπείρων οὐκ ἐνδέχεται ἅψασθαι ἐν πεπερασμένῳ χρόνῳ, τῶν δὲ κατὰ διαίρεσιν ἐνδέχεται· καὶ γὰρ αὐτὸς ὁ χρόνος οὕτως ἄπειρος. ὥστε ἐν τῷ ἀπείρῳ καὶ οὐκ ἐν τῷ πεπερασμένῳ συμβαίνει διιέναι τὸ ἄπειρον, καὶ ἅπτεσθαι τῶν ἀπείρων τοῖς ἀπείροις, οὐ τοῖς πεπερασμένοις.

> **318** ... The first asserts the non-existence of motion on the ground that that which is in locomotion must arrive at the half-way stage before it arrives at the goal... (*Tr. Gaye*)
>
> **319** For we have many arguments contrary to accepted opinion, such as Zeno's that motion is impossible and that you cannot traverse the stadium.
>
> **320** Hence Zeno's argument makes a false assumption in asserting that it is impossible for a thing to pass over or come in contact with infinite things individually in a finite time. For there are two senses in which length and time and generally anything continuous are called 'infinite': they are called so either in respect of divisibility or in respect of their extremities. So while a thing in a finite time cannot come in contact with things quantitatively infinite, it can come in contact with things infinite in respect of divisibility: for in this sense the time itself is also infinite; and so we find that the time occupied by the passage over the infinite is not a finite but an infinite time, and the contact with the infinites is made in times not finite but infinite in number. (*After Gaye*)

Aristotle's account of this puzzle (sometimes known as the Dichotomy) is brief and allusive in the extreme: it is even unclear whether the task of the runner in the stadium is to reach the half-way point *before* the half-way point of the course (and then the half-way point before that, etc.) or rather the half-way point *past* the half-way point (etc.). But we can extract the following argument:

(1) To reach his goal, a runner must touch infinitely many points ordered in the sequence $\frac{1}{2}$, $\frac{1}{4}$, $\frac{1}{8}$, ...
(2) It is impossible to touch infinitely many points in a finite time. So
(3) the runner cannot reach his goal.

Aristotle thinks we can easily resist the absurd conclusion (3) by rejecting (2): a finite time is infinitely divisible, and an infinitely divisible time is sufficient for the runner to traverse an infinitely divisible distance and touch the points which mark its divisions.

321 Aristotle *Phys.* Θ8, 263a15–18, b3–9   ἀλλ' αὕτη ἡ λύσις πρὸς μὲν ἐρωτῶντα ἱκανῶς ἔχει (ἠρωτᾶτο γὰρ εἰ ἐν πεπερασμένῳ ἄπειρα ἐνδέχεται διεξελθεῖν ἢ ἀριθμῆσαι), πρὸς δὲ τὸ πρᾶγμα καὶ τὴν ἀλήθειαν οὐχ ἱκανῶς... ὥστε λεκτέον πρὸς τὸν ἐρωτῶντα εἰ ἐνδέχεται ἄπειρα διεξελθεῖν ἢ ἐν χρόνῳ ἢ ἐν μήκει, ὅτι ἔστιν ὡς, ἔστιν δ' ὡς οὔ. ἐντελεχείᾳ μὲν γὰρ ὄντα οὐκ ἐνδέχεται, δυνάμει δὲ ἐνδέχεται· ὁ γὰρ συνεχῶς κινούμενος κατὰ συμβεβηκὸς ἄπειρα διελήλυθεν, ἁπλῶς δ' οὔ· συμβέβηκε γὰρ τῇ γραμμῇ ἄπειρα ἡμίσεα εἶναι, ἡ δ' οὐσία ἐστὶν ἑτέρα καὶ τὸ εἶναι.

> **321**   But although this solution is an adequate reply to the questioner (for the question was whether it is possible to traverse or count infinite things in a finite time), it is inadequate to the facts and the truth... So when someone asks the question whether it is possible to traverse infinite things – either in time or in distance – we must reply that in a way it is but in a way it is not. For if they exist actually, it is not possible, but if potentially, it is; for someone in continuous movement has traversed infinite things incidentally, not without qualification; for it is incidental to the line to be infinitely many halves, but its essence and being are different.

Aristotle now has second thoughts. The solution in **320** provides a reply to Zeno adequate *ad hominem*. But (2) is less easily dismissed if reformulated as:

(2′) It is impossible to get through the task of touching infinitely many points.

Aristotle responds to the reformulated argument by observing that (2′) would be true only if 'infinitely many points' meant 'infinitely many actually existent points'; he apparently believes it would then be true because he thinks it would be impossible to perform an infinite number of discrete physical acts which counted as 'touching' or 'coming into contact with' each of an actual infinity of points (263a19–b3). But in fact, Aristotle supposes, a weaker interpretation of 'infinitely many points' is required by (1): the runner must traverse a finite distance divided by an infinity of points whose existence is only potential (i.e., as we might say, a distance which may simply be mathematically represented as divided according to the infinite series $\frac{1}{2}, \frac{1}{4}, \frac{1}{8}, \ldots$). And if this weaker reading is adopted in (2′), (2′) is false.

Aristotle's second solution brings to light the fundamental issues which the paradox raises and which are still the subject of intense and unconcluded debate. In particular, philosophers cannot agree whether the impossibility of completing the performance of an infinite number of discrete physical acts (if indeed that *is* impossible) is a logical or merely a physical impossibility, nor what in either case the impossibility consists in.

(ii) *Achilles and the Tortoise*

322 Aristotle *Phys.* Z9, 239b14   δεύτερος δ' ὁ καλούμενος Ἀχιλλεύς. ἔστι δ' οὗτος ὅτι τὸ βραδύτατον οὐδέποτε καταληφθήσεται θέον ὑπὸ τοῦ ταχίστου· ἔμπροσθεν γὰρ ἀναγκαῖον ἐλθεῖν τὸ διῶκον ὅθεν ὥρμησε τὸ φεῦγον, ὥστ' ἀεί τι προέχειν ἀναγκαῖον τὸ βραδύτερον. ἔστι δὲ καὶ οὗτος ὁ αὐτὸς λόγος τῷ διχοτομεῖν, διαφέρει δ' ἐν τῷ διαιρεῖν μὴ δίχα τὸ προσλαμβανόμενον μέγεθος.

> **322** The second is the so-called 'Achilles', and it amounts to this, that in a race the quickest runner can never overtake the slowest, since the pursuer must first reach the point whence the pursued started, so that the slower must always hold a lead. This argument is the same in principle as that which depends on bisection, though it differs from it in that the added magnitudes are not divided into halves. (*After Gaye*)

Where the runner in **318–19** was required to reach a succession of half-way points, Achilles has to reach the point from which the tortoise started, and then the point the tortoise had reached when he reached its starting-point, and so on *ad infinitum*. If we assume that pursuer and pursued run at uniform speeds, then Achilles' series of runs again constitutes a geometrical progression which converges on zero. As Aristotle comments (239b24–5), the Achilles is simply a theatrical version of the Stadium.

(iii) *The Arrow*

323 Aristotle *Phys.* Z9, 239b30–3, 5–9 (DK 29 A 27)
(a) τρίτος δ' ὁ νῦν ῥηθείς, ὅτι ἡ ὀιστὸς φερομένη ἔστηκεν. συμβαίνει δὲ παρὰ τὸ λαμβάνειν τὸν χρόνον συγκεῖσθαι ἐκ τῶν νῦν· μὴ διδομένου γὰρ τούτου οὐκ ἔσται ὁ συλλογισμός.
(b) Ζήνων δὲ παραλογίζεται· εἰ γὰρ αἰεί, φησίν, ἠρεμεῖ πᾶν [ἢ κινεῖται]¹ ὅταν ᾖ κατὰ τὸ ἴσον, ἔστιν δ' αἰεὶ τὸ φερόμενον ἐν τῷ νῦν, ἀκίνητον τὴν φερομένην εἶναι ὀιστόν. τοῦτο δ' ἐστὶ ψεῦδος· οὐ γὰρ σύγκειται ὁ χρόνος ἐκ τῶν νῦν τῶν ἀδιαιρέτων, ὥσπερ οὐδ' ἄλλο μέγεθος οὐδέν.

¹ ἢ κινεῖται seclusit Zeller; cf. Ross *ad loc.*

324   Fr. 4, Diogenes Laertius IX, 72   Ζήνων δὲ τὴν κίνησιν ἀναιρεῖ λέγων 'τὸ κινούμενον οὔτ' ἐν ᾧ ἔστι τόπῳ κινεῖται οὔτ' ἐν ᾧ μὴ ἔστι.'

323   (a) Third is the one just mentioned, that the arrow in locomotion is at rest. This follows from assuming that time is composed of 'nows'; for if that is not granted, the conclusion will not follow.

(b) Zeno argues fallaciously; for if, he says, everything always rests when it is against what is equal, and what is in locomotion is always in the now, the arrow in locomotion is motionless. But this is false: for time is not composed of indivisible 'nows', no more than is any other magnitude.

324   Zeno abolishes motion, saying: 'What is in motion moves neither in the place it is in nor in one in which it is not.'

The report in **323** (b) is textually uncertain and again very condensed; it does not disclose that the argument of the Arrow probably formed the first limb of the antinomy ascribed to Zeno in **324** and later borrowed by Diodorus Cronus (Sextus *adv. math.* x, 87). Here is a reconstruction of the reasoning Aristotle summarizes:

(1) Anything occupying a place just its own size is at rest.
(2) In the present, what is moving occupies a place just its own size.
So   (3) in the present, what is moving is at rest.
Now   (4) what is moving always moves in the present.
So   (5) what is moving is always – throughout its movement – at rest.

Aristotle objects to the inference from (3) and (4) to (5). He treats Zeno as meaning by 'the now' what he himself means by it, viz. the present conceived as an indivisible instant; and he suggests that we may judge the inference valid only if we assume falsely with Zeno that a period of time is the sum of the indivisible instants within it. Aristotle's suggestion is mistaken, and it is responsible for the equally mistaken notion that Zeno assumes in the Arrow that space and time are not infinitely divisible. His argument requires no determinate assumption about the structure of space and time; and all he requires for the validity of his inference is that what is true of something *at every moment* of a period of time (whether or not moments are indivisible instants) is true of it *throughout* the period.

The paradox in fact poses an incisive challenge to the attractive idea that motion must occur – if it occurs at all – in the present. It shows that it is hard to reconcile this idea with the equally attractive notion that in the present what moves cannot be traversing any distance. Perhaps there are two incompatible conceptions of the 'now' at work here – one that of a present duration, the other that of an indivisible instant, as it were a line dividing past from future. If so, that does not make Zeno's argument any the less impressive. For it is such arguments which force the distinction upon us. And the choice between the alternatives hinges on one's deep-seated predilections in the philosophy of time, as is shown by J. D. Lear (*Phronesis* 26 (1981), 91–104).

(iv) *The Moving Rows*

325 Aristotle *Phys.* 239b33 (DK 29 A 28) τέταρτος δ' ὁ περὶ τῶν ἐν σταδίῳ κινουμένων ἐξ ἐναντίας ἴσων ὄγκων παρ' ἴσους, τῶν μὲν ἀπὸ τέλους τοῦ σταδίου τῶν δ' ἀπὸ μέσου, ἴσῳ τάχει, ἐν ᾧ συμβαίνειν οἴεται ἴσον εἶναι χρόνον τῷ διπλασίῳ τὸν ἥμισυν. ἔστι δ' ὁ παραλογισμὸς ἐν τῷ τὸ μὲν παρὰ κινούμενον τὸ δὲ παρ' ἠρεμοῦν τὸ ἴσον μέγεθος ἀξιοῦν τῷ ἴσῳ τάχει τὸν ἴσον φέρεσθαι χρόνον. τοῦτο δ' ἐστὶ ψεῦδος. οἷον ἔστωσαν οἱ ἑστῶτες ἴσοι ὄγκοι ἐφ' ὧν τὰ ΑΑ, οἱ δ' ἐφ' ὧν τὰ ΒΒ ἀρχόμενοι ἀπὸ τοῦ μέσου,[1] ἴσοι τὸν ἀριθμὸν τούτοις ὄντες καὶ τὸ μέγεθος, οἱ δ' ἐφ' ὧν τὰ ΓΓ ἀπὸ τοῦ ἐσχάτου, ἴσοι τὸν ἀριθμὸν ὄντες τούτοις καὶ τὸ μέγεθος, καὶ ἰσοταχεῖς τοῖς Β. συμβαίνει δὴ τὸ πρῶτον Β ἅμα ἐπὶ τῷ ἐσχάτῳ εἶναι καὶ τὸ πρῶτον Γ, παρ' ἄλληλα κινουμένων. συμβαίνει δὲ καὶ τὸ Γ παρὰ πάντα [τὰ Α][2] διεξεληλυθέναι, τὸ δὲ Β παρὰ τὰ ἡμίση· ὥστε ἥμισυν εἶναι τὸν χρονον· ἴσον γὰρ ἑκάτερόν ἐστιν παρ' ἕκαστον. ἅμα δὲ συμβαίνει τὸ πρῶτον Β[3] παρὰ πάντα τὰ Γ παρεληλυθέναι· ἅμα γὰρ ἔσται τὸ πρῶτον Γ καὶ τὸ πρῶτον Β ἐπὶ τοῖς ἐναντίοις ἐσχάτοις [ἴσον χρόνον παρ' ἕκαστον γινόμενον τῶν Β ὅσον περ τῶν Α, ὥς φησι],[4] διὰ τὸ ἀμφότερα ἴσον χρόνον παρὰ τὰ Α γίγνεσθαι. ὁ μὲν οὖν λόγος οὗτός ἐστιν, συμβαίνει δὲ παρὰ τὸ εἰρημένον ψεῦδος.

[1] Post μέσου habent FJ²K τῶν Α: om. EHIJ¹, Ross; cf. Simpl. *in Phys.* 1017, 4.
[2] τὰ Α: E²FJK, Simpl. *in Phys.* 1018, 1, Alex. apud Simpl. 1019, 28; τὰ Β: E¹HI; seclusit Ross.
[3] τὸ πρῶτον Β Cornford: τὸ ΑΒ E; τὰ Β cett.
[4] Seclusit Ross.

326 Diagram of Alexander *ap.* Simplicium *in Phys.* 1016, 14

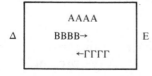

Α ὄγκοι ἑστῶτες
Β ὄγκοι κινούμενοι ἀπὸ τοῦ Δ ἐπὶ τὸ Ε
Γ ὄγκοι κινούμενοι ἀπὸ τοῦ Ε ἐπὶ τὸ Δ
Δ ἀρχὴ τοῦ σταδίου
Ε τέλος τοῦ σταδίου

325   The fourth is the one about equal bodies which move in opposite directions past equal bodies in a stadium at equal speed, the one row from the end of the stadium [towards us] and the other from the middle [away from us] – in which he thinks it follows that half the time is equal to [its] double. The fallacy consists in requiring that things which move at equal speed past a moving body and past a body at rest of equal magnitude take an equal time. But this is false. For example, let the stationary equal bodies be A, A ...; let B, B ... be those starting from the middle, equal in number and magnitude to them; let Γ, Γ ... be those starting from the end, equal in number and magnitude to them [*sc.* the As], and equal in speed to the Bs. Now it follows that the first B and the first Γ are at the end at the same time, as they [*sc.* the Bs and Γs] move past each other. And it follows that the Γ [*sc.* the first Γ] has gone right past all of them [*sc.* the Bs], but the B [*sc.* the first B] past only half [what it passes, *sc.* the As]: so the time is half, for each is alongside each for an equal time. And at the same time it follows that the first B has gone past all the Γs; for the first Γ and the first B will be at opposite ends at the same time, because both are an equal time alongside the As. This then is his argument, and it depends on the falsehood we have mentioned.[1]

326   A = stationary bodies.
   B = bodies moving from Δ towards E.
   Γ = bodies moving from E towards Δ.
   Δ = starting-place.
   E = goal.

[1] As the square brackets here (and our notes to the Greek text) indicate, **325** bristles with difficulties and uncertainties. For full discussion see e.g. H. D. P. Lee, *Zeno of Elea* (Cambridge, 1936), 83–102, W. D. Ross, *Aristotle's Physics* (Oxford, 1936), 660–6. Aristotle's unsatisfactory exposition is plainly a set of notes originally intended for use in an oral presentation aided by reference to diagrams such as **326**.

The diagram in **326** represents the starting-position of the bodies (presumably contiguous) in the three rows which Aristotle posits in his illustration of Zeno's argument; he apparently assumes, without telling us, that the As are in the middle of the stadium and that the leading Γ begins at the midpoint like the leading B. Aristotle then focuses on a subsequent position that must indeed be reached by the bodies, given the initial hypothesis about their size, speed and direction set out in the first sentence of **325**: viz. the position in which the three rows are all exactly aligned with each other ('the first B and the first Γ are at the end [presumably of each other's rows] at the same time'). He points out two simple truths: when the first Γ has passed all the Bs, the first B (i) has passed only two As, but (ii) has passed all the Γs. Zeno's mistake, according to Aristotle, was to go on to assume that each moving body must be opposite every body it passes for an equal time. This led him to conclude that (i') the first B takes only half the time to pass half the As as the first Γ takes to pass all the Bs. But from (i') and (ii) it follows that (ii') the time it takes it to pass half the As is also half what it takes it to pass all the Γs. So the first B's passage past half the As takes both the same time and half the time as its passage past the Γs.

It has often been supposed (as in KR) that, despite Aristotle's failure to say so, Zeno must have postulated that his bodies were minimal, indivisible bodies, each of which took a minimal, indivisible time to pass a stationary body. The paradox then constitutes a powerful objection to the postulate, since each B must pass each Γ in half an indivisible time. Yet Aristotle's own version of the argument yields a more satisfying puzzle than he allows. Baldly stated, the assumption he attributes to Zeno does look like a banal mistake. But in order to force us to the conclusion he comes to in **325**, Zeno needs only to get us to accept the plausible idea that if a body moves past n bodies of size m, it moves a distance of mn units; simple arithmetic will then show that moving mn units will take half the time of moving $2mn$ units at the same speed. Nor is this idea about the measurement of movement easily abandoned in favour of a relative theory. For if the distance a body moves is simply a function of its positions relative to other bodies, is there any absolute basis for ascribing movement to *it* at all?

A comparison with the Arrow suggests itself. Both paradoxes expose difficulties in our ordinary unreflective thought about motion: we often assume that if real and accessible to experience, it must occur in the present moment and be subject to an absolute measure. An obvious alternative in each case is to make the motion of a body a matter of relative position: whether its own earlier and later positions at indivisible instants (as perhaps the arrow) or these relative to those of other bodies (as perhaps the moving rows). But in each case motion is then apparently no longer accessible to direct experience, and as such lacks at any rate the reality we thought it had.

ZENO'S AIMS

327 Plato *Parmenides* 128c (DK29A12) ...ἔστι δὲ τό γε ἀληθὲς
βοήθειά τις ταῦτα [τὰ γράμματα] τῷ Παρμενίδου λόγῳ πρὸς τοὺς
ἐπιχειροῦντας αὐτὸν κωμῳδεῖν ὡς, εἰ ἕν ἐστι, πολλὰ καὶ γελοῖα
συμβαίνει πάσχειν τῷ λόγῳ καὶ ἐναντία αὑτῷ. ἀντιλέγει δὴ οὖν
τοῦτο τὸ γράμμα πρὸς τοὺς τὰ πολλὰ λέγοντας, καὶ ἀνταποδίδωσι
ταὐτὰ καὶ πλείω, τοῦτο βουλόμενον δηλοῦν, ὡς ἔτι γελοιότερα
πάσχοι ἂν αὐτῶν ἡ ὑπόθεσις, εἰ πολλά ἐστιν, ἢ ἡ τοῦ ἓν εἶναι, εἴ τις
ἱκανῶς ἐπεξίοι. διὰ τοιαύτην δὴ φιλονικίαν ὑπὸ νέου ὄντος ἐμοῦ
ἐγράφη...

327 ...In reality the book is a sort of defence of Parmenides'
argument against those who try to make fun of it by showing that,
if there is a One, many absurd and contradictory consequences
follow for his argument. This book is a retort against those who
believe in plurality; it pays them back in their own coin, and with
something to spare, by seeking to show that, if anyone examines
the matter thoroughly, yet more absurd consequences follow from
their hypothesis of plurality than from that of the One. In such
a spirit of contention I wrote it while I was a young man...

The *Parmenides* devotes considerable space (127D–128E) to discussion
of the point of Zeno's work, evidently because Zeno himself did not
declare his own purposes. Plato's assessment in **327** has usually, if not
universally, been accepted. It may be that some of Zeno's arguments
(e.g. the paradoxes of motion) were not directed at the specific belief
that there are many things. But they all assault common sense; and
Plato's essential point is that Zeno defended Parmenides against
outraged common sense.[1] Again, monism was not Parmenides'
central tenet, but as we have seen (pp. 249ff.) he is certainly
committed to some form of monism. It is true that some of Zeno's
arguments in fact undermine Parmenidean positions as much as
pluralistic common sense (pp. 267–9).[2] From this we should not
conclude that Zeno was not a Parmenidean, but perhaps that he was
a Parmenidean in method rather than in doctrine. That is, his
paradoxes should be interpreted as showing that it is no conclusive
objection to a philosophical thesis that it leads or seems to lead to
absurd conclusions – or if it is, common sense is as vulnerable as
Eleatic logic. And the general moral intended will have been the
thoroughly Parmenidean exhortation (cf. **294** above): 'Don't just
think about conclusions: apply your critical powers to the arguments
which produce them.' This interpretation may be supported by
Aristotle's assessment of Zeno:

328 Diogenes Laertius VIII, 57 (DK 29 A 10) Ἀριστοτέλης δ' ἐν τῷ Σοφιστῇ φησι πρῶτον Ἐμπεδοκλέα ῥητορικὴν εὑρεῖν, Ζήνωνα δὲ διαλεκτικήν.

328 Aristotle in the *Sophist* says that Empedocles was the first to discover rhetoric and Zeno dialectic.

By dialectic Aristotle has in mind the sort of philosophical interrogation pursued by Socrates in the early Platonic dialogues: the questioner elicits from his interlocutor assent to an *endoxon*, a belief in good standing accepted by everyone or most people or the experts, which he then forces him to abandon whether by reducing it to absurdity or by showing that it conflicts with other beliefs the interlocutor holds. If one suspects the motives or the tactics of the questioner, one will be inclined to charge him with being a mere controversialist (*antilogikos*), which is what Plato had in mind when he described Zeno in the *Phaedrus* thus:

329 Plato *Phaedrus* 261D (DK 29 A 13) τὸν οὖν Ἐλεατικὸν Παλαμήδην λέγοντα οὐκ ἴσμεν τέχνῃ ὥστε φαίνεσθαι τοῖς ἀκούουσι τὰ αὐτὰ ὅμοια καὶ ἀνόμοια, καὶ ἓν καὶ πολλά, μένοντά τε αὖ καὶ φερόμενα;

329 Do we not then know that this Eleatic Palamedes argues with such skill that the same things appear to his listeners to be both like and unlike, both one and many, both at rest and in motion?

¹ KR supported the once popular view that Zeno's principal target was not common sense, but a particular school of philosophical pluralists, namely the Pythagoreans. But there is no solid evidence that the Pythagoreans of this period held any distinctive philosophical views about the pluralities constituted by the contents of the universe (other than that they exhibited *harmonia*), or that Zeno had any such special position in mind.
² It is not likely that Zeno explicitly attacked monism, as Simplicius thought Eudemus supposed: **330** Eudemus *ap.* Simplicium *in Phys.* 97, 12 (DK 29 A 16) καὶ Ζήνωνά φασι λέγειν, εἴ τις αὐτῷ τὸ ἓν ἀποδοίη τί ποτέ ἐστιν, ἕξειν τὰ ὄντα λέγειν. (*They say that Zeno used to say that, if anyone would explain to him what the one was, he would then be able to account for existing things.*) **331** Simplicius *in Phys.* 99, 7 (DK 29 A 21) ἐν ᾗ ὁ μὲν Ζήνωνος λόγος ἄλλος τις ἔοικεν οὗτος εἶναι παρ' ἐκεῖνον τὸν ἐν βιβλίῳ φερόμενον, οὗ καὶ ὁ Πλάτων ἐν τῷ Παρμενίδῃ μέμνηται. ἐκεῖ μὲν γὰρ ὅτι πολλὰ οὐκ ἔστι δείκνυσι βοηθῶν ἐκ τοῦ ἀντικειμένου τῷ Παρμενίδῃ ἓν εἶναι λέγοντι· ἐνταῦθα δέ, ὡς ὁ Εὔδημός φησι, καὶ ἀνῇρει τὸ ἓν (τὴν γὰρ στιγμὴν ὡς τὸ ἓν λέγει), τὰ δὲ πολλὰ εἶναι συγχωρεῖ. ὁ μέντοι Ἀλέξανδρος καὶ ἐνταῦθα τοῦ Ζήνωνος ὡς τὰ πολλὰ ἀναιροῦντος μεμνῆσθαι τὸν Εὔδημον οἴεται. 'ὡς γὰρ ἱστορεῖ, φησίν, Εὔδημος, Ζήνων ὁ Παρμενίδου γνώριμος ἐπειρᾶτο δεικνύναι, ὅτι μὴ οἷόν τε τὰ ὄντα πολλὰ εἶναι τῷ μηδὲν εἶναι ἐν τοῖς οὖσιν ἕν, τὰ δὲ πολλὰ πλῆθος εἶναι ἑνάδων.' (*Zeno's argument in this passage seems to be different from the one in his*

book to which Plato refers in the Parmenides. *For there, arguing in support of Parmenides' monism from the opposite point of view, he shows that there is no plurality: but here, as Eudemus says, he both does away with the one (for he speaks of the point as the one), and allows the existence of plurality. However, Alexander thinks that here too Eudemus is referring to Zeno as doing away with plurality. He says: 'As Eudemus records, Zeno the friend of Parmenides tried to show that it is not possible for there to be plurality because there is no "one" among existing things, and plurality is a collection of units.')* Alexander's alternative interpretation of Eudemus is probably correct (cf. Simplicius *in Phys.* 97, 13 (DK 29A21)): Eudemus was merely attributing to Zeno the idea that no coherent account can be given of the units of which a plurality must presumably consist - for if the units are indivisible (like points), they have no real existence, but if they are divisible (like ordinary perceptible things) they are not units but pluralities (cf. **316** (a) above).

ZENO'S INFLUENCE

It is unclear whether Zeno's work preceded and influenced the philosophizing of Melissus and Anaxagoras or whether the reverse is the case. A much more decisive impact is evident in the atomism of Leucippus and Democritus, and we discuss it below (pp. 408–9). Among the sophists Gorgias' curious work *On What Is Not* is deeply imbued with Zenonian methods of argument and echoes a number of specific Zenonian trains of thought, while in his advocacy of the construction of contradictory arguments on every subject Protagoras must surely have drawn inspiration from Zeno. Plato's interest in Zeno flowered relatively late in his philosophical life: it resulted in the elaborate and forbidding antinomies which fill the last thirty pages of the *Parmenides* with seminal arguments about motion, place and time (*inter alia*), arguments that were to provide Aristotle in the *Physics* with much stimulus when he came to treat of these topics himself. The discussion of the continuity of motion in the *Physics* clearly owes a more direct debt to Zeno, too, as do the arguments against motion of the early Hellenistic dialectician Diodorus Cronus (Sextus *adv. math.* x, 85ff.). But philosophers have never discussed the paradoxes more intensely than in our own century, ever since Russell succumbed to their fascination in its first decade. Of all the Presocratics Zeno has most life in him today.

CHAPTER X

Empedocles of Acragas

DATE

332 Diogenes Laertius VIII, 51 (DK31A1) Ἐμπεδοκλῆς, ὥς φησιν Ἱππόβοτος, Μέτωνος ἦν υἱὸς τοῦ Ἐμπεδοκλέους Ἀκραγαντῖνος ...λέγει δὲ καὶ Ἐρατοσθένης ἐν τοῖς Ὀλυμπιονίκαις τὴν πρώτην καὶ ἑβδομηκοστὴν ὀλυμπιάδα νενικηκέναι τὸν τοῦ Μέτωνος πατέρα, μάρτυρι χρώμενος Ἀριστοτέλει. Ἀπολλόδωρος δ' ὁ γραμματικὸς ἐν τοῖς Χρονικοῖς φησιν ὡς

> ἦν μὲν Μέτωνος υἱός, εἰς δὲ Θουρίους
> αὐτὸν νεωστὶ παντελῶς ἐκτισμένους
> ⟨ὁ⟩ Γλαῦκος ἐλθεῖν φησιν.

εἶθ' ὑποβάς·

> οἱ δ' ἱστοροῦντες, ὡς πεφευγὼς οἴκοθεν
> εἰς τὰς Συρακούσας μετ' ἐκείνων ἐπολέμει
> πρὸς Ἀθηναίους ἐμοὶ ⟨γε⟩ τελέως ἀγνοεῖν
> δοκοῦσιν· ἢ γὰρ οὐκέτ' ἦν ἢ παντελῶς
> ὑπεργεγηρακώς, ὅπερ οὐχὶ φαίνεται.

Ἀριστοτέλης γὰρ αὐτόν, ἔτι τε Ἡρακλείδης, ἐξήκοντα ἐτῶν φησὶ τετελευτηκέναι.

333 Diogenes Laertius VIII, 74 (DK31A1) ἤκμαζε δὲ κατὰ τὴν τετάρτην καὶ ὀγδοηκοστὴν ὀλυμπιάδα.

334 Aristotle *Met.* A3, 984a11 (DK31A6) Ἀναξαγόρας δὲ ὁ Κλαζομένιος τῇ μὲν ἡλικίᾳ πρότερος ὢν τούτου (*sc.* Ἐμπεδοκλέους) τοῖς δ' ἔργοις ὕστερος...

335 Simplicius *in Phys.* 25, 19, quoting Theophrastus (DK31A7) Ἐμπεδοκλῆς ὁ Ἀκραγαντῖνος οὐ πολὺ κατόπιν τοῦ Ἀναξαγόρου γεγονώς, Παρμενίδου δὲ ζηλωτὴς καὶ πλησιαστὴς καὶ ἔτι μᾶλλον τῶν Πυθαγορείων...

336 Diogenes Laertius VIII, 58 (DK31A1) φησὶ δὲ Σάτυρος ἐν τοῖς Βίοις ὅτι καὶ ἰατρὸς ἦν καὶ ῥήτωρ ἄριστος. Γοργίαν γοῦν τὸν Λεοντῖνον αὐτοῦ γενέσθαι μαθητήν.

332 Empedocles, according to Hippobotus, was the son of Meton, himself son of Empedocles, and came from Acragas... Eratosthenes, in his *Olympic victors*, says that the father of Meton won a victory in the seventy-first Olympiad, and he cites Aristotle as evidence. Apollodorus the grammarian writes in his *Chronicles* that 'He was the son of Meton, and Glaucus says that he came to Thurii very soon after its foundation.' Then further on: 'Those who relate that in exile from his home he went to Syracuse and fought with them against the Athenians seem to me to be completely mistaken; for either he was no longer alive or in extreme old age, which he does not seem to have reached.' For according to Aristotle, and also Heraclides, he died at the age of sixty.

333 He flourished in the eighty-fourth Olympiad.

334 Anaxagoras of Clazomenae, who, though older than Empedocles, was later in his philosophical activity... (*Tr. Ross*)

335 Empedocles of Acragas was born not long after Anaxagoras, and was an emulator and associate of Parmenides, and even more of the Pythagoreans...

336 Satyrus in his *Lives* says that he was also a physician and an excellent orator – at all events, he says, Gorgias of Leontini became his pupil.

If Anaxagoras was born *c.* 500 B.C. (see p. 353 below) and Gorgias *c.* 485 (cf. DK 82 A 6, 7), then Empedocles may have lived *c.* 495–35. These dates fit well with what we are told of his philosophical affiliations by Theophrastus (**335**), and with the story of his visit to Thurii (founded 445/4 B.C.). That story presumably led Apollodorus (whom Diogenes is doubtless following in **333**) to put his *floruit* in 444–1 B.C., which seems at the very least a decade too late.

LIFE

Empedocles, like Pythagoras and Heraclitus, was a favourite subject (cf. p. 182) for apocryphal biographical tales. A considerable number of them, drawn from numerous sources, are preserved by Diogenes. For the most part they are concerned either with his political activities or with his death, and it is the former group alone which may perhaps contain a germ of truth, although the tale of his leap into the crater of Etna (Diog. L. VIII, 67–72, DK 31 A 1) is what has always captured the imagination. He is said on Aristotle's authority to have been an ardent democrat (Diog. L. VIII, 63, DK 31 A 1); we hear of his refusing the kingship of his city, and of his breaking up an otherwise unknown organization called the Thousand (Diog. L. VIII, 63 and 66, DK 31 A 1; cf. Plutarch *adv. Colot.* 1126B, DK 31 A 14). Here at least we do seem to have something other than a misguided embellishment of his own words in his poems, which might indeed rather lead one to suppose that he held anti-democratic views (as the historian Timaeus remarked, *ap.* Diog. L. VIII, 66, DK 31 A 1). We may at any rate infer that Empedocles took a leading part as a democrat in the affairs of his city, as might be expected of a man of distinguished family as interested and accomplished in oratory as he seems to have been (**336**; Aristotle went so far as to call him the inventor of rhetoric, **328**). His later reputation as a doctor (**336**; cf. e.g. Celsus *Proem.* 2, 11; Galen *Meth. med.* 1, 1) has sometimes been viewed as an illegitimate inference from claims to healing powers made in the poems (**399**, 9–11; **345**, 1–2, 9), which no doubt did give rise to fictitious anecdotes like the story of his revival of the woman who stopped breathing (Diog. L. VIII, 60–1, DK 31 A 1). But his evident admiration for physicians (cf. also **409**, 1) is probably partly self-admiration.

WRITINGS

337 Diogenes Laertius VIII, 77 (DK 31 A 1)   τὰ μὲν οὖν Περὶ φύσεως αὐτῷ καὶ οἱ Καθαρμοὶ εἰς ἔπη τείνουσι πεντακισχίλια, ὁ δὲ Ἰατρικὸς λόγος εἰς ἔπη ἑξακόσια. περὶ δὲ τῶν τραγῳδιῶν προειρήκαμεν.

338 Suda s.v. Ἐμπεδοκλῆς (DK 31 A 2)   καὶ ἔγραψε δι' ἐπῶν Περὶ φύσεως τῶν ὄντων βιβλία β̄ (καί ἐστιν ἔπη ὡς δισχίλια), Ἰατρικὰ καταλογάδην καὶ ἄλλα πολλά.

337 His *On Nature* and *Purifications* extend to 5,000 lines, and his *Discourse of Medicine* to 600. Of the tragedies we have spoken above [in VIII, 58].

338 He wrote in verse *On the Nature of Things*, in two books (and about 2,000 lines), in prose *Medicine* and many other works.

The surviving fragments come from the poems called (but probably not by Empedocles himself) *On Nature* and *Purifications*. The extant verses even of *On Nature* represent (if we may believe **337** and **338**)[1] less than a fifth of the original whole, while those of the *Purifications* are even scrappier. But Empedocles' fragments are more extensive than those of any other Presocratic, and consequently give us a strong basis for interpretation. Very few of them are assigned in the sources to one poem rather than the other, let alone to a specific book. Nonetheless it is possible to distribute the great majority between the two works with varying degrees of confidence – high in the case of the most important extracts (see M. R. Wright, *Empedocles: the Extant Fragments* (New Haven, Conn., 1981) ch. iv). It is much harder to reconstruct the original sequence of fragments within the poems or to divine the plan of either work. In this chapter fragments will be presented mostly in the order we believe most likely to represent Empedocles' own ordering.

Empedocles' decision to write in hexameter verse is more easily explained than Parmenides'. In the first place he was (in Theophrastus' words, **335**) an emulator of Parmenides. The fragments of *On Nature* show that in metaphysics and cosmology he wrote out of a deep preoccupation with Parmenides' thought, both in what he denied and what he asserted; verbal echoes of Parmenides' poem and allusions to it are correspondingly frequent in Empedocles' verses. It is therefore not surprising that he should adopt the same verbal medium as the older thinker and like him claim the didactic authority traditionally associated with epic. Secondly, the un-Parmenidean subject matter of *Purifications* – the fall of man and the practices necessary for his restoration – is naturally suited to an epic treatment in the manner of Hesiod, to whom Empedocles is here heavily indebted. Thirdly, most readers agree with Plutarch against Aristotle in admiring Empedocles' poetic gifts.[2] These are better illustrated than catalogued. But it is worth observing that he exploited his chosen medium to express and reinforce the complex unity of his vision of the world by means of two devices in particular: a novel employment of the Homeric technique of repeated lines and half-lines, and an equally individual use of simile and metaphor.

---

[1] It is very doubtful whether the other writings mentioned in **337–8** (or at Diog. L. viii, 57–8) ever existed, and what they say about the two authentic poems may be wrong. In apparent conflict with **338** Tzetzes quotes a fragment (**397**) as belonging to the third book of *On Nature* (*Chil.* vii, 514); scholarly opinion now supports three books for *On Nature*, two for *Purifications*, fortified by a reference to 'Book 2 of the *Purifications*' in a recently published palimpsest of Herodian (fr. 152 in Wright, *Empedocles*; see in general her discussion at pp. 17–21). It has also been doubted whether (as **337** and **338** taken together imply) *Purifications* was the longer poem. Diels accordingly emended **337** to read πάντα τρισχίλια, '3,000 in all', not πεντακισχίλια (*Sitz. Ber. d. Berlin Akad.* 63 (1898), 398); G. Zuntz (*Persephone*, 236–9) more plausibly supposes that in **338** the words γ΄· καὶ ἔστιν ἔπη ὡς τρισχίλια· καὶ τοὺς Καθαρμούς, βιβλία have dropped out (i.e. *On Nature* 3 books, 3,000 lines; *Purifications* 2 books, 2,000 lines).

[2] **339** Aristotle *Poet.* 1, 1447b17 (DK31A22) οὐδὲν δὲ κοινόν ἐστιν Ὁμήρῳ καὶ Ἐμπεδοκλεῖ πλὴν τὸ μέτρον, διὸ τὸν μὲν ποιητὴν δίκαιον καλεῖν, τὸν δὲ

φυσιολόγον μᾶλλον ἢ ποιητήν. *(Homer and Empedocles have nothing in common but metre; so while it is right to call the one a poet, the other should be called a physicist rather than a poet.)* 340 Plutarch *Quaest. conv.* 683E καὶ μάλιστα τοῦ ἀνδρὸς οὐ καλλιγραφίας ἕνεκα τοῖς εὐπροσωποτάτοις τῶν ἐπιθέτων ὥσπερ ἀνθηροῖς χρώμασι τὰ πράγματα γανοῦν εἰωθότος, ἀλλ' ἕκαστον οὐσίας τινὸς ἢ δυνάμεως δήλωμα ποιοῦντος οἷον ἀμφιβρότην χθόνα τὸ τῇ ψυχῇ περικείμενον σῶμα, καὶ νεφεληγερέτην τὸν ἀέρα καὶ πολυαίματον τὸ ἧπαρ. *(...especially since Empedocles is not in the habit of polishing up facts with the showiest epithets he can find for the sake of fine writing, as if he were laying on gaudy colours; instead he makes each expression reveal an essence or a power of something, as for example 'mortal-enclosing earth' (of the body surrounding the soul), 'cloud-gatherer' (of the air), and 'rich in blood' (of the liver).)* For further discussion see Guthrie, *HGP* II, 134–6, and (more extensively) J. Bollack, *Empédocle* I (Paris, 1965), 277–323.

ON NATURE: GENERAL PRINCIPLES

341   Fr. 1, Diogenes Laertius VIII, 60
   Παυσανίη, σὺ δὲ κλῦθι, δαΐφρονος 'Αγχίτεω υἱέ.

341   And you, Pausanias, son of wise Anchites, hear me.

Nothing is known (despite ancient fabrications, e.g. Diog. L. VIII, 67–9, 71) about Pausanias, to whom *On Nature* is addressed.

(i) *Defence of the senses*

342   Fr. 2, Sextus *adv. math.* VII, 123
   στεινωποὶ μὲν γὰρ παλάμαι κατὰ γυῖα κέχυνται·
   πολλὰ δὲ δείλ' ἔμπαια, τά τ' ἀμβλύνουσι μέριμνας.
   παῦρον δ' ἐν ζωῇσι βίου μέρος ἀθρήσαντες
   ὠκύμοροι καπνοῖο δίκην ἀρθέντες ἀπέπταν
5   αὐτὸ μόνον πεισθέντες, ὅτῳ προσέκυρσεν ἕκαστος
   πάντοσ' ἐλαυνόμενοι· τὸ δ' ὅλον ⟨τίς ἄρ'⟩¹ εὔχεται εὑρεῖν;
   οὕτως οὔτ' ἐπιδερκτὰ τάδ' ἀνδράσιν οὔτ' ἐπακουστὰ
   οὔτε νόῳ περιληπτά. σὺ δ' οὖν, ἐπεὶ ὧδ' ἐλιάσθης,
   πεύσεαι· οὐ πλεῖόν γε² βροτείη μῆτις ὄρωρεν.

¹ τίς ἄρ' H. Fränkel: πᾶς Bergk, Diels.
² πλεῖόν γε Sextus: πλέον ἠὲ Stein, Diels.

343   Fr. 3, line 9, Sextus *adv. math.* VII, 125
   ἀλλ' ἄγ' ἄθρει πάσῃ παλάμῃ, πῇ δῆλον ἕκαστον,
10   μήτε τιν' ὄψιν ἔχων πίστει πλέον ἢ κατ' ἀκουήν
   ἢ ἀκοὴν ἐπίδουπον ὑπὲρ τρανώματα γλώσσης,
   μήτε τι τῶν ἄλλων, ὁπόσῃ πόρος ἐστὶ νοῆσαι,
   γυίων πίστιν ἔρυκε, νόει δ' ᾗ δῆλον ἕκαστον.

342 Narrow are the powers that are spread through the body, and many are the miseries that burst in, blunting thought. Men behold in their span but a little part of life, then swift to die are carried off and fly away like smoke, persuaded of one thing only, that which each has chanced on as they are driven every way: who, then, boasts that he has found the whole? Not so are these things to be seen or heard by men, or grasped by the understanding. You then, since you have turned aside to this place, shall learn: no further can mortal wit reach. (*After Guthrie*)

343 Come now, observe with all your powers how each thing is clear, neither holding sight in greater trust compared with hearing, nor noisy hearing above the passages of the tongue, nor withhold trust from any of the other limbs [organs, parts of the body], by whatever way there is a channel to understanding, but grasp each thing in the way in which it is clear. (*After Guthrie*)

The early position of these lines in the poem (suggested by the invocation of the Muse in fr. 3, 1–8) and their echoes of Parmenides (e.g. 'mortal wit' in **342**, and compare **343** with **294**) make it probable that Empedocles recognized in Parmenides' work a radical epistemological challenge to cosmology which required him to stake out his own position at the outset. He responds here in strongly Heraclitean spirit. He bewails the very limited understanding of things most men achieve through their senses (cf. pp. 187f. above), but he promises that an intelligent use of all the sensory evidence available to mortals, aided by his own instruction, will (contrary to Parmenides' claims) make each thing clear to us (cf. **194**, **197**, **198**).[1]

[1] Line 10 may contain also an implied criticism of **344** Heraclitus fr. 101a, Polybius XII, 27 ὀφθαλμοὶ [τῶν] ὤτων ἀκριβέστεροι μάρτυρες. (*Eyes are more accurate witnesses than ears.*) Perhaps, however, Heraclitus only meant that seeing something for oneself is better than hearing second-hand reports; but cf. pp. 205ff.

(ii) *The power of knowledge*

345 Fr. 111, Diogenes Laertius VIII, 59

φάρμακα δ᾽ ὅσσα γεγᾶσι κακῶν καὶ γήραος ἄλκαρ
πεύσῃ, ἐπεὶ μούνῳ σοὶ ἐγὼ κρανέω τάδε πάντα.
παύσεις δ᾽ ἀκαμάτων ἀνέμων μένος οἵ τ᾽ ἐπὶ γαῖαν
ὀρνύμενοι πνοιαῖσι καταφθινύθουσιν ἀρούρας·
5 καὶ πάλιν, ἢν ἐθέλησθα, παλίντιτα πνεύματ⟨α⟩ ἐπάξεις·
θήσεις δ᾽ ἐξ ὄμβροιο κελαινοῦ καίριον αὐχμόν
ἀνθρώποις, θήσεις δὲ καὶ ἐξ αὐχμοῖο θερείου
ῥεύματα δενδρεόθρεπτα, τά τ᾽ αἰθέρι ναιετάουσιν,
ἄξεις δ᾽ ἐξ Ἀίδαο καταφθιμένου μένος ἀνδρός.

345 You shall learn all the remedies that there are for ills and defence against old age, since for you alone will I accomplish all this. And you shall stay the force of the unwearied winds which sweep over the earth and lay waste the fields with their blasts; and then, if you wish, you shall bring back breezes in requital. After black rain you shall cause drought for men in due season, and then after summer drought cause air-inhabiting tree-nourishing streams. And you shall bring from Hades the strength of a dead man.

Man's natural powers may be narrow, but Empedocles promises to make him capable of feats which can only be described as magical, even though the actual discussion in the poem of the four elements (lines 3–8) and the composition and functioning of the human body (lines 1–2, 9) is properly philosophical.

(iii) *The four roots*

346 Fr. 6, Aetius I, 3, 20

τέσσαρα γὰρ πάντων ῥιζώματα πρῶτον ἄκουε·
Ζεὺς ἀργὴς Ἥρη τε φερέσβιος ἠδ᾽ Ἀιδωνεὺς
Νῆστίς θ᾽ ἣ δακρύοις τέγγει κρούνωμα βρότειον.

347 Aristotle *Met.* A4, 985a31–3 (DK31A37)   ἔτι δὲ τὰ ὡς ἐν ὕλης εἴδει λεγόμενα στοιχεῖα τέτταρα πρῶτος εἶπεν.

346 Hear first the four roots of all things: shining Zeus, life-bringing Hera, Aidoneus and Nestis who with her tears waters mortal springs.

347 Moreover, he was the first to make the material 'elements' four.

The four 'roots' are now formally introduced. The name marks them as basic and mutually irreducible elements from which all other things are formed (cf. Parmenides' light and night, **302–3**). The idea of a quartet of elements seems (as **347** claims) to be original with Empedocles. His argument for the four he chooses is given in **355**. Their initial characterization as gods is presumably designed both to indicate what is sound in traditional conceptions of divinity and to claim for them powers and properties, as yet undefined, which make them worthy of awe. Nestis is plainly water, but already in antiquity there was disagreement over the other three (see DK31A33). Theophrastus seems to have identified Zeus as fire, Hera as air, and Aidoneus (i.e. Hades) as earth (Aetius I, 3, 20).

(iv) *The cycle of change*

348 Fr. 17, 1–13, Simplicius *in Phys.* 158, 1

δίπλ' ἐρέω· τοτὲ μὲν γὰρ ἓν ηὐξήθη μόνον εἶναι
ἐκ πλεόνων, τοτὲ δ' αὖ διέφυ πλέον' ἐξ ἑνὸς εἶναι.
δοιὴ δὲ θνητῶν γένεσις, δοιὴ δ' ἀπόλειψις·
τὴν μὲν γὰρ πάντων σύνοδος τίκτει τ' ὀλέκει τε,
5   ἡ δὲ πάλιν διαφυομένων θρεφθεῖσα διέπτη.
καὶ ταῦτ' ἀλλάσσοντα διαμπερὲς οὐδαμὰ λήγει,
ἄλλοτε μὲν Φιλότητι συνερχόμεν' εἰς ἓν ἅπαντα,
ἄλλοτε δ' αὖ δίχ' ἕκαστα φορεύμενα Νείκεος ἔχθει.
⟨οὕτως ᾗ μὲν ἓν ἐκ πλεόνων μεμάθηκε φύεσθαι⟩
10   ἠδὲ πάλιν διαφύντος ἑνὸς πλέον' ἐκτελέθουσι,
τῇ μὲν γίγνονταί τε καὶ οὔ σφισιν ἔμπεδος αἰών·
ᾗ δὲ διαλλάσσοντα διαμπερὲς οὐδαμὰ λήγει,
ταύτῃ δ' αἰὲν ἔασιν ἀκίνητοι κατὰ κύκλον.[1]

---

[1] Lines 7–8 and 10–13 are almost identical with lines 5–6 and 9–12 of fr. 26, which is also preserved by Simpl. at *in Phys.* 33, 19. Line 9 above, which is needed to complete the sense, is line 8 of fr. 26 inserted here by Diels.

348 A twofold tale I shall tell: at one time they [*i.e.* the roots] grew to be one alone out of many, at another again they grew apart to be many out of one. Double is the birth of mortal things and double their failing; for the one is brought to birth and destroyed by the coming together of all things, the other is nurtured and flies apart as they grow apart again. And these things never cease their continual interchange, now through Love all coming together into one, now again each carried apart by the hatred of Strife. So insofar as they have learned to grow one from many, and again as the one grows apart grow many, thus far do they come into being and have no stable life; but insofar as they never cease their continual interchange, thus far they exist always changeless in the cycle.

348 presents the principal doctrine of Empedocles' philosophy. Its beginning deliberately echoes and defiantly contradicts Parmenides: 'a twofold tale' (contrast **295**, 1), 'at one time' (contrast **296**, 5), 'grew' (contrast **296**, 7), etc. Yet it culminates (lines 12–13) in an assertion which seems designed to preserve something of Parmenides' metaphysical position.

The fragment divides into three sections. Lines 1–5 tell us of a dual process constituted by the creation of one from many, and then many from one (lines 1–2; further described in the obscure lines 3–5). Lines

6–8 assert that this dual process is ceaselessly repeated, and explain it as due to the alternate activity of Love and Strife. In lines 9–13 these two points are taken up and contrasted in a surprising and rather Heraclitean conclusion. Lines 9–11 infer from the double birth of things that they come to be and (or, but) have no stable life; lines 12–13, however, assert that in virtue of their ceaseless alternation between unity and plurality, they are for ever changeless.

Empedocles nowhere argues for this doctrine. It accordingly seems best to understand the passage as offering a hypothesis whose object is to reconcile the apparently contradictory notions that birth, death and in general change exist, and yet that, as Parmenides held, being is unchanging and everlasting or eternal. The crucial idea of the reconciliation is that insofar as the dual process described in lines 1–5 recurs ceaselessly, the things involved in the process have a sort of changelessness. A unity will always form from a plurality and vice versa; and it will always be the same unity and the same plurality. (No doubt unity and plurality are chosen as the simplest conceivable poles between which change can occur.) As in Heraclitus, 'there is local change', to use Barnes' words, 'but global stability' (*The Presocratic Philosophers* ii, 13).

Empedocles' conception of everlasting recurrence is sometimes called his 'cosmic cycle'. But it is propounded here as an entirely general metaphysical thesis. Its clearest and most important application is undoubtedly in his theory of the birth and death of the universe, but he applied it also to the life-cycle of animals (as in fr. 26).[1]

[1] It is therefore wrong in principle to attempt to interpret lines 3–5 as specifically concerned with the creation and dissolution of the universe or of formations within the universe, as many scholars do. *A fortiori*, it is a mistake to rely on them, as did KR and as do most recently D. O'Brien (*Empedocles' Cosmic Cycle* (Cambridge, 1969)) and M. R. Wright (*Empedocles: the Extant Fragments*), to support the idea that Empedocles posited the creation and destruction of one world, as things grew to be one from many (supposedly referred to in line 4), and those of another, distinct world as things grew apart once more from unity (line 5). Lines 3–5 are to be understood in the light of lines 9–11. They suggest that Empedocles is saying simply that the coming together of all things brings the one to birth and destroys the many (line 4), and again that when they grow apart the many are brought to birth and the one perishes (it is lines 3–5, not 1–2, which introduce the notions of birth and destruction exploited in lines 9–11). τήν (line 4) is best understood as an ambiguous internal accusative, referring to both γένεσις and ἀπόλειψις (line 3), and to be taken with both τίκτει and ὀλέκει; and ἡ (line 5) should be read in similar fashion: 'The one birth [of the one] is brought to birth and [is identical with] the one death [of the many, which] is destroyed by the coming together of all things; as things grow apart again, the other birth [of the many] is nurtured and [is identical with] the other death [of

the one, which] is died [*lit.* flies away].' (Cf. Guthrie, *HGP* II, 153 *ad loc.*) It has sometimes been held that Empedocles reserves the word 'mortal' (line 3) for compounds of the elements which fall short of total unity (e.g. **349**, 22; **388**, 3), and would in any case be loath to describe the one (understood as the Sphere, **357-8** below) or the many (identified with the elements) as mortal. But at **360**, 14 the elements are explicitly credited with mortality; and the Sphere evidently *is* mortal.

(v) *Agents and materials of the cycle*

349   Fr. 17, line 14, Simplicius *in Phys.* 158, 13 (continuing **348**)

ἀλλ' ἄγε μύθων κλῦθι· μάθη γάρ τοι φρένας αὔξει·
15   ὡς γὰρ καὶ πρὶν ἔειπα πιφαύσκων πείρατα μύθων,
δίπλ' ἐρέω· τοτὲ μὲν γὰρ ἓν ηὐξήθη μόνον εἶναι
ἐκ πλεόνων, τοτὲ δ' αὖ διέφυ πλέον' ἐξ ἑνὸς εἶναι,
πῦρ καὶ ὕδωρ καὶ γαῖα καὶ ἠέρος ἄπλετον ὕψος,
Νεῖκός τ' οὐλόμενον δίχα τῶν, ἀτάλαντον ἁπάντη,
20   καὶ Φιλότης ἐν τοῖσιν, ἴση μῆκός τε πλάτος τε·
τὴν σὺ νόῳ δέρκευ, μηδ' ὄμμασιν ἧσο τεθηπώς·
ἥτις καὶ θνητοῖσι νομίζεται ἔμφυτος ἄρθροις,
τῇ τε φίλα φρονέουσι καὶ ἄρθμια ἔργα τελοῦσι,
Γηθοσύνην καλέοντες ἐπώνυμον ἠδ' Ἀφροδίτην·
25   τὴν οὔ τις μετὰ τοῖσιν ἑλισσομένην δεδάηκε
θνητὸς ἀνήρ· σὺ δ' ἄκουε λόγου στόλον οὐκ ἀπατηλόν.
ταῦτα γὰρ ἶσά τε πάντα καὶ ἥλικα γένναν ἔασι,
τιμῆς δ' ἄλλης ἄλλο μέδει, πάρα δ' ἦθος ἑκάστῳ,
ἐν δὲ μέρει κρατέουσι περιπλομένοιο χρόνοιο.
30   καὶ πρὸς τοῖς οὔτ' ἄρ τι ἐπιγίγνεται οὐδ' ἀπολήγει·
33   πῇ δέ κε κἠξαπόλοιτο, ἐπεὶ τῶνδ' οὐδὲν ἔρημον;
31   εἴτε γὰρ ἐφθείροντο διαμπερές, οὐκέτ' ἂν ἦσαν.
32   τοῦτο δ' ἐπαυξήσειε τὸ πᾶν τί κε; καὶ πόθεν ἐλθόν; [1]
ἀλλ' αὔτ' ἔστιν ταῦτα, δι' ἀλλήλων δὲ θέοντα
35   γίγνεται ἄλλοτε ἄλλα καὶ ἠνεκὲς αἰὲν ὁμοῖα.

[1] 33 ante 31 transposui.

349   But come, hear my words, for learning increases wisdom. As I said before in declaring the limits of my words, I shall tell a twofold tale: at one time they grew to be one alone out of many, at another again they grew apart to be many out of one – fire and water and earth and the immense height of air, and cursed Strife apart from them, equal in every direction, and Love among them, equal in length and breadth. Her must you contemplate with your mind, and not sit with eyes dazed: she it is who is thought innate even in mortal limbs, because of her they think friendly thoughts and accomplish harmonious deeds, calling her Joy by name and Aphrodite. She is perceived by no mortal man as she circles among them: but you must listen to the undeceitful ordering of my discourse.

All these are equal and coeval, but each has a different prerogative and each its own character, and they prevail in turn as time comes round. And besides them nothing further comes into being nor does anything pass away. How could it in fact be utterly destroyed, since nothing is empty of these? For only if they were continually perishing would they no longer exist. And what could increase this all? Whence could it have come? No, there are just these, but running through one another they become different things at different times and yet ever and always the same.

Empedocles now descends a little from the high level of abstraction in **348** to identify the entities involved in the cycle of birth as the four roots, and to make some specific claims about them and about Love and Strife, the motive forces of the cycle.

A hymn to Love occupies most of the space he devotes to this last theme. Its burden is epistemological. Love cannot be seen; but in language unusually full of Parmenidean reminiscence Pausanias is bidden to infer its presence and power in general from its effects in the human sphere. In lines 19–20 Empedocles hints that Strife is at odds with the roots, but Love is in harmony with them. His talk here of their equality is probably not intended to imply that Love and Strife are bodies. Its point emerges at lines 27–9 in the second paragraph, where he enunciates his theory of the alternate dominance of the elements (cf. **365–6**) and of Love and Strife (cf. **359**). The theory states the mechanism by which global stability is maintained through continual change. Its core idea goes back to Anaximander (**110** and **111**) and Heraclitus (**211, 217–19**). Empedocles specifies a precondition of the mechanism not explicitly mentioned by his predecessors and indeed implicitly denied by Heraclitus in the pre-eminence he accords to fire: each of the elements involved in the alternation must be equal to each of the others (cf. p. 120 above); and if the process is to be regulated by Love and Strife they must each be in some sense the equal of all the elements together. How precisely these equalities are to be understood is of much less concern to him than the formal requirement *that* there be equal elements and equal forces controlling them.

In the final lines of **349** (30–5) Empedocles indicates what he takes to be the other principal attraction of the doctrine of four elements.

By supposing that they intermingle ('run through one another') to form mortal compounds, we can dispense with the idea, shown to be troublesome by Parmenides (296), that there is any absolute coming into being or any destruction into nothing. This consequence of the doctrine is worked out in explicit detail in the fragments of the next section.

(vi) Birth and death

350   Fr. 8, Plutarch adv. Colotem 1111F

ἄλλο δέ τοι ἐρέω· φύσις οὐδενὸς ἔστιν ἁπάντων
θνητῶν, οὐδέ τις οὐλομένου θανάτοιο τελευτή,
ἀλλὰ μόνον μίξις τε διάλλαξίς τε μιγέντων
ἔστι, φύσις δ' ἐπὶ τοῖς ὀνομάζεται ἀνθρώποισιν.

351   Fr. 9, Plutarch adv. Colotem 1113A–B

οἱ δ' ὅτε μὲν κατὰ φῶτα μιγέντ' εἰς αἰθέρ' ἵ⟨κωνται⟩[1]
ἢ κατὰ θηρῶν ἀγροτέρων γένος ἢ κατὰ θάμνων
ἠὲ κατ' οἰωνῶν, τότε μὲν τὸ ⟨λέγουσι⟩ γενέσθαι,[2]
εὖτε δ' ἀποκρινθῶσι, τὸ δ' αὖ δυσδαίμονα πότμον·
5   ἧ θέμις ⟨οὐ⟩ καλέουσι, νόμῳ δ' ἐπίφημι καὶ αὐτός.

> [1] Diels dubitanter: μιγὲν φῶς αἰθέρι lac. 6–8 litt. codd.
> [2] Reiske: τὸν lac. 7–8 litt. codd.

352   Fr. 11, Plutarch adv. Colotem 1113C

νήπιοι· οὐ γάρ σφιν δολιχόφρονές εἰσι μέριμναι,
οἳ δὴ γίγνεσθαι πάρος οὐκ ἐὸν ἐλπίζουσιν
ἤ τι καταθνήσκειν τε καὶ ἐξόλλυσθαι ἁπάντη.

353   Fr. 12 [Aristotle] M.X.G. 2, 975b1

ἔκ τε γὰρ οὐδάμ' ἐόντος ἀμήχανόν ἐστι γενέσθαι
καί τ' ἐὸν ἐξαπολέσθαι ἀνήνυστον καὶ ἄπυστον·
αἰεὶ γὰρ τῇ γ' ἔσται, ὅπῃ κέ τις αἰὲν ἐρείδῃ.

350   Another thing will I tell you: of all mortal things none has birth, nor any end in accursed death, but only mingling and interchange of what is mingled – birth is the name given to these by men.

351   And when they [sc. the roots] are mixed in the form of a man and come to the air, or in the form of the race of wild beasts or of plants or of birds, then they say that this comes into being; but when they are separated, they call this wretched fate: they do not name them as is right, but I myself comply with custom.

352   Fools – for they have no far-reaching thoughts, since they think that what before did not exist comes into being, or that a thing dies and is completely destroyed.

353 For it is impossible for anything to come to be from what is not, and it cannot be brought about or heard of that what is should be utterly destroyed; for wherever one may ever set it, there indeed it will always be.

The new point ('another thing', **350**) is a corollary about language, expressed as an attack on the substantives 'birth' and 'death' (**349**, 30–5, is couched in terms exclusively of the verbs which underlie them). **352–3** show that it is because 'birth', 'death', etc. in their common meaning involve the idea of creation from and destruction into what is not that Empedocles objects to them. Elsewhere (cf. **351**, 5) he is happy to use the words without commitment to these implications, as when in **348**, 11, he speaks of the roots as coming into being – inasmuch as they grow from many into one and from one into many.

Very soon after quoting **350–2** Plutarch quotes a further fragment, which it is accordingly natural to suppose belonged to this same context of *On Nature*:

354 Fr. 15, Plutarch *adv. Colotem* 1113D
οὐκ ἂν ἀνὴρ τοιαῦτα σοφὸς φρεσὶ μαντεύσαιτο,
ὡς ὄφρα μέν τε βιῶσι, τὸ δὴ βίοτον καλέουσι,
τόφρα μὲν οὖν εἰσίν, καί σφιν πάρα δειλὰ καὶ ἐσθλά,
πρὶν δὲ πάγεν τε βροτοὶ καὶ ⟨ἐπεὶ⟩ λύθεν, οὐδὲν ἄρ᾽ εἰσιν.

354 A man wise in such matters would not surmise in his mind that while they live what they call life, so long do they exist, and good and ill befall them, but that before they were formed as mortals and once they are dissolved, they do not exist at all.

Empedocles indicates that the common understanding of 'life', too, is wrong, and (as Plutarch rightly interprets the lines) that our real existence extends before 'birth' and after 'death'. Thus **354** hints at the doctrine of reincarnation expounded in *Purifications*, although the connexion between it and the theory of the mixture of the roots is a lot less intelligible, in the present state of the evidence, than the corollary explained in **350–1**.

(vii) *Mixture of roots*

355 Fr. 21, Simplicius *in Phys.* 159, 13
ἀλλ᾽ ἄγε, τῶνδ᾽ ὀάρων προτέρων ἐπιμάρτυρα δέρκευ,
εἴ τι καὶ ἐν προτέροισι λιπόξυλον ἔπλετο μορφῇ,

ἠέλιον μὲν θερμὸν ὁρᾶν καὶ λαμπρὸν ἁπάντη,
ἄμβροτα δ᾽ ὅσσ᾽ εἴδει τε καὶ ἀργέτι δεύεται αὐγῇ,
ὄμβρον δ᾽ ἐν πᾶσι δνοφόεντά τε ῥιγαλέον τε·
ἐκ δ᾽ αἴης προρέουσι θελεμνά τε καὶ στερεωπά.
ἐν δὲ Κότῳ διάμορφα καὶ ἄνδιχα πάντα πέλονται,
σὺν δ᾽ ἔβη ἐν Φιλότητι καὶ ἀλλήλοισι ποθεῖται.
ἐκ τῶν πάνθ᾽ ὅσα τ᾽ ἦν ὅσα τ᾽ ἔστι καὶ ἔσται ὀπίσσω,[1]
δένδρεά τ᾽ ἐβλάστησε καὶ ἀνέρες ἠδὲ γυναῖκες,
θῆρές τ᾽ οἰωνοί τε καὶ ὑδατοθρέμμονες ἰχθῦς,
καί τε θεοὶ δολιχαίωνες τιμῇσι φέριστοι.
αὐτὰ γὰρ ἔστιν ταῦτα, δι᾽ ἀλλήλων δὲ θέοντα
γίγνεται ἀλλοιωπά· τόσον διὰ κρῆσις ἀμείβει.

[1] ἐκ τῶν...ὀπίσσω coniecit Wright ex Arist. *Met.* 1000a29; ἐκ τούτων γὰρ πάνθ᾽...ἔσται Simpl.

356 Fr. 23, Simplicius *in Phys.* 159, 27 (following **355**)   καὶ παρά-
δειγμα δὲ ἐναργὲς παρέθετο τοῦ ἐκ τῶν αὐτῶν γίνεσθαι τὰ διάφορα·

ὡς δ᾽ ὁπόταν γραφέες ἀναθήματα ποικίλλωσιν
ἀνέρες ἀμφὶ τέχνης ὑπὸ μήτιος εὖ δεδαῶτε,
οἵτ᾽ ἐπεὶ οὖν μάρψωσι πολύχροα φάρμακα χερσίν,
ἁρμονίῃ μείξαντε τὰ μὲν πλέω, ἄλλα δ᾽ ἐλάσσω,
ἐκ τῶν εἴδεα πᾶσιν ἀλίγκια πορσύνουσι,
δένδρεά τε κτίζοντε καὶ ἀνέρας ἠδὲ γυναῖκας
θῆράς τ᾽ οἰωνούς τε καὶ ὑδατοθρέμμονας ἰχθῦς
καί τε θεοὺς δολιχαίωνας τιμῇσι φερίστους·
οὕτω μή σ᾽ ἀπάτη φρένα καινύτω ἄλλοθεν εἶναι
θνητῶν, ὅσσα γε δῆλα γεγάκασιν ἄσπετα, πηγήν,
ἀλλὰ τορῶς ταῦτ᾽ ἴσθι, θεοῦ πάρα μῦθον ἀκούσας.

355   But come, look upon the witnesses to this former discourse
of mine, should beauty have been lacking in it earlier: the sun,
hot to see and dazzling all over; all the immortals[1] that are bathed
in heat and brilliant rays; rain in all things dark and chill; and
from the earth pour forth things rooted and solid. In Anger all are
of different forms and separate, but in Love they come together
and are desired by each other. From them comes all that was and
is and will be in future – trees have sprung up and men and
women, beasts and birds and water-bred fish, and long-lived gods,
too, highest in honour. For there are just these, but running
through each other they assume different appearances: so much
does mixture change them.
356   Moreover he added a clear model of the way different things
come from the same: 'As when painters are decorating offerings

[*i.e.* votive tablets], men through cunning well skilled in their craft – when they actually seize pigments of many colours in their hands, mixing in harmony more of some and less of others, they produce from them forms resembling all things, creating trees and men and women, beasts and birds and water-bred fish, and long-lived gods, too, highest in honour: so let not deception overcome your mind and make you think there is any other source of all the countless mortal things that are plain to see, but know this clearly, for the tale you hear comes from a god.'

[1] Probably breezes and expanses of air are intended; Empedocles perhaps hints at a rationalistic explanation of *ambrosia*, 'food of the immortals', as vapours that provide fuel for the sun, which consequently steeps them in its heat and light. Cf. Democritus fr. 25.

355 and **356** are chiefly of interest because they show Empedocles employing more empirical modes of argument than the metaphysical reasoning of **352–3**. To support his identification of the four roots as the fundamental materials of which things are made, he appeals to our sensory awareness of their basic qualities, as of something pervasively and beautifully present in the world around us (**355**, 1–6). To support the idea that the immense variety of the world is adequately explained by the theory of the mixture of so small a number of elements, he introduces in Homeric style an analogy with the painter's creation of an imaginary world from pigments few in number but many-coloured in their potentialities (**356**). These two passages probably come from near the end of the first section of the poem, which evidently concluded with a full statement of the theory of the cycle of change, particularly as it applies to living compounds, in verses that almost all repeat or adapt lines from **348** and **349** (fr. 26).

SPHERE AND COSMOS

It is unclear and much disputed how Empedocles disposed the material in the next section of *On Nature*. Probably he began with a general outline of the cycle of change as it unfolds on the cosmic stage (roughly frr. 27–36 DK), followed by a detailed but now very fragmentary cosmogony and zoogony (roughly frr. 37–70).

(i) *The Sphere*

357 Fr. 29, Hippolytus *Ref.* vii, 29, 13 καὶ περὶ μὲν τῆς τοῦ κόσμου ἰδέας, ὁποία τίς ἐστιν ὑπὸ τῆς φιλίας κοσμουμένη, λέγει τοι-οῦτόν τινα τρόπον·

οὐ γὰρ ἀπὸ νώτοιο δύο κλάδοι ἀίσσονται,
οὐ πόδες, οὐ θοὰ γοῦν᾽, οὐ μήδεα γεννήεντα
ἀλλὰ 'σφαῖρος ἔην' καὶ ἶσος ἐστιν αὐτῷ.

358 Frr. 27 and 31, Simplicius *in Phys.* 1183, 28 Εὔδημος δὲ τὴν
ἀκινησίαν ἐν τῇ τῆς φιλίας ἐπικρατείᾳ κατὰ τὸν σφαῖρον ἐκδέχεται,
ἐπειδὰν ἅπαντα συγκριθῇ·
ἔνθ᾽ οὔτ᾽ ἠελίοιο διείδεται ὠκέα γυῖα
ἀλλ᾽, ὥς φησιν,
οὕτως ἁρμονίης πυκινῷ κρυφῷ ἐστήρικται
σφαῖρος κυκλοτερὴς μονίῃ περιγηθέι γαίων.
ἀρξαμένου δὲ πάλιν τοῦ νείκους ἐπικρατεῖν τότε πάλιν κίνησις ἐν τῷ
σφαίρῳ γίνεται·
πάντα γὰρ ἐξείης πελεμίζετο γυῖα θεοῖο.

359 Fr. 30, Aristotle *Met.* B4, 1000b12 καὶ ἅμα δὲ αὐτῆς τῆς
μεταβολῆς αἴτιον οὐθὲν λέγει, ἀλλ᾽ ἢ ὅτι οὕτως πέφυκεν·
αὐτὰρ ἐπεὶ μέγα νεῖκος ἐνὶ μελέεσσιν ἐθρέφθη,
ἐς τιμάς τ᾽ ἀνόρουσε τελειομένοιο χρόνοιο,
ὅς σφιν ἀμοιβαῖος πλατέος παρ᾽ ἐλήλαται ὅρκου...

357 And as to the form of the cosmos, he describes what it is like
when ordered by Love in the following manner: 'No twin
branches spring from its back, it has no feet, no nimble knees, no
fertile parts', but 'it was a sphere', and is equal to itself.

358 Eudemus understands the immobility [*sc.* of which Aristotle
speaks at *Phys.* 252a9] to apply to the Sphere in the supremacy
of Love, when all things are combined – 'there neither are the swift
limbs of the sun distinguished', but, as he says, 'thus it is held fast
in the close obscurity of Harmonia, a rounded sphere rejoicing in
its joyous solitude'. But as Strife begins to win supremacy once
more, then once more motion occurs in the Sphere: 'For one by
one all the limbs of the god began to quiver.'

359 And at the same time he mentions no cause of the change
itself, except that things are so by nature: 'But when great Strife
had grown strong in the limbs, and sprang to its prerogatives as
the time was fulfilled which is marked for them in turn by a broad
oath...'

When the four roots are completely united by Love throughout their
entire extent, they give rise to the Sphere, which (as Simplicius tells
us, *de an.* 70, 17) Empedocles 'hymns as a god' (cf. **358**). His
description of it, while doubtless reflecting the influence of Xenophanes' attack upon anthropomorphic gods (see pp. 168ff.), is in-

disputably modelled on Parmenides' verses in **299**, 42–4. His Sphere differs from Parmenides' in its mortality; perhaps he implies that Parmenides' conception of perfection is sound, but mistakenly represented as a general condition of existence.

(ii) *The vortex*

360 Fr. 35, Simplicius *de caelo* 529, 1 (lines 1–15), *in Phys.* 32, 13 (lines 3–17)

αὐτὰρ ἐγὼ παλίνορσος ἐλεύσομαι ἐς πόρον ὕμνων
τὸν πρότερον κατέλεξα λόγῳ λόγον ἐξοχετεύων,
κεῖνον· ἐπεὶ Νεῖκος μὲν ἐνέρτατον ἵκετο βένθος
δίνης, ἐν δὲ μέσῃ Φιλότης στροφάλιγγι γένηται,
5 ἐν τῇ δὴ τάδε πάντα συνέρχεται ἓν μόνον εἶναι,
οὐκ ἄφαρ, ἀλλὰ θελημὰ συνιστάμεν' ἄλλοθεν ἄλλα.
τῶν δέ τε μισγομένων χεῖτ' ἔθνεα μυρία θνητῶν·
πολλὰ δ' ἄμικτ' ἔστηκε κεραιομένοισιν ἐναλλάξ,
ὅσσ' ἔτι Νεῖκος ἔρυκε μετάρσιον· οὐ γὰρ ἀμεμφέως
10 πω πᾶν ἐξέστηκεν ἐπ' ἔσχατα τέρματα κύκλου,
ἀλλὰ τὰ μέν τ' ἐνέμιμνε μελέων τὰ δέ τ' ἐξεβεβήκει.
ὅσσον δ' αἰὲν ὑπεκπροθέοι, τόσον αἰὲν ἐπῄει
ἠπιόφρων Φιλότητος ἀμεμφέος ἄμβροτος ὁρμή·
αἶψα δὲ θνήτ' ἐφύοντο τὰ πρὶν μάθον ἀθάνατ' εἶναι,
15 ζωρά τε τὰ πρὶν ἄκρητα διαλλάξαντα κελεύθους·
τῶν δέ τε μισγομένων χεῖτ' ἔθνεα μυρία θνητῶν
παντοίαις ἰδέῃσιν ἀρηρότα, θαῦμα ἰδέσθαι.

360 But I shall turn back again to the path of song I traced before, as I draw off one discourse after another – to that path. When Strife reached the lowest depth of the whirl, and when Love comes to be in the middle of the vortex, there it is that all these things come together to be one only, not suddenly, but combining from different directions at will. And as they mingled countless tribes of mortal things poured forth; but many remained unmixed, alternating with those that were being mixed – all those that Strife still held back from above, for it had not all yet retired blamelessly to the furthest limits of the circle, but in some of the limbs it remained while from others it had withdrawn. As much as it was always running ahead in escape, so much was it always pursued by a gentle immortal impulse of blameless Love. Then straightway those things grew mortal that before had learned to be immortal, and those that were unmixed before became mixed as they exchanged their paths. And as they mingled countless tribes of mortal things poured forth, fitted with forms of all kinds, a wonder to look upon.

As **358–9** describe the time when Love's dominance in the cycle is first weakened, so **360** tells of the time, at exactly the opposite pole of the cycle, when Strife, having reached the xenith of its power, begins to retreat before Love's advance from the centre of the cosmic whirlpool (where it has been confined) to its outer limits. After Strife has separated the roots, Love starts to unite them once more. Love's principal achievement in this period of the cycle is evidently zoogony, the formation of 'countless tribes of mortal things' (i.e. compounds). Cosmogony proper was presumably something achieved by Strife in the period of its dominance prior to the critical point described in **360**. The vortex separating the four roots will have caused the four world-masses (see **365**) to form – hence the basic structure of the universe, if not its present form, will already be established at the crisis of Strife's dominance, which therefore should not be thought of as a time of random, chaotic movement (whirlpools are, after all, organized). Empedocles' metaphysical doctrine of the alternation of Love and Strife thus has attractive explanatory properties. It can account both for the separation fundamental to cosmogony (something not explained nor explicable in Parmenides' cosmogony, in which Love is the only cosmic cause, pp. 259–60 above) and for the mixtures of the living world (something very inadequately treated by the Milesians, wedded as they were to separation as the basic causal mechanism at work in the cosmos).[1]

---

[1] This interpretation of the cosmic roles of Love and Strife is broadly supported by Aristotle: **361** Aristotle *Met.* A4, 985a25 (DK 31 A 37) ὅταν μὲν γὰρ εἰς τὰ στοιχεῖα διίστηται τὸ πᾶν ὑπὸ τοῦ Νείκους, τότε τὸ πῦρ εἰς ἓν συγκρίνεται καὶ τῶν ἄλλων στοιχείων ἕκαστον· ὅταν δὲ πάλιν ὑπὸ τῆς Φιλίας συνίωσιν εἰς τὸ ἕν, ἀναγκαῖον ἐξ ἑκάστου τὰ μόρια διακρίνεσθαι πάλιν. (*When the universe is dissolved into its elements by Strife, fire is aggregated into one, and so is each of the other elements; but when again under the influence of Love they come together into one, the parts must again be segregated out of each element.*) (After Ross)

But Aristotle on one occasion writes as if he thinks Empedocles was committed to the hypothesis of a distinct cosmogony (not merely a zoogony) in the post-critical as well as the pre-critical period:

362 Aristotle *de caelo* Γ2, 301a14 ἐκ διεστώτων δὲ καὶ κινουμένων οὐκ εὔλογον ποιεῖν τὴν γένεσιν. διὸ καὶ Ἐμπεδοκλῆς παραλείπει τὴν ἐπὶ τῆς Φιλότητος· οὐ γὰρ ἂν ἠδύνατο συστῆσαι τὸν οὐρανὸν ἐκ κεχωρισμένων μὲν κατασκευάζων, σύγκρισιν δὲ ποιῶν διὰ τὴν Φιλότητα· ἐκ διακεκριμένων γὰρ συνέστηκεν ὁ κόσμος τῶν στοιχείων, ὥστ' ἀναγκαῖον γίνεσθαι ἐξ ἑνὸς καὶ συγκεκριμένου.

362 It is not reasonable to make generation begin with bodies that are separated and in movement. This is why Empedocles passes over the generation under Love, for he could not have built up the universe by constructing it from separated elements and combining them through Love; for the cosmos consists of elements in a state of separation, so that it would have to come to be from what is one and combined.

Yet if (as **362** complains) Empedocles did not describe a complete post-critical cosmogony, that was no doubt because he did not believe in one. We may diagnose the source of Aristotle's error by considering a further criticism he makes:

363 Aristotle *de caelo* B13, 295a29   ἔτι δὲ πρὸς Ἐμπεδοκλέα κἂν ἐκεῖνό τις εἴπειεν. ὅτε γὰρ τὰ στοιχεῖα διειστήκει χωρὶς ὑπὸ τοῦ Νείκους, τίς αἰτία τῇ γῇ τῆς μονῆς ἦν; οὐ γὰρ δὴ καὶ τότε αἰτιάσεται τὴν δίνην. ἄτοπον δὲ καὶ τὸ μὴ συννοεῖν ὅτι πρότερον μὲν διὰ τὴν δίνησιν ἐφέρετο τὰ μόρια τῆς γῆς πρὸς τὸ μέσον, νῦν δὲ διὰ τίν' αἰτίαν πάντα τὰ βάρος ἔχοντα φέρεται πρὸς αὐτήν; οὐ γὰρ ἥ γε δίνη πλησιάζει πρὸς ἡμᾶς.

363 Again, one might make the following objection against Empedocles: when the elements have been brought into a state of separation by Strife, what was the cause [*sc.* then] of the immobility of the earth? For assuredly he cannot hold the vortex responsible then too. And it is odd also that he did not see that, if formerly the parts of earth were borne to the centre by the vortex, he must explain by what cause all things which have weight are borne towards the earth now. For it cannot be the vortex which brings them into our neighbourhood.

Aristotle supposes that after Strife has achieved complete separation of the elements in the pre-critical period, there is no more (because no more separation) for the vortex to do; yet Empedocles should but does not explain what keeps the elements separated in the present post-critical period. But Simplicius plainly thinks Aristotle only reaches this judgement through misunderstanding, and quotes **360** to show that the vortex continues to operate in the post-critical period of Love's increasing domination (see *de cael.* 528, 11–14; 530, 16–22). In **362** and **363** alike, what Aristotle has failed to appreciate is the degree of causal and structural continuity Empedocles posits between pre- and post-critical phases.

No other ancient writer on Empedocles attests both pre- and

post-critical cosmogonies, although they have sometimes been thought to be implied by another text of Aristotle:

364 Aristotle *de gen. et corr.* B7, 334a5 ἅμα δὲ καὶ τὸν κόσμον ὁμοίως ἔχειν φησὶν ἐπί τε τοῦ Νείκους νῦν καὶ πρότερον ἐπὶ τῆς Φιλίας.

364 At the same time he asserts that the cosmos is in a similar state now under Strife as it was earlier under Love.

Yet Empedocles probably meant only that the basic ordering of the universe established by the vortex continues under increasing Love. (The curious contrast between now and then must be a slip of Aristotle's: it flatly contradicts **363**, which assumes that now is the post-critical period increasingly dominated by Love, as its association with zoogony would lead one to conclude anyway.)

(iii) *Cosmogony: the first stages*

365 Aetius II, 6, 3 (DK31A49) Ἐμπεδοκλῆς τὸν μὲν αἰθέρα πρῶτον διακριθῆναι, δεύτερον δὲ τὸ πῦρ, ἐφ᾽ ᾧ τὴν γῆν, ἐξ ἧς ἄγαν περισφιγγομένης τῇ ῥύμῃ τῆς περιφορᾶς ἀναβλύσαι τὸ ὕδωρ.

366 Ps.-Plutarch *Strom. ap.* Eusebium *P.E.* I, 8, 10 (DK31A30) Ἐμπεδοκλῆς ὁ Ἀκραγαντῖνος...ἐκ πρώτης φησὶ τῆς τῶν στοιχείων κράσεως ἀποκριθέντα τὸν ἀέρα περιχυθῆναι κύκλῳ· μετὰ δὲ τὸν ἀέρα τὸ πῦρ ἐκδραμὸν καὶ οὐκ ἔχον ἑτέραν χώραν ἄνω ἐκτρέχειν ὑπὸ τοῦ περὶ τὸν ἀέρα πάγου.

367 Fr. 27, Plutarch *de fac. in orbe lun.* 12, 926E
    ἔνθ᾽ οὔτ᾽ ἠελίοιο δεδίσκεται[1] ἀγλαὸν εἶδος,
    οὐδὲ μὲν οὐδ᾽ αἴης λάσιον μένος,[2] οὐδὲ θάλασσα.

    [1] δεδίσκεται Karsten: δεδίττεται codd.
    [2] μένος Bergk: γένος codd.

365 Empedocles holds that aither was the first to be separated off, next fire, and after that earth. From the earth, as it was excessively constricted by the force of the rotation, sprang water. **366** Empedocles of Acragas...holds that the air that was separated off from the original mixture of the elements flowed around in a circle; and after the air fire ran outwards and, having nowhere else to go, ran upwards under the solidified periphery around the air.
367 There the shining form of the sun is not shown, nor the shaggy might of earth, nor sea.

Each of the four elements, beginning with *aither* (the clear upper air, wrongly identified with vaporous lower air, *aer*, in **366**), is separated in turn (cf. **349**, 28–9) – presumably by the action of the vortex initiated by Strife, with which the references to rotation here should be connected. Although the basic structure of our world is thus established, there is as yet no sun nor any distinction between dry land and sea on the earth's surface.

(iv) *Cosmogony: the present world*

368 Fr. 38, Clement *Strom.* v, 48, 3

εἰ δ' ἄγε τοι λέξω πρῶτ' ἐξ ὧν ἥλιος ἀρχήν
τἆλλά τε δῆλ'¹ ἐγένοντο τὰ νῦν ἐσορῶμεν ἅπαντα,
γαῖά τε καὶ πόντος πολυκύμων ἠδ' ὑγρὸς ἀήρ
Τιτὰν ἠδ' αἰθὴρ σφίγγων περὶ κύκλον ἅπαντα.

¹ Coniecit Wright: πρῶθ' ἥλιον ἀρχήν / ἐξ ὧν δή codd.

369 Aetius II, 6, 3 (DK 31 A 49; continuing **365**) ἐξ οὗ θυμιαθῆναι τὸν ἀέρα, καὶ γενέσθαι τὸν μὲν οὐρανὸν ἐκ τοῦ αἰθέρος, τὸν δὲ ἥλιον ἐκ τοῦ πυρός, πιληθῆναι δὲ ἐκ τῶν ἄλλων τὰ περίγεια.

370 Ps.-Plutarch *Strom. ap.* Eusebium *P.E.* I, 8, 10 (DK 31 A 30; continuing **366**) εἶναι δὲ κύκλῳ περὶ τὴν γῆν φερόμενα δύο ἡμισφαίρια τὸ μὲν καθόλου πυρός, τὸ δὲ μικτὸν ἐξ ἀέρος καὶ ὀλίγου πυρός, ὅπερ οἴεται τὴν νύκτα εἶναι. τὴν δὲ ἀρχὴν τῆς κινήσεως συμβῆναι ἀπὸ τοῦ τετυχηκέναι κατὰ ⟨τι⟩ τὸν ἀθροισμὸν ἐπιβρίσαντος τοῦ πυρός. ὁ δὲ ἥλιος τὴν φύσιν οὔκ ἐστι πῦρ, ἀλλὰ τοῦ πυρὸς ἀντανάκλασις ὁμοία τῇ ἀφ' ὕδατος γινομένῃ. σελήνην δέ φησιν συστῆναι καθ' ἑαυτὴν ἐκ τοῦ ἀποληφθέντος ἀέρος ὑπὸ τοῦ πυρός. τοῦτον γὰρ παγῆναι καθάπερ καὶ τὴν χάλαζαν. τὸ δὲ φῶς αὐτὴν ἔχειν ἀπὸ τοῦ ἡλίου. (Cf. Aetius II, 20, 13 (DK 31 A 56).)

371 Aristotle *Meteor.* B3, 357a24 (DK 31 A 25) and B1, 353b11
(a) ὁμοίως δὲ γελοῖον καὶ εἴ τις εἰπών
γῆς ἱδρῶτα θάλασσαν
οἴεταί τι σαφὲς εἰρηκέναι, καθάπερ Ἐμπεδοκλῆς.
(b) ἔνιοι δ' αὐτῶν θερμαινομένης φασὶν ὑπὸ τοῦ ἡλίου τῆς γῆς οἷον ἱδρῶτα γίγνεσθαι, διὸ καὶ ἁλμυρὰν εἶναι· καὶ γὰρ ὁ ἱδρὼς ἁλμυρός.

372 Aristotle *de gen. et corr.* B6, 334a1 διέκρινε μὲν γὰρ τὸ Νεῖκος, ἠνέχθη δ' ἄνω ὁ αἰθὴρ οὐχ ὑπὸ τοῦ Νείκους, ἀλλ' ὁτὲ μέν φησιν ὥσπερ ἀπὸ τύχης
(Fr. 53) οὕτω γὰρ συνέκυρσε θέων τοτέ, πολλάκι δ' ἄλλως
ὁτὲ δέ φησι πεφυκέναι τὸ πῦρ ἄνω φέρεσθαι, ὁ δ' αἰθήρ, φησί,
(Fr. 54) μακρῇσι κατὰ χθόνα δύετο ῥίζαις.

368 Come now, I shall tell you first from what [origins] in the beginning the sun and all those others which we now see became distinct – earth and swelling sea and moist air and Titan sky [*lit.* aither] fastening his circle tight round everything.

369 From water air came by evaporation. The heavens came into being from aither, the sun from fire, and the bodies about the earth from the others.

370 There are two hemispheres revolving round the earth, one entirely of fire and the other a mixture of air and a little fire. This he supposes is the night. The start of the motion is due to the accident that there was a concentration in one region because fire pressed heavily there. The sun is not in its nature fire, but a reflexion of fire like that which comes from water. The moon, he says, was formed separately of the air cut off by the fire; for this air solidified, like hail. It has its light from the sun.

371 (a) Similarly it is ridiculous for someone who talks of 'sea, sweat of earth' to suppose that he has said anything clear, like Empedocles.

(b) Some of them say that when the earth is heated by the sun, the sea comes into being like sweat – which is also the reason why it is salty, for sweat is salty.

372 For though Strife was segregating the elements, it was not by Strife that aither was borne upwards; on the contrary, he sometimes speaks as if it happened by mere chance 'for so, at the time, it chanced to be running, though often otherwise' – while sometimes he says that it is the nature of fire to be borne upwards, but aither, he says, 'sank beneath the earth with long roots'.

368 announces the second phase of the cosmogony. Its focus was plainly the sun. First comes the formation of diurnal and nocturnal hemispheres as a result of misty air rising into the region hitherto totally dominated by fire. The sun is then explained as a reflexion of fire (perhaps on the analogy of the moon's light); probably it is cast by the earth from the fiery hemisphere back to that hemisphere (despite Aetius II, 20, 13, DK 31 A 56) 'in one concentrated flash' (Burnet, *EGP* 238; cf. Plutarch *de Pyth. or.* 12, 400B, DK 31 B 44). The other heavenly bodies are more conventionally explained. Then follows the emergence of the sea and presumably of the earth in its present form.

These events – in contrast to those of **365–6** – are to be placed in the post-critical period of the cycle. For we hear of trees growing (i.e. some of the 'countless tribes of mortal things') even before night and day were distinguished (Aetius V, 26, 4; DK 31 A 70). It is to that same early phase of the period that we must assign such associations of different elements as the penetration of earth by *aither*, plunging downwards in what puzzles Aristotle as an unnatural direction. He has missed a sign of Love's influence, indeed one of the preconditions of the origin of life from earth. But we may infer that the cosmogony was described mostly in physical and biological terms, with constant references to chance but few to Love or even Strife.

(v) *Zoogony*

It seems likely that, after reminding his reader that zoogony is Love's special province, Empedocles turned first to account for the generation of the parts of animals (cf. Aristotle *de caelo* 300b25ff., DK 31 B 57; **374** apparently came earlier in the poem than **381**: see Simpl. *in Phys.* 300, 20; 381, 29). Fragments on blood and flesh and on bones are preserved. Their use of numerical ratios perhaps reflects Pythagorean influence.

373　Fr. 98, Simplicius *in Phys.* 32, 6

ἡ δὲ χθών τούτοισιν ἴση συνέκυρσε μάλιστα,
'Ηφαίστῳ τ' ὄμβρῳ τε καὶ αἰθέρι παμφανόωντι,
Κύπριδος ὁρμισθεῖσα τελείοις ἐν λιμένεσσιν,
εἴτ' ὀλίγον μείζων εἴτ' ἐν πλεόνεσσιν ἐλάσσων
ἐκ τῶν αἷμά τε γέντο καὶ ἄλλης εἴδεα σαρκός.

374　Fr. 96, Simplicius *in Phys.* 300, 21

ἡ δὲ χθὼν ἐπίηρος ἐν εὐστέρνοις χοάνοισι
τὰς δύο τῶν ὀκτὼ μοιράων λάχε Νήστιδος αἴγλης,
τέσσαρα δ' 'Ηφαίστοιο· τὰ δ' ὀστέα λευκὰ γένοντο
'Αρμονίης κόλλησιν ἀρηρότα θεσπεσίηθεν.

373　And earth chanced in about equal quantity upon these, Hephaestus [*i.e.* fire], rain and gleaming air [*lit.* aither], anchored in the perfect harbours of Cypris [*i.e.* Love], either a little more of it or less of it among more of them. From these arose blood and the various forms of flesh.

374　And kindly earth received in its broad melting-pots two parts of the glitter of Nestis out of eight, and four of Hephaestus; and they became white bones, marvellously joined by the gluing of Harmonia.

The creatures to which these parts belong were described subsequently, in Empedocles' remarkable theory of evolution:

375　Aetius v, 19, 5 (DK 31 A 72) 'Εμπεδοκλῆς τὰς πρώτας γενέσεις τῶν ζῴων καὶ φυτῶν μηδαμῶς ὁλοκλήρους γενέσθαι, ἀσυμφυέσι δὲ τοῖς μορίοις διεζευγμένας, τὰς δὲ δευτέρας συμφυομένων τῶν μερῶν εἰδωλοφανεῖς, τὰς δὲ τρίτας τῶν ὁλοφυῶν, τὰς δὲ τετάρτας οὐκέτι ἐκ τῶν ὁμοίων οἷον ἐκ γῆς καὶ ὕδατος, ἀλλὰ δι᾽ ἀλλήλων ἤδη, τοῖς μὲν πυκνωθείσης [τοῖς δὲ καὶ τοῖς ζῴοις] τῆς τροφῆς, τοῖς δὲ καὶ τῆς εὐμορφίας τῶν γυναικῶν ἐπερεθισμὸν τοῦ σπερματικοῦ κινήματος ἐμποιησάσης· τῶν δὲ ζῴων πάντων τὰ γένη διακριθῆναι διὰ τὰς ποιὰς κράσεις...

375 Empedocles held that the first generations of animals and plants were not complete but consisted of separate limbs not joined together; the second, arising from the joining of these limbs, were like creatures in dreams; the third was the generation of whole-natured forms; and the fourth arose no longer from the homogeneous substances such as earth or water, but by intermingling, in some cases as the result of the condensation of their nourishment, in others because feminine beauty excited the sexual urge; and the various species of animals were distinguished by the quality of the mixture in them...

In the first stage, according to Simplicius (*de caelo* 587, 18–19), solitary limbs wandered in search of mutual mixture:

376 Fr. 57, Aristotle *de caelo* Γ2, 300b30 (line 1) and Simplicius *de caelo* 587, 1 (lines 2–3)

ᾗ πολλαὶ μὲν κόρσαι ἀναύχενες ἐβλάστησαν,
γυμνοὶ δ᾽ ἐπλάζοντο βραχίονες εὔνιδες ὤμων,
ὄμματά τ᾽ οἶ᾽ ἐπλανᾶτο πενητεύοντα μετώπων.

376 Here sprang up many faces without necks, arms wandered without shoulders, unattached, and eyes strayed alone, in need of foreheads.

Union, mostly unsatisfactory, was achieved at the second stage:

377 Fr. 59, Simplicius *de caelo* 587, 20

αὐτὰρ ἐπεὶ κατὰ μεῖζον ἐμίσγετο δαίμονι δαίμων
ταῦτά τε συμπίπτεσκον, ὅπῃ συνέκυρσεν ἕκαστα,
ἄλλα τε πρὸς τοῖς πολλὰ διηνεκῆ ἐξεγένοντο.

378 Fr. 60, Plutarch *adv. Colot.* 28, 1123B

...εἰλίποδ᾽ ἀκριτόχειρα...

379 Fr. 61, Aelian *Nat. anim.* XVI, 29

πολλὰ μὲν ἀμφιπρόσωπα καὶ ἀμφίστερνα φύεσθαι,
βουγενῆ ἀνδρόπρωρα, τὰ δ᾽ ἔμπαλιν ἐξανατέλλειν
ἀνδροφυῆ βούκρανα, μεμειγμένα τῇ μὲν ἀπ᾽ ἀνδρῶν
τῇ δὲ γυναικοφυῆ σκιεροῖς ἠσκημένα γυίοις.

377 But as one divine element mingled further with another, these things fell together as each chanced to meet other, and many other things besides these were constantly resulting.

378 ...with rolling gait and countless hands...

379 Many creatures were born with faces and breasts on both sides, man-faced ox-progeny, while others again sprang forth as ox-headed offspring of man, creatures compounded partly of male, partly of the nature of female, and fitted with shadowy parts.

Although this stage is dominated by monsters, those creatures that were accidently fitted to survive did so (i.e. they presumably reproduced), while the rest perished:

380 Aristotle *Phys.* B8, 198b29 (DK 31 B61) ὅπου μὲν οὖν ἅπαντα συνέβη ὥσπερ κἂν εἰ ἕνεκά του ἐγίνετο, ταῦτα μὲν ἐσώθη ἀπὸ τοῦ αὐτομάτου συστάντα ἐπιτηδείως· ὅσα δὲ μὴ οὕτως, ἀπώλετο καὶ ἀπόλλυται, καθάπερ Ἐμπεδοκλῆς λέγει τὰ 'βουγενῆ ἀνδρόπρωρα'.

380 Wherever, then, everything turned out as it would have if it were happening for a purpose, there the creatures survived, being accidentally compounded in a suitable way; but where this did not happen, the creatures perished and are perishing still, as Empedocles says of his 'man-faced ox-progeny'.

A third stage follows:

381 Fr. 62, Simplicius *in Phys.* 381, 31
νῦν δ' ἄγ', ὅπως ἀνδρῶν τε πολυκλαύτων τε γυναικῶν
ἐννυχίους ὅρπηκας ἀνήγαγε κρινόμενον πῦρ,
τῶνδε κλύ'· οὐ γὰρ μῦθος ἀπόσκοπος οὐδ' ἀδαήμων.
οὐλοφυεῖς μὲν πρῶτα τύποι χθονὸς ἐξανέτελλον,
ἀμφοτέρων ὕδατός τε καὶ εἴδεος αἶσαν ἔχοντες·
τοὺς μὲν πῦρ ἀνέπεμπε θέλον πρὸς ὁμοῖον ἱκέσθαι,
οὔτε τί πω μελέων ἐρατὸν δέμας ἐμφαίνοντας
οὔτ' ἐνοπὴν οἵη τ' ἐπιχώριον ἀνδράσι γυίων.

381 Come now, hear how fire as it was separated raised up the nocturnal shoots of men and pitiable women: it is no erring nor ignorant tale. Whole-natured shapes first sprang up from the earth, having a portion of both water and heat. These fire sent up, wishing to come to its like: they did not yet display the desirable form of limbs nor voice, which is the part proper to men. (*After Guthrie*)

These shapes are presumably called 'whole-natured' because they, unlike the creatures of **376–9**, are both complete beings (not mere fragments) and organic wholes (not adventitious collections of parts), although they are represented as larval in comparison with the animals of Aetius' fourth stage (**375**). They are doubtless the product largely of Love's workmanship, although their emergence from the earth is due to behaviour of fire not yet subject to her powers of mixture.[1]

[1] Proponents of a double cosmogony in Empedocles hold that while the first two stages of the zoogony belong in the post-critical period, the second two are early stages of the pre-critical period; and they suppose the whole-natured creatures to manifest Love's power to a higher degree than the men and women of our present world. But there is no independent evidence of such a division of the stages of **375**. And lines 7–8 strongly suggest that Love has not yet achieved as much at the third stage as she will at the fourth.

382 Aetius v, 18, 1 (DK 31 A 75) Ἐμπεδοκλῆς ὅτε ἐγεννᾶτο τὸ τῶν ἀνθρώπων γένος ἐκ τῆς γῆς, τοσαύτην γενέσθαι τῷ μήκει τοῦ χρόνου διὰ τὸ βραδυπορεῖν τὸν ἥλιον τὴν ἡμέραν, ὁπόση νῦν ἐστιν ἡ δεκάμηνος· προϊόντος δὲ τοῦ χρόνου τοσαύτην γενέσθαι τὴν ἡμέραν, ὁπόση νῦν ἐστιν ἡ ἑπτάμηνος· διὰ τοῦτο καὶ τὰ δεκάμηνα καὶ τὰ ἑπτάμηνα, τῆς φύσεως τοῦ κόσμου οὕτω μεμελετηκυίας, αὔξεσθαι ἐν μιᾷ ἡμέρᾳ ᾗ τίκτεται [νυκτὶ] τὸ βρέφος.

382 Empedocles says that when the race of men were produced from the earth, the day lasted as long as a period of ten months does now, because of the slowness of the sun's motion. But as time went on the day lasted as long as a seven-month period now. For this reason ten-month and seven-month babies develop in a single day – the one on which the child is born – since the nature of the cosmos has provided for this.

382 seems to be concerned with the 'whole-natured' shapes, unless Empedocles posited a later generation of earth-born giants. It shows that the first three stages of evolution must have occurred in very early phases of the post-critical period.

BIOLOGY

The last part of *On Nature* was devoted to detailed (and subsequently often influential) discussions of many topics in the biology of our present world, including the reproduction of plants and animals and the physiology of respiration and perception. It is possible to include here only fragments and testimonia of most general interest.

(i) *Principles of explanation*

383   Fr. 82, Aristotle *Meteor*. Δ9, 387b4
ταὐτὰ τρίχες καὶ φύλλα καὶ οἰωνῶν πτερὰ πυκνά
καὶ φλονίδες γίγνονται ἐπὶ στιβαροῖσι μέλεσσιν.

384   Fr. 83, Plutarch *de fortuna* 3, 98D   τὰ μὲν γὰρ ὥπλισται κέρασι
καὶ ὀδοῦσι καὶ κέντροις,

αὐτὰρ ἐχίνοις
ὀξυβελεῖς χαῖται νώτοις ἐπιπεφρίκασι.

385   Fr. 79, Aristotle *de gen. animalium* A23, 731a4   καὶ τοῦτο καλῶς
λέγει Ἐμπεδοκλῆς ποιήσας
οὕτω δ᾽ ᾠοτοκεῖ μακρὰ δένδρεα· πρῶτον ἐλαίας
τό τε γὰρ ᾠὸν κύημά ἐστι, καὶ ἔκ τινος αὐτοῦ γίγνεται τὸ ζῷον,
τὸ δὲ λοιπὸν τροφή.

383   The same things are hair and leaves and the close-packed
feathers of birds and the scales which come into being on sturdy
limbs.
384   For some things are equipped with horns and teeth and
stings, 'but hedgehogs have sharp hairs bristling on their backs'.
385   And Empedocles puts this well in his poem, when he says:
'Thus do tall trees bear eggs: first olives...'; for the egg is a foetus,
and the animal is produced out of part of it, while the remainder
is nutrient.

Aristotle not only praised but systematically exploited the most
striking feature of Empedocles' biology, his perception of homologous
functions in apparently dissimilar parts of very different sorts of living
being. 383 is an explicit statement of the theme; 384–5 show how
Empedocles used it to arresting descriptive effect, making his reader
see the unexpected kinship of all nature.

For the rest, Aristotle is a harsh critic of Empedocles' explanatory
framework:

386   Aristotle *de part. animalium* A1, 640a18 (DK31B97)   ἡ γὰρ
γένεσις ἕνεκα τῆς οὐσίας ἐστίν, ἀλλ᾽ οὐχ ἡ οὐσία ἕνεκα τῆς γενέσεως.
διόπερ Ἐμπεδοκλῆς οὐκ ὀρθῶς εἴρηκε λέγων ὑπάρχειν πολλὰ τοῖς
ζῷοις διὰ τὸ συμβῆναι οὕτως ἐν τῇ γενέσει οἷον καὶ τὴν ῥάχιν
τοιαύτην ἔχειν ὅτι στραφέντος καταχθῆναι συνέβη.

386   Coming to be is for the sake of being, not being for the sake
of coming to be. Hence Empedocles was wrong in saying that many
attributes belong to animals because it happened so in their

coming to be, for instance that their backbone is such because it happened to get broken by bending.

Aristotle objects to the extent of Empedocles' use of chance (his unexplained use: *Phys.* 196a19–24) in accounting for regular biological phenomena. We may rather praise him as the first thinker to see that biology needs both randomness and principles of organization in its explanatory equipment.

387 Aristotle *de gen. et corr.* B6, 333b30 ταύτην οὖν ἡ Φιλία κινεῖ; ἢ οὔ; τοὐναντίον γὰρ τὴν γῆν κάτω, καὶ διακρίσει ἔοικεν, καὶ μᾶλλον τὸ Νεῖκος αἴτιον τῆς κατὰ φύσιν κινήσεως ἢ ἡ Φιλία, ὥστε καὶ ὅλως παρὰ φύσιν ἡ Φιλία ἂν εἴη μᾶλλον. ἁπλῶς δέ, εἰ μὴ ἡ Φιλία ἢ τὸ Νεῖκος κινεῖ, αὐτῶν τῶν σωμάτων οὐδεμία κίνησίς ἐστιν οὐδὲ μονή· ἀλλ' ἄτοπον.

387 Is it, then, Love that is cause of natural motion? Or not? For – contrary to the idea that it is Love – natural motion moves earth downwards, and resembles separation, and Strife is rather its cause than is Love, so that in general Love would be the cause rather of motion contrary to nature. And if Love or Strife do not cause motion, then there is simply no motion nor yet rest inherent in the bodies themselves: but that is absurd.

The relation between the activity of Love and Strife and the 'natural' motion of the elements in Empedocles is indeed obscure, as consideration of the following fragment will show:

388 Fr. 22, Simplicius *in Phys.* 160, 26
ἄρθμια μὲν γὰρ ταῦτα ἑαυτῶν πάντα μέρεσσιν,
ἠλέκτωρ τε χθών τε καὶ οὐρανὸς ἠδὲ θάλασσα,
ὅσσα φιν ἐν θνητοῖσιν ἀποπλαχθέντα πέφυκεν·
ὡς δ' αὔτως ὅσα κρῆσιν ἐπαρκέα μᾶλλον ἔασιν,
5   ἀλλήλοις ἔστερκται ὁμοιωθέντ' Ἀφροδίτῃ·
ἐχθρὰ μάλισθ' ⟨ὅσα⟩ πλεῖστον ἀπ' ἀλλήλων διέχουσι[1]
γέννῃ τε κρήσει τε καὶ εἴδεσιν ἐκμάκτοισι,
πάντῃ συγγίνεσθαι ἀήθεα καὶ μάλα λυγρά
Νείκεος ἐννεσίῃσιν, ὅτι σφίσι γένναν ἔοργεν.

> [1] coniecit Wright: ἐχθρὰ πλεῖστον...διέχουσι μάλιστα codd.

388 For all these – shining sun and earth and sky and sea – are one with their own parts which are scattered in mortal things. But in the same way all that are fitted rather for mixture are made like by Aphrodite and are loved by one another, whereas most hostile are all that are farthest apart from each other in birth, in mixture, and in moulded forms, altogether unaccustomed to come together and very grim at the biddings of Strife, because it has brought about their birth.

The natural affinity of (for example) fire with fire (lines 1–3) is apparently contrasted (μέν...δέ) with the assimilation of different elements to each other achieved by Love (lines 4–5); and that affinity is given fullest realization under Strife's dominance (cf. **361**). On the other hand it is described in terms which irresistibly recall the activity of Love (cf. line 1 with **349**, 23; and NB **381**, 6). That may suggest that *all* attraction whether of likes or of unlikes is due to Love, although the latter will be a more complete and noteworthy exercise of her powers. It is hard to avoid concluding that Empedocles' metaphors of love and strife have got the better of him.

Analogy and metaphor are, for better or worse, the most pervasive explanatory devices in Empedocles' armoury. We may conclude this section with a memorable extended simile in the Homeric manner.[1]

[1] Part of Empedocles' even more elaborate simile of the clepsydra is included below as **471**.

389   Fr. 84, Aristotle *de sensu*, 2, 437b23
ὡς δ' ὅτε τις πρὸ ὁδὸν νοέων ὡπλίσσατο λύχνον
χειμερίην διὰ νύκτα, πυρὸς σέλας αἰθομένοιο,
ἅψας παντοίων ἀνέμων λαμπτῆρας ἀμοργούς,
οἵ τ' ἀνέμων μὲν πνεῦμα διασκιδνᾶσιν ἀέντων,
5 φῶς δ' ἔξω διαθρῷσκον, ὅσον ταναώτερον ἦεν,
λάμπεσκεν κατὰ βηλὸν ἀτειρέσιν ἀκτίνεσσιν·
ὣς δὲ τότ' ἐν μήνιγξιν ἐελμένον ὠγύγιον πῦρ
λεπτῇσίν ⟨τ'⟩ ὀθόνῃσι λοχεύσατο[1] κύκλοπα κούρην·
αἳ δ' ὕδατος μὲν βένθος ἀπέστεγον ἀμφιναέντος,
10 πῦρ δ' ἔξω δίεσκον, ὅσον ταναώτερον ἦεν.

[1] λοχεύσατο Förster: λοχάζετο Arist. EM, ἐχεύατο cet. codd., Alex *ad loc.*

389   As when someone planning a journey through the wintry night prepares a light, a flame of blazing fire, kindling for whatever the weather a linen lantern, which scatters the breath of the winds when they blow, but the finer light leaps through outside and shines across the threshold with unyielding beams: so at that time did she [*sc.* Aphrodite] give birth to the round eye, primeval fire confined within membranes and delicate garments, and these held back the deep water that flowed around, but they let through the finer fire to the outside.

(ii) *Sense-perception and thought*

390   Plato *Meno* 76c (DK 31 A 92)

Σ.   Οὐκοῦν λέγετε ἀπορροάς τινας τῶν ὄντων κατὰ Ἐμπεδοκλέα;

Μ.   Σφόδρα γε.

Σ.   Καὶ πόρους εἰς οὓς καὶ δι᾽ ὧν αἱ ἀπορροαὶ πορεύονται;

Μ.   Πάνυ γε.

Σ.   Καὶ τῶν ἀπορροῶν τὰς μὲν ἁρμόττειν ἐνίοις τῶν πόρων, τὰς δὲ ἐλάττους ἢ μείζους εἶναι;

Μ.   Ἔστι ταῦτα.

Σ.   Οὐκοῦν καὶ ὄψιν καλεῖς τι;

Μ.   Ἔγωγε.

Σ.   Ἐκ τούτων δὴ ʽσύνες ὅ τοι λέγωʼ, ἔφη Πίνδαρος· ἔστιν γὰρ χρόα ἀπορροὴ σχημάτων ὄψει σύμμετρος καὶ αἰσθητός.

Μ.   Ἄριστά μοι δοκεῖς, ὦ Σώκρατες, ταύτην τὴν ἀπόκρισιν εἰρηκέναι.

Σ.   Ἴσως γάρ σοι κατὰ συνήθειαν εἴρηται· καὶ ἅμα, οἶμαι, ἐννοεῖς ὅτι ἔχοις ἂν ἐξ αὐτῆς εἰπεῖν καὶ φωνὴν ὅ ἐστι, καὶ ὀσμὴν καὶ ἄλλα πολλὰ τῶν τοιούτων.

Μ.   Πάνυ μὲν οὖν.

391   Theophrastus *de sensu* 7 (DK 31 A 86)   Ἐμπεδοκλῆς δὲ περὶ ἁπασῶν (*sc.* αἰσθήσεων) ὁμοίως λέγει καί φησι τῷ ἐναρμόττειν εἰς τοὺς πόρους τοὺς ἑκάστης αἰσθάνεσθαι· διὸ καὶ οὐ δύνασθαι τὰ ἀλλήλων κρίνειν, ὅτι τῶν μὲν εὐρύτεροί πως, τῶν δὲ στενώτεροι τυγχάνουσιν οἱ πόροι πρὸς τὸ αἰσθητόν, ὡς τὰ μὲν οὐχ ἁπτόμενα διευτονεῖν τὰ δ᾽ ὅλως εἰσελθεῖν οὐ δύνασθαι.

390   *Socrates* Do you agree with Empedocles that existing things give off certain effluences? *Meno* Certainly. *S.* And that they have passages into which and through which the effluences travel? *M.* Yes. *S.* And of the effluences some fit some of the passages while others are too small or too big? *M.* That is so. *S.* And there is something you call sight? *M.* There is. *S.* From all this, then, ʽgrasp what I say to youʼ, as Pindar puts it: colour is an effluence of shapes which is commensurate with sight and perceptible. *M.* This answer of yours, Socrates, is in my view quite excellent. *S.* Perhaps it is the one you are used to. And at the same time, I suppose, you have it in mind that it will put you in a position to say also what voice is, and smell, and many other such things. *M.* Yes indeed.

391   Empedocles has the same theory about all the senses, maintaining that perception arises when something fits into the passages of any of the senses. This is why one sense cannot judge the objects of another, since the passages of some are too wide, of others too narrow for the object perceived, so that some things pass straight through without making contact while others cannot enter at all.

Theophrastus goes on to describe quite fully Empedocles' accounts of the individual senses, especially sight[1] and hearing, and to criticize the theory at still greater length. Other texts make it clear that Empedocles used the ingenious doctrine of pores and effluences to give the first detailed explanations offered by a Greek philosopher not only of perception, but of many other phenomena too (cf. **545**), including chemical mixture (Aristotle *de gen. et corr.* 324b26–35, DK 31 A 87; examples in frr. 91–2) and magnetism (Alexander *Quaest.* II, 23; DK 31 A 89). Theophrastus accordingly complains that he has no means of distinguishing between mixture, perception and growth (*de sensu* 12, DK 31 A 86). Empedocles plainly supposed that only like things (or things made like by Love) could have symmetrical pores and effluences, since he posits fire in the eye for perception of light colours, a resounding bell in the ear to explain hearing, and breath in the nose for smelling (*de sensu* 7 and 9; for the general principle see **388**, 1–5).

[1] He begins his treatment of sight by summarizing **389**, which he rightly interprets not as an account (at odds with the theory of effluences) of sight as the emission of fire from the eye (so Aristotle *de sensu* 437b9–14, 438a4–5), but as explaining how the eye is so structured and composed as to receive effluences of colour.

392 Theophrastus *de sensu* 9 (DK 31 A 86) ὡσαύτως δὲ λέγει καὶ περὶ φρονήσεως καὶ ἀγνοίας. (10) τὸ μὲν γὰρ φρονεῖν εἶναι τοῖς ὁμοίοις, τὸ δ' ἀγνοεῖν τοῖς ἀνομοίοις, ὡς ἢ ταὐτὸν ἢ παραπλήσιον ὂν τῇ αἰσθήσει τὴν φρόνησιν. διαριθμησάμενος γὰρ ὡς ἕκαστον ἑκάστῳ γνωρίζομεν, ἐπὶ τέλει προσέθηκεν ὡς
(Fr. 107)   ἐκ τούτων ⟨γὰρ⟩ πάντα πεπήγασιν ἁρμοσθέντα
         καὶ τούτοις φρονέουσι καὶ ἥδοντ' ἠδ' ἀνιῶνται.
διὸ καὶ τῷ αἵματι μάλιστα φρονεῖν· ἐν τούτῳ γὰρ μάλιστα κεκρᾶσθαι [ἐστὶ] τὰ στοιχεῖα τῶν μερῶν.

393 Fr. 109, Aristotle *Met.* B4, 1000b6
         γαίῃ μὲν γὰρ γαῖαν ὀπώπαμεν, ὕδατι δ' ὕδωρ,
         αἰθέρι δ' αἰθέρα δῖον, ἀτὰρ πυρὶ πῦρ ἀίδηλον,
         στοργὴν δὲ στοργῇ, νεῖκος δέ τε νείκεϊ λυγρῷ.

394 Fr. 105, Porphyrius *ap*. Stobaeum *Anth*. 1, 49, 53

αἵματος ἐν πελάγεσσι τεθραμμένη ἀντιθορόντος,
τῇ τε νόημα μάλιστα κικλήσκεται ἀνθρώποισιν·
αἷμα γὰρ ἀνθρώποις περικάρδιόν ἐστι νόημα.

392 And he has the same theory about thought and ignorance. Thinking is of like by like, ignorance of unlike by unlike, thought being either identical with or closely akin to perception. For having enumerated how we know each thing by its equivalent, he added at the end that 'out of these things are all things fitted together and constructed, and by these do they think and feel pleasure or pain'. So it is especially with the blood that they think; for in the blood above all other parts the elements are blended.
393 For with earth do we see earth, with water water, with air bright air, with fire consuming fire; with Love do we see Love, Strife with dread Strife.
394 ...[The heart] dwelling in the sea of blood which surges back and forth, where especially is what is called thought by men; for the blood around men's hearts is their thought.

393 gives the enumeration spoken of in **392**; and **394** (together with **373**) must be Theophrastus' evidence for his final statement. The texts are sometimes understood as implying that the elements literally perceive and the blood they constitute literally thinks. It is better to stress the 'we' of **393** and the 'they' of **392**, noting the datives 'with earth' etc., and to read Empedocles as holding that it is *in virtue of* our possession of a substance in which the elements are mixed in equal proportions that *we* can think (cf. Plutarch *de exil.* 607D). No doubt he believes equal mixture so important because only then, in his view, can we attain an unbiased judgement of what the world is like. A further fragment indicates that such judgement is best derived from what is present to our senses (cf. **343**):

395 Fr. 106, Aristotle *de anima* Γ3, 427a21

πρὸς παρεὸν γὰρ μῆτις ἀέξεται ἀνθρώποισιν.

395 Men's wit grows according as they encounter what is present.

Empedocles may have concluded *On Nature* with a description of the 'holy mind' of a god who has some of the physical properties of the Sphere, yet whose existence is apparently contemporaneous with the cosmos:

396   Fr. 133, Clement *Strom.* v, 81, 2

οὐκ ἔστιν πελάσασθαι ἐν ὀφθαλμοῖσιν ἐφικτὸν
ἡμετέροις ἢ χερσὶ λαβεῖν, ἧπέρ τε μεγίστη
πειθοῦς ἀνθρώποισιν ἁμαξιτὸς εἰς φρένα πίπτει.

397   Fr. 134, Ammonius *de interpretatione* 249, 6 Busse

οὐδὲ γὰρ ἀνδρομέη κεφαλῇ κατὰ γυῖα κέκασται,
οὐ μὲν ἀπὸ νώτοιο δύο κλάδοι ἀΐσσονται,
οὐ πόδες, οὐ θοὰ γοῦν', οὐ μήδεα λαχνήεντα,
ἀλλὰ φρὴν ἱερὴ καὶ ἀθέσφατος ἔπλετο μοῦνον,
φροντίσι κόσμον ἅπαντα καταΐσσουσα θοῇσιν.

396   It is impossible to bring [the divine] near to us within reach of our eyes or to grasp him with the hands – although this is the main road of persuasion entering the minds of men.

397   For he is not furnished with a human head upon limbs, nor do two branches spring from his back, he has no feet, no nimble knees, no shaggy genitals, but he is mind alone, holy and beyond description, darting through the whole cosmos with swift thoughts.

As the body of the god exhibits a perfection our bodies lack, so the power of his mind transcends the limitations of our minds.

EPILOGUE

398   Fr. 110, Hippolytus *Ref.* vii, 29, 25

εἰ γὰρ καί σφ' ἀδινῇσιν ὑπὸ πραπίδεσσιν ἐρείσας
εὐμενέως καθαρῇσιν ἐποπτεύσεις μελέτῃσιν,
ταῦτά τέ σοι μάλα πάντα δι' αἰῶνος παρέσονται,
ἄλλα τε πόλλ' ἀπὸ τῶνδε κτήσεαι· αὐτὰ γὰρ αὔξει
5   ταῦτ' εἰς ἦθος ἕκαστον, ὅπη φύσις ἐστὶν ἑκάστῳ.
εἰ δὲ σύ γ' ἀλλοίων ἐπορέξεαι, οἷα κατ' ἄνδρας
μυρία δειλὰ πέλονται ἅ τ' ἀμβλύνουσι μερίμνας,
ἦ σ' ἄφαρ ἐκλείψουσι περιπλομένοιο χρόνοιο
σφῶν αὐτῶν ποθέοντα φίλην ἐπὶ γένναν ἱκέσθαι·
10   πάντα γὰρ ἴσθι φρόνησιν ἔχειν καὶ νώματος αἶσαν.

398   If you plant them in your stout understanding and contemplate them with good will in pure exercises, these will assuredly all be with you throughout your life: and you will gain many other things from them; for of themselves they will cause each to grow in his own way, according to the nature of each. But if you reach for things of a different kind, such as come in their thousands among men, evils that blunt their thoughts, then at once they will abandon you as time comes round, longing to find their own dear kind; for know that they all have intelligence and a share of thought.

The poem concludes with encouragement and warning for Pausanias, dispensed in equal quantities. What he is bidden to contemplate is presumably the instruction he has been given. Empedocles' teachings are the things which, intelligent as they are, will have the sense to leave Pausanias and find more congenial company if he engages in pursuits inimical to philosophy.

PURIFICATIONS

399 Fr. 112, Diogenes Laertius VIII, 62 (lines 1–10) and Clement *Strom.* VI, 30 (lines 9–11)

> ὦ φίλοι, οἳ μέγα ἄστυ κάτα ξανθοῦ 'Ακράγαντος
> ναίετ' ἀν' ἄκρα πόλεος, ἀγαθῶν μελεδήμονες ἔργων,
> χαίρετ'· ἐγὼ δ' ὑμῖν θεὸς ἄμβροτος, οὐκέτι θνητὸς
> πωλεῦμαι μετὰ πᾶσι τετιμένος, ὥσπερ ἔοικα,
> 5 ταινίαις τε περίστεπτος στέφεσίν τε θαλείοις·
> ⟨πᾶσι δὲ⟩ τοῖς ἂν ἵκωμαι ἐς ἄστεα τηλεθάοντα,
> ἀνδράσιν ἠδὲ γυναιξί, σεβίζομαι· οἱ δ' ἅμ' ἔπονται
> μυρίοι ἐξερέοντες, ὅπη πρὸς κέρδος ἀταρπός,
> οἱ μὲν μαντοσυνέων κεχρημένοι, οἱ δ' ἐπὶ νούσων
> 10 παντοίων ἐπύθοντο κλύειν εὐηκέα βάξιν,
> δηρὸν χαλεπῆσι πεπαρμένοι ⟨ἀμφ' ὀδύνησιν⟩.

399 Friends, who live in the great city of the yellow Acragas, up on the heights of the citadel, caring for good deeds, I give you greetings. An immortal god, mortal no more, I go about honoured by all, as is fitting, crowned with ribbons and fresh garlands; and by all whom I come upon as I enter their prospering towns, by men and women, I am revered. They follow me in their thousands, asking where lies the road to profit, some desiring prophecies, while others ask to hear the word of healing for every kind of illness, long transfixed by harsh pains.

The first line of *Purifications* establishes it as a poem addressed, unlike *On Nature*, to an extended group of people (conceivably a Pythagorean *hetaireia*), if not to the general public. Empedocles evidently writes away from home. Diels and Wilamowitz, indeed, pictured him in exile (cf. Diog. L. VIII, 52 and 57; DK 31 A 1), a recent convert from the sober materialist philosophy of *On Nature* to the spiritual intoxication of Pythagoreanism or mystery religion. But the grounds for this biographical speculation have been proved flimsy, although there is general agreement that *Purifications* is the later poem. It contains numerous references to themes and concepts (e.g. Love, Strife, the four elements, the oath) which assume in it a key function fully explicable only within the theoretical framework of *On Nature*.

Empedocles' claim to divinity (line 3) echoes Hermes' self-disclosure to Priam in the last book of the *Iliad* (xxiv, 460; cf. also Demeter's words of address, *Hym. Dem.* 120). It also resembles the greeting with which the deceased initiate of the mystery cults is received (apparently by Persephone) in the 'golden plates' of Thurii (dated to the fourth century B.C. and later; cf. p. 29 above):

400 *Inscriptiones Graecae*² xiv, 641, 1 (line 10), DK1B18 (= A1 Zuntz)

ὄλβιε καὶ μακαριστέ, θεὸς δ' ἔσῃ ἀντὶ βροτοῖο.

400 Happy and blessed one, you shall be a god instead of a mortal.

In the main body of the poem Empedocles taught that like other divine spirits (*daimones*) he has been condemned to mortality, but that divinity is once more attainable after a cycle of incarnations. And he added an explanation of the sin by which he and they fall from grace, and of the ritual practices necessary for pure religion.

THE CYCLE OF INCARNATION

(i) *The decree*

401 Fr. 115, Hippolytus *Ref.* vii, 29, 14 (ll. 1–2, 4–14) and Plutarch *de exilio* 17, 607c (lines 1, 3, 5, 6, 13)

ἔστι τι Ἀνάγκης χρῆμα, θεῶν ψήφισμα παλαιόν,
ἀίδιον, πλατέεσσι κατεσφρηγισμένον ὅρκοις·
εὖτέ τις ἀμπλακίῃσι φόνῳ φίλα γυῖα μιήνῃ,
ὅς κεν τὴν ἐπίορκον ἁμαρτήσας ἐπομόσσῃ,
5 δαίμονες οἵτε μακραίωνος λελάχασι βίοιο,
τρίς μιν μυρίας ὥρας ἀπὸ μακάρων ἀλάλησθαι,
φυόμενον παντοῖα διὰ χρόνου εἴδεα θνητῶν,
ἀργαλέας βιότοιο μεταλλάσσοντα κελεύθους.
αἰθέριον μὲν γάρ σφε μένος πόντονδε διώκει,
10 πόντος δ' ἐς χθονὸς οὖδας ἀπέπτυσε, γαῖα δ' ἐς αὐγὰς
ἠελίου φαέθοντος, ὁ δ' αἰθέρος ἔμβαλε δίναις·
ἄλλος δ' ἐξ ἄλλου δέχεται, στυγέουσι δὲ πάντες.
τῶν καὶ ἐγὼ νῦν εἰμι, φυγὰς θεόθεν καὶ ἀλήτης,
Νείκεϊ μαινομένῳ πίσυνος.

401 There is an oracle of Necessity, ancient decree of the gods, eternal, sealed with broad oaths: when anyone sins and pollutes his own limbs with bloodshed, who by his error makes false the oath he swore – spirits whose portion is long life – for thrice ten thousand years he wanders apart from the blessed, being born throughout that time in all manner of forms of mortal things, exchanging one hard path of life for another. The force of the air [*lit.* aither] pursues him into the sea, the sea spews him out onto the floor of the earth, the earth casts him into the rays of the blazing sun, and the sun into the eddies of the air; one takes him from the other, but all abhor him. Of these I too am now one, an exile from the gods and a wanderer, having put my trust in raving Strife.

The law which ordains a series of incarnations as the consequence of sin is described in terms almost identical to those used in specifying the law which governs disruption of the Sphere by Strife; sin is explicitly associated with 'trust in raving Strife'; and the round of the elements made by the *daimones* recalls the successive domination of different elements which in *On Nature* follows the fragmentation of the Sphere. But **401** is at the same time modelled on some lines of the *Theogony* (775–806) which tell of the fate of any god who engages in quarrel and strife and then forswears the oath to desist: 'the banished god described by Hesiod is – Man' (Zuntz, *Persephone*, 267). And Empedocles apparently went on to elaborate his account of the fall of the *daimones* in decidedly mythical terms, derived from Homer and Hesiod (perhaps especially the descent to the underworld in the *Odyssey*).

(ii) *The misery of incarnation*

402 Fr. 118, Clement *Strom.* iii, 14, 2 (line 1) and fr. 121, Hierocles *ad carmina aurea* 24 (ll. 2 and 3)

κλαῦσά τε καὶ κώκυσα ἰδὼν ἀσυνήθεα χῶρον,
ἔνθα Φόνος τε Κότος τε καὶ ἄλλων ἔθνεα Κηρῶν

.   .   .   .

Ἄτης ἂν λειμῶνα κατὰ σκότος ἠλάσκουσιν.

403 Fr. 124, Clement *Strom.* iii, 14, 2

ὢ πόποι, ὢ δειλὸν θνητῶν γένος, ὢ δυσάνολβον,
τοίων ἔκ τ' ἐρίδων ἔκ τε στοναχῶν ἐγένεσθε.

404 Fr. 119, Clement *Strom.* iv, 13, 1

ἐξ οἵης τιμῆς τε καὶ ὅσσου μήκεος ὄλβου...

405 Fr. 120, Porphyrius *de antro nymph.* 8

ἠλύθομεν τόδ' ὑπ' ἄντρον ὑπόστεγον...

406 Fr. 122, Plutarch *de tranqu. an.* 15, 474B

ἔνθ᾽ ἦσαν Χθονίη τε καὶ Ἡλιόπη ταναῶπις,
Δῆρίς θ᾽ αἱματόεσσα καὶ Ἁρμονίη θεμερῶπις,
Καλλιστώ τ᾽ Αἰσχρή τε, Θόωσά τε Δηναίη τε,
Νημερτής τ᾽ ἐρόεσσα μελάγκουρός τ᾽ Ἀσάφεια.

407 Fr. 126, Stobaeus *Anth.* 1, 49, 60

σαρκῶν ἀλλογνῶτι περιστέλλουσα χιτῶνι.

402 I wept and wailed when I saw the unfamiliar place where Murder and Anger and tribes of other Deaths...they [*sc.* the *daimones*] wander in darkness over the meadow of Doom.

403 Alas, poor unhappy race of mortals, from what strifes and groanings were you born.

404 From what high rank and from what a height of bliss...

405 We came under this roofed cave...

406 There were Earth and far-seeing Sun, bloody Discord and serene Harmonia, Beauty and Ugliness, Haste and Tarrying, lovely Truth and blind Obscurity.

407 ...clothing [*sc.* the *daimon*] in an alien garment of flesh.

These disconnected fragments constitute most of the surviving scraps of a passage in which Empedocles seems to have told first of his descent to a place of misery where other fallen *daimones* were assembled, and then of being led to a cave where *daimones* were clothed in alien flesh and made subject to the contrary forces which rule mortal existence. Is the scene set throughout in the underworld? Or is Empedocles speaking metaphorically of the nature of mortal life here on earth? Scholars have strangely supposed these two possibilities to exclude each other. Probably Empedocles was using eschatological myth (of which we have seen evidence in Pythagoreanism) both to give intense expression to his conviction of the alien and pitiful condition of mortal existence, and to bring home as vividly as possible the idea that life is set in more than merely human dimensions of space and time.

(iii) *The hope of release*

408 Fr. 127, Aelian *Nat. anim.* XII, 7

ἐν θήρεσσι λέοντες ὀρειλεχέες χαμαιεῦναι
γίγνονται, δάφναι δ᾽ ἐνὶ δένδρεσιν ἠυκόμοισιν.

409 Frr. 146 and 147, Clement *Strom.* IV, 150, 1 and V, 122, 3

εἰς δὲ τέλος μάντεις τε καὶ ὑμνοπόλοι καὶ ἰητροὶ
καὶ πρόμοι ἀνθρώποισιν ἐπιχθονίοισι πέλονται,

ἔνθεν ἀναβλαστοῦσι θεοὶ τιμῆσι φέριστοι,
ἀθανάτοις ἄλλοισιν ὁμέστιοι, αὐτοτράπεζοι
†ἐόντες†, ἀνδρείων ἀχέων ἀπόκληροι, ἀτειρεῖς.

408 Among beasts they are born as lions with lairs in the hills and beds on the ground, and as laurels among fair-tressed trees.

409 But at the end they come among men on earth as prophets, bards, doctors and princes; and thence they arise as gods highest in honour, sharing with the other immortals their hearth and their table, without part in human sorrows or weariness.

These lines probably derive from a passage in which Empedocles explained how in each successive life a *daimon* might ascend through ever higher realms of creation (plants, beasts, man), undergo the best form of incarnation possible within each, and finally regain his original status as a god. It is often and plausibly supposed that Empedocles believed the Apolline vocations specified in **409** were all united in his own person. In the description of forms of life and of gods alike we find echoes of the phraseology used in *On Nature* to specify the 'countless tribes of mortal things' (cf. e.g. **355–6**); and the reference to divine feasting recalls once more the return to the banquets of the gods which Hesiod promises the banished god after his 9 years of exile (*Theog.* 801–4). But Empedocles is probably drawing also on the eschatology of Pythagorean mystery religion, as comparison with a famous fragment of Pindar will show (cf. pp. 236–8 above):

410 Pindar fr. 133 Snell (Plato *Meno* 81 B)
οἶσι δὲ Φερσεφόνα ποινὰν παλαιοῦ πένθεος
δέξεται, ἐς τὸν ὕπερθεν ἅλιον κείνων ἐνάτῳ ἔτεϊ
ἀνδιδοῖ ψυχὰς πάλιν, ἐκ τᾶν βασιλῆες ἀγαυοὶ
καὶ σθένει κραιπνοὶ σοφίᾳ τε μέγιστοι
ἄνδρες αὔξοντ'· ἐς δὲ τὸν λοιπὸν χρόνον ἥροες ἁ-
γνοὶ πρὸς ἀνθρώπων καλέονται.

410 Those from whom Persephone receives requital for ancient grief, in the ninth year she restores again their souls to the sun above. From them arise noble kings, and those men swift in strength, and greatest in wisdom; and for the rest of time they are called heroes and sanctified by mankind. (*After Guthrie*)

SACRIFICE

(i) *The primal state*

411 Fr. 128, Porphyrius *de abstinentia* II, 21

  οὐδέ τις ἦν κείνοισιν ῎Αρης θεὸς οὐδὲ Κυδοιμὸς
  οὐδὲ Ζεὺς βασιλεὺς οὐδὲ Κρόνος οὐδὲ Ποσειδῶν,
  ἀλλὰ Κύπρις βασίλεια.
  τὴν οἵ γ᾽ εὐσεβέεσσιν ἀγάλμασιν ἱλάσκοντο
5 γραπτοῖς τε ζῴοισι μύροισί τε δαιδαλεόδμοις
  σμύρνης τ᾽ ἀκρήτου θυσίαις λιβάνου τε θυώδους,
  ξανθῶν τε σπονδὰς μελίτων ῥίπτοντες ἐς οὖδας·
  ταύρων τ᾽ ἀρρήτοισι φόνοις οὐ δεύετο βωμός,
  ἀλλὰ μύσος τοῦτ᾽ ἔσκεν ἐν ἀνθρώποισι μέγιστον,
10 θυμὸν ἀπορραίσαντας ἐέδμεναι ἠέα γυῖα.

412 Fr. 130, Schol. *in Nic. Ther.* 453

  ἦσαν δὲ κτίλα πάντα καὶ ἀνθρώποισι προσηνῆ,
  θῆρές τ᾽ οἰωνοί τε, φιλοφροσύνη τε δεδῄει.

411 Among them was no war-god Ares worshipped nor the battle-cry, nor was Zeus their king nor Kronos nor Poseidon, but Cypris [*i.e.* Aphrodite] was queen. Her they propitiated with holy images, with paintings of living creatures, with perfumes of varied fragrance and sacrifices of pure myrrh and sweet-scented frankincense, throwing to the ground libations of yellow honey. Their altar was not drenched by the unspeakable slaughters of bulls, but this was held among men the greatest defilement – to tear out the life from noble limbs and eat them.

412 All things were tame and gentle to men, both beasts and birds, and their friendship burned bright.

Theophrastus tells us (*ap.* Porph. *de abstinentia.* II, 21) that **411** occurred in Empedocles' account of 'sacrifices and theogony'. These lines certainly show the poet again employing myth, although at this point he is drawing on the portrayal of the Golden Age in Hesiod's *Works and Days* (109ff.) rather than the *Theogony*. Empedocles corrects traditional theology in asserting that Love (not Kronos) was originally the supreme god; and we are once more reminded of *On Nature*, on this occasion of the period of the Sphere when Love exerts complete dominance over the roots.

(ii) *Bloodshed and cannibalism*

413 Fr. 135, Aristotle *Rhetoric* A13, 1373b6
ἀλλὰ τὸ μὲν πάντων νόμιμον διά τ' εὐρυμέδοντος
αἰθέρος ἠνεκέως τέταται διά τ' ἀπλέτου αὐγῆς.

414 Fr. 136, Sextus *adv. math.* IX, 129
οὐ παύσεσθε φόνοιο δυσηχέος; οὐκ ἐσορᾶτε
ἀλλήλους δάπτοντες ἀκηδείῃσι νόοιο;

415 Fr. 137, Sextus *adv. math.* IX, 129
μορφὴν δ' ἀλλάξαντα πατὴρ φίλον υἱὸν ἀείρας
σφάζει ἐπευχόμενος μέγα νήπιος· οἰκτρὰ τορεῦντα[1]
λισσόμενον θύοντος·[2] ὁ δὲ νήκουστος ὁμοκλέων
σφάξας ἐν μεγάροισι κακὴν ἀλεγύνατο δαῖτα.
ὣς δ' αὔτως πατέρ' υἱὸς ἑλὼν καὶ μητέρα παῖδες
θυμὸν ἀπορραίσαντε φίλας κατὰ σάρκας ἔδουσιν.

[1] οἰκτρὰ τορεῦντα Zuntz: οἱ δὲ πορεῦνται Sextus LE, οἶδα πορεῦντα N.
[2] θύοντος Hermann: θύοντες codd.

416 Fr. 139, Porphyrius *de abstinentia* II, 31
οἴμοι ὅτι οὐ πρόσθεν με διώλεσε νηλεὲς ἦμαρ,
πρὶν σχέτλι' ἔργα βορᾶς περὶ χείλεσι μητίσασθαι.

417 Fr. 117, Diogenes Laertius VIII, 77
ἤδη γάρ ποτ' ἐγὼ γενόμην κοῦρός τε κόρη τε
θάμνος τ' οἰωνός τε καὶ ἔξαλος ἔμπορος ἰχθύς.

413 But this, the law for all, extends unendingly throughout wide-ruling air and the immense light [of the sun].

414 Will you not cease from the din of slaughter? Do you not see that you are devouring each other in the heedlessness of your minds?

415 The father lifts up his own son changed in form and slaughters him with a prayer, blind fool, as he shrieks piteously, beseeching as he sacrifices. But he, deaf to his cries, slaughters him and makes ready in his halls an evil feast. In the same way son seizes father and children their mother, and tearing out the life they eat the flesh of those they love.

416 Alas that the pitiless day did not destroy me first, before I contrived the wretched deed of eating flesh with my lips.

417 For I have already been once a boy and a girl, a bush and a bird and a leaping journeying fish.

It was already apparent in **411** that bloody sacrifices and the consumption of flesh are the primal sins (cf. **401**, 3–4). Aristotle explains (*ad loc.*) that the 'law of nature' proclaimed in **413** proscribed in absolute terms the killing of living things. **414–15** attempt to bring home to us the horror of bloodshed and flesh-eating by drawing upon a consequence of the theory of reincarnation already remarked in jocular spirit by Xenophanes (**260** above): if you kill what you take to be just a dumb animal, you may in fact be murdering a reincarnation of your son or your father. In **416–17** Empedocles bewails, in the urgent personal accents so distinctive of *Purifications*, his own fall from grace, and bizarrely records his own history of incarnation.

(iii) *Ritual injunctions*

418   Fr. 140, Plutarch *Quaest. conviv.* III, 1, 646D
δάφνης φύλλων ἄπο πάμπαν ἔχεσθαι.

419   Fr. 141, Aulus Gellius IV, 11, 9
δειλοί, πάνδειλοι, κυάμων ἄπο χεῖρας ἔχεσθαι.

418   ...keep completely from leaves of laurel.
419   Wretches, utter wretches, keep your hands from beans.

Empedocles probably concluded *Purifications* (hence its ancient title) with instructions about proper ritual. Few of these survive (but cf. **411**). The rationale of **418** is to be found, no doubt, in **408**. **419**, a floating tag attributed to several authors, at least gives memorable expression to the Pythagoreans' notorious aversion to beans (cf. pp. 230–1 above).

THE RELATION BETWEEN THE TWO POEMS

Empedocles makes no attempt to justify the teaching of *Purifications* in terms of the theories of *On Nature*. But he clearly indicates that the same powers and the same pattern of change govern human destiny as prevail in the cosmos at large. It is tempting, if hazardous, to connect the doctrines of the two poems yet more closely than Empedocles himself cared to do.

If he thinks of man as fallen god (or divine spirit), this is surely because he sees an affinity between him and the god of *On Nature*, the Sphere, which transcends the difference between them. The affinity doubtless lies in their shared capacity for thought. It is in this that Empedocles sees perfection, as is suggested both by his association of 'holy mind' with divinity (**397**) and by his notion that blood, the stuff with which we think (**394**), is a nearly equal mixture of the four elements (**373**), which are of course perfectly mixed in the Sphere. Perhaps, indeed, the god in each of us is actually a fragment of the Sphere: currently subject to strife among the elements, but one day to be united with all its other fragments and with all other things in one perfect thinker. This conjecture points to an explanation of why Empedocles does not talk about the soul (*psuchē*) in *Purifications*, even though his belief in reincarnation is obviously a version of the Pythagorean doctrine of metempsychosis. His own concept of man as an exiled god improves upon Pythagorean teaching in identifying the subject of the cycle of human destiny in such a way as to hint (if no more than hint) at its place in the cosmic scheme.

It has often been thought that *Purifications* is in conflict with *On Nature* on this very issue of the nature of the soul. For *On Nature* has been read as proposing a wholly reductive materialist account of all psychological functions, whereas *Purifications* has been interpreted as holding or implying that the soul (or the *daimon*) can and will one day enjoy an incorporeal existence as it did before the fall. We have argued against both these interpretations. The *daimon* is always embodied: it is condemned to an unsuitable and unnatural body of human flesh; it longs for the perfect body of the Sphere. The psychology of *On Nature* is not purely reductive, although it leaves in obscurity what is the 'I' which thinks and perceives *with* the elements.

It remains similarly obscure what the continuing identity of a *daimon* consists in, as it is tossed from element to element and transformed from plant to beast to man. What is clear is the force of Empedocles' conviction *that* there is an 'I' which survives such changes, whose perspective on life and death and everything else can never be entirely subsumed within a cosmic perspective, whether that of the divine Sphere or that of the philosopher constructing a metaphysics of the cosmos. Empedocles conveys an acute sense of personal guilt in all he says about bloodshed: not least about his own fall from grace, which he plainly does not feel to be just an inevitable episode in the cosmic havoc wrought by the impersonal force of Strife. 'I' is ineliminable.

CHAPTER XI

Philolaus of Croton and Fifth-Century Pythagoreanism

INTRODUCTION

After studying the comparatively rich store of actual fragments of such towering intellectual figures as Parmenides, Zeno and Empedocles, it is disappointing to have next to turn once again to evidence mostly of doxographical character for the teaching of fifth-century Pythagoreanism. Its general nature has been described above (pp. 214–16). Fortunately there do survive a few authentic fragments of the leading Pythagorean philosopher of the latter half of the fifth century, Philolaus. And we shall begin our consideration of Pythagorean doctrine with an examination of the most important of these. Then we shall discuss their relationship with the philosophy which Aristotle attributes to 'the so-called Pythagoreans' – and which forms the main subject of this chapter.

PHILOLAUS OF CROTON

(i) Date and life

420 Plato *Phaedo* 61D, DK44B15   τί δέ, ὦ Κέβης; οὐκ ἀκηκόατε σύ τε καὶ Σιμμίας περὶ τῶν τοιούτων Φιλολάῳ συγγεγονότες;

οὐδέν γε σαφές, ὦ Σώκρατες...ἤδη γὰρ ἔγωγε, ὅπερ νυνδὴ σὺ ἤρου, καὶ Φιλολάου ἤκουσα, ὅτε παρ' ἡμῖν διῃτᾶτο, ἤδη δὲ καὶ ἄλλων τινῶν, ὡς οὐ δέοι τοῦτο ποιεῖν· σαφὲς δὲ περὶ αὐτῶν οὐδενὸς πώποτε οὐδὲν ἀκήκοα.

421 Diogenes Laertius VIII, 46, DK44A4   τελευταῖοι γὰρ ἐγένοντο τῶν Πυθαγορείων, οὓς καὶ Ἀριστόξενος εἶδε, Ξενόφιλός τε ὁ Χαλκιδεὺς ἀπὸ Θράκης καὶ Φάντων ὁ Φλιάσιος καὶ Ἐχεκράτης καὶ Διοκλῆς καὶ Πολύμναστος Φλιάσιοι καὶ αὐτοί. ἦσαν δὲ ἀκροαταὶ Φιλολάου καὶ Εὐρύτου τῶν Ταραντίνων.

422 Diogenes Laertius IX, 38, DK44A2   φησὶ δὲ καὶ Ἀπολλόδωρος ὁ Κυζικηνὸς Φιλολάῳ αὐτὸν (*sc.* Δημόκριτον) συγγεγονέναι.

420 Let me ask you something, Cebes: have not you and Simmias heard about this [*sc.* the wrongness of suicide] in your association with Philolaus? – Nothing clear, Socrates... I've certainly heard before now both from Philolaus, when he lived among us [*sc.* in Thebes], and from others that – to take up the question you just now asked – one ought not to do it; but I have never heard anything clear on this matter from anyone.

421 For the last of the Pythagoreans, whom Aristoxenus saw, were Xenophilus the Chalcidian from Thrace, and Phanton, Echecrates, Diocles and Polymnastos, all of Phleious. They were pupils of Philolaus and Eurytus, the Tarentines.[1]

422 Apollodorus of Cyzicus,[2] too, says that Democritus and Philolaus were contemporaries.

[1] Aristoxenus may be right in making Philolaus a Tarentine; on the other hand Aristotle's pupil Menon, the medical historian, made him a Crotoniate (**445**), as does Diogenes Laertius in **423**. Perhaps he was born in Croton, but philosophized and lived his adult life mostly in Tarentum (cf. **268**).

[2] A philosopher (to be distinguished from the chronographer), perhaps of the latter part of the fourth century B.C. (cf. Clem. *Strom.* II, 130 (DK 68 B 4), with Burkert, *Lore*, 229 n. 51).

420 indicates that Philolaus has been living in Thebes and teaching there not long before the death of Socrates in 399 B.C. Echecrates, like Simmias and Cebes, is among the *dramatis personae* of the *Phaedo*, and so **421** broadly confirms the chronological indications of **420**, besides suggesting that Philolaus was a leading figure in what sounds like a Pythagorean community at Phleious, near Corinth. **422** is a less reliable testimony, brief in the extreme and from an obscure source. From **420–2** and **542** below (which states that Democritus was born *c.* 460–57 B.C.) we can infer that Philolaus' life was roughly contemporary with Socrates' (born 470 B.C.). There is no other reliable evidence about Philolaus' life.

(ii) *Writings*

423 Diogenes Laertius VIII, 84 (DK 44 A 1) Φιλόλαος Κροτωνιάτης Πυθαγορικός. παρὰ τούτου Πλάτων ὠνήσασθαι τὰ βιβλία τὰ Πυθαγορικὰ Δίωνι γράφει....γέγραφε δὲ βιβλίον ἕν. (ὅ φησιν Ἕρμιππος λέγειν τινὰ τῶν συγγραφέων Πλάτωνα τὸν φιλόσοφον παραγενόμενον εἰς Σικελίαν πρὸς Διονύσιον ὠνήσασθαι παρὰ τῶν συγγενῶν τοῦ Φιλολάου ἀργυρίου Ἀλεξανδρινῶν μνῶν τεττεράκοντα καὶ ἐντεῦθεν μεταγεγραφέναι τὸν Τίμαιον. ἕτεροι δὲ λέγουσι τὸν Πλάτωνα λαβεῖν αὐτά, παρὰ Διονυσίου παραιτησάμενον ἐκ τῆς φυλακῆς νεανίσκον ἀπηγμένον τῶν τοῦ Φιλολάου μαθητῶν.)

423 Philolaus of Croton, a Pythagorean. It was from him that Plato, in a letter, told Dion to buy the Pythagorean books...He wrote one book. (Hermippus says that according to one writer the philosopher Plato went to Sicily, to the court of Dionysius, bought this book from Philolaus' relatives for 40 Alexandrian *minae*, and from it copied out the *Timaeus*. Others say that Plato acquired the books by securing from Dionysius the release from prison of a young man who had been one of Philolaus' pupils.)

Hermippus' story was evidently designed (like many other anecdotes about Plato) to blacken his reputation, in this instance by impugning his originality. His source is perhaps a writer of the fourth century B.C. (he himself, as a pupil of Callimachus, belongs to the following century). The letter referring to 'Pythagorean treatises' which is mentioned in the variant of the tale may have actually existed as a forgery devised to defend the authenticity of further forged documents, perhaps the three books ascribed to Pythagoras himself (cf. Diog. L. VIII, 6, DK 14, 19, Iambl. *V.P.* 199, DK 14, 17, with Burkert, *Lore*, 223–5). **423** at any rate shows how Philolaus' name was early associated with a written form of Pythagorean teaching; and the existence of a book by him is confirmed by Menon's report of his biological theories (**445** below).

There survive in late authors a number of extracts which purport to be fragments of works by Philolaus. Their authenticity has been much debated; but Burkert has rightly persuaded most subsequent writers of the genuineness of the main metaphysical and cosmological texts (ch. III). Burkert also argued the further theses (*a*) that Philolaus' book is the main source of Aristotle's account of Pythagoreanism in **430** and elsewhere, and (*b*) that Philolaus actually *created* 'the philosophy of Limit and Unlimited and their harmony achieved through number', in its abstract form, in an effort 'to formulate anew, with the help of fifth-century φυσιολογία, a view of the world that came to him, somehow, from Pythagoras' (*Lore*, 298). These further theses have not been generally accepted (see e.g. J. A. Philip, *Pythagoras and Early Pythagoreanism* (Toronto, 1966), 32–3, 121–2; C. J. de Vogel, *Philosophia* I (Assen, 1970), 33–4, 84–5; J. Barnes, *The Presocratic Philosophers* II, 88, 92–3). Our verdict will be more sympathetic to Burkert.

(iii) *Limiters and unlimiteds*

424 Fr. 1, Diogenes Laertius VIII, 85   ἁ φύσις δ' ἐν τῷ κόσμῳ[1] ἁρμόχθη ἐξ ἀπείρων τε καὶ περαινόντων, καὶ ὅλος ⟨ὁ⟩ κόσμος καὶ τὰ ἐν αὐτῷ πάντα.

¹ ἐν τῷ κόσμῳ codd.: τῶ κόσμω Heidel.

425 Fr. 2, Stobaeus *Anth.* 1, 21, 7*a*   ἀνάγκα τὰ ἐόντα εἶμεν πάντα
ἢ περαίνοντα ἢ ἄπειρα ἢ περαίνοντά τε καὶ ἄπειρα· ἄπειρα δὲ μόνον
οὔ κα εἴη.¹ ἐπεὶ τοίνυν φαίνεται οὔτ' ἐκ περαινόντων πάντων ἐόντα
οὔτ' ἐξ ἀπείρων πάντων, δῆλον τἄρα ὅτι ἐκ περαινόντων τε καὶ
ἀπείρων ὅ τε κόσμος καὶ τὰ ἐν αὐτῷ συναρμόχθη. δηλοῖ δὲ καὶ τὰ ἐν
τοῖς ἔργοις. τὰ μὲν γὰρ αὐτῶν ἐκ περαινόντων περαίνοντι, τὰ δ' ἐκ
περαινόντων τε καὶ ἀπείρων περαίνοντί τε καὶ οὐ περαίνοντι, τὰ δ'
ἐξ ἀπείρων ἄπειρα φανέονται.

¹ Something has apparently been omitted from the text at this point, since we
expect an argument for the claim just made, and then a discussion of limiters.
Very likely **426** belongs here.

426   Fr. 3, Iamblichus *in Nicomachum* p. 7, 24 Pist.   ἀρχὰν γὰρ οὐδὲ
τὸ γνωσούμενον ἐσσεῖται πάντων ἀπείρων ἐόντων.

424   Nature in the universe was harmonized from both unlimiteds
and limiters – both the universe as a whole and everything in it.
425   It is necessary for the things that exist to be all either limiters
or unlimiteds or both limiters and unlimiteds. But they could not
be only unlimiteds...¹ Since, then, they appear to have their
existence neither from things that are all limiters nor from things
that are all unlimiteds, it is clear thus that both the universe and
the things in it were harmonized from both limiters and unlimiteds.
And things as they are in fact also make this clear. For some of
them, coming from limiters, limit; others, coming from both
limiters and unlimiteds, both limit and do not limit; and others,
coming from unlimiteds, are evidently unlimited.
426   For there will not be anything that will know in the first place
if all things are unlimited.

¹ See note to the Greek text.

424, which according to Diogenes constituted the beginning
of Philolaus' book, introduces the main concepts and the main
thesis of his system. The laborious reasoning of **425** is obscure.¹ It
interestingly divides into (*a*) an *a priori* section followed by (*b*)
what purports to be an appeal to experience. From (*b*) it appears
that the conclusion it seeks to establish is that there must be
limiters *and* unlimiteds *and* compounds of the two. The argument
of (*a*) may accordingly be read as claiming that because it is not the
case that all things are limiters or that all things are unlimited, there
must also be some things (viz. the cosmos and its contents) which are
compounds of the two; and so as obliquely defending the thesis of

424 (only obliquely, since the 'viz.' of our paraphrase remains altogether unsupported). This is a blatant *non sequitur* as it stands – but the text is admittedly incomplete.

Neither here nor elsewhere does Philolaus explain why *limiter* and *unlimited* should be taken to be the basic concepts we need in philosophical analysis. Indeed, he fails to disclose even the identity of the limiters and unlimiteds he has in mind, and thereby emasculates the argument in (*b*). Barnes (*The Presocratic Philosophers* II, 85–7) thinks that limiters are shapes (pre-eminently geometrical shapes) and unlimiteds stuffs (e.g. copper, tin, oil, vinegar), and that Philolaus is glimpsing Aristotle's distinction between form and matter. It is more likely that he assumes acquaintance on the part of his readers with Pythagorean number doctrine (note the unexpected expression 'limit and do not limit'). Limiters will then be odd numbers, unlimiteds even, and their products ('things from limiters', etc.) the sorts of figure referred to in **437**. This hypothesis is supported by the existence of two fragments explicitly concerned with number, which Stobaeus quotes immediately after **425**.

[1] Its disjunctive form is apparently Eleatic in inspiration; cf. Melissus (**533**) and Gorgias (*ap.* [Arist.] *M.X.G.* 979a11f.). Philolaus' preoccupation with the concepts *limiter* and *unlimited* may also owe something to Melissus (**526–31**).

(iv) *Number*

427 Fr. 4, Stobaeus *Anth.* I, 21, 7*b* καὶ πάντα γα μὰν τὰ γιγνωσκόμενα ἀριθμὸν ἔχοντι· οὐ γὰρ οἷόν τε οὐδὲν οὔτε νοηθῆμεν οὔτε γνωσθῆμεν ἄνευ τούτου.

428 Fr. 5, Stobaeus *Anth.* I, 21, 7*c* ὅ γα μὰν ἀριθμὸς ἔχει δύο μὲν ἴδια εἴδη, περισσὸν καὶ ἄρτιον, τρίτον δὲ ἀπ' ἀμφοτέρων μειχθέντων ἀρτιοπέριττον· ἑκατέρω δὲ τῶ εἴδεος πολλαὶ μορφαί, ἃς ἕκαστον αὐταυτὸ σημαίνει.

427 And indeed all the things that are known have number; for it is not possible for anything to be thought of or known without this.

428 Number, indeed, has two kinds peculiar to it, odd and even, and a third derived from the mixture of the two, even–odd. Each of the two kinds has many forms, which each thing in itself indicates.[1]

[1] **428** is very close in wording and doctrine to Arist. *Met.* A5, 986a17 (**430** *ad fin.*); with **427** compare Alexander *in Met.* 40, 12 (Aristotle fr. 203).

427 shows that if limiter and unlimited are Philolaus' fundamental concepts, number also plays a central role in his thought. He probably means to claim that if things are not *countable* we cannot think of them nor be acquainted with them. His words are perhaps reminiscent of Parmenides (e.g. **291**), but we should not interpret them as a deliberate attempt to state (let alone argue) against the Eleatics that it is pluralism, not monism, which reasoning establishes to be the necessary condition of knowledge and thought.[1] They are intended rather to buttress an old Pythagorean idea with new epistemological supports.

[1] So M. C. Nussbaum, 'Eleatic Conventionalism and Philolaus on the Conditions of Thought', *HSCP* 83 (1979), 64–6, 81–93, who implausibly finds Eleatic echoes and preoccupations at every turn in **425–9**.

(v) *Nature and harmony*

429 Fr. 6, Stobaeus *Anth.* 1, 21, 7*d* περὶ δὲ φύσιος καὶ ἁρμονίας ὧδε ἔχει· ἁ μὲν ἐστὼ τῶν πραγμάτων ἀίδιος ἔσσα καὶ αὐτὰ μὲν ἁ φύσις θείαν τε καὶ οὐκ ἀνθρωπίνην ἐνδέχεται γνῶσιν πλάν γα ἢ ὅτι οὐχ οἷόν τ' ἦν οὐθενὶ τῶν ἐόντων καὶ γιγνωσκομένων ὑφ' ἀμῶν γεγενῆσθαι μὴ ὑπαρχούσας τᾶς ἐστοῦς τῶν πραγμάτων, ἐξ ὧν συνέστα ὁ κόσμος, καὶ τῶν περαινόντων καὶ τῶν ἀπείρων. ἐπεὶ δὲ ταὶ ἀρχαὶ ὑπᾶρχον οὐχ ὁμοῖαι οὐδ' ὁμόφυλοι ἔσσαι, ἤδη ἀδύνατον ἦς κα αὐταῖς κοσμηθῆναι, εἰ μὴ ἁρμονία ἐπεγένετο ὡτινιῶν ἅδε τρόπῳ ἐγένετο. τὰ μὲν ὦν ὁμοῖα καὶ ὁμόφυλα ἁρμονίας οὐδὲν ἐπεδέοντο, τὰ δὲ ἀνόμοια μηδὲ ὁμόφυλα μηδὲ ἰσοταγῆ ἀνάγκα τὰ τοιαῦτα ἁρμονίᾳ συγκεκλεῖσθαι, αἰ μέλλοντι ἐν κόσμῳ κατέχεσθαι.

429 About nature and harmony this is the position. The being of the objects, being eternal, and nature itself admit of divine, not human, knowledge – except that it was not possible for any of the things that exist and are known by us to have come into being, without there existing the being of those things from which the universe was composed, the limiters and the unlimiteds. And since these principles existed being neither alike nor of the same kind, it would have been impossible for them to be ordered into a universe if harmony had not supervened – in whatever manner this came into being. Things that were alike and of the same kind had no need of harmony, but those that were unlike and not of the same kind and of unequal order – it was necessary for such things to have been locked together by harmony, if they are to be held together in an ordered universe.

429 is much the most interesting of Philolaus' fragments. Its sceptical reflections on human knowledge stand in a tradition represented by

Xenophanes (**186**), Heraclitus (**205**) and Alcmaeon (**439**). Quite original, however, is its subtle argument that what we can know about the real being of things (which – following the Eleatics – Philolaus takes to be everlasting) is only, but at least, this: it must be such as to supply the necessary conditions of the existence of the temporal things with which we are acquainted. Philolaus evidently supposes that on this basis we are licensed to infer the existence of limiters and unlimiteds as ultimate principles of things. Then by a further *a priori* argument he infers that if a thing (or more particularly, the universe) is put together from limiters and unlimiteds, these must have been subject to a process of *harmonia* or mutual adjustment.

(vi) *Conclusion*

Philolaus supplies for Pythagorean doctrine what we looked for but did not find in our chapter on Pythagoras' teaching: philosophical argument. He thus brings Pythagoreanism closer to the mainstream of Presocratic thought of the fifth century, whose ontological and epistemological preoccupations he shares, as we have seen. Indeed he presents Pythagoreanism in full Presocratic dress, in a panoply of characteristically philosophical concepts like nature, cosmos, being, principle, etc. How many of these concepts were already part of his distinctively Pythagorean inheritance we can only guess. Harmony and number were probably among Pythagoras' own key ideas. But it may well have been Philolaus and his contemporaries who introduced the other main notions of **424–9** into Pythagoreanism, or at any rate first exploited their systematic potential. Examination of Aristotle's principal account of Pythagorean doctrine (**430**) will support the judgement that limiter (or limit) and unlimited, in particular, were not viewed by Pythagoreans in general as the master concepts of their system. They assume that role only in Philolaus – and, perhaps, in another (anonymous) Pythagorean tradition reported by Aristotle (**438**). It is time now to turn to the Aristotelian evidence about the 'so-called' Pythagoreans. We shall present texts pertaining to other aspects of Philolaus' work as we explore it.

ARISTOTLE'S PRINCIPAL ACCOUNT OF PYTHAGOREANISM

430 Aristotle *Met.* A5, 985b23 (DK 58 B 4 and 5) ἐν δὲ τούτοις καὶ πρὸ τούτων (*sc.* Λευκίππου καὶ Δημοκρίτου) οἱ καλούμενοι Πυθαγόρειοι τῶν μαθημάτων ἁψάμενοι πρῶτοι ταῦτα προήγαγον, καὶ ἐντραφέντες ἐν αὐτοῖς τὰς τούτων ἀρχὰς τῶν ὄντων ἀρχὰς ᾠήθησαν εἶναι πάντων. ἐπεὶ δὲ τούτων οἱ ἀριθμοὶ φύσει πρῶτοι, ἐν δὲ τοῖς ἀριθμοῖς ἐδόκουν θεωρεῖν ὁμοιώματα πολλὰ τοῖς οὖσι καὶ γιγνομένοις, μᾶλλον ἢ ἐν πυρὶ καὶ γῇ καὶ ὕδατι, ὅτι τὸ μὲν τοιονδὶ τῶν ἀριθμῶν πάθος δικαιοσύνη, τὸ δὲ τοιονδὶ ψυχὴ καὶ νοῦς, ἕτερον δὲ καιρὸς καὶ τῶν ἄλλων ὡς εἰπεῖν ἕκαστον ὁμοίως, ἔτι δὲ τῶν ἁρμονιῶν ἐν ἀριθμοῖς ὁρῶντες τὰ πάθη καὶ τοὺς λόγους, ἐπεὶ δὴ τὰ μὲν ἄλλα τοῖς ἀριθμοῖς ἐφαίνετο τὴν φύσιν ἀφωμοιῶσθαι πᾶσαν, οἱ δ᾽ ἀριθμοὶ πάσης τῆς φύσεως πρῶτοι, τὰ τῶν ἀριθμῶν στοιχεῖα τῶν ὄντων στοιχεῖα πάντων ὑπέλαβον εἶναι, καὶ τὸν ὅλον οὐρανὸν ἁρμονίαν εἶναι καὶ ἀριθμόν· καὶ ὅσα εἶχον ὁμολογούμενα δεικνύναι ἔν τε τοῖς ἀριθμοῖς καὶ ταῖς ἁρμονίαις πρὸς τὰ τοῦ οὐρανοῦ πάθη καὶ μέρη καὶ πρὸς τὴν ὅλην διακόσμησιν, ταῦτα συνάγοντες ἐφήρμοττον. κἂν εἴ τί που διέλειπε, προσεγλίχοντο τοῦ συνειρομένην πᾶσαν αὐτοῖς εἶναι τὴν πραγματείαν. λέγω δ᾽ οἷον, ἐπειδὴ τέλειον ἡ δεκὰς εἶναι δοκεῖ καὶ πᾶσαν περιειληφέναι τὴν τῶν ἀριθμῶν φύσιν, καὶ τὰ φερόμενα κατὰ τὸν οὐρανὸν δέκα μὲν εἶναί φασιν, ὄντων δὲ ἐννέα μόνον τῶν φανερῶν διὰ τοῦτο δεκάτην τὴν ἀντίχθονα ποιοῦσιν. διώρισται δὲ περὶ τούτων ἐν ἑτέροις ἡμῖν ἀκριβέστερον... (986a15) φαίνονται δὴ καὶ οὗτοι τὸν ἀριθμὸν νομίζοντες ἀρχὴν εἶναι καὶ ὡς ὕλην τοῖς οὖσι καὶ ὡς πάθη τε καὶ ἕξεις, τοῦ δὲ ἀριθμοῦ στοιχεῖα τό τε ἄρτιον καὶ τὸ περιττόν, τούτων δὲ τὸ μὲν ἄπειρον, τὸ δὲ πεπερασμένον, τὸ δ᾽ ἓν ἐξ ἀμφοτέρων εἶναι τούτων (καὶ γὰρ ἄρτιον εἶναι καὶ περιττόν), τὸν δ᾽ ἀριθμὸν ἐκ τοῦ ἑνός, ἀριθμοὺς δέ, καθάπερ εἴρηται, τὸν ὅλον οὐρανόν.

430 Contemporaneously with these philosophers [*sc.* Leucippus and Democritus], and before them, the Pythagoreans, as they are called, took up mathematics; they were the first to advance this study, and having been brought up in it they thought its principles were the principles of all things. Since of these principles numbers are by nature the first, and in numbers they thought they saw many resemblances to the things that exist and come into being – more than in fire and earth and water (such and such a modification of numbers being justice, another being soul and intellect, another being opportunity – and similarly almost all other things being numerically expressible); since, again, they saw that the attributes and the ratios of the attunements were expressible in numbers; since, then, all other things in the whole of nature seemed to be modelled after numbers, and numbers seemed to be the first things in the whole of nature, they supposed the elements of numbers to be the elements of all things, and the whole heaven to be an attunement and a number. And all the properties of numbers and attunements they could show to agree with the attributes and parts and the whole arrangement of the heavens, they collected and fitted into their scheme; and if there was a gap anywhere, they readily made additions so as to make their whole theory coherent. E.g. as the number 10 is thought to be perfect and to comprise the whole nature of numbers, they say that the bodies which move through the heavens are ten, but as the visible bodies are only nine, to meet this they invent a tenth – the 'counter-earth'. We have discussed these matters more exactly elsewhere...[1]

Evidently, then, these thinkers also consider that number is the principle both as matter for things and as forming their modifications and their permanent states, and hold that the elements of number are the even and the odd, and of these the former is unlimited, and the latter limited; and the 1 proceeds from both of these (for it is both even and odd), and number from the 1; and the whole heaven, as has been said, is numbers.

[1] Alexander, in his comments on this passage (*in Met.* 41, 1, DK 58 B 4), refers to the *de caelo* (i.e. **446**) and the lost writings on the Pythagoreans for Aristotle's fuller treatment of this topic.

Here as elsewhere Aristotle speaks not of Pythagoras but of the Pythagoreans when he is concerned with the speculations he associates with 'the Italians' (*Met.* 987a31, *de caelo* 293a20, *Meteor.* 342b30). This must be due to scepticism about how much of that teaching was Pythagoras' own.[1] Probably Aristotle means the qualifying expression 'so-called' to convey his scepticism. He leaves the antiquity of the doctrines he presents deliberately vague. If we are right to date the atomists' philosophical activity to *c.* 440 B.C. onwards (see p. 404 below), then Aristotle makes them belong to the latter half of the fifth century or even earlier (cf. also *Met.* 1078b19, DK 58 B 4).

[1] No doubt all such speculations were already by Aristotle's time attributed to Pythagoras himself, perhaps by means of the celebrated phrase αὐτὸς ἔφα, 'he himself said so' (Diog. L. VIII, 46; cf. Iambl. *Comm. math. sc.* p. 77, 22–4). But Aristotle was well aware how thoroughly Pythagoras' name was enveloped in the mist of legend: see **273–4** above.

This studied vagueness regarding both chronology and authorship of the doctrines of **430** already weighs against Burkert's contention that Aristotle's account derives mainly from Philolaus, who is named only once, and then incidentally, in the entire corpus (*Eth. Eudem.* 1225a30, DK 44 B 16). And in fact, despite obvious points of similarity, there are considerable differences of emphasis between **430** and **424–9** which further weaken the credibility of Burkert's hypothesis. **430** makes number and its principles odd and even the focus of Pythagorean speculation, whereas **424–9** take limiter and unlimited (which are, of course, more general concepts) to be fundamental. In **430** *harmonia* is constituted by musical ratios, in **429** it is a matter of the mutual adjustment of limiters and unlimiteds.[1] **430** dwells mostly on the Pythagoreans' pretty arbitrary use of resemblances (cf. *Met.* 1092b26ff, DK 58 B 27), whereas **425** and **429**, in particular, present abstract arguments. **430** does, of course, make odd limited and even unlimited; and the notions of limit and unlimited figure more prominently in Aristotle's reports of Pythagorean doctrine elsewhere (e.g. **438** and **442–4**; also *Met.* 987a9ff., DK58B8), where they assume the sort of roles that **424–9** lead one to expect. Again, it is highly probable that the example in **430** of the strange theory of the counter-earth takes up a doctrine especially associated with the name of Philolaus (cf. **447** below). But the proper conclusion to draw from the evidence as a whole is that Aristotle found himself turning to Philolaus' book when he needed explicit and detailed accounts of (for example) Pythagorean cosmogony or astronomy: when he wanted (as in **430**) to present a sketch of the general motive and character of Pythagorean teaching, on the other hand, he no doubt relied on other (perhaps mostly oral) sources as well as, and indeed in preference to, Philolaus.

---

[1] Philolaus certainly did develop an account of *harmonia* as expressed by musical ratios (cf. e.g. Nicomachus *Arithm.* 26, 2, DK 44 A 24); indeed a fragment is preserved in the passage Stobaeus quotes immediately after **429** (*Ecl.* I, 21, 7d cont., DK 44 B 6). But it bears no direct relation to the employment of the concept in **424–5** and **429**.

There is in fact nothing in **430** (as opposed to **424–9** and **438** below) which cannot be explained simply as an elaboration of the doctrine about number and *harmonia* which we found reason to attribute to Pythagoras himself (pp. 232–5 above). It is not, like **438**, pre-occupied with a dualistic view of reality. It is largely devoid of the technical concepts of **424–9**, at any rate in the uses they are put to there, which are consequently best interpreted as original importations of Philolaus' own. Aristotle struggles at the end of **430** to express the relation of numbers and things in terms of his own metaphysical concepts of matter and of affections and states. His earlier talk of resemblances seems nearer the mark (just as in marriage the two sexes are joined, so in the number 5 odd and even are added; the relations of the heavenly bodies are like those of the sounds in a concord). But it does not fit all cases (the number of right time is 7, because births occur in the seventh month after conception, teeth appear in the seventh after birth, etc.: Aristotle fr. 203 *ap.* Alex. *in Met.* 38, 16). The point of the doctrine as a whole is surely to teach that the cosmos – and everything that happens in it – exhibits a wholly intelligible order. The chief function of the Pythagorean identification of things with numbers is accordingly to give symbolic expression to that order. Particular numbers (chosen on a variety of grounds) are used to express the essence of particular things; and this makes it possible to express the order of all things by the membership of each such number in an ordered series (in fact the sequence 1 to 10; 10 is conceived of as including and perfecting all the others).

ARISTOTLE'S PRINCIPAL CRITICISM OF PYTHAGOREANISM

431 Aristotle *Met.* M6, 1080b16 (DK 58 B 9) καὶ οἱ Πυθαγόρειοι δ᾽ ἕνα, τὸν μαθηματικόν (*sc.* ἀριθμόν), πλὴν οὐ κεχωρισμένον ἀλλ᾽ ἐκ τούτου τὰς αἰσθητὰς οὐσίας, συνεστάναι φασίν. τὸν γὰρ ὅλον οὐρανὸν κατασκευάζουσιν ἐξ ἀριθμῶν, πλὴν οὐ μοναδικῶν, ἀλλὰ τὰς μονάδας ὑπολαμβάνουσιν ἔχειν μέγεθος· ὅπως δὲ τὸ πρῶτον ἓν συνέστη ἔχον μέγεθος, ἀπορεῖν ἐοίκασιν.

432 Aristotle *Met.* M8, 1083b8 (DK 58 B 10) ὁ δὲ τῶν Πυθαγορείων τρόπος τῇ μὲν ἐλάττους ἔχει δυσχερείας τῶν πρότερον εἰρημένων, τῇ δὲ ἰδίας ἑτέρας. τὸ μὲν γὰρ μὴ χωριστὸν ποιεῖν τὸν ἀριθμὸν ἀφαιρεῖται πολλὰ τῶν ἀδυνάτων· τὸ δὲ τὰ σώματα ἐξ ἀριθμῶν εἶναι συγκείμενα, καὶ τὸν ἀριθμὸν τοῦτον εἶναι μαθηματικόν, ἀδύνατόν ἐστιν. οὔτε γὰρ ἄτομα μεγέθη λέγειν ἀληθές, εἴ θ᾽ ὅτι μάλιστα τοῦτον ἔχει τὸν τρόπον, οὐχ αἵ γε μονάδες μέγεθος ἔχουσιν. μέγεθος δὲ ἐξ ἀδιαιρέτων πῶς δυνατόν; ἀλλὰ μὴν ὅ γ᾽ ἀριθμητικὸς ἀριθμὸς μοναδικός ἐστιν. ἐκεῖνοι δὲ τὸν ἀριθμὸν τὰ ὄντα λέγουσιν. τὰ γοῦν θεωρήματα προσάπτουσι τοῖς σώμασιν ὡς ἐξ ἐκείνων ὄντων τῶν ἀριθμῶν.[1]

[1] Aristotle has been discussing before this passage, and in the second sentence quoted is referring to, the theory held by Plato and some of the Platonists that number exists as a separate entity apart from sensible things. On this theory see Ross, *Aristotle's Metaphysics* (Oxford, 1924), liii–lvii.

431 Now the Pythagoreans also believe in one kind of number – the mathematical; only they say it is not separate, but sensible substances are formed out of it. For they construct the whole universe out of numbers – only not numbers consisting of abstract units; they suppose the units to have spatial magnitude. But how the first unit with magnitude was constructed, they seem at a loss to describe. (*Tr. Ross*)

432 The doctrine of the Pythagoreans in one way affords fewer difficulties than those before named, but in another way has others peculiar to itself. For not thinking of number as capable of existing separately removes many of the impossible consequences; but that bodies should be composed of numbers, and that this should be mathematical number, is impossible. For it is not true to speak of indivisible spatial magnitudes; and however much there might be magnitudes of this sort, units at least have not magnitude; and how can a magnitude be composed of indivisibles? But arithmetical number, at least, consists of abstract units, while these thinkers identify number with real things; at any rate they apply their propositions to bodies as if they consisted of those numbers. (*Tr. Ross*)

Less sympathetically than in **430**, Aristotle here takes the Pythagoreans to be literally identifying numbers and things, and on this basis charges them with gross error. It seems unlikely that the Pythagoreans in general wanted to be understood in this way, or that they held the view Aristotle supposes to be a consequence of the identification, viz. that magnitudes are indivisible units (cf. e.g. D. J. Furley, *Two Studies in the Greek Atomists* 1, ch. 3). In **431** Aristotle aims some well-directed criticisms at Philolaus' cosmogony (see pp. 340f. below), but in **432** he is simply making dialectical but unhistorical use of Pythagoreanism in discussions principally concerned with Platonism. Elsewhere he reveals by his own complaints that the Pythagorean position was much less determinate than **431–2** suggest:

433 Aristotle *Met.* N5, 1092b8 (DK 45, 3) οὐθὲν δὲ διώρισται οὐδὲ ὁποτέρως οἱ ἀριθμοὶ αἴτιοι τῶν οὐσιῶν καὶ τοῦ εἶναι, πότερον ὡς ὅροι, οἷον αἱ στιγμαὶ τῶν μεγεθῶν, καὶ ὡς Εὔρυτος ἔταττε τίς ἀριθμὸς τίνος, οἷον ὁδὶ μὲν ἀνθρώπου ὁδὶ δὲ ἵππου, ὥσπερ οἱ τοὺς ἀριθμοὺς ἄγοντες εἰς τὰ σχήματα τρίγωνον καὶ τετράγωνον, οὕτως ἀφομοιῶν ταῖς ψήφοις τὰς μορφὰς τῶν φυτῶν, ἢ ὅτι [ὁ] λόγος ἡ συμφωνία ἀριθμῶν, ὁμοίως δὲ καὶ ἄνθρωπος καὶ τῶν ἄλλων ἕκαστον;

433 Once more, it has in no sense been determined in which way numbers are the causes of substances and of being – whether (1) as limits (as points are of spatial magnitudes): this is how Eurytus decided what was the number of what (e.g. of man, or of horse), viz. by imitating the figures of living things with pebbles, as some people bring numbers into the forms of triangle and square; or (2) is it because harmony is a ratio of numbers, and so is man and everything else?

Eurytus, working towards the end of the fifth century (cf. **421**), evidently attempted to make Pythagorean teaching more precise by extending the doctrine that geometrical figures are determined by natural numbers (as could be shown by representing numbers in configurations of pebbles: cf. 437) to account for substances like man or horse.

MATHEMATICS AND PHILOSOPHY

434 Diogenes Laertius VIII, 12   φησὶ δ᾽ Ἀπολλόδωρος ὁ λογιστικὸς ἑκατόμβην θῦσαι αὐτόν, εὑρόντα ὅτι τοῦ ὀρθογωνίου τριγώνου ἡ ὑποτείνουσα πλευρὰ ἴσον δύναται ταῖς περιεχούσαις. καὶ ἔστιν ἐπίγραμμα οὕτως ἔχον·

ἡνίκα Πυθαγόρης τὸ περικλεὲς εὕρετο γράμμα,
κεῖν᾽ ἐφ᾽ ὅτῳ κλεινὴν ἤγαγε βουθυσίην.

435 Proclus *in Euclidem* I, 44 (p. 419 Friedl.; DK 58 B 20)   ἔστι μὲν ἀρχαῖα, φασὶν οἱ περὶ τὸν Εὔδημον, καὶ τῆς τῶν Πυθαγορείων μούσης εὑρήματα ταῦτα ἥ τε παραβολὴ τῶν χωρίων καὶ ἡ ὑπερβολὴ καὶ ἡ ἔλλειψις.

436 Proclus *in Euclidem* I, 32 (p. 379 Friedl.; DK 58 B 21)   Εὔδημος δὲ ὁ Περιπατητικὸς εἰς τοὺς Πυθαγορείους ἀναπέμπει τὴν τοῦδε τοῦ θεωρήματος εὕρεσιν, ὅτι τρίγωνον ἅπαν δυσὶν ὀρθαῖς ἴσας ἔχει τὰς

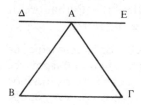

ἐντὸς γωνίας, καὶ δεικνύναι φησὶν αὐτοὺς οὕτω τὸ προκείμενον· ʼἔστω τρίγωνον τὸ ΑΒΓ, καὶ ἤχθω διὰ τοῦ Α τῇ ΒΓ παράλληλος ἡ ΔΕ. ἐπεὶ οὖν παράλληλοί εἰσιν αἱ ΒΓ ΔΕ, καὶ αἱ ἐναλλὰξ ἴσαι εἰσίν· ἴση ἄρα ἡ μὲν ὑπὸ ΔΑΒ τῇ ὑπὸ ΑΒΓ, ἡ δὲ ὑπὸ ΕΑΓ τῇ ὑπὸ ΑΓΒ. κοινὴ προσκείσθω ἡ ⟨ὑπὸ⟩ ΒΑΓ. αἱ ἄρα ὑπὸ ΔΑΒ ΒΑΓ ΓΑΕ, τουτέστιν αἱ ὑπὸ ΔΑΒ ΒΑΕ, τουτέστιν αἱ δύο ὀρθαί, ἴσαι εἰσὶ ταῖς τοῦ ΑΒΓ τριγώνου τρισὶ γωνίαις. αἱ ἄρα τρεῖς τοῦ τριγώνου δύο ὀρθαῖς εἰσιν ἴσαι.ʼ

434 Apollodorus the calculator says that he [*sc.* Pythagoras] sacrificed a hundred oxen when he discovered that the square on the hypotenuse of a right-angled triangle is equal to the squares on the sides containing the right angle. And there is an epigram which runs as follows: 'When Pythagoras discovered the famous figure, the one on account of which he made his renowned sacrifice of oxen.'

435 These things, according to Eudemus and his followers, are ancient, and discoveries of the Muse of the Pythagoreans – the application of areas, their exceeding and their falling short.

436 Eudemus the Peripatetic attributes to the Pythagoreans the discovery of this theorem, that every triangle has its interior angles equal to two right angles, and he says they proved the proposition as follows: 'Let ABΓ be a triangle, and let ΔE be drawn through A parallel to BΓ. Then, since BΓ, ΔE are parallel, the alternate angles are equal. So ΔAB is equal to ABΓ, and EAΓ to AΓB. Let the angle BAΓ be added in common. Then the angles ΔAB, BAΓ, ΓAE, i.e. the angles ΔAB, BAE, i.e. two right angles, are equal to the three angles of the triangle ABΓ. So the three angles of the triangle are equal to two right angles.'

There can be little doubt that from the fifth century on the Pythagoreans made a substantial contribution to the development of Greek mathematics. In geometry, besides the important technique of application of areas (**435**) and some isolated theorems such as **436**, discovery of the theorems of the fourth book of Euclid is credited to them by the scholia (Schol. Eucl. 273, 3; 13). Archytas in particular, active in the early fourth century (cf. **268**), was an important mathematician who worked out a serious arithmetical theory of music (cf. Ptolemaeus *Harm.* I, 13, DK47A16, Boethius *de mus.* III, 11, DK47A19), which is of course the sort of mathematics Plato leads us to expect of a Pythagorean (**253**), and which seems a natural development of the original Pythagorean concept of harmony. What is hard to gauge is the total extent and overall character of Pythagorean work in mathematics. For example, various late sources associate the Pythagoreans with the discovery of the irrationality of the diagonal of a square (e.g. Schol. Eucl. 417, 12ff., Iambl. *V.P.* 246ff., DK18, 4), but there is no good reason to believe them (see Burkert, *Lore*, 455–65; also J. A. Philip, *Pythagoras and Early Pythagoreanism*, Appendix 2). And the evidence connecting the discovery of 'Pythagoras' theorem' with Pythagoras all derives from late anecdotal material like **434**. It is tempting to guess that in this case the Pythagoreans originally at least had no thought of geometrical proof, but had recognized the corresponding properties of specific sets of numbers such as 3, 4, 5. They may have arranged pebbles (cf. **433** and **437**) to represent right-angled triangles, and so hit on a general method for calculating their rational sides (cf. Burkert, *Lore*, 427–30). Such an arithmetical technique was already known to the Babylonians (see O. Neugebauer, *The Exact Sciences in Antiquity* (2nd ed., Providence, R.I., 1957) ch. II).

From Aristotle's first sentence in **430**[1] one might infer that the Pythagoreans virtually *created* Greek mathematics, a view exploded by modern scholarship, although it still has popular currency. It was in fact the Ionian Greeks who laid the foundations of geometry and were responsible for most of its major advances well into the fourth century, as is clear from Proclus' famous summary of Eudemus' history of the subject (*in Eucl.* p. 65, 3ff.).[2] Still less plausible is Aristotle's suggestion that it was their work in mathematics which led the Pythagoreans to their speculations about number and *harmonia*. This puts the cart before the horse. It is fascination with the imagined symbolic powers of numbers, individually and as a system, not more profound mathematical study, which finds expression in the ideas of **430**. What leads the Pythagoreans to identify marriage (for example) with the number 5, as the sum of the first female and the first male numbers (Aristotle *ap.* Alex. *in Met.* 39, 8 (fr. 203)), is reflection on the simple truth that $2 + 3 = 5$.

[1] But its syntax and interpretation are disputed. For example, Burkert, *Lore*, 412–14 takes Aristotle to mean that the Pythagoreans 'were first to see the relevance of the "principles of mathematics" to the general question of "principles"'.

[2] See W. A. Heidel, 'The Pythagoreans and Greek Mathematics', in D. J. Furley and R. E. Allen, *Studies in Presocratic Philosophy* I, 350ff.; Burkert, *Lore*, ch. VI. Burkert shows that the section on Pythagoras in the summary derives not from Eudemus but from the Neoplatonist Iamblichus (pp. 409–12).

Further evidence for this interpretation of the motivation of Pythagorean metaphysics is supplied, by Aristotle himself again, in a text which also bears witness to their fondness for representing numbers in the form of patterns similar to those now found on dominoes or dice:

437 Aristotle *Physics* Γ4, 203a10 (DK 58 B 28)   καὶ οἱ μὲν (*sc.* φασὶ) τὸ ἄπειρον εἶναι τὸ ἄρτιον (τοῦτο γὰρ ἐναπολαμβανόμενον καὶ ὑπὸ τοῦ περιττοῦ περαινόμενον παρέχειν τοῖς οὖσι τὴν ἀπειρίαν· σημεῖον δ' εἶναι τούτου τὸ συμβαῖνον ἐπὶ τῶν ἀριθμῶν· περιτιθεμένων γὰρ τῶν γνωμόνων περὶ τὸ ἓν καὶ χωρὶς ὅτε μὲν ἄλλο ἀεὶ γίγνεσθαι τὸ εἶδος, ὅτε δὲ ἕν).

437 The Pythagoreans say that the unlimited is the even. For this, they say, when it is enclosed and limited by the odd provides the unlimited element in the things there are. An indication of this is what happens with numbers. If the gnomons are placed round the one, and without the one, in the one case the figure produced varies continually, in the other it is always the same.

Both the doctrine of **437** and its supporting illustration are obscure (especially the words καὶ χωρίς, here translated 'and without the one'). The two figures to which Aristotle refers are apparently these. Either of these figures can, of course, be extended, by the addition of more 'gnomons' (on which see p. 103 above), *ad infinitum*. In Figure 1, where 'the gnomons are being placed around the one', each

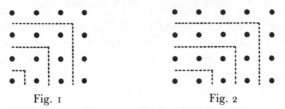

Fig. 1   Fig. 2

successive addition marks the next in the series of odd numbers, while Figure 2 similarly represents the series of even numbers. But whereas Figure 1 remains, with each addition, always the same figure, a square, Figure 2 on the contrary changes with each addition the ratio of its length to its height. Hence the inclusion of *square* and *oblong* in **438** below.

This illustration certainly succeeds in forging a connexion of sorts between odd and limited (via uniformity) and even and unlimited (via infinite variability). But it does not explain why even *accounts for* the unlimitedness of things, nor what is meant by its being taken in and limited by the odd. Probably no precise explanation of the Pythagoreans' thought processes here is possible, despite the unpersuasive efforts of ancient commentators to supply one (Simpl. *in Phys.* 455, 20–456, 15). The Pythagoreans evidently wanted to use as principles *both* odd and even *and* limit and unlimited, and to connect the two sets of principles. But it is obvious from the evidence that they never settled on any determinate way of making the connexion. In **437**, like **430** but unlike **424–9** and **443–4**, it is odd and even, not limit and unlimited, that are taken to be the fundamental principles of number and so of all else.

THE TABLE OF OPPOSITES

438 Aristotle *Met.* A5, 986a22 (DK 58 B 5; continues **430**) ἕτεροι δὲ τῶν αὐτῶν τούτων τὰς ἀρχὰς δέκα λέγουσιν εἶναι τὰς κατὰ συστοιχίαν λεγομένας·

πέρας καὶ ἄπειρον
περιττὸν καὶ ἄρτιον
ἓν καὶ πλῆθος
δεξιὸν καὶ ἀριστερόν
ἄρρεν καὶ θῆλυ

ἠρεμοῦν καὶ κινούμενον
εὐθὺ καὶ καμπύλον
φῶς καὶ σκότος
ἀγαθὸν καὶ κακόν
τετράγωνον καὶ ἑτερόμηκες·

ὅνπερ τρόπον ἔοικε καὶ ᾿Αλκμαίων ὁ Κροτωνιάτης ὑπολαβεῖν, καὶ ἤτοι οὗτος παρ᾿ ἐκείνων ἢ ἐκεῖνοι παρὰ τούτου παρέλαβον τὸν λόγον τοῦτον· καὶ γὰρ ᾿Αλκμαίων ἀπεφήνατο παραπλησίως τούτοις.¹ φησὶ γὰρ εἶναι δύο τὰ πολλὰ τῶν ἀνθρωπίνων, λέγων τὰς ἐναντιότητας οὐχ ὥσπερ οὗτοι διωρισμένας ἀλλὰ τὰς τυχούσας, οἷον λευκὸν μέλαν, γλυκὺ πικρόν, ἀγαθὸν κακόν, μέγα μικρόν. οὗτος μὲν οὖν ἀδιορίστως ἀπέρριψε περὶ τῶν λοιπῶν, οἱ δὲ Πυθαγόρειοι καὶ πόσαι καὶ τίνες αἱ ἐναντιώσεις ἀπεφήναντο. παρὰ μὲν οὖν τούτων ἀμφοῖν τοσοῦτον ἔστι λαβεῖν ὅτι τἀναντία ἀρχαὶ τῶν ὄντων· τὸ δὲ ὅσαι, παρὰ τῶν ἑτέρων, καὶ τίνες αὗταί εἰσιν. πῶς μέντοι πρὸς τὰς εἰρημένας αἰτίας ἐνδέχεται συναγαγεῖν, σαφῶς μὲν οὐ διήρθρωται παρ᾿ ἐκείνων, ἐοίκασι δ᾿ ὡς ἐν ὕλης εἴδει τὰ στοιχεῖα τάττειν· ἐκ τούτων γὰρ ὡς ἐνυπαρχόντων συνεστάναι καὶ πεπλάσθαι φασὶ τὴν οὐσίαν.

¹ Some manuscripts write this clause as καὶ γὰρ ἐγένετο τὴν ἡλικίαν ᾿Αλκμαίων ἐπὶ γέροντι Πυθαγόρᾳ, ἀπεφήνατο δὲ κτλ. 'Alcmaeon was ⟨? a young man⟩ in Pythagoras' old age'. So written it is obviously corrupt, and Ross (ad loc.) is doubtless right to follow A^b and Alexander in omitting the additional phrases as marginal notes wrongly incorporated into the text, although conceivably containing true information.

438 Other members of this same school say there are ten principles, which they arrange in two columns of cognates – limit and unlimited, odd and even, one and plurality, right and left, male and female, resting and moving, straight and curved, light and darkness, good and bad, square and oblong. In this way Alcmaeon of Croton seems also to have conceived the matter, and either he got this view from them or they got it from him; for he expressed himself similarly to them. For he says most human affairs go in pairs, meaning not definite contrarieties such as the Pythagoreans speak of, but any chance contrarieties, e.g. white and black, sweet and bitter, good and bad, great and small. He threw out indefinite suggestions about the other contrarieties, but the Pythagoreans declared both how many and which their contrarieties are.

From both these schools, then, we can learn this much, that the contraries are the principles of things; and how many these principles are and which they are, we can learn from one of the two schools. But how these principles can be brought together under the causes we have named has not been clearly and articulately stated by them; they seem, however, to range the elements under the head of matter; for out of these as immanent parts they say substance is composed and moulded. (*Tr. Ross*)

Aristotle evidently derived the table of opposites from a Pythagorean source different from those he employed in **430**, as also from Philolaus' book. The table reminds him of the use of opposites by the philosopher–physician Alcmaeon of Croton (cf. **310** above), who perhaps wrote in the early fifth century (see note on the Greek text).[1] On this reminiscence he bases his suggestion about the relationship between Alcmaeon's view and theirs, and in so doing betrays his vagueness about the antiquity of the table. Unlike the speculations reported in **430**, the table of opposites does not recall any of the original Pythagorean ideas discussed in ch. VII. It looks like the work of someone who has been impressed by Parmenides' cosmological dualism and by the figures referred to in **437**, which he has then attempted to connect with other Eleatic and mathematical concepts and to subsume under the Pythagorean principles of limit and unlimited and odd and even. The table has very little internal structure, but it is tempting to infer that limit and unlimited are intended to be the basic opposites which in some sense underlie all the others, odd and even included.[2]

---

[1] Aristotle's choice of words in **438** suggests that Alcmaeon was not himself a Pythagorean, although the friends to whom his book was addressed were probably members of the sect: **439** Alcmaeon fr. 1, Diog. L. VIII, 83 Ἀλκμαίων Κροτωνιήτης τάδε ἔλεξε Πειρίθου υἱὸς Βροτίνῳ καὶ Λέοντι καὶ Βαθύλλῳ· περὶ τῶν ἀφανέων [περὶ τῶν θνητῶν] σαφήνειαν μὲν θεοὶ ἔχοντι, ὡς δὲ ἀνθρώποις τεκμαίρεσθαι... (*Alcmaeon of Croton, son of Peirithous, spoke these words to Brotinus and Leon and Bathyllus: 'Concerning things unseen the gods see clearly, but so far as men may conjecture...'*)

[2] Cf. **440** Aristotle *Eth. Nic.* B5, 1106b29 (DK 58 B 7) τὸ γὰρ κακὸν τοῦ ἀπείρου, ὡς οἱ Πυθαγόρειοι εἴκαζον, τὸ δ' ἀγαθὸν τοῦ πεπερασμένου. (*For evil belongs to the unlimited, as the Pythagoreans conjectured, and good to the limited.*)

COSMOGONY

441 Philolaus fr. 7, Stobaeus *Anth.* I, 21, 8 τὸ πρᾶτον ἁρμοσθέν, τὸ ἕν, ἐν τῷ μέσῳ τᾶς σφαίρας ἑστία καλεῖται.

442 Aristotle *Met.* N3, 1091a12 (DK 58 B 26) ἄτοπον δὲ καὶ γένεσιν ποιεῖν ἀιδίων ὄντων, μᾶλλον δ' ἕν τι τῶν ἀδυνάτων. οἱ μὲν οὖν Πυθαγόρειοι πότερον οὐ ποιοῦσιν ἢ ποιοῦσι γένεσιν οὐδὲν δεῖ διστάζειν· φανερῶς γὰρ λέγουσιν ὡς τοῦ ἑνὸς συσταθέντος, εἴτ' ἐξ ἐπιπέδων εἴτ' ἐκ χροιᾶς εἴτ' ἐκ σπέρματος εἴτ' ἐξ ὧν ἀποροῦσιν εἰπεῖν, εὐθὺς τὸ ἔγγιστα τοῦ ἀπείρου ὅτι εἵλκετο καὶ ἐπεραίνετο ὑπὸ τοῦ πέρατος.

443 Aristotle *Phys.* Δ6, 213b22 (DK 58 B 30) εἶναι δ' ἔφασαν καὶ οἱ Πυθαγόρειοι κενόν, καὶ ἐπεισιέναι αὐτὸ τῷ οὐρανῷ ἐκ τοῦ ἀπείρου πνεύματος ὡς ἀναπνέοντι καὶ τὸ κενόν, ὃ διορίζει τὰς φύσεις, ὡς ὄντος τοῦ κενοῦ χωρισμοῦ τινος τῶν ἐφεξῆς καὶ τῆς διορίσεως· καὶ τοῦτ' εἶναι πρῶτον ἐν τοῖς ἀριθμοῖς· τὸ γὰρ κενὸν διορίζειν τὴν φύσιν αὐτῶν.

444 Stobaeus *Anth.* 1, 18, 1c (quoting Aristotle; DK 58 B 30) ἐν δὲ τῷ περὶ τῆς Πυθαγόρου φιλοσοφίας πρώτῳ γράφει τὸν μὲν οὐρανὸν εἶναι ἕνα, ἐπεισάγεσθαι δὲ ἐκ τοῦ ἀπείρου χρόνον τε καὶ πνοὴν καὶ τὸ κενόν, ὃ διορίζει ἑκάστων τὰς χώρας ἀεί.

441 The first thing to be harmonized – the one – in the middle of the sphere is called the hearth.

442 It is strange also to attribute generation to eternal things, or rather this is one of the things that are impossible. There need be no doubt whether the Pythagoreans attribute generation to them or not; for they plainly say that when the one had been constructed, whether out of planes or of surface or of seed or of elements which they cannot express, immediately the nearest part of the unlimited began to be drawn in and limited by the limit. (*After Ross*)

443 The Pythagoreans, too, held that void exists, and that it enters the heaven from the unlimited breath – it so to speak breathes in void also [*sc.* as well as breath]. The void distinguishes the natures of things, since it is the thing that separates and distinguishes the successive terms in a series. This happens in the first instance in the case of numbers; for the void distinguishes their nature.

444 In the first book of his work *On the Philosophy of Pythagoras* he writes that the universe is one, and that from the unlimited there are drawn into it time, breath and the void, which always distinguishes the places of each thing.

Aristotle writes in **442** as though he is drawing on at least one written account of Pythagorean doctrine for the point he is making. His principal source here (in contrast e.g. to **430**) was very likely Philolaus' book – although of Philolaus' cosmogony hardly any authentic fragments survive, perhaps only **441**, which happily presents the same doctrine as **442**. Philolaus was no doubt unwilling to claim to know more than his general theory demanded (cf. the prudent reticence of **429** about the means by which *harmonia* was achieved), and so laid himself open to Aristotle's strictures in **442** (also **431**). As for **443-4**, their account of 'respiration' in cosmogony is phrased in terms which recall those used in the theory of respiration in Philolaus' biology.[1] Whether this cosmogony was largely Philolaus' own creation or a more ancient doctrine is a matter of dispute. Its crudity may be thought to suggest that it originally belonged in a sixth-century intellectual environment, echoing as it does the cosmogonical concepts of Anaximander and Anaximenes (cf. also **172** above; and see e.g. Philip, *Pythagoras*, 68-70, 93-5; C. H. Kahn, 'Pythagorean philosophy before Plato', in *The Presocratics*, ed. A. P. D. Mourelatos (Garden City, N.Y., 1974), 183-4). But crudity is endemic in Pythagoreanism; and the appearance in **443-4** of the concept of void (probably an Eleatic invention), distinguished from that of air (cf. **470** below), points to a date well into the fifth century.[2]

---

[1] **445** Meno *ap*. Anon. Londinensem xviii, 8 (DK 44 A 27) Φιλόλαος δὲ Κροτωνιάτης συνεστάναι φησὶν τὰ ἡμέτερα σώματα ἐκ θερμοῦ. ἀμέτοχα γὰρ αὐτὰ εἶναι ψυχροῦ, ὑπομιμνήσκων ἀπό τινων τοιούτων· τὸ σπέρμα εἶναι θερμόν, κατασκευαστικὸν δὲ τοῦτο τοῦ ζῴου· καὶ ὁ τόπος δέ, εἰς ὃν ἡ καταβολή (μήτρα δὲ αὕτη), ἐστὶν θερμοτέρα καὶ ἐοικυῖα ἐκείνῳ· τὸ δὲ ἐοικός τινι ταὐτὸ δύναται ᾧ ἔοικεν· ἐπεὶ δὲ τὸ κατασκευάζον ἀμέτοχόν ἐστιν ψυχροῦ, καὶ ὁ τόπος δέ, ἐν ᾧ ἡ καταβολή, ἀμέτοχός ἐστι ψυχροῦ, δῆλον ὅτι καὶ τὸ κατασκευαζόμενον ζῷον τοιοῦτον γίνεται. εἰς δὲ τούτου τὴν κατασκευὴν ὑπομνήσει προσχρῆται τοιαύτῃ· μετὰ γὰρ τὴν ἔκτεξιν εὐθέως τὸ ζῷον ἐπισπᾶται τὸ ἐκτὸς πνεῦμα ψυχρὸν ὄν· εἶτα πάλιν καθαπερεὶ χρέος ἐκπέμπει αὐτό. διὰ τοῦτο δὴ καὶ ὄρεξις τοῦ ἐκτὸς πνεύματος, ἵνα τῇ ἐπεισάκτῳ τοῦ πνεύματος ὁλκῇ θερμότερα ὑπάρχοντα τὰ ἡμέτερα σώματα πρὸς αὐτοῦ καταψύχηται. *(Philolaus of Croton holds that our bodies are composed of the hot; for they have no share in the cold, as he reasons from considerations such as the following: the sperm is warm, and it is the sperm that produces the living thing; and the place in which it is deposited (i.e. the womb) is, like it, warm; and what is like something has the same power as that which it resembles. Since, then, the productive factor has no share in the cold, and also the place in which it is deposited has no share in the cold, clearly the living thing produced will also be of the same nature. With regard to its production, he makes use of the following reasoning: immediately after its birth the living thing draws in the breath outside, which is cold; and then, as if of necessity, it expels it again. This desire for the breath outside arises in order that, as the result of the inhalation of the breath, our bodies, which are by nature too warm, may be cooled by it.)*

[2] It has sometimes (as in KR) been supposed that fifth-century Pythagoreans should be credited with a much more specific set of cosmogonical ideas, involving first the generation of numbers, then that of geometrical figures from numbers, and finally that of physical bodies from geometrical figures (see e.g. Guthrie, *HGP* I, 239-82). Such detailed constructions are hard to square with **442** (cf. also **431**); and they place heavy reliance on texts (e.g. Aristotle *Met.* 1028b16, 1090b5, DK 58 B 23-4 which are almost certainly not Pythagorean (so e.g. Cherniss,

ACPA, 132ff., Burkert, *Lore*, 42–3), or others (e.g. Aristotle *de an.* 409a4, Sextus *adv. math.* x, 281, [Iambl.] *Theolog. arithm.* p. 84, 10, DK44A13) which originate in the Pythagorizing Platonism of the early Academy (cf. e.g. Burkert, *Lore*, 66–71).

The cosmogony Aristotle reports is of considerable interest. It embodies the perception that both time and discrete bodies are (in different ways, as we would insist) countable, and that this is a fundamental fact about them. Where the theory becomes fantastical is in its treatment of numerical and in general formal concepts as amenable to physical explanation: thus numbers are to be kept separate in their proper sequence by void.

ASTRONOMY

(i) *The planetary system*

446 Aristotle *de caelo* B13, 293a18 (DK58B37)   τῶν πλείστων ἐπὶ τοῦ μέσου κεῖσθαι λεγόντων (*sc.* τὴν γῆν)...ἐναντίως οἱ περὶ τὴν Ἰταλίαν, καλούμενοι δὲ Πυθαγόρειοι, λέγουσιν. ἐπὶ μὲν γὰρ τοῦ μέσου πῦρ εἶναί φασι, τὴν δὲ γῆν ἓν τῶν ἄστρων οὖσαν κύκλῳ φερομένην περὶ τὸ μέσον νύκτα τε καὶ ἡμέραν ποιεῖν. ἔτι δ᾽ ἐναντίαν ἄλλην ταύτῃ κατασκευάζουσι γῆν, ἣν ἀντίχθονα ὄνομα καλοῦσιν, οὐ πρὸς τὰ φαινόμενα τοὺς λόγους καὶ τὰς αἰτίας ζητοῦντες, ἀλλὰ πρός τινας λόγους καὶ δόξας αὐτῶν τὰ φαινόμενα προσέλκοντες καὶ πειρώμενοι συγκοσμεῖν. πολλοῖς δ᾽ ἂν καὶ ἑτέροις συνδόξειε μὴ δεῖν τῇ γῇ τὴν τοῦ μέσου χώραν ἀποδιδόναι, τὸ πιστὸν οὐκ ἐκ τῶν φαινομένων ἀθροῦσιν ἀλλὰ μᾶλλον ἐκ τῶν λόγων. τῷ γὰρ τιμιωτάτῳ οἴονται προσήκειν τὴν τιμιωτάτην ὑπάρχειν χώραν, εἶναι δὲ πῦρ μὲν γῆς τιμιώτερον, τὸ δὲ πέρας τοῦ μεταξύ, τὸ δ᾽ ἔσχατον καὶ τὸ μέσον πέρας· ὥστ᾽ ἐκ τούτων ἀναλογιζόμενοι οὐκ οἴονται ἐπὶ τοῦ μέσου τῆς σφαίρας κεῖσθαι αὐτήν, ἀλλὰ μᾶλλον τὸ πῦρ. (b1) ἔτι δ᾽ οἵ γε Πυθαγόρειοι καὶ διὰ τὸ μάλιστα προσήκειν φυλάττεσθαι τὸ κυριώτατον τοῦ παντός· τὸ δὲ μέσον εἶναι τοιοῦτον· ὃ Διὸς φυλακὴν ὀνομάζουσι, τὸ ταύτην ἔχον τὴν χώραν πῦρ, ὥσπερ τὸ μέσον ἁπλῶς λεγόμενον καὶ τὸ τοῦ μεγέθους μέσον καὶ τοῦ πράγματος ὂν μέσον καὶ τῆς φύσεως. καίτοι καθάπερ ἐν τοῖς ζῴοις οὐ ταὐτὸν τὸ τοῦ ζῴου καὶ τοῦ σώματος μέσον, οὕτως ὑποληπτέον μᾶλλον καὶ περὶ τὸν ὅλον οὐρανόν.

447 Aetius ιι, 7, 7 (DK44A16)   Φιλόλαος πῦρ ἐν μέσῳ περὶ τὸ κέντρον ὅπερ ἑστίαν τοῦ παντὸς καλεῖ καὶ Διὸς οἶκον καὶ μητέρα θεῶν βωμόν τε καὶ συνοχὴν καὶ μέτρον φύσεως. καὶ πάλιν πῦρ ἕτερον ἀνωτάτω τὸ περιέχον. πρῶτον δ᾽ εἶναι φύσει τὸ μέσον, περὶ δὲ τοῦτο δέκα σώματα θεῖα χορεύειν, [οὐρανόν] ⟨μετὰ τὴν τῶν ἀπλανῶν σφαῖραν⟩ τοὺς ε̄ πλανήτας, μεθ᾽ οὓς ἥλιον, ὑφ᾽ ᾧ σελήνην, ὑφ᾽ ᾗ τὴν γῆν, ὑφ' ᾗ τὴν ἀντίχθονα, μεθ' ἃ σύμπαντα τὸ πῦρ ἑστίας περὶ τὰ κέντρα τάξιν ἐπέχον.

446 Most people say that the earth lies at the centre of the universe,...but the Italian philosophers known as Pythagoreans take the contrary view. At the centre, they say, is fire, and the earth is one of the stars, creating night and day by its circular motion about the centre. They further construct another earth in opposition to ours to which they give the name counter-earth. In all this they are not seeking for theories and causes to account for observed facts, but rather forcing their observations and trying to accommodate them to certain theories and opinions of their own. But there are many others who would agree that it is wrong to give the earth the central position, looking for confirmation rather to theory than to the facts of observation. Their view is that the most precious place befits the most precious thing: but fire, they say, is more precious than earth, and the limit than the intermediate, and the circumference and the centre are limits. Reasoning on this basis they take the view that it is not earth that lies at the centre of the sphere, but rather fire. The Pythagoreans have a further reason. They hold that the most important part of the world, which is the centre, should be most strictly guarded, and name it, or rather the fire which occupies that place, the 'guardhouse of Zeus', as if the word 'centre' were quite unequivocal, and the centre of the mathematical figure were always the same with that of the thing or the natural centre. But it is better to conceive of the case of the whole heaven as analogous to that of animals, in which the centre of the animal and that of the body are different. (*After Stocks*)

447 Philolaus places fire around the centre of the universe, and calls it the 'hearth of the world', the 'house of Zeus', 'mother of the gods', 'altar, bond and measure of nature'. Then again there is another fire enveloping the universe at the circumference. But he says that the centre is by nature primary, and around the centre ten divine bodies dance – first the sphere of the fixed stars, then the five planets, next the sun, then the moon, then the earth, then the counter-earth, and finally the fire of the 'hearth', which has its station around the centre.

447 is trustworthy evidence that Philolaus was the author of the Pythagorean theory described in **446**. Does his displacement of the earth from the centre of the universe make him a precursor of the Copernican revolution? That depends on the questions his system was designed to answer and the sorts of grounds he offered in its defence. The only astronomical phenomenon Aristotle mentions is the alternation of day and night, which the theory explains as due to the rotation of the earth (axial rotation would presumably have served as well as revolution about the central fire). An astronomer might then have seen that he need not make the fixed stars move; but Philolaus has them dancing. In general, he seems to have tried to account for phenomena like eclipses and the origin of the sun's light by his theory, in characteristic Presocratic style,[1] but not for others with which Greek astronomy was to be most typically concerned, such as the annual paths of the heavenly bodies. Aristotle took the system to be motivated by veneration of fire and of the number ten (cf. **430**), and by a religious conviction that the earth is too unimportant to occupy the central position in the cosmos.[2]

[1] **448** Aetius II, 20, 12 (DK44A19) Φιλόλαος ὁ Πυθαγόρειος ὑαλοειδῆ τὸν ἥλιον, δεχόμενον μὲν τοῦ ἐν τῷ κόσμῳ πυρὸς τὴν ἀνταύγειαν, διηθοῦντα δὲ πρὸς ἡμᾶς τό τε φῶς καὶ τὴν ἀλέαν, ὥστε τρόπον τινὰ διττοὺς ἡλίους γίνεσθαι, τό τε ἐν τῷ οὐρανῷ πυρῶδες καὶ τὸ ἀπ' αὐτοῦ πυροειδὲς κατὰ τὸ ἐσοπτροειδές, εἰ μή τις καὶ τρίτον λέξει τὴν ἀπὸ τοῦ ἐνόπτρου κατ' ἀνάκλασιν διασπειρομένην πρὸς ἡμᾶς αὐγήν· καὶ γὰρ ταύτην προσονομάζομεν ἥλιον οἱονεὶ εἴδωλον εἰδώλου. *(Philolaus the Pythagorean holds that the sun is like glass, receiving the reflection of the cosmic fire and filtering its light and warmth to us, so that in a sense there are two suns, the fiery region in the heaven and the mirror-like fire it produces – if one is not to add as a third the rays which are scattered in our direction from the mirror by reflexion: for this too we name the sun, an image, as it were, of an image.)* This account is evidently inspired by Empedocles' theory about the sun (**370** above; also Aetius II, 20, 13, DK31A56). The counter-earth was invoked to explain eclipses (Aetius II, 29, 4, DK58B36; the style of explanation is borrowed from Anaxagoras: Hippolytus *Ref.* I, 8, 6 and 9, DK59A42 (= **502**), Aetius II, 29, 7, DK59A77).

[2] Probably, therefore, Philolaus was as usual drawing on older Pythagorean tradition; Hippasus (see pp. 234–5) is credited with belief in fire as the basic substance (Aristotle *Met.* 984a7, Simpl. *in Phys.* 23, 33, DK 18, 7). Yet the specific idea of a central fire is attested as a feature of Parmenides' cosmology (albeit an obscure one: see **307** above), and most details of the system can hardly be earlier than the latter part of the fifth century (cf. n. 1 above).

(ii) *The harmony of the spheres*

449 Aristotle *de caelo* B9, 290b12 (DK58B35) φανερὸν δ' ἐκ τούτων ὅτι καὶ τὸ φάναι γίνεσθαι φερομένων (*sc.* τῶν ἄστρων) ἁρμονίαν, ὡς συμφώνων γινομένων τῶν ψόφων, κομψῶς μὲν εἴρηται καὶ περιττῶς ὑπὸ τῶν εἰπόντων, οὐ μὴν οὕτως ἔχει τἀληθές. δοκεῖ γάρ τισιν ἀναγκαῖον εἶναι τηλικούτων φερομένων σωμάτων γίγνεσθαι ψόφον, ἐπεὶ καὶ τῶν παρ' ἡμῖν οὔτε τοὺς ὄγκους ἐχόντων ἴσους οὔτε τοιούτῳ τάχει φερομένων· ἡλίου δὲ καὶ σελήνης, ἔτι τε τοσούτων τὸ πλῆθος ἄστρων καὶ τὸ μέγεθος φερομένων τῷ τάχει τοιαύτην φοράν, ἀδύνατον μὴ γίγνεσθαι ψόφον ἀμήχανόν τινα τὸ μέγεθος. ὑποθέμενοι δὲ ταῦτα καὶ τὰς ταχυτῆτας ἐκ τῶν ἀποστάσεων ἔχειν τοὺς τῶν συμφωνιῶν λόγους, ἐναρμόνιόν φασι γίγνεσθαι τὴν φωνὴν φερομένων κύκλῳ τῶν ἄστρων. ἐπεὶ δ' ἄλογον δοκεῖ τὸ μὴ συνακούειν ἡμᾶς τῆς φωνῆς ταύτης, αἴτιον τούτου φασὶν εἶναι τὸ γιγνομένοις εὐθὺς ὑπάρχειν τὸν ψόφον, ὥστε μὴ διάδηλον εἶναι πρὸς τὴν ἐναντίαν σιγήν· πρὸς ἄλληλα γὰρ φωνῆς καὶ σιγῆς εἶναι τὴν διάγνωσιν, ὥστε καθάπερ τοῖς χαλκοτύποις διὰ συνήθειαν οὐθὲν δοκεῖ διαφέρειν, καὶ τοῖς ἀνθρώποις ταὐτὸ συμβαίνειν.

449 From all this it is clear that the theory that the movement of the stars produces a harmony, because the sounds they make are concordant, in spite of the ingenuity and originality with which it has been stated, is nevertheless untrue. Some thinkers suppose that the motion of bodies of that size must produce a noise, since on our earth the motion of bodies far inferior in size and in speed of movement has that effect. Also, when the sun and the moon, they say, and all the stars, so great in number and in size, are moving with so rapid a motion, how should they not produce a sound immensely great? Starting from this argument and from the hypothesis that their speeds, as measured by their distances, are in the same ratios as musical concordances, they assert that the sound given forth by the circular movement of the stars is a harmony. Since, however, it appears unaccountable that we should not hear this music, they explain this by saying that the sound is in our ears from the very moment of birth and is thus indistinguishable from its contrary silence, since sound and silence are discriminated by mutual contrast. What happens to mankind, then, is just what happens to coppersmiths, who are so accustomed to the noise of the smithy that it makes no difference to them. (*After Stocks*)

449 attests an attempt to work out in some detail the old Pythagorean doctrine of the harmony of the spheres (see p. 233 above). Aristotle was impressed by the ingenuity of its authors (whom it is tempting to suppose members of Philolaus' circle). There is no evidence, however, that exact observations were made, nor any use of observations, which could support their view.

THE SOUL

(i) *Its nature*

450 Aristotle *de anima* A2, 404a16 (DK58B40) ἔοικε δὲ καὶ τὸ παρὰ τῶν Πυθαγορείων λεγόμενον τὴν αὐτὴν ἔχειν διάνοιαν· ἔφασαν γάρ τινες αὐτῶν ψυχὴν εἶναι τὰ ἐν τῷ ἀέρι ξύσματα, οἱ δὲ τὸ ταῦτα κινοῦν. περὶ δὲ τούτων εἴρηται, διότι συνεχῶς φαίνεται κινούμενα, κἂν ᾖ νηνεμία παντελής.

451 Aristotle *de anima* A4, 407b27 (DK44A23) καὶ ἄλλη δέ τις δόξα παραδέδοται περὶ ψυχῆς...ἁρμονίαν γάρ τινα αὐτὴν λέγουσι· καὶ γὰρ τὴν ἁρμονίαν κρᾶσιν καὶ σύνθεσιν ἐναντίων εἶναι καὶ τὸ σῶμα συγκεῖσθαι ἐξ ἐναντίων. (Cf. Aristotle *Pol.* Θ5, 1340b18 (DK58B41).)

452 Plato *Phaedo* 88D θαυμαστῶς γάρ μου ὁ λόγος οὗτος ἀντιλαμβάνεται καὶ νῦν καὶ ἀεί, τὸ ἁρμονίαν τινὰ ἡμῶν εἶναι τὴν ψυχήν, καὶ ὥσπερ ὑπέμνησέν με ῥηθεὶς ὅτι καὶ αὐτῷ μοι ταῦτα προυδέδοκτο.

450 The theory held by the Pythagoreans seems to have the same purport; for some of them said that the soul is the motes in the air, others that it is what moves them. They spoke of motes because they are evidently in continual motion, even when there is a complete calm.

451 Another theory has been handed down to us about the soul...They say that it is a kind of attunement; for attunement is a blending and composing of opposites, and the body is constituted of opposites.

452 This theory has and always has had a remarkable hold on me [*sc.* Echecrates], that our soul is a kind of attunement (*harmonia*), and when it was formulated it reminded me, so to speak, that I myself formerly came to hold this view.

450 reports a primitive belief (comparable with the idea that the sound of a gong is the voice of a *daimon* (281)), together with a rationalizing interpretation of it. 451 presumably represents an explanation inspired by general Pythagorean number theory.[1] Aristotle's specification of the sort of *harmonia* involved obviously depends on Plato's *Phaedo*, and may not be what the Pythagoreans originally had in mind (one would have expected them to identify the soul with a numerical ratio: cf. 430). 452 serves to remind us of the difficulty of reconciling the doctrine with the theory of transmigration.

[1] Its Pythagorean credentials are suggested by Echecrates' endorsement of it in 452 (cf. 421), but it would be rash to attribute it to any particular Pythagorean.

(ii) *Its immortality*

453 Aristotle *de anima* A2, 405a29 (DK 24 A 12) παραπλησίως δὲ τούτοις καὶ ᾽Αλκμαίων ἔοικεν ὑπολαβεῖν περὶ ψυχῆς· φησὶ γὰρ αὐτὴν ἀθάνατον εἶναι διὰ τὸ ἐοικέναι τοῖς ἀθανάτοις· τοῦτο δ᾽ ὑπάρχειν αὐτῇ ὡς ἀεὶ κινουμένῃ· κινεῖσθαι γὰρ καὶ τὰ θεῖα πάντα συνεχῶς ἀεί, σελήνην, ἥλιον, τοὺς ἀστέρας καὶ τὸν οὐρανὸν ὅλον.

454 Aetius IV, 2, 2 (DK 24 A 12) ᾽Αλκμαίων φύσιν αὐτοκίνητον κατ᾽ ἀΐδιον κίνησιν καὶ διὰ τοῦτο ἀθάνατον αὐτὴν καὶ προσεμφερῆ τοῖς θείοις ὑπολαμβάνει.

455 Alcmaeon fr. 2, [Aristotle] *Problemata* XVII, 3, 916a33 τοὺς ἀνθρώπους φησὶν ᾽Αλκμαίων διὰ τοῦτο ἀπόλλυσθαι, ὅτι οὐ δύνανται τὴν ἀρχὴν τῷ τέλει προσάψαι.

453 Alcmaeon also seems to have held much the same view about the soul as these others [*sc.* Thales, Diogenes of Apollonia and Heraclitus]; for he says that it is immortal owing to its similarity to the immortal; and it has this quality because it is always in motion; for everything divine is in continual motion – the sun, the moon, the stars and the whole heavens.

454 Alcmaeon supposes the soul to be a substance self-moved in eternal motion, and for that reason immortal and similar to the divine.

455 Alcmaeon says that men die for this reason, that they cannot join the beginning to the end.

Alcmaeon was probably not himself a Pythagorean (cf. p. 339 above), but these texts contain the first actual arguments known to us (exploiting, interestingly, a connexion between soul and movement: cf. **450**) for the immortality of the soul (cf. **285** above). **454** suggests that Alcmaeon moved directly from the premiss that the soul is always in motion to the conclusion that it is immortal, and cited the evidence of the heavenly bodies merely (*pace* **453**) as a supporting analogy. What lies behind the premiss is perhaps the thought that only animate beings move themselves, in virtue of having soul. But if it is soul's essence to move itself, it cannot ever cease to move itself, and so cannot cease to live: it is therefore immortal (cf. Plato *Phaedr.* 245C–246A, a passage apparently inspired by Alcmaeon). **455** is yet harder to interpret. Conceivably Alcmaeon alludes to the fact that the means by which the heavenly bodies continue in everlasting motion, viz. by repetition of revolutions, is not open to man because the process of ageing is irreversible. A person cannot change from old age to babyhood ('cannot join the beginning to the end') while present in one and the same body. So if he is immortal, as the argument of 453–4 teaches, he must undergo physical death followed by incarnation in a new body.

ETHICS

456 Iamblichus *Vita Pythagorae* 137 (DK58D2) βούλομαι δὲ ἄνωθεν τὰς ἀρχὰς ὑποδεῖξαι τῆς τῶν θεῶν θρησκείας, ἃς προεστήσατο Πυθαγόρας τε καὶ οἱ ἀπ' αὐτοῦ ἄνδρες. ἅπαντα ὅσα περὶ τοῦ πράττειν ἢ μὴ πράττειν διορίζουσιν, ἐστόχασται τῆς πρὸς τὸ θεῖον ὁμιλίας, καὶ ἀρχὴ αὕτη ἐστὶ καὶ βίος ἅπας συντέτακται πρὸς τὸ ἀκολουθεῖν τῷ θεῷ καὶ ὁ λόγος οὗτος ταύτης ἐστὶ τῆς φιλοσοφίας, ὅτι γελοῖον ποιοῦσιν ἄνθρωποι ἄλλοθέν ποθεν ζητοῦντες τὸ εὖ ἢ παρὰ τῶν θεῶν, καὶ ὅμοιον, ὥσπερ ἂν εἴ τις ἐν βασιλευομένῃ χώρᾳ τῶν πολιτῶν τινα ὕπαρχον θεραπεύσαι, ἀμελήσας αὐτοῦ τοῦ πάντων ἄρχοντος καὶ βασιλεύοντος. τοιοῦτον γὰρ οἴονται ποιεῖν καὶ τοὺς ἀνθρώπους. ἐπεὶ γὰρ ἔστι τε θεὸς καὶ οὗτος πάντων κύριος, δεῖν δὲ ὡμολόγηται παρὰ τοῦ κυρίου τἀγαθὸν αἰτεῖν, πάντες τε, οὓς μὲν ἂν φιλῶσι καὶ οἷς ἂν χαίρωσι, τούτοις διδόασι τἀγαθά, πρὸς δὲ οὓς ἐναντίως ἔχουσι, τἀναντία, δῆλον ὅτι ταῦτα πρακτέον, οἷς τυγχάνει ὁ θεὸς χαίρων.

457 Iamblichus *Vita Pythagorae* 175 (DK58D3) μετὰ δὲ τὸ θεῖόν τε καὶ τὸ δαιμόνιον πλεῖστον ποιεῖσθαι λόγον γονέων τε καὶ νόμου, καὶ τούτων ὑπήκοον αὐτὸν κατασκευάζειν, μὴ πλαστῶς, ἀλλὰ πεπεισμένως. καθόλου δὲ ᾤοντο δεῖν ὑπολαμβάνειν, μηδὲν εἶναι μεῖζον κακὸν ἀναρχίας· οὐ γὰρ πεφυκέναι τὸν ἄνθρωπον διασώζεσθαι μηδενὸς ἐπιστατοῦντος. (176) τὸ μένειν ἐν τοῖς πατρίοις ἔθεσί τε καὶ νομίμοις ἐδοκίμαζον οἱ ἄνδρες ἐκεῖνοι, κἂν ᾖ μικρῷ χείρω ἑτέρων· τὸ γὰρ ῥᾳδίως ἀποπηδᾶν ἀπὸ τῶν ὑπαρχόντων νόμων καὶ οἰκείους εἶναι καινοτομίας οὐδαμῶς εἶναι σύμφορον καὶ σωτήριον.

458 Plato *Phaedo* 62B (DK44B15) ὁ μὲν οὖν ἐν ἀπορρήτοις λεγόμενος περὶ αὐτῶν λόγος, ὡς ἔν τινι φρουρᾷ ἐσμεν οἱ ἄνθρωποι καὶ οὐ δεῖ δὴ ἑαυτὸν ἐκ ταύτης λύειν οὐδ' ἀποδιδράσκειν, μέγας τέ τίς μοι φαίνεται καὶ οὐ ῥᾴδιος διιδεῖν· οὐ μέντοι ἀλλὰ τόδε γέ μοι δοκεῖ, ὦ Κέβης, εὖ λέγεσθαι, τὸ θεοὺς εἶναι ἡμῶν τοὺς ἐπιμελουμένους καὶ ἡμᾶς τοὺς ἀνθρώπους ἓν τῶν κτημάτων τοῖς θεοῖς εἶναι.

456 I want to indicate the first principles of the worship of the gods which Pythagoras and his followers put forward. All the rules they define for action or refraining from action are devised with a view to our relationship with the divine. This is their principle. All of life is ordered with the object of following god. And this is the theory of this philosophy, that men behave ludicrously if they look for the good anywhere other than from the hands of the gods – it is as if, in a monarchy, one were to pay court to some subordinate officer among the citizens, neglecting the king and ruler of all himself. They think that mankind should behave as one would in a monarchy. For since there is a god, and he has authority over all, and it is agreed that one must ask for the good from the one who is in authority, and all give goods to those whom they love and in whom they delight, but the opposite to those whom they hate – it is clear that we should do those things in which god happens to delight.

457 After the gods and the divine spirits [*i.e. daimons*] they devote most discussion to one's parents and the law, and they say that one must make oneself subject to them, not in pretence but out of conviction. In general they thought one should take for granted that there is no greater evil than anarchy; for it is not in human nature to survive if nobody is in charge. These philosophers approved of a city's remaining in its ancestral customs and laws, even if they were a little worse than those of other cities; for to skip easily out of the existing laws and to be at home with innovation is not at all advantageous or salutary.

458 The theory about this which is imparted as a secret doctrine – that we men are in a prison, and that no one may set himself free from it and run away – this seems to me a great matter, in which the truth is not easy to make out. But at any rate *this* is something that in my opinion is well said, Cebes, that those who have us in their care are gods, and that we men are one of the gods' possessions.

456–7 probably derive from Aristoxenus (cf. Stobaeus *Anth.* IV, 25, 45 and IV, 1, 40, DK 58 D 4). His detailed account of Pythagorean ethics is full of Platonic echoes, and (if historical and not just an attempt to make Plato a plagiarist) probably represents the views of the 'last generation of Pythagoreans' in the middle of the fourth century B.C. (cf. **421**). Nonetheless these men were pupils of Philolaus, and comparison with **458** (Philolaus' teaching: see **420**) makes it likely that Aristoxenus preserves the main emphases of the Pythagorean ethics of the late fifth century. In any event these texts remind us that a good part of the continuing attraction of Pythagoreanism lay in the religious and moral certainties it offered.

CONCLUSION

The Pythagoreanism Aristotle reports in **430** (probably on the basis largely of oral sources) is very similar in its central ideas and emphases and in its general lack of sophistication to the teachings we have ascribed to Pythagoras himself. It is in other texts that the distinctive contribution of fifth-century Pythagoreans (above all Philolaus, but doubtless not him alone) becomes apparent. They gave more abstract and sometimes more detailed accounts of metaphysical and cosmological topics which take their origin from the oldest Pythagorean speculations. They did so in a style derived partly from earlier natural philosophers (and from Eleatics) of the same century. There is something rather magnificent about their attempt to show how the governing concept of *harmonia* unlocks the key to every area of philosophy: cosmology, astronomy, psychology; even their obsession with order in ethics and politics can be read as reflecting this central preoccupation. In the project of mathematicizing science they got scarcely beyond numerological fancy, despite the boldness and ingenuity of some of their thinking. But the idea at the heart of the project – if it is legitimate to regard it as the same idea as the Pythagoreans conceived – has now borne astonishingly abundant fruit.

THE IONIAN RESPONSE

Parmenides' metaphysics dominated fifth-century Ionian philosophy, which constitutes the last stage of Presocratic speculation. Individual, ingenious and often creative as the leading Ionian thinkers were, each of them is appropriately seen as responding to his radical critique of common-sense belief in the world about us. This is immediately obvious in the case of Melissus, whose fragments present a revised version of Parmenides' arguments. It is no less true of the pluralisms of Anaxagoras and of the atomists Leucippus and Democritus. And the reworked material monism of Diogenes, which is perhaps the fifth-century system closest in spirit to those of the Milesians, is yet founded on a determination to avoid transgressing the Eleatic principle that what is cannot come to be from what is not, a principle accepted by all these writers, as also by Empedocles. It is not easy to specify any other Eleatic canons which they were all agreed in upholding. For example, Anaxagoras, Melissus and the atomists (Empedocles, too) held that plurality cannot come from an original unity: if there is to be plurality, it, like reality, must be ultimate. But would Diogenes have concurred? Most of them (and again, Empedocles also) no longer take motion as something they can just assume in their cosmogonies (as the Milesians had done); they endeavour to account for its existence. But the atomists were apparently content to say that there had always been motion, without further elaboration. It would therefore be wrong to try to paint too tidy a picture of the Eleatic impact on Ionian thought. Yet since one of the most interesting and important aspects of the history of early Greek philosophy – and it is an aspect that can easily be lost from sight – is its peculiar continuity, a part of each of the main chapters that follow will be devoted to showing, where possible in the philosophers' own words, how these post-Parmenidean systems are deliberately designed to take account of the findings of the *Truth* (mediated, in the atomists' case, by Melissus).

CHAPTER XII

Anaxagoras of Clazomenae

DATE AND LIFE

459 Diogenes Laertius II, 7 (DK 59 A 1) λέγεται δὲ κατὰ τὴν Ξέρξου διάβασιν εἴκοσιν ἐτῶν εἶναι, βεβιωκέναι δὲ ἑβδομήκοντα δύο. φησὶ δ' Ἀπολλόδωρος ἐν τοῖς Χρονικοῖς γεγενῆσθαι αὐτὸν τῇ ἑβδομηκοστῇ ὀλυμπιάδι (i.e. 500–497 b.c.), τεθνηκέναι δὲ τῷ πρώτῳ ἔτει τῆς ἑβδομηκοστῆς ὀγδόης (i.e. 468/7; ὀγδοηκοστῆς ὀγδόης Scaliger, i.e. 428/7). ἤρξατο δὲ φιλοσοφεῖν Ἀθήνησιν ἐπὶ Καλλίου (i.e. 456/5) ἐτῶν εἴκοσι ὤν, ὥς φησι Δημήτριος ὁ Φαληρεὺς ἐν τῇ τῶν Ἀρχόντων ἀναγραφῇ, ἔνθα καί φασιν αὐτὸν ἐτῶν διατρῖψαι τριάκοντα...(12)...περὶ δὲ τῆς δίκης αὐτοῦ διάφορα λέγεται. Σωτίων μὲν γάρ φησιν ἐν τῇ Διαδοχῇ τῶν φιλοσόφων ὑπὸ Κλέωνος αὐτὸν ἀσεβείας κριθῆναι, διότι τὸν ἥλιον μύδρον ἔλεγε διάπυρον· ἀπολογησαμένου δὲ ὑπὲρ αὐτοῦ Περικλέους τοῦ μαθητοῦ, πέντε ταλάντοις ζημιωθῆναι καὶ φυγαδευθῆναι. Σάτυρος δ' ἐν τοῖς Βίοις ὑπὸ Θουκυδίδου φησὶν εἰσαχθῆναι τὴν δίκην ἀντιπολιτευομένου τῷ Περικλεῖ· καὶ οὐ μόνον ἀσεβείας, ἀλλὰ καὶ μηδισμοῦ· καὶ ἀπόντα καταδικασθῆναι θανάτῳ...(14)...καὶ τέλος ἀποχωρήσας εἰς Λάμψακον αὐτόθι κατέστρεψεν. ὅτε καὶ τῶν ἀρχόντων τῆς πόλεως ἀξιούντων τί βούλεται αὐτῷ γενέσθαι, φάναι, τοὺς παῖδας ἐν ᾧ ἂν ἀποθάνῃ μηνὶ κατ' ἔτος παίζειν συγχωρεῖν. καὶ φυλάττεται τὸ ἔθος καὶ νῦν. (15) τελευτήσαντα δὴ αὐτὸν ἔθαψαν ἐντίμως οἱ Λαμψακηνοί....

460 Aristotle *Met.* A3, 984a11 (= **334**) Ἀναξαγόρας δὲ ὁ Κλαζομένιος τῇ μὲν ἡλικίᾳ πρότερος ὢν τούτου (*sc.* Ἐμπεδοκλέους), τοῖς δ' ἔργοις ὕστερος...

461 Plato *Phaedrus* 270A (DK 59 A 15) ὃ (*sc.* τὸ ὑψηλόνουν) καὶ Περικλῆς πρὸς τῷ εὐφυὴς εἶναι ἐκτήσατο· προσπεσὼν γὰρ οἶμαι τοιούτῳ ὄντι Ἀναξαγόρᾳ, μετεωρολογίας ἐμπλησθεὶς καὶ ἐπὶ φύσιν νοῦ τε καὶ ἀνοίας ἀφικόμενος, ὧν δὴ πέρι τὸν πολὺν λόγον ἐποιεῖτο Ἀναξαγόρας, ἐντεῦθεν εἵλκυσεν ἐπὶ τὴν τῶν λόγων τέχνην τὸ πρόσφορον αὐτῇ.

459 He is said to have been twenty years old at the time of Xerxes' crossing, and to have lived to seventy-two. Apollodorus says in his *Chronicles* that he was born in the seventieth Olympiad (500–497 B.C.) and died in the first year of the eighty-eighth (428/7). He began to be a philosopher at Athens in the archonship of Callias (456/5), at the age of twenty, as Demetrius Phalereus tells us in his *Register of Archons*, and they say he spent thirty years there.... There are different accounts given of his trial. Sotion, in his *Succession of Philosophers*, says that he was prosecuted by Cleon for impiety, because he maintained that the sun was a red-hot mass of metal, and that after Pericles, his pupil, had made a speech in his defence, he was fined five talents and exiled. Satyrus in his *Lives*, on the other hand, says that the charge was brought by Thucydides in his political campaign against Pericles; and he adds that the charge was not only for impiety but for Medism as well; and he was condemned to death in absence...Finally he withdrew to Lampsacus, and there died. It is said that when the rulers of the city asked him what privilege he wished to be granted, he replied that the children should be given a holiday every year in the month in which he died. The custom is preserved to the present day. When he died the Lampsacenes buried him with full honours.

460 Anaxagoras of Clazomenae, who, though older than Empedocles, was later [*or*: inferior] in his philosophical activity... (*Tr. Ross*)

461 Pericles acquired high-mindedness in addition to his natural talents; for he fell in, I believe, with Anaxagoras, who already possessed this quality, and steeping himself in natural speculation, and grasping the true nature of mind and folly (which were the subjects of much of Anaxagoras' discussion), he drew from that source anything that could contribute towards the art of debate.

These passages suffice to show the difficulty of determining the dates of Anaxagoras' life. The first section of **459**, most of which probably represents mere conjecture by Apollodorus based on a statement of Demetrius Phalereus which it is impossible to reconstruct, immediately presents acute problems of chronology; for even if we accept, as we apparently must, the emendation of Scaliger and conclude that Anaxagoras lived from *c.* 500 to 428 B.C., it is still necessary, in order to make the passage consistent, to suppose that the words ἐπὶ Καλλίου, 'in the archonship of Callias', should rather read ἐπὶ Καλλιάδου, 'in the archonship of Calliades', i.e. 480 B.C. That would give the following outline:

Born	500/499 B.C.
Came to Athens and began his philosophical activities	480/79 B.C.
Died at Lampascus	428/7 B.C.

All that can be said is that these dates may well be approximately right; for **460**, which might have thrown some light on the problem, is robbed of most of its value, not only by our ignorance of the exact dates of Empedocles (see pp. 281f.), but also by the ambiguity of its last phrase, which may mean either that Anaxagoras wrote his book after Empedocles (the more obvious interpretation), or that he was more up-to-date (or even, by Alexander's interpretation, inferior) in his views.[1]

[1] For discussion of **460** see Ross *ad loc.*, Kahn, *Anaximander*, 163–5 and D. O'Brien, *JHS* 88 (1968), 93–113.

The problem of the date of his trial is even more difficult. Its historicity has sometimes been doubted (as e.g. by K. J. Dover, *Talanta* 7 (1975), 24–54), but most scholars accept Plutarch's story[1] that Anaxagoras was the victim of a decree against atheists introduced by one Diopeithes *c.* 433 B.C., whether or not he was actually brought to trial, and on that account left Athens. A. E. Taylor, however, held that 'the account given by Satyrus (cf. **459**) was right in placing his prosecution at the beginning and not at the close of Pericles' political career', i.e. *c.* 450 B.C. (*CQ* 11 (1917), 81–7). Certainly there is a fair amount of evidence which cumulatively supports the conclusion that Anaxagoras' immediate impact as a philosopher was made mostly in Athens[2] before 450 B.C. Plato gives the impression that in the years directly preceding the Peloponnesian War (431–404 B.C.) the city's intellectual life was dominated by the sophists, with whom he contrasts Anaxagoras as the last of the old philosophers (*Hipp. Maj.* 281C, 282E–283B); and he represents Socrates as hearing of Anaxagoras' views only by a reading of his book (*Phaedo* 97B–99C). Likewise the story of the honours accorded to Anaxagoras after his death by the Lampsacenes[3] suggests a considerable period of residence there, and not in Athens, in his later life. On the other hand Anaxagoras' name is associated with the fall of a large meteorite at Aegospotami in Thrace *c.* 467 B.C. (taken, so we are told, as fulfilling a prediction of his: **503** below). Aeschylus echoes Anaxagorean theories in the *Supplices* (?463 B.C.: the causes of the flooding of the Nile, *Suppl.* 559–61; cf. **502** below) and the *Eumenides* (458 B.C.: the mother contributes nothing to the generation of offspring but a place where the father's seed may grow, *Eum.* 657–66;

cf. Aristotle *de gen. animalium* Δ1, 763b30–3, DK59A107). The only fifth-century philosopher whose ideas have clearly influenced Anaxagoras is Parmenides (see pp. 358ff.), although it is possible that he reacts against both Zeno (see pp. 360ff.) and Empedocles (see e.g. pp. 370, 384). All this points to a *floruit* around 470–460 B.C.[4]

[1] **462** Plutarch *Pericles* 32 (DK59A17) περὶ δὲ τοῦτον τὸν χρόνον...καὶ ψήφισμα Διοπείθης ἔγραψεν εἰσαγγέλλεσθαι τοὺς τὰ θεῖα μὴ νομίζοντας ἢ λόγους περὶ τῶν μεταρσίων διδάσκοντας ἀπερειδόμενος εἰς Περικλέα δι᾽ Ἀναξαγόρου τὴν ὑπόνοιαν...Ἀναξαγόραν δὲ φοβηθεὶς ἐξέπεμψεν ἐκ τῆς πόλεως. (*At about this time [sc. the beginning of the Peloponnesian War]...Diopeithes introduced a decree to impeach those who did not believe in religion or who taught theories about the heavens, in an attempt to direct suspicion against Pericles via Anaxagoras...And Pericles in fear helped Anaxagoras leave the city.*)

[2] Anaxagoras is said to have taught both Archelaus (see ch. XIII) and Euripides. Cf. **463** Strabo 14, p. 645 Cas. Κλαζομένιος δ᾽ ἦν ἀνὴρ ἐπιφανὴς Ἀναξαγόρας ὁ φυσικός, Ἀναξιμένους ὁμιλητὴς τοῦ Μιλησίου· διήκουσαν δὲ τούτου Ἀρχέλαος ὁ φυσικὸς καὶ Εὐριπίδης ὁ ποιητής. (*Anaxagoras the natural philosopher was a distinguished Clazomenian, an associate of Anaximenes of Miletus; and his own pupils included Archelaus the natural philosopher and Euripides the poet.*) Since the statement that Anaxagoras was an associate of Anaximenes can mean no more than that he reproduced elements of Anaximenes' cosmology (cf. p. 372), it could be argued that the tradition of Anaxagoras' own influence on Archelaus and Euripides need imply no more. But even by 450 B.C. Euripides was at least thirty years old, and it seems almost certain that, in a society as small as the intellectual circle at Athens, he would already have made the acquaintance of Anaxagoras. For passages in Euripides in which the influence of Anaxagoras is said to be manifest see DK59A20a–c, 30, 33, 48 and 112, the last of which seems on the whole to be a good deal the most convincing.

[3] Cf. **464** Alcidamas *ap.* Aristotelem *Rhet.* B23, 1398b15 (DK59A23) καὶ Λαμψακηνοὶ Ἀναξαγόραν ξένον ὄντα ἔθαψαν καὶ τιμῶσιν ἔτι καὶ νῦν. (*The inhabitants of Lampsacus buried Anaxagoras although he was a foreigner and even to this day still honour him.*)

[4] For a recent review of the disputed issues in Anaxagorean chronology see the judicious remarks of D. Sider, *The Fragments of Anaxagoras* (Meisenheim an Glan, 1981), 1–11. Debate continues: Taylor's views are broadly endorsed by L. Woodbury, *Phoenix* 35 (1981), 295–315, but a late date for Anaxagoras' arrival in Athens (456 B.C.) is supported by J. Mansfeld, *Mnemosyne* ser. 4, 32 (1979), 39–60, 33 (1980), 17–95.

WRITINGS

465 Plato *Apology* 26D μὰ Δί᾽, ὦ ἄνδρες δικασταί, ἐπεὶ τὸν μὲν ἥλιον λίθον φησὶν εἶναι, τὴν δὲ σελήνην γῆν. Ἀναξαγόρου οἴει κατηγορεῖν, ὦ φίλε Μέλητε, καὶ οὕτω καταφρονεῖς τῶνδε καὶ οἴει αὐτοὺς ἀπείρους γραμμάτων εἶναι, ὥστε οὐκ εἰδέναι ὅτι τὰ Ἀναξαγόρου βιβλία τοῦ Κλαζομενίου γέμει τούτων τῶν λόγων;

καὶ δὴ καὶ οἱ νέοι ταῦτα παρ' ἐμοῦ μανθάνουσιν ἃ ἔξεστιν ἐνίοτε, εἰ πάνυ πολλοῦ, δραχμῆς ἐκ τῆς ὀρχήστρας πριαμένους Σωκράτους καταγελᾶν, ἐὰν προσποιῆται ἑαυτοῦ εἶναι, ἄλλως τε καὶ οὕτως ἄτοπα ὄντα.

466 Diogenes Laertius I, 16 οἱ δὲ ἀνὰ ἓν σύγγραμμα Μέλισσος, Παρμενίδης, 'Αναξαγόρας.

465 'By Zeus, gentlemen of the jury, it is because he says that the sun is a stone, the moon earth.' Do you imagine, friend Meletus, that you are accusing Anaxagoras, and do you despise the jury, and think them so illiterate that they do not know that the rolls of Anaxagoras of Clazomenae are packed with such theories? The young, I suppose, learn these things from me – things which you can sometimes buy for a drachma, dear as that may be, in the *orchestra*, and then mock Socrates if he claims them as his own, particularly when they are so absurd.

466 Those who wrote only one book include Melissus, Parmenides and Anaxagoras.

Very probably Anaxagoras did indeed write only the one book; various other writings attributed to him by late and unreliable authorities – a treatise on perspective, another on the squaring of the circle and a book of problems – if they ever existed at all, are most unlikely to be the genuine work of Anaxagoras. His one book, moreover, though it is said by Burnet (apparently on the strength of the plural βιβλία in **465**, which 'perhaps implies that it filled more than one roll')[1] to have been 'of some length', would seem more probably to have been quite short. Not only do the fragments preserved by Simplicius seem to give us, with considerable repetitions, the whole basis of his system; but also the statement in **465** that the book could be bought for a drachma is a strong indication that it ran to no great length. The economics of Athens in 399 B.C. are by no means easy to reconstruct, but what evidence there is shows that the purchasing power of a drachma was by then quite small. No doubt in the latter part of his book Anaxagoras pursued his general principles into such detailed topics as astronomy, meteorology, physiology and sense-perception – subjects on which there is plenty of second-hand evidence but very few and scanty fragments. But he must in that case have dealt with them with the same summary brevity that characterizes some of the fragments surviving from the earlier part. The extant fragments, which together comprise about a thousand words, can hardly represent less than an eighth of the original whole and may well represent a considerably larger fraction.[2]

[1] Simplicius also implies that in his day Anaxagoras' work was divided into more than one part: at e.g., *in Phys.* 34, 29 (DK 59 B 4) and 155, 26 (DK 59 B 1) he speaks of 'the first part' (or 'book') of the work *On Nature*. This certainly seems to tell in favour of Burnet's view. But there is nothing in Socrates' words in **465** to suggest that the book was a long one except the plural βιβλία, 'books'; and the word βιβλίον, even in the plural, carries (at this date at least) no definite implication of length. It seems more likely, for the reasons given in this section, that if the work was originally divided, as it was in Simplicius' time, into more than one part, they were very short parts.

[2] Prof. A. H. M. Jones very kindly corroborated this calculation with the following note: 'The simplest calculation is on the assumption that the copyist would be a slave χωρὶς οἰκῶν. His owner would expect an ἀποφορά from a skilled slave of at least 2 obols a day; Timarchus' σκυτοτόμοι (Aeschines I, 97) paid him 2 obols and their foreman 3 obols; Nicias and others in the fifth century got 1 obol a day for unskilled mine slaves, but this included amortization (the hirer had to replace those who died) (Xenophon *Poroi* IV, 14–15). Food is reckoned at 2 obols a day by Dem. IV, 28, but this is probably an underestimate, as Dem. is trying to prove that his scheme could be run quite cheaply. The Eleusinian accounts (*I.G.*[2] II and III 1672–3, of 329–327 B.C.) allow 3 obols a day for public slaves for τροφή. One must also allow for clothes and other extras, and for the slave's own profit (he would have to allow for slack times when he had no work, and he also expected to put by to pay for his freedom); also for the cost of papyrus (I fear this cannot be calculated as we do not know in what units it was bought). However, a man's time alone would amount to at least a drachma a day; skilled men (carpenters, stonemasons etc.) are paid 2 to 2½ drachmae a day in the Eleusinian accounts.

A book sold for a drachma would, therefore, be such as could be copied in well under a day.'

ANAXAGORAS' REACTION TO PARMENIDES AND THE EARLIER PLURALISTS

467 Fr. 1, Simplicius *in Phys.* 155, 26   ὁμοῦ χρήματα πάντα ἦν, ἄπειρα καὶ πλῆθος καὶ σμικρότητα· καὶ γὰρ τὸ σμικρὸν ἄπειρον ἦν. καὶ πάντων ὁμοῦ ἐόντων οὐδὲν ἔνδηλον ἦν ὑπὸ σμικρότητος· πάντα γὰρ ἀήρ τε καὶ αἰθὴρ κατεῖχεν, ἀμφότερα ἄπειρα ἐόντα· ταῦτα γὰρ μέγιστα ἔνεστιν ἐν τοῖς σύμπασι καὶ πλήθει καὶ μεγέθει.

468 Fr. 4 (latter half), *ibid.* 34, 21 (for rest of fr. 4 see **483** and **498**) πρὶν δὲ ἀποκριθῆναι ταῦτα πάντων ὁμοῦ ἐόντων οὐδὲ χροιὴ ἔνδηλος ἦν οὐδεμία· ἀπεκώλυε γὰρ ἡ σύμμιξις ἁπάντων χρημάτων, τοῦ τε διεροῦ καὶ τοῦ ξηροῦ καὶ τοῦ θερμοῦ καὶ τοῦ ψυχροῦ καὶ τοῦ λαμπροῦ καὶ τοῦ ζοφεροῦ, καὶ γῆς πολλῆς ἐνεούσης καὶ σπερμάτων ἀπείρων πλῆθος οὐδὲν ἐοικότων ἀλλήλοις. οὐδὲ γὰρ τῶν ἄλλων οὐδὲν ἔοικε τὸ ἕτερον τῷ ἑτέρῳ. τούτων δὲ οὕτως ἐχόντων ἐν τῷ σύμπαντι χρὴ δοκεῖν ἐνεῖναι πάντα χρήματα.

467 All things were together, infinite in respect of both number and smallness; for the small too was infinite. And while all things were together, none of them were plain because of their smallness; for air and aither held all things in subjection, both of them being infinite; for these are the greatest ingredients in the mixture of all things, both in number and in size.

468 But before these things were separated off, while all things were together, there was not even any colour plain; for the mixture of all things prevented it, of the moist and the dry, the hot and the cold, the bright and the dark, since there was much earth in the mixture and seeds countless in number and in no respect like one another. For none of the other things either are like one to the other. And since this is so, we must suppose that all things were in the whole.

Simplicius, to whom we owe the preservation of almost all the fragments, tells us that **467** was the opening of Anaxagoras' book. It shows at the outset how extreme was the reaction of Anaxagoras against the Eleatic monism. Whereas Parmenides had written (in **296**):

οὐδέ ποτ' ἦν οὐδ' ἔσται, ἐπεὶ νῦν ἐστιν ὁμοῦ πᾶν,
ἕν, συνεχές·

('nor was it at some time past, nor shall it be, since it *is* now all at once, one, continuous'), Anaxagoras in his very first sentence starts by substituting ὁμοῦ πάντα χρήματα for ὁμοῦ πᾶν, ἕν; next admits the forbidden 'was', and finally, in the words 'infinite in smallness', denies also the implication of indivisibility in Parmenides' 'continuous'. The world, according to Anaxagoras, arose from a universal mixture of every single thing that was ultimately to emerge; only by putting 'all things together' into this original mixture could coming into being and perishing be effectually eliminated. This is put very clearly in the following passage:

469 Fr. 17, Simplicius *in Phys.* 163, 20   τὸ δὲ γίνεσθαι καὶ ἀπόλλυσθαι οὐκ ὀρθῶς νομίζουσιν οἱ Ἕλληνες· οὐδὲν γὰρ χρῆμα γίνεται
οὐδὲ ἀπόλλυται, ἀλλ' ἀπὸ ἐόντων χρημάτων συμμίσγεταί τε καὶ
διακρίνεται. καὶ οὕτως ἂν ὀρθῶς καλοῖεν τό τε γίνεσθαι συμμίσγεσθαι
καὶ τὸ ἀπόλλυσθαι διακρίνεσθαι.

469 The Greeks are wrong to recognize coming into being and perishing; for nothing comes into being nor perishes, but is rather compounded or dissolved from things that are. So they would be right to call coming into being composition and perishing dissolution.

358

Here it cannot be doubted that Anaxagoras is explicitly accepting one of the Parmenidean demands. There can be little doubt either that the rejection of the other demands, in **467**, is equally deliberate.

The original mixture, as Anaxagoras says in both **467** and **468**, was so uniform a mixture of so many diverse ingredients that nothing would have been perceptible to an imaginary observer except perhaps 'air[1] and aither' (see pp. 372ff.). The list of ingredients in the long sentence in **468**, which has been a source of difficulty to modern commentators, is probably not intended to be exhaustive. Apart from the 'numberless seeds', of which more will be said later, the other ingredients listed can be reasonably explained by reference to the views of others of Anaxagoras' predecessors. There had in the past been two main types of pluralism. There had been those who, like Anaximander and Heraclitus, had in one way or another regarded the world as a battlefield of the opposites; and Empedocles (if his work preceded Anaxagoras') had solidified the warring opposites into the four eternal and immutable elements. Neither type of pluralism, to Anaxagoras' mind, went far enough. His own original mixture must contain, not only the traditional opposites nor only the Empedoclean elements – here probably exemplified by earth, because two of the others, air and aither (or fire), have already been mentioned as ingredients in **467**; it must contain also 'innumerable seeds in no way like each other'.

---

[1] Cf. **470** Aristotle *Phys.* Δ6, 213a22 οἱ μὲν οὖν δεικνύναι πειρώμενοι ὅτι οὐκ ἔστιν (*sc.* τὸ κενόν), οὐχ ὃ βούλονται λέγειν οἱ ἄνθρωποι κενόν, τοῦτ' ἐξελέγχουσιν, ἀλλ' ἁμαρτάνοντες λέγουσιν, ὥσπερ Ἀναξαγόρας καὶ οἱ τοῦτον τὸν τρόπον ἐλέγχοντες. ἐπιδεικνύουσι γὰρ ὅτι ἔστι τι ὁ ἀήρ, στρεβλοῦντες τοὺς ἀσκοὺς καὶ δεικνύντες ὡς ἰσχυρὸς ὁ ἀήρ, καὶ ἐναπολαμβάνοντες ἐν ταῖς κλεψύδραις. (*Those who try to show that the void does not exist do not disprove what people really mean by it, but argue erroneously; this is true of Anaxagoras and of those who refute the existence of the void in this way. They merely give an ingenious demonstration that air is something – by straining wine-skins and showing the resistance of the air, and by cutting it off in clepsydras.*) (After Hardie.) In Anaxagoras, therefore, air, being corporeal, is clearly distinguished from the non-existent void. Cf. also Aristotle *de caelo* Δ2, 309a19 (DK59A68), where Aristotle groups Empedocles and Anaxagoras together as (1) denying the existence of the void (cf. Empedocles, **536** below), (2) giving no explanation of differences of weight. The clepsydra was a metal vessel with a narrow neck and with its base perforated, like a modern coffee-strainer, with numerous small holes. For details of Anaxagoras' experiments with it see [Aristotle] *Problemata* XVI, 8, 914b9 (DK59A69). It is described, not to show that air is corporeal, but to illuminate the nature of respiration, in a famous passage of Empedocles, from which we quote the relevant lines: **471** Empedocles fr. 100, Aristotle *de respiratione* 7, 473b9

ἔνθεν ἔπειθ' ὁπόταν μὲν ἀπαίξῃ τέρεν αἷμα,
αἰθὴρ παφλάζων καταίσσεται οἴδματι μάργῳ,

εὖτε δ' ἀναθρῴσκῃ, πάλιν ἐκπνέει, ὥσπερ ὅταν παῖς
κλεψύδρῃ παίζουσα διειπετέος χαλκοῖο –
10   εὖτε μὲν αὐλοῦ πορθμὸν ἐπ' εὐειδεῖ χερὶ θεῖσα
εἰς ὕδατος βάπτῃσι τέρεν δέμας ἀργυφέοιο,
οὐδεὶς ἄγγοσδ' ὄμβρος ἐσέρχεται, ἀλλά μιν εἴργει
ἀέρος ὄγκος ἔσωθε πεσὼν ἐπὶ τρήματα πυκνά,
εἰσόκ' ἀποστεγάσῃ πυκινὸν ῥόον· αὐτὰρ ἔπειτα
15   πνεύματος ἐλλείποντος ἐσέρχεται αἴσιμον ὕδωρ.
ὡς δ' αὕτως, ὅθ' ὕδωρ μὲν ἔχῃ κατὰ βένθεα χαλκοῦ
πορθμοῦ χωσθέντος βροτέῳ χροῒ ἠδὲ πόροιο,
αἰθὴρ δ' ἐκτὸς ἔσω λελιημένος ὄμβρον ἐρύκει,
ἀμφὶ πύλας ἠθμοῖο δυσήχεος ἄκρα κρατύνων,
20   εἰσόκε χειρὶ μεθῇ, τότε δ' αὖ πάλιν, ἔμπαλιν ἢ πρίν,
πνεύματος ἐμπίπτοντος ὑπεκθέει αἴσιμον ὕδωρ.

(Then, when the fluid blood rushes away thence, the bubbling air rushes in with violent surge ; and when the blood leaps up, the air is breathed out again, just as when a girl plays with a clepsydra of gleaming brass. When she puts the mouth of the pipe against her shapely hand and dips it into the fluid mass of shining water, no liquid enters the vessel, but the bulk of the air within, pressing upon the frequent perforations, holds it back until she uncovers the dense stream; but then, as the air yields, an equal bulk of water enters. In just the same way, when water occupies the depths of the brazen vessel and the passage of its mouth is blocked by human hand, the air outside, striving inwards, holds the water back, holding its surface firm at the gates of the ill-sounding neck until she lets go with her hand; and then again (the reverse of what happened before), as the breath rushes in, an equal bulk of water runs out before it.)

ANAXAGORAS' REACTION TO ZENO

472   Fr. 3, Simplicius *in Phys.* 164, 17   οὔτε γὰρ τοῦ σμικροῦ
ἔστι τό γε ἐλάχιστον, ἀλλ' ἔλασσον ἀεί (τὸ γὰρ ἐὸν οὐκ ἔστι τὸ μὴ
οὐκ εἶναι) – ἀλλὰ καὶ τοῦ μεγάλου ἀεί ἐστι μεῖζον. καὶ ἴσον ἐστὶ τῷ
σμικρῷ πλῆθος, πρὸς ἑαυτὸ δὲ ἕκαστόν ἐστι καὶ μέγα καὶ σμικρόν.

473   Fr. 5, *ibid.* 156, 10   τούτων δὲ οὕτω διακεκριμένων γινώσκειν
χρὴ ὅτι πάντα οὐδὲν ἐλάσσω ἐστὶν οὐδὲ πλείω· οὐ γὰρ ἀνυστὸν
πάντων πλείω εἶναι, ἀλλὰ πάντα ἴσα ἀεί.

472   Neither is there a smallest part of what is small, but there
is always a smaller (for it is impossible that what is should cease
to be). Likewise there is always something larger than what is
large. And it is equal in respect of number to what is small, each
thing, in relation to itself, being both large and small.

473   And when these things have been thus separated, we must
know that all things are neither more nor less; for it is not possible
that there should be more than all, but all things are always equal.

There is reason to suppose that in these two brief fragments
Anaxagoras is explicitly responding to Zeno.[1] It is at any rate a

striking coincidence that, of the only two of Zeno's arguments against plurality which have survived in his own words, one should end as follows:

474 Zeno fr. 1, Simplicius *in Phys.* 141, 6 (= **316**) οὕτως εἰ πολλά ἐστιν, ἀνάγκη αὐτὰ μικρά τε εἶναι καὶ μεγάλα· μικρὰ μὲν ὥστε μὴ ἔχειν μέγεθος, μεγάλα δὲ ὥστε ἄπειρα εἶναι.

474 So if there is a plurality, things must be both small and great; so small as to have no magnitude at all, so great as to be infinite.

And the other should begin thus:

475 Zeno fr. 3, Simplicius *in Phys.* 140, 29 (= **315**) εἰ πολλά ἐστιν, ἀνάγκη τοσαῦτα εἶναι ὅσα ἐστὶ καὶ οὔτε πλείονα αὐτῶν οὔτε ἐλάττονα.

475 If there is a plurality, things must be just as many as they are, neither more nor less.

Since both these statements are of a somewhat unusual character, it seems most likely that, when Anaxagoras echoes them both so exactly as he does, he is doing so quite deliberately.

¹ Both philosophers probably wrote in the decade 470–460 b.c., and any guess as to which wrote first is a little hazardous. See further M. Schofield, *An Essay on Anaxagoras* (Cambridge, 1980), 81–2 (arguing against the view that Anaxagoras precedes Zeno).

473 is of comparatively little importance within the overall framework of Anaxagoras' system. Its point is presumably that, whatever changes occur in the world, the number of things (or kinds of thing) must remain constant. But it gains in interest if written in response to **475**. For Zeno had inferred from his proposition that pluralities must be limited in number. Anaxagoras, believing as he does that reality consists of an infinite number of things (**467**), will be correctly rejecting that inference. Just because there are neither more nor less than the things there are, it does not follow that their number is finite. This insight suggests that Anaxagoras had a clearer view of the nature of infinity than Zeno.

The same is indicated by **472**. The second limb of the argument whose conclusion is given in **474** had been designed to show that the notion of infinite divisibility is intolerably paradoxical – if a thing is divisible into an infinite number of parts each of which has positive magnitude, it must be infinitely large. The atomists Leucippus and Democritus accepted this argument, and concluded that the idea that things are infinitely divisible must therefore be rejected. They accordingly posited as a fundamental principle of their physics that reality is composed of indivisible bodies or atoms (545-6 below). Anaxagoras, by contrast, shows in 472 that he finds nothing paradoxical in the notion of infinite divisibility. Here again, if he knew Zeno's argument for the thesis of 474, he was clear-headed enough to reject it: however small the pieces into which something is divided (Zeller's reading τομῇ, 'by cutting', for τὸ μή is attractive) they have positive magnitude (not the null size of Zeno's first limb), but there is no reason to fear that, from the fact that the division has no last term, it follows that the sum of its terms is infinitely large (as Zeno's second limb concluded). Each thing may in fact be described as large or small indifferently, since whatever a thing's size it contains a portion of everything (481-2). Thus Anaxagoras' theory of matter may be read as devised, like that of the atomists, to answer Zeno; and when that answer is added to his answer to Parmenides, one half of the basis of his system is now complete. He is enabled to devise a cosmogony and to give an account of change which does indeed eliminate the forbidden coming-into-being of what was not.

MIND

476 Fr. 12, Simplicius *in Phys.* 164, 24 and 156, 13 τὰ μὲν ἄλλα παντὸς μοῖραν μετέχει, νοῦς δέ ἐστιν ἄπειρον καὶ αὐτοκρατὲς καὶ μέμεικται οὐδενὶ χρήματι, ἀλλὰ μόνος αὐτὸς ἐφ' ἑαυτοῦ ἐστιν. εἰ μὴ γὰρ ἐφ' ἑαυτοῦ ἦν, ἀλλά τεῳ ἐμέμεικτο ἄλλῳ, μετεῖχεν ἂν ἁπάντων χρημάτων, εἰ ἐμέμεικτό τεῳ· ἐν παντὶ γὰρ παντὸς μοῖρα ἔνεστιν, ὥσπερ ἐν τοῖς πρόσθεν μοι λέλεκται· καὶ ἂν ἐκώλυεν αὐτὸν τὰ συμμεμειγμένα, ὥστε μηδενὸς χρήματος κρατεῖν ὁμοίως ὡς καὶ μόνον ἐόντα ἐφ' ἑαυτοῦ. ἔστι γὰρ λεπτότατόν τε πάντων χρημάτων καὶ καθαρώτατον, καὶ γνώμην γε περὶ παντὸς πᾶσαν ἴσχει καὶ ἰσχύει μέγιστον· καὶ ὅσα γε ψυχὴν ἔχει, καὶ τὰ μείζω καὶ τὰ ἐλάσσω, πάντων νοῦς κρατεῖ. καὶ τῆς περιχωρήσιος τῆς συμπάσης νοῦς ἐκράτησεν, ὥστε περιχωρῆσαι τὴν ἀρχήν. καὶ πρῶτον ἀπό του σμικροῦ ἤρξατο περιχωρεῖν, ἐπὶ δὲ πλέον περιχωρεῖ, καὶ περιχωρήσει ἐπὶ πλέον. καὶ τὰ συμμισγόμενά τε καὶ ἀποκρινόμενα καὶ διακρινόμενα πάντα ἔγνω νοῦς. καὶ ὁποῖα ἔμελλεν ἔσεσθαι καὶ ὁποῖα ἦν καὶ ὅσα νῦν ἔστι καὶ ὁποῖα ἔσται, πάντα διεκόσμησε νοῦς, καὶ τὴν περιχώρησιν ταύτην ἣν νῦν περιχωρεῖ τά τε ἄστρα καὶ ὁ ἥλιος καὶ ἡ σελήνη καὶ ὁ ἀὴρ καὶ ὁ αἰθὴρ οἱ ἀποκρινόμενοι. ἡ δὲ περιχώρησις αὕτη ἐποίησεν ἀποκρίνεσθαι. καὶ ἀποκρίνεται ἀπό τε τοῦ ἀραιοῦ τὸ πυκνὸν καὶ ἀπὸ τοῦ ψυχροῦ τὸ θερμὸν καὶ ἀπὸ τοῦ ζοφεροῦ τὸ λαμπρὸν καὶ ἀπὸ τοῦ διεροῦ τὸ ξηρόν. μοῖραι δὲ πολλαὶ πολλῶν εἰσι. παντάπασι δὲ οὐδὲν ἀποκρίνεται οὐδὲ διακρίνεται ἕτερον ἀπὸ τοῦ ἑτέρου πλὴν νοῦ. νοῦς δὲ πᾶς ὅμοιός ἐστι καὶ ὁ μείζων καὶ ὁ ἐλάττων. ἕτερον δὲ οὐδέν ἐστιν ὅμοιον οὐδενί, ἀλλ' ὅτων πλεῖστα ἔνι, ταῦτα ἐνδηλότατα ἓν ἕκαστόν ἐστι καὶ ἦν.

477 Fr. 13, Simplicius *in Phys.* 300, 31 καὶ ἐπεὶ ἤρξατο ὁ νοῦς κινεῖν, ἀπὸ τοῦ κινουμένου παντὸς ἀπεκρίνετο, καὶ ὅσον ἐκίνησεν ὁ νοῦς πᾶν τοῦτο διεκρίθη· κινουμένων δὲ καὶ διακρινομένων ἡ περιχώρησις πολλῷ μᾶλλον ἐποίει διακρίνεσθαι.

478 Fr. 9, *ibid.* 35, 14 ...οὕτω τούτων περιχωρούντων τε καὶ ἀποκρινομένων ὑπὸ βίης τε καὶ ταχυτῆτος. βίην δὲ ἡ ταχυτὴς ποιεῖ. ἡ δὲ ταχυτὴς αὐτῶν οὐδενὶ ἔοικε χρήματι τὴν ταχυτῆτα τῶν νῦν ἐόντων χρημάτων ἐν ἀνθρώποις, ἀλλὰ πάντως πολλαπλασίως ταχύ ἐστι.

479 Fr. 14, *ibid.* 157, 7 ὁ δὲ νοῦς, ὃς ἀεί ἐστι, τὸ κάρτα [so Diels: ὅσα ἐστί τε κάρτα Simplic. MSS] καὶ νῦν ἐστιν ἵνα καὶ τὰ ἄλλα πάντα, ἐν τῷ πολλῷ περιέχοντι καὶ ἐν τοῖς προσκριθεῖσι καὶ ἐν τοῖς ἀποκεκριμένοις.

476 All other things have a portion of everything, but Mind is infinite and self-ruled, and is mixed with nothing but is all alone by itself. For if it was not by itself, but was mixed with anything else, it would have a share of all things if it were mixed with any; for in everything there is a portion of everything, as I said earlier; and the things that were mingled with it would hinder it so that it could control nothing in the same way as it does now being alone by itself. For it is the finest of all things and the purest, it has all knowledge about everything and the greatest power; and Mind controls all things, both the greater and the smaller, that have life. Mind controlled also the whole rotation, so that it began to rotate in the beginning. And it began to rotate first from a small area, but it now rotates over a wider and will rotate over a wider area still. And the things that are mingled and separated and divided off, all are known by Mind. And all things that were to be – those that were and those that are now and those that shall be – Mind arranged them all, including this rotation in which are now rotating the stars, the sun and moon, the air and the aither that are being separated off. And this rotation caused the separating off. And the dense is separated off from the rare, the hot from the cold, the bright from the dark and the dry from the moist. But there are many portions of many things, and nothing is altogether

separated off nor divided one from the other except Mind. Mind is all alike, both the greater and the smaller quantities of it, while nothing else is like anything else, but each single body is and was most plainly those things of which it contains most.

477 And when Mind initiated motion, from all that was moved Mind was separated, and as much as Mind moved was all divided off; and as things moved and were divided off, the rotation greatly increased the process of dividing.

478 ...as these things rotated thus and were separated off by the force and speed (of their rotation). And the speed creates the force. Their speed is like the speed of nothing that now exists among men, but it is altogether many times as fast.

479 But Mind, which ever is, is assuredly even now where everything else is too, in the surrounding mass and in the things that have been either aggregated or separated.

Another Parmenidean demand with which Anaxagoras had to comply was that motion should not be simply taken for granted but explained. In place of Empedocles' Love and Strife (**349**) Anaxagoras substitutes the single intellectual motive force of Mind. It too, like Love and Strife, has many of the qualities of an abstract principle. 'It has all knowledge about everything, and the greatest strength; it controls all things that have life'; and 'it set in order all things that were to be', including, of course, the cosmic revolution. Yet at the same time it is 'the finest of all things and the purest'; it is 'all alike, both the larger and the smaller quantities'; and though it is 'mixed with nothing', it is none the less present 'there, where everything else is, in the surrounding mass, and in what has been united and separated off'. Anaxagoras in fact is striving, as had several of his predecessors, to imagine and describe a truly incorporeal entity. But as with them, so still with him, the only ultimate criterion of reality is extension in space. Mind, like everything else, is corporeal, and owes its power partly to its fineness, partly to the fact that it alone, though present in the mixture, yet remains unmixed.

How Mind imparted the first rotatory movement is by no means obvious; it may be that even Anaxagoras himself had no clear mental picture of the process. It appears, however, that the area affected was at first small but is still steadily increasing. The speed of the revolution is immense, and therefore its effect on the original mixture is very powerful (**478**). The immediate consequence is progressive separation: the moment the rotation takes in a new area, as it is doing all the time, the ingredients of that area begin at once to separate off (477). It is in fact the rotation which is directly responsible for the separation, which leads in turn to cosmogony. Mind, having initiated the rotation, remains alone ultimately responsible; but at the same time, as is evident from the statement at the end of 477, once the original motion has been imparted, purely mechanical factors begin to operate and the agency of Mind itself becomes less direct. This is a feature of Anaxagoras' system which, to the irritation of Plato and Aristotle (see 495 and note), becomes more pronounced as his cosmogony proceeds.

With the introduction of Mind the basis of the system is complete. Anaxagoras is, like Philolaus and the atomists after him, a dualist; and his dualism is in a sense a dualism of Mind and matter.[1] But both members of this dualism are peculiar. Mind, like matter, is corporeal and owes its power over matter to its fineness and purity. Matter itself, so far from being pure, is originally at least an infinitely divisible mixture of every form of substance that the world is ultimately to contain.

[1] Cf. 480 Theophrastus *Phys. op.* fr. 4 *ap.* Simplicium *in Phys.* 27, 17 (DK 59 A 41) καὶ οὕτω μὲν λαμβανόντων δόξειεν ἂν ὁ Ἀναξαγόρας τὰς μὲν ὑλικὰς ἀρχὰς ἀπείρους ποιεῖν, τὴν δὲ τῆς κινήσεως καὶ τῆς γενέσεως αἰτίαν μίαν τὸν νοῦν· εἰ δέ τις τὴν μίξιν τῶν ἁπάντων ὑπολάβοι μίαν εἶναι φύσιν ἀόριστον καὶ κατ' εἶδος καὶ κατὰ μέγεθος, συμβαίνει δύο τὰς ἀρχὰς αὐτὸν λέγειν τήν τε τοῦ ἀπείρου φύσιν καὶ τὸν νοῦν. *(Such being their theory, Anaxagoras would appear to make his material principles infinite, but the cause of motion and coming into being one only, namely Mind. But if we were to suppose that the mixture of all things was a single substance, indefinite both in form and in extent, then it follows that he is really affirming two first principles only, namely the substance of the infinite and Mind.)*

IN EVERYTHING A PORTION OF EVERYTHING

481 Fr. 6, Simplicius *Phys.* 164, 26 καὶ ὅτε δὲ ἴσαι μοῖραί εἰσι τοῦ τε μεγάλου καὶ τοῦ σμικροῦ πλῆθος, καὶ οὕτως ἂν εἴη ἐν παντὶ πάντα· οὐδὲ χωρὶς ἔστιν εἶναι, ἀλλὰ πάντα παντὸς μοῖραν μετέχει. ὅτε τοὐλάχιστον μὴ ἔστιν εἶναι, οὐκ ἂν δύναιτο χωρισθῆναι, οὐδ' ἂν ἐφ' ἑαυτοῦ γενέσθαι, ἀλλ' ὅπωσπερ ἀρχὴν εἶναι καὶ νῦν πάντα ὁμοῦ. ἐν πᾶσι δὲ πολλὰ ἔνεστι καὶ τῶν ἀποκρινομένων ἴσα πλῆθος ἐν τοῖς μείζοσί τε καὶ ἐλάσσοσι.

482 Fr. 11, *ibid.* 164, 23 ἐν παντὶ παντὸς μοῖρα ἔνεστι πλὴν νοῦ, ἔστιν οἷσι δὲ καὶ νοῦς ἔνι.

481 And since the portions of the great and of the small are equal in number, so too all things would be in everything. Nor is it

possible that they should exist apart, but all things have a portion of everything. Since it is not possible that there should be a smallest part, nothing can be put apart nor come-to-be all by itself, but as things were originally, so they must be now too, all together. In all things there are many ingredients, equal in number in the greater and in the smaller of the things that are being separated off.

482   In everything there is a portion of everything except Mind; and there are some things in which there is Mind as well.

These two fragments say what they want to say briefly, emphatically and, one might have thought clearly. **481** tells us that, as in the original mixture, so now in everything, of whatever size, that is being separated off, *all things* are together; while **482**, by its addition of the words πλὴν νοῦ, drives home the point that, just as the original mixture contained not only the traditional opposites and the Empedoclean elements but 'countless seeds' as well, so now everything contains a portion of *everything except Mind*. That is unquestionably what Anaxagoras himself says; and he repeats it more than once in a later fragment which has already been quoted, **476**. Those who maintain, as for example Cornford and Vlastos do, that when Anaxagoras said: 'in everything there is a portion of everything' he can only have meant that in everything there is a portion of all the opposites, can only do so at the expense of accusing Anaxagoras of saying what he did not mean. It is surely inconceivable that any Greek, let alone a practised thinker like Anaxagoras, should have written ἐν παντὶ παντὸς μοῖρα ἔνεστι if by παντός he really meant to signify something quite different from παντί. Whatever παντί and παντός are or are not intended to include, it must in fairness to Anaxagoras be assumed that they include the same things. And that those things comprise other things than the opposites seems to follow inevitably from a comparison of fr. 6, **481**, with fr. 4, **468**.

When Anaxagoras adds at the end of **482** that there are some things also in which Mind is present, the statement is to be compared with that other sentence in **476** which tells us that Mind controls everything that has life. If there are some things in which Mind is present, there are obviously other things in which it is not. Mind is presumably therefore to be imagined as discontinuously distributed throughout the world in living things; which would explain how Anaxagoras could speak, as he does near the end of **476**, of 'both the greater and the smaller quantities' of it.

'SEEDS' AND 'PORTIONS'

The chief problem in any reconstruction which assumes that Anaxagoras meant what he said is to determine the relation of the σπέρματα, 'seeds', of **468** to the μοῖραι of **476**, **481** and **482**. If Anaxagoras really believed (and this at least is never disputed) in the infinite divisibility of matter, how is it that there are already 'seeds' present in the original mixture? To answer this crucial question, it will be easiest first to consider what precisely Anaxagoras means by the word μοῖρα and only then to consider why the 'seeds' need be introduced at all.

μοῖρα is not, of course, in the way in which σπέρμα is, employed by Anaxagoras as a semi-technical term; but for all that, he seems to have used the word in a sense that requires careful consideration. An Anaxagorean μοῖρα is a 'portion' in the sense of a 'share' rather than of a 'piece' or 'particle'. The essential characteristic of such a 'portion' seems to be that it is something which neither in theory nor in practice can ever be actually reached and separated out from that which contains it. However far you may subdivide matter, and however infinitesimal a piece of it you may thereby reach, Anaxagoras will always reply that so far from being irreducible, it still contains an infinite number of 'portions'. This indeed is precisely the nature of Anaxagoras' reaction to Zeno; and it is probably what he means when he says in **481** that 'the portions of the great and of the small are equal in number'. Both the infinitely great and the infinitesimally small alike contain an infinite number of 'portions'. In effect, of course, such a theory is indistinguishable from a theory of fusion such as Bailey (*Greek Atomists and Epicurus* (Oxford, 1928), App. 1) attributes to Anaxagoras; but it differs from the modern conception of chemical fusion in two radical ways. In a cup of coffee, water, milk, sugar and coffee-bean extract may all be thoroughly mixed so that any visible drop of the liquid appears wholly homogeneous. But we believe that such a drop consists of a variety of quite distinct elemental molecular structures, whereas Anaxagoras, by virtue of his commitment to the principle of infinite divisibility, rejects any possibility of reaching such elements. And we believe it contains only a limited number of substances, whereas Anaxagoras holds that it contains 'portions' or proportions of all the substances and opposites there are.

How, then, can cosmogony begin, if in the original state of things reality consisted simply of a thoroughly uniform mixture of all substances and opposites? Where is there any determinate and discrete entity which could provide the basis for the small-scale and large-scale processes of differentiation necessary for the creation of an ordered cosmos? Perhaps Anaxagoras thought such entities were not required by those processes. But it may be that his answer was supplied by the 'seeds' he posits in the original mixture. **467–8** may be read as holding that at the microscopic level the original mixture was not uniform. Matter, infinitely divisible though it is, was from the first coagulated into particles or 'seeds', and there is therefore a natural unit from which cosmogony can begin (hence, perhaps, the word 'seed', since a seed is that from which larger things develop).[1]

[1] For development of the interpretation of Anaxagoras' 'portions' offered here see e.g. C. Strang, 'The Physical Theory of Anaxagoras', in *Studies in Presocratic Philosophy* II, ed. R. E. Allen and D. J. Furley (London, 1975), 361–80; Barnes, *The Presocratic Philosophers* II, ch. 2; Schofield, *An Essay on Anaxagoras*, 75–8, 107–21. The nature and role of 'seeds' in his system remains controversial. For a clear alternative to the view sketched here see Barnes, *op. cit.* II, 21–4; the question is discussed in detail in Schofield, *op. cit.*, 68–79, 121–33 (which refers to further bibliography).

'SEEDS' AND OPPOSITES

483   Fr. 4 (first sentence), Simplicius *in Phys.* 34, 29   τούτων δὲ οὕτως ἐχόντων χρὴ δοκεῖν ἐνεῖναι πολλά τε καὶ παντοῖα ἐν πᾶσι τοῖς συγκρινομένοις καὶ σπέρματα πάντων χρημάτων καὶ ἰδέας παντοίας ἔχοντα καὶ χροιὰς καὶ ἡδονάς... (Continues at **498**.)

484   Fr. 10, scholion *in* Gregor. Naz. xxxvi, 911 Migne   πῶς γὰρ ἂν ἐκ μὴ τριχὸς γένοιτο θρὶξ καὶ σὰρξ ἐκ μὴ σαρκός;

485   Aristotle *Phys.* A4, 187a23   διαφέρουσι δὲ ἀλλήλων τῷ τὸν μὲν (*sc.* Ἐμπεδοκλέα) περίοδον ποιεῖν τούτων, τὸν δ' (*sc.* Ἀναξαγόραν) ἅπαξ, καὶ τὸν μὲν (*sc.* Ἀναξαγόραν) ἄπειρα, τά τε ὁμοιομερῆ καὶ τἀναντία, τὸν δὲ τὰ καλούμενα στοιχεῖα μόνον. ἔοικε δὲ Ἀναξαγόρας ἄπειρα οὕτως οἰηθῆναι διὰ τὸ ὑπολαμβάνειν τὴν κοινὴν δόξαν τῶν φυσικῶν εἶναι ἀληθῆ, ὡς οὐ γιγνομένου οὐδενὸς ἐκ τοῦ μὴ ὄντος (διὰ τοῦτο γὰρ οὕτω λέγουσιν, ἦν ὁμοῦ πάντα, καὶ τὸ γίγνεσθαι τοιόνδε καθέστηκεν ἀλλοιοῦσθαι, οἱ δὲ σύγκρισιν καὶ διάκρισιν)· ἔτι δ' ἐκ τοῦ γίγνεσθαι ἐξ ἀλλήλων τἀναντία· ἐνυπῆρχεν ἄρα· εἰ γὰρ πᾶν μὲν τὸ γιγνόμενον ἀνάγκη γίγνεσθαι ἢ ἐξ ὄντων ἢ ἐκ μὴ ὄντων, τούτων δὲ τὸ μὲν ἐκ μὴ ὄντων γίγνεσθαι ἀδύνατον (περὶ γὰρ ταύτης ὁμο-γνωμονοῦσι τῆς δόξης ἅπαντες οἱ περὶ φύσεως), τὸ λοιπὸν ἤδη συμβαίνειν ἐξ ἀνάγκης ἐνόμισαν, ἐξ ὄντων μὲν καὶ ἐνυπαρχόντων γίγνεσθαι, διὰ μικρότητα δὲ τῶν ὄγκων ἐξ ἀναισθήτων ἡμῖν. διὸ φασι πᾶν ἐν παντὶ μεμῖχθαι, διότι πᾶν ἐκ παντὸς ἑώρων γιγνόμενον· φαίνεσθαι δὲ διαφέροντα καὶ προσαγορεύεσθαι ἕτερα ἀλλήλων ἐκ τοῦ μάλισθ' ὑπερέχοντος διὰ πλῆθος ἐν τῇ μίξει τῶν ἀπείρων· εἰλικρινῶς μὲν γὰρ ὅλον λευκὸν ἢ μέλαν ἢ γλυκὺ ἢ σάρκα ἢ ὀστοῦν οὐκ εἶναι, ὅτου δὲ πλεῖστον ἕκαστον ἔχει, τοῦτο δοκεῖν εἶναι τὴν φύσιν τοῦ πράγματος.

483 And since these things are so, we must suppose that there are many things of all sorts in everything that is being aggregated, seeds of all things with all sorts of shapes and colours and tastes...

484 How could hair come from what is not hair or flesh from what is not flesh?

485 These two, however, differ from each other in that Empedocles imagines a cycle of such changes, Anaxagoras a single series. Anaxagoras again posited an infinity of principles, namely the homoeomerous substances and the opposites together, while Empedocles posits only the so-called 'elements'. The theory of Anaxagoras that the principles are infinite in number was probably due to his acceptance of the common opinion of the physicists that nothing comes into being from not-being. For this is the reason why they use the phrase 'all things were together', and the coming into being of such and such a kind of thing is reduced to change of quality, while others speak of combination and separation. Moreover, the fact that the opposites proceed from each other led them to the same conclusion. The one, they reasoned, must have already existed in the other; for since everything that comes into being must arise either from what is or from what is not, and it is impossible for it to arise from what is not (on this point all the physicists agree), they thought that the truth of the alternative necessarily followed, namely that things come into being out of existent things, i.e. out of things already present, but imperceptible to our senses because of the smallness of their bulk. So they assert that everything is mixed in everything, because they saw everything arising out of everything. But things, as they say, appear different from one another and receive different names according to the nature of the thing that is numerically predominant among the innumerable constituents of the mixture. For nothing, they say, is purely and entirely white or black or sweet or flesh or bone, but the nature of a thing is held to be that of which it contains the most. (*After Hardie*)

Unfortunately the only two surviving sentences of Anaxagoras himself that give us any clue concerning the composition of the 'seeds' are those in **483** and **484**; and of these the latter may well represent, not Anaxagoras' own exact words, but a paraphrase by the scholiast on Gregorius Nazianzenus who preserves the argument. At this point, therefore, we are compelled to invoke secondary sources. But at least our secondary authorities (one of whom, Simplicius, certainly had Anaxagoras' book or extensive extracts from it before him) are unanimous in attributing to Anaxagoras the views voiced by Aristotle in **485**.

It is fairly evident from **483**, where the 'seeds' are said to have diverse colours and tastes, that some at least of the opposites, such as bright and dark or sweet and bitter, were actually ingredients in the 'seeds'; and there can be little doubt that Aristotle is therefore right when he attributes to Anaxagoras the general argument that, since opposites 'come out of one another' – since, in other words, a thing becomes hotter from having been cooler and vice versa – they must have been present in one another all the time. But that does not seem to be, as it is sometimes taken to be, the end of the matter. **484** equally suggests, if somewhat less directly, that natural substances are on an equal footing with the opposites. For if hair cannot come from what is not hair nor flesh from what is not flesh, hair and flesh too, just like the opposites, must have been there all the time. Again, moreover, this inference is supported by Aristotle; for in the last sentence of **485**, in the list of examples of the things the predominance of which determines the apparent character of a whole body, there appear, besides the opposites, white, black and sweet, the natural substances, flesh and bone. The 'seeds' in fact contain, like the original mixture in which they were present, not only the opposites, nor only natural substances, but both together.

It is significant that Aristotle should so often, as he does in **485**, compare and contrast Empedocles and Anaxagoras. Anaxagoras seems to have felt, as has already become evident from the list of the ingredients of the original mixture in **468**, that Empedocles had not gone far enough. If everything consisted solely of the four elements, then in putting together the four elements in different proportions to form, say, flesh or bone, Empedocles had not, to Anaxagoras' mind, succeeded in eliminating the coming-into-being of something new. The only way to do that was to posit in everything the presence *ab initio* of everything which might emerge from it. Since there was no end to the apparent changes that might take place in the world, there must be, not only in the original mixture as a whole but in every constituent 'seed', a 'portion' not only of all the opposites but of every natural substance as well. In that way alone can hair and flesh come from the wheat which nourishes them without the coming-into-being of something new.

THE OPPOSITES

486 Fr. 8, Simplicius *in Phys.* 175, 12 and 176, 29   οὐ κεχώρισται ἀλλήλων τὰ ἐν τῷ ἑνὶ κόσμῳ οὐδὲ ἀποκέκοπται πελέκει οὔτε τὸ θερμὸν ἀπὸ τοῦ ψυχροῦ οὔτε τὸ ψυχρὸν ἀπὸ τοῦ θερμοῦ.

486 The things in the one world-order are not separated one from the other nor cut off with an axe, neither the hot from the cold nor the cold from the hot.

This fragment should be compared with the last few sentences of **476** (beginning καὶ ἀποκρίνεται, 'And the dense'). The two passages together are often taken, along with those in the next section, as indicating that Anaxagoras did indeed regard the opposites as primary elements of superior status to natural substances. It seems more likely, however, in view of the evidence to the contrary, that he merely regarded the opposites as providing the best illustration of his general theory that 'in everything there is a portion of everything'. Heraclitus had already shown that one of a pair of opposites cannot exist without the other; while the very fact that they are opposites means that the existence of a close relation between them, whatever it may be, is more obvious than in the case of such substances as, say, gold and flesh. Indeed a particular argument which Anaxagoras is said to have used, the paradox that snow must really be black,[1] may well be no more than a later distortion of a statement to the effect that there is a 'portion' of 'the black' in snow. But even though the opposites do unquestionably, for this reason, figure very prominently in the fragments, the evidence still seems to suggest that, just as the hot and the cold cannot be cut off from one another with a hatchet, so are flesh, hair, gold, and every other natural substance equally inseparable one from another.

[1] **487** Sextus *Pyrrh.* 1, 33 (DK 59 A 97)   νοούμενα δὲ φαινομένοις (*sc.* ἀντιτίθεμεν), ὡς ὁ Ἀναξαγόρας τῷ λευκὴν εἶναι τὴν χιόνα ἀντετίθει ὅτι ἡ χιὼν ὕδωρ ἐστὶ πεπηγός, τὸ δὲ ὕδωρ ἐστὶ μέλαν, καὶ ἡ χιὼν ἄρα μέλαινά ἐστιν. (*We oppose the objects of thought to those of the senses, as Anaxagoras used to oppose to the view that snow is white the argument that snow is frozen water, and water is black, whence it follows that snow is black.*)

THE BEGINNINGS OF COSMOGONY

488 Fr. 2, Simplicius *in Phys.* 155, 31   καὶ γὰρ ἀήρ τε καὶ αἰθὴρ ἀποκρίνονται ἀπὸ τοῦ πολλοῦ τοῦ περιέχοντος, καὶ τό γε περιέχον ἄπειρόν ἐστι τὸ πλῆθος.

489 Fr. 15, *ibid.* 179, 3 τὸ μὲν πυκνὸν καὶ ⟨τὸ⟩ διερὸν καὶ τὸ ψυχρὸν καὶ τὸ ζοφερὸν ἐνθάδε συνεχώρησεν, ἔνθα νῦν γῆ, τὸ δὲ ἀραιὸν καὶ τὸ θερμὸν καὶ τὸ ξηρὸν ⟨καὶ τὸ λαμπρὸν⟩ ἐξεχώρησεν εἰς τὸ πρόσω τοῦ αἰθέρος.

490 Fr. 16, *ibid.* 179, 8 and 155, 21 ἀπὸ τουτέων ἀποκρινομένων συμπήγνυται γῆ· ἐκ μὲν γὰρ τῶν νεφελῶν ὕδωρ ἀποκρίνεται, ἐκ δὲ τοῦ ὕδατος γῆ, ἐκ δὲ τῆς λίθοι συμπήγνυνται ὑπὸ τοῦ ψυχροῦ, οὗτοι δὲ ἐκχωρέουσι μᾶλλον τοῦ ὕδατος.

488 For air and aither are being separated off from the surrounding mass, which is infinite in number.

489 The dense and the moist and the cold and the dark came together here, where the earth now is, while the rare and the hot and the dry and the bright went outwards to the further part of the aither.

490 From these things, as they are separated off, the earth is solidified; for water is separated off from the clouds, earth from water, and from earth stones are solidified by the cold; and stones tend to move outwards more than water.

Comparison of **490** with **140–1** shows that Anaxagoras' scheme of transformations[1] is borrowed comprehensively from Anaximenes,[2] although of course he does not subscribe to Anaximenes' belief in a single underlying principle of air. Anaxagoras' own view of air and aither (or fire)[3] is not clear. We have already been told, in the opening sentences of the book, **467**, that in the original mixture 'none of them were plain because of their smallness; for air and aither held all things in subjection'. Why, then, if air and aither are already evident in the original mixture, do they need to be separated off when the rotation begins? One speculative answer will emerge from a consideration of **489**.[4]

[1] **490** actually specifies a general pattern of change in the cosmos as it is (see M. C. Stokes, 'On Anaxagoras', *AGP* 47 (1965), 229–44); but it is clearly based on the same principles as the cosmogonical separation described in **489**.

[2] Cf. p. 355 n. 2.

[3] Cf. **491** Aristotle *de caelo* A3, 270b24 Ἀναξαγόρας δὲ καταχρῆται τῷ ὀνόματι τούτῳ οὐ καλῶς· ὀνομάζει γὰρ αἰθέρα ἀντὶ πυρός. (*Anaxagoras employs this name (i.e. aither) incorrectly. For he speaks of aither in place of fire.*) Cf. e.g. Aristotle *Meteor.* B9, 369b14 (DK 59A84) and **494**.

[4] For further discussion of this difficult issue see Schofield, *An Essay on Anaxagoras*, 70–8 (esp. n. 6 at p. 155), 128, 131–2.

The opposites, as we have already seen, exist in the form of 'portions' in the 'seeds', each 'seed' being characterized by that of which it has most in it. When, therefore, **489** tells us that 'the dense, the moist, the cold and the dark came together where the earth now is', it means that the 'seeds' in which there was a preponderance of the dense, the moist, the cold and the dark over their respective opposites tended towards the centre of the rotation. They obeyed, in other words, two laws which Anaxagoras seems to have regarded as virtually axiomatic, the attraction of like to like and the tendency of the heavy to the centre, of the light to the circumference of a whirl.[1] The Empedoclean elements were not to Anaxagoras primary substances, but rather mixtures of 'seeds' of all sorts.[2] At this stage in cosmogony at least, earth is earth rather than anything else simply because of the predominance in its constituent 'seeds' of the dense and the rest over their opposites. Aither, on the other hand, consists of 'seeds' that are characterized by the rare, the hot and the dry. All that is happening, therefore, at this very early stage in the world's evolution is that the 'seeds' that are characterized by the same combination of opposites are tending together towards their appropriate place in the universe.

[1] **492** Simplicius *in Phys.* 27, 11 (DK 59 A 41) καὶ ταῦτά φησιν ὁ Θεόφραστος παραπλησίως τῷ Ἀναξιμάνδρῳ λέγειν τὸν Ἀναξαγόραν· ἐκεῖνος (*sc.* Ἀναξαγόρας) γάρ φησιν ἐν τῇ διακρίσει τοῦ ἀπείρου τὰ συγγενῆ φέρεσθαι πρὸς ἄλληλα, καὶ ὅτι μὲν ἐν τῷ παντὶ χρυσὸς ἦν, γίνεσθαι χρυσόν, ὅτι δὲ γῆ, γῆν. (*Theophrastus says that the theory of Anaxagoras resembles that of Anaximander; for Anaxagoras says that, in the dividing up of the infinite, things of a like kind tend together, and what was gold or earth in the original whole becomes gold and earth respectively.*)
493 Diog. L. II, 8 (DK 59 A 1) καὶ νοῦν μὲν ἀρχὴν κινήσεως· τῶν δὲ σωμάτων τὰ μὲν βαρέα τὸν κάτω τόπον, τὰ δὲ κοῦφα τὸν ἄνω ἐπισχεῖν... Cf. **117**. (*Mind, he says, initiates motion, and heavy bodies occupy the lower position, light bodies the upper...*)
[2] **494** Aristotle *de caelo* Γ 3, 302a28 Ἀναξαγόρας δὲ Ἐμπεδοκλεῖ ἐναντίως λέγει περὶ τῶν στοιχείων. ὁ μὲν γὰρ πῦρ καὶ τὰ σύστοιχα τούτοις στοιχεῖά φησιν εἶναι τῶν σωμάτων καὶ συγκεῖσθαι πάντ' ἐκ τούτων, Ἀναξαγόρας δὲ τοὐναντίον· τὰ γὰρ ὁμοιομερῆ στοιχεῖα, λέγω δ' οἷον σάρκα καὶ ὀστοῦν καὶ τῶν τοιούτων ἕκαστον· ἀέρα δὲ καὶ πῦρ μείγματα τούτων καὶ τῶν ἄλλων σπερμάτων πάντων· εἶναι γὰρ ἑκάτερον αὐτῶν ἐξ ἀοράτων [τῶν ὁμοιομερῶν πάντων] ἠθροισμένων. διὸ καὶ γίνεσθαι πάντ' ἐκ τούτων· τὸ γὰρ πῦρ καὶ τὸν αἰθέρα προσαγορεύει ταὐτό. (*Anaxagoras and Empedocles hold opposite views on the elements. Empedocles holds that fire and the rest of the list are the elements of bodies and that everything is made up of these; but Anaxagoras opposes this. He maintains that the homoeomerous substances (e.g. flesh, bone and so on) are the elements, while air or fire are mixtures of these and all other seeds; each of them consists of invisible particles collected together. For this reason everything comes into being from these two – fire and aither being in Anaxagoras synonymous.*)

But if that is so, then the problem raised by the comparison of fr. 1, **467**, with fr. 2, **488**, is easily solved. All that the crucial sentence in fr. 1 is intended to tell us is that, in Cornford's words (*CQ* 24 (1930),

25), 'Aether and Air are merely collective names for the sets of hotter and colder (etc.) Seeds respectively. Both sets exist in the Mixture, and indeed together make up the whole Mixture; but originally they were completely jumbled together and coextensive.' Fr. 2, on the other hand, describes how these sets of 'seeds', originally inter-mingled, began to be separated one from the other to form two distinctive masses. Anaxagoras, true to his Ionian upbringing, has in fact allowed the traditional opposites, even though they are now reduced to the status of 'portions' in 'seeds' and are therefore on an equal footing with natural substances, to retain their traditional part in cosmogony; and at the same time he has found a place in his system for the Empedoclean elements.[1]

[1] This is another illustration of the way in which the responsibility of Mind becomes less direct as cosmogony proceeds. It is clearly the ground for Socrates' famous criticism of Anaxagoras' use of Mind in *Phaedo* 97Bff. Cf. especially **495** Plato *Phaedo* 98B7 (DK 59A47) ἀπὸ δὴ θαυμαστῆς ἐλπίδος, ὦ ἑταῖρε, ᾠχόμην φερόμενος, ἐπειδὴ προϊὼν καὶ ἀναγιγνώσκων ὁρῶ ἄνδρα τῷ μὲν νῷ οὐδὲν χρώμενον οὐδέ τινας αἰτίας ἐπαιτιώμενον εἰς τὸ διακοσμεῖν τὰ πράγματα, ἀέρας δὲ καὶ αἰθέρας καὶ ὕδατα αἰτιώμενον καὶ ἄλλα πολλὰ καὶ ἄτοπα. (*From this wonderful hope, my friend, I was at once cast down: as I went ahead and read the book I found a man who made no use at all of Mind, nor invoked any other real causes to arrange the world, but explained things by airs and aithers and waters and many other absurdities.*) This criticism is echoed by Aristotle *Met.* A4, 985a18 and Eudemus *ap.* Simpl. *in Phys.* 327, 26 (both DK 59A47).

So Anaxagoras' cosmogony is launched; and the process begun in **488** and **489** is continued in **490**. First air, which is at this stage the opposite of aither, is solidified into clouds; from clouds comes water; from water comes earth; and finally from earth are solidified stones. Not only is like continuing to be attracted by like, but also, evidently, the pressure at the centre of the rotation (cf. the βίη, 'force', of **478**) is compressing the 'seeds' into ever more solid bodies. Of the ingredients in the 'seeds' it is still apparently the opposites that are the operative factor: stones are solidified from earth under the agency of the cold. But by now the opposites have fulfilled their main function; from now onwards their place will be largely taken by the substances with which they are mixed in the 'seeds'.

NOURISHMENT AND GROWTH

496 Aetius I, 3, 5 (DK 59A46) Ἀναξαγόρας Ἡγησιβούλου ὁ Κλαζομένιος ἀρχὰς τῶν ὄντων τὰς ὁμοιομερείας ἀπεφήνατο. ἐδόκει γὰρ αὐτῷ ἀπορώτατον εἶναι, πῶς ἐκ τοῦ μὴ ὄντος δύναταί τι γίνεσθαι ἢ φθείρεσθαι εἰς τὸ μὴ ὄν. τροφὴν γοῦν προσφερόμεθα

ἁπλῆν καὶ μονοειδῆ, ἄρτον καὶ ὕδωρ, καὶ ἐκ ταύτης τρέφεται θρὶξ
φλὲψ ἀρτηρία σὰρξ νεῦρα ὀστᾶ καὶ τὰ λοιπὰ μόρια. τούτων οὖν
γιγνομένων ὁμολογητέον ὅτι ἐν τῇ τροφῇ τῇ προσφερομένῃ πάντα
ἐστὶ τὰ ὄντα, καὶ ἐκ τῶν ὄντων πάντα αὔξεται. καὶ ἐν ἐκείνῃ ἐστὶ
τῇ τροφῇ μόρια αἵματος γεννητικὰ καὶ νεύρων καὶ ὀστέων καὶ
τῶν ἄλλων· ἃ ἦν λόγῳ θεωρητὰ μόρια. οὐ γὰρ δεῖ πάντα ἐπὶ τὴν
αἴσθησιν ἀνάγειν, ὅτι ἄρτος καὶ τὸ ὕδωρ ταῦτα κατασκευάζει, ἀλλ'
ἐν τούτοις ἐστὶ λόγῳ θεωρητὰ μόρια. Cf. Simplicius *in Phys.* 460,
12 (DK 59 A 45).

496 Anaxagoras of Clazomenae, son of Hegesiboulos, held that
the first principles of things were the homoeomeries. For it seemed
to him quite impossible that anything should come into being from
the non-existent or be dissolved into it. Anyhow we take in
nourishment that is simple and homogeneous, such as bread or
water, and by this are nourished hair, veins, arteries, flesh, sinews,
bones and all the other parts of the body. Which being so, we must
agree that everything that exists is in the nourishment we take in,
and that everything derives its growth from things that exist. There
must be in that nourishment some parts that are productive of
blood, some of sinews, some of bones, and so on – parts which
reason alone can apprehend. For there is no need to refer the fact
that bread and water produce all these things to sense-perception;
rather, there are in bread and water parts which only reason can
apprehend.

This passage and others like it, along with fr. 10 (**484**), suggest that
Anaxagoras was particularly interested in the problem of nutrition.
His general principles, 'a portion of everything in everything' and
the attraction of like to like, provide him with a simple solution – so
simple, indeed, that he may well have arrived at those general
principles from consideration of this very problem. For though there
are certain inevitable differences of detail, the analogy between
macrocosm – the world in which we live – and microcosm – the
individual living thing – is in Anaxagoras especially plain.

Bread and water, like all other substances, consist of 'seeds'; and
each of those 'seeds' contains a 'portion' of everything. (It is true,
of course, that bread is not a natural substance, while water, as we
have already seen, is a collection of 'seeds' of every sort; but if we
substitute wheat, which is a natural substance, for the bread which
both Aetius and Simplicius actually cite, it makes no difference to the
argument.) When the bread (or wheat) is eaten, it is presumably
broken up into its constituent 'seeds'; and since these are themselves

infinitely divisible, some of them at least will probably be broken down, by the processes of mastication and digestion, into still smaller seeds. Thereupon those seeds in which flesh predominates proceed, by the attraction of like to like, to join the flesh of the body, hair joins hair, and so on. But since no such thing as a particle of pure substance can ever exist, the flesh from the bread that goes to join the flesh of the body must always carry with it a 'portion' of everything else, and so ensures that the flesh, like the loaf, will continue to contain a 'portion' of everything. Meanwhile, of course, those ingredients in the loaf that are irrelevant to nutrition, copper, for instance, or cork,[1] are for the most part – that is, all except the few 'portions' which are carried to join the flesh or hair of the body – eliminated by the digestive processes.

[1] The examples are Cornford's. Commenting on this passage from Aetius, he writes (*CQ* 24 (1930), 20): 'Corn feeds flesh and bones; therefore it contains particles of flesh and bone. It does not nourish silver or rubies; so why should it contain particles of these?...There is no motive here for asserting "a portion of *every substance*" in bread or corn or any other food as such. The assertion would be gratuitous as well as absurd.' But the argument that the contention 'a portion of everything in everything' is absurdly uneconomical, true as it may be in one way, overlooks the fact, on which comment has already been made above (p. 370), that it is at least economical of effort. It would have been an unending task for Anaxagoras to determine what could and what could not come from what; and it is perhaps characteristic of Presocratic dogmatism that, rather than face that unending task, he should simply have asserted, as we have seen he several times did, 'a portion of everything in everything'.

HOMOEOMERIES

Three of the passages already quoted have used one or other of the words ὁμοιομερῆ or ὁμοιομέρειαι ('homoeomeries' or 'things with like parts'). None of these passages comes from Anaxagoras himself; two, **485** and **494**, come from Aristotle; one, **496**, to which many parallels could be found in Simplicius and others, comes from Aetius. It is actually very unlikely that Anaxagoras himself ever used either word; what the later commentators called ὁμοιομέρειαι, he himself seems to have called 'seeds'. Aristotle, who was probably the first to apply the phrase τὰ ὁμοιομερῆ to the theories of Anaxagoras, seems at least to have used it consistently. But in the later writers the precise meaning of either term is open to question.

Perhaps the most significant of the passages in Aristotle is that at the beginning of **485**, in which he tells us that Anaxagoras regarded as primary elements both the opposites and τὰ ὁμοιομερῆ, 'the things with like parts'. Now Aristotle frequently uses the phrase τὰ ὁμοιομερῆ for his own purposes: τὰ ὁμοιομερῆ in his own system were natural substances, such as flesh or bone, metals, or the four elements, every part of which, in his own view, was exactly like the whole. It seems hardly likely that, when he used the phrase in connexion with the theories of Anaxagoras, he should have used it in a different sense. What 485 therefore tells us is that Anaxagoras regarded both the opposites and natural substances as primary elements. It is true that elsewhere in Aristotle, as in 494, the homoeomerous substances appear alone as the primary elements of Anaxagoras; but that after all does not contradict the fuller statement in 485. Our own reconstruction of Anaxagoras' system suggests that the fuller statement is correct. For in that system as reconstructed the opposites and the natural substances do indeed together comprise the 'everything' of which everything contains a 'portion'. Even if, therefore, the strictest possible interpretation is placed upon the phrase τὰ ὁμοιομερῆ in Aristotle, that still does not in the slightest degree undermine any arguments adduced in earlier sections of this chapter. It may be that Aristotle uses the phrase in a sense which Anaxagoras himself would not have allowed; whatever the natural substances were or were not in Anaxagoras' system, they were certainly not, as they were in Aristotle's own, homogeneous: no one seed is like any other (468). But that does not invalidate the truth of the statement that in the system of Anaxagoras the primary elements were the opposites and the natural substances together.

Only in the later writers, when the term ὁμοιομέρεια creeps in alongside τὰ ὁμοιομερῆ, does the problem become more complicated. It is evident from, for instance, Lucretius I, 830 (DK 59 A 44) that the word ὁμοιομέρεια had by now become a catchword that was almost automatically applied to Anaxagoras' physical theories; and it seems very probable that many of those who used it did so without understanding its exact significance.[1] Simplicius, thanks to his familiarity with Anaxagoras' book, is probably our safest guide as to its correct usage. In the passages of Simplicius where either τὰ ὁμοιομερῆ or ὁμοιομέρειαι figure, the former can always be understood in the sense in which Aristotle used it, whereas the latter can usually, if not always, be taken to mean the 'seeds'. The fact is, of course, that the problem is somewhat academic. Not only did Anaxagoras himself apparently never use the words, but also, whatever interpretation be put upon them (except only the impossible interpretation of homogeneity), there is no difficulty in fitting them into the system as reconstructed. But if we have to speculate on why

Anaxagoras' 'seeds' came to be called ὁμοιομέρειαι, then the most likely explanation is that, since every 'seed' contains a 'portion' of everything, not only every individual 'seed' but also everything composed of 'seeds' will contain similar 'portions'.

¹ Aetius, e.g., is clearly uncertain of the exact implications of the word ὁμοιομέρεια. **496** continues thus: **497** Aetius I, 3, 5 (DK59A46) ἀπὸ τοῦ οὖν ὅμοια τὰ μέρη εἶναι ἐν τῇ τροφῇ τοῖς γεννωμένοις ὁμοιομερείας αὐτὰς ἐκάλεσε καὶ ἀρχὰς τῶν ὄντων ἀπεφήνατο... *(Since, therefore, the nourishment contains parts that are like the things which it produces, he called them homoeomeries and said that they were the first principles of existing things...)*

SUMMARY OF THE PHYSICAL SYSTEM

Before proceeding to certain special doctrines, it will be as well to add a few last observations on the above reconstruction of the basis of Anaxagoras' system.

The problem which faced Anaxagoras was, of course, exactly the same as faced the atomists. He had to give an account of the origin of the world without either deriving a plurality from an original unity or allowing the coming-into-being or change of anything real. Given the same problem, the two solutions could hardly have been more different. Whereas Anaxagoras made matter, like magnitude, infinitely divisible, the atomists maintained that it was composed of indivisible minima; and whereas Anaxagoras eliminated both coming-into-being and the derivation of plurality from unity by postulating *ab initio* an infinite variety of substances, the atomists regarded all substance as absolutely homogeneous and accounted for the apparent variety of phenomena by mere differences of shape, size, position and arrangement. Both solutions are full of ingenuity, in outline and in detail. But for all their ingenuity, and for all the difference between them, they are each the outcome as much of the Eleatic paradox as of the inventiveness of their respective authors.

SPECIAL DOCTRINES

(i) *Innumerable worlds?*

498 Fr. 4, Simplicius *in Phys.* 35, 3 (continuing **483**) ...καὶ ἀνθρώπους τε συμπαγῆναι καὶ τὰ ἄλλα ζῷα ὅσα ψυχὴν ἔχει. καὶ τοῖς γε ἀνθρώποισιν εἶναι καὶ πόλεις συνῳκημένας καὶ ἔργα κατεσκευασμένα, ὥσπερ παρ' ἡμῖν, καὶ ἠέλιόν τε αὐτοῖσιν εἶναι καὶ σελήνην καὶ τὰ ἄλλα, ὥσπερ παρ' ἡμῖν, καὶ τὴν γῆν αὐτοῖσι φύειν πολλά τε καὶ παντοῖα, ὧν ἐκεῖνοι τὰ ὀνῆστα συνενεγκάμενοι εἰς τὴν οἴκησιν χρῶνται. ταῦτα μὲν οὖν μοι λέλεκται περὶ τῆς ἀποκρίσιος, ὅτι οὐκ ἂν παρ' ἡμῖν μόνον ἀποκριθείη, ἀλλὰ καὶ ἄλλη. (**468** follows.)

499 Simplicius *in Phys.* 157, 9 καὶ μέντοι εἰπὼν 'ἐνεῖναι πολλά...ἡδονάς' (from **483**), καὶ 'ἀνθρώπους γε συμπαγῆναι... ψυχὴν ἔχει', ἐπάγει 'καὶ τοῖς γε ἀνθρώποισιν...χρῶνται' (from **498**). καὶ ὅτι μὲν ἑτέραν τινὰ διακόσμησιν παρὰ τὴν παρ' ἡμῖν αἰνίττεται, δηλοῖ τὸ 'ὥσπερ παρ' ἡμῖν' οὐχ ἅπαξ μόνον εἰρημένον. ὅτι δὲ οὐδὲ αἰσθητὴν μὲν ἐκείνην οἴεται, τῷ χρόνῳ δὲ ταύτης προηγησαμένην, δηλοῖ τὸ 'ὧν ἐκεῖνοι τὰ ὀνῆστα συνενεγκάμενοι εἰς τὴν οἴκησιν χρῶνται'. οὐ γὰρ 'ἐχρῶντο' εἶπεν, ἀλλὰ 'χρῶνται'. ἀλλ' οὐδὲ ὡς νῦν κατ' ἄλλας τινὰς οἰκήσεις ὁμοίας οὔσης καταστάσεως τῇ παρ' ἡμῖν. οὐ γὰρ εἶπε 'τὸν ἥλιον καὶ τὴν σελήνην εἶναι παρ' ἐκείνοις ὥσπερ καὶ παρ' ἡμῖν', ἀλλ' 'ἥλιον καὶ σελήνην, ὥσπερ παρ' ἡμῖν', ὡς δὴ περὶ ἄλλων λέγων. ἀλλὰ ταῦτα μὲν εἴτε οὕτως εἴτε ἄλλως ἔχει, ζητεῖν ἄξιον.

498 (We must suppose that) men have been formed and the other animals that have life; and that the men have inhabited cities and cultivated fields, just as we have here; and sun and moon and so on, just as we have; and that the earth brings forth for them all manner of produce, of which they garner the best into their houses and use it. So much, then, have I said about the process of separating off – that separation would have taken place not only here with us but elsewhere too.

499 Having said, however, 'there are many things...and tastes' [*from* **483**] and 'men have been formed...have life', he adds 'the men have...and use it' [*from* **498**]. That he is hinting at another world in addition to our own is clear from the phrase, which he uses more than once, 'just as we have'. And that he does not regard this other world as a perceptible world which preceded this world in time is clear from the words 'of which they garner the best into their houses and use it'. For he did not say 'used' but 'use'. Nor does he mean that they are now inhabiting other regions of the same world as our own. For he did not say 'they have the sun and the moon just as we too have' but 'sun and moon, as we have' – as if he were talking of a different sun and moon. But it is debatable whether or not these considerations are valid.

Many scholars have maintained, on the strength of **498**, that Anaxagoras must have believed in a plurality of contemporary worlds. Yet some of the ancient evidence seems to suggest that he believed in one world only. Admittedly Aetius at one point (II, 4, 6,

DK 59A65) lists Anaxagoras among those who held that the world was perishable, thereby suggesting that he believed in a succession of worlds; but Aetius, as was shown in the case of Anaximander (p. 124), was confused on this issue, and elsewhere (II, 1, 2, DK 59A63) lists Anaxagoras instead among those who believed in one world only. Simplicius is probably our most reliable witness, since he certainly had the relevant part of Anaxagoras' book before him; and though elsewhere in his commentary on the *Physics* (e.g. 154, 29, DK 59A64) he speaks of Anaxagoras' world in the singular, that need mean no more than that he was there concerned only with the world we know.[1] **499** gives us his considered view, and clearly acknowledges his uncertainty on the point. It is perhaps just possible that, as Cornford maintained, Anaxagoras is referring in **498** not to other worlds, but to distant and unknown parts of this earth's surface, comparable with the 'hollows in the earth' in the myth in Plato's *Phaedo* (109Aff.). But since the question was anyhow not for Anaxagoras (as it was for the atomists, see p. 419) one which arose inevitably from his first principles and consequently demanded a definite answer, it seems wisest to follow the guidance of Simplicius in **499** and leave the question open.

[1] Aristotle's remarks about Anaxagoras at, e.g., *Phys.* A4, 187a23ff., Θ1, 250b18ff., though they have been used as evidence that Anaxagoras believed in only one world, are either so generalized that they are of little value as evidence on this particular question, or else suggest only that in Aristotle's opinion Anaxagoras regarded this world (irrespective of the existence of others) as imperishable.

(ii) *Astronomy and meteorology*

500 Fr. 18, Plutarch *de fac. in orbe lun.* 16, 929B ἥλιος ἐντίθησι τῇ σελήνῃ τὸ λαμπρόν.

501 Fr. 19, scholion BT *in Iliadem* 17, 547 Ἶριν δὲ καλέομεν τὸ ἐν τῇσι νεφέλῃσιν ἀντιλάμπον τῷ ἡλίῳ.

502 Hippolytus *Ref.* 1, 8, 3–10 (DK 59A42) τὴν δὲ γῆν τῷ σχήματι πλατεῖαν εἶναι καὶ μένειν μετέωρον διὰ τὸ μέγεθος καὶ διὰ τὸ μὴ εἶναι κενὸν καὶ διὰ τὸ τὸν ἀέρα ἰσχυρότατον ὄντα φέρειν ἐποχουμένην τὴν γῆν. (4) τῶν δ' ἐπὶ γῆς ὑγρῶν τὴν μὲν θάλασσαν ὑπάρξαι ⟨ἔκ⟩ τε τῶν ἐν αὐτῇ ὑδάτων, ⟨ὧν⟩ ἐξατμισθέν⟨των⟩ τὰ ὑποστάντα οὕτως γεγονέναι, καὶ ἀπὸ τῶν καταρρευσάντων ποταμῶν. (5) τοὺς δὲ ποταμοὺς καὶ ἀπὸ τῶν ὄμβρων λαμβάνειν τὴν ὑπόστασιν καὶ ἐξ ὑδάτων τῶν ἐν τῇ γῇ. εἶναι γὰρ αὐτὴν κοίλην καὶ ἔχειν ὕδωρ ἐν τοῖς κοιλώμασιν. τὸν δὲ Νεῖλον αὔξεσθαι κατὰ τὸ θέρος καταφερομένων εἰς αὐτὸν ὑδάτων ἀπὸ τῶν ἐν τοῖς ἀνταρκτικοῖς χιόνων. (6) ἥλιον δὲ καὶ σελήνην καὶ πάντα τὰ ἄστρα λίθους εἶναι ἐμπύρους συμπεριληφθέντας ὑπὸ τῆς αἰθέρος περιφορᾶς. εἶναι δ' ὑποκάτω τῶν ἄστρων ἡλίῳ καὶ σελήνῃ σώματά τινα συμπεριφερό-μενα ἡμῖν ἀόρατα. (7) τῆς δὲ θερμότητος μὴ αἰσθάνεσθαι τῶν ἄστρων διὰ τὸ μακρὰν εἶναι [καὶ διὰ] τὴν ἀπόστασιν τῆς γῆς· ἔτι δὲ οὐχ ὁμοίως θερμὰ τῷ ἡλίῳ διὰ τὸ χώραν ἔχειν ψυχροτέραν. εἶναι δὲ τὴν σελήνην κατωτέρω τοῦ ἡλίου πλησιώτερον ἡμῶν. (8) ὑπερέχειν δὲ τὸν ἥλιον μεγέθει τὴν Πελοπόννησον. τὸ δὲ φῶς τὴν σελήνην μὴ ἴδιον ἔχειν, ἀλλὰ ἀπὸ τοῦ ἡλίου. τὴν δὲ τῶν ἄστρων περιφορὰν ὑπὸ γῆν γίνεσθαι. (9) ἐκλείπειν δὲ τὴν σελήνην γῆς ἀντιφραττούσης, ἐνίοτε δὲ καὶ τῶν ὑποκάτω τῆς σελήνης, τὸν δὲ ἥλιον ταῖς νουμηνίαις σελήνης ἀντιφραττούσης...(10)...ἔφη δὲ γηίνην εἶναι τὴν σελήνην ἔχειν τε ἐν αὐτῇ πεδία καὶ φάραγγας. Cf. Diog. L. II, 8–9 (DK 59 A 1).

500 The sun indues the moon with brightness.

501 We call the reflexion of the sun in the clouds a rainbow.

502 The earth (he thinks) is flat in shape, and stays suspended where it is because of its size, because there is no void and because the air, which is very strong, keeps the earth afloat on it. Of the moisture on the earth, the sea came from the waters in the earth, the evaporation of which gave rise to all that has emerged, and from the rivers that flow into it. Rivers owe their origin partly to rain, partly to the waters in the earth; for the earth is hollow, and in its hollows contains water. The Nile rises in summer because waters are carried down into it from the snows in the south. The sun, the moon and all the stars are red-hot stones which the rotation of the aither carries round with it. Beneath the stars are certain bodies, invisible to us, that are carried round with the sun and moon. We do not feel the heat of the stars because they are so far from the earth; moreover, they are not as hot as the sun because they occupy a colder region. The moon is beneath the sun and nearer to us. The sun exceeds the Peloponnese in size. The moon has not any light of its own but derives it from the sun. The stars in their revolution pass beneath the earth. Eclipses of the moon are due to its being screened by the earth, or, sometimes, by the bodies beneath the moon; those of the sun to screening by the moon when it is new...He held that the moon was made of earth, and had plains and ravines on it.

500 and **501** are included mainly to show that Anaxagoras did indeed concern himself with the usual astronomical and meteorological questions. It is from the long passage of which **502** is a part that we get most of our information on the subject; and **502** for the most part speaks for itself. Clearly Anaxagoras' astronomy is much more rational than most of his predecessors', especially perhaps the view that the sun, moon and stars are huge incandescent stones. There is a story preserved by Diogenes Laertius[1] and Pliny that Anaxagoras predicted the fall of the large meteorite which fell at Aegospotami in 467 B.C. (cf. p. 446). Certainly this event caused a considerable stir; and though the suggestion that Anaxagoras predicted it is absurd, it may well have contributed towards his belief that the heavenly bodies were made of stone. It is because of their solidity, as **490** has already suggested, that they were originally thrown off from the earth at the centre of the cosmic revolution to take up their positions nearer the periphery. Presumably meteorites are heavenly bodies which, despite the speed of the revolution which normally keeps them aloft, have been drawn back to the earth by the familiar tendency of the heavy to move towards the centre of the revolution.

[1] **503** Diog. L. II, 10 (DK 59 A 1) φασὶ δ' αὐτὸν προειπεῖν τὴν περὶ Αἰγὸς ποταμοὺς γενομένην τοῦ λίθου πτῶσιν, ὃν εἶπεν ἐκ τοῦ ἡλίου πεσεῖσθαι. *(They say that he foretold the fall of the stone at Aegospotami, saying that it would fall from the sun.)* Cf. Marmor Parium 57 and Pliny *N.H.* II, 149 (both DK 59 A 11).

(iii) *Biology*

504 Fr. 22, Athenaeus II, 57D τὸ καλούμενον ὄρνιθος γάλα τὸ ἐν τοῖς ᾠοῖς λευκόν.

505 Hippolytus *Ref.* I, 8, 12 (DK 59 A 42) ζῷα δὲ τὴν μὲν ἀρχὴν ἐν ὑγρῷ γενέσθαι, μετὰ ταῦτα δὲ ἐξ ἀλλήλων. Cf. Diog. L. II, 9 *ad fin.* (DK 59 A 1).

506 Theophrastus *Hist. plant.* III, 1, 4 'Αναξαγόρας μὲν τὸν ἀέρα πάντων φάσκων ἔχειν σπέρματα καὶ ταῦτα συγκαταφερόμενα τῷ ὕδατι γεννᾶν τὰ φυτά...

504 What is called 'birds' milk' is the white of the egg.
505 Animals (he says) originally arose in the moisture, but later from one another.
506 Anaxagoras, when he says that the air contains the seeds of all things and that it is these seeds which, when carried down with the rain, give rise to plants...

504 is again quoted merely to show that Anaxagoras did include detailed doctrines in his book: its point presumably is that the white of an egg is the embryo's food. Several equally detailed theories are attributed to him by the ancient authorities, including Aristotle; but they are of no great importance for present purposes. The two most important of his biological theories are those in **505** and **506**. In his belief that life originated in 'the moist' he followed Anaximander (see pp. 141f.), but the notion that it was brought down to the earth with the rain is curious.[1] All living things, of course, from plants at the bottom of the scale to man at the top,[2] have a portion of Mind (see **476** and **482**). Before living things came into existence Mind was presumably dispersed evenly throughout the mixture; but from the time when life originated it evidently began to localize itself in living things, so that there are now, according to **482**, only '*some* things in which there is Mind also'.

[1] This may be a development of the popular idea, exemplified in Aeschylus (see **33**), that rain is the semen of Ouranos, by which Gaia is fertilized.

[2] **507** Plutarch *Quaest. phys.* I, 911D ζῷον γὰρ ἔγγειον τὸ φυτὸν εἶναι οἱ περὶ Πλάτωνα καὶ Ἀναξαγόραν καὶ Δημόκριτον οἴονται. (*The followers of Plato, Anaxagoras and Democritus regard a plant as an animal fixed in the earth.*) Also **508** Ar. *de part. animalium* Δ10, 687a7 (DK59A102) Ἀναξαγόρας μὲν οὖν φησι διὰ τὸ χεῖρας ἔχειν φρονιμώτατον εἶναι τῶν ζῴων ἄνθρωπον. (*Anaxagoras says, then, that it is his possession of hands that makes man the wisest of living things.*)

(iv) *Sensation*

509 Fr. 21, Sextus *adv. math.* VII, 90 ὑπ' ἀφαυρότητος αὐτῶν (*sc.* τῶν αἰσθήσεων) οὐ δυνατοί ἐσμεν κρίνειν τἀληθές.

510 Fr. 21a, *ibid.* VII, 140 ὄψις γὰρ τῶν ἀδήλων τὰ φαινόμενα.

511 Theophrastus *de sensu* 27ff. (DK59A92) Ἀναξαγόρας δὲ γίνεσθαι μὲν (*sc.* τὰ αἰσθητὰ) τοῖς ἐναντίοις· τὸ γὰρ ὅμοιον ἀπαθὲς ὑπὸ τοῦ ὁμοίου..., τὸ γὰρ ὁμοίως θερμὸν καὶ ψυχρὸν οὔτε θερμαίνειν οὔτε ψύχειν πλησιάζον οὐδὲ δὴ τὸ γλυκὺ καὶ τὸ ὀξὺ δι' αὐτῶν γνωρίζειν, ἀλλὰ τῷ μὲν θερμῷ τὸ ψυχρόν, τῷ δ' ἁλμυρῷ τὸ πότιμον, τῷ δ' ὀξεῖ τὸ γλυκὺ κατὰ τὴν ἔλλειψιν τὴν ἑκάστου· πάντα γὰρ ἐνυπάρχειν φησὶν ἐν ἡμῖν...ἅπασαν δ' αἴσθησιν μετὰ λύπης, ὅπερ ἂν δόξειεν ἀκόλουθον εἶναι τῇ ὑποθέσει· πᾶν γὰρ τὸ ἀνόμοιον ἁπτόμενον πόνον παρέχει. φανερὸν δὲ τοῦτο τῷ τε τοῦ χρόνου πλήθει καὶ τῇ τῶν αἰσθητῶν ὑπερβολῇ.

509 From the weakness of our senses we cannot judge the truth.

510 Appearances are a glimpse of the obscure.

511 Anaxagoras thinks that perception is by opposites, for like is not affected by like...A thing that is as warm or as cold as we are does not either warm us or cool us by its approach, nor can we recognize sweetness or bitterness by their like; rather we know cold by warm, fresh by salt and sweet by bitter in proportion to our deficiency in each. For everything, he says, is in us already...Every perception is accompanied by pain, a consequence that would seem to follow from his hypothesis; for everything unlike produces pain by its contact; and the presence of this pain becomes clear either from too long a duration or from an excess of sensation.

Like the other post-Parmenidean pluralists, Anaxagoras had to give an account of perception that would re-establish its validity. These three passages are all concerned with the senses, but otherwise they have little in common. 509, as we are told by Sextus, who preserved it, was concerned with imperceptible gradations of colour, and its general point seems to have been that though our senses show us what 'portions' predominate in a thing they are not adequate to reveal all the other 'portions' which that thing must contain. 510, on the other hand (which may perhaps come from a discussion of epistemology rather than of perception), suggests that from what we can see we are enabled to imagine also what we cannot see. 511 contains only the most important excerpts from a detailed account of Anaxagoras' theories of perception. These few sentences suffice to show that in this field too Anaxagoras marks an advance upon most of his predecessors. His theory may have been developed in conscious opposition to that of Empedocles, who believed in perception of like by like (see 393); but the notion that the perception of unlike by unlike is, as it were, an imperceptible pain is original and subtle.

CHAPTER XIII

Archelaus of Athens

DATE AND LIFE

512 Diogenes Laertius II, 16 (DK 60 A 1) Ἀρχέλαος Ἀθηναῖος ἢ Μιλήσιος, πατρὸς Ἀπολλοδώρου, ὡς δέ τινες, Μίδωνος, μαθητὴς Ἀναξαγόρου, διδάσκαλος Σωκράτους· οὗτος πρῶτος ἐκ τῆς Ἰωνίας τὴν φυσικὴν φιλοσοφίαν μετήγαγεν Ἀθήναζε, καὶ ἐκλήθη φυσικός, παρὸ καὶ ἔληξεν ἐν αὐτῷ ἡ φυσικὴ φιλοσοφία, Σωκράτους τὴν ἠθικὴν εἰσαγαγόντος. ἔοικεν δὲ καὶ οὗτος ἅψασθαι τῆς ἠθικῆς. καὶ γὰρ περὶ νόμων πεφιλοσόφηκε καὶ καλῶν καὶ δικαίων.

> **512** Archelaus, of Athens or else Miletus, son of Apollodorus or, according to some accounts, of Midon, was a pupil of Anaxagoras and teacher of Socrates; it was he who first transferred physical philosophy from Ionia to Athens, and he was called a physicist. Moreover, physical philosophy came to an end with him, owing to Socrates' introduction of ethics. Archelaus too seems to have touched upon ethical questions, for he speculated as well about law, goodness and justice.

The precise date of Archelaus is uncertain. Diogenes is almost certainly wrong in saying that Archelaus first brought physical speculation to Athens; that distinction probably belongs to Anaxagoras. Likewise the statement that physical philosophy ended with him is very dubious;[1] even Leucippus, let alone Democritus, was probably later than Archelaus. But the tradition that Archelaus was a pupil of Anaxagoras and teacher of Socrates is too well attested to be doubted,[2] and it gives us at least an approximate date. His importance lies chiefly in these distinguished associations; in comparison with either his master or his pupil his direct contribution to philosophy is very small. But he is of a certain interest as indicating the straits to which all but the very greatest of the later physicists were driven in their search for an original cosmology.

[1] This is doubtless merely an instance of the passion for organizing history into 'Ages'. Socrates introduces the 'Age of Ethics', so the 'Age of Physical Philosophy' must stop abruptly.

² See 514, and also 513 Diogenes Laertius ii, 23 Ἴων δὲ ὁ Χῖος (see p. 398) καὶ νέον ὄντα (*sc.* Σωκράτην) εἰς Σάμον σὺν Ἀρχελάῳ ἀποδημῆσαι. *(Ion of Chios says that in his youth Socrates went away with Archelaus to Samos.)* Cf. also Porphyry *Hist. phil.* fr. 12 Nauck² (DK60A3).

COSMOLOGY AND ZOOGONY

514 Simplicius *in Phys.* 27, 23 καὶ Ἀρχέλαος ὁ Ἀθηναῖος, ᾧ καὶ Σωκράτη συγγεγονέναι φασὶν Ἀναξαγόρου γενομένῳ μαθητῇ, ἐν μὲν τῇ γενέσει τοῦ κόσμου καὶ τοῖς ἄλλοις πειρᾶταί τι φέρειν ἴδιον, τὰς ἀρχὰς δὲ τὰς αὐτὰς ἀποδίδωσιν ἅσπερ Ἀναξαγόρας. οὗτοι μὲν οὖν ἀπείρους τῷ πλήθει καὶ ἀνομογενεῖς τὰς ἀρχὰς λέγουσι, τὰς ὁμοιομερείας τιθέντες ἀρχάς...

515 Hippolytus *Ref.* 1, 9, 1 Ἀρχέλαος τὸ μὲν γένος Ἀθηναῖος, υἱὸς δὲ Ἀπολλοδώρου. οὗτος ἔφη τὴν μίξιν τῆς ὕλης ὁμοίως Ἀναξαγόρᾳ τάς τε ἀρχὰς ὡσαύτως. οὗτος δὲ τῷ νῷ ἐνυπάρχειν τι εὐθέως μῖγμα. (2) εἶναι ⟨δ'⟩ ἀρχὴν τῆς κινήσεως ⟨τὸ⟩ ἀποκρίνεσθαι ἀπ' ἀλλήλων τὸ θερμὸν καὶ τὸ ψυχρόν, καὶ τὸ μὲν θερμὸν κινεῖσθαι, τὸ δὲ ψυχρὸν ἠρεμεῖν. τηκόμενον δὲ τὸ ὕδωρ εἰς μέσον ῥεῖν, ἐν ᾧ καὶ κατακαιόμενον ἀέρα γίνεσθαι καὶ γῆν, ὧν τὸ μὲν ἄνω φέρεσθαι, τὸ δὲ ὑφίστασθαι κάτω. (3) τὴν μὲν οὖν γῆν ἠρεμεῖν καὶ γενέσθαι διὰ ταῦτα, κεῖσθαι δ' ἐν μέσῳ οὐδὲν μέρος οὖσαν, ὡς εἰπεῖν, τοῦ παντός. ⟨τὸν δ' ἀέρα κρατεῖν τοῦ παντός⟩ [Roeper, Diels] ἐκδεδομένον ἐκ τῆς πυρώσεως, ἀφ' οὗ πρῶτον ἀποκαιομένου τὴν τῶν ἀστέρων εἶναι φύσιν, ὧν μέγιστον μὲν ἥλιον, δεύτερον δὲ σελήνην, τῶν δὲ ἄλλων τὰ μὲν ἐλάττω τὰ δὲ μείζω. (4) ἐπικλιθῆναι δὲ τὸν οὐρανόν φησι καὶ οὕτως τὸν ἥλιον ἐπὶ τῆς γῆς ποιῆσαι φῶς καὶ τόν τε ἀέρα ποιῆσαι διαφανῆ καὶ τὴν γῆν ξηράν. λίμνην γὰρ εἶναι τὸ πρῶτον, ἅτε κύκλῳ μὲν οὖσαν ὑψηλήν, μέσον δὲ κοίλην. σημεῖον δὲ φέρει τῆς κοιλότητος ὅτι ὁ ἥλιος οὐχ ἅμα ἀνατέλλει τε καὶ δύεται πᾶσιν, ὅπερ ἔδει συμβαίνειν εἴπερ ἦν ὁμαλή. (5) περὶ δὲ ζῴων φησίν, ὅτι θερμαινομένης τῆς γῆς τὸ πρῶτον ἐν τῷ κάτω μέρει, ὅπου τὸ θερμὸν καὶ τὸ ψυχρὸν ἐμίσγετο ἀνεφαίνετο τά τε ἄλλα ζῷα πολλὰ καὶ οἱ ἄνθρωποι, ἅπαντα τὴν αὐτὴν δίαιταν ἔχοντα ἐκ τῆς ἰλύος τρεφόμενα (ἦν δὲ ὀλιγοχρόνια), ὕστερον δὲ αὐτοῖς ἡ ἐξ ἀλλήλων γένεσις συνέστη. (6) καὶ διεκρίθησαν ἄνθρωποι ἀπὸ τῶν ἄλλων καὶ ἡγεμόνας καὶ νόμους καὶ τέχνας καὶ πόλεις καὶ τὰ ἄλλα συνέστησαν. νοῦν δὲ λέγει πᾶσιν ἐμφύεσθαι ζῴοις ὁμοίως. χρῆσθαι γὰρ ἕκαστον καὶ τῶν ζῴων τῷ νῷ, τὸ μὲν βραδυτέρως, τὸ δὲ ταχυτέρως.

514 Archelaus of Athens, the pupil of Anaxagoras with whom Socrates is said to have associated, tries to introduce something original of his own into cosmogony and other subjects, but still gives the same first principles as Anaxagoras had. Both hold that the first principles are infinite in number and different in kind, and they posit the homoeomeries as principles...

515 Archelaus was by birth an Athenian, the son of Apollodorus. He believed in a material mixture like that of Anaxagoras and his first principles were the same; but he maintained that from the outset there was a certain mixture immanent in Mind. The origin of motion was the separation one from the other of the hot and the cold, of which the former moves, the latter stays still.[1] When water is liquefied it flows to the centre, and there it is burnt up to become air and earth, the former of which is borne upwards, while the latter takes up a position below. For these reasons, then, the earth came into being, and lies at rest in the centre, forming no appreciable fraction of the whole universe. ⟨The air⟩ produced by the conflagration ⟨controls the universe⟩, and from its original combustion comes the substance of the heavenly bodies. Of these the sun is the biggest, the moon the second, and of the rest some are smaller, some larger. He says that the heavens are inclined, with the result that the sun gave light on the earth, made the air transparent, and the earth dry. For it was originally a marsh, being lofty around the edge and hollow in the middle. He adduces as a proof of this hollowness the fact that the sun does not rise and set at the same time for all men, as would inevitably happen if the earth were flat. On the subject of animals, he holds that when the earth was originally getting warm in the lower region, where the hot and the cold were mingled, many animals began to appear, including men, all with the same manner of life and all deriving their nourishment from the slime. These were short-lived; but later they began to be born from one another. Men were distinguished from animals, and established rulers, laws, crafts, cities and so on. Mind, he says, is inborn in all animals alike; for each of the animals, as well as man, makes use of Mind, though some more rapidly than others.

[1] Cf. the only surviving fragment of Archelaus, *ap.* Plut. *de prim. frig.* 21 954F: ἡ ψυχρότης δεσμός ἐστιν ('coldness is the bond').

It would appear from these passages, which of course derive ultimately from Theophrastus,[1] that Archelaus took over the system of Anaxagoras but at numerous points, some fundamental, some superficial, made his own modifications or corrections. The following are the most interesting features of the revised cosmology:

(1) *Mind.* Whereas Mind in the system of Anaxagoras had been 'mixed with nothing' and had derived its power from its purity (see

476), in Archelaus it seems to be deprived of its purity (**515**, § 1)[2] and therewith, perhaps, of its creative power.

(2) *Primary substance*. Though some of the ancient authorities suggest that Archelaus made air the primary substance (and one, Epiphanius, even that he chose earth), there can be little doubt that **514** and **515** preserve the most reliable tradition and that he started, like Anaxagoras, with 'seeds' or 'homoeomeries'. Whereas, however, Anaxagoras had made Mind initiate motion and so cause the separating off of 'the dense, the moist, the cold and the dark' from 'the rare, the hot and the dry' (see **489**), Archelaus seems (though the evidence is conflicting: cf. DK60A10 and 18) to make the apparently automatic separation of the hot from the cold the cause of movement (**515**, §2). Thereby he exaggerates the tendency in Anaxagoras, to which Plato so strongly objected (see p. 374 n.), to delegate the responsibility of Mind to the opposites.

(3) *The four world-masses*. The method by which Archelaus brought the four world-masses into being from the opposites is somewhat obscure and very peculiar. Water seems to have been 'melted' or 'liquefied' from 'the cold' in its interaction with 'the hot' (which suggests, perhaps, that 'the cold' was conceived of as ice), and when it thereupon flowed to the centre, it was 'burnt up', again in its interaction with 'the hot', to form earth and air. The mobility of 'the hot' (i.e. fire), and the immobility of 'the cold' (i.e. perhaps ice, producing first water, and thence not only the stationary earth but also fluid air[3]), and the reaction between them, seem to constitute an essential and, so far as we can judge, an original feature of Archelaus' cosmogony.[4] There is no obvious motive for this revision of Anaxagoras except perhaps the desire to bring the Empedoclean 'elements' into greater prominence.

(4) *Zoogony*. The zoogony of Archelaus seems to represent a reversion from that of Anaxagoras, in which seeds were carried down to earth with the rain (see **506**), to that of Anaximander, in which 'living things arose from the moist element as it was evaporated by the sun' (see **136**).

---

[1] Diog. L. v, 42 lists among the writings of Theophrastus Περὶ τῶν ᾿Αρχελάου ᾱ ('1 book on the theories of Archelaus'); cf. pp. 3f.

[2] The relevant sentence of **515**, §1 is, however, so curiously expressed if this is really what it means that Zeller suggested reading τῷ νῷ συνυπάρχειν.

[3] Cf. **516** Diog. L. II, 17 (DK60A1)   τηκόμενόν φησι τὸ ὕδωρ ὑπὸ τοῦ θερμοῦ, καθὸ μὲν εἰς τὸ ⟨κάτω διὰ τὸ⟩ πυρῶδες συνίσταται, ποιεῖν γῆν· καθὸ δὲ περιρρεῖ, ἀέρα γεννᾶν. (*He holds that water is liquefied by the hot; and in so far as it comes together to the lower region owing to the fiery element, it forms earth; in so far as it flows around, it creates air.*) The supplement by Diels, or something very like it, seems essential.

[4] This theory is extended in the Hippocratic *de victu*, an eclectic and very superficial quasi-philosophical treatise written, probably, toward the end of the fourth century B.C.

CONCLUSION

In general, it is hard to resist the conclusion that Archelaus was a second-rate thinker, motivated by the desire to revise the system of Anaxagoras by the inclusion of as many as possible of the doctrines of his most eminent predecessors. From Anaximander he borrowed, besides his biological theories, the primacy of the hot and the cold; from Anaximenes he apparently borrowed the doctrine of the condensation and rarefaction of air (see **140**);[1] from Empedocles he seems to have taken the four 'elements'; and from Anaxagoras he inherited, with a number of modifications of detail such as that concerning the shape of the earth (**515**, §4), almost everything else. It is hardly surprising that the resulting synthesis is lacking in great interest or importance.[2]

[1] Cf. **517** Aetius I, 3, 6 (DK 60 A 7) Ἀρχέλαος...ἀέρα ἄπειρον (*sc.* ἀρχὴν ἔφη εἶναι), καὶ τὴν περὶ αὐτὸν πυκνότητα καὶ μάνωσιν. τούτων δὲ τὸ μὲν εἶναι πῦρ τὸ δ' ὕδωρ. (*Archelaus...[held that the first principle was] infinite air, with its condensation and rarefaction, the former of which was water, the latter fire.*)

[2] If more were known of Archelaus' ethical doctrines, this evaluation might possibly have to be revised. Almost all we are told about them is summarized in the following sentence, which comes very soon after **512**: **518** Diogenes Laertius II, 16 (DK 60 A 1) καὶ τὸ δίκαιον εἶναι καὶ τὸ αἰσχρὸν οὐ φύσει, ἀλλὰ νόμῳ. (*[He maintained that] right and wrong exist only by convention, not by nature.*) This is of course the well-known sophistic view, which may well have been read into Archelaus (perhaps, as Zeller suggested, because he had said something to the effect that men were at first without laws or morals and had only attained to them in course of time (cf. **515**, §6)) in a misguided attempt to credit the teacher of Socrates with a decent minimum of ethical teaching.

CHAPTER XIV

Melissus of Samos

DATE AND LIFE

519 Plutarch *Pericles* 26 (DK 30 A 3) πλεύσαντος γὰρ αὐτοῦ (*sc.*
Περικλέους) Μέλισσος ὁ ᾽Ιθαγένους, ἀνὴρ φιλόσοφος στρατηγῶν τότε
τῆς Σάμου, καταφρονήσας τῆς ὀλιγότητος τῶν νεῶν ἢ τῆς ἀπειρίας
τῶν στρατηγῶν, ἔπεισε τοὺς πολίτας ἐπιθέσθαι τοῖς ᾽Αθηναίοις. καὶ
γενομένης μάχης νικήσαντες οἱ Σάμιοι καὶ πολλοὺς μὲν αὐτῶν ἄνδρας
ἑλόντες πολλὰς δὲ ναῦς διαφθείραντες ἐχρῶντο τῇ θαλάσσῃ καὶ
παρετίθεντο τῶν ἀναγκαίων πρὸς τὸν πόλεμον ὅσα μὴ πρότερον
εἶχον. ὑπὸ δὲ τοῦ Μελίσσου καὶ Περικλέα φησὶν αὐτὸν ᾽Αριστοτέλης
ἡττηθῆναι ναυμαχοῦντα πρότερον.

520 Plutarch *Themistocles* 2 (DK 30 A 3) καίτοι Στησίμβροτος
᾽Αναξαγόρου τε διακοῦσαι τὸν Θεμιστοκλέα φησὶ καὶ περὶ
Μέλισσον σπουδάσαι τὸν φυσικόν, οὐκ εὖ τῶν χρόνων ἁπτόμενος.
Περικλεῖ γάρ, ὃς πολὺ νεώτερος ἦν Θεμιστοκλέους, Μέλισσος μὲν
ἀντεστρατήγει πολιορκοῦντι Σαμίους, ᾽Αναξαγόρας δὲ συνδιέτριβε.

> **519** For when Pericles had set sail, Melissus, son of Ithagenes,
> a philosopher who was then in command of Samos, was so
> contemptuous of the small number of the Athenian ships or of their
> commanders' inexperience that he persuaded the Samians to
> attack. A battle took place which the Samians won. They took so
> many prisoners and destroyed so many ships that they had
> command of the sea, and they devoted to the prosecution of the
> war certain supplies which they did not till then possess. Pericles
> himself, according to Aristotle,[1] had also been defeated by Melissus
> in an earlier naval battle.
>
> **520** Yet Stesimbrotus says that Themistocles sat at the feet of
> Anaxagoras and was enthusiastic in his regard for the physicist
> Melissus. His grasp of chronology here is deficient. For Pericles was
> much younger than Themistocles. And it was against Pericles,
> when he was besieging the Samians, that Melissus fought as
> general, and it was with him that Anaxagoras used to consort.

[1] I.e. in the lost *Constitution of the Samians*.

519 provides our only solid information about Melissus' life and date. The battle in which he defeated the Athenian fleet was fought in 441 B.C., and it is probably for that reason that Apollodorus fixed his *floruit* in the eighty-fourth Olympiad, i.e. 444–441 (Diog. L. IX, 24, DK 30 A 1). It is therefore conceivable that Melissus was no younger than Anaxagoras (born 500); and it may be that Stesimbrotus had some evidence to support his story of Themistocles' associations with the two philosophers.[1] If so, Melissus must have acquired some reputation by the mid-460s, when Themistocles' death is usually dated.

[1] So e.g. Gomme, *A Historical Commentary on Thucydides* I (Oxford, 1945), 37 n. 1 (but he notes the unreliability of Stesimbrotus, a late fifth-century sophist and pamphleteer, *ibid.* 37–8). Plutarch is no doubt right if he is implying in **520** that Themistocles could not have sat as a young man at the feet of either Anaxagoras or Melissus. But despite the difficulties both of Anaxagoras' chronology (pp. 353f. above) and of Themistocles' (cf. Gomme *ad* Thuc. I, 138, 4), it would be rash to rule out the possibility that Themistocles knew Anaxagoras and took an interest in his philosophy. And he perhaps became acquainted with Melissus during his last years in Magnesia on the Ionian coast.

MELISSUS' BOOK

521 Simplicius *in Phys.* 70, 16 (DK 30 A 4) ὁ Μέλισσος καὶ τὴν ἐπιγραφὴν οὕτως ἐποιήσατο τοῦ συγγράμματος Περὶ φύσεως ἢ περὶ τοῦ ὄντος.

522 Simplicius *de caelo* 557, 10 (DK 30 A 4) καὶ εἰ Περὶ φύσεως ἢ περὶ τοῦ ὄντος ἐπέγραψε Μέλισσος, δῆλον ὅτι τὴν φύσιν ἐνόμιζεν εἶναι τὸ ὄν.

> **521** Melissus in fact entitled his treatise in this way *On Nature or on What Exists*.
> **522** And if Melissus used the title *On Nature or on What Exists*, it is clear that he thought that nature is what exists.

A single book is evidently the source of the surviving fragments of Melissus (cf. **466**), which are all preserved by Simplicius. The title reported in **521** and **522** is probably as usual not the author's.[1]

There is no doubt that Melissus wrote after Parmenides, whose pupil he is said to have been (Diog. L. IX, 24, DK 30 A 1), and with whose name his philosophy is associated from Plato (*Theaet.* 180D) and Aristotle (e.g. *Phys.* 186a6, *de caelo* 298b14) on. We would dearly love to know whether his book was composed and in circulation before or after those of his Presocratic contemporaries. As we shall see, there are perhaps signs in **537** that he had read both Anaxagoras and Empedocles; Leucippus, on the other hand, is said in one testimony to have been a pupil of Melissus (Tzetzes *Chil.* II, 980, DK 67 A 5), and Aristotle's general account of the motivation of atomism (**545** below) certainly bears out the idea that he was influenced by Melissus at least as much as by Zeno.[2]

[1] It is sometimes suggested that Gorgias entitled his own work *On Nature, or on What Is Not* in parody of Melissus' title. But the practice of giving titles to prose books seems to have begun only in the sophistic age (see e.g. E. Schmalzriedt, Περὶ φύσεως: *zur Frühgeschichte der Buchtitel* [Munich, 1970]), so the most we could with any safety conjecture is that Melissus' work was known to Gorgias by the title recorded in **521** and **522**. Cf. p. 102 n. 1.

[2] Melissus' stature as a philosopher has often been judged far inferior to that of Parmenides or Zeno, ever since Aristotle declared his thought 'uncouth' (*Phys.* A2, 186a8–10) and 'rather lacking in sophistication (*Met.* A5, 986b25–7). But latterly it has been stoutly defended by Reale (*op. cit.* in n. 1 below) and Barnes, *The Presocratic Philosophers*.

MELISSUS' DEDUCTION

Paraphrases of the argument of Melissus' book are preserved in the pseudo-Aristotelian treatise *On Melissus, Xenophanes and Gorgias* 974a1ff., DK 30 A 5), and by Simplicius (*in Phys.* 103.13ff., DK vol. I pp. 268–70), who curiously represents the schematic version of it which he there reports as Melissus' own work, even though a few pages later he cites genuine fragments of what Melissus actually wrote on the same topics. The paraphrases indicate that the argument proceeded principally by a rigorous deduction of the consequences of assuming simply that something exists.[1] This evidence is confirmed by the actual fragments we possess.

[1] The author of *M.X.G.* takes this to be an unargued assumption: **523** [Aristotle] *M.X.G.* 974a2–3, 975a34–5 (DK 30 A 5) Ἀίδιον εἶναί φησιν εἴ τι ἔστιν, εἴπερ μὴ ἐνδέχεσθαι γενέσθαι μηδὲν ἐκ μηδενός...ἀλλὰ γὰρ τοῦ μὲν εἶναί τι ὡς ὄντος καὶ κειμένου διαλέγεται. (*He says that if there exists something it is eternal, since it is impossible for anything to come to be from nothing...For he talks of there being something that exists as that which is the case and has been assumed.*) Simplicius' paraphrase, on the other hand, represents Melissus as arguing for it: **524** Simplicius *in Phys.* 103, 18 (DK 1 p. 268) εἰ μὲν μηδὲν ἔστι, περὶ τούτου τί ἂν λέγοιτο ὡς ὄντος τινός; εἰ δέ τι ἔστιν, ἤτοι γινόμενόν ἐστιν ἢ ἀεὶ ὄν. (*If it is nothing, what could be said about this – as though it were something? But if it is something, either it is something that comes into being or it always exists.*) Then follows a schematic account of the reasoning preserved in **525**. Some scholars (e.g. Burnet, *EGP*, 321 n. 5; G. Reale, *Melisso* (Florence, 1970), 34–6, 368–9) make the first sentence of **524** the first actual fragment of Melissus. But we should suppose that *M.X.G.* sticks closer to the original here, as we can observe elsewhere.

(i) *Ungenerated and indestructible*

525 Fr. 1, Simplicius *in Phys.* 162, 24 ἀεὶ ἦν ὅ τι ἦν καὶ ἀεὶ ἔσται. εἰ γὰρ ἐγένετο, ἀναγκαῖόν ἐστι πρὶν γενέσθαι εἶναι μηδέν· εἰ τοίνυν μηδὲν ἦν, οὐδαμὰ ἂν γένοιτο οὐδὲν ἐκ μηδενός.

525 It always was whatever it was and it always will be. For if it came to be, it is necessary that before it came into being it was nothing. Now if it was nothing, in no way could anything come to be from nothing.

Like Parmenides, Melissus begins his deduction of the properties entailed by existence with a proof that if something exists, it cannot have come into existence. Like him, he argues that coming into being requires antecedent non-existence, and that nothing could come to be from what is not. And he too leaves us to construct an isomorphic proof against destruction. Parmenides, however, had obscurely concluded that what is never was nor will be, but exists in an eternal present. Melissus firmly rejects this conclusion: he allows the tenses 'was' and 'will be', and ascribes a more readily intelligible everlasting existence to what is.

(ii) *Unlimited extension*

526 Fr. 2, Simplicius *in Phys.* 29, 22 and 109, 20 ὅτε τοίνυν οὐκ ἐγένετο, ἔστι δέ, ἀεὶ ἦν καὶ ἀεὶ ἔσται καὶ ἀρχὴν οὐκ ἔχει οὐδὲ τελευτήν, ἀλλ᾽ ἄπειρόν ἐστιν. εἰ μὲν γὰρ ἐγένετο, ἀρχὴν ἂν εἶχεν (ἤρξατο γὰρ ἄν ποτε γινόμενον) καὶ τελευτήν (ἐτελεύτησε γὰρ ἄν ποτε γινόμενον)· ὅτε δὲ μήτε ἤρξατο μήτε ἐτελεύτησεν, ἀεί τε ἦν καὶ ἀεὶ ἔσται ⟨καὶ⟩ οὐκ ἔχει ἀρχὴν οὐδὲ τελευτήν· οὐ γὰρ ἀεὶ εἶναι ἀνυστόν, ὅ τι μὴ πᾶν ἔστι.

527 Fr. 3, *ibid.* 109, 31 ἀλλ᾽ ὥσπερ ἔστιν ἀεί, οὕτω καὶ τὸ μέγεθος ἄπειρον ἀεὶ χρὴ εἶναι.

528 Fr. 4, *ibid.* 110, 3 ἀρχήν τε καὶ τέλος ἔχον οὐδὲν οὔτε ἀίδιον οὔτε ἄπειρόν ἐστιν.

526 Since, then, it did not come to be, but is, it always was and always will be, and it has no beginning nor end but is unlimited. For if it had come to be, it would have a beginning (for it would have begun coming into being at some time) and an end (for it would have ended coming into being at some time). But since it neither began nor ended, it always was and always will be and it has no beginning nor end; for what is not entire cannot be always.

527 But as it is always, so too it must always be unlimited in magnitude.

528 Nothing that has both beginning and end is either eternal or unlimited.

Melissus now infers that, lacking a beginning and an ending, what is is unlimited in spatial extension just as it is everlasting. It is clear that he means once again to move from Parmenidean premises to a conclusion which flatly contradicts those of the *Truth*: Parmenides' opaque talk of limits is abandoned for the thesis of infinite extension. Unfortunately Melissus' own argument in **526** is itself tortuous and murky. Indeed, some scholars have thought that he intended to argue there only for unlimited *temporal* extension. But ἀίδιον and ἀεί are the words he uses to express that idea (**527** and **528**), and **526** is altogether too complicated a piece of reasoning to be aimed towards a conclusion already simply and adequately argued in **525**.

Melissus apparently assumes that if a thing were to come into existence, there would be a part of it which comes to be first in time and is (thereby) the bit of it first in spatial position (e.g. its front edge); and another part which comes to be last in time and is the bit of it last in position (e.g. its back edge). His argument is then that, since what is cannot begin or finish coming into existence, it can have no such first and last parts – and so is unlimited in extension. Aristotle was appalled at the bad logic of this[1] (cf. also *Soph. elen.* 5, 167b13; 6, 168b35; 28, 181a27):

529 Aristotle *Physics* A3, 186a10 ὅτι μὲν οὖν παραλογίζεται Μέλισσος, δῆλον· οἴεται γὰρ εἰληφέναι, εἰ τὸ γενόμενον ἔχει ἀρχὴν ἅπαν, ὅτι καὶ τὸ μὴ γενόμενον οὐκ ἔχει. εἶτα καὶ τοῦτο ἄτοπον, τὸ παντὸς εἶναι ἀρχήν – τοῦ πράγματος καὶ μὴ τοῦ χρόνου, καὶ γενέσεως μὴ τῆς ἁπλῆς ἀλλὰ καὶ ἀλλοιώσεως, ὥσπερ οὐκ ἀθρόας γιγνομένης μεταβολῆς.

529 It is clear that Melissus' reasoning is fallacious. For he thinks that he can assume, if everything which came into being has a beginning, that what did *not* come into being does *not* have a beginning. And then this too is absurd, the assumption that *everything* has a beginning – the thing and not [just] the time, and coming into being, not [just] unqualified coming into being but alteration too: as though change could not occur all at once.

[1] It is sometimes supposed that Melissus also presented a more plausible argument for unlimited extension: **530** Aristotle *de gen. et corr.* A8, 325a13 (DK 30A8) ἐκ μὲν οὖν τούτων τῶν λόγων ὑπερβάντες τὴν αἴσθησιν καὶ παριδόντες αὐτὴν ὡς τῷ λόγῳ δέον ἀκολουθεῖν ἓν καὶ ἀκίνητον τὸ πᾶν εἶναί φασι

καὶ ἄπειρον ἔνιοι· τὸ γὰρ πέρας περαίνειν ἂν πρὸς τὸ κενόν. *(From these arguments, then – transgressing what the senses say and ignoring them on the grounds that one must follow the argument – they conclude that the universe is one and motionless; and some add that it is unlimited, for its limit would limit it against the void.)* But neither *M.X.G.* nor Simplicius' paraphrase records this proof, which is not easy to reconcile with **531**. Probably it is not genuine Melissus, but something concocted by Aristotle from Melissan materials.

(iii) *One*

531   Fr. 6, Simplicius *de caelo* 557, 16   εἰ γὰρ ⟨ἄπειρον⟩ εἴη, ἓν εἴη ἄν· εἰ γὰρ δύο εἴη, οὐκ ἂν δύναιτο ἄπειρα εἶναι, ἀλλ' ἔχοι ἂν πείρατα πρὸς ἄλληλα.

531   For if it were ⟨infinite⟩, it would be one; for if it were two, the two could not be infinite, but would be limited by one another.

Melissus' tactic here is the opposite of the one he used in **525** and **526–8**. He argues a Parmenidean *conclusion* (monism) from a premiss (unlimited extension) which Parmenides *rejected* (although of course unlimited extension is itself derived from a Parmenidean rejection of generation).

531 expresses what was the most influential of all Melissus' propositions. It is natural to read Parmenides as committed to the idea that if there is something, then there can be only one thing. But he offered no clear proof or statement of it (see p. 251 above), and he certainly did not make it his central preoccupation. So when Plato and Aristotle represent monism as the principal thesis of the Eleatics (e.g. **327**, **530** above, *Phys.* 184b25ff., 186a4ff.), they must be reading Parmenides through Melissan spectacles.

(iv) *Homogeneous*

532   [Aristotle] *M.X.G.* 974a12–14 (DK30A5)   ἓν δὲ ὂν ὅμοιον εἶναι πάντη· εἰ γὰρ ἀνόμοιον, πλείω ὄντα οὐκ ἂν ἔτι ἓν εἶναι, ἀλλὰ πολλά.

532   Being one it is alike in every way; for if it were unlike, being plural it would no longer be one but many.

The words in which Melissus himself inferred homogeneity from uniqueness are lost (**533** *ad init.* makes it certain that he made the inference). No doubt he was inspired at this point by Parmenides' lines in **297**, although he has introduced a characteristic variation, inferring Parmenides' premiss from Parmenides' conclusion.

(v) *Unchangeable*

533 Fr. 7, Simplicius *in Phys.* 111, 18 (1) οὕτως οὖν ἀίδιόν ἐστι καὶ ἄπειρον καὶ ἓν καὶ ὅμοιον πᾶν. (2) καὶ οὔτ' ἂν ἀπόλλύοι τι[1] οὔτε μεῖζον γίνοιτο οὔτε μετακοσμέοιτο οὔτε ἀλγεῖ οὔτε ἀνιᾶται· εἰ γάρ τι τούτων πάσχοι, οὐκ ἂν ἔτι ἓν εἴη. εἰ γὰρ ἑτεροιοῦται, ἀνάγκη τὸ ἐὸν μὴ ὁμοῖον εἶναι, ἀλλὰ ἀπόλλυσθαι τὸ πρόσθεν ἐόν, τὸ δὲ οὐκ ἐὸν γίνεσθαι. εἰ τοίνυν τριχὶ μιῇ μυρίοις ἔτεσιν ἑτεροῖον γίνοιτο, ὀλεῖται πᾶν ἐν τῷ παντὶ χρόνῳ. (3) ἀλλ' οὐδὲ μετακοσμηθῆναι ἀνυστόν· ὁ γὰρ κόσμος ὁ πρόσθεν ἐὼν οὐκ ἀπόλλυται οὔτε ὁ μὴ ἐὼν γίνεται. ὅτε δὲ μήτε προσγίνεται μηδὲν μήτε ἀπόλλυται μήτε ἑτεροιοῦται, πῶς ἂν μετακοσμηθείη τι τῶν ἐόντων; εἰ μὲν γάρ τι ἐγίνετο ἑτεροῖον, ἤδη ἂν καὶ μετακοσμηθείη. (4) οὐδὲ ἀλγεῖ· οὐ γὰρ ἂν πᾶν εἴη ἀλγέον· οὐ γὰρ ἂν δύναιτο ἀεὶ εἶναι χρῆμα ἀλγέον· οὐδὲ ἔχει ἴσην δύναμιν τῷ ὑγιεῖ· οὐδ' ἂν ὁμοῖον εἴη, εἰ ἀλγέοι· ἀπογινομένου γάρ τευ ἂν ἀλγέοι ἢ προσγινομένου, κοὐκ ἂν ἔτι ὁμοῖον εἴη. (5) οὐδ' ἂν τὸ ὑγιὲς ἀλγῆσαι δύναιτο· ἀπὸ γὰρ ἂν ὄλοιτο [τὸ ὑγιὲς καὶ] τὸ ἐόν, τὸ δὲ οὐκ ἐὸν γένοιτο. (6) καὶ περὶ τοῦ ἀνιᾶσθαι ὡυτὸς λόγος τῷ ἀλγέοντι.

[1] ἀπολλύοι τι Covotti: ἀπόλοιτο Simplicius F, ἀπόλλοιτο E.

533 In this way, then, it is eternal and unlimited and one and all alike. And it will not lose anything nor become larger nor be rearranged, nor does it suffer pain or anguish; for if it were affected by any of these, it would no longer be one. For if it alters, it is necessary that what is should not be alike, but that what was earlier perishes and what is not comes into being. Indeed, if it were to become different by a single hair in ten thousand years, it will all perish in the whole of time. But neither is it possible for it to be rearranged. For the order (*kosmos*) which was earlier does not perish, nor does an order which is not come into being. And since nothing is added or destroyed or alters, how might anything that is be rearranged? For if it became different in any respect, it would thereby be rearranged. Nor does it suffer pain. For it would not be entire if it were in pain, for a thing in pain could not be always; nor has it equal power with what is healthy; nor would it be alike if it were in pain, for it would be in pain in virtue of something's passing from it or being added to it, and it would no longer be alike. Nor could what is healthy be in pain, for then what is would perish and what is not would come into being. And the same argument applies to anguish as to pain.

This long extract is packed with interesting arguments. Some of them turn on considerations about homogeneity; others rely on the fundamental argument of **525** against generation and destruction; others again introduce quite fresh trains of thought, as for example when it is observed that what is in pain does not have the same power as what is healthy. This example is puzzling, and indeed belongs to a sequence of reasoning that is little understood. Why should Melissus be so concerned to deny that what is suffers pain and grief? Does he have some special philosophical target in mind, which his first readers would have recognized as a well-known doctrine but we do not? Are his denials the counterpart of a positive belief (conceivably derived from Xenophanes) in the divinity of reality? Perhaps it is rather that Melissus wanted to emphasize the perfection of what is in terms which would point up most tellingly and poignantly its difference from the animate beings ordinary mortals believe in and believe themselves to be. His arguments may therefore have been inspired by Xenophanes (**166–9**), but he will not have intended us to think of reality as sentient or intelligent (contrast **170–2**).

(vi) *Motionless*

534 Fr. 7, Simplicius *in Phys.* 112, 6[1] (7) οὐδὲ κενεόν ἐστιν οὐδέν· τὸ γὰρ κενεὸν οὐδέν ἐστιν· οὐκ ἂν οὖν εἴη τό γε μηδέν. οὐδὲ κινεῖται· ὑποχωρῆσαι γὰρ οὐκ ἔχει οὐδαμῇ, ἀλλὰ πλέων ἐστίν. εἰ μὲν γὰρ κενεὸν ἦν, ὑπεχώρει ἂν εἰς τὸ κενόν· κενοῦ δὲ μὴ ἐόντος οὐκ ἔχει ὅκη ὑποχωρήσει. (8) πυκνὸν δὲ καὶ ἀραιὸν οὐκ ἂν εἴη. τὸ γὰρ ἀραιὸν οὐκ ἀνυστὸν πλέων εἶναι ὁμοίως τῷ πυκνῷ, ἀλλ᾽ ἤδη τὸ ἀραιόν γε κενεώτερον γίνεται τοῦ πυκνοῦ. (9) κρίσιν δὲ ταύτην χρὴ ποιήσασθαι τοῦ πλέω καὶ τοῦ μὴ πλέω· εἰ μὲν οὖν χωρεῖ τι ἢ εἰσδέχεται, οὐ πλέων· εἰ δὲ μήτε χωρεῖ μήτε εἰσδέχεται, πλέων. (10) ἀνάγκη τοίνυν πλέων εἶναι, εἰ κενὸν μὴ ἔστιν. εἰ τοίνυν πλέων ἐστίν, οὐ κινεῖται.

534 And nothing of it is empty. For what is empty is nothing. Well, what is nothing could not very well exist. Nor does it move. For it cannot give way at any point, but is full. For if there were such a thing as empty it would give way into what was empty; but since there is no such thing as empty, it has nowhere to give way. (Dense and rare will not exist. For what is rare cannot be as full as what is dense, but what is rare thereby becomes emptier than what is dense.) And this is the criterion for distinguishing between what is full and what is not full: if something gives way or accommodates, it is not full; but if it neither gives way nor accommodates, it is full. So it must be full, if there is no such thing as empty. Now if it is full, it does not move. (*After D. N. Sedley*)

[1] Simplicius makes **534** continuous with **533**; but it introduces a topic not

promised in the introduction to 533, so it is right to make 534 a separate section of the argument, whether or not any intervening matter has been lost.

The argument of 534 is Melissus' greatest achievement. In these lines he not only improves enormously on Parmenides' obscure remarks about change and motion (298), but creates[1] one of the classic notions of Greek physical thought: void is the precondition of motion. This notion, together with the idea (possibly also Melissus' invention) that void is nothing,[2] was to be borrowed by Leucippus as one of the foundations of his physical system. Melissus no doubt thought his claim that what is nothing does not exist incontrovertible, but the atomists were prepared to advance the paradoxical thesis that what is exists no more than what is not (555), so turning the refutation of the possibility of motion in 534 to unexpected positive effect.

[1] Unless priority should be ascribed to the obscure Xuthus: 535 Aristotle *Phys.* Δ9, 216b22   εἰσὶ δέ τινες οἳ διὰ τοῦ μανοῦ καὶ πυκνοῦ οἴονται φανερὸν εἶναι ὅτι ἔστι κενόν. εἰ μὲν γὰρ μὴ ἔστι μανὸν καὶ πυκνόν, οὐδὲ συνιέναι καὶ πιλεῖσθαι οἷόν τε. εἰ δὲ τοῦτο μὴ εἴη, ἢ ὅλως κίνησις οὐκ ἔσται ἢ κυμανεῖ τὸ ὅλον, ὥσπερ ἔφη Ξοῦθος. *(There are some who think that the existence of rarity and density shows that there is a void. If rarity and density do not exist, they say, neither can things contract and be compressed. But if this were not to take place, either there would be no movement at all, or the universe would swell like the sea, as Xuthus said.* (After Hardie) This Xuthus, called a Pythagorean by Simplicius (*ad loc., in Phys.* 683, 24), may be the Xuthus who was father of Ion of Chios (Harpocration, s.v. ῎Ιων, DK 36A1; cf. p. 218 above). If so, Xuthus is an early fifth-century figure (the Suda, s.v. ῎Ιων Χῖος, DK 36A3, dates Ion's first tragedy to the eighty-second Olympiad, i.e. 452–449 B.C.). In his speculation about the swelling of the universe it is tempting to see a reply to Parmenides: if reality is finite and full, then even if there can be no motion proper (i.e. no change of position either within the limits or through them), what is may still expand and push its limits out. Melissus is, of course, not liable to this curious line of objection.

[2] But Anaxagoras had probably already distinguished the concept of void from that of air (cf. 470 above), and Empedocles had employed the word κένεον, 'empty', again probably before Melissus, in such a way as to imply recognition of the distinction: 536 Empedocles fr. 13, Aetius I, 18, 2   οὐδέ τι τοῦ παντὸς κενεὸν πέλει οὐδὲ περισσόν. *(Nor is any part of the all empty nor yet overfull.)*

CONFUTATION OF COMMON SENSE

537   Fr. 8, Simplicius *de caelo* 558, 21   μέγιστον μὲν οὖν σημεῖον οὗτος ὁ λόγος, ὅτι ἓν μόνον ἐστιν· ἀτὰρ καὶ τάδε σημεῖα. εἰ γὰρ ἦν πολλά, τοιαῦτα χρὴ αὐτὰ εἶναι οἷόν περ ἐγώ φημι τὸ ἓν εἶναι. εἰ γὰρ ἔστι γῆ καὶ ὕδωρ καὶ ἀὴρ καὶ πῦρ καὶ σίδηρος καὶ χρυσός, καὶ τὸ μὲν ζῶον τὸ δὲ τεθνηκός, καὶ μέλαν καὶ λευκὸν καὶ τὰ ἄλλα ὅσα φασὶν οἱ ἄνθρωποι εἶναι ἀληθῆ, εἰ δὴ ταῦτα ἔστι, καὶ ἡμεῖς ὀρθῶς ὁρῶμεν καὶ ἀκούομεν, εἶναι χρὴ ἕκαστον τοιοῦτον οἷόν περ τὸ πρῶτον ἔδοξεν

ἡμῖν, καὶ μὴ μεταπίπτειν μηδὲ γίνεσθαι ἑτεροῖον, ἀλλὰ ἀεὶ εἶναι
ἕκαστον οἷόν πέρ ἐστιν. νῦν δέ φαμεν ὀρθῶς ὁρᾶν καὶ ἀκούειν καὶ
συνιέναι· δοκεῖ δὲ ἡμῖν τό τε θερμὸν ψυχρὸν γίνεσθαι καὶ τὸ ψυχρὸν
θερμὸν καὶ τὸ σκληρὸν μαλθακὸν καὶ τὸ μαλθακὸν σκληρὸν καὶ τὸ
ζῶον ἀποθνήσκειν καὶ ἐκ μὴ ζῶντος γίνεσθαι, καὶ ταῦτα πάντα
ἑτεροιοῦσθαι, καὶ ὅ τι ἦν τε καὶ ὃ νῦν οὐδὲν ὁμοῖον εἶναι, ἀλλ' ὅ τε
σίδηρος σκληρὸς ἐὼν τῷ δακτύλῳ κατατρίβεσθαι ὁμουρέων [Bergk
Diels; ὁμοῦ ῥέων MSS], καὶ χρυσὸς καὶ λίθος καὶ ἄλλο ὅ τι ἰσχυρὸν
δοκεῖ εἶναι πᾶν,[1] ἐξ ὕδατός τε γῆ καὶ λίθος γίνεσθαι. οὐ τοίνυν ταῦτα
ἀλλήλοις ὁμολογεῖ. φαμένοις γὰρ εἶναι πολλὰ καὶ ἀίδια καὶ εἴδη τε καὶ
ἰσχὺν ἔχοντα, πάντα ἑτεροιοῦσθαι ἡμῖν δοκεῖ καὶ μεταπίπτειν ἐκ τοῦ
ἑκάστοτε ὁρωμένου. δῆλον τοίνυν, ὅτι οὐκ ὀρθῶς ἑωρῶμεν οὐδὲ ἐκεῖνα
πολλὰ ὀρθῶς δοκεῖ εἶναι· οὐ γὰρ ἂν μετέπιπτεν, εἰ ἀληθῆ ἦν· ἀλλ'
ἦν οἷόν περ ἐδόκει ἕκαστον τοιοῦτον. τοῦ γὰρ ἐόντος ἀληθινοῦ
κρεῖσσον οὐδέν. ἢν δὲ μεταπέσῃ, τὸ μὲν ἐὸν ἀπώλετο, τὸ δὲ οὐκ ἐὸν
γέγονεν. οὕτως οὖν, εἰ πολλὰ εἴη, τοιαῦτα χρὴ εἶναι οἷόν περ τὸ ἕν.

[1] Then in the MSS follow the words ὥστε συμβαίνει μήτε ὁρᾶν μήτε τὰ ὄντα
γινώσκειν, transposed after γίνεσθαι by Karsten but rightly deleted as a gloss
by Barnes, *The Presocratic Philosophers* I, 340 n. 3.

537 This argument, then, is the greatest proof that it is one alone;
but the following are proofs of it also. If there were a plurality,
things would have to be of the same kind as I say that the one is.
For if there is earth and water, and air and fire, and iron and gold,
and if one thing is living and another dead, and if things are black
and white and all that men say they really are – if that is so, and
if we see and hear aright, each one of these must be such as we
first decided, and they cannot be changed or altered, but each must
be always just as it is. But, as it is, we say that we see and hear
and understand aright, and yet we believe that what is warm
becomes cold, and what is cold warm; that what is hard turns soft,
and what is soft hard; that what is living dies, and that things are
born from what lives not; and that all those things are changed,
and that what they were and what they are now are in no way
alike. We think that iron, which is hard, is rubbed away by contact
with the finger, and so with gold and stone and everything which
we fancy to be strong; and that earth and stone are made out of
water. Now these things do not agree with one another. We said
that there were many things that were eternal and had forms and
strength of their own, and yet we fancy that they all suffer
alteration, and that they change from what we see each time. It
is clear, then, that we did not see aright after all, nor are we right
in believing that all these things are many. They would not change

if they were real, but each thing would be just what we believed it to be; for nothing is stronger than true reality. But if it has changed, what is has passed away and what is not has come into being. So then, if there were a plurality, things would have to be of just the same nature as the one. (*After Burnet*)

This skilful attack upon the validity of the senses is plainly directed at the basic assumptions all men make about reality, just as Parmenides and Zeno levelled their critiques against mortal opinions in general.[1] The strategy of the argument is simple but ingenious: if men believe that the things in the catalogue Melissus itemizes are real, they do so because they trust in the reliability of their senses; but if they also accept the argument of **533** that nothing real can change, then they are committed to a contradiction. For our senses also lead us to believe that the things in the catalogue change. Consequently **533** compels us to abandon the initial assumption that our senses are reliable. We thus lose reason to believe in a plurality of the kind our senses disclose to us. If there were a plurality, its members would have to be just the sort of things Melissus claims the one to be – changeless, ungenerated and indestructible. This conclusion, intended by Melissus as a *reductio ad absurdum* of belief in a plurality of things, was accepted by the atomists and made into another fundamental thesis of their system.

[1] Nonetheless Melissus' catalogue perhaps betrays acquaintance with Empedocles' work (he seems to know the canonical list of four elements, which is probably due to Empedocles) and above all Anaxagoras' (in its listing of both substances and opposites (cf. **485**) and in its choice of black and white from the latter (cf. **487**)).

THE INCORPOREAL

538 Simplicius *in Phys.* 109, 34 and 87, 6   ὅτι γὰρ ἀσώματον εἶναι βούλεται τὸ ὄν, ἐδήλωσεν εἰπών· (fr. 9) εἰ μὲν οὖν εἴη, δεῖ αὐτὸ ἓν εἶναι· ἓν δ' ἐὸν δεῖ αὐτὸ σῶμα μὴ ἔχειν. εἰ δὲ ἔχοι πάχος, ἔχοι ἂν μόρια, καὶ οὐκέτι ἓν εἴη.

538 That he wants what exists to be incorporeal he makes clear when he says [fr. 9]: 'If, then, it were, it must be one; and being one, it must not have body. But if it had solidity, it would have parts, and be no longer one.'

538 is a deeply puzzling text. Simplicius quotes it to show that Melissus believed reality to be incorporeal. But this proof pretty clearly did not form part of the deduction of **525ff.** (it is unknown to the *M.X.G.* and does not appear in Simplicius' paraphrase); and it is natural to read 534 as ascribing solidity to reality, when it claims that what is is full and therefore cannot admit the movement of anything into it or within it. It is accordingly tempting to suppose either that 538 is not a genuine text of Melissus at all[1] or that it belongs to the polemical part of Melissus' book already represented by 537. Perhaps after 537 Melissus went on to argue that each member of the sorts of plurality men ordinarily believe in must be one – but therefore (so 538) incorporeal, which is *contrary* to ordinary belief.[2] But in that case, it is hard to see how his *reductio* does not damage equally his own conception of reality as one but full throughout infinite extension.

[1] Simplicius may be drawing on a *selection* of Eleatic texts (hence his confusion about the status of the paraphrase of 103.13ff.), and may have been misled by it into attributing to Melissus a fragment of Zeno: note Zeno's use of the term πάχος, 'solidity' or 'thickness', in 316; and note how neatly 538 would supply an argument needed in the first limb of 316.

[2] Simplicius may then have become muddled about the bearing of Melissus' remark, as he was in the case of the observation of Zeno discussed in 330–1.

CONCLUSION

Melissus was not a great original metaphysician like Parmenides nor a brilliant exponent of paradox like Zeno. But he was inventive in argument, and his deduction of the properties of reality is in general much clearer than Parmenides'. It is his version of Eleatic doctrine to which the atomists chiefly responded and which shaped its presentation by Plato and Aristotle.

CHAPTER XV

The Atomists: Leucippus of Miletus and Democritus of Abdera

INDIVIDUAL CONTRIBUTIONS, AND DATES

539 Simplicius *in Phys.* 28, 4 (= Theophrastus *Phys. op.* fr. 8) Λεύκιππος δὲ ὁ Ἐλεάτης ἢ Μιλήσιος (ἀμφοτέρως γὰρ λέγεται περὶ αὐτοῦ), κοινωνήσας Παρμενίδῃ τῆς φιλοσοφίας, οὐ τὴν αὐτὴν ἐβάδισε Παρμενίδῃ καὶ Ξενοφάνει περὶ τῶν ὄντων ὁδόν, ἀλλ' ὡς δοκεῖ τὴν ἐναντίαν.

540 Diogenes Laertius x, 13 τοῦτον (*sc.* Ἐπίκουρον) Ἀπολλόδωρος ἐν Χρονικοῖς Ναυσιφάνους ἀκοῦσαί φησι καὶ Πραξιφάνους· αὐτὸς δὲ οὔ φησιν, ἀλλ' ἑαυτοῦ ἐν τῇ πρὸς Εὐρύλοχον ἐπιστολῇ. ἀλλ' οὐδὲ Λεύκιππόν τινα γεγενῆσθαί φησι φιλόσοφον οὔτε αὐτὸς οὔτε Ἕρμαρχος, ὃν ἔνιοί φασι (καὶ Ἀπολλόδωρος ὁ Ἐπικούρειος) διδάσκαλον Δημοκρίτου γεγενῆσθαι.

541 Cicero *Academica priora* II, 37, 118 Leucippus plenum et inane; Democritus huic in hoc similis, uberior in ceteris.

542 Diogenes Laertius IX, 34 Δημόκριτος Ἡγησιστράτου, οἱ δὲ Ἀθηνοκρίτου, τινὲς Δαμασίππου, Ἀβδηρίτης ἤ, ὡς ἔνιοι, Μιλήσιος. ...ὕστερον δὲ Λευκίππῳ παρέβαλε καὶ Ἀναξαγόρᾳ κατά τινας, ἔτεσιν ὢν αὐτοῦ νεώτερος τετταράκοντα... (41) γέγονε δὲ τοῖς χρόνοις, ὡς αὐτός φησιν ἐν τῷ Μικρῷ διακόσμῳ, νέος κατὰ πρεσβύτην Ἀναξαγόραν, ἔτεσιν αὐτοῦ νεώτερος τετταράκοντα. συντετάχθαι δέ φησι τὸν Μικρὸν διάκοσμον ἔτεσιν ὕστερον τῆς Ἰλίου ἁλώσεως τριάκοντα καὶ ἑπτακοσίοις. γεγόνοι δ' ἄν, ὡς μὲν Ἀπολλόδωρος ἐν Χρονικοῖς, κατὰ τὴν ὀγδοηκοστὴν ὀλυμπιάδα (460–457 B.C.), ὡς δὲ Θρασύλος, ἐν τῷ ἐπιγραφομένῳ Τὰ πρὸ τῆς ἀναγνώσεως τῶν Δημοκρίτου βιβλίων, κατὰ τὸ τρίτον ἔτος τῆς ἑβδόμης καὶ ἑβδομηκοστῆς ὀλυμπιάδος (470/69), ἐνιαυτῷ, φησί, πρεσβύτερος ὢν Σωκράτους.

539 Leucippus of Elea or Miletus (both accounts are current) had associated with Parmenides in philosophy, but in his view of reality he did not tread the same path as Parmenides and Xenophanes, but rather, it seems, the opposite path.

540 Apollodorus in the *Chronicles* says that Epicurus was instructed by Nausiphanes and Praxiphanes; but Epicurus himself denies this, saying in the letter to Eurylochus that he instructed himself. He and Hermarchus both maintain that there never was a philosopher Leucippus, who some (including Apollodorus the Epicurean) say was the teacher of Democritus.

541 Leucippus postulated atoms and void, and in this respect Democritus resembled him, though in other respects he was more productive.

542 Democritus, son of Hegesistratus (or by other accounts of Athenocritus or Damasippus), a citizen of Abdera or, as some say, of Miletus... Later he met Leucippus and, according to some, Anaxagoras also, whose junior he was by forty years...As he himself says in the *Little World-system*, he was a young man in the old age of Anaxagoras, being forty years younger. He says that the *Little World-system* was composed 730 years after the capture of Troy. He would have been born, according to Apollodorus in the *Chronicles*, in the eightieth Olympiad; according to Thrasylus, in his book entitled *Preparation for Reading the Works of Democritus*, in the third year of the seventy-seventh, being one year (as he says) older than Socrates.

Leucippus was generally agreed to have evolved his theory of atoms in answer to the Eleatic elenchus: so Aristotle in **545** below. He was even assumed by late sources to have been an Eleatic; according to Diogenes Laertius IX, 30 (DK 67 A 1) he was a pupil of Zeno. This we need not believe: it is not suggested by Aristotle, and is the kind of thing which might easily be asserted by Sotion and the other succession-writers. Miletus is given as his alternative birth-place; the *a priori* reasons for this are not so strong, though he obviously revived some Milesian astronomical theories; it might therefore be true. He may of course have visited Elea, but the Eleatic doctrines were known in Athens, and Melissus, against whom Leucippus perhaps chiefly reacted (cf. pp. 398ff., 408f.), was an Ionian. Singularly little was known about Leucippus, in any case, and in **540** his very existence seems to be denied by Epicurus and Hermarchus. But Epicurus is intent on proving his own originality; Burnet (*EGP*, 330 n. 2) suggested that all Epicurus said was something like Λεύκιππον οὐδ' εἰ γέγονεν οἶδα, meaning 'I don't consider Leucippus worth discussing'. Alternatively, the emphasis might have been on the word φιλόσοφον: there was no *philosopher* Leucippus (i.e. Leucippus was no philosopher).

Unlike Leucippus, Democritus was the subject of a large number of anecdotes told by ancient writers (see e.g. Diog. L. IX, 34ff., DK68A1; selections below, p. 406 n. 1). But he remains a scarcely less shadowy figure: the stories are mere fictions. All we can be sure of is that he came from Abdera, the city of his elder contemporary Protagoras, and that he did indeed associate with Leucippus.

It is clear from **545** that Aristotle considered Leucippus to be the inventor of atomism, and this is accepted by Theophrastus (in the continuation of **539**, Simpl. *in Phys.* 28, 7ff.). Much harder to assess is Democritus' contribution to the theory. In his reports of it Aristotle normally writes simply of 'Leucippus and Democritus' and when later doxographical passages refer to one of the philosophers only, it is in general unsafe to infer that the doctrine in question is special to him.[1] But we have evidence that Democritus was particularly preoccupied with the epistemological basis of atomism; and no doubt he was responsible for working out many of its detailed applications, as for example in the theory of perception, which Theophrastus presents as his without any mention of Leucippus (*de sensu* 49ff., DK68A135). Otherwise, as Cicero implies (**541**), Democritus wrote on a wide range of topics presumably left untouched by Leucippus (cf. pp. 405–6 below), showing himself in this variety of interests a typical author of the sophistic age.

[1] The attempt of C. Bailey, in *The Greek Atomists and Epicurus*, to distinguish the views of the two thinkers, has not found much support. See the criticisms of Guthrie, *HGP* II, 382 n. 2, and (on particular points) of Furley, *Two Studies in the Greek Atomists*, 94–5, and M. C. Stokes, *One and Many in Presocratic Philosophy* (Washington, D.C., 1971), 334 n. 15, 335 n. 20.

The date of Leucippus is not known independently, except from such guesses as that he was a pupil of Zeno. Democritus, however, evidently gave a clue to his own age in his work the *Little World-system*: he was about forty years younger than Anaxagoras. This fits Apollodorus' date in **542** (born 460–457 B.C.) better than Thrasylus', of some ten years earlier. In any case, if Democritus accepted 1184 B.C. as the year of the capture of Troy (and this, the Eratosthenic epoch-year, was merely the commonest of several dates), then the composition of the *Little World-system* (on which see the next section) would be placed too early, in 454. The probability is that it was written after 430. Leucippus, presumably, was somewhat older, and his *floruit* (i.e. the composition of the *Great World-system*) might be put around 440–435. A possible *terminus ante quem* is provided by Theophrastus' statement (**598**) that Diogenes of Apollonia derived some of his ideas from Leucippus; for Diogenes was already parodied in the *Clouds* of 423 B.C. (**614**).

WRITINGS

543 Diogenes Laertius IX, 45 (DK68A33) τὰ δὲ βιβλία αὐτοῦ (sc. Δημοκρίτου) καὶ Θρασύλος ἀναγέγραφε κατὰ τάξιν οὕτως ὡσπερεὶ καὶ τὰ Πλάτωνος κατὰ τετραλογίαν. (46) ἔστι δὲ ἠθικὰ μὲν τάδε·...φυσικὰ δὲ τάδε· [tetralogy III] Μέγας διάκοσμος (ὃν οἱ περὶ Θεόφραστον Λευκίππου φασὶν εἶναι), Μικρὸς διάκοσμος, Κοσμογραφίη, Περὶ τῶν πλανητῶν...

543 Thrasylus listed his books in order by tetralogies, just as he did Plato's books. His ethical works comprised the following... The physical books were these: The *Great World-system* (which Theophrastus' followers say was by Leucippus), the *Little World-system*, the *Cosmography* and *On the Planets*...

It is true that the *Great World-system* is usually assigned to Democritus, since he was the elaborator of atomism and, apart from Epicurus, its chief exponent. Epicurus himself would presumably have credited it to Democritus. But Theophrastus' opinion in **543** counts for much: Aristotle came from a city in Thrace, and both he and his pupil Theophrastus devoted special works to Democritus. They were evidently aware of the distinction between Leucippus and Democritus, whereas it is natural that when the distinction became forgotten all early atomistic works should be attributed to Democritus. We may therefore provisionally accept Theophrastus' view that Leucippus wrote the *Great*, Democritus the *Little World-system*[1]; with the possible modification that the former may have been a compendium of Leucippus' cosmological work with other, later, atomistic additions. One other work is attributed to Leucippus, namely *On Mind*: the quotation from him by Aetius (**569**) is assigned to this work, which may, of course, have been a section of the *Great World-system*. The content of this fragment would certainly not be foreign to that work, and might have formed part of an attack on the concept of Mind in Anaxagoras.

[1] It seems probable that this work contained a description of the origin of civilization and culture, and that part of the description in Diodorus I, 7–8 (DK68B5, I) goes back to Democritus by way of Hecataeus of Abdera (see G. Vlastos, *AJP* 67 (1946), 51ff.). However, Diodorus certainly used more than one Ionian source for this section, and it can be conceded that the account of cosmogony in I, 7 is not primarily atomistic.

Democritus, on the other hand, must have been one of the most prolific of all ancient authors. Thrasylus (or Thrasyllus), who arranged Plato's dialogues in tetralogies, did the same for Democritus according to **543**: there were thirteen tetralogies (comprising fifty-two separate works, some no doubt quite short) divided between the following general headings: Ethics (2 tetralogies), Physics (4), Mathematics (3), Music, including literature and language (2), Technical subjects (2). There were additional works which were probably not genuine.[1] It is a tantalizing misfortune, and a reflexion of later taste, that the considerable number of fragments that have survived (not all of which are certainly genuine) are nearly all taken from the ethical works.

[1] Among the works classed as Ὑπομνήματα and not included by Thrasylus (Diog. L. ix, 49, DK68a33) are five concerned with foreign travel, for example a Chaldaean and a Phrygian dissertation. The attribution is perhaps related to the many stories in our ancient biographical sources that Democritus travelled extensively: for example **544** Diog. L. ix, 35 φησὶ δὲ Δημήτριος ἐν Ὁμωνύμοις καὶ Ἀντισθένης ἐν Διαδοχαῖς ἀποδημῆσαι αὐτὸν καὶ εἰς Αἴγυπτον πρὸς τοὺς ἱερέας γεωμετρίαν μαθησόμενον καὶ πρὸς Χαλδαίους εἰς τὴν Περσίδα, καὶ εἰς τὴν Ἐρυθρὰν θάλασσαν γενέσθαι. τοῖς τε Γυμνοσοφισταῖς φασί τινες συμμῖξαι αὐτὸν ἐν Ἰνδίᾳ καὶ εἰς Αἰθιοπίαν ἐλθεῖν. *(Demetrius in his* Homonyms *and Antisthenes in his* Successions *say that he travelled to Egypt to visit the priests and learn geometry, and that he went also to Persia, to visit the Chaldaeans, and to the Red Sea. Some say that he associated with the 'naked philosophers' in India; also that he went to Aethiopia.)* Another story is that Xerxes left Chaldaean overseers in Democritus' father's household, from whom Democritus learned much. There may have been some basis in fact for these stories of foreign contact. According to another anecdote Democritus said that he visited Athens, but that no one recognized him.

METAPHYSICAL PRINCIPLES

545 Aristotle *de gen. et corr.* A8, 325a2 (DK67a7; first part of extract is continued at **530**)   ἐνίοις γὰρ τῶν ἀρχαίων ἔδοξε τὸ ὂν ἐξ ἀνάγκης ἓν εἶναι καὶ ἀκίνητον· τὸ μὲν γὰρ κενὸν οὐκ ὄν, κινηθῆναι δ' οὐκ ἂν δύνασθαι μὴ ὄντος κενοῦ κεχωρισμένου, οὐδ' αὖ πολλὰ εἶναι μὴ ὄντος τοῦ διείργοντος – τοῦτο δ' οὐδὲν διαφέρειν, εἴ τις οἴεται μὴ συνεχὲς εἶναι τὸ πᾶν ἀλλ' ἅπτεσθαι διῃρημένον, τοῦ φάναι πολλὰ καὶ μὴ ἓν εἶναι καὶ κενόν. εἰ μὲν γὰρ πάντῃ διαιρετόν, οὐθὲν εἶναι ἕν, ὥστε οὐδὲ πολλά, ἀλλὰ κενὸν τὸ ὅλον· εἰ δὲ τῇ μὲν τῇ δὲ μή, πεπλασμένῳ τινὶ τοῦτ' ἐοικέναι. μέχρι πόσου γάρ, καὶ διὰ τί τὸ μὲν οὕτως ἔχει τοῦ ὅλου καὶ πλῆρές ἐστι, τὸ δὲ διῃρημένον; ἔτι δ' ὁμοίως ἀναγκαῖον μὴ εἶναι κίνησιν... (a23) Λεύκιππος δ' ἔχειν ᾠήθη λόγους οἵτινες πρὸς τὴν αἴσθησιν ὁμολογούμενα λέγοντες οὐκ ἀναιρήσουσιν οὔτε γένεσιν οὔτε φθορὰν οὔτε κίνησιν καὶ τὸ πλῆθος τῶν ὄντων. ὁμολογήσας δὲ ταῦτα μὲν τοῖς φαινομένοις, τοῖς δὲ τὸ ἓν κατασκευάζουσιν ὡς οὐκ ἂν κίνησιν οὖσαν ἄνευ κενοῦ, τό τε κενὸν μὴ ὂν καὶ τοῦ ὄντος οὐθὲν μὴ ὂν φησιν εἶναι· τὸ γὰρ κυρίως ὂν παμπλῆρες ὄν. ἀλλ' εἶναι τὸ τοιοῦτον οὐχ ἕν, ἀλλ' ἄπειρα τὸ πλῆθος καὶ ἀόρατα διὰ σμικρότητα τῶν

ὄγκων. ταῦτα δ' ἐν τῷ κενῷ φέρεσθαι (κενὸν γὰρ εἶναι), καὶ
συνιστάμενα μὲν γένεσιν ποιεῖν, διαλυόμενα δὲ φθοράν. ποιεῖν δὲ καὶ
πάσχειν ᾗ τυγχάνουσιν ἁπτόμενα (ταύτῃ γὰρ οὐχ ἓν εἶναι), καὶ
συντιθέμενα δὲ καὶ περιπλεκόμενα γεννᾶν. ἐκ δὲ τοῦ κατ' ἀλήθειαν ἑνὸς
οὐκ ἂν γενέσθαι πλῆθος οὐδ' ἐκ τῶν ἀληθῶς πολλῶν ἕν, ἀλλ' εἶναι
τοῦτ' ἀδύνατον· ἀλλ', ὥσπερ Ἐμπεδοκλῆς καὶ τῶν ἄλλων τινές φασι
πάσχειν διὰ τῶν πόρων, οὕτω πᾶσαν ἀλλοίωσιν καὶ πᾶν τὸ πάσχειν
τοῦτον γίνεσθαι τὸν τρόπον, διὰ τοῦ κενοῦ γινομένης τῆς διαλύσεως
καὶ τῆς φθορᾶς, ὁμοίως δὲ καὶ τῆς αὐξήσεως, ὑπεισδυομένων στερεῶν.

546 Aristotle *Phys.* A3, 187a1 (DK 29 A 22) ἔνιοι δ' ἐνέδοσαν τοῖς
λόγοις ἀμφοτέροις, τῷ μὲν ὅτι πάντα ἕν, εἰ τὸ ὂν ἓν σημαίνει, ὅτι ἔστι
τὸ μὴ ὄν, τῷ δὲ ἐκ τῆς διχοτομίας, ἄτομα ποιήσαντες μεγέθη.

545 For some of the ancients thought that what is must necessarily
be one and motionless, since the void is non-existent and there
could be no motion without a separately existing void, and again
there could not be a plurality without something to separate them.
And if someone thinks the universe is not continuous but consists
of divided pieces in contact with each other, this is no different,
they held, from saying that it is many, not one, and is void. For
if it is divisible everywhere, there is no unit, and therefore no many,
and the whole is void. If on the other hand it is divisible in one
place and not another, this seems like a piece of fiction. For how
far is it divisible, and why is one part of the whole like this –
full – and another part divided? Again, it is necessary similarly
that there be no motion... But Leucippus thought he had arguments which would assert what is consistent with sense-perception
and not do away with coming into being or perishing or motion,
or the plurality of existents. He agrees with the appearances to this
extent, but he concedes, to those who maintain the One, that there
would be no motion without void, and says that the void is
non-existent, and that no part of what is is non-existent – for what
is in the strict sense is wholly and fully being. But such being, he
says, is not one; there is an infinite number, and they are invisible
because of the smallness of the particles. They move in the void
(for there *is* void), and when they come together they cause coming
to be, and when they separate they cause perishing. They have
effects and are affected wherever they happen to be in contact
(contact does not make them one), but when they are compounded
together and entangled they create something. From what is truly
one no plurality could come into being, nor a unity from what is
truly a plurality – that is impossible. But as Empedocles and some

of the other philosophers say that things are affected through their pores, so in his view all alteration and all being affected comes about in this way: dissolution and destruction, and similarly growth, occur when solid objects slip in through the void.

546 Some gave in to both of these arguments – to the argument that all is one if what is signifies one thing, by saying that what is not exists, and to the argument from dichotomy, by positing atomic magnitudes.

Aristotle plausibly presents Leucippus' theory of infinitely numerous invisible particles moving in a void as intended to reconcile the evidence of our senses with Eleatic metaphysics. Accordingly neither the reliability of sensory evidence nor the validity of Eleatic reasoning is accepted by Leucippus without qualification. The atomists' chief disagreements with the Eleatics are succinctly (but anonymously) described in **546**.[1] (i) Leucippus posited the existence of not-being, which (following Melissus) he identified as void. As **545** stresses, he was thus able to account for the possibility of motion and plurality (the two principal features of sensory experience he regarded as veridical), by endorsing the Eleatic thesis that they can exist only if void does.[2] (ii) The atomists rejected Zeno's attempt to show that the members of a plurality are infinitely divisible, and therefore subject to absurd consequences. **545** does not make it very clear exactly how Leucippus phrased his response to the version of Zeno's argument it reproduces. His attitude to it is perhaps indicated by the sentence beginning: 'From what is truly one...' If so, it looks as though he accepted that the notion of divisibility – whether divisibility 'everywhere' or only 'up to a point' – is indeed intolerable, and accordingly declared that none of *his* infinite plurality of particles is divisible, but each is a true unity.[3] This stress on the unity of his particles suggests that in reacting thus to Zeno he was exploiting Melissus' conclusion in **537**: 'So, then, if there were a plurality, things would have to be of just the same nature as the one.' Leucippus presumably agreed both with Melissus' premiss, that our senses are misleading guides to the nature of pluralities, and with his conclusion, that if there is to be a plurality, each of its members must be such as Melissus' one being is. And indeed, he goes on to endow his own particles with some of the properties which Melissus in **533** and **534** holds to derive ultimately from unity and being – notably being full, lack of internal change, and impassivity (cf. **555–7**).[4] (It is curiously hard to find a text which explicitly calls the atoms uncreated and imperishable, although this is implied by the frequent description of atoms and void as elements and principles: e.g. **555**.)

[1] This passage was construed as referring to Plato and Xenocrates by the ancient Greek commentators (see Simplicius *ad loc.*). But Ross (*ad loc.*), followed e.g. by Furley, *Two Studies*, 81–2, convincingly argues that Aristotle is thinking of the atomists.

[2] This thesis is reliably attested elsewhere for Melissus alone among the Eleatics, and only for the case of motion. Leucippus' own assumption of a connexion between void and plurality has to be inferred from Aristotle's text, as it was by Philoponus *ad loc.* (DK67A7). Perhaps it is more a deduction from such a text as Parmenides fr. 8, 22–5 (**297**) than an explicit Eleatic doctrine. It is worth noting that Anaxagoras and Empedocles apparently thought they could construct physical systems impervious to Parmenides' critique of mortal opinions without employing the concept of void, perhaps because they wrote before Melissus (see **470, 536**). But Empedocles' theory of pores in the body actually presupposed the existence of the void which he formally denied, according to Aristotle (*de gen. et corr.* 325b1).

[3] This train of thought is also ascribed to Democritus: Aristotle *Met.* 1039a9, DK68A42 (cf. **579**). Elsewhere Aristotle suggests that Democritus reacted to the Eleatic argument by agreeing that division at every point entails absurdities, but that he therefore accepted the second horn of the dilemma: division must come to a stop when it reaches indivisible magnitudes or atoms (*de gen. et corr.* 316a33–317a2, DK68A48b; discussed e.g. by Furley, *Two Studies* 1, ch. 6, Stokes, *One and Many*, 222–4, Barnes, *Presocratic Philosophers* 11, 50–8. It is very unclear how much of this actually goes back to Democritus or the Eleatics).

[4] Where Eleatic positions described in **545** can be precisely identified they are invariably Melissan: thus the inference 'not divided, therefore not in motion' apparently envisaged in the sentence 'Again,...' recalls **547** Melissus fr. 10, Simplicius *in Phys.* 109, 32 εἰ γὰρ διήρηται, φησί, τὸ ἐόν, κινεῖται· κινούμενον δὲ οὐκ ἂν εἴη. ('*If what is has been divided*', he says, '*it is in motion; but it would not be in motion.*') And **530** (the continuation of the first part of **545**) makes a specific reference to Melissus' doctrine of the unlimited extent of what is. So there is little doubt that in Aristotle's eyes it is particularly Melissus' version of Eleatic doctrine which influenced Leucippus. Later accounts which make atomism a development of Eleaticism, and Leucippus, for example, a pupil of Zeno (Diog. L. IX, 30, DK67A1, Hippolytus *Ref.* I, 12, 1, DK67A10), were probably derived from the Aristotelian assessment; cf. Theophrastus in **539**. But this is a case in which Aristotle's essential judgement makes such excellent historical sense that we cannot attribute it to over-schematization of the relations between his philosophical forebears.

THE EVIDENCE OF THE SENSES

(i) *Scepticism*

548 Aristotle *Met.* Γ5, 1009b7   ἔτι δὲ καὶ πολλοῖς 3ῴων ὑγιαίνουσι τἀναντία περὶ τῶν αὐτῶν φαίνεσθαι καὶ ἡμῖν, καὶ αὐτῷ δὲ ἑκάστῳ πρὸς αὐτὸν οὐ ταὐτὰ κατὰ τὴν αἴσθησιν ἀεὶ δοκεῖν. ποῖα οὖν τούτων ἀληθῆ ἢ ψευδῆ, ἄδηλον· οὐθὲν γὰρ μᾶλλον τάδε ἢ τάδε ἀληθῆ, ἀλλ' ὁμοίως. διὸ Δημόκριτός γέ φησιν ἤτοι οὐθὲν εἶναι ἀληθὲς ἢ ἡμῖν γ' ἄδηλον.

549 Democritus fr. 9, Sextus *adv. math.* VII, 135 Δημόκριτος δὲ ὁτὲ μὲν ἀναιρεῖ τὰ φαινόμενα ταῖς αἰσθήσεσι καὶ τούτων λέγει μηδὲν φαίνεσθαι κατ' ἀλήθειαν, ἀλλὰ μόνον κατὰ δόξαν, ἀληθὲς δὲ ἐν τοῖς οὖσιν ὑπάρχειν τὸ ἀτόμους εἶναι καὶ κενόν· 'νόμῳ' γάρ φησι 'γλυκύ, [καὶ] νόμῳ πικρόν, νόμῳ θερμόν, νόμῳ ψυχρόν, νόμῳ χροιή, ἐτεῇ δὲ ἄτομα καὶ κενόν'.

550 Democritus frr. 10 and 6–8, Sextus *adv. math.* VII, 136 (continues **553**) καὶ πάλιν φησίν (fr. 10)· 'ἐτεῇ μέν νυν ὅτι οἶον ἕκαστον ἔστιν ⟨ἢ⟩ οὐκ ἔστιν οὐ συνίεμεν, πολλαχῇ δεδήλωται'. ἐν δὲ τῷ Περὶ ἰδεῶν (fr. 6)· 'γιγνώσκειν τε χρή, φησίν, ἄνθρωπον τῷδε τῷ κανόνι, ὅτι ἐτεῆς ἀπήλλακται'. καὶ πάλιν (fr. 7)· 'δηλοῖ μὲν δὴ καὶ οὗτος ὁ λόγος, ὅτι ἐτεῇ οὐδὲν ἴσμεν περὶ οὐδενός, ἀλλ' ἐπιρρυσμίη ἑκάστοισιν ἡ δόξις'. καὶ ἔτι (fr. 8)· 'καίτοι δῆλον ἔσται, ὅτι ἐτεῇ οἶον ἕκαστον γιγνώσκειν ἐν ἀπόρῳ ἐστί.'

548 Again, the same things appear quite the opposite to many of the animals when they are in good health as they do to us, nor does one individual always make the same judgements about how things appear to him so far as sense-perception is concerned. Which of them, then, are true or false is unclear, for these are no more true than those, but of equal standing. This is why Democritus, at any rate, says that either nothing is true, or it is unclear to *us*.

549 Democritus sometimes does away with what appears to the senses, and says that none of these appears according to truth but only according to opinion: the truth in real things is that there are atoms and void. 'By convention sweet', he says, 'by convention bitter, by convention hot, by convention cold, by convention colour: but in reality atoms and void.'

550 And again he says (fr. 10): 'Now that in reality we do not grasp what each thing is or is not in character, has been made clear in many ways'. And in *On Forms* (fr. 6): 'A man must know by this yardstick that he is separated from reality.' And again (fr. 7): 'This argument too shows that in reality we know nothing about anything; but for each of us there is a reshaping – belief.' And further (fr. 8): 'Yet it will be clear that to know in reality what each thing is in character is baffling.'

Although Leucippus held that the senses reliably report that there are many things and that there is motion, nonetheless he must have believed false much of what they tell us, particularly as concerns the nature of such pluralities. For his commitment to Eleatic principles required him to hold that nothing which truly is can change or come into being or perish. It was evidently Democritus, however, who developed a thorough critique of the trustworthiness of the senses.

In **548** Aristotle explains that Democritus was persuaded to take up his own position by the sorts of consideration which led Protagoras to the alternative view that every appearance is true, but true relatively to the man who experiences it: thus one and the same wind *is* hot (for you) if it appears hot to you, and *is* cold (for me) if it appears cold to me.[1] Whereas Protagoras concludes that both appearances are true, Democritus, not prepared to abandon an objective conception of truth, decides that neither can be. Aristotle thus attributes to him a reason for distrusting the senses independent of Melissus' critique in **537**. The attribution is supported by independent evidence that Democritus rejected Protagoras' theory of truth, and took issue with him over his use of the οὐ μᾶλλον principle (the principle 'no more this than that').[2] And it is attractive to interpret Democritus' treatment of secondary qualities in **549** in this light: the contradictions in appearances exemplified in the case of the wind show not that the appearances are relatively true, but rather that it could only be an arbitrary decision on our part to call the wind hot *or* cold. In any event, **549–50** supply ample evidence (cf. also fr. 117) that, as Aristotle and Sextus maintained, Democritus did indeed commit himself to a far-reaching scepticism about the reliability of the senses – if not, indeed, about the possibility of knowledge of any kind whatsoever.

[1] Cf. **551** Protagoras fr. 1, Sextus *adv. math.* VII, 60   πάντων χρημάτων μέτρον ἐστὶν ἄνθρωπος, τῶν μὲν ὄντων ὡς ἔστιν, τῶν δὲ οὐκ ὄντων ὡς οὐκ ἔστιν. (*Man is the measure of all things, of those that are that they are, of those that are not that they are not.*) The wind example, taken from Plato *Theaet.* 151Eff., is very likely original.

[2] See fr. 156, Plutarch *adv. Colot.* 1108F; Sextus *adv. math.* VII, 389, DK68A114. The atomists employed the principle more widely than Plutarch allows: see e.g. p. 415 n. 2; cf. Barnes. *The Presocratic Philosophers* II, 251–7.

(ii) *Confirmation*

552 Democritus fr. 125, Galen *de Med. empir.* p. 113 Walzer τάλαινα φρήν, παρ' ἡμέων λαβοῦσα τὰς πίστεις ἡμέας καταβάλλεις; πτῶμά τοι τὸ κατάβλημα.

553 Democritus fr. 9, Sextus *adv. math.* VII, 136 (after **549**)   ἐν δὲ τοῖς Κρατυντηρίοις, καίπερ ὑπεσχημένος ταῖς αἰσθήσεσι τὸ κράτος τῆς πίστεως ἀναθεῖναι, οὐδὲν ἧττον εὑρίσκεται τούτων καταδικάζων. φησὶ γάρ· 'ἡμεῖς δὲ τῷ μὲν ἐόντι οὐδὲν ἀτρεκὲς συνίεμεν, μεταπῖπτον δὲ κατά τε σώματος διαθήκην καὶ τῶν ἐπεισιόντων καὶ τῶν ἀντιστηριζόντων.'

554 Democritus fr. 11, Sextus *adv. math.* VII, 138 (after **550**) ἐν δὲ τοῖς Κανόσι δύο φησὶν εἶναι γνώσεις· τὴν μὲν διὰ τῶν αἰσθήσεων τὴν δὲ διὰ τῆς διανοίας, ὧν τὴν μὲν διὰ τῆς διανοίας γνησίην καλεῖ προσμαρτυρῶν αὐτῇ τὸ πιστὸν εἰς ἀληθείας κρίσιν, τὴν δὲ διὰ τῶν αἰσθήσεων σκοτίην ὀνομάζει ἀφαιρούμενος αὐτῆς τὸ πρὸς διάγνωσιν τοῦ ἀληθοῦς ἀπλανές. λέγει δὲ κατὰ λέξιν· 'γνώμης δὲ δύο εἰσὶν ἰδέαι, ἡ μὲν γνησίη, ἡ δὲ σκοτίη· καὶ σκοτίης μὲν τάδε σύμπαντα, ὄψις, ἀκοή. ὀδμή, γεῦσις, ψαῦσις. ἡ δὲ γνησίη, ἀποκεκριμένη δὲ ταύτης.' εἶτα προκρίνων τῆς σκοτίης τὴν γνησίην ἐπιφέρει λέγων· 'ὅταν ἡ σκοτίη μηκέτι δύνηται μήτε ὁρῆν ἐπ' ἔλαττον μήτε ἀκούειν μήτε ὀδμᾶσθαι μήτε γεύεσθαι μήτε ἐν τῇ ψαύσει αἰσθάνεσθαι, ἀλλ' ἐπὶ λεπτότερον...'

552 Wretched mind, do you take your assurances from us and then overthrow us [*sc.* the senses]? Our overthrow is your downfall.

553 In the *Confirmations*, although he had promised to assign the power of assurance to the senses, he is none the less found condemning them, for he says: 'But we in actuality grasp nothing for certain, but what shifts in accordance with the condition of the body and of the things which enter it and press upon it.'

554 But in the *Canons* he says there are two kinds of knowing, one through the senses and the other through the intellect. Of these he calls the one through the intellect 'legitimate', attesting its trustworthiness for the judgement of truth, and that through the senses he names 'bastard', denying it inerrancy in the discrimination of what is true. To quote his actual words: 'Of knowledge there are two forms, one legitimate, one bastard. To the bastard belong all this group: sight, hearing, smell, taste, touch. The other is legitimate, and separate from that.' Then, preferring the legitimate to the bastard, he continues: 'When the bastard can no longer see any smaller, or hear, or smell, or taste, or perceive by touch, but finer...'[1] (*After Barnes*)

[1] Here the text breaks off in mid-sentence.

552 and **553** indicate that Democritus' scepticism was not so thoroughgoing that he denied the senses any positive role at all in epistemology. His title *Confirmations* suggests he would have envisaged the mind as replying thus to the senses' complaint that in **549–50** they are rejected entirely: 'Not so. You *tell* us very few truths about the world (except that it contains many things in motion). In particular, you tell us nothing objectively true about what individual things are like (NB ἕκαστον 550). But you do *confirm* the truth of the theory of atoms and void which I have worked out using the genuine sort of judgement constituted by *a priori* Eleatic reasoning (554). For example, my theory holds that combinations of atoms *must* be merely temporary because of the constant collisions to which atoms are subject: you falsely report births and deaths, but in so reporting you confirm the actual existence of the events which the theory says must occur. Again, my theory holds that perception involves an interaction between object and observer which depends on the character of each and *must* therefore vary from case to case (553). One of you says: "the wind is hot", another in another person says: "the wind is cold": again you lie, but what you say shows that my theory predicts what actually happens.'[1]

[1] This valuation of the senses as supplying confirmation of the truth is probably what underlies Aristotle's claim that the atomists hold that 'truth lies in the appearances' (562); cf. *Met.* 1009b12 (DK68A112), *de an.* 427a21–b6.

ATOMS AND THE VOID

555 Aristotle *Met.* A4, 985b4 (DK67A6) Λεύκιππος δὲ καὶ ὁ ἑταῖρος αὐτοῦ Δημόκριτος στοιχεῖα μὲν τὸ πλῆρες καὶ τὸ κενὸν εἶναί φασι, λέγοντες τὸ μὲν ὂν τὸ δὲ μὴ ὄν, τούτων δὲ τὸ μὲν πλῆρες καὶ στερεόν, τὸ ὄν, τὸ δὲ κενὸν καὶ μανόν, τὸ μὴ ὄν· διὸ καὶ οὐθὲν μᾶλλον τὸ ὂν τοῦ μὴ ὄντος εἶναί φασιν, ὅτι οὐδὲ τὸ κενὸν ⟨ἔλαττον⟩ τοῦ σώματος· αἴτια δὲ τῶν ὄντων ταῦτα ὡς ὕλην. καὶ καθάπερ οἱ ἐν ποιοῦντες τὴν ὑποκειμένην οὐσίαν τἆλλα τοῖς πάθεσιν αὐτῆς γεννῶσι, τὸ μανὸν καὶ τὸ πυκνὸν ἀρχὰς τιθέμενοι τῶν παθημάτων, τὸν αὐτὸν τρόπον καὶ οὗτοι τὰς διαφορὰς αἰτίας τῶν ἄλλων εἶναί φασιν. ταύτας μέντοι τρεῖς εἶναι λέγουσι, σχῆμά τε καὶ τάξιν καὶ θέσιν· διαφέρειν γάρ φασι τὸ ὂν ῥυσμῷ καὶ διαθιγῇ καὶ τροπῇ μόνον. τούτων δὲ ὁ μὲν ῥυσμὸς σχῆμά ἐστιν, ἡ δὲ διαθιγὴ τάξις, ἡ δὲ τροπὴ θέσις· διαφέρει γὰρ τὸ μὲν Α τοῦ Ν σχήματι, τὸ δὲ ΑΝ τοῦ ΝΑ τάξει, τὸ δὲ Ζ τοῦ Ν θέσει.

556 Aristotle *On Democritus ap.* Simplicium *de caelo* 295, 1 (DK68A37) Δημόκριτος... προσαγορεύει δὲ τὸν μὲν τόπον τοῖσδε τοῖς ὀνόμασι, τῷ τε κενῷ καὶ τῷ οὐδενὶ καὶ τῷ ἀπείρῳ, τῶν δὲ οὐσιῶν ἑκάστην τῷ τε δενὶ καὶ τῷ ναστῷ καὶ τῷ ὄντι. νομίζει δὲ εἶναι οὕτω μικρὰς τὰς οὐσίας ὥστε ἐκφυγεῖν τὰς ἡμετέρας αἰσθήσεις· ὑπάρχειν δὲ αὐταῖς παντοίας μορφὰς καὶ σχήματα παντοῖα καὶ κατὰ μέγεθος διαφοράς. ἐκ τούτων οὖν ἤδη καθάπερ ἐκ στοιχείων γεννᾷ καὶ συγκρίνει τοὺς ὀφθαλμοφανεῖς καὶ τοὺς αἰσθητοὺς ὄγκους. [δὲ Α, δενὶ Diels, cf. DK68Β156.]

557 Simplicius *de caelo* 242, 18 (DK67A14) οὗτοι γὰρ (*sc.* Λεύκιππος, Δημόκριτος, Ἐπίκουρος) ἔλεγον ἀπείρους εἶναι τῷ πλήθει τὰς ἀρχάς, ἃς καὶ ἀτόμους καὶ ἀδιαιρέτους ἐνόμιζον καὶ ἀπαθεῖς διὰ τὸ ναστὰς εἶναι, καὶ ἀμοίρους τοῦ κενοῦ· τὴν γὰρ διαίρεσιν κατὰ τὸ κενὸν τὸ ἐν τοῖς σώμασι ἔλεγον γίνεσθαι...

555 Leucippus and his associate Democritus hold that the elements are the full and the void; they call them what is and what is not respectively. What is is full and solid, what is not is void and rare. Since the void exists no less than body, it follows that what is not exists no less than what is. The two together are the material causes of existing things. And just as those who make the underlying substance one generate other things by its modifications, and postulate rarefaction and condensation as the origin of such modifications, in the same way these men too say that the differences [*sc.* in their elements] are the causes of other things. They hold that these differences are three – shape, arrangement and position; being, they say, differs only in 'rhythm, touching and turning', of which 'rhythm' is shape, 'touching' is arrangement and 'turning' is position; for A differs from N in shape, AN from NA in arrangement, and Z from N in position.

556 Democritus...calls space by these names – 'the void', 'nothing', and 'the infinite', while each individual substance he calls 'thing' [*i.e.* 'nothing' *without* 'no'], the 'compact' and 'being'. He thinks that substances are so small as to elude our senses, but they have all sorts of forms and shapes and differences in size. So he is already enabled from them, as from elements, to create by aggregation bulks that are perceptible to sight and the other senses.

557 They [*sc.* Leucippus, Democritus, Epicurus] said that the first principles were infinite in number, and thought they were indivisible atoms and impassible owing to their compactness, and without any void in them; divisibility comes about because of the void in compound bodies...

Having considered the atomists' attitude both to Eleatic principles and to the senses, we are now in a position to explore the system they erected on the bases laid in 545-6, 548-50, and 554. 555-7 (cf. also Simpl. *in Phys.* 28, 7-27, from Theophrastus) give fuller information about atoms and void. Reality is assigned to what is corporeal or solid, which is held to be equivalent with the full (cf. Melissus, 534), and hence excludes void or interstices of any sort. But according to 557 what is full and solid must be indivisible, or in other words an atom (presumably only physically, not notionally, indivisible, since for example atoms differ in size (556)).[1] Atoms are conceived of as very small, in fact so small as to be invisible (556), although Democritus may have held that 'it is possible for there to be an atom the size of the universe' (Aetius I, 12, 6, DK68A47). They are scattered throughout infinite void, and are infinite in number and shape.[2] It is above all in shape and arrangement that they differ from each other (555–6): all 'qualitative' differences in objects (which are conglomerates of atoms), therefore, are dependent on quantitative and local differences alone. Void, although it is identified as what is not, is accorded existence. It is hard to see how the atomists justified this paradox. Perhaps their point was that, when a place is occupied by nothing, then insofar as the occupant – 'the empty' – is nothing it does not exist, but insofar as it occupies a place it does exist. On this interpretation, void is not (as 556 assumes) 'space' or 'place' but a more mysterious entity, the negation of substance.[3]

---

[1] Other texts give other reasons for the indivisibility of atoms: e.g. 558 Simplicius *in Phys.* 925, 10 (DK67A13) Λεύκιππος μὲν καὶ Δημόκριτος οὐ μόνον τὴν ἀπάθειαν αἰτίαν τοῖς πρώτοις σώμασι τοῦ μὴ διαιρεῖσθαι νομίζουσιν, ἀλλὰ καὶ τὸ σμικρὸν καὶ ἀμερές, Ἐπίκουρος δὲ ὕστερον ἀμερῆ μὲν οὐχ ἡγεῖται, ἄτομα δὲ αὐτὰ διὰ τὴν ἀπάθειαν εἶναί φησι *(Leucippus and Democritus hold that it is not only their impassibility which is the reason why the primary bodies cannot be divided, but the fact that they are small and partless. But Epicurus in the later period does not think them partless, but says that they are indivisible because of their impassibility.)* The notion that smallness could make anything indivisible is extremely curious, and has often been taken for doxographical confusion by scholars unwilling to believe anything but good of Leucippus and Democritus. Certainly Simplicius' attempt to gloss 'small' by 'partless' smacks of an attempt to read Epicurean preoccupations back into the earlier atomists; and this same doctrine of Leucippus is reported elsewhere without the gloss (Galen *de elem. sec. Hippocr.* I, 2 (DK68A49)). But this very divergence of testimony points to the authenticity of the basic idea. It remains obscure, however, and it is unsafe to adduce it in support of the thesis that atoms were conceived by Leucippus and Democritus as *notionally* indivisible (as is maintained by Guthrie, *HGP* II, 396, 503–7 and Furley, *Two Studies* I, ch. 6; cf. also Stokes, *One and Many*, 225ff.; *contra* Barnes, *The Presocratic Philosophers* II, 50–8).

[2] The distribution of bodies throughout the infinite void was probably inferred by use of the οὐ μᾶλλον principle: 559 (= 112) Aristotle *Phys.* Γ4, 203b25 ἀπείρου δ' ὄντος τοῦ ἔξω, καὶ σῶμα ἄπειρον εἶναι δοκεῖ καὶ κόσμοι· τί γὰρ μᾶλλον τοῦ κενοῦ ἐνταῦθα ἢ ἐνταῦθα; *(If what lies outside [sc. the heavens] is infinite, so too, it seems, is body, and worlds too. For why should they be here rather than there in the void?)* The same principle was employed in arguing that they were infinite in number and shape: 560 Simplicius *in Phys.* 28, 8 (from Theophrastus), DK67A8 οὗτος ἄπειρα καὶ ἀεὶ κινούμενα ὑπέθετο στοιχεῖα τὰς ἀτόμους καὶ τῶν

ἐν αὐτοῖς σχημάτων ἄπειρον τὸ πλῆθος διὰ τὸ μηδὲν μᾶλλον τοιοῦτον ἢ τοιοῦτον εἶναι. *(Leucippus posited an infinite number of elements in perpetual motion – the atoms – and held that the number of their shapes was infinite, on the ground that nothing is such rather than such.)* Perhaps Democritus then concluded that there was no reason not to apply it also to the question of the size of atoms, too: **561** Dionysius *ap.* Eusebium *P.E.* xiv, 23, 3 (DK68A43) τοσοῦτον δὲ διεφώνησαν *(sc.* ᾿Επίκουρος καὶ Δημό-κριτος) ὅσον ὁ μὲν ἐλαχίστας πάσας καὶ διὰ τοῦτο ἀνεπαισθήτους, ὁ δὲ καὶ μεγίστας εἶναί τινας ἀτόμους, ὁ Δημόκριτος, ὑπέλαβεν. *(To this extent they [sc. Epicurus and Democritus] differed, that one supposed that all atoms were very small, and on that account imperceptible; the other, Democritus, that there are some atoms that are very large.)* No doubt he would have explained that very large atoms are to be found only in parts of space distant from our universe. The atomists took the hypothesis of an infinity of shapes to account for the infinite variety of sensory appearances: **562** Aristotle *de gen. et corr.* A1, 315b6 (DK67A9) ἐπεὶ δ᾿ ᾤοντο τἀληθὲς ἐν τῷ φαίνεσθαι, ἐναντία δὲ καὶ ἄπειρα τὰ φαινόμενα, τὰ σχήματα ἄπειρα ἐποίησαν, ὥστε ταῖς μεταβολαῖς τοῦ συγκειμένου τὸ αὐτὸ ἐναντίον δοκεῖν ἄλλῳ καὶ ἄλλῳ, καὶ μετακινεῖσθαι μικροῦ ἐμμειγνυμένου καὶ ὅλως ἕτερον φαίνεσθαι ἑνὸς μετα-κινηθέντος· ἐκ τῶν αὐτῶν γὰρ τραγῳδία καὶ κωμῳδία γίνεται γραμμάτων. *(Since they thought that the truth lies in appearance, but the appearances are contrary and infinite, they made the shapes infinite, so that the same thing will appear contrary to one man and to another through changes in the compound, and it will be altered by a small admixture and appear altogether different because of that single alteration. For tragedies and comedies are composed from the same letters.)*

³ The interpretation is advanced by D. N. Sedley, 'Two conceptions of vacuum', *Phronesis* 27 (1982), 179–83. On the more usual view, void is not absolute Newtonian space, but the empty space which exists only where atoms are not, thus forming gaps between them. Sedley argues that the atomists had no reason to call *that* non-existent, and observes that by parity of treatment 'the full' would have to be full space – whereas we know that it is what fills space, the moving atoms. With his interpretation the atomists' use of 'nothing' echoes precisely Parmenides' paradoxical use of it to refer to what negative existentials would be about if they were about anything (**293**, **296**), and 'void' or 'empty' is just another designation of that.

THE FORMATION OF WORLDS

563 Diogenes Laertius IX, 31 (DK67A1) τὸ μὲν πᾶν ἄπειρόν φησιν *(sc.* Λεύκιππος)...τούτου δὲ τὸ μὲν πλῆρες εἶναι, τὸ δὲ κενόν...κόσμους τε ἐκ τούτου ἀπείρους εἶναι καὶ διαλύεσθαι εἰς ταῦτα. γίνεσθαι δὲ τοὺς κόσμους οὕτω· φέρεσθαι 'κατὰ ἀποτομὴν ἐκ τῆς ἀπείρου' πολλὰ σώματα παντοῖα τοῖς σχήμασιν εἰς μέγα κενόν, ἅπερ ἀθροισθέντα δίνην ἀπεργάζεσθαι μίαν, καθ᾿ ἣν προσκρούοντα ⟨ἀλλήλοις⟩ καὶ παντοδαπῶς κυκλούμενα διακρίνεσθαι χωρὶς τὰ ὅμοια πρὸς τὰ ὅμοια. ἰσορρόπων δὲ διὰ τὸ πλῆθος μηκέτι δυναμένων περιφέρεσθαι, τὰ μὲν λεπτὰ χωρεῖν εἰς τὸ ἔξω κενόν, ὥσπερ διαττώ-μενα· τὰ δὲ λοιπὰ 'συμμένειν' καὶ περιπλεκόμενα συγκατατρέχειν ἀλλήλοις καὶ ποιεῖν πρῶτόν τι σύστημα σφαιροειδές. (32) τοῦτο δ᾿

οἷον 'ὑμένα' ἀφίστασθαι περιέχοντα ἐν ἑαυτῷ παντοῖα σώματα· ὧν κατὰ τὴν τοῦ μέσου ἀντέρεισιν περιδινουμένων λεπτὸν γενέσθαι τὸν πέριξ ὑμένα, συρρεόντων ἀεὶ τῶν συνεχῶν κατ' ἐπίψαυσιν τῆς δίνης. καὶ οὕτω γενέσθαι τὴν γῆν, συμμενόντων τῶν ἐνεχθέντων ἐπὶ τὸ μέσον. αὐτόν τε πάλιν τὸν περιέχοντα οἷον ὑμένα αὔξεσθαι κατὰ τὴν ἐπέκκρισιν [Heidel, ἐπέκρυσιν MSS] τῶν ἔξωθεν σωμάτων· δίνῃ τε φερόμενον αὐτόν, ὧν ἂν ἐπιψαύσῃ, ταῦτα ἐπικτᾶσθαι. τούτων δέ τινα συμπλεκόμενα ποιεῖν σύστημα, τὸ μὲν πρῶτον κάθυγρον καὶ πηλῶδες, ξηρανθέντα δὲ καὶ περιφερόμενα σὺν τῇ τοῦ ὅλου δίνῃ εἶτ' ἐκπυρωθέντα τὴν τῶν ἀστέρων ἀποτελέσαι φύσιν. (Cf. also Aetius I, 4, 1–4, DK67a24.)[1]

564 Aetius II, 7, 2 Λεύκιππος καὶ Δημόκριτος 'χιτῶνα' κύκλῳ καὶ 'ὑμένα' περιτείνουσι τῷ κόσμῳ διὰ τῶν ἀγκιστροειδῶν ἀτόμων συμπεπλεγμένον.

565 Hippolytus *Ref.* I, 13, 2 (DK68a40) λέγει δὲ ὁμοίως Λευκίππῳ (*sc.* Δημόκριτος) περὶ στοιχείων, πλήρους καὶ κενοῦ...ἔλεγε δὲ ὡς ἀεὶ κινουμένων τῶν ὄντων ἐν τῷ κενῷ· ἀπείρους δ' εἶναι κόσμους καὶ μεγέθει διαφέροντας. ἐν τισὶ δὲ μὴ εἶναι ἥλιον μηδὲ σελήνην, ἐν τισὶ δὲ μείζω τῶν παρ' ἡμῖν καὶ ἐν τισὶ πλείω. (3) εἶναι δὲ τῶν κόσμων ἄνισα τὰ διαστήματα καὶ τῇ μὲν πλείους, τῇ δὲ ἐλάττους, καὶ τοὺς μὲν αὔξεσθαι, τοὺς δὲ ἀκμάζειν, τοὺς δὲ φθίνειν, καὶ τῇ μὲν γίνεσθαι, τῇ δ' ⟨ἐκ⟩λείπειν. φθείρεσθαι δὲ αὐτοὺς ὑπ' ἀλλήλων προσπίπτοντας. εἶναι δὲ ἐνίους κόσμους ἐρήμους ζῴων καὶ φυτῶν καὶ παντὸς ὑγροῦ.

563 Leucippus holds that the whole is infinite...part of it is full and part void...Hence arise innumerable worlds, and are resolved again into these elements. The worlds come into being as follows: many bodies of all sorts of shapes move 'by abscission from the infinite' into a great void; they come together there and produce a single whirl, in which, colliding with one another and revolving in all manner of ways, they begin to separate apart, like to like. But when their multitude prevents them from rotating any longer in equilibrium, those that are fine go out towards the surrounding void as if sifted, while the rest 'abide together' and, becoming entangled, unite their motions and make a first spherical structure. This structure stands apart like a 'membrane' which contains in itself all kinds of bodies; and as they whirl around owing to the resistance of the middle, the surrounding membrane becomes thin, while contiguous atoms keep flowing together owing to contact with the whirl. So the earth came into being, the atoms that had been borne to the middle abiding together there. Again, the containing membrane is itself increased, owing to the attraction of bodies outside; as it moves around in the whirl it takes in anything it touches. Some of these bodies that get entangled form a structure that is at first moist and muddy, but as they revolve with the whirl of the whole they dry out and then ignite to form the substance of the heavenly bodies.

564 Leucippus and Democritus envelop the world in a circular 'cloak' or 'membrane', which was formed by the hooked atoms becoming entangled.

565 Democritus holds the same view as Leucippus about the elements, full and void...he spoke as if the things that are were in constant motion in the void; and there are innumerable worlds, which differ in size. In some worlds there is no sun and moon, in others they are larger than in our world, and in others more numerous. The intervals between the worlds are unequal; in some parts there are more worlds, in others fewer; some are increasing, some at their height, some decreasing; in some parts they are arising, in others failing. They are destroyed by collision one with another. There are some worlds devoid of living creatures or plants or any moisture.

[1] It looks as though συμμένειν, ὑμήν, and (in **564**) χιτών were actually derived from atomist contexts. The phrase κατὰ ἀποτομὴν ἐκ τῆς ἀπείρου (*sc.* χώρας) is closely paralleled in the Epicurean letter to Pythocles (*Ep.* II, 88; DK67A24). Diogenes might have derived it from Democritus; but it is also possible that συμμένειν, ὑμήν, χιτών, as well as κατὰ ἀποτομήν, are merely Epicurean.

The account in **563** of the formation of worlds (formally attributed to Leucippus, but no doubt representing the general views of Democritus also) is fairly detailed, but full of difficulties. The first stage is when a large collection of atoms becomes isolated, as it were, in a large patch of void. The second stage is when they form a whirl or vortex. How this occurs we cannot tell; it must happen 'by necessity',[1] as the result of a particular combination of their separate atomic movements, and a vortex would presumably not necessarily or commonly arise out of the circumstances of the first stage alone. The vortex-action causes like atoms to tend towards like.[2] (There is a good deal of reminiscence of Anaxagoras in all this: in him *Nous* started a vortex and similar particles came together to form bodies, **476** and pp. 372f.)[3] The larger atoms congregate towards the middle, the smaller ones are squeezed out (**575**). A kind of membrane or garment (**564**) encloses the whole: whether this is formed by the smaller and extruded atoms (as suggested by Aetius, DK67A24), or whether these are thrust right out of the σύστημα into the void (as suggested in 563), is uncertain. Other atoms come into contact with the extremity of the revolving mass and are drawn within the membrane. Certain of these atoms become ignited by the speed of the revolution (563 *ad fin.*) and so form the heavenly bodies; the bulkier ones at the centre 'stay together' (συμμένειν) to form the earth. Diogenes Laertius continues, after the end of 563, with a description of cosmological details which are not particularly enlightening, but show us that here Leucippus tended to accept, not very critically, the old Ionian theories. One important and highly conservative idea of Leucippus is that the earth is flat, shaped like a tambourine (τυμπανοειδής, Aetius III, 10, 4); Democritus slightly emended this (*ibid.* 10, 5), but retained the overall flatness. Both appear to have held that the earth was tilted downward towards the south.[4] Since there are innumerable atoms and an infinite void, there is no reason why only one such world should be formed; Leucippus and Democritus therefore postulated innumerable worlds, coming-to-be and passing away throughout the void (563 *init.*, 565). They are the first to whom we can with absolute certainty attribute the concept of innumerable worlds (as opposed to successive states of a continuing organism), one which is reached entirely on the *a priori* grounds described above.[5] The doxographers, however, certainly attributed the idea of plural worlds (whether coexistent or successive) to some Ionians, conceivably by an error initiated by Theophrastus (see pp. 123ff., also pp. 379f.). Democritus, according to 565, seems to have embellished the idea by observing that there is no need for each world to have a sun and moon, and so on, or to have waters and give rise to life: the random nature of the cosmogonical process 563 would not always produce the same result. For example, if there were no futher atoms to be attracted close to the outer membrane of a world, that world would presumably have no heavenly bodies.[6]

---

[1] So 566 Diogenes Laertius IX, 45 (on Democritus) πάντα τε κατ᾽ ἀνάγκην γίνεσθαι, τῆς δίνης αἰτίας οὔσης τῆς γενέσεως πάντων, ἣν ἀνάγκην λέγει. (*Everything happens according to necessity; for the cause of the coming-into-being of all things is the whirl, which he calls necessity.*) The whirl or vortex is called necessity because it produces the necessary (mechanical and *theoretically* determinable) collisions and unions of atoms: so 567 Aetius I, 26, 2 (Π. οὐσίας ἀνάγκης) Δημόκριτος τὴν ἀντιτυπίαν καὶ φορὰν καὶ πληγὴν τῆς ὕλης. (*[On the nature of necessity] Democritus means by it the resistance and movement and blows of matter.*) In Aristotelian terms, combinations can be said to take place by *chance*: so 568 Aristotle *Phys.* B4, 196a24 εἰσὶ δέ τινες οἳ καὶ τοὐρανοῦ τοῦδε καὶ τῶν κόσμων πάντων αἰτιῶνται τὸ αὐτόματον· ἀπὸ ταὐτομάτου γὰρ γενέσθαι τὴν δίνην καὶ τὴν κίνησιν τὴν διακρίνασαν καὶ καταστήσασαν εἰς ταύτην τὴν τάξιν τὸ πᾶν. (*There are some who make chance the cause both of these heavens and of all the worlds: for from chance arose*

the whirl and the movement which, by separation, brought the universe into its present order.)
For Aristotle they are chance events because they do not fulfil any final cause;
but the atomists emphasized the other aspect of non-planned mechanical
sequences, i.e. as necessity. So in the only extant saying of Leucippus himself:
569 Fr. 2, Aetius I, 25, 4 οὐδὲν χρῆμα μάτην γίνεται, ἀλλὰ πάντα ἐκ λόγου τε
καὶ ὑπ' ἀνάγκης. (*Nothing occurs at random, but everything for a reason and by necessity.*)
Every object, every event, is the result of a chain of collisions and reactions, each
according to the shape and particular motion of the atoms concerned.

² Democritus illustrates this traditional rule of the behaviour of things, both
animate and inanimate, in **570** Fr. 164, Sextus *adv. math.* VII, 117 καὶ γὰρ ζῷα,
φησίν, ὁμογενέσι ζῴοις συναγελάζεται ὡς περιστεραὶ περιστεραῖς καὶ γέρανοι
γεράνοις καὶ ἐπὶ τῶν ἄλλων ὡσαύτως. ⟨ὡς⟩ δὲ καὶ ἐπὶ τῶν ἀψύχων, καθάπερ
ὁρᾶν πάρεστιν ἐπί τε τῶν κοσκινευομένων σπερμάτων καὶ ἐπὶ τῶν παρὰ ταῖς
κυματωγαῖς ψηφίδων... (*For creatures (he says) flock together with their kind, doves
with doves, cranes with cranes and so on. And the same happens even with inanimate things,
as can be seen with seeds in a sieve and pebbles on the sea-shore...*) (similar grains, he
continues, and pebbles of the same shape, congregate under the action of sieve
or waves). The mechanical tendency of objects of similar shape and size to sort
together under the influence of motion is especially relevant to atomism, of course,
and goes beyond the naïve view of Homer, *Od.* XVII, 218, that 'god always leads
like to like'.

³ According to Simplicius, Democritus held that the vortex was 'separated off':
571 Fr. 167, Simplicius *in Phys.* 327, 24 ἀλλὰ καὶ Δημόκριτος, ἐν οἷς φησι 'δῖνον
ἀπὸ τοῦ παντὸς ἀποκριθῆναι παντοίων ἰδεῶν' (πῶς δὲ καὶ ὑπὸ τίνος αἰτίας μὴ
λέγει), ἔοικεν ἀπὸ ταὐτομάτου καὶ τύχης γεννᾶν αὐτόν. (*When Democritus says
that 'a whirl was separated off from the whole, of all sorts of shapes' (and he does not say
how or through what cause), he seems to generate it by accident or chance.*) The idea of
the initiator of the cosmogonical process being 'separated off' may go back to
Anaximander (see **121** and pp. 131ff.).

⁴ So **572** Diogenes Laertius IX, 33 (on Leucippus) ἐκλείπειν δ' ἥλιον καὶ
σελήνην τῷ κεκλίσθαι τὴν γῆν πρὸς μεσημβρίαν· τὰ δὲ πρὸς ἄρκτῳ ἀεί τε νίφεσθαι
καὶ κατάψυχρα εἶναι καὶ πήγνυσθαι. (*Eclipses of sun and moon are due to the tilting
of the earth towards the south; the regions towards the north are always under snow and
are very cold and hard-frozen.*) Most scholars have assumed a gap after σελήνην,
'moon', so that some other phenomenon than eclipse is explained by the tilting
of the earth. The order of subjects in Diogenes is against a gap; but the tilting
of the earth would be so utterly unsuitable as an explanation of eclipses that it
seems reasonable to postulate either a textual displacement or a total misunderstanding by Diogenes or his sources. The tilting of the earth remains; it
explains both the slant of the zodiac and the differences of climate, and is
conceivably related to, though very different from, Anaximenes' theory that the
sun is hidden behind high northern parts at night. Eclipses had already been
correctly explained by Empedocles and Anaxagoras. Cf. also Aetius III, 12, 1–2
(DK 67 A 27 and 68 A 96).

⁵ Compare the well-known saying of Democritus' pupil Metrodorus of Chios,
that it is strange for one ear of corn to be produced in a great plain, and for one
world in the boundless.

⁶ It looks as though there is a reference here to Anaxagoras fr. 4 (**498**; the
recurrence of the phrase παρ' ἡμῖν may be accidental). It is not at all certain,
however, that that fragment described entirely separate worlds with separate suns

and moons; *if* it did, then the fact that every world had the same structure justifies G. Vlastos' reference (*Philos. Rev.* 55 (1946), 53f.) to 'the teleological streak in Anaxagorean physics', and his suggestion that Democritus' theory may be a 'conscious refutation' of it.

THE BEHAVIOUR OF ATOMS

(*a*) *Weight*

573 Aristotle *de gen. et corr.* A8, 326a9 καίτοι βαρύτερόν γε κατὰ τὴν ὑπεροχήν φησιν εἶναι Δημόκριτος ἕκαστον τῶν ἀδιαιρέτων.

574 Theophrastus *de sensu* 61 (DK68A135) βαρὺ μὲν οὖν καὶ κοῦφον τῷ μεγέθει διαιρεῖ Δημόκριτος... οὐ μὴν ἀλλ' ἕν γε τοῖς μεικτοῖς κουφότερον μὲν εἶναι τὸ πλέον ἔχον κενόν, βαρύτερον δὲ τὸ ἔλαττον. ἐν ἐνίοις μὲν οὕτως εἴρηκεν· (62) ἐν ἄλλοις δὲ κοῦφον εἶναί φησιν ἁπλῶς τὸ λεπτόν.

575 Simplicius *de caelo* 712, 27 (DK68A61) ...οἱ περὶ Δημόκριτον οἴονται πάντα μὲν ἔχειν βάρος, τῷ δὲ ἔλαττον ἔχειν βάρος τὸ πῦρ ἐκθλιβόμενον ὑπὸ τῶν προλαμβανόντων ἄνω φέρεσθαι καὶ διὰ τοῦτο κοῦφον δοκεῖν.

576 Aetius I, 3, 18 (DK68A47) Δημόκριτος μὲν γὰρ ἔλεγε δύο (*sc.* ταῖς ἀτόμοις συμβεβηκέναι), μέγεθός τε καὶ σχῆμα, ὁ δὲ Ἐπίκουρος τούτοις καὶ τρίτον βάρος προσέθηκεν... I, 12, 6 Δημόκριτος τὰ πρῶτά φησι σώματα (ταῦτα δ' ἦν τὰ ναστά) βάρος μὲν οὐκ ἔχειν, κινεῖσθαι δὲ κατ' ἀλληλοτυπίαν ἐν τῷ ἀπείρῳ.

573 Yet Democritus says that each of the indivisible bodies is heavier in proportion to its excess [*sc.* of size].

574 Democritus distinguishes heavy and light by size... Nevertheless in compound bodies the lighter is that which contains more void, the heavier that which contains less. Sometimes he expressed it thus, but elsewhere he says simply that the fine is light.

575 ...Democritus' school thinks that everything possesses weight, but that because it possesses less weight fire is squeezed out by things that possess more, moves upwards and consequently appears light.

576 Democritus named two [*sc.* properties of atoms], size and shape; but Epicurus added a third to these, namely weight... – Democritus says that the primary bodies (that is, the solid atoms) do not possess weight but move in the infinite as the result of striking one another.

The texts in which Aristotle and Simplicius discuss the basic properties of atoms (e.g. **555–7**) are silent on the question whether they possess weight; and indeed reports of the views of Anaxagoras and Empedocles are similarly uninformative on this topic (**493** is obviously no more than interpretation of **489**, inspired by Aristotle's general remarks in **117**). **573–6** present apparently contradictory opinions about Democritus' position, which has in consequence been the subject of disagreement among scholars. (Leucippus is not mentioned in these passages, and presumably did not think that the subject demanded special treatment.)

Aristotle in **573** is quite clear that for Democritus the atoms *had* weight, and that the weight depended on their size; his opinion is supported by Theophrastus (**574**) and (on the first point) by Simplicius (**575**). Indeed it is difficult to see how the atomists could have avoided holding some form of this view, since bodies in our world do as a matter of experience seem to have weight, and since the fullness and homogeneity of atoms means that difference in size is the only conceivable determinant of difference in weight. But it looks as though **576** contradicts **573–5**. How is the contradiction to be explained? (i) One popular solution, advocated e.g. by Burnet (*EGP*, 341–6) and adopted in KR, holds that the testimonies in **573–5** should be referred only to bodies located in a world, or more generally bodies subject to a vortex. Larger objects tend to move towards the centre of a whirl, and it is then convenient to express the fact that their 'downward' motion is a function of their greater size by saying that they are heavier than smaller objects closer to the circumference. But in themselves bodies have no weight, i.e. no tendency to move 'downwards'; in a vortex-free void their movements are solely determined by collisions (and, of course, size and shape), and there is no reason to describe them as heavy or light. It is just this point which is adverted to by Aetius in **576**. (ii) Explanation (i) accords great respect to **576**, and has to import a considerable theoretical apparatus to sustain such confidence in Aetius. It is altogether simpler to take **573–5**, which are after all the opinions of more trustworthy authorities, at their face value, as descriptions true of Democritean atoms without restriction. Weight, then, is an absolute property of atoms, albeit not one on which Democritus had a great deal to say. It is true that he would probably have no ready answer to the question of what weight in a vortex-free void consists in, where it is not expressed in a tendency to move downwards. But that very difficulty suggests a reason why Aetius came to misrepresent Democritus' view as he did in **576**. He has just mentioned Epicurus' view (1, 12, 5), according to which atoms move downwards through the void in virtue of their weight, but in other directions as a result of collisions (which in turn were notoriously explained as the consequence of random swerves: cf. e.g. Diog. L. x, 61, Lucretius II, 216–42). He may have found Epicurus' position so obvious that he inferred: since Democritus' atoms do *not* move downwards in a void, they cannot have weight.[1]

[1] See further on weight D. O'Brien, 'Heavy and light in Democritus and Aristotle', *JHS* 97 (1977), 64–74; or (more voluminously) O'Brien, *Democritus, weight and size* (Paris, 1981).

(b) Motion

577 Aristotle *de caelo* Γ2, 300b8   διὸ καὶ Λευκίππῳ καὶ Δημοκρίτῳ, τοῖς λέγουσιν ἀεὶ κινεῖσθαι τὰ πρῶτα σώματα ἐν τῷ κενῷ καὶ τῷ ἀπείρῳ, λεκτέον τίνα κίνησιν καὶ τίς ἡ κατὰ φύσιν αὐτῶν κίνησις.

578 Aristotle *On Democritus ap.* Simplicium *de caelo* 295, 9 (continuing **556**)   στασιάζειν δὲ καὶ φέρεσθαι ἐν τῷ κενῷ διά τε τὴν ἀνομοιότητα καὶ τὰς ἄλλας εἰρημένας διαφοράς, φερομένας δὲ ἐμπίπτειν καὶ περιπλέκεσθαι...

579 Aristotle *de caelo* Γ4, 303a5   φασὶ γὰρ (*sc.* Λεύκιππος καὶ Δημόκριτος) εἶναι τὰ πρῶτα μεγέθη πλήθει μὲν ἄπειρα, μεγέθει δὲ ἀδιαίρετα, καὶ οὔτ' ἐξ ἑνὸς πολλὰ γίγνεσθαι οὔτε ἐκ πολλῶν ἕν, ἀλλὰ τῇ τούτων συμπλοκῇ καὶ περιπαλάξει πάντα γεννᾶσθαι.

580 Alexander *in Met.* 36, 21   οὗτοι γὰρ (*sc.* Λεύκιππος καὶ Δημόκριτος) λέγουσιν ἀλληλοτυπούσας καὶ κρουομένας πρὸς ἀλλήλας κινεῖσθαι τὰς ἀτόμους.

581 Aetius I, 23, 3   Δημόκριτος ἓν γένος κινήσεως τὸ κατὰ παλμὸν ἀπεφαίνετο.

582 Simplicius *in Phys.* 1318, 35 (DK68A58)   καὶ ἔλεγον κατὰ τὴν ἐν αὐτοῖς βαρύτητα κινούμενα ταῦτα διὰ τοῦ κενοῦ εἴκοντος καὶ μὴ ἀντιτυποῦντος κατὰ τόπον κινεῖσθαι· περιπαλάσσεσθαι[1] γὰρ ἔλεγον αὐτά.

[1] περιπαλαίσεσθαι MSS, em. Diels.

577 So Leucippus and Democritus, who say that their primary bodies are always in motion in the infinite void, ought to specify what kind of motion – that is, what is the motion natural to them. **578** They struggle and move in the void because of the dissimilarities between them and the other differences already mentioned; and as they move they collide and become entangled...

579   For they [*sc.* Leucippus and Democritus] say that their primary magnitudes are infinite in number and indivisible in magnitude; the many does not come from one nor one from many, but rather all things are generated by the intertwining and scattering around of these primary magnitudes.

580   For they [*sc.* Leucippus and Democritus] say that the atoms move by mutual collisions and blows.

581   Democritus said there was only one kind of motion, that due to vibration.

582   They said that, moving by virtue of the weight in them, they [*sc.* the atoms] move through the void which yields and does not resist them; for they said that they are 'scattered around'.

It is evident from **577** and other similar complaints by Aristotle, as well as from the lack of positive information on this point, that neither Leucippus nor Democritus gave any full account of an *original* motion of atoms – the motion, that is, which causes collisions, not that which is caused by collisions. Indeed, since atoms and the void have always existed, there is every reason to suppose that there must always have been motion, and consequent collisions. For atoms are in motion now: why should they ever not have been (cf. Parmenides' argument from sufficient reason against coming into being at **296**, 7–9, which the atomists may have had in mind in the present context; see also Aristotle *Phys.* 252a32, *de gen. animalium* 742b17)? To enquire, therefore, as Aristotle does, what was the 'natural' motion of atoms is less pertinent than at first appears. However, if the atomists were forced to define an 'original' motion they could presumably say that it was a random motion, with no tendency in any atom to move in one direction rather than another. It is clear that collisions would very soon take place, and that the original motion would progressively be supplanted by the secondary motions which result from collision and rebound.

The regular motion of atoms, and perhaps the only one which Leucippus and Democritus fully envisaged, is due to rebounds of atoms after collision. The character of the ensuing motion will be determined, no doubt, by the weight, shape, and antecedent motions of the colliding bodies. Collisions of atoms result either in 'intertwining' (συμπλοκή), if the atoms are of congruent shape, or in 'being scattered around' (περιπάλαξις), if not – that is, in rebounding in one direction or another. This is what is meant by Aristotle in **579** (cf. **582**). Aetius in **581** assigns a special type of motion to Democritus, namely παλμός or 'vibration' (the verbal root of which is the same as that of περιπάλαξις; Bailey (*The Greek Atomists and Epicurus*) actually interpreted περιπάλαξις in **579** in the sense of παλμός, though not very plausibly). There is little doubt that Aetius is here reading an Epicurean idea into Democritus; Epicurus used this word to describe the invisible oscillation which, as he conceived, atoms underwent when confined in a complex body (Epicurus *Ep.* I, 43; cf. Bailey, p. 332).[1]

[1] LSJ gives the meaning of περιπάλαξις as 'collision, combination' of atoms, though that of περιπαλάσσεσθαι is given as 'to be hurled around'. Both translations are imperfect. The meaning of παλάσσεσθαι is 'to be shaken about, or sprinkled', and that of its simpler form πάλλειν is 'to shake'. A transitional stage to the Epicurean παλμός-interpretation is perhaps seen at Theophrastus *de sensu* 66 *fin.* (DK 68 A 135). In **579** Aristotle simply means that things are produced by the entanglement and rebound of atoms; the latter does not of itself produce γένεσις, but is necessary for its continuity.

(c) *The formation of bodies*

583 Aristotle *On Democritus ap.* Simplicium *de caelo* 295, 11 (continuing **578**)   ...φερομένας δὲ (*sc.* τὰς ἀτόμους) ἐμπίπτειν καὶ περιπλέκεσθαι περιπλοκὴν τοιαύτην ἢ συμψαύειν μὲν αὐτὰ καὶ πλησίον ἀλλήλων εἶναι ποιεῖ, φύσιν μέντοι μίαν ἐξ ἐκείνων κατ' ἀλήθειαν οὐδ' ἡντιναοῦν γεννᾷ· κομιδῇ γὰρ εὔηθες εἶναι τὸ δύο ἢ τὰ πλείονα γενέσθαι ἄν ποτε ἕν. τοῦ δὲ συμμένειν τὰς οὐσίας μετ' ἀλλήλων μέχρι τινὸς αἰτιᾶται τὰς ἐπαλλαγὰς καὶ τὰς ἀντιλήψεις τῶν σωμάτων· τὰ μὲν γὰρ αὐτῶν εἶναι σκαληνά, τὰ δὲ ἀγκιστρώδη, τὰ δὲ κοῖλα, τὰ δὲ κυρτά, τὰ δὲ ἄλλας ἀναρίθμους ἔχοντα διαφοράς· ἐπὶ τοσοῦτον οὖν χρόνον σφῶν αὐτῶν ἀντέχεσθαι νομίζει καὶ συμμένειν ἕως ἰσχυροτέρα τις ἐκ τοῦ περιέχοντος ἀνάγκη παραγενομένη διασείσῃ καὶ χωρὶς αὐτὰς διασπείρῃ.

584 Simplicius *de caelo* 242, 21 (continuing **557**)   ...ταύτας δὲ τὰς ἀτόμους ἐν ἀπείρῳ τῷ κενῷ κεχωρισμένας ἀλλήλων καὶ διαφερούσας σχήμασί τε καὶ μεγέθεσι καὶ θέσει καὶ τάξει φέρεσθαι ἐν τῷ κενῷ καὶ ἐπικαταλαμβανούσας ἀλλήλας συγκρούεσθαι, καὶ τὰς μὲν ἀποπάλλεσθαι, ὅπη ἂν τύχωσιν, τὰς δὲ περιπλέκεσθαι ἀλλήλαις κατὰ τὴν τῶν σχημάτων καὶ μεγεθῶν καὶ θέσεων καὶ τάξεων συμμετρίαν καὶ συμμένειν [Diels, συμβαίνειν MSS] καὶ οὕτως τὴν τῶν συνθέτων γένεσιν ἀποτελεῖσθαι.

583 ...As they [*sc.* the atoms] move they collide and become entangled in such a way as to cling in close contact to one another, but not so as to form one substance of them in reality of any kind whatever; for it is very simple-minded to suppose that two or more could ever become one. The reason he gives for atoms staying together for a while is the intertwining and mutual hold of the primary bodies; for some of them are angular, some hooked, some concave, some convex, and indeed with countless other differences; so he thinks they cling to each other and stay together until such time as some stronger necessity comes from the surrounding and shakes and scatters them apart.

584 ...these atoms move in the infinite void, separate one from the other and differing in shapes, sizes, position and arrangement; overtaking each other they collide, and some are shaken away in any chance direction, while others, becoming intertwined one with another according to the congruity of their shapes, sizes, positions and arrangements, stay together and so effect the coming into being of compound bodies.

These passages state more precisely what has been outlined in earlier extracts, e.g. **545** and **563**, namely how atoms make up the visible complex bodies of our experience. As a result of collision between atoms those which are of congruous shape do not rebound but remain temporarily attached to one another: for example a hook-shaped atom may become involved with an atom into whose shape the hook fits. Other congruous atoms colliding with this two-atom complex then become attached, until a visible body of a certain character is formed. It is emphasized that no real coalescence of atoms takes place: they simply come into contact with each other, and always retain their own shape and individuality. When a complex of atoms collides with another complex it may be broken up into smaller complexes or into its constituent atoms, which then resume their motion through the void until they collide with a congruous atom, or complex, once again.

There are considerable difficulties in this account. What part does the principle of like-to-like play? This principle, illustrated by Democritus in **570**, is used in the description of world-formation; for in **563** atoms of all shapes come together in a great void, and like tends to like when the smaller atoms go to the periphery, the bulkier ones to the centre. It is likeness of size rather than shape that seems to be primarily in question here; and it is only in a vortex that the sorting of sizes takes place. In the collisions of atoms *not* primarily subject to a vortex, i.e. either outside the scattered areas of world-formation, or within a formed world where the vortex-action may be modified, coalescence is due to congruence (which implies difference, so far as συμπλοκή is concerned, and not similarity) rather than to the principle of like-to-like. **584** tells us that this congruence must operate in respect of shape, size, position, and order. But this is not a complete solution, since we are told of one particular shape of atom that cannot be subject to any obvious type of congruence with others of its shape, but which does nevertheless combine to make up a single type of complex (or rather two different but connected types). This is the spherical atom, of which both soul and fire were evidently held to be composed.[1] Soul, it might be argued, is regarded (as elsewhere in the fifth century) as scattered throughout the whole body; but even so some conjunction of soul-atoms seems necessary. Fire is a clearer case, for it is distinctly visible, and must be composed of spherical atoms and no (or very few) atoms of another shape. How did these atoms come together? They cannot have become implicated with or hooked on to one another, as a result of collision; rather they must have become conjoined by the operation of the principle of like-to-like. It seems, therefore, that Aristotle in 583 is misleading in implying that all examples of συμμένειν, i.e. of the formation of apparently stable complex bodies, are due to *implication* of atoms: there are occasions when other types of συμμετρία (see 584), especially *similarity* of shape and size, are more relevant.

[1] Aristotle asserts in several passages that for the atomists soul- and fire-atoms were spherical, because they had to be mobile and penetrative: e.g. 585 *de an.* A2, 405a11   τῶν δὲ σχημάτων εὐκινητότατον τὸ σφαιροειδὲς λέγει (*sc.* Δημόκριτος)· τοιοῦτον δ᾽ εἶναι τόν τε νοῦν καὶ τὸ πῦρ. (*Democritus says that the spherical is the most mobile of shapes; and such is mind and fire.*) Compare *ibid.* 404a5 (DK 67 A 28), where soul is said to be recruited by the inhalation of spherical atoms from the atmosphere – an idea analogous perhaps, to that of Heraclitus in 234. Aristotle occasionally implies that the soul *is* fire, because of this community of shape; but the truth is that a spherical atom is neither soul nor fire, it is just a spherical atom. It takes on secondary properties only in association with other atoms; in the context of an animal body it is soul, in other contexts it is fire (cf. Cherniss, *Aristotle's Criticism of Presocratic Philosophy*, 290 n.). Nevertheless, the similarity of shape explains how soul can be nurtured from the atmosphere (which is not besouled, but contains some fire). Apart from soul (equivalent to mind according to Aristotle's account of atomism) and fire, no details have survived about which shape of atom gave rise to which secondary characteristics, except in the case of sensation – sharp atoms produce salty tastes, etc. (see 591 below). Aristotle understood that air and water (and earth, probably) were conglomerations of all shapes of atoms, πανσπερμίαι: 586 *de caelo* Γ4, 303a12   ποῖον δὲ καὶ τί ἑκάστου τὸ σχῆμα τῶν στοιχείων οὐθὲν ἐπιδιώρισαν (*sc.* Λεύκιππος καὶ Δημόκριτος), ἀλλὰ μόνον τῷ πυρὶ τὴν σφαῖραν ἀπέδωκαν· ἀέρα δὲ καὶ ὕδωρ καὶ τἆλλα μεγέθει καὶ μικρότητι διεῖλον, ὡς οὖσαν αὐτῶν τὴν φύσιν οἷον πανσπερμίαν πάντων τῶν στοιχείων. (*They [sc. Leucippus and Democritus] did not further define what particular shape belonged to each of the elements but merely attributed the sphere to fire; air, water and the rest they distinguished by magnitude and smallness, as if their substance was a sort of mixture of seeds of all the elements.*) If this is accurate, then the atomists may have taken over the idea from Anaxagoras (see p. 373).

SENSATION AND THOUGHT

587 Aristotle *de sensu* 4, 442a29   Δημόκριτος δὲ καὶ οἱ πλεῖστοι τῶν φυσιολόγων ὅσοι λέγουσι περὶ αἰσθήσεως ἀτοπώτατόν τι ποιοῦσιν· πάντα γὰρ τὰ αἰσθητὰ ἁπτὰ ποιοῦσιν.

588 Aetius IV, 8, 10   Λεύκιππος Δημόκριτος Ἐπίκουρος τὴν αἴσθησιν καὶ τὴν νόησιν γίνεσθαι εἰδώλων ἔξωθεν προσιόντων· μηδενὶ γὰρ ἐπιβάλλειν μηδετέραν χωρὶς τοῦ προσπίπτοντος εἰδώλου.

589 Theophrastus *de sensu* 50 (DK 68 A 135)   ὁρᾶν μὲν οὖν ποιεῖ (*sc.* Δημόκριτος) τῇ ἐμφάσει· ταύτην δὲ ἰδίως λέγει· τὴν γὰρ ἔμφασιν οὐκ εὐθὺς ἐν τῇ κόρῃ γίνεσθαι, ἀλλὰ τὸν ἀέρα τὸν μεταξὺ τῆς ὄψεως καὶ τοῦ ὁρωμένου τυποῦσθαι συστελλόμενον ὑπὸ τοῦ ὁρωμένου καὶ τοῦ ὁρῶντος· ἅπαντος γὰρ ἀεὶ γίνεσθαί τινα ἀπορροήν. ἔπειτα τοῦτον στερεὸν ὄντα καὶ ἀλλόχρων ἐμφαίνεσθαι τοῖς ὄμμασιν †ὑγροῖς†· καὶ τὸ μὲν πυκνὸν οὐ δέχεσθαι τὸ δὲ ὑγρὸν διιέναι...

590 Alexander *de sensu* 56, 12   εἴδωλα γάρ τινα ὁμοιόμορφα ἀπὸ τῶν ὁρωμένων συνεχῶς ἀπορρέοντα καὶ ἐμπίπτοντα τῇ ὄψει τοῦ ὁρᾶν ἠτιῶντο. τοιοῦτοι δὲ ἦσαν οἱ περὶ Λεύκιππον καὶ Δημόκριτον...

587 Democritus and the majority of natural philosophers who discuss perception are guilty of a great absurdity; for they represent all perception as being by touch.

588 Leucippus, Democritus and Epicurus say that perception and thought arise when images enter from outside; neither occurs to anybody without an image impinging.

589 Democritus explains sight by the visual image, which he describes in a peculiar way; the visual image does not arise directly in the pupil, but the air between the eye and the object of sight is contracted and stamped by the object seen and the seer; for from everything there is always a sort of effluence proceeding. So this air, which is solid and variously coloured, appears in the eye, which is moist(?); the eye does not admit the dense part, but the moist passes through...

590 They attributed sight to certain images, of the same shape as the object, which were continually streaming off from the objects of sight and impinging on the eye. This was the view of the school of Leucippus and Democritus...

It is a necessary consequence of the atomist doctrine, that everything consists of atoms and void, that all sensation should be explained as a form of contact or touch (**587**). The soul consists of spherical atoms (**585**) spread through the body, and the mind was presumably regarded as a concentration of soul-atoms. Thus thought is a process analogous to sensation, and takes place when the soul- or mind-atoms are set in motion by the impingement of congruent atoms from outside (**588**). A full account of Democritus' detailed explanation of the different senses is given by Theophrastus in his *de sensu*, §§49–83 (DK68A135); this account may contain some Peripatetic distortion and elaboration, but shows that Democritus, on this and on other subjects, went to great pains to work out the detailed mechanism of the atomic theory. The fullest, and least satisfactory, description is of vision. Leucippus had evidently (**590**) taken over the Empedoclean theory (pp. 309f.) that effluences, now described as images, εἴδωλα, are given off by objects and affect the sense-organs. Democritus then held (**589**) that the visual image (ἔμφασις) in the pupil is the result of effluences (ἀπορροαί) both from the seen object and from the observer; these meet and form a solid impression (ἐντύπωσις) in the air, which then enters the pupil of the eye. The other senses are explained more simply, and with emphasis on the different effects of different sizes and shapes of atom;[1] none of the explanations stands close examination, and Aristotle and Theophrastus were able to make some very pertinent criticisms. We do not know, for example, how Democritus explained the sense of touch: as all senses depend ultimately on this sense, it is obviously a problem how sight or taste, for example, differ from it.

[1] E.g. of *taste*, **591** Theophrastus *de sensu* 66 (DK68A135) τὸν δὲ πικρὸν (*sc.* χυλὸν) ἐκ μικρῶν καὶ λείων καὶ περιφερῶν, τὴν περιφέρειαν εἰληχότων [-α MSS, Diels; -ων scripsi] καὶ καμπὰς ἔχουσαν· διὸ καὶ γλίσχρον εἶναι καὶ κολλώδη. ἁλμυρὸν δὲ τὸν ἐκ μεγάλων καὶ οὐ περιφερῶν, ἀλλ' ἐπ' ἐνίων μὲν σκαληνῶν... (*Bitter taste is caused by small, smooth, rounded atoms, whose circumference is actually sinuous; therefore it is both sticky and viscous. Salt taste is caused by large, not rounded atoms, but in some cases jagged ones...*) *Sound* is transferred when the particles of voice or noise mingle with similar particles in the air (and thus, presumably, form εἴδωλα): **592** Aetius IV, 19, 3 (DK68A128; probably from Poseidonius, according to Diels) Δημόκριτος καὶ τὸν ἀέρα φησὶν εἰς ὁμοιοσχήμονα θρύπτεσθαι σώματα καὶ συγκαλινδεῖσθαι τοῖς ἐκ τῆς φωνῆς θραύσμασι. (*Democritus says that the air is broken up into bodies of like shape and is rolled along together with the fragments of the voice.*)

ETHICS

593 Democritus fr. 3, Stobaeus *Anth.* IV, 39, 25 τὸν εὐθυμεῖσθαι μέλλοντα χρὴ μὴ πολλὰ πρήσσειν, μήτε ἰδίῃ μήτε ξυνῇ, μηδὲ ἄσσ' ἂν πράσσῃ, ὑπέρ τε δύναμιν αἱρεῖσθαι τὴν ἑωυτοῦ καὶ φύσιν· ἀλλὰ τοσαύτην ἔχειν φυλακήν, ὥστε καὶ τῆς τύχης ἐπιβαλλούσης καὶ ἐς τὸ πλέον ὑπηγεομένης, τῷ δοκεῖν κατατίθεσθαι καὶ μὴ πλέω προσάπτεσθαι τῶν δυνατῶν. ἡ γὰρ εὐογκίη ἀσφαλέστερον τῆς μεγαλογκίης.

594 Democritus fr. 191, Stobaeus *Anth.* III, 1, 210 ἀνθρώποισι γὰρ εὐθυμίη γίνεται μετριότητι τέρψιος καὶ βίου συμμετρίη· τὰ δ᾽ ἐλλείποντα καὶ ὑπερβάλλοντα μεταπίπτειν τε φιλεῖ καὶ μεγάλας κινήσιας ἐμποιεῖν τῇ ψυχῇ· αἱ δ᾽ ἐκ μεγάλων διαστημάτων κινούμεναι τῶν ψυχέων οὔτε εὐσταθέες εἰσὶν οὔτε εὔθυμοι. ἐπὶ τοῖς δυνατοῖς οὖν δεῖ ἔχειν τὴν γνώμην καὶ τοῖς παρεοῦσιν ἀρκέεσθαι, τῶν μὲν ζηλουμένων καὶ θαυμαζομένων ὀλίγην μνήμην ἔχοντα καὶ τῇ διανοίᾳ μὴ προσεδρεύοντα, τῶν δὲ ταλαιπωρεόντων τοὺς βίους θεωρέειν ἐννοούμενον ἃ πάσχουσι κάρτα, ὅκως ἂν τὰ παρεόντα σοι καὶ ὑπάρχοντα μεγάλα καὶ ζηλωτὰ φαίνηται, καὶ μηκέτι πλειόνων ἐπιθυμέοντι συμβαίνῃ κακοπαθεῖν τῇ ψυχῇ. ὁ γὰρ θαυμάζων τοὺς ἔχοντας καὶ μακαριζομένους ὑπὸ τῶν ἄλλων ἀνθρώπων καὶ τῇ μνήμῃ πᾶσαν ὥραν προσεδρεύων ἀεὶ ἐπικαινουργεῖν ἀναγκάζεται καὶ ἐπιβάλλεσθαι δι᾽ ἐπιθυμίην τοῦ τι πρήσσειν ἀνήκεστον ὧν νόμοι κωλύουσιν. διόπερ τὰ μὲν μὴ δίζεσθαι χρεών, ἐπὶ δὲ τοῖς εὐθυμέεσθαι χρεών, παραβάλλοντα τὸν ἑαυτοῦ βίον πρὸς τὸν τῶν φαυλότερον πρησσόντων, καὶ μακαρίζειν ἑωυτὸν ἐνθυμεύμενον ἃ πάσχουσιν, ὁκόσῳ αὐτέων βέλτιον πρήσσει τε καὶ διάγει· ταύτης γὰρ ἐχόμενος τῆς γνώμης εὐθυμότερόν τε διάξεις καὶ οὐκ ὀλίγας κῆρας ἐν τῷ βίῳ διώσεαι, φθόνον καὶ ζῆλον καὶ δυσμενίην.

593 The man who is going to be in good spirits must not do too much, neither in private nor in public, nor, whatever he does, must he aspire beyond his natural power. But rather he must be so much on his guard that, even when chance comes his way and points to more, in his judgement he can lay it aside and not put his hand to more than what lies in his power. The right load is a safer thing than a large load.

594 For good spirits come to men through temperate enjoyment and a life commensurate. Deficiencies and excesses tend to turn into their opposites and to make large motions in the soul. And such souls as are in large-scale motion are neither in good balance nor in good spirits.

One should keep one's mind, then, on things in one's power, and be quite satisfied with things at hand, taking little notice of those who are envied or admired and not dwelling in thought upon them. One should look at the lives of those in trouble, bearing in mind how mightily they are suffering. In this way, things at hand

and at your disposal may well appear great and enviable; yours will no longer be a case of suffering in soul through desire for more.

For he who admires those blessed with possessions and the congratulations of other men and who dwells every hour on the memory is ever compelled to plot something new and to throw himself, through desire, into doing something irremediable and illegal.

That is why one must not seek things there; one must be in good spirits over things here, comparing one's own life with that of those doing worse. One must congratulate oneself, laying their sufferings to heart, on how much better one is doing and carrying on than they are. For if you keep to this mind, you will both carry on in better spirits, and you will ward off some considerable curses in life – envy, jealousy and malice.

Of the sixty works ascribed to Democritus in Thrasyllus' catalogue (DK 68 A 33) only eight were classified as 'ethical', the best-known of these being one Περὶ εὐθυμίης or *On Good Spirits*. But over four-fifths of his surviving *verbatim* fragments are concerned with ethics. Most of them, including the most substantial pieces, have come down to us in the vast anthology compiled by John of Stobi in the fifth century A.D. There is also a collection of 86 *gnomai* ascribed to 'Democrates', which overlap with Democritean material in Stobaeus and are generally regarded, with five exceptions, as genuine fragments of Democritus.

The fragments in DK cover a wide range of subjects – good spirits and how to avoid depression (3, 189, 191, 285), fortune (119, 172–4) and folly (197–206), child-rearing (275–80) and education (178–82, 228), pleasure and prudence (74, 188, 207, 232–5), favours (92–6) and friendship (97–101, 106), political questions (245, 248–55, 265–6) and the punishment of wrongdoers (356–62), to name only a few. They vary in style from the verbosely ornate to the graphic and gnomic, with some of the shorter fragments showing signs of abbreviation by anthologists. The content of some seems embarrassingly close to Socratic or later doctrines. The authenticity of almost any fragment can usually be attacked on some ground or other.

A notable exception is fragment 3 (**593**), a much quoted sentence which probably began the *Peri Euthumies*. Its message is one of traditional common sense: it is safer to reject the blandishments of good luck and to stay within the limits of one's own natural ability. Other fragments (176, compare 210, 197) draw the same contrast between chance and nature. But 'nature' is not for Democritus the overriding moral authority that it was for some contemporary sophists, since one's nature can be 'transformed' by teaching (fr. 33). Men can extend their natural abilities; faced with deep water, for instance, they can take swimming-lessons (fr. 172). None the less, restricting oneself to what is in one's power must often mean renouncing much that, unfortunately, is not in one's power. Fragment 191 (**594**), almost certainly from the same work *On Good Spirits*, shows how to make the renunciation bearable. Men attain good spirits through enjoyment that avoids extremes of want and satiety (unlike the debauchery described in fr. 235) and through a life 'commensurate' with such enjoyment or perhaps with their own natural abilities; anything else makes for upheavals in the soul, precluding stability and good spirits. The opening of the fragment bristles with abstract terms all of which might just have some technical, scientific meaning. It constitutes our principal evidence for the view that Democritus based his ethical doctrines upon his physics. But a literal interpretation of the paragraph in terms of atomistic psychology leaves a confusing picture; and it seems easier, in view of what follows, to interpret the 'large-scale motions' and so forth as metaphorical. What is certain, and highly important, is that Democritus here is directing our moral attention inwards, as Socrates did, to the state of our souls. Only, the Democritean 'care of the soul' is not a quest for universal truths. His concern, in this fragment as in others (283, 284, 219), is with our subjective well-being, that 'what you have may *seem* great and enviable to you'. Democritus' work *On Good Spirits* thus belongs to the literature of undogmatic practical ethics, alongside the treatises on curing anger and the 'consolations' designed to cure grief. His main advice, that you should gain contentment by taking those worse off than yourself as your point of reference, was to be a stock-in-trade of such literature. Its tone, rational, paradoxical and a bit unfeeling, recurs elsewhere in the fragments – for instance, in the argument that it is wiser to adopt than to beget a child, because only then can you choose the sort you want (fr. 277). A political motive for the advice appears in the third paragraph, with the claim that disregard of it can lead to crime and revolutionary politics (ἐπικαινουργεῖν has the implications of νεωτερίʒειν). Fragment 252 expresses the view, common in the fifth century, that the well-being of the state should be the paramount consideration. But this, as other fragments (notably 255) make clear, depends on the voluntary public-spiritedness of its citizens. Law can only be of benefit, if people are willing to obey it (fr. 248). An external constraint, it cannot on its own prevent their 'sinning in secret' (fr.

181). Hence Democritus' interest in the inner, psychological motives for right conduct, in 'conviction, understanding and knowledge' (fr. 181), in the sanctions of guilty conscience (frr. 262, 297), in 'respect for oneself' – and not just for other people's opinion – as a 'law for the soul' (fr. 264). Hence, too, his interest in remedies for antisocial attitudes, such as envy which can lead to civil strife (fr. 245) and so to the ruin of the whole community (fr. 249). By following the advice of **594**, Democritus' reader might not only put himself into better spirits; he might also become less of a menace to his fellow-citizens. In thus encouraging a certain civic virtue, Democritus was carrying on the work of poets and moralists before him.[1]

---

[1] Some of the pithier sayings have a specifically Heraclitean ring, e.g. fr. 171: 'Happiness does not reside in cattle or gold; the soul is the dwelling-place of one's good or evil genius (*daimon*)' (cf. Heraclitus frr. 9 and 119 [= **247**]), or fr. 246: 'Service abroad teaches self-sufficiency; barleybread and a straw mattress are the pleasantest medicines for hunger and fatigue' (cf. Heraclitus fr. 111 [= **201**]). The Heraclitean echoes are doubtless intentional.

CONCLUSION

Atomism is in many ways the crown of Greek philosophical achievement before Plato. It fulfilled the ultimate aim of Ionian material monism by cutting the Gordian knot of the Eleatic elenchus. Much as it owed not only to Parmenides, Zeno and Melissus, but also to the pluralist systems of Empedocles and Anaxagoras, atomism was not, however, an eclectic philosophy like that of Diogenes of Apollonia. It was in essence a new conception, one which was widely and skilfully applied by Democritus, and which through Epicurus and Lucretius was to play an important part in Greek thought even after Plato and Aristotle. It also, of course, eventually gave a stimulus to the development of modern atomic theory – the real nature and motives of which, however, are utterly distinct.

CHAPTER XVI

Diogenes of Apollonia

LIFE AND DATE

595 Diogenes Laertius ix, 57 Διογένης Ἀπολλοθέμιδος Ἀπολλωνιάτης, ἀνὴρ φυσικὸς καὶ ἄγαν ἐλλόγιμος. ἤκουσε δέ, φησὶν Ἀντισθένης, Ἀναξιμένους. ἦν δὲ τοῖς χρόνοις κατ' Ἀναξαγόραν.

595 Diogenes son of Apollothemis, an Apolloniate, a physicist and a man of exceptional repute. He was a pupil of Anaximenes, as Antisthenes says. His period was that of Anaxagoras.

The Apollonia of which Diogenes was a citizen was probably the Milesian foundation on the Pontus, rather than the Cretan city.[1] The statement that he was roughly contemporary with Anaxagoras must be taken together with Theophrastus' judgement in **598** that he was 'almost the youngest' of the physical philosophers, and with Aristophanes' parody in the *Clouds* (**614**), produced in 423 B.C. All this is consonant with a *floruit* around 440–430. The statement that the succession-writer Antisthenes made Diogenes a *pupil* of Anaximenes may be due to a misunderstanding by Laertius rather than by Antisthenes: Diogenes would naturally be placed in the Milesian tradition and associated with Anaximenes because of his material principle, but his relative lateness in date does not seem to have been in doubt.

[1] So Aelian, *V.H.* ii, 31 (DK 64A 3), who mentioned 'Diogenes the Phrygian' in a list of 'atheists'. Stephanus of Byzantium, on the other hand, associates 'Diogenes the physicist' with the Cretan city, the former Eleutherna (DK *ibid.*).

WRITINGS

596 Diogenes Laertius ix, 57 ἀρχὴ δὲ αὐτῷ τοῦ συγγράμματος ἥδε· (Fr. 1) λόγου παντὸς ἀρχόμενον δοκεῖ μοι χρεὼν εἶναι τὴν ἀρχὴν ἀναμφισβήτητον παρέχεσθαι, τὴν δὲ ἑρμηνείαν ἁπλῆν καὶ σεμνήν.

597 Simplicius *in Phys.* 151, 20 ἐπειδὴ δὲ ἡ μὲν τῶν πλειόνων ἱστορία Διογένην τὸν Ἀπολλωνιάτην ὁμοίως Ἀναξιμένει τὸν ἀέρα τίθεσθαι τὸ πρῶτον στοιχεῖόν φησι, Νικόλαος δὲ ἐν τῇ περὶ θεῶν πραγματείᾳ τοῦτον ἱστορεῖ τὸ μεταξὺ πυρὸς καὶ ἀέρος τὴν ἀρχὴν ἀποφήνασθαι..., ἱστέον ὡς γέγραπται μὲν πλείονα τῷ Διογένει τούτῳ συγγράμματα (ὡς αὐτὸς ἐν τῷ Περὶ φύσεως ἐμνήσθη καὶ πρὸς φυσιολόγους ἀντειρηκέναι λέγων, οὓς καλεῖ καὶ αὐτὸς σοφιστάς, καὶ Μετεωρολογίαν γεγραφέναι, ἐν ᾗ καὶ λέγει περὶ τῆς ἀρχῆς εἰρηκέναι, καὶ μέντοι καὶ Περὶ ἀνθρώπου φύσεως), ἐν δέ γε τῷ Περὶ φύσεως, ὃ τῶν αὐτοῦ μόνον εἰς ἐμὲ ἦλθε, προτίθεται μὲν διὰ πολλῶν δεῖξαι ὅτι ἐν τῇ ὑπ' αὐτοῦ τεθείσῃ ἀρχῇ ἐστι νόησις πολλή.

596 This is the beginning of his book: 'It is my opinion that the author, at the beginning of any account, should make his principle or starting-point indisputable, and his explanation simple and dignified.'

597 Since the generality of enquirers say that Diogenes of Apollonia made air the primary element, similarly to Anaximenes, while Nicolaus in his theological investigation relates that Diogenes declared the material principle to be between fire and air[1]..., it must be realized that several books were written by this Diogenes (as he himself mentioned in *On Nature*, where he says that he had spoken also against the physicists – whom he calls 'sophists' – and written a *Meteorology*, in which he also says he spoke about the material principle, as well as *On the Nature of Man*); in the *On Nature*, at least, which alone of his works came into my hands, he proposes a manifold demonstration that in the material principle posited by him is much intelligence.

[1] According to Simplicius (*in Phys.* 149, 18) the references by Aristotle in **103** to an 'intermediate' substance were interpreted by Nicolaus of Damascus and by Porphyry as referring to Diogenes of Apollonia. See p. 439 n. 1 below.

There has been much debate about whether Diogenes wrote a single book which, like Anaxagoras' work, for example, covered different but nevertheless interrelated subjects, or whether, as Simplicius thought (**597**), he wrote at least four books: *Against the Sophists*, *Meteorologia* (a highly dubious form of book-title), and *On the Nature of Man*, as well as the *On Nature* which Simplicius himself saw and from which he quoted nearly all our extant fragments. Diels held the former view, which is supported by **596**, and thought that a subdivision of the book in the Hellenistic period (suggested by a reference by Rufus in Galen, DK64B9, to the *second* book of Diogenes' *On Nature*) could have misled Simplicius. Burnet (*EGP*, 353) and W. Theiler, on the other hand, argued that Simplicius is unlikely to be wrong on this point. Yet Simplicius' argument in **597**, that what he took to be a divergence in the ancient interpretation of Diogenes' primary substance must have arisen from the existence of different and not entirely consistent accounts by Diogenes, is rendered invalid because Nicolaus could have derived his interpretation from the book available to Simplicius himself (see p. 439 n.). Further, that same book certainly included a great deal on the 'nature of man'; for the long and detailed fr. 6 (extracts in **615**), quoted by Aristotle, seems to give precisely what Simplicius claims (*in Phys.* 153, 13, DK 64 B 6) to have found in *On Nature*, namely 'an accurate anatomy of the veins', and not to have come from a separate work on the nature of man. Similarly the subjects of the other separate books postulated by Simplicius could have been comprehended in one original work, and Simplicius might easily have mistaken references to other parts of this work for references to separate books; modern scholars are sometimes confronted by a similar ambiguity in Aristotle's references to his treatment of particular subjects elsewhere. Yet perhaps Diogenes *did* write at least one book other than Simplicius' *On Nature*: for it is stated by Galen, *de med. empir.* XXII, 3 (in R. Walzer's translation from the Arabic), that 'Diogenes, writing more briefly and compendiously than you (*sc.* Asclepiades), has collected the diseases and their causes and remedies in one treatise'. This Diogenes (mentioned also *ibid.* XIII, 4) may well be the Apolloniate, whom we know from Theophrastus (*de sensu* 43, DK 64 A 19) and from another medical author ([Galen] *de humor.* XIX, 495 Kühn, DK 64 A 29 a) to have held views about diagnosis by the tongue and colour of the patient. He was, therefore, perhaps a professional doctor, who may have published a technical medical treatise as well as a general exposition of his cosmic theory.

The opening sentence of the latter, quoted in **596**, reminds one of the methodological claims made at the beginning of some of the older and more philosophically-inclined works of the Hippocratic corpus, notably *Ancient Medicine*, *Airs Waters Places*, and *The Nature of Man*. It must be admitted to Diogenes' credit that his exposition and argumentation is, for his period, clear, simple and dignified.

THE ECLECTIC, BUT NOT VALUELESS, NATURE OF DIOGENES' THOUGHT

598 Theophrastus *Phys. op.* fr. 2 *ap.* Simplicium *in Phys.* 25, 1 (DK 64 A 5) καὶ Διογένης δὲ ὁ Ἀπολλωνιάτης, σχεδὸν νεώτατος γεγονὼς τῶν περὶ ταῦτα σχολασάντων, τὰ μὲν πλεῖστα συμπεφορημένως γέγραφε, τὰ μὲν κατὰ Ἀναξαγόραν, τὰ δὲ κατὰ Λεύκιππον

λέγων· τὴν δὲ τοῦ παντὸς φύσιν ἀέρα καὶ οὗτός φησιν ἄπειρον εἶναι
καὶ ἀίδιον, ἐξ οὗ πυκνουμένου καὶ μανουμένου καὶ μεταβάλλοντος τοῖς
πάθεσι τὴν τῶν ἄλλων γίνεσθαι μορφήν. καὶ ταῦτα μὲν Θεόφραστος
ἱστορεῖ περὶ τοῦ Διογένους, καὶ τὸ εἰς ἐμὲ ἐλθὸν αὐτοῦ σύγγραμμα
Περὶ φύσεως ἐπιγεγραμμένον ἀέρα σαφῶς λέγει τὸ ἐξ οὗ πάντα
γίνεται τὰ ἄλλα.

598 Diogenes the Apolloniate, almost the youngest of those who
occupied themselves with these matters (*i.e.* physical studies),
wrote for the most part in an eclectic fashion, following Anaxagoras
in some things and Leucippus in others. He, too, says that the
substance of the universe is infinite and eternal air, from which,
when it is condensed and rarefied and changed in its dispositions,
the form of other things comes into being. This is what Theophrastus relates about Diogenes; and the book of Diogenes which
has reached me, entitled *On Nature*, clearly says that air is that
from which all the rest come into being.

Simplicius here obligingly distinguishes Theophrastus' judgement on
Diogenes from his own appended comments. According to Theophrastus, then, most of Diogenes' theories were eclectic, being derived
from Anaxagoras, from Leucippus, or, in the important matter of the
material principle, from Anaximenes. This seems to be true so far as
it goes; but it seems probable that Heraclitus should be added to the
list of important influences (pp. 440f., 443ff., 449).[1] Although an
eclectic, Diogenes seems to have been far more effective than Hippon
of Samos, for example, or even Archelaus; he used elements from
earlier systems as material for a unitary theory of the world which
was more self-consistent, less complicated, more explicit and more
widely applicable than its monistic forebears. He adapted Anaxagoras' 'Mind' to his own monistic conception, and thereby showed,
perhaps more clearly than his predecessors, how the basic substance
(which is itself, in certain forms, νόησις or intelligence) could control
the operation of natural change; and in the explicitly teleological
fragment (**601**, which must have been further expanded in other parts
of Diogenes' work) he fully worked out an idea which seems to have
been foreshadowed in Heraclitus and left uncompleted in
Anaxagoras.

[1] H. Diller, *Hermes* 76 (1941), 359ff., argued that the Leucippean elements are
negligible; and that *Melissus* was criticizing both Diogenes and Leucippus (the
normal view being, of course, that Leucippus reacted to suggestions in Melissus,
see pp. 408f.). The chronology of these three thinkers is admittedly loose enough
to allow that they were all active, as Diller suggests, in the decade 440–430 B.C.;

and we cannot be absolutely certain about their relationship. Yet Diller bases his theory of the priority of Diogenes to Melissus largely on similarities of diction and vocabulary, and overlooks the fact that words like μετακοσμεῖσθαι were liable to be used in any philosophical writing of the latter half of the fifth century B.C. There *are* verbal similarities between Melissus fr. 7 (**533**) and Diogenes fr. 2 (**599** below); but it seems clear, not that Melissus is rebuffing Diogenes, or even vice versa, but that both are reacting in different ways to pluralist explanations of the world.

ALL THINGS MUST BE MODIFICATIONS OF ONE BASIC SUBSTANCE

599 Fr. 2, Simplicius *in Phys.* 151, 31 ἐμοὶ δὲ δοκεῖ τὸ μὲν ξύμπαν εἰπεῖν πάντα τὰ ὄντα ἀπὸ τοῦ αὐτοῦ ἑτεροιοῦσθαι καὶ τὸ αὐτὸ εἶναι. καὶ τοῦτο εὔδηλον· εἰ γὰρ τὰ ἐν τῷδε τῷ κόσμῳ ἐόντα νῦν, γῆ καὶ ὕδωρ καὶ ἀὴρ καὶ πῦρ καὶ τὰ ἄλλα ὅσα φαίνεται ἐν τῷδε τῷ κόσμῳ ἐόντα, εἰ τούτων τι ἦν ἕτερον τοῦ ἑτέρου, ἕτερον ὂν τῇ ἰδίᾳ φύσει, καὶ μὴ τὸ αὐτὸ ἐὸν μετέπιπτε πολλαχῶς καὶ ἑτεροιοῦτο, οὐδαμῇ οὔτε μίσγεσθαι ἀλλήλοις ἠδύνατο, οὔτε ὠφέλησις τῷ ἑτέρῳ οὔτε βλάβη, οὐδ' ἂν οὔτε φυτὸν ἐκ τῆς γῆς φῦναι οὔτε ζῷον οὔτε ἄλλο γενέσθαι οὐδέν, εἰ μὴ οὕτω συνίστατο ὥστε ταὐτὸ εἶναι. ἀλλὰ πάντα ταῦτα ἐκ τοῦ αὐτοῦ ἑτεροιούμενα ἄλλοτε ἀλλοῖα γίνεται καὶ εἰς τὸ αὐτὸ ἀναχωρεῖ.

599 My opinion, in sum, is that all existing things are differentiated from the same thing, and *are* the same thing. And this is manifest: for if the things that exist at present in this world-order – earth and water and air and fire and all the other things apparent in this world-order – if any of these were different from the other (different, that is, in its own proper nature), and did not retain an essential identity while undergoing many changes and differentiations, it would be in no way possible for them to mix with each other, or for one to help or harm the other, or for a growing plant to grow out of the earth or for a living creature or anything else to come into being, unless they were so composed as to be the same thing. But all these things, being differentiated from the same thing, become of different kinds at different times and return into the same thing.

This statement, which according to Simplicius' introductory remark (DK 64 B 2) came 'immediately after the proem' – that is, immediately or shortly after **596** – is a reaffirmation of monism in face, presumably, of the pluralist systems of Empedocles and Anaxagoras. It is based on a new argument: not that it is *simpler* to have a single originative and basic substance (which may have been the chief Milesian motive, partly consciously, but partly unconsciously through the influence of the mythical–genealogical tradition), but that interaction of any kind between absolutely and essentially distinct substances would be impossible. Of the interactions named, 'helping' and 'harming' (probably), and plant and animal growth, are taken from the animate sphere; which suggests that Diogenes' view of the world is influenced by his physiological interests, much as Anaxagoras' theory seems to have been intimately connected with his reflections on nutrition. Biological change cannot arise from the mere juxtaposition of totally different substances, as for example in Empedocles' 'recipes' for bone and flesh (**373** and **374**). This principle is extended by Diogenes to the inanimate world, too, which is analysed in terms of the four now recognized world-masses and the other natural substances, thus showing the effect of Anaxagoras' extension of natural substance beyond Empedocles' four 'roots' (**346**). **599** concludes with the earliest certain enunciation (cf. pp. 118ff.) of a principle assigned by Aristotle to the Presocratics in general, that things are destroyed into that from which they came.[1]

[1] Simplicius, in his connecting comment (DK64B2) between **599** and **601**, found it odd that air, which is to be identified as the single underlying substance, is mentioned in **599** as one of several world-constituents. And Barnes (*Presocratic Philosophers* II, 272–4) on this basis develops a powerful argument for the thesis that Diogenes' ἀρχή is in fact not air, but body, conceived as a basic stuff underlying but distinct from the four 'elements', having no determinate character of its own: a precursor of Aristotelian matter. Yet if he is right it is strange that Theophrastus (**598**) did not seize on this interpretation, or at least on one like Nicolaus' (**597**). Perhaps we should suppose that atmospheric air is not the basic form of air, but a close derivative. The basic form of air is presumably the warm air that is intelligence, cf. **603** – if, that is, Diogenes distinguished any such 'basic' or true form.

599 may also be taken as a limitation of the principle expressed in Anaxagoras fr. 17 (**469**), that all coming-to-be is mixture, all passing-away is separation. Diogenes accepted this, but only if the elements of the mixture were of one kind and not, as Anaxagoras thought, of many different kinds. In this respect Diogenes may have been following Leucippus. The direct evidence for dependence on Leucippus, however, apart from Theophrastus' bare assertion in **598**, is slight.[1]

[1] Cf. **600** Diogenes Laertius IX, 57 (after **595**) ἐδόκει δὲ αὐτῷ τάδε· στοιχεῖον εἶναι τὸν ἀέρα, κόσμους ἀπείρους καὶ κενὸν ἄπειρον· τόν τε ἀέρα πυκνούμενον καὶ ἀραιούμενον γεννητικὸν εἶναι τῶν κόσμων· οὐδὲν ἐκ τοῦ μὴ ὄντος γίνεσθαι οὐδὲ εἰς τὸ μὴ ὂν φθείρεσθαι· τὴν γῆν στρογγύλην, ἠρεισμένην ἐν τῷ μέσῳ, τὴν

σύστασιν εἰληφυῖαν κατὰ τὴν ἐκ τοῦ θερμοῦ περιφορὰν καὶ πῆξιν ὑπὸ τοῦ ψυχροῦ. (Cf. 607.) *(His opinions were as follows. Air is the element, and there are innumerable worlds and infinite void. Air is generative of the worlds through being condensed and rarefied. Nothing comes to be from that which is not, nor is anything destroyed into that which is not. The earth is circular, supported in the centre [sc. of the world], having received its formation in accordance with the revolution proceeding from the hot and coagulation produced by the cold.)* This brief summary is indirectly derived from Theophrastus, but through a third-rate biographical source. There is only one other mention of the void in connexion with Diogenes (DK 64 A 31). It might appear that its presence here is due to doxographical conjecture. Yet Theophrastus evidently credited Diogenes with innumerable worlds of atomistic type (see 607, as well as the present passage), and Diogenes could certainly have taken this theory from Leucippus. If so, then he might also have followed Leucippus in postulating the void – a postulate intimately connected, for the atomists, with that of innumerable worlds.

THE BASIC SUBSTANCE CONTAINS DIVINE INTELLIGENCE, WHICH DIRECTS ALL THINGS FOR THE BEST

601 Fr. 3, Simplicius *in Phys.* 152, 13 οὐ γὰρ ἄν, φησίν, οἷόν τε ἦν οὕτω δεδάσθαι ἄνευ νοήσιος ὥστε πάντων μέτρα ἔχειν,[1] χειμῶνός τε καὶ θέρους καὶ νυκτὸς καὶ ἡμέρας καὶ ὑετῶν καὶ ἀνέμων καὶ εὐδιῶν· καὶ τὰ ἄλλα, εἴ τις βούλεται ἐννοεῖσθαι, εὑρίσκοι ἂν οὕτω διακείμενα ὡς ἀνυστὸν κάλλιστα.

[1] Were it not for the difficulty of providing a subject for πάντων μέτρα ἔχειν, it would be natural to understand πάντα as the subject of δεδάσθαι. As it is, it seems preferable to understand something like the underlying substance referred to in 599 *fin.* as the subject both of δεδάσθαι and of ἔχειν.

601 For, he says, it would not be possible without intelligence for it [*sc.* the underlying substance] so to be divided up that it has measures of all things –of winter and summer and night and day and rains and winds and fair weather. The other things, too, if one wishes to consider them, one would find disposed in the best possible way.

According to Simplicius, **601** followed very closely upon **599**, and was itself followed by **602**. Diogenes set out his teleological belief in a prominent position, therefore, before the basic substance had been fully identified as air. According to that belief the world and its parts are arranged by a divine intelligence in the best possible way. This intelligence, according to Simplicius and to fr. 5 (**603**), is implicit in the basic substance. It is postulated because otherwise it would have been impossible for things to be divided up, and to be measured, as they patently are, into winter and summer, night and day, rain and wind and fair weather. It is the regularity of natural events, therefore, of year- and day-cycles and of the weather, which impressed Diogenes;[1] here he was surely to some extent dependent on Heraclitus, who stressed that the *measures* (217-20) of all natural change were preserved by the Logos, itself an expression or aspect of the archetypal substance, fire. Heraclitus had instanced these same natural oppositions and cycles (cf. 202, 204 and fr. 57) as evincing a basic unity because of the regularity of their measures. Diogenes' concept of the conscious purposefulness of nature, however, goes beyond Heraclitus; the latter, although he considered all things to be 'steered' by fire (220), held that this was in accordance with an objective natural rule (which could be regarded materially as Logos or fire itself) implicit in the constitution of things – a development, perhaps, of Anaximander's idea that natural interchanges were governed by a natural law of justice. Thus for Heraclitus pure fire was intelligent, but the regularity of natural events was achieved not so much by the deliberate exercise of this intelligence on every occasion as by the incorporation of the Logos (fire in a systematically metric function) in each separate thing, leading it to behave in a regular or measured way. For Diogenes, on the other hand, every natural event was evidently due directly to the intelligence of the pure form of the basic substance; and thus occasional local anomalies, which were permitted in the systems of Anaximander and Heraclitus, providing they were eventually corrected and counterbalanced, should not really take place. The difference in Diogenes' view is undoubtedly due to the influence of Anaxagoras' Mind, νοῦς (476ff.); the effect of which, however, as Socrates complained in 495, was only too often merely mechanical.

[1] No doubt he was also impressed by the significant functions of the organs of living creatures. We know that he gave considerable attention to methods of sensation (see 613) and breathing in different species – for example in fish (DK 64 A 31); and that such differences were explained by differences in natural structure, which might thus appear to be purpose-serving.

INTELLIGENCE AND LIFE ARE DUE TO AIR, WHICH IS THERE-
FORE THE BASIC FORM OF MATTER. AIR IS DIVINE AND
CONTROLS ALL THINGS; IT TAKES DIFFERENT FORMS
ACCORDING TO ITS DIFFERENCES IN HEAT, MOTION AND
SO ON

602 Fr. 4, Simplicius *in Phys.* 152, 18 ἔτι δὲ πρὸς τούτοις καὶ τάδε μεγάλα σημεῖα. ἄνθρωποι γὰρ καὶ τὰ ἄλλα ζῷα ἀναπνέοντα ζώει τῷ ἀέρι. καὶ τοῦτο αὐτοῖς καὶ ψυχή ἐστι καὶ νόησις, ὡς δεδηλώσεται

ἐν τῇδε τῇ συγγραφῇ ἐμφανῶς, καὶ ἐὰν τοῦτο ἀπαλλαχθῇ ἀποθνήσκει καὶ ἡ νόησις ἐπιλείπει.

603 Fr. 5, Simplicius *in Phys.* 152, 22 καί μοι δοκεῖ τὸ τὴν νόησιν ἔχον εἶναι ὁ ἀὴρ καλούμενος ὑπὸ τῶν ἀνθρώπων, καὶ ὑπὸ τούτου πάντας καὶ κυβερνᾶσθαι καὶ πάντων κρατεῖν· αὐτὸ γάρ μοι τοῦτο θεὸς δοκεῖ εἶναι καὶ ἐπὶ πᾶν ἀφῖχθαι καὶ πάντα διατιθέναι καὶ ἐν παντὶ ἐνεῖναι. καὶ ἔστιν οὐδὲ ἓν ὅ τι μὴ μετέχει τούτου· μετέχει δὲ οὐδὲ ἓν ὁμοίως τὸ ἕτερον τῷ ἑτέρῳ, ἀλλὰ πολλοὶ τρόποι καὶ αὐτοῦ τοῦ ἀέρος καὶ τῆς νοήσιός εἰσιν· ἔστι γὰρ πολύτροπος, καὶ θερμότερος καὶ ψυχρότερος καὶ ξηρότερος καὶ ὑγρότερος καὶ στασιμώτερος καὶ ὀξυτέρην κίνησιν ἔχων, καὶ ἄλλαι πολλαὶ ἑτεροιώσιες ἔνεισι καὶ ἡδονῆς καὶ χροιῆς ἄπειροι. καὶ πάντων τῶν ζῴων δὲ ἡ ψυχὴ τὸ αὐτό ἐστιν, ἀὴρ θερμότερος μὲν τοῦ ἔξω ἐν ᾧ ἐσμεν, τοῦ μέντοι παρὰ τῷ ἡλίῳ πολλὸν ψυχρότερος. ὅμοιον δὲ τοῦτο τὸ θερμὸν οὐδενὸς τῶν ζῴων ἐστίν (ἐπεὶ οὐδὲ τῶν ἀνθρώπων ἀλλήλοις), ἀλλὰ διαφέρει μέγα μὲν οὔ, ἀλλ᾽ ὥστε παραπλήσια εἶναι. οὐ μέντοι ἀτρεκέως γε ὅμοιον οὐδὲν οἷόν τε γενέσθαι τῶν ἑτεροιουμένων ἕτερον τῷ ἑτέρῳ, πρὶν τὸ αὐτὸ γένηται. ἅτε οὖν πολυτρόπου ἐούσης τῆς ἑτεροιώσιος πολύτροπα καὶ τὰ ζῷα καὶ πολλὰ καὶ οὔτε ἰδέαν ἀλλήλοις ἐοικότα οὔτε δίαιταν οὔτε νόησιν ὑπὸ τοῦ πλήθεος τῶν ἑτεροιώσεων. ὅμως δὲ πάντα τῷ αὐτῷ καὶ ζῇ καὶ ὁρᾷ καὶ ἀκούει, καὶ τὴν ἄλλην νόησιν ἔχει ἀπὸ τοῦ αὐτοῦ πάντα.

604 Fr. 7, Simplicius *in Phys.* 153, 19 καὶ αὐτὸ μὲν τοῦτο καὶ ἀίδιον καὶ ἀθάνατον σῶμα, τῶν δὲ τὰ μὲν γίνεται, τὰ δὲ ἀπολείπει.

605 Fr. 8, Simplicius *in Phys.* 153, 20 ἀλλὰ τοῦτό μοι δῆλον δοκεῖ εἶναι, ὅτι καὶ μέγα καὶ ἰσχυρὸν καὶ ἀίδιόν τε καὶ ἀθάνατον καὶ πολλὰ εἰδός ἐστι.

602 Further, in addition to those, these too are important indications. Men and the other living creatures live by means of air, through breathing it. And this is for them both soul [*i.e.* life-principle] and intelligence, as will be clearly shown in this work; and if this is removed, then they die and intelligence fails.

603 And it seems to me that that which has intelligence is what men call air, and that all men are steered by this and that it has power over all things. For this very thing seems to me to be a god and to have reached everywhere and to dispose all things and to be in everything. And there is no single thing that does not have a share of this; but nothing has an equal share of it, one with another, but there are many fashions both of air itself and of intelligence. For it is many-fashioned, being hotter and colder and drier and moister and more stationary and more swiftly mobile, and many other differentiations are in it both of taste and of colour, unlimited in number. And yet of all living creatures the soul is the same, air that is warmer than that outside, in which we exist, but much cooler than that near the sun. But in none of living creatures is this warmth alike (since it is not even so in individual men); the difference is not great, but as much as still allows them to be similar. Yet it is not possible for anything to become truly alike, one to the other, of the things undergoing differentiation, without becoming the same. Because, then, the differentiation is many-fashioned, living creatures are many-fashioned and many in number, resembling each other neither in form nor in way of life nor in intelligence, because of the number of differentiations. Nevertheless they all live and see and hear by the same thing, and have the rest of their intelligence from the same thing.

604 And this very thing is both eternal and immortal body, but of the rest some come into being, some pass away.[1]

605 But this seems to me to be plain, that it is both great and strong and eternal and immortal and much-knowing.

[1] This is the old contrast between god and man, or god and the world: the perfect and the imperfect (cf. p. 179). Simplicius noted (DK 64 B 7) that both the divine and the world are made of the same thing, air, for Diogenes. It is nevertheless legitimate to contrast the pure, divine form of air with its derivative, corporeal forms; the severity of this contrast is due to its traditional formulation.

Simplicius obviously omitted something that came between **601** and **602** in Diogenes' book, so that we do not know the 'signs' (cf. Melissus fr. 8 *init.*, **537**) mentioned in **602**: presumably they too were signs that the basic substance was air. Perhaps the gradual diminution of decaying bodies, 'into thin air', might have been one such indication, the nature of semen (see p. 451 and **616**) another. The sign that is mentioned, that all creatures live by breathing air, which is both soul (life-principle) and intelligence, is obviously the most important of all; it was probably stated in Anaximenes, indeed (cf. pp. 161f.), but would occur naturally to anyone of pronounced physiological interests like Diogenes. That breath is the life-substance is deduced in **602** from the fact that life leaves the body with the breath, and was implicit in some Homeric uses of θυμός and ψυχή. The connexion of πνεῦμα, breath, with πνεῦμα, wind, was perhaps first made by Anaximenes. That air is also intelligence is, on the one hand, an inference from its *divinity* as the life-principle; on the other it may be a reasonable development of a view like Heraclitus', that the intelligent substance (in his case Logos or fire) is inhaled by

443

breathing.[1] But even in Homer the distinction between life (ψυχή) and intelligence or feeling (θυμός) was blurred.

[1] Diogenes succeeded in accounting for the dual function of air (as life, and as intelligence and perception) in his detailed physiological theory; for air as sensation see p. 449 below, for air as life cf. 606 Aetius v, 24, 3 (DK 64 A 29) Διογένης (sc. φησὶ) ἐὰν ἐπὶ πᾶν τὸ αἷμα διαχεόμενον πληρώσῃ μὲν τὰς φλέβας, τὸν δὲ ἐν αὐταῖς περιεχόμενον ἀέρα ὤσῃ εἰς τὰ στέρνα καὶ τὴν ὑποκειμένην γαστέρα, ὕπνον γεγενῆσθαι καὶ θερμότερον ὑπάρχειν τὸν θώρακα· ἐὰν δὲ ἅπαν τὸ ἀερῶδες ἐκ τῶν φλεβῶν ἐκλίπῃ, θάνατον συντυγχάνειν. (Diogenes says that if the blood, pouring into every part, fills the veins and pushes the air enclosed in them into the chest and the stomach below, then sleep occurs and the middle part of the body is warmer; but if all the airy part goes away from the veins, death occurs simultaneously.) This is analogous to Heraclitus' theory of waking, sleeping and death as descending stages of consciousness, due to the diminution of soul-fire.

Air is god; it steers, has power over, inheres in, and disposes all things (603 init.); it is eternal and immortal (604, 605). In these descriptions, whose hieratic quality (particularly 603 with its repetition of πάντας, πάντων, πᾶν etc.) has been rightly remarked, Diogenes seems to collect together all the phraseology of his predecessors – of Anaximander (108), Heraclitus (220) and Anaxagoras (476) in particular. His emphasis in 603 that all things absolutely participate in air may be intended as a correction of Anaxagoras, for whom Mind only existed in animate things. For Diogenes all things are made of air, but the inanimate is divided from the animate world by the fact that only in some things is warm air found. In 603 the animate is chiefly in question; differences are explained by air changing in accordance with its warmth, dryness, motion, and other characteristics, which give it different 'tastes and colours'. It may be noted here that, in spite of Theophrastus' assessment in 598, Diogenes does not appear to be interested in explaining all changes of air as being due solely to rarefaction and condensation; at least he describes some alteration in terms of what should be derivative and secondary changes, like those of temperature. In fact, the distinguishing mark of the divine is its temperature, not its density; Diogenes has clearly overlooked, or at least failed to stress, the elegant consistency of Anaximenes.

Intelligence is *warm* air, warmer than the atmosphere (which is presumably air verging towards water), but cooler than the air round the sun (which is verging towards fire). There are indefinite slight variations in the temperature-range of intelligence-producing air, thus accounting for countless variations in perception, intelligence, and way of life. Moderate warmth is the *differentia* of soul-air; thus Diogenes achieves a rational distinction between the animate and the inanimate world, while retaining (unlike Anaxagoras) a common substance for both, and thus keeping his monistic conception intact. Neatness, rather than originality, is his contribution here. Anaximenes had already assumed that both soul and the world were made of air, and that they were nevertheless distinguished, presumably by degree of concentration – though this is not explicitly stated; and for Heraclitus, too, the archetypal form of matter, fire, was also, in certain forms, soul-substance – which acted not only within animate creatures but also, as noetic and directive, on the world as a whole.

DETAILED PHYSICAL DOCTRINES

(i) *Cosmogony and cosmology*

607 Ps.-Plutarch *Strom.* 12 Διογένης ὁ Ἀπολλωνιάτης ἀέρα ὑφίσταται στοιχεῖον· κινεῖσθαι δὲ τὰ πάντα ἀπείρους τε εἶναι τοὺς κόσμους. κοσμοποιεῖ δὲ οὕτως· ὅτι τοῦ παντὸς κινουμένου, καὶ ᾗ μὲν ἀραιοῦ ᾗ δὲ πυκνοῦ γινομένου, ὅπου συνεκύρησεν τὸ πυκνὸν συστροφῇ ⟨τὴν γῆν⟩ ποιῆσαι καὶ οὕτως τὰ λοιπὰ κατὰ τὸν αὐτὸν λόγον, τὰ ⟨δὲ⟩ κουφότατα τὴν ἄνω τάξιν λαβόντα τὸν ἥλιον ἀποτελέσαι. [συστροφὴν ποιῆσαι MSS, em. Kranz, cf. **600**. ⟨δὲ⟩ Diels.]

608 Aetius II, 13, 5 + 9 Διογένης κισηροειδῆ τὰ ἄστρα, διαπνοὰς δὲ αὐτὰ νομίζει τοῦ κόσμου· εἶναι δὲ διάπυρα. συμπεριφέρεσθαι δὲ τοῖς φανεροῖς ἄστροις ἀφανεῖς λίθους καὶ παρ' αὐτὸ τοῦτ' ἀνωνύμους· πίπτοντας δὲ πολλάκις ἐπὶ τῆς γῆς σβέννυσθαι καθάπερ τὸν ἐν Αἰγὸς ποταμοῖς πυροειδῶς κατενεχθέντα ἀστέρα πέτρινον.

607 Diogenes the Apolloniate premises that air is the element, and that all things are in motion and the worlds innumerable. He gives this account of cosmogony: the whole was in motion, and became rare in some places and dense in others; where the dense ran together centripetally it made the earth, and so the rest by the same method, while the lightest parts took the upper position and produced the sun.
608 Diogenes says that the heavenly bodies are like pumice-stone, and he considers them as the breathing-holes of the world; and they are fiery. With the visible heavenly bodies are carried round invisible stones, which for this reason have no name: they often fall on the earth and are extinguished, like the stone star that made its fiery descent at Aegospotami.

Diogenes' cosmogony is unoriginal, and is dependent on Anaxagoras (for the idea of the noetic substance starting a vortex) and on the

Milesian tradition (the dense coalescing at the centre to form earth, the rarer material going to the extremity, by like-to-like and differentiation). Both **607** and **600** assign innumerable worlds to Diogenes (see n. on pp. 439f.); these were of atomistic type, presumably after Leucippus – coming-to-be, that is, and passing away throughout the boundless void (cf. also Aetius II, 1, 3, DK64A10). Aristotle's comment (**132**) that according to some natural philosophers the world was drying up was referred by Alexander to Diogenes as well as to Anaximander; Alexander adds (DK64A17) that Diogenes explained the saltness of the sea by the sun's evaporating the sweet water, which may suggest that this drying of the sea was a simple meteorological comment not necessarily concerned with cosmic cycles or innumerable worlds.[1] The heavenly bodies (of which the sun is probably farther away than the stars, cf. **607** *fin.*) are like pumice-stone, and glowing; doubtless their pumice-like consistency is postulated so that they can be very light, and interpenetrated by fire. The great Aegospotami meteorite of 467 B.C. had evidently impressed Diogenes (as it had Anaxagoras, cf. p. 382), who inferred that there must be other such bodies revolving unseen in the sky. This may be Diogenes' own idea (cf. p. 156). Other astronomical details are derivative: that the sun is a concentration of rays from the aither (Aetius II, 20, 10, DK64A13) is from Empedocles (p. 301); that the earth, which is a circle, presumably a round disc, is tilted toward the south (Aetius II, 8, 1, DK59A67) is ascribed also to Anaxagoras and Leucippus; whether or not it is derived from Anaximenes is questionable (see pp. 156f.).

[1] It is probable that Diogenes is referred to (though perhaps not exclusively; for this kind of detail he was classed with Anaximenes) in **609** Aristotle *Meteor.* B2, 355a21 τὸ δ' αὐτὸ συμβαίνει καὶ τούτοις ἄλογον καὶ τοῖς φάσκουσι τὸ πρῶτον ὑγρᾶς οὔσης καὶ τῆς γῆς, καὶ τοῦ κόσμου τοῦ περὶ τὴν γῆν ὑπὸ τοῦ ἡλίου θερμαινομένου, ἀέρα γενέσθαι καὶ τὸν ὅλον οὐρανὸν αὐξηθῆναι, καὶ τοῦτον πνεύματά τε παρέχεσθαι καὶ τὰς τροπὰς αὐτοῦ ποιεῖν. *(The same illogicality results both for these and for those who say that when the earth, too, was at first moist, and the part of the world round the earth was being heated by the sun, air was produced and the whole heaven was increased, and that air causes winds and makes the turnings of the sun.)* That the drawing up of vapour by the sun was mentioned by Diogenes is proved by his solution of that popular natural problem (cf. **502**), the cause of the flooding of the Nile: **610** Scholion *in* Apollonium Rhod. IV, 269 Διογένης δὲ ὁ Ἀπολλωνιάτης ὑπὸ ἡλίου ἁρπάζεσθαι τὸ ὕδωρ τῆς θαλάσσης, ὃ τότε εἰς τὸν Νεῖλον καταφέρεσθαι· οἴεται γὰρ πληροῦσθαι τὸν Νεῖλον ἐν τῷ θέρει διὰ τὸ τὸν ἡλίον εἰς τοῦτον τὰς ἀπὸ γῆς ἰκμάδας τρέπειν. *(Diogenes the Apolloniate says that the water of the sea is snatched up by the sun, and then comes down into the Nile; for he thinks that the Nile floods in summer through the sun turning into it the emanations from earth.)* Diogenes used ἰκμάδες, moist secretions or emanations, to explain another popular

natural problem too (cf. **89, 90**), that of magnetism: **611** Alexander *Quaest.* II, 23 (DK 64 A 33)   (περὶ τῆς Ἡρακλείας λίθου, διὰ τί ἕλκει τὸν σίδηρον.) Διογένης δὲ ὁ Ἀπολλωνιάτης πάντα τὰ ἐλατά φησιν καὶ ἀφιέναι τινὰ ἰκμάδα ἀφ᾽ αὑτῶν πεφυκέναι καὶ ἕλκειν ἔξωθεν τὰ μὲν πλείω τὰ δὲ ἐλάττω, πλείστην δὲ ἀφιέναι χαλκόν τε καὶ σίδηρον... *((On why the Heraclean stone* [i.e. *the magnet*] *attracts iron.) Diogenes the Apolloniate says that all ductile metals naturally discharge from themselves, and draw in from outside, a kind of emanation, some more and others less; but that bronze and iron discharge it in the greatest quantity...)* (The magnet, on the contrary, absorbs more emanations than it discharges, and therefore draws in the superfluous emanations of iron and bronze, which are 'akin' to it – and so also attracts the metals themselves.) Similarly Empedocles, DK 31 A 89.

(ii) *Physiology:* (a) *Cognition*

612 Theophrastus *de sensu* 39ff. (DK 64 A 19)   Διογένης δ᾽ ὥσπερ τὸ 3ῆν καὶ τὸ φρονεῖν τῷ ἀέρι καὶ τὰς αἰσθήσεις ἀνάπτει· διὸ καὶ δόξειεν ἂν τῷ ὁμοίῳ ποιεῖν (οὐδὲ γὰρ τὸ ποιεῖν εἶναι καὶ πάσχειν, εἰ μὴ πάντα ἦν ἐξ ἑνός)· τὴν μὲν ὄσφρησιν τῷ περὶ τὸν ἐγκέφαλον ἀέρι·...(40) τὴν δ᾽ ἀκοήν, ὅταν ὁ ἐν τοῖς ὠσὶν ἀὴρ κινηθεὶς ὑπὸ τοῦ ἔξω διαδῷ πρὸς τὸν ἐγκέφαλον. τὴν δὲ ὄψιν [ὁρᾶν] ἐμφαινομένων εἰς τὴν κόρην, ταύτην δὲ μειγνυμένην τῷ ἐντὸς ἀέρι ποιεῖν αἴσθησιν· σημεῖον δέ· ἐὰν γὰρ φλεγμασία γένηται τῶν φλεβῶν, οὐ μείγνυσθαι τῷ ἐντὸς οὐδ᾽ ὁρᾶν ὁμοίως τῆς ἐμφάσεως οὔσης. τὴν δὲ γεῦσιν τῇ γλώττῃ διὰ τὸ μανὸν καὶ ἁπαλόν. περὶ δὲ ἁφῆς οὐδὲν ἀφώρισεν οὔτε πῶς οὔτε τίνων ἐστίν. ἀλλὰ μετὰ ταῦτα πειρᾶται λέγειν διὰ τί συμβαίνει τὰς αἰσθήσεις ἀκριβεστέρας εἶναι καὶ τῶν ποίων. (41) ὄσφρησιν μὲν οὖν ὀξυτάτην οἷς ἐλάχιστος ἀὴρ ἐν τῇ κεφαλῇ· τάχιστα γὰρ μείγνυσθαι· καὶ πρὸς τούτοις ἐὰν ἕλκῃ διὰ μακροτέρου καὶ στενωτέρου· θᾶττον γὰρ οὕτω κρίνεσθαι· διόπερ ἔνια τῶν 3ῴων ὀσφραντικώτερα τῶν ἀνθρώπων εἶναι· οὐ μὴν ἀλλὰ συμμέτρου γε οὔσης τῆς ὀσμῆς τῷ ἀέρι πρὸς τὴν κρᾶσιν μάλιστα ἂν αἰσθάνεσθαι τὸν ἄνθρωπον...ὅτι δὲ ὁ ἐντὸς ἀὴρ αἰσθάνεται μικρὸν ὢν μόριον τοῦ θεοῦ, σημεῖον εἶναι, διότι πολλάκις πρὸς ἄλλα τὸν νοῦν ἔχοντες οὔθ᾽ ὁρῶμεν οὔτ᾽ ἀκούομεν. (43) ἡδονὴν δὲ καὶ λύπην γίνεσθαι τόνδε τὸν τρόπον· ὅταν μὲν πολὺς ὁ ἀὴρ μίσγηται τῷ αἵματι καὶ κουφίζῃ κατὰ φύσιν ὢν καὶ κατὰ πᾶν τὸ σῶμα διεξιών, ἡδονήν· ὅταν δὲ παρὰ φύσιν καὶ μὴ μίσγηται συνιζάνοντος τοῦ αἵματος καὶ ἀσθενεστέρου καὶ πυκνοτέρου γινομένου, λύπην. ὁμοίως καὶ θάρσος καὶ ὑγίειαν καὶ τἀναντία... (44) φρονεῖν δ᾽, ὥσπερ ἐλέχθη, τῷ ἀέρι καθαρῷ καὶ ξηρῷ· κωλύειν γὰρ τὴν ἰκμάδα τὸν νοῦν· διὸ καὶ ἐν τοῖς ὕπνοις καὶ ἐν ταῖς μέθαις καὶ ἐν ταῖς πλησμοναῖς ἧττον φρονεῖν· ὅτι δὲ ἡ ὑγρότης ἀφαιρεῖται τὸν νοῦν, σημεῖον, διότι τὰ ἄλλα 3ῷα χείρω τὴν διάνοιαν· ἀναπνεῖν τε γὰρ τὸν ἀπὸ τῆς γῆς ἀέρα καὶ τροφὴν ὑγροτέραν προσφέρεσθαι. τοὺς δὲ ὄρνιθας ἀναπνεῖν μὲν καθαρόν, φύσιν δὲ ὁμοίαν ἔχειν τοῖς ἰχθύσι· καὶ γὰρ τὴν σάρκα στιφράν, καὶ τὸ πνεῦμα οὐ διιέναι διὰ

447

παντός, ἀλλὰ ἱστάναι περὶ τὴν κοιλίαν...τὰ δὲ φυτὰ διὰ τὸ μὴ εἶναι κοῖλα μηδὲ ἀναδέχεσθαι τὸν ἀέρα παντελῶς ἀφηρῆσθαι τὸ φρονεῖν.

612 Diogenes atttributes thinking and the senses, as also life, to air. Therefore he would seem to do so by the action of similars (for he says that there would be no action or being acted upon, unless all things were from one). The sense of smell is produced by the air round the brain...Hearing is produced whenever the air within the ears, being moved by the air outside, spreads toward the brain. Vision occurs when things are reflected on the pupil, and it, being mixed with the air within, produces a sensation. A proof of this is that, if there is an inflammation of the veins (*i.e.* those in the eye), there is no mixture with the air within, nor vision, although the reflexion exists exactly as before. Taste occurs to the tongue by what is rare and gentle. About touch he gave no definition, either about its nature or its objects. But after this he attempts to say what is the cause of more accurate sensations, and what sort of objects they have. Smell is keenest for those who have least air in their heads, for it is mixed most quickly; and, in addition, if a man draws it in through a longer and narrower channel; for in this way it is more swiftly assessed. Therefore some living creatures are more perceptive of smell than are men; yet nevertheless, if the smell were symmetrical with the air, with regard to mixture, man would smell perfectly...That the air within perceives, being a small portion of the god, is indicated by the fact that often, when we have our mind on other things, we neither see nor hear. Pleasure and pain come about in this way: whenever air mixes in quantity with the blood and lightens it, being in accordance with nature, and penetrates through the whole body, pleasure is produced; but whenever the air is present contrary to nature and does not mix, then the blood coagulates and becomes weaker and thicker, and pain is produced. Similarly confidence and health and their opposites...Thought, as has been said, is caused by pure and dry air; for a moist emanation inhibits the intelligence; for this reason thought is diminished in sleep, drunkenness and surfeit. That moisture removes intelligence is indicated by the fact that other living creatures are inferior in intellect, for they breathe the air from the earth and take to themselves moister sustenance. Birds breathe pure air, but have a constitution similar to that of fishes; for their flesh is solid, and the breath does not penetrate all through but stays around the abdomen...Plants, through not being hollow and not receiving air within them, are completely devoid of intelligence.

Slightly over half of Theophrastus' description is given in **612**; for the remainder see DK. Some of Theophrastus' explanations show his own interpretation, notably like-to-like as a principle of sensation, and 'symmetry', which has apparently been superimposed on Diogenes' idea of κρᾶσις, correct mixture. All sensation is caused by air, air from the outside meeting and mixing with, or simply agitating, air in the sense-organ itself or in the brain, whither it is led by blood-channels from the sense-organ. Clarity of perception depends on the fineness of the air in the body and the fineness and directness of the blood-channel by which the air is conveyed. Apparently the air is mixed with blood on its journeys through the head; when air naturally permeates the blood throughout the whole body, pleasure is produced. Thinking (φρονεῖν) depends on pure, dry air; it is not clear from **612** exactly where or how this functions,[1] but Simplicius tells us in **616** that air mixed with blood and pervading the body through the blood-channels produces thought (being distinguished from pleasure, presumably, by its purity, dryness and warmth). One may compare Anaxagoras' Mind, which was 'purest and finest of all substances' (**476**), and Heraclitus' soul-fire; in Diogenes, as in Heraclitus, moisture (ἰκμάς again) quenches or inhibits intelligence. Differences of intelligence and of animation are explained partly by differences of surrounding air (that near the ground is moist and heavy, therefore plants have a very low degree of life),[2] partly by differences of bodily structure (birds cannot properly assimilate their pure surrounding air).

---

[1] However, a theory is advanced, in one of the earlier Hippocratic treatises, which seems probably to be derived from Diogenes: **613** [Hippocrates] *de morbo sacro* 16 (DK 64 c 3a) κατὰ ταῦτα νομίζω τὸν ἐγκέφαλον δύναμιν ἔχειν πλείστην ἐν τῷ ἀνθρώπῳ. οὗτος γὰρ ἡμῖν ἐστι τῶν ἀπὸ τοῦ ἠέρος γινομένων ἑρμηνεὺς ἢν ὑγιαίνων τυγχάνῃ· τὴν δὲ φρόνησιν ὁ ἀὴρ παρέχεται. οἱ δ' ὀφθαλμοὶ καὶ τὰ ὦτα καὶ ἡ γλῶσσα καὶ αἱ χεῖρες καὶ οἱ πόδες, οἷα ἂν ὁ ἐγκέφαλος γινώσκῃ, τοιαῦτα πρήσσουσι· γίνεται γὰρ ἐν ἅπαντι τῷ σώματι τῆς φρονήσιός τι, ὡς ἂν μετέχῃ τοῦ ἠέρος, ἐς δὲ τὴν ξύνεσιν ὁ ἐγκέφαλός ἐστιν ὁ διαγγέλλων. ὅταν γὰρ σπάσῃ τὸ πνεῦμα ὤνθρωπος ἐς ἑωυτόν, ἐς τὸν ἐγκέφαλον πρῶτον ἀφικνεῖται καὶ οὕτως ἐς τὸ λοιπὸν σῶμα σκίδναται ὁ ἀὴρ καταλελοιπὼς ἐν τῷ ἐγκεφάλῳ ἑωυτοῦ τὴν ἀκμὴν καὶ ὅ τι ἂν ᾖ φρόνιμόν τε καὶ γνώμην ἔχον. *(Accordingly I consider that the brain has the most power in man. For, if it is in sound condition, it is our interpreter of the things that come into being through air; and air provides intelligence. The eyes and ears and tongue and hands and feet do whatsoever the brain determines; for there is an element of intelligence in the whole body, according as each part partakes of air, but it is the brain that is the messenger to the understanding. For whenever man draws breath into himself it arrives first at the brain, and thus the air spreads into the rest of the body after leaving behind its choicest part in the brain, and whatever of it is intelligent and possesses judgement.)* This writer attaches particular importance to the brain.

² Diogenes is undoubtedly the source of Socrates' remarks in the *Clouds*: **614**
Aristophanes *Clouds* 227

οὐ γὰρ ἄν ποτε
ἐξηῦρον ὀρθῶς τὰ μετέωρα πράγματα,
εἰ μὴ κρεμάσας τὸ νόημα καὶ τὴν φροντίδα
λεπτὴν καταμείξας ἐς τὸν ὅμοιον ἀέρα·
εἰ δ' ὢν χαμαὶ τἄνω κάτωθεν ἐσκόπουν,
οὐκ ἄν ποθ' ηὗρον· οὐ γὰρ ἀλλ' ἡ γῆ βίᾳ
ἕλκει πρὸς αὑτὴν τὴν ἰκμάδα τῆς φροντίδος.

(For never would I have correctly discovered the affairs on high, except by hanging up my thought and mingling my rarefied intelligence with air of like kind. If I had stayed on the ground and considered from beneath the things above, never would I have discovered them; for the truth is that the earth draws to itself by force the emanation of intelligence.) – Aristotle (*de respir.* 2, 471a2, DK64A31) criticized Diogenes for his theory that fish breathed a small amount of air in water, but that fresh air was too much for them.

(b) Anatomy and reproduction

615 Fr. 6, Aristotle *Hist. animalium* Γ2, 511b31 (DK64B6) αἱ δὲ φλέβες ἐν τῷ ἀνθρώπῳ ὧδ' ἔχουσιν· εἰσὶ δύο μέγισται· αὗται τείνουσι διὰ τῆς κοιλίας παρὰ τὴν νωτιαίαν ἄκανθαν, ἡ μὲν ἐπὶ δεξιά, ἡ δ' ἐπ' ἀριστερά, εἰς τὰ σκέλη ἑκατέρα τὰ παρ' ἑαυτῇ καὶ ἄνω εἰς τὴν κεφαλὴν παρὰ τὰς κλεῖδας διὰ τῶν σφαγῶν. ἀπὸ δὲ τούτων καθ' ἅπαν τὸ σῶμα φλέβες διατείνουσιν, ἀπὸ μὲν τῆς δεξιᾶς εἰς τὰ δεξιά, ἀπὸ δὲ τῆς ἀριστερᾶς εἰς τὰ ἀριστερά, μέγισται μὲν δύο εἰς τὴν καρδίαν περὶ αὐτὴν τὴν νωτιαίαν ἄκανθαν, ἕτεραι δ' ὀλίγον ἀνωτέρω διὰ τῶν στηθῶν ὑπὸ τὴν μασχάλην εἰς ἑκατέραν τὴν χεῖρα τὴν παρ' ἑαυτῇ· καὶ καλεῖται ἡ μὲν σπληνῖτις, ἡ δὲ ἡπατῖτις... (512b1) ἕτεραι δ' εἰσὶν αἱ ἀπὸ ἑκατέρας τείνουσαι διὰ τοῦ νωτιαίου μυελοῦ εἰς τοὺς ὄρχεις λεπταί· ἕτεραι δ' ὑπὸ τὸ δέρμα καὶ διὰ τῆς σαρκὸς τείνουσιν εἰς τοὺς νεφροὺς καὶ τελευτῶσιν εἰς τοὺς ὄρχεις τοῖς ἀνδράσι, ταῖς δὲ γυναιξὶν εἰς τὰς ὑστέρας. (αἱ δὲ φλέβες αἱ μὲν πρῶται ἐκ τῆς κοιλίας εὐρύτεραί εἰσιν, ἔπειτα λεπτότεραι γίγνονται, ἕως ἂν μεταβάλωσιν ἐκ τῶν δεξιῶν εἰς τὰ ἀριστερὰ καὶ ἐκ τούτων εἰς τὰ δεξιά.) αὗται δὲ σπερματίτιδες καλοῦνται. τὸ δ' αἷμα τὸ μὲν παχύτατον ὑπὸ τῶν σαρκωδῶν ἐκπίνεται· ὑπερβάλλον δὲ εἰς τοὺς τόπους τούτους λεπτὸν καὶ θερμὸν καὶ ἀφρῶδες γίνεται.

616 Simplicius *in Phys.* 153, 13 καὶ ἐφεξῆς (after **603**) δείκνυσιν ὅτι καὶ τὸ σπέρμα τῶν ζῴων πνευματῶδές ἐστι, καὶ νοήσεις γίνονται τοῦ ἀέρος σὺν τῷ αἵματι τὸ ὅλον σῶμα καταλαμβάνοντος διὰ τῶν φλεβῶν, ἐν οἷς καὶ ἀνατομὴν ἀκριβῆ τῶν φλεβῶν παραδίδωσιν. ἐν δὴ τούτοις σαφῶς φαίνεται λέγων ὅτι ὃν ἄνθρωποι λέγουσιν ἀέρα, τοῦτό ἐστιν ἡ ἀρχή.

615 The veins in man are as follows. There are two veins

pre-eminent in magnitude. These extend through the belly along
the backbone, one to right, one to left; either one to the leg on
its own side, and upwards to the head, past the collar-bones,
through the throat. From these, veins extend all over the body,
from that on the right hand to the right side and from that on the
left hand to the left side; the most important ones, two in number,
to the heart in the region of the backbone; two others a little higher
up through the chest underneath the armpit, each to the hand
on its own side: of these two, one being termed the spleen-vein,
and the other the liver-vein... There is also another pair, running
from each of these through the spinal marrow to the testicles, thin
and delicate. There is, further, a pair running a little underneath
the cuticle through the flesh to the kidneys, and these with men
terminate at the testicle, and with women at the womb. (The veins
that leave the stomach are comparatively broad just as they leave;
but they become gradually thinner, until they change over from
right to left and from left to right.) These veins are termed the
spermatic veins. The blood is thickest when it is imbibed by the
fleshy parts; when it is transmitted to these regions it becomes thin,
warm, and frothy. (*After D'Arcy Thompson*)

616 And in the continuation he shows that also the sperm of
living creatures is aerated, and acts of intelligence take place when
the air, with the blood, gains possession of the whole body through
the veins; in the course of which he gives an accurate anatomy of
the veins. Now in this he clearly says that what men call air is the
material principle.

616 seems to show that the long fragment on the blood-channels, **615**,
actually came in the book called by Simplicius *On Nature*. That the
semen is aerated is stated in both **615** and **616**; this is important, since
semen produces new life, and its aerated nature (conceivably noted
by Pherecydes, though see p. 58) is an important indication that air
is the vital substance. Semen, for Diogenes and for other early
theorists on the anatomy of the body, was a product of the blood,
which was also, of course, aerated (thought not so conspicuously),
and thus conveyed sensation and thought. The great detail of the
account of the blood-channels (the central part of which is omitted
here) shows that Diogenes' physiological interests,[1] which connected
with and perhaps partly motivated the general theory, were of no
merely incidental importance to him; in this we may compare
Empedocles (also a doctor of some kind, cf. p. 282) and Anaxagoras
(p. 375). There is no doubt that from Alcmaeon and Empedocles

onwards the more easily determinable structure of the human body was used as a clue to that of the whole world. The assumption of a parallelism between the two seems to have been held in some form by Anaximenes, probably as a development of the entirely unscientific tendency to treat the outside world as a person, to animate it and regard it as a living organism. This assumption was grounded in reason as a result of integrations like that of Heraclitus, who had emphasized very strongly that the Logos or arrangement of *all* things, of men and of the world as a whole, was essentially the same.

[1] Diogenes, like Empedocles and Anaxagoras, also paid attention to embryology (cf. DK 64 A 25–8) ; treating, for example, the old problem of whether the embryo is produced from the male contribution only, or from both male and female (cf. pp. 354f.).

CONCLUSION

With Diogenes and Democritus, who were little if at all older than Socrates, the Presocratic period is legitimately held to end. During the second half of the fifth century B.C., particularly during the Peloponnesian War and under the influence of the mature Socrates and the Sophists, the old cosmological approach – by which the primary aim was to explain the outside world as a whole, man being considered only incidentally – was gradually replaced by a humanistic approach to philosophy, by which the study of man became no longer subsidiary but the starting-point of all enquiry. This reorientation was a natural development: in part it was determined by social factors, but in part, as will have become apparent, it was the product of tendencies in the Presocratic movement itself.

Selective Bibliography

The most conveniently accessible large-scale bibliography of work on the Presocratics published in recent years is that in J. Barnes, *The Presocratic Philosophers* (details below). Good bibliographies are also to be found in W. K. C. Guthrie's *History* and A. P. D. Mourelatos' collection *The Presocratics*. See also G. B. Kerferd, 'Recent Work on Presocratic Philosophy', *American Philosophical Quarterly* 2 (1965), 130–40. The following periodicals together give details of most work published in the field as it appears: *L'Année Philologique, Repertoire bibliographique de la Philosophie de Louvain, The Philosopher's Index*.

Text

DIELS, H., *Die Fragmente der Vorsokratiker*, 6th ed. revised with additions and index by W. Kranz (Berlin, 1952; often reprinted).

Assessment of sources

(i) *Aristotle*

CHERNISS, H. F., *Aristotle's Criticism of Presocratic Philosophy* (Baltimore, 1935).
GUTHRIE, W. K. C., 'Aristotle as an historian of philosophy', *JHS* 77 (1957), 35–41 (repr. in Furley and Allen).
STEVENSON, J. G., 'Aristotle as historian of philosophy', *JHS* 94 (1974), 138–43.

See also the classic commentaries on Aristotle by W. D. Ross, notably the *Metaphysics* (Oxford, 1924) and the *Physics* (Oxford, 1936), and by R. D. Hicks, on *de anima* (Cambridge, 1907).

(ii) *Theophrastus*

McDIARMID, J. B., 'Theophrastus on the Presocratic causes', *HSCP* 61 (1953), 85–156 (repr. in Furley and Allen).
STEINMETZ, P., *Die Physik des Theophrasts* (Bad Homburg, 1964).
STRATTON, G. M., *Theophrastus and the Greek Physiological Psychology before Aristotle* (London, 1917).

(iii) *General*

DIELS, H., *Doxographi Graeci* (Berlin, 1879); includes *inter alia* Book I of
Hippolytus' *Refutation* and a reconstruction of the text of Aetius.
JACOBY, F., *Apollodors Chronik* (Berlin, 1903).

Discussion of sources is apt to occur in any treatment of the Presocratics.
See in particular the major editions of individual Presocratics listed below,
and also Kahn's *Anaximander* and Burkert's *Lore and Science*.

General works

BARNES, J., *The Presocratic Philosophers*, in 2 vols. (London, 1979; revised
1-vol. ed., 1982).
BURNET, J., *Early Greek Philosophy*, 4th ed. (London, 1930).
CHERNISS, H. F., 'The characteristics and effects of Presocratic philosophy',
Journal of the History of Ideas 12 (1951), 319–45 (repr. in Furley and
Allen).
DODDS, E. R., *The Greeks and the Irrational* (Berkeley, 1951).
FRÄNKEL, H., *Early Greek Poetry and Philosophy*, English trans. (Oxford, 1975).
GUTHRIE, W. K. C., *A History of Greek Philosophy*, in 6 vols. (Cambridge,
1962–81).
'The Greek world picture', *Harvard Theological Review* 45 (1952), 87–104.
HUSSEY, E., *The Presocratics* (London, 1972).
LLOYD, G. E. R., *Polarity and Analogy* (Cambridge, 1966).
Magic, Reason and Experience (Cambridge, 1979).
POPPER, K. R., 'Back to the Presocratics', in his *Conjectures and Refutations*,
3rd ed. (London, 1969); reprinted in Furley and Allen together with
G. S. Kirk's reply: 'Popper on science and the Presocratics', *Mind* 69
(1960), 318–39.
REINHARDT, K., *Parmenides und die Geschichte der griechischen Philosophie* (Bonn,
1916).
ROBIN, L., *Greek Thought*, English trans. (London, 1928).
SAMBURSKY, S., *The Physical World of the Greeks*, English trans. (London,
1956).
SNELL, B., *The Discovery of Mind*, English trans. (Oxford, 1953).
STOKES, M. C., *One and Many in Presocratic Philosophy* (Washington, D.C.,
1971).
VERNANT, J. P., *The Origins of Greek Thought*, English trans. (London, 1982).
VLASTOS, G., 'Theology and philosophy in early Greek thought', *Philosophical
Quarterly* 2 (1952), 97–123 (repr. in Furley and Allen).
ZELLER, E., *Die Philosophie der Griechen* I, i, and I, ii, respectively 7th and 6th
eds. (Leipzig, 1923 and 1920), edited and enlarged by W. Nestle.
La Filosofia dei Greci I, i, and I, ii, ed. and enlarged by R. Mondolfo
(Florence, 1932 and 1938).

Special studies

BEARE, J. I., *Greek Theories of Elementary Cognition* (Oxford, 1906).
DICKS, D. R., *Early Greek Astronomy to Aristotle* (London, 1970).
   'Solstices, equinoxes and the Presocratics', *JHS* 86 (1966), 26–40.
EDELSTEIN, L., *Ancient Medicine*, ed. O. and C. L. Temkin (Baltimore, 1967).
VON FRITZ, K., 'Νοῦς, νοεῖν and their derivatives in Presocratic philosophy',
   Classical Philology 40 (1945), 223–42 and 41 (1946), 12–34 (repr. in
   Mourelatos).
GUTHRIE, W. K. C., *In the Beginning* (Ithaca, N.Y., 1957).
HEATH, T. L., *Aristarchus of Samos* (Oxford, 1913) (pp. 1–133 on pre-Platonic
   astronomy).
   A History of Greek Mathematics, 2 vols. (Oxford, 1921).
HEINIMANN, F., *Nomos und Physis* (Basel, 1945).
JONES, W. H. S., *Philosophy and Medicine in Ancient Greece* (Baltimore, 1946).
KAHN, C. H., 'The Greek verb "to be" and the concept of being',
   Foundations of Language 2 (1966), 245–65.
   The Verb 'Be' in Ancient Greek (Dordrecht, 1973).
   'On early Greek astronomy', *JHS* 90 (1970), 99–116.
KERFERD, G. B., *The Sophistic Movement* (Cambridge, 1981).
KNORR, W. R., *The Evolution of the Euclidean Elements* (Dordrecht and Boston,
   1975).
LONGRIGG, J., 'Philosophy and medicine: some early interactions', *HSCP*
   67 (1963), 147–75.
NEUGEBAUER, O., *The Exact Sciences in Antiquity*, 2nd ed. (Providence R.I.,
   1957).
   A History of Ancient Mathematical Astronomy, 3 vols. (Berlin and New York,
   1975).
ROHDE, E., *Psyche*, English trans. (London, 1925).
SZABO, A., *The Beginnings of Greek Mathematics*, English transl. (Dordrecht,
   1978).
TANNERY, P., *Pour l'histoire de la science Hellène*, 2nd ed. (Paris, 1930).
VAN DER WAERDEN, B. L., *Science Awakening*, English trans. (New York,
   1961).

Collections of articles

FURLEY, D. J. and ALLEN, R. E. (eds.), *Studies in Presocratic Philosphy*, 2 vols.
   (London, 1970, 1975).
MOURELATOS, A. P. D. (ed.), *The Pre-Socratics* (Garden City, N.Y., 1974).

Mythical cosmogony and cosmology

BURKERT, W., 'Orpheus und die Vorsokratiker', *Antike und Abendland* 14
   (1968), 93–114.

'La genèse des choses et des mots. Le papyrus de Derveni entre Anaxagore et Cratyle', *Études philosophiques* 25 (1970), 443–55.

Griechische Religion der archaischen und klassischen Epoche (Stuttgart, 1977).

CORNFORD, F. M., 'Mystery religions and Pre-Socratic philosophy', *Cambridge Ancient History* IV (Cambridge, 1939), ch. 15.

Principium Sapientiae (Cambridge, 1952).

DETIENNE, M. and VERNANT, J. P., *Cunning Intelligence in Greek Culture and Society* (Hassocks, 1978).

FRANKFORT, H., *et al.*, *Before Philosophy* (Harmondsworth, 1949).

GUTHRIE, W. K. C., *The Greeks and their Gods* (London, 1950).

HÖLSCHER, U., *Anfängliches Fragen* (Göttingen, 1968).

KIRK, G. S., *Myth, its Meaning and Functions in Ancient and Other Cultures* (Berkeley and Cambridge, 1970).

The Nature of Greek Myths (Harmondsworth, 1974).

LINFORTH, I. M., *The Arts of Orpheus* (Berkeley, 1941).

NILSSON, M. P., *Geschichte der griechischen Religion* I, 3rd ed. (Munich, 1967). (See Index II, s.v. 'Kosmogonie', 'Kosmogonische Mythen'.)

PRITCHARD, J. B., ed., *Ancient Near Eastern Texts relating to the Old Testament*, 3rd ed. (Princeton, 1969).

SCHWABL, H., 'Weltschöpfung', in Pauly-Wissowa, *Realencyclopädie* suppl. 9 (1962), 1433–1589.

STOKES, M. C., 'Hesiodic and Milesian cosmogonies', *Phronesis* 7 (1963), 1–35, and 8 (1964), 1–34.

VERNANT, J. P., *Myth and Society in Ancient Greece*, English trans. (London, 1980).

WALCOT, P., *Hesiod and the Near East* (Cardiff, 1966).

WEST, M. L., 'Three Presocratic cosmologies', *CQ* N.S. 13 (1963), 154–76. 'Alcman and Pythagoras', *CQ* N.S. 17 (1967), 1–15.

See also the same author's editions of Hesiod's *Theogony* (Oxford, 1966) and *Works and Days* (Oxford, 1978).

Thales

CLASSEN, C. J., 'Thales', in Pauly-Wissowa, *Realencyclopädie* suppl. 10 (1965), 930–47.

DICKS, D. R., 'Thales', *CQ* N.S. 9 (1959), 294–309.

SNELL, B., 'Die Nachrichten über die Lehren des Thales', *Philologus* 96 (1944), 170–82.

Anaximander

BURKERT, W., 'Iranisches bei Anaximandros', *Rh.M.* 106 (1963), 97–134.

CLASSEN, C. J., 'Anaximandros', in Pauly-Wissowa, *Realencyclopädie* suppl. 12 (1970), 30–69.

HÖLSCHER, U., 'Anaximander and the beginnings of Greek philosophy', in

Furley and Allen (English trans. of an article in *Anfängliches Fragen* first published in *Hermes* 81 (1953), 255–77 and 358–417).

KAHN, C. H., *Anaximander and the Origins of Greek Cosmology* (New York, 1960).

KIRK, G. S., 'Some problems in Anaximander', *CQ* N.S. 5 (1955), 21–38 (repr. in Furley and Allen).

VLASTOS, G., 'Equality and justice in early Greek cosmologies', *C.P.* 42 (1957), 156–78 (repr. in Furley and Allen).

Xenophanes

DEICHGRÄBER, K., 'Xenophanes περὶ φύσεως', *Rh.M.* 87 (1938), 1–31.

FRÄNKEL, H., 'Xenophanes' Empiricism and his critique of knowledge', in Mourelatos (English trans. of a German original in the author's collected articles: *Wege und Forme frühgriechischen Denkens*, 2nd ed. (Munich, 1960)).

VON FRITZ, K., 'Xenophanes', in Pauly-Wissowa's *Realencyclopädie* 9A (1967), 1541–62.

HEIDEL, W. A., 'Hecataeus and Xenophanes', *AJP* 64 (1943), 257–77.

LESHER, J. H., 'Xenophanes' scepticism', *Phronesis* 23 (1978), 1–21.

STEINMETZ, P., 'Xenophanesstudien', *Rh.M.* 109 (1966), 13–73.

WIESNER, J., *Ps.-Aristoteles, MXG: der historische Wert des Xenophanesreferats* (Amsterdam, 1976).

Heraclitus

FRÄNKEL, H., 'A thought pattern in Heraclitus', *AJP* 59 (1938), 309–37 (repr. in Mourelatos).

HÖLSCHER, U., 'Paradox, simile, and gnomic utterance in Heraclitus', English trans., in Mourelatos (from the German of *Anfängliches Fragen*).

KAHN, C. H., *The Art and Thought of Heraclitus* (Cambridge, 1979).

KIRK, G. S., 'Heraclitus and death in battle (fr. 24D)', *AJP* 70 (1949), 384–93.

'Natural change in Heraclitus', *Mind* 60 (1951), 35–42 (repr. in Mourelatos).

Heraclitus, the Cosmic Fragments (Cambridge, 1954).

MARCOVICH, M., *Heraclitus* (Merida, 1967).

NUSSBAUM, M. C., 'ψυχή in Heraclitus', *Phronesis* 17 (1972), 1–16 and 153–70.

RAMNOUX, C., *Héraclite, ou l'homme entre les choses et les mots* (Paris, 1959).

REINHARDT, K., 'Heraklits Lehre vom Feuer', *Hermes* 77 (1942), 1–27.

VLASTOS, G., 'On Heraclitus', *AJP* 76 (1955), 337–68 (repr. in Furley and Allen).

WIGGINS, D., 'Heraclitus' conceptions of flux, fire and material persistence', in *Language and Logos*, ed. M. Schofield and M. C. Nussbaum (Cambridge, 1982), 1–32.

Pythagoras and Pythagoreanism

BURKERT, W., *Lore and Science in Ancient Pythagoreanism*, English trans. (Cambridge, Mass., 1972).
'Craft versus sect: the problem of Orphics and Pythagoreans', in *Jewish and Christian Self-definition*, ed. B. E. Meyer and E. P. Sanders, III (London, 1982), 1–22.
CORNFORD, F. M., 'Mysticism and science in the Pythagorean tradition', *CQ* 16 (1922), 137–50 and 17 (1923), 1–12 (repr. in Mourelatos).
DELATTE, A., *Études sur la littérature pythagoricienne* (Paris, 1915).
VON FRITZ, K., *Pythagorean Politics in South Italy* (New York, 1940).
VON FRITZ, K., *et al.*, 'Pythagoras', in Pauly-Wissowa's *Realencyclopädie* 24 (1963), 171–300, with a further contribution (by B. L. van der Waerden) in suppl. 10 (1965), 843–64.
HEIDEL, W. A., 'The Pythagoreans and Greek mathematics', *AJP* 61 (1940), 1–33 (repr. in Furley and Allen).
KAHN, C. H., 'Pythagorean philosophy before Plato', in Mourelatos.
MORRISON, J. S., 'Pythagoras of Samos', *CQ* N.S. 6 (1956), 133–56.
NUSSBAUM, M. C., 'Eleatic conventionalism and Philolaus on the conditions of thought', *HSCP* 83 (1979), 63–108.
PHILIP, J. A., *Pythagoras and early Pythagoreanism* (Toronto, 1966).
RAVEN, J. E., *Pythagoreans and Eleatics* (Cambridge, 1948).
THESLEFF, H., *An Introduction to the Pythagorean Writings of the Hellenistic Period* (Åbo, 1961).
The Pythagorean Texts of the Hellenistic Period (Åbo, 1965).

Parmenides

CORNFORD, F. M., *Plato and Parmenides* (London, 1939), ch. 2.
DIELS, H., *Parmenides Lehrgedicht* (Berlin, 1897).
FRÄNKEL, H., 'Studies in Parmenides', English trans., in Furley and Allen (from the German of *Wege und Formen frühgriechischen Denkens*).
FURLEY, D. J., 'Notes on Parmenides', in *Exegesis and Argument*, ed. E. N. Lee, A. P. D. Mourelatos and R. Rorty (Assen, 1973), 1–15.
GALLOP, D., '"Is" or "Is not"?', *The Monist* 62 (1979), 61–80.
HÖLSCHER, U., *Parmenides: vom Wesen des Seiendes* (Frankfurt am Main, 1969).
KAHN, C. H., 'The thesis of Parmenides', *Review of Metaphysics* 22 (1969–70), 700–24.
LONG, A. A., 'The principles of Parmenides' cosmogony', *Phronesis* 8 (1963), 90–107 (repr. in Furley and Allen).
MACKENZIE, M. M., 'Parmenides' dilemma', *Phronesis* 27 (1982), 1–12.
MANSFELD, J., *Die Offenbarung des Parmenides* (Assen, 1964).
MOURELATOS, A. P. D., *The Route of Parmenides* (New Haven, 1970).
OWEN, G. E. L., 'Eleatic questions', *CQ* N.S. 10 (1960), 84–102 (repr. in Furley and Allen).

'Plato and Parmenides on the timeless present', *The Monist* 50 (1966), 317–40 (repr. in Mourelatos).

VLASTOS, G., 'Parmenides' theory of knowledge', *Transactions of the American Philological Association* 77 (1946), 66–77.

Zeno

FRÄNKEL, H., 'Zeno of Elea's attacks on plurality', *AJP* 63 (1942), 1–25 and 193–206 (repr. in Furley and Allen).

GRÜNBAUM, A., *Modern Science and Zeno's Paradoxes* (London, 1968).

LEAR, J. D., 'A note on Zeno's Arrow', *Phronesis* 26 (1981), 91–104.

LEE, H. D. P., *Zeno of Elea* (Cambridge, 1936).

OWEN, G. E. L., 'Zeno and the mathematicians', *Proceedings of the Aristotelian Society* 58 (1957–8), 199–222 (repr. in Furley and Allen and in Salmon, listed below.)

ROSS, W. D., *Aristotle's Physics* (Oxford, 1936), 71–85 and 655–66.

SALMON, W. C., ed., *Zeno's Paradoxes* (Indianapolis, 1970).

VLASTOS, G., 'Zeno of Elea', in *The Encyclopedia of Philosophy*, ed. P. Edwards (New York, 1967).

The same author has composed many detailed studies of Zenonian arguments, the most important of which are reprinted in Furley and Allen.

Empedocles

BIGNONE, E., *Empedocle* (Turin, 1916).

BOLLACK, J., *Empédocle*, 4 vols. (Paris, 1965–9). (See also C. H. Kahn's review, in *Gnomon* 41 (1969), 439–47.)

KAHN, C. H., 'Religion and natural philosophy in Empedocles' doctrine of the soul', *AGP* 42 (1960), 3–35 (repr. in Mourelatos).

LONG, A. A., 'Thinking and sense-perception in Empedocles', *CQ* n.s. 16 (1966), 256–76.

MILLERD, C., *On the Interpretation of Empedocles* (Chicago, 1908).

O'BRIEN, D., 'Empedocles' cosmic cycle', *CQ* n.s. 17 (1967), 29–40. *Empedocles' Cosmic Cycle* (Cambridge, 1969).

SOLMSEN, F., 'Love and strife in Empedocles' cosmology', *Phronesis* 10 (1965), 123–45 (repr. in Furley and Allen). 'Eternal and temporary beings in Empedocles' physical poem', *AGP* 57 (1975), 123–45.

WRIGHT, M. R., *Empedocles: the Extant Fragments* (New Haven, 1981).

ZUNTZ, G., *Persephone* (Oxford, 1971), 181–274 (re-edits the *Katharmoi*).

Anaxagoras

CORNFORD, F. M., 'Anaxagoras' Theory of Matter', *CQ* 24 (1930), 14–30 and 83–95 (repr. in Furley and Allen).

FURLEY, D. J., 'Anaxagoras in response to Parmenides', in *New Essays on Plato and the Presocratics*, ed. R. A. Shiner and J. King-Farlow (Guelph, 1976).

KERFERD, G. B., 'Anaxagoras and the concept of matter before Aristotle', *Bulletin of the John Rylands Library* 52 (1969), 129–43 (repr. in Mourelatos).

LANZA, D., *Anassagora – testimonianze e frammenti* (Florence, 1966).

SCHOFIELD, M., *An Essay on Anaxagoras* (Cambridge, 1980).

SIDER, D., *The Fragments of Anaxagoras* (Meisenheim an Glan, 1981).

STRANG, C., 'The physical theory of Anaxagoras', *AGP* 45 (1963), 101–18 (repr. in Furley and Allen).

VLASTOS, G., 'The physical theory of Anaxagoras', *Philosophical Review* 59 (1950), 31–57 (repr. in Furley and Allen and in Mourelatos).

Melissus

REALE, G., *Melisso – testimonianze e frammenti* (Florence, 1970).

Leucippus and Democritus

ALFIERI, V., *Atomos Idea* (Florence, 1953).

BAILEY, C., *The Greek Atomists and Epicurus* (Oxford, 1928).

COLE, A. T., *Democritus and the Sources of Greek Anthropology* (Cleveland, 1967).

FURLEY, D. J., *Two Studies in the Greek Atomists* (Princeton, 1967).
'The Greek theory of the infinite universe', *Journal of the History of Ideas* 42 (1981), 571–85.

LANGERBECK, H., Δόξις ἐπιρρυσμίη (Berlin, 1935).

LURIA, S., *Democritea* (Leningrad, 1970). (The most complete edition of Democritean fragments and testimonia.)

O'BRIEN, D., 'Heavy and light in Democritus and Aristotle', *JHS* 97 (1977), 64–74.

ROMANO, F., ed., *Democrite e l'atomismo antico* (Catania, 1980).

SEDLEY, D. N., 'Two conceptions of vacuum', *Phronesis* 27 (1982), 175–93.

TAYLOR, C. C. W., 'Pleasure, knowledge, and sensation in Democritus', *Phronesis* 12 (1967), 6–27.

VLASTOS, G., 'Ethics and physics in Democritus', *Philosophical Review* 54 (1945), 578–92 and 55 (1946), 53–64 (repr. in Furley and Allen).

Diogenes of Apollonia

LAKS, A., *Diogène d'Apollonie* (Lille, 1983).

INDEX OF PASSAGES

A page number in bold type indicates that the passage in question is quoted in full, with translation, on that page. Other, ordinary-type, page-references to such a passage will normally be to citations of the *passage*-number, which should be found by turning to the bold-type page-reference first.

E.g. Aetius 1, 3, 20 is quoted on p. 286, where its passage-number is seen to be **346** and the reference on p. 439 is simply to this passage-number, **346**.

Usually, only the first line is specified in the references to passages quoted.

ACHILLES
Isag. in Arati Phaen.
  (3) 60n.
  (4 p. 33 Maass) **29**
  (4 p. 34 Maass) **175**, 176
AELIAN
Nat. anim.
  (XII, 7) **316–17**
  (XVI, 29) **303–4**, 305
V.H.
  (II, 26) **228**, 229, 233 n.
    I, 330 n. I
  (II, 31) 434n.
  (III, 17) 105
  (IV, 17) 228 n. I, **235–6**,
    238
AESCHINES
(I, 97) 357 n. 2
AESCHYLUS
Ag.
  (1382) 110 n. I
Eum.
  (657–66) 354
Pr.
  (351ff.) 60
Suppl.
  (96–103) **171 n. 4**
  (559–60) 354
fr.
  (44, 1–5) **39**, 382 n. I
AETIUS
I
  (3, 1) **79**
  (3, 4) 115n., 146, **158–9**,
    162n.

(3, 5) **374–5**, 376, **378n.**
(3, 6) **389 n. I**
(3, 18) **421**, 422
(3, 20) **286**, 439
(7, 11) **97 nn. I and 2**
(7, 12) 124, 151n.
(7, 13) **150**, 151
(12, 5) 422
(12, 6) 415, **421**, 422
(18, 2) 359n., **398 n. 2**
  (23, 3) **123–4**
(25, 4) 405, **420 n. I**
(26, 2) **419 n. I**
II
(1, 2) 380
(1, 3) 124, 151 n. I, 446
(4, 6) 379
(6, 3) 290, 297, **299**,
  300–1
(7, 1) 257, **258–9**, 344 n.
  2
(7, 2) **417–18 and n.**
(7, 7) 259, 331, **342–3**
(8, 1) 446
(13, 5 and 9) 156, **445**
(13, 10) **154**, 155, 156
(14, 3–4) **154**, 155, 156
(16, 5) **135**, 136, 138, 259
(18, 1) 174
(20, 1) **135**, 136, 259
(20, 3) **172–3**
(20, 10) 446
(20, 12) **344 n. I**
(20, 13) 300, 301, 344 n.I
(21, 1) **135**, 259
(22, 1) **154**, 155

(23, 1) **154**, 155
(24, 1) 82
(24, 4) 175 n. I
(24, 9) **173**, 174
(29, 4) 344 n. I
(29, 7) 344 n. I
III
(3, 1–2) **137–8 and n.**, 158
(3, 2) 138, **157–8**
(10, 2) 133 n. I
(10, 3) 153
(10, 4) 419
(12, 1–2) 420 n. 4
(15, 8) 153
(16, 1) 139
IV
(1, 1) **79–80**
(2, 2) **347**, 348
(3, 12) 206
(8, 10) **428**, 429
(19, 3) **429n.**
V
(18, 1) **305**, 306
(19, 4) 133 n. I, 138,
  140–1, 142
(19, 5) **302–3**, 305 *and n.*
(24, 3) **444n.**
(26, 4) 301
(30, 1) **260**, 339
AGATHEMERUS
I
  (1) **104**
ALCIDAMAS
ap. Arist. *Rhet.*
  B23, 1398b15, **355 n. 3**

ALCMAEON

fr.

(1) 179, 328, **339 n. 1**

(2) **347**

ALCMAN

fr.

(1 (Page), 13) 48

(1, 13f.) 49

(3, col. ii, 7–20) **47–8**, 49

(3, col. ii, 24f.) 48

**ALEXANDER OF
APHRODISIAS**

in Met.

(36, 21) **423–4**

(38, 16) 331

(39, 8) 336

(40, 12) 326 n. 1

(41, 1) 330 n. 1

in Meteor.

(67, 11) 133, 137, **139**,
140

Quaest.

(II, 23) 310, **447n.**

de sensu

(56, 12) **428**, 429

AMMONIUS

de interpretatione

(249, 6 Busse) 159n.,
283n., **312**

ANAXAGORAS

fr.

(1) 111n., **357–8**, 359,
361, 368, 372, 373

(2) 111n., 115n., **371–2**,
373, 374

(3) **360**, 361, 362

(4) **357–8**, 359, 366, 367,
368–9, 370, 377,
378–9, 380, 420 n. 6

(5) **360**, 361, 362

(6) 362, **365–6**, 367

(8) **371**

(9) 132 n. 2, **363–4**, 374

(10) **368–9**, 370, 375

(11) 362, **365–6**, 367, 383

(12) **362–4**, 366, 367,
371, 383, 388, 418,
441, 444, 449

(13) **363–4**, 365

(14) **363–4**

(15) **372**, 373, 374, 388,
422

(16) **372**, 374, 382

(17) **358**, 439

(18) 156 n. 1, **380–1**

(19) **380–1**

(21) **383**, 384

(21a) **383**, 384

(22) **382**

ANAXIMANDER

fr.

(1) 57 n. 1, 114, **117–18**,
130, 139, 144, 194,
244, 290

ANAXIMENES

fr.

(2) 115n., 146, **158–9**,
162n.

ANONYMUS LONDINENSIS

XI

(22) 91 n. 1

XVIII

(8) 323 n. 1, 324, **341 n. 1**

**APOLLODORUS
MYTHOGRAPHUS**

Bibl. III

(4, 2) 62 n. 3

**APOLLONIUS
PARADOXOGRAPHUS**

Hist. Mir.

(6) **228–9**, 330 n. 1

APOLLONIUS RHODIUS

I

(496) **42**, 43, 66, 68 n. 1

(503) **66**, 67, 69, 70

Σ on IV

(269) **446n.**

ARATUS

Phaen.

(39) 82

Σ on *Phaen.*

(39) 84

(172) 88

ARCHELAUS

ap. Plut. *de prim. frig.*

(21, 954F) 387n.

ARISTOCRITUS

Theosophia

(68) 182, **209**

ARISTOPHANES

Birds

(693) **26–7**, 37

(697) 28 n. 2

(1218) 37

(1737ff.) 63 n. 4

Clouds

(227) 404, 434, **450n.**

(424) 37

(627) 37

Frogs

(1030–2) 221

(1032) 222

Peace

(832f.) 199n.

Σ on *Clouds*

(247) 67

ARISTOTLE

A. po.

B11 (94b32–4) **236**, 238

de an.

A2 (404a5) 427n., 429;
(404a16) **346**, 347;
(405a11) **427n.**, 429;
(405a19) 87, 89, **95**,
161, 447n.; (405a21)
161n.; (405a24)
204n.; (405a29) **347**,
348; (405b1) **91 n. 1**

A4 (407b27) **346**;
(409a4) 342n.

A5 (411a7) 89, **95**, 96

Γ3 (427a21) **311**;
(427a21–b6) 413n.

de caelo

A3 (270b24) **372 n. 3**

A9 (278b9) 117

A10 (279b12) 151n.;
(279b14) 200n.

B1 (284a11) **199n.**

B9 (290b12) 233, **344–5**

B13 (293a18) 259, 330 n.
1, **342–3**; (293a20)
330; (294a21) 175;
(294a28) 87, **88–9**,
175; (294b13) 145,
153, 157, 175; (295a7)
126–7, 128, 152–3n.,
373 n. 1, 422;
(295a29) **298**, 299;
(295b10) 64, 128,
133–4, 137

Γ1 (298b14) 391

Γ2 (300b8) **423**, 424;
(300b25ff.) 302;
(300b30) 290, **295**,
297; (301a14) **297–8**

Γ3 (302a28) 372 n. 3, **373
n. 2**, 376, 377

Γ4 (303a5) 409 n. 3,
423–4, 425 *and* n.;
(303a12) **427n.**

Γ5 (303b10) 109, 112,
113 n. 1, **115**, 116,
125

Δ2 (309a19) 395n.

ARISTOTLE (cont.)
On Democritus
ap. Simpl. *de caelo* (295,
  1) 408, **413–14**, 415,
  422; (295, 9) **423**;
  (295, 11) **425–6**, 427
Eth. Eud.
  B8 (1225a30) 330
  H1 (1235a25) **194n.**, 208
    n. 1
Eth. Nic.
  B5 (1106b29) **339 n. 2**
  H8 (1150b25) 183
de gen. animal.
  A23 (731a4) **306**
  B3 (736b33ff.) 58;
    (742b17) 424
  Γ11 (762a21) 96 n. 1
  Δ1 (763b30–3) 355
de gen. et corr.
  A1 (315b6) 413n., **416 n.
    2**
  A2 (316a33–317a2) 409
    n. 3
  A8 (324b26–35) 310;
    (325a2) 310, 362, 392,
    403, 404, **406–8**, 409 n.
    4, 414; (325a13) 326
    n. 1, **394–5n.**, 395, 409
    n. 4; (325b1) 409 n. 2;
    (326a9) **421**, 422
  B1 (328b35) 113 n. 1
  B5 (332a19) **111**, 112,
    113 n. 1, 435n.
  B6 (333b30) **307**;
    (334a1) **300–1**
  B7 (334a5) **299**
Hist. animal.
  Γ2 (511b31) 436, **450–1**
  Z10 (565b1) 141n.
Met.
  A3 (983b6) 76, 87, **88–9**,
    90, 91 *and* n. 1, 93,
    118; (983b27) **15**, 96;
    (984a5) **144–5**;
    (984a7) 344 n. 2;
    (984a11) **280–1**, **352–3**,
    354 *and* n.
  A4 (985a18) 374n.;
    (985a25) **297n.**, 308;
    (985a31–3) **286**;
    (985b4) 398, 408,
    413–14, 415, 422
  A5 (985b23) 324, **328–30**,
    331, 333, 335, 336,
    337, 339, 340, 344,

  346, 350; (985b25–7)
    392 n. 2; (986a22)
    328, 331, **337–9** *and* n.;
    (986b18) **165**, 166,
    171; (986b21) 167n.,
    171; (987a9ff.) 331
  A6 (987a31) 330;
    (987a32) 186, 195
  A7 (988a30) 113 n. 1;
    (989a14) 113 n. 1
  B4 (1000b6) **310–11**,
    384; (1000b12) 290,
    295, 297
  Γ5 (1009b7) **409–10**, 411,
    414; (1009b12) 413n.;
    (1010a13) 196
  Z2 (1028b16) 341 n. 2
  Z13 (1039a9) 409 n. 2
  Λ1 (1069b20) **130 n. 1**
  Λ6 (1071b27) 15, **17–18**,
    20, 32; (1072a8) 17
  M4 (1078b19) 330
  M6 (1080b16) **332**, 333,
    341 *and* n.
  M8 (1083b8) **332–3**
  N3 (1090b5) 341 n. 2;
    (1091a12) 331, **339–40**,
    341 *and* n. 2
  N4 (1091b4) 15, **17–18**,
    20, 32; (1091b8) **50**,
    59 n. 1, 71
  N5 (1092b8) **333**, 335
Meteor.
  A6 (342b30) 330
  A14 (352a17) 139
  B1 (353b5) 155; (353b6)
    133, 137, **138–9**, 140,
    446; (353b11) **300–1**;
    (354a28) **154**, 157
  B2 (355a13) **201**;
    (355a21) 155, **446n.**;
    (355a22) 139n.
  B3 (356b10) 139;
    (357a24) **300–1**
  B7 (365b6) 145, **157–8**
  B9 (369b14) 372 n. 3
  Δ9 (387b4) **306**
de part. animal.
  A1 (640a18) **306–7**
  Δ10 (687a7) **383 n. 2**
Phys.
  A2 (184b25ff.) 395
  A3 (186a4ff.) 395;
    (186a6) 391;
    (186a8–10) 392 n. 2;
    (186a10) 326 n. 1,

  394; (187a1) 362,
    407–8, 414
  A4 (187a12) 94n., **111**,
    112, 113 n. 1, 129;
    (187a20) 119, **128–9**,
    130 n. 1, 132;
    (187a23) **368–9**, 370,
    376, 377, 400n.;
    (187a23ff.) 380n.
  A6 (189b1) 113 n. 1
  B4 (196a19–24) 307;
    (196a24) **419–20n.**
  B8 (198b29) **304**
  Γ4 (203a10) 326, 334,
    335, **336**, 337, 339;
    (203a16) **109** *and* n.,
    112, 113 n. 1; (203b7)
    109, 110, 112, **115**,
    116, 117, 125, 127,
    146, 150, 159, 160,
    444; (203b15) **113**,
    114, 116; (203b23)
    123, 124, **415 n. 2**
  Γ5 (204b22) 112, **113**,
    114; (204b33) 118
  Γ8 (208a8) **114**
  Δ1 (208b29) 36;
    (209a23ff.) 265
  Δ3 (210b22ff.) 265
  Δ6 (213a22) 341, **359n.**,
    398 n. 2, 409 n. 2;
    (213b22) 331, 337,
    340, 341
  Δ9 (216b22) **398 n. 1**
  Z2 (233a21) 264, 265,
    270
  Z9 (239b5–9) 264, 265,
    272–3; (239b9) 264,
    269; (239b11) 264,
    265, **269–70**, 272;
    (239b14) 264, 265,
    272; (239b24–5) 272;
    (239b30–3) 264, 265,
    272–3; (239b33) 264,
    265, **274–5** *and* n., 276
  H5 (250a19ff.) 264
  Θ1 (250b11) 98, 123,
    126–7; (250b18ff.)
    380n.; (252a9) 295;
    (252a32) 424
  Θ3 (253b9) **195**
  Θ8 (263a15–18) 264, 265,
    271; (263b3–9) 264,
    265, **271**
Poet.
  1 (1447b17) **283–4n.**

ARISTOTLE (*cont.*)
Pol.
A11 (1259a9) **80–1**, 84
Θ5 (1340b18) 346
de respir.
2 (471a2) 450n.
7 (473b9) 146, 308 n. 1,
359–60n.
Rhet.
A13 (1373b6) **319**, 320
B23 (1398b15) **355 n. 3**
de sensu
2 (437b9–14) 310n.;
(438a4–5) 310n.
4 (442a29) **428**, 429
5 (444a22) 208 n. 3
7 310
9 310
12 310
Soph. elen.
5 (167b13) 394
6 (168b35) 394
28 (181a27) 394
Top.
Θ8 (160b7) 264, 265,
269–70, 272
fr.
(191 Rose) **228–9**, 233 n.
1, 330 n. 1
(192) 238
(194) 231
(195) **230–1**, 233, 236
(196) 232 n. 1, **235–6**,
238, 346
(197) **231–2**, 233, 236
(201) 331, 337, **340**, 341
(203) 326 n. 1, 331, 336

[ARISTOTLE]
de mundo
5 (396b20) **190**, 193
M.X.G.
1 (974a1ff.) 392;
(974a2–3) **392 n. 1**;
(974a12–14) **395**;
(975a11) 35 n. 1
2 (975b1) **291–2**, 294;
(979a11f.) 326 n. 1
Problemata
XVI (8, 914b9) 359n.
XVII (3, 916a33) **347**
XXXIV (7, 964a10) 148
ARISTOXENUS
fr.
(11A Wehrli) **222–3**, 224
(14) **222–3**, 224
(15) **233 n. 1**

(16) **222–3**, 224
(18) **222–3**, **224–5**, 323 n.
1, 335
(31) 228
(90) 234
ARIUS DIDYMUS
ap. Euseb. *P.E.*
XV (20) **194–5** *and* n. 1,
196–7
ATHENAEUS
II
(57D) **382**
ATHENAGORAS
pro Christianis
18 (p. 20 Schwartz) 25, 28
AUGUSTINE, S.
de civ. dei
VIII (2) **124–5**, **150**
BACCHYLIDES
fr.
(5, 27 Snell) 37
BOETHIUS
de mus.
III (11) 335
CALLIMACHUS
Iambus
1 (52) (fr. 191 Pfeiffer)
77, **84**, 88
CELSUS
Proem.
2 (11) 282
ap. Origen *c. Celsum*
VI (42) 57, 64n., 65 n. 1,
66–7, 68 n. 1, 69
CENSORINUS
de die nat.
(4, 7) **140–1**
CHALCIDIUS
in Tim.
(122) 35 n. 1
(251) 207n.
CICERO
Academica priora
II (37, 118) 147, **402–3**,
404
de divinatione
I (49, 111) 80; (50, 112)
105n.
de fin.
II (5, 15) 183
ND
I (10, 25) 97 n. 1, 125n.,
151n.; (10, 26) **150**,
151n.

Tusc.
I (16, 38) 50n.
CLEANTHES
Hymn to Zeus
(34f.) 202 n. 1
CLEMENT OF
ALEXANDRIA
Protrepticus
(22) **209**
(34) **209**
Stromateis
I (64, 2) **163–4**, 165;
(131) **220–1**
II (17, 4) **193 n. 1**, 244;
(130) 323 n. 2
III (14, 2) **315–16**
IV (13, 1) **315–16**; (49, 3)
207; (141, 2) **205**,
206; (150, 1) 282,
316–17
V (15, 5) **262**; (48, 3)
300–1; (59, 5) **211n.**;
(81, 2) **312**, 321; (104,
1) 56, 159 n. 1, 170,
197–8 *and* n., 200n.,
290, 441; (104, 3) 146,
192n., **197–8**, 199, 201,
204, 208, 290, 441;
(109, 1) **169**, 170, 171,
179, 241, 397; (109, 2)
166, **168–9** *and* n. 1,
397; (109, 3) **168–9**
and n. 1, 397; (115, 1)
202, 203; (122, 3)
316–17; (138) **257–8**,
259
VI (9, 4) 61n.; (17, 2)
182, **203**, 204 *and* n.,
206, 207; (23) **246 n.
2**; (30) 282, **313**; (53,
5) 62, **63**, 65 n. 2
VII (22, 1) **168**, 169 n. 1,
397
CLEOSTRATUS
fr.
(4 Diels) 88
DAMASCIUS
de principiis
(123) **23–4**, 28
(123 *bis*) **24**, 25 n. 1, 27,
28
(124) 15, **18**, 19 *and* n. 2,
20 n. 4, 22, **27**
(124 *bis*) 51, 52n., **56**, 58,
60, 69, 70

DEMOCRITUS
fr.
(3) **429–30**, 431
(6) **410**, 411, 412, 413, 414
(7) **410**, 411, 412, 413, 414
(8) **410**, 411, 412, 413, 414
(9) **410**, **411–12**, 413, 414
(10) **410**, 411, 412, 413, 414
(11) **412**, 413, 414
(25) 294n.
(33) 432
(117) 411
(125) **411–12**
(156) 411 n. 2
(164) **420 n. 2**, 426
(167) 132, **420 n. 3**
(171) 433n.
(172) 432
(181) 432, 433
(191) **430–1**, 432, 433
(235) 432
(245) 433
(246) 433n.
(248) 432
(249) 432
(252) 432
(255) 432
(262) 433
(264) 433
(277) 432
(283) 432
(284) 432
(285) 432
(297) 433

DEMOSTHENES
(IV, 28) 357 n. 2

DERCYLLIDES
ap. Theon. Smyrn.
(p. 198, 14 Hiller) **81–2**, 83, 87, 88, 104n., 156

DICAEARCHUS
fr.
(33 Wehrli) **226–7**

DIODORUS SICULUS
I
(7, 1) **42**, 43
(7–8) 405n.
X (3, 4) 52

DIOGENES OF APOLLONIA
fr.
(1) **434–5**, 436, 438

(2) **438** *and* n. 1, 440 *and* n. 1
(3) 437, 439 n. 1, **440**, 443
(4) 162n., 440, **441–2**, 443
(5) 116n., 439 n. 1, 440, **442–3**, 444
(6) 436, **450–1**
(7) **442–3**, 444
(8) **442–3**, 444

DIOGENES LAERTIUS
I
(16) 241, **356**, 391
(22) 76n., **76–7**
(23) **81–2**, 83, 84 *and* n., **86–7**, 88
(24) 83, 86n., 89, **95**, 97 n. 2, 447n.
(26) 80
(27) 79, **84–5**
(34) 87
(37–8) 76n.
(42) 50n.
(116) **51**
(118) 50n., 52, 265
(119) **51**, 52, **54**, **56**, 61, 83
(120) **53**, **217–18**, 220
(121) 50n.
II
(1–2) 83, **100**, 101, 102 *and* n. 1, 103, 104, 105n.
(3) **143** *and* n., 144, 159
(7) **352–3**, 354
(8) **373 n. 1**, 433
(9) 382
(10) 354, **382n.**
(16) **385**, **389 n. 2**
(17) **388 n. 3**
(23) **386n.**
V
(42) 388 n. 1
VIII
(1) **222–3**, 224
(6) 182n., 188 n. 1, 216, **217**, 218, 324
(8) 222n. 1, **233 n. 1**
(12) **334**, 335
(15) 238
(19) 231
(34–5) **230–1**, 233, 236
(36) 164, 180, **219**, 220, 320
(46) 224, **322–3** *and* n. 1,

330 n. 1, 333, 346n., 349
(48) 159n.
(51) **280–1**
(52) 313
(57) **278**, 282, 313
(58) **280–1**, 282
(59) 282, **285–6**
(60) **284**
(60–1) 282
(62) 282, **313**
(63) 281, 282
(66) 282
(67–9) 284
(67–72) 281
(71) 284
(74) **280–1**
(77) **282**, 283, **319**, 320
(79) 223
(83) 179, 328, **339 n. 1**
(84) **323–4**
(85) 234, **324–5**, 326, 328, 330, 331 *and* n., 337
IX
(1) 13, 116n., 164, 168, **181**, 182n., 188 n. 1, **202**, 203, 211, **216–17**, 218
(2) **210–11**, 212
(5) 182n., **183–4**
(6) 183, **183n.**, 211n.
(7) 192n., **203**, 204, 211
(8) 192n.
(9–10) **200–1**
(11) 201
(16) 207
(18) **163**, 164, 166
(19) 169 n. 1
(20) 166
(21–3) **239–40**
(24) 391
(29) 263
(30) 394, 409 n. 4
(31) **416–18**, 419, 426
(33) **420 n. 4**
(34) 323, **402–3**, 404
(34ff.) 404
(35) **406n.**
(38) **322–3**
(45) **405**, **419n.**
(49) 406n.
(57) **434–5**, 436, 438, **439–40n.**, 446
(72) 264, 265, **273**
X
(13) **402–3**
(61) 423

DIONYSIUS
  ALEXANDRINUS
ap. Euseb. *P.E.*
  XIV (23, 3) **416 n. 2**

*DK references not further
  specified*
4B1–5 (Athenaeus *et alii*)
  88
6B4 (Censorinus) 88
7A1*a* (Eusebius) 5on.
7A2 (Suda) 5on., 6on.
7A10 (Sextus) 6on.
7B1*a* (Achilles) 47
7B7 (Porphyrius) 6on.
7B9 (Herodian) 57, 6on.
7B12 (Diog. L.) 57
11A5 (Eusebius) 76n.
13A2 (Suda) 143
13A7 (Hippolytus) 144n.
14, 7 (Apollonius) 52
14, 9 (Porphyrius *et alii*)
  231
21A20–3 (Strabo *et alii*) 166
21B21 (Σ *in* Aristophanem)
  164
22A1 (Diog. L.) 201
22A5 (Aristotle *et alii*) 147n.
22A13 (Aetius, Censorinus)
  200n.
28A42 (Anonym. Byzant.)
  156n.
29A1, 2, 6, 7, 8, 9, (Diog. L.
  et alii) 263
31A33 (Aetius *et alii*) 286
31A89 (Alexander, Psellus)
  447n.
58E (Theocritus *et alii*) 231
59A20*a–c*, 30, 33, 48, 112
  (Σ *in* Pindarum *et alii*)
  355 n. 2
64A3 (Stephanus Byz.)
  434n.
64A17 (Alexander) 446
64A25–8 (Aristoph. Byz. *et
  alii*) 452n.
64A31 (Aristotle) 440, 441n.
64B2 (Simplicius) 438, 439
  n. 1
64B7 (Simplicius) 443n.
64B9 (Galen) 435
67A24 (Aetius) 418
68A33 (Diog. L.) 431
68B156 (Plutarch) 414
82A6–7 ([Plutarch] *et alii*)
  281

EMPEDOCLES
fr.
  (1) **284**
  (2) **284–5**
  (3, 9) **284–5**, 311
  (6) **286**, 439
  (8) **291**, 292
  (9) **291**, 292
  (11) **291–2**, 294
  (12) **291–2**, 294
  (13) 359n., **398 n. 2**, 409
    n. 2
  (15) **292**
  (17, 1–13) 234, **287**, 290,
    292, 294
  (17, 14) 234, **289–90**,
    292, 294, 300, 308, 364
  (21) 286, **292–3**, 294, 317
  (22) 234, 289n., **307–8**,
    310
  (23) **293–4**, 317
  (26) 288
  (27) 289n., **295**, 297, **299**
  (29) 289n., **294–5**
  (30) 290, **295**, 297
  (31) 289n., **295**, 297
  (35) 289, **296–7**, 298
  (38) **300–1**
  (53) **300–1**
  (54) **300–1**
  (57) **303**, 305
  (59) **303–4**, 305
  (60) **303–4**, 305
  (61) **303–4**, 305
  (62) 301, **304**, 308
  (79) **306**
  (82) **306**
  (83) **306**
  (84) **308–9**, 310n.
  (91) 310
  (92) 310
  (96) 234, **302**, 439
  (98) 234, **302**, 311, 321,
    439
  (100) 146, 308 n. 1,
    359–6on.
  (105) **311**, 321
  (106) **311**
  (107) **310–11**
  (109) **310–11**, 384
  (110) **312–13**
  (111) 282, **285–6**
  (112) 282, **313**
  (115) 220, **314–15**, 320
  (117) **319**, 320
  (118) **315–16**

  (119) **315–16**
  (120) **315–16**
  (121) **315–16**
  (122) 316
  (124) **315–16**
  (126) 316
  (127) **316–17**, 320
  (128) **318**, 320
  (129) **218–19**
  (130) **318**
  (133) **312**, 321
  (134) 159n., 283n., **312**
  (135) **319**, 320
  (136) **319**, 320
  (137) **319**, 320
  (139) **319**, 320
  (146) 282, **316–17**
  (147) **316–17**
  (152 Wright) 283 n. 1

EPICHARMUS
fr.
  (1 Diels) 56

EPICTETUS
Σ Bodl. *ad* Epictetum
    (p. lxxxiii Schenkl)
    194, **207**

EPICURUS
Ep.
  (I, 43) 425
  (II, 88) 418n.

ETYMOLOGICUM MAGNUM
(772.50) 58n.

EUCLID
Σ Eucl.
  (273, 3 *and* 13) 335
  (417, 12ff.) 335

EUDEMUS
ap. Simplic. *in Phys.*
  (97, 12) **278 n. 2**, 401 n.
    2
  (327, 26) 374n.
  (732, 30) 238

EURIPIDES
Helen
  (1014ff.) 199n.
Hipp.
  (952) 222
  (953–4) 221
Phoen.
  (1605) 40
fr.
  (282 Nauck²) 168
  (448) 37
  (484) **42**, 43

EURIPIDES (*cont.*)
(839, 9ff.) 199n.
(910) 117n.
(941) 199n.

EUSEBIUS
Praeparatio Evangelica
I (8, 10) 156 n. 1, 234,
    299, **300–1**, 344 n. 1;
    (10) 41n.; (10, 36) 25
    n. 1; (10, 50) 53, **68**
XIV (23, 3) **416 n. 2**
XV (20) **194–5** *and* n. 1,
    196–7

GALEN
de elem. sec. Hippocr.
I (2) 415 n. 1
in Epid.
VI (48) **260**
de medic. empir.
XIII (4 Walzer) 436
XXII (3) 436
    (p. 113 Walzer) **411–12**
Meth. med.
I (1) 282
Plac. Hipp. et Plat.
    (495 M) 216

[GALEN]
de humor.
XIX (495 Kühn) 436

GORGIAS
ap [Arist] *M X G*
    (979a11f.) 326 n. 1

GREGORIUS NAZ.
Σ *in* Gregor. Naz.
    (XXXVI 911 Migne)
    368–9, 370, 375

HARPOCRATION
s.v.
    Ἴων 398 n. 1

HERACLITUS
fr.
  (1) 182, 184, **186–7**, 188
    n. 1, 203, 205, 206,
    211, 212, 285
  (2) 185, **187**, 188 n. 1,
    198n., 206, 212
  (3) 174
  (5) 182, **209**
  (6) **201**
  (9) 189
  (10) **190**, 193
  (12) **194–5** *and* n. 1,
    196–7
  (13) 189

  (14) **209**
  (15) **209**
  (17) 188 n. 1
  (18) **193 n. 1**, 244
  (19) 188 n. 1
  (21) 205
  (22) 193 n. 1
  (23) 189
  (24) 207
  (25) **207**
  (26) **205**, 206
  (28) 188 n. 1
  (29) **211n.**
  (30) 56, 159 n. 1, 170,
    197–8 *and* n., 200n.,
    290, 441
  (31) 146, 192n., **197–8**,
    199, 201, 204, 208,
    290, 441
  (32) **202**, 203
  (34) 188 n. 1
  (35) 218
  (36) 182, **203**, 204 *and* n.,
    206, 207
  (40) 164, 168, **181**, 182n.,
    188 n. 1, **216-17**,
    218
  (41) 13, 116n., **202**, 203,
    211
  (43) **210–11**, 212
  (44) **210–11**, 212
  (45) **203**, 204, 211
  (48) 190
  (49) 211n.
  (50) **187**, 188 *and* n. 1,
    203, 211, 212
  (51) **192**, 210, 234
  (53) **193**, 194
  (54) **192**, 210, 234
  (55) **188 n. 2**, 195 n. 1,
    285
  (56) 182
  (57) 189, 441
  (58) 182, 189
  (59) 189 *and* n.
  (60) **188**, 189
  (61) **188**, 189
  (62) 194, **208 n. 1**, 210
  (63) **207**, 209
  (64) **197–8**, 202, 203,
    441, 444
  (67) **190**, 191, 209, 441
  (67a) 160, 205 n. 2
  (72) 188 n. 1
  (75) 205
  (76) 204n.

  (78) 179, 184, **191n.**, 244,
    328
  (80) 118, 119, **193**, 194,
    290
  (82) 191n.
  (83) 191n.
  (85) **208 n. 2**
  (86) 193 n. 1
  (88) **188–9**, 210, 441
  (90) **197–8**, 200n., 290,
    441
  (91) **194–5** *and* n. 1, 196–7
  (92) **210 n. 2**
  (93) 193 n. 1, **209**, 210,
    233
  (94) **201**, 202
  (96) 182
  (98) 208 n. 3
  (99) 190, 202 n. 1
  (101) **210–11**
  (101a) **285n.**
  (102) 184, **191n.**, 203, 244
  (103) 190, **244n.**
  (107) **188 n. 2**, 195 n. 1,
    285
  (111) **188**, 189
  (114) 188 n. 2, 210 n. 2,
    210–11, 212
  (117) **203**, 204
  (118) **203**, 204, 212
  (119) **210–11**
  (121) 211n.
  (122) 206n., 211n.
  (123) **192**, 210, 234
  (126) 120, 189, 190
  (129) 182n., 188 n. 1,
    217, 218
  (136) 194, **207**

HERACLITUS HOMERICUS
Quaest. Hom.
  (22) **92 n. 2**

HERODIAN
π. μον. λέξ.
  (30, 30) **177**, 178
  (41, 5) **179**, 180, 241

HERODOTUS
I
  (29) **83 n. 1**
  (74) 76, 78, **81–2**, 83 n. 2
  (75) **77–8**
  (146) **77n.**
  (170) **76–7**, **77–8**
II
  (4) 83n.
  (20) **79**

HERODOTUS (*cont.*)
(21) 10
(23) 10
(81) 30, **220–1**
(109) **79**, 83 *and* n., **103**
(123) **219–20**
III
(125) 224
(131–2) 224
IV
(8) **10**, 11
(15) 229
(36) **104–5**
(78–80) 30
(95) **217–18**, 220
VII
(6) 20 n. 3

HESIOD
Theogony
(20) 18
(26–7) 255n.
(27–8) 262
(106f.) 18
(116) 18, 19, 20, 24 n. 2,
    34–5, 38, 40, 45
(123) 36
(123ff.) 38
(125) 36
(126) 36
(126ff.) 38
(132) 36
(154) 32, 33, 35 n. 2, 38,
    43, **44–5**, 58
(211ff.) 35 n. 2
(213) 36
(215) 12
(274) 12
(294) 12
(295ff.) 68 n. 2
(306ff.) 68 n. 1
(358) 68 n. 2
(468ff.) 46
(632) 38
(669) 36
(681ff.) 38
(695) **37**
(700) 38
(720) 9, 175
(720ff.) 40
(726) **9**, 20, 40, 64, 175
(734–819) 20
(736) 20, 24 n. 1, 28,
    39–40
(742) 28 n. 2
(775–806) 315
(801–4) 317

(811) **40**
(814) 37
Works and Days
(109ff.) 318
(121ff.) **208 n. 1**
(252ff.) 97 n. 1

HIPPIAS
fr.
(6) 96 n. 2

HIPPOCRATIC CORPUS
de carnibus
(2) **199n.**
(16) 208 n. 3
de morbo sacro
(16) 441n., **449n.**
Περὶ ἑβδομάδων
(1–11) 59 n. 2

HIPPOLYTUS
Refutatio
I (2, 12) 65 n. 2; (6, 1–2)
    106–8, 117; (6, 2)
    126–7, 129; (6, 3) 64,
    133–4, 137; (6, 4–5)
    131, 133, **134–5**, 136
    and n., 259; (6, 6) **141**,
    388; (6, 7) 101n.,
    137–8, 139; (7, 1)
    144–5, 146, 147, 149,
    150, 372; (7, 4) 153,
    154, 155; (7, 5) **152**,
    155; (7, 6) **154**, 155,
    156; (7, 7–8) 158;
    (7, 9) 143, (8, 3–10)
    153, 354, **380–1**, 382,
    446n.; (8, 6) 156, 344
    n. 1; (8, 9) 344 n. 1;
    (8, 12) **382**, 383; (9, 1)
    386–7, 388 *and* n. 2,
    389 *and* n.; (12, 1) 409
    n. 4; (13, 2) **417–18**, 419;
    (14, 3) **172–3**, 174; (14, 5)
    176–7, 178 *and* n.
VII (29, 13) 289n., **294–5**;
    (29, 14) 220, **314–15**,
    320; (29, 25) **312–13**
IX (9, 1) **187**, 188 *and* n.,
    192, 203, 210, 211,
    212, 234; (9, 4) **193**,
    194; (9, 5) **188 n. 2**,
    192, 195 n. 1, 210, 234,
    285; (10, 4) **188**, 189;
    (10, 5) **188**, 189; (10,
    6) 194, **197–8**, 202,
    203, **207**, **208 n. 1**, 209,
    210, 441, 444; (10, 8)
    190, 191, 212, 441

HOMER
Iliad
I (530) 171 n. 3
II (447) 117; (485ff.) 179
V (6) 13 n. 1; (504) 9
VII (422) 13 n. 1
VIII (13) **9**, 40, 90, 175;
    (13ff.) 14 n. 1; (15)
    40; (16) 67; (116)
    175; (478–9) 40;
    (478ff.) 14 n. 1
IX (600) 170 n. 3
XI (574) 98n.
XIV (153–360) 14; (200)
    11, **13–14**, 16, 19, 67,
    93; (203f.) 14 n. 1, 67;
    (244) **13–14**, 16, 19,
    67, 93; (258) **17**, 18,
    19; (271) 14 n. 1;
    (274) 14 n. 1; (279) 14
    n. 1; (288) 9; (296)
    70; (328) 65
XV (*init.*) 14; (37f.) 14 n.
    1; (189–93) 14 n. 1;
    (225) 14 n. 1
XVII (425) 9
XVIII (107) **194 n. 1**;
    (398ff.) 68 n. 2; (489)
    13 n. 1; (607) **10**, 11
XX (444ff.) 137
XXI (194) **10**, 11, 14, 94,
    176; (549) 137
XXII (235) 171 n. 3
XXIV (460) 314
Odyssey
III (2) 9
V (123) 55 n. 2; (218)
    117
X (191) 13 n. 1
XV (329) 9; (403–4) **54**,
    55 n. 2; (455) 55 n. 2
XVII (218) 420 n. 2;
    (565) 9
XXIV (11) 12 n. 3
Σ *in Il.*
II (783) 27, 58n., **59**,
    70
XI (27) **173**, 174
XVII (547) **380–1**
XXI (196) **176**, 178
Σ *in Od.*
XV (403–4) **54**

[**HOMER**]
Hymn to Apollo
(16) 55 n. 2
(351f.) 58n.

[HOMER] (cont.)
Hymn to Demeter
(120) 314
(480–2) 236
IAMBLICHUS
Comm. math. sc.
(p. 76, 16–77, 2 Festa) **234**
(p. 77, 22–4) 330 n. 1
in Nic.
(p. 7, 24 Pistelli) **325** and
n. 1, 327n., 328, 330,
331, 337
Protrepticus
(21) 232 n. 1
Vita Pythagorae
(11–19) 224
(82) **232**, 236
(85) 236
(115ff.) 235
(127) 228
(137) **348–9**
(142) 228 n. 2
(175) **348–9**
(197) 224
(199) 324
(233–7) 228
(239) 228
(246ff.) 335
(248–9) **222–3**, 224
(249–51) **224–5**, 323 n. 1,
335
(251) 224
[IAMBLICHUS]
Theolog. arithm.
(p. 84, 10) 342n.
INSCRIPTIONS
Gold plate from
Hipponion **29–30**
IG I (945, 6) **199n.**; II–III
(1672–3) 357 n. 2; XIV
(641, 1.10) **314**
Marmor Parium (57)
382n.
ION OF CHIOS
fr.
(4) 53, **217–18**, 220
ISIDORUS GNOSTICUS
ap. Clem. Strom.
VI (53, 5) 62, **63**, 65 n. 2
IUSTINUS
ap. Pomp. Trog. Hist. Phil.
Epit.
XX (4, 1–2 and 5–8)
225–6, 227; (4, 14)
227, 228

JOSEPHUS
Ant.
I (94) 25 n. 1
contra Apionem
I (163) **216n.**
LEUCIPPUS
fr.
(2) 405, **420 n. 1**
LUCIAN
Amores
(32) 36
LUCRETIUS
I (830) 377
II (216–42) 423
MACROBIUS
S. Scip.
(14, 19) 205 n. 3
II (1, 9ff.) 235
MAXIMUS TYRIUS
IV, 4
(p. 45, 5 Hobein) 62, **63**,
67, 69, 70
MELISSUS
fr.
(1) 392, **393**, 394, 395,
397, 400
(2) 326 n. 1, **393**, 394,
395
(3) 326 n. 1, **393–4**, 395
(4) 326 n. 1, **393–4**, 395
(6) 326 n. 1, **395**
(7) 326 n. 1, 395, **396**,
397, 397–8n., 398 and
n. 1, 400, 401, 408,
415, 438n.
(8) 195 n. 1, 391,
398–400, 401, 408,
411, 443
(9) 268, **400**, 401
(10) **409 n. 4**
MENO
ap. Anon. Londinensem
XVIII (8) 323 n. 1, 324,
341 n. 1
MIMNERMUS
fr.
(10 Diehl) **12–13**, 92,
201
NICANDER
Σ in Nic. Ther.
(453) **318**
NICOMACHUS
Arithm.
(26, 2) 331n.

ORIGEN
c. Celsum
VI (12) 179, 184, **191n.**,
244, 328; (42) 57,
64n., **66–7**, 68 n. 1, 69,
118, 119, **193**, 194, 290
ORPHICA
fr.
(66 Kern) **24 n. 2**, 28 n. 2
(68) 28 n. 1, 57 n. 1
(70) **24 n. 2**, 27, **29**
(78) 28 n. 2
(89) 23 n. 2
(91–3) 23 n. 2
(94) 23 n. 2
(96) 23 n. 2
(101) **19 n. 1**
(107) 24 n. 1
(109) **23**
(167) 32
PAPYRUS DERVENI
18, 19 and n. 1, 23 n. 1, 24
n. 3, 26, 30, **31–2**
PARMENIDES
fr.
(1) 241, **242–3**, 244
(1, 28–32) **254–5**, 255n.,
256
(2) **244–5**, 246 n. 2, 247
and n., 327
(3) **246 n. 2**
(4) **262**
(5) **244**
(6) 182, 192n., 246,
247n., **247**, 248, 249,
254, 416 n. 3
(7) 244, **248**, 277, 285
(8, 1–4) **248**, 249, 287
(8, 5–21) 245, 246, 247n.,
249–50 and n., 251,
253, 259, 287, 291,
358, 416 n. 3, 424
(8, 22–5) 246, **250–1**,
395, 409 n. 2
(8, 26–31) 249, **251**, 253,
259, 398
(8, 32–49) 170 n. 1, 246,
251, **252–3**, 259, 296
(8, 50–2) **254**
(8, 53–61) 182, **255–6** and
n., 260, 286
(9) **255–6**, 256n., 260,
286
(10) **257–8**, 259
(12) 116n., 240, **257–8**,
259

PARMENIDES (*cont.*)
(13) 240
(14) **259**
(16) **261**, 262
(17) **260**
(19) **262**

PHERECYDES
fr.
(1) **56**
(1a) 36, 60n.
(2) 57 *and* n. 2, 59 n. 1,
62, **63**, 65 n. 2
(3) **62**
(4) 53, 57, **66**, 67, **68** *and*
n. 1
(5) 64n., 65 n. 1, **66–7**,
69
(6) **59 n. 3**
(7) 60n.
(9) 57, 60n.
(12) 57

PHILO OF BYBLOS
ap. Euseb. *P.E.*
I (10) 41n.; (10, 50) 53,
68

PHILODEMUS
de pietate
(47a) 15 n. 1, **18–19** *and*
n. 3, 27
(137, 5) **18–19**, 37

PHILOLAUS
fr.
(1) 234, **324–5**, 326, 328,
330, 331 *and* n., 337
(2) **325**, 326, 327 n. 1,
328, 330, 331 *and* n.,
337
(3) 325 n. 1, **325**, 327n.,
328, 330, 331, 337
(4) **326** *and* n., 327n.,
328, 330, 331, 337
(5) **326** *and* n., 327n.,
328, 330, 331, 337
(6) 234, **327**, 328, 330,
331 *and* n., 337, 341
(7) **339–40**

PHILOPONUS
in Arist. *de gen. et corr.*
(158, 26) 409 n. 2

PINDAR
Nem.
VI (3–4) 9
Ol.
II (17) 57 n. 1; (56–77)
236–7, 238

Pyth.
I (16ff.) 60
Paean
VI (51ff.) 179
fr.
(131b Snell) 207n.
(133) 237, 238, **317**
Σ *in Ol.*
X (53) 84

PLATO
Apology
(26D) **355–6**, 357 n. 1
Cratylus
(400B–C) 221–2
(402A) **195**
(402B) 14, **15–16**, 196 n.
2
(440C) 183
Gorgias
(523A–B) 238
Hippias Major
(281C) 354
(282E–283B) 354
Laws
VI (782C) 222
X (899B) **95n.**
Meno
(76C) **309**
(81B) 237, 238, **317**
Parmenides
(127A) **239**, 263
(127D–128A) **263–4**
(127D–128E) 277
(128C) **277**, 395
Phaedo
(61D) **322–3**, 349
(62B) **348–9**
(88D) **346** *and* n.
(96ff.) 3
(96B) 161n.
(97B–99C) 354
(98Bff.) 374n.
(98B7) 365, **374n.**,
441
(99B) 153
(109Aff.) 380
Phaedrus
(245C–246A) 347
(261D) **278**
(270A) **352–3**
Republic
(363C–E) 222
(364E) 221
(530D) **214**
(600A–B) **214**
(616B–617E) 222

Sophist
(237A), 244, **248**, 277,
285
(242C–D) **71n.**
(242D) **165**, 200n., 241
Symposium
(178B) 35 n. 1
(187A) 192n.
Theaetetus
(151Eff.) 411 n. 1
(152D–E) 165
(152E) **14–15**
(160D) 165
(174A) **80**, 81, 84
(179D) **185n.**
(180D) 319
Timaeus
(22C–E) 122
(40D–E) **15–16**
Σ *in Phaedrum*
(108D) 234
(279C) **227**

PLINY
N.H.
II (31) 103 n. 3; (53)
76n.; (149) 382n.;
(187) 104n.
VII (205) 50 n. 1
XVIII (213) 88
XXXVI (82) 85

PLOTINUS
V
(1, 8) **246 n. 2**

PLUTARCH
adv. Colotem
(1108F) 411 n. 2
(1111F) **291**, 292
(1113C) **291–2**, 294
(1113D) **291–2**, 294
(1114B) **257**, 259
(1116A) **259**
(1118C) **210–11**
(1123B) **303–4**, 305
(1126B) 282
Alex. fort.
(328A) 216
Aud. poet.
(2, 17E) 179
Coriol.
(22) **208 n. 2**
de E
(8, 388D) **197–8**, 200n.,
290, 441
(18, 392B) **194–5**, 195 n.
1, 196–7

PLUTARCH (*cont.*)
de exil.
(11, 604A) **201**, 202
(17, 607C) 220, **314–15**,
320
de fac. in orb.
(12, 926E) 299
(16, 929B) 156 n. 1,
380–1
de fortuna
(3, 98D) **306**
de Is. et Osir.
(32) 57 n. 1
(34, 364D) 15 n. 1
de prim. frig.
(7, 947F) **148**, 149
(21, 954F) **387n.**
de Pyth. or.
(6, 397A) **210 n. 2**
(12, 400B) 301
(21, 404E) 193 n. 1, **209**,
210, 233
de soll. an.
(33, 982A) 141n.
Pericles
(26) **390**, 391
(32) **355 n. 1**
Phocion
(12) 159n.
Quaest. conv.
(683E) **284n.**
Quaest. phys.
(1, 911D) **383 n. 2**
Sept. sap. conv.
(2, 147A) 85
Symp.
VIII (730E) **141**
IX (7, 746B) **179**, 180,
241
Themistocles
(2) **390**, 391n.
[PLUTARCH]
Cons. ad Apoll.
(10, 106E) **188–9**, 210,
441
Strom.
(2) 64, **106–8**, 119–29,
130, **131**, **133** and n. 1,
134, 136, 139n., **140–1**,
142, 420 n. 3
(3) 145, **151–2**, 153
(4) **172–3**
(12) 440 n. 1, **445**, 446
ap. Euseb. *P.E.* 1 (8, 10)
156 n. 1, 234, **299**,
300–1, 344 n. 1

POLYBIUS
II
(39) 224
(39, 1) 228
XII
(27) 285n.
POMPEIUS TROGUS
Hist. Phil. Epit.
XX (4, 1–2 and 5–8)
225–6, 227; (4, 14)
227, 228
PORPHYRIUS
de abstinentia
(II, 21) **318**, 320
(II, 31) **319**, 320
de antro nymph.
(8) **315–16**
(31) 59 n. 3
Hist. phil.
(fr. 12 Nauck) 386n.
in Ptol.
(30, 2ff.) 234
Quaest. Hom. ad Il.
IV (4) 184, **191n.**, 203,
244
XIV (200) **244n.**
Vita Pythagorae
(9) **222–3**, 224
(18) **226–7**
(19) **238**, 347
(30) **218–19**
(41) 232 n. 1, **235–6**, 238,
346
(42) **231–2**, 233, 236
ap. Stob. *Anth.*
I (49, 53) **311**, 321
PROCLUS
in Cratylum
(p. 55 Pasquali) **19 n. 1**,
28 n. 1
in Euclidem
(p. 65 Friedl.) **79**, 336
(p. 352) **85**, 87
(p. 379) **334–5**
(p. 419) **334**, 335
in Parm.
(I, p. 708, 16 Cousin)
244
in Tim.
(I, p. 345, 18 Diehl)
244–5, 246 n. 2, 247
and n., 327
(II, p. 54, 28) **62**
PROTAGORAS
fr.
(1) **411 n. 1**

PTOLEMAEUS
Harm.
I (13) 335
SENECA
Quaest. nat.
II (18) **137–8**
III (14) 92 n. 2, **93 n. 2**
SEXTUS EMPIRICUS
adv. math.
VII (3) 241, **242–3**, 244;
(49) 175, **179**, 180,
241, 328; (60) **411 n.**
1; (90) **383**, 384;
(94–5) **233–4n.**, 235;
(110) 175, **179**, 180,
241, 328; (114) 244,
248, 277, 285; (117)
411–12, 413; (123)
284–5; (125) **284–5**,
311; (126) **188 n. 2**,
195 n. 1, 285; (129)
205, 206, 211, 427n.;
(132) 182, 184, **186–7**,
188 n. 1, 203, 205, 206,
211, 212, 285; (133)
185, **187**, 188 n. 1,
198n., 206, 212; (135)
410, 411, 412, 414;
(136) **410**, **411–12**,
413, 414; (138) **412**,
413, 414; (140) **383**,
384; (389) 411 n. 2
IX (129) **319**, 320; (144)
169–70 and n. 1, 341,
397; (193) 167, **168**,
175, 397
X (34) **175–6**, 178; (85ff.)
279; (281) 342n.
Pyrrh.
I (33) **371n.**, 400n.
SIMPLICIUS
de an.
(p. 70, 17 Hayduck) 295
de caelo
(p. 242, 18 Heiberg) 408,
414, 415, 422
(242, 21) **425–6**, 427
(295, 1) 408, **413–14**,
415, 422
(295, 9) **423**
(295, 11) **425–6**, 427
(522, 7) 166
(528, 11–14) 298
(529, 1) 289, **296–7**, 298
(530, 16–22) 298

SIMPLICIUS (*cont.*)

(557, 10) **391**, 392 n. 1

(557, 16) 326 n. 1, **395**

(557, 25ff.) 241, **242–3**, 244

(558, 8) **262**

(558, 21) 195 n. 1, 391, **398–400**, 401, 408, 411, 433

(587, 20) **303–4**, 305

(615, 15) 114

(712, 27) 418, **421**, 422

in Phys.

(p. 22, 26 Diels) 165, **167n.**, 172

(23, 11) **169–70**, 171, 172, 241, 397

(23, 20) **169–70**, 171, 172, 241, 397

(23, 21) 91 n. 1

(23, 23) 108

(23, 29) **86**, 87, 88

(23, 33) 344 n. 2

(24, 1) 198

(24, 4ff.) 200n.

(24, 13) 101, 102, 105, **106–8**, 109, 110, 112

(24, 17) 57 n. 1, 114, **117–18**, 130, 139, 144, 194, 244, 290

(24, 21) **128–9**, 130

(24, 26) 143, **144–5**, 146, 147, 152, 155, 158, 372, 389

(25, 1) 404, 434, **436–7**, 439 *and* n. 1, 444

(25, 19) **280–1**, 283

(27, 11) 130 n. 2, **373 n. 1**

(27, 17) **365n.**

(27, 23) **386–7**, 388

(28, 4) **402–3**, 404, 426

(28, 7ff.) 404

(28, 7–27) 414

(28, 8) **415–16n.**

(29, 22) 326 n. 1, **393**, 394, 395

(30, 14) **254**, 255n.

(31, 13) 116n., **257–8**

(32, 6) 234, **302**, 311, 321, 439

(32, 13) 289, **296–7**, 298

(34, 21) **357–8**, 359, 366, 367, 368, 370, 377

(34, 29) 357 n. 1, **368–9**, 370

(35, 14) 132 n. 2, **363–4**, 374

(38, 28) 182, **255–6** *and* n., 260, 286

(39, 14) 116n., **257–8**

(39, 18) 240

(70, 16) **391**, 392 n. 1

(78, 5) 245, 246, 247n., **248**, **249–50** *and* n., 251, 253, 259, 287, 291, 358, 416 n. 3, 424

(86, 27–8) 12, 192n., 246, **247** *and* n., 248, 249, 254, 416n.

(87, 6) 268, **400**, 401

(97, 12) **278 n. 2**, 401 n. 2

(97, 13) 279n.

(99, 7) **278–9n.**, 401 n. 2

(103, 13ff.) 392, 401 n. 1

(103, 18) **392 n. 1**

(109, 31) 326 n. 1, **393–4**, 395

(109, 32) **409 n. 4**

(109, 34) 268, **400**, 401

(110, 3) 326 n. 1, **393–4**, 395

(111, 18) 326 n. 1, 395, **396**, 397–8n., 400, 408, 438n.

(112, 6) **397** *and* n., 398 *and* n. 1, 401, 408, 415

(116, 28) **244–5**, 246 n. 2, 247 *and* n., 327

(117, 4) 182, 192n., 246, **247** *and* n., 248, 249, 254, 416n.

(139, 9) 265, **266–7**, 268, 269, 401 n. 1

(140, 28) 264, **265–6**, 267, 268, **361**

(140, 34) 265, **266–7**, 268, 269, 279n., **361**, 362, 401 n. 1

(144, 29) 246, **250–1**, 395, 409 n. 2

(145, 1) **248**, 249, 287

(145, 5) 245, 246, 247n., **249–50** *and* n., 251, 253, 259, 287, 291, 358, 416 n. 3, 424

(145, 27) 249, **251**, 253, 259, 398

(146, 5) 170 n. 1, 246, 251, **252–3**, 259, 296

(149, 18) 435n.

(149, 32) 94n., **147n.**

(150, 22) 129

(151, 20) **434–5**, 439 n. 1

(152, 13) 437, 439 n. 1, **440**, 443

(152, 18) 162n., **441–2**

(152, 22) 116n., **442–3**

(153, 13) 443, 449, **450–1**

(153, 19) **442–3**

(155, 21) **372**, 374, 382

(155, 26) 111n., 357 n. 1, **357–8**, 359, 361, 368, 372, 373

(155, 31) 111n., 115n., **371–2**, 373, 374

(156, 10) **360**, 361, 362

(156, 13) **362–4**, 366, 367, 371, 383, 388, 418, 441, 444, 449

(157, 7) **363–4**

(157, 9) **379**, 380

(158, 1) 234, **287**, 290, 292, 294

(158, 13) 234, **289–90**, 292, 294, 300, 308, 364

(159, 13) 286, **292–3**, 294, 317, 436

(159, 27) **293–4**, 317

(160, 26) 234, 289n., **307–8**, 310

(162, 24) 392, **393**, 394, 395, 397, 400

(163, 20) **358**, 439

(164, 17) **360**, 361, 362

(164, 23) 362, **365–6**, 367, 283

(164, 24) **362–3**, 366, 367, 371, 383, 388, 418, 441, 444, 449

(164, 26) 362, **365–6**, 367

(175, 12) **371**

(176, 29) **371**

(179, 3) **372**, 373, 374, 388, 422

(179, 8) **372**, 374, 382

(180, 8) **255–6**, 256n., 260, 286

(180, 14) 94n.

SIMPLICIUS (*cont.*)
  (189, 1) **175–6**, 178
  (300, 20) 302
  (300, 21) 234, **302**,
    439
  (300, 31) **363–4**, 365
  (327, 24) **420 n. 3**
  (327, 26) 374 n.
  (381, 29) 302
  (381, 31) 301, **304**, 308
  (455, 20–456, 15) 337
  (458, 23) 94n.
  (460, 12) 375
  (479, 33) 114
  (683, 24) 398 n. 1
  (732, 30) 238
  (925, 10) **415 n. 1**
  (1016, 14) 264, 265
  (1121, 5) **124**, 125
  (1121, 12) 125, **151n.**
  (1183, 28) 289n., **295**,
    297
  (1318, 35) **423–4**

SOLON
fr.
  (16 Diehl) 202 n. 1
  (24) 57 n. 1, **121**, 290

STESICHORUS
fr.
  (8, 1–4 Page) 13
ap. Et. Mag. (772.50) 58n.

STOBAEUS
I
  (8, 2) 170, **179**, 193 n. 1,
    241
  (18, 1*c*) 331, 337, **340**,
    341
  (21, 7*a*) **325**, 326, 327 n.
    1, 328, 330, 331 and n.,
    337
  (21, 7*b*) **326** and n.,
    327n., 328, 330, 331,
    337
  (21, 7*c*) **326** and n.,
    327n., 328, 330, 331,
    337
  (21, 7*d*) 234, **327**, 328,
    330, 331 and n., 337,
    341
  (49, 53) **311**, 321
  (49, 60) **316**
III
  (1, 172) 96 n. 1
  (1, 177) **188**, 189

  (1, 179) 188 n. 2, 210 n.
    2, **210–11**, 212
  (1, 210) **430–1**, 432, 433
  (5, 7) **203**, 204
  (5, 8) **203**, 204, 212
IV
  (1, 40) 349
  (25, 45) 349
  (39, 25) **429–30**, 431
  (40, 23) **210–11**, 433

STRABO
  (1, p. 7 Casaubon) **104**
  (1, 12) 10
  (14, 633) 183n.
  (14, 645) **355 n. 2**

SUDA
s.v.
  Ἀναξίμανδρος **100–1**,
    102, 103, 230
  Ἐμπεδοκλῆς **282**, 283n.
  Θαλῆς **86–7**, 88
  Ἴων Χῖος 398 n. 1
  Ὀρφεύς 23 n. 1
  Φερεκύδης 51, **53**, 68

TERTULLIAN
de corona
  (7) 67

THEMISTIUS
Or.
  (5, p. 69 Dindorf) **192**,
    210, 234
  (26, p. 383) 87, **102 n. 1**

THEO SMYRNAEUS
  (p. 198, 14 Hiller) **81–2**, 83,
    87, 88, 104n., 156 n. 1

THEOPHRASTUS
Hist. plant.
  III (1, 4) **382**, 383, 388
Phys. op.
  fr. (1) 91 n. 1; (2) 404,
    434, **436–7**, 439 and n.
    1, 444; (4) **365n.**; (8)
    402–3, 404, 426
de sensu
  (1ff.) **260–1**
  (7) **309–10**
  (9) **310–11**
  (27ff.) **383–4**
  (39ff.) **447–8**, 449
  (43) 436
  (49ff.) 404
  (50) **428**, 429
  (61) **421**, 422
  (66) 425n., 527n., **429n.**

ap. Porph. *de abst.*
  (11, 21) 318
ap. Simpl. *in Phys.*
  (p. 23, 29 Diels) **86**, 87
  (24, 1) 198
  (24, 4ff.) 200n.
  (24, 26) 143, **144–5**, 146,
    147, 152, 155, 158,
    372, 389
  (25, 19) **280–1**, 283

TIMAEUS
fr.
  (13a Jacoby) **227**
ap. Diog. L. VIII
  (66) 282

TIMON
fr.
  (59) 170 n. 1

TZETZES
Chil.
  II (980) 392
  VII (514) 283n.

VIRGIL
Aen.
  IV (166) 58n.

XENOCRATES
fr.
  (9 Heinze) 234

XENOPHANES
fr.
  (1) 164
  (2) 168
  (7) 164, 180, **219**, 220,
    320
  (8) **163**, 164
  (10) 169
  (11) 167, **168**, 175, 397
  (14) 166, **168–9 n. 1**,
    397
  (15) **168–9** and n. 1,
    397
  (16) **168**, 169 n. 1, 397
  (18) 170, **179**, 193 n. 1,
    241
  (23) **169**, 170, 171, 179,
    241, 397
  (24) **169–70** and n. 1,
    341, 397
  (25) **169–70**, 171, 172,
    241, 397
  (26) **169–70**, 171, 172,
    241, 397
  (28) **10**, 90, 110, **175**, 176
  (29) **175–6**, 178

XENOPHANES (*cont.*)
(30) **176**, 178
(32) **173**, 174
(33) **175–6**, 178
(34) 175, **179**, 180, 241, 328
(35) **179**, 180, 241
(37) **177**, 178
(38) **179**, 180, 241

XENOPHON
Poroi
IV (14–15) 357 n. 2
Symp.
(3, 6) 230
ZENO OF CITIUM
(*SVF* I, 103) 36
(*SVF* I, 104–5) 35 n. 1

ZENO OF ELEA
fr.
(1) 265, **266–7**, 268, 269, 361, 362, 401 n. 1
(2) 265, **266–7**, 268, 269, 279n., 401 n. 1
(3) 264, **265–6**, 267, 268, **361**
(4) 264, 265, **273**

GENERAL INDEX

For ancient authors see also the Index of Passages (pp. 461ff.). Reference is not normally made in this General Index to the content of passages quoted or cited, unless this is the subject of further comment.

Abaris, 229

Abstinence: Pythagorean rules of, 230–1; rules in Empedocles, 320

Academy, Platonic, 215, 342n.

Acusilaus of Argos: cosmogony associated with, 19–20; his interpretation of χάος, 37

Acusmata (ἀκούσματα): Pythagorean, 229–36; antiquity, 229–30; rationale, 229, 236; explanations, 231, 232; classification, 233

Acusmatici (ἀκουσματικοί), 234–5

Aegospotami, fall of meteor at, 156, 354, 382, 445–6

Aer (ἀήρ, mist): between earth and sky, 9; distinguished from 'air', 19; but assimilated to it, 146; distinguished from aither, 9, 300; associated with Night in Orphic and Hesiodic cosmogony, 19; one of Epimenides' first principles, 19 n.; compared with ψυχή by Anaximenes, 158–62; synonymous with πνεῦμα, 159, 160; as exhalation from the sea, source of fire, 204n.; see also Air

Aeschylus: on impregnation of earth by rain, 383n.; Xenophanes' influence on, 167, 170; affinities with Heraclitus, 71, 210n.; knows theories of Anaxagoras, 354

Aetius, 2, 124; and the Vetusta Placita, 4–5; on Thales, 79–80, 97n.; on Anaximander, 106, 114; on Anaximenes, 158; on Heraclitus, 206; on Empedocles, 301; on Anaxagoras, 378n., 379–80; on the atomists, 418–19, 422–3, 424–5

Aia, identified with Colchis, 56n.

ἀίδιον, in cosmogony of Anaximander, 131, 132n.

Aidoneus, in cosmology of Empedocles, 286

Air: in post-Hesiodic cosmogony, 18; distinguished from ἀήρ, 19; in Anaximander, 131, 132–3; in Anaximenes, 143–62; in Empedocles, 286, 299–302; in cosmogony of Anaxagoras, 359, 372–4; distinguished from void (Anaxagoras, Empedocles), 359n.; in Archelaus, 388; in theory of atomists, 427n.; in system of Diogenes, 441–5, 448–51; see also Aer

Aisa, in Alcman, 48–9

Aither (αἰθήρ), the upper air, 9; in Orphic cosmogony, 23–4, 27; generation from Erebos (Hesiod), 36; identified with fire (Heraclitus), 161, 198; popularly regarded as divine, 199n., 204; distinguished from aer, 300; in cosmogony of Anaxagoras, 372–4

Alcmaeon of Croton, 119, 179, 328, 451–2; date, 338n.; contact with Pythagoreans, 339n.; book, 339n.; theory of health and dualism, 260, 339; on immortality of soul, 347–8

Alcman, 7; theogonical cosmogony, 47–9

Alexander of Aphrodisias: as source for Simplicius, 3, 105; on Anaximander, 112, 139, 177; on Zeno, 279n.; on Pythagoreans, 326n., 330n.; on Anaxagoras, 354; on Diogenes, 446

Alt, K., 162n.

Ameinias, and Parmenides, 240

Anacalypteria (Unveiling of the bride), 62

Anatomy: Diogenes' views, 450–2; used as parallel with cosmos, 451–2

Anaxagoras of Clazomenae, 111, 115n., 119, 152, 162, 199n., 281, 390–1, 400n.
sources for, 1, 3–4, 5
date and life, 352–5; the trial, 354; pupils and associates, 355n. *(and* 385)
writings, 355–7
reaction to Parmenides, 351, 357–9, 364, 378; to earlier pluralists (? including Empedocles, *cf.* 354), 359, 370, 373, 439 *(and cf.* 130 n. 2); to Zeno, 360–2 *(cf.* 279)
composition of the original mixture, 358–9, 370, 372–4
on void, 359n., 398n.
Mind, 362–6; and the single god of Xenophanes, 171–2; and motion, 364–5 *(cf.* 132n.); and Empedocles' Love and Strife, 364; dualism of mind and matter, 365; Archelaus' modifications, 387–8
'in everything a portion of everything', 365–7; significance of πλὴν νοῦ, 366; application to nourishment, 375–6
'seeds' and 'portions', 367–8
'seeds' and opposites, 368–71; extension of Empedocles' views, 370, 373, 439
the opposites, 371 *(and cf.* 190)
beginnings of cosmogony, 372–4
nourishment and growth, 375–6, 439
homoeomeries, 376–8
summary, and contrast with atomists, 378; their debt to him, 418, 427n., 433
special doctrines, 378–84; astronomy and meteorology, 380–2, 420nn. *(cf.* 344n.), 446 *(cf.* 152n., 153, 156, 157); biology, 382–3, 451, 452n. *(cf.* 354–5); sensation, 383–4
influence on Archelaus, 386–9; on Diogenes, 437, 439, 441, 444; on author of Derveni papyrus, 30
Anaximander of Miletus (philosopher), 26, 50, 51–2, 143, 194, 212, 388–9, 441, 444
Hippolytus as source for, 5
life and date, 100–25; association with Sparta, 49, 100–3, 104n.; relation to Thales, 102–3, 106; slight evidence for connexion with Pythagoras, 102n.; colonization of Apollonia, 105
his book, 102–3, 106
scientific activities, 103–5; the map, 64, 100, 104–5; astronomy and the *gnomon*, 83, 100, 103, 104n.
τὸ ἄπειρον, 105–17; origin of, 41n., 49; of ἀρχή, 106, 108–9, 112; meaning of ἄπειρον, 109–11; Aristotle's

interpretation, 109; Anaximander's use (spatially indefinite or indefinite in kind), 109–11; as an intermediate substance (Aristotle), 111–13; reasons for postulating, 113–15; characteristics, 115–17; change in, 114–15, 127–8
the extant fragment, 117–22; extent, 118; meaning, 118–19; original and Theophrastean elements, 118–20, 121–2; the opposites, 119–20, *and cf.* 359; justice and injustice, 118–22, 193–4; the 'assessment of time', 120–1 *(and cf.* 57n.)
the innumerable worlds, 122–6, 380; a cycle of worlds rejected, 122–3; atomist arguments applied to Anaximander, 123; atomistic worlds assigned to Anaximander, 124–6, 127–8; elements in his cosmology encouraging innumerable-world interpretation, 126
cosmogony, 126–33; doubtful relevance of 'eternal motion' and vortex, 127–30, 132; opposites, 114–15, 119–21; Theophrastus' misinterpretation, 121, 126; separation of opposites, 128–30, 131–3, 420n.; formation of the cosmos, 131–3
cosmology, 133–40; the earth, 83, 133–4, *and cf.* 63–4; the heavenly bodies, 135–7; mathematical basis, 135–6, 137; possible influence on Pythagoras, 136; meteorological phenomena, 137–8; the earth drying up, 139–40, 178; the cyclical process, 139–40
zoogony and anthropogony, 140, 141–2
influence on Anaximenes, 162; on Parmenides, 244, 254, 259; on Empedocles, 290; on Philolaus, 341
Anaximander of Miletus (interpreter of Pythagoreanism), 229–30
Anaximenes of Miletus, 56, 94n., 115n., 124, 134, 181–2, 198, 204, 205n., 372, 434, 444
sources for, 3, 5
date, life, book, 143–4; style, 144
his view of change, 144, 146, 149, 161, 162
air, 144–53; as basic form of matter, 144–8; reason for the choice, 144–7, 161; nature of ἀήρ and πνεῦμα, 146–7 *(and cf.* 58); condensation and rarefaction, 147; as cause of heat and cold, 148–50; gives life to matter, 147; assumption of other basic forms

Anaximenes of Miletus (*cont.*)
  unlikely, 147–8; air is divine, 150–1;
  attribution to Anaximenes of
  innumerable worlds, 151n. (*and cf.*
  126)
  attitude to doctrine of opposites, 147, 149
  attitude to conventional religion, 150 1
  cosmogony, 151–3; air as origin of earth,
  152; origin of heavenly bodies, 152;
  confusion with other thinkers, 152
  cosmology, 153–8; earth, flat, floats on
  air, 153, 154; the heavenly bodies,
  154–7; inaccuracy of doxographical
  attributions, 155–6; explanation of
  setting of sun and stars, 156–7, 446;
  meteorological phenomena, 157–8
  ἀήρ–ψυχή comparison, 158–62, 443 (*and
  cf.* 205n.); explanations of the
  comparison, 160–2
  his debt to predecessors and later
  influence, 162, 172, 341, 372, 389, 434,
  437, 443
  and parallel between human body and
  cosmos, 452
Androclus, founder of Ephesus, 183n.
Andron of Ephesus, on Pherecydes, 52
Animism, primitive: contrasted with
  Thales' view of the soul, 96; in
  Homer, 98n.
Anonymus Londinensis: on Hippon, 91n.; on
  Philolaus, 341n.
Antisthenes: on Heraclitus, 189n.; on
  travels of Democritus, 406n.; on
  Diogenes, 434
Anu, Hittite sky god, 45–6
ἄπειρος, ἀπείρων, 109–11; applied to air,
  146; *see also* Anaximander (τὸ
  ἄπειρον)
Aphrodite, 44, 72, 211; equated by
  Empedocles with cosmic Love, 290; *see
  also* Kupris, Love and Strife
ἀποκρίνεσθαι, applied to opposites, 129–
  30
ἀπόκρισις, use of in embryology, 133n.
Apollo: Orphic cult of, 21; Heraclitus and
  the oracle at Delphi, 209, 210, 211;
  Pythagoras identified with, 228–9; cult
  of Apollo and Pythagoreanism, 233n.;
  and Empedocles, 317
Apollodorus of Athens, his dates:
  Pherecydes, 50; Thales, 76n.;
  Anaximander, 100, 101, 102, 144n.;
  Xenophanes, 164; Heraclitus, 181–2;
  Parmenides, 240; Zeno, 263;
  Empedocles, 281; Anaxagoras, 353;
  Melissus, 391; Democritus, 404

Apollodorus of Cyzicus, 323
Apollonia (Pontic): colonized by
  Anaximander, 105; and Diogenes, 434
Apollonius Paradoxographus, on connexion
  between Pythagoras and Pherecydes,
  52
Apollonius Rhodius: on separation of earth
  and sky, 42–3; on the fight between
  Kronos and Ophioneus, 66–7, 69;
  non-Orphic elements attributed to
  Orpheus, 68n.
ἀπορρήγνυσθαι, use of in biology, 133n.
Apsu, in Babylonian Creation-epic, 12n.,
  43, 92
Apuleius, on Anaximander, 102n.
ἀρχή: Aristotle's use of, 90, 93–4, 98–9;
  Anaximander's, 106, 108–9, 112
Archelaus of Athens, 124
  sources for, 4, 5, 388n.
  date and life, 385; association with
    Anaxagoras and Socrates, 335n., 385,
    386
  cosmology and zoogony, 386–8;
    modification of Anaxagoras' Mind,
    387–8; primary substance, 388; the
    four world-masses, 388; zoogony, 388–9
  his lack of originality, 389
Archippus, 224–5
Archytas, 216, 223, 225, 335
Ares, 72, 318
ἀρέσκοντα, *see Placita*
Arimon, 59, 60
Aristeas, 229
Aristophanes, 131, 199n.; meaning of χάος
  in, 37; cosmogonical concepts in, 26–8,
  63n.; and Thales, 78; use of ἄπειρος,
  110n.; on Orphic books, 221–2; on
  Diogenes, 404, 434, 450n.
Aristotle
  as source for Presocratic thought:
    quotations, 1; his surveys of
    Presocratic opinions, 3; Simplicius'
    commentary on *Physics*, 3; his
    influence on Theophrastus, 3–4, 6;
    and non-Theophrastean judgements in
    the doxographical tradition, 6
  on cosmogonical concepts: Okeanos and
    Tethys, 14–15; Night, 17–18, 20;
    interpretation of χάος, 36
  Aristotelian commentator on Alcman, 48,
    49
  on Pherecydes of Syros, 50, 71
  on σπέρμα, 58
  on Thales' cosmology, 88–98 *passim*; use
    of ἀρχή, 90, 93–4, 98–9; not
    acquainted with his writings, 87

Aristotle (*cont.*)
on Hippon, 91n.
on 'hylozoism', 98
on Anaximander: and Theophrastus'
account of originative substance, 106,
108; Peripatetic interpretation of τὸ
ἄπειρον, 109; the Indefinite as an
intermediate substance, 111–13;
reasons for choice of the Indefinite,
113–15; the Indefinite 'enfolds all and
steers all', 115–17; and application of
atomist-type arguments, 123–6; and
relevance of eternal motion and vortex,
127–8; on separating out of opposites,
128–30; the earth drying up, 139
on Anaximenes: air as originative
substance, 145; air as divine, 151;
cosmology, 153, 155; meteorology,
158; the soul as air, 161n.
on Xenophanes: and connexion with
Parmenides, 165–6; on single god,
171–2; cosmology, 175
on Heraclitus, 184; defects in his
assessment, 185–6; extension of
Platonic interpretation of flux, 195,
196; his dual exhalation and
Heraclitus' meteorological views,
202n., 204n.; soul as the fiery
exhalation, 204n.
on Pythagoreanism, 215–16; lost
monographs, 216, 230, 330n., 340 (*and
cf.* 228–9, 230–1, 235–6); Pythagoras
miracle stories, 228–9; collects and
explains *acusmata*, 229–32, 235–6;
perhaps classifies them, 233; his
summary of Pythagorean teaching and
its sources, 328–32, 350; his principal
criticism, 332–3; on their interest in
mathematics, 335–7; table of
opposites, 337–9; cosmogony, 339–42;
astronomy, 342–5; the soul, 346–7
on Parmenides, 256n.
on Zeno's paradoxes of motion, 264–5,
269; the stadium argument, 269–72;
Achilles and the tortoise, 272; the
arrow, 272–4; the moving rows,
274–6; Zeno's dialectic, 277–8;
influence on Aristotle, 279
on Empedocles, 281–2; evaluation as
poet, 283; cosmogony, 297–9, 302; his
criticisms of Empedocles' explanatory
framework, 306–7; misinterprets
lantern simile, 310n.
on Philolaus: mentions once only, 330;
possible use of his book, 324, 328,
330–2, 340–1, 343; criticism of

cosmogony, 333, 340–1; his
astronomy, 344, 345
on Anaxagoras: equation of void with
not-being, 359n.; seeds and opposites,
370; comparison with Empedocles,
370; and Socrates' criticism of Mind,
374n.; on homoeomeries, 376–7; and
Anaxagoras' belief in only one world,
380n.
on Melissus, 391–2; his lack of
sophistication, 392n.; his bad logic,
394; unlimited extension, 395n.;
monism, 395
on Xuthus, 398n.
on the atomists: metaphysical principles,
406–9; scepticism, 409–11; truth,
413n.; chance, 419n.; weight, 421–2;
motion, 424–5; formation of bodies,
425–7; soul and fire atoms, 427n.;
sensation and touch, 429
on Diogenes: the soul as air, 161n.;
attribution of intermediate substance,
435n., 439n.; anatomical work, 436
[Aristotle], *M.X.G.*: on Xenophanes,
165–6; on Melissus, 392, 395n.
Aristoxenus: his biographies, 6; on
Pherecydes, 50n., 52, 223–4; on
Pythagoras, 65n., 216, 223–4, 233n.;
on Hippasus, 234; on Pythagoreans,
224–5, 323n., 348–9
Arnobius, 4
Assyrian thought, reflected in Greek art,
22n.
Astronomy: heavenly bodies as bowls, 12,
13, 157, 201; Thales, 81–4; his
nautical star-guide, 87–8; Babylonian,
82, 83 *and* n.; stellar observation in
archaic times, 88; Anaximander,
100–4, 133–7; Anaximenes, 154–7,
420n.; Heraclitus, 173–4, 200–2;
Parmenides, 257–9, 344n.;
Empedocles, 299–302, 344n., 420n.;
Pythagoreans, 331, 342–5;
Anaxagoras, 334n., 381–2, 420nn.;
atomists, 418–19, 420n.; Diogenes,
446; *see* Moon, Navigation, Planets,
Stars, Sun, Eclipses
Ἄτη, as instrument of divine power,
170
Athenaeus, 2
Athenagoras, 5; on Orphic cosmogony,
25–6
Athene, 63, 64n.
Athens: Parmenides' and Zeno's visit, 240,
263; Anaxagoras at, 354–5, 385; naval
battle against Samos, 391

Atomists (Leucippus and Democritus)
Hippolytus as source for, 5
Aristotle and atomist arguments applied
to Anaximander, 123; Anaximander
and atomist-type worlds, 124–6
Ionian elements in their cosmology, 153;
improbability of Anaximenes as
forerunner, 148n.; foreshadowed by
Melissus, 398, 400 (cf. 392, 401, 408–9,
415); cosmology contrasted with
Anaxagoras', 378
attitude to Eleatic demands, 351, 406–9
individual contributions, and dates,
402–4
writings, 405–6
metaphysical principles, 406–9
evidence of the senses, 409–13
atoms and the void, 413–16; the shape
and size of atoms, 415nn., 427n.
formation of worlds, 416–21; chance and
necessity, 419n.; innumerable worlds,
415n., 419; the earth and heavenly
bodies, 419, 420n.
behaviour of atoms, 421–7; weight,
421–3; motion, 423–5; formation of
bodies, 425–7
sensation and thought, 428–9
ethics, 429–33; possible connexion with
physics, 432
their position in Presocratic thought,
433; and modern atomic theory, 433
Atum, in Babylonian creation-epic, 12n., 58
Augustine, S., as source for Presocratic
thought, 4, 124–5

Babylon: mythology, similarities with
Greek, 7–8, 11–12, 16–17, 33, 43, 59,
71, 92–3; thought of, reflected in
Greek art, 22n.; prediction of eclipses,
82, 84, 98; invention of the gnomon,
83; Greek scientists' debt to, 82, 103,
335
Bacchylides, meaning of χάος in, 37
Bailey, C.: on Anaxagoras, 367; on the
atomists, 404n.; on περιπάλαξις, 425
Baldry, H. C., on cosmogony of
Anaximander, 133n.
Barnes, J.: on Anaximander's cosmogony,
132n.; on Anaximenes' physics, 148;
on Xenophanes' theology, 170 with n.;
and his scepticism, 180n.; and his
testimony on Pythagorean
metempsychosis, 220; on Zeno's
difficulty, 268; on Empedocles' cycle of
change, 288; on Aristotle's use of
Philolaus, 324; on Philolaus' limiters

and unlimiteds, 326; on Anaxagoras'
'seeds' and 'portions', 368n.; on
Melissus as a philosopher, 392n.; on
text of Melissus fr. 8, 399n.; on the
atomists' οὐ μᾶλλον principle, 411n.;
on the indivisibility of atoms, 415n.;
on Diogenes' basic substance, 439n.
Barnett, R.D., on the Kumarbi-Tablet, 46n.
Basilides, father of Isidorus the Gnostic,
65n.
Bathyllus, Pythagorean, 339n.
Biology: biological language in
cosmogonical explanation, 133n.; in
Anaximander, 141–2; in Empedocles,
305–12 (cf. 302–5); Anaxagoras'
theories, 382–3; influence on thought
of Diogenes, 441n.; see also
Embryology, Physiology
Birds, in cosmogony, 26–7; and see
Aristophanes
Blood, and Empedocles' views on
consciousness, 302, 310–11; its
products, in Diogenes, 451
Bollack, J., on Empedocles as poet, 284n.
Books, use of standard titles, 102 and n.,
282, 392n.; contents of papyrus rolls,
103n.; prices in 4th-century Athens,
356 and n. (and cf. 324)
Brain, as instrument of intelligence, 449n.
Brotinus (Brontinus), 221, 339n.
Burkert, W.: on Derveni papyrus, 30, 32;
on Alcman, 48; on Pythagoreanism,
214–15; and its relation to Orphism,
222n.; on the social structure of
Croton, 227; on the cult of Apollo at
Metapontum, 229; on the harmonious
blacksmith, 235; on the fragments of
Philolaus, 324; and Aristotle's account
of Pythagoreanism, 330–1; on
Pythagorean mathematics, 335,
336nn.; on Pythagorean cosmogony,
341n.
Burnet, J., xii; on Thales 86n., 97; on
6th-century meteorological interest,
91; on Anaximander, 101, 108, 122,
128; on Anaximenes, 151n.; on
Xenophanes, 166, 167; on
Empedocles, 301; on Plato's Phaedo,
215; on date of foundation of Elea,
240; on Anaxagoras, 356; on the
atomists, 403; on concept of weight,
422; on the writings of Diogenes, 435

Cadmeians, among Ionian colonists, 77n.
Cadmus, marriage-gift to Harmonia, 62n.;
ancestor of Thales, 77

Calendar, determination of in archaic period, 88
Calliades, archonship of, 353
Callimachus, 51; on Thales' work in navigation, 84, 88; teacher of Hermippus, 324
Callir(r)hoe, 68n.
Cartography: map of Anaximander, 64, 100, 104–5; of Hecataeus, 104–5
Casius, Mt, as scene of fight between Zeus and Typhoeus, 68
χαλαρός, used by Anaximenes, 149
Chalcidius, 35n., 205n.
Chance: in Empedocles, 306–7; in atomism, 419 *and* n.
Change: in Anaximander, 114–15, 116, 119–21, 127–8; Anaximenes, 144 9, 152, 162; Xenophanes, 176, 177–8; Heraclitus, 186, 190–202, 204; Parmenides, 247, 251–3; Empedocles, 287–94; Anaxagoras, 358, 368–70; Melissus, 396–7, 398–400 (*cf. also* 195n.); atomists, 406–8, 425–7; Diogenes, 438–9
Chaos
    archaic cosmogonical position of, according to Aristotle, 17–18; primary in Hesiod's cosmogony, 36–41; later elaborations of Hesiod's concept, 20, 39–41; role in Orphic cosmogony, 26–8, 33; and Alcman's Poros, 49
    interpretations of χάος, 36–7; etymology, 37; use in literature, 37; in *Theogony*, 37ff.; Cornford's interpretation as gap between earth and sky, 38–9, 41; comparison with Nordic *ginnunga-gap*, 38n.; description of underworld in variants appended to Titanomachy, 20, 39–41; nature of the gap and relation to Tartaros, 41; interpretations of Vlastos and Hölscher, 41n.; in Pherecydes, 57, 60n.
χάσμα, the windy gap, location of Night, 20, 24n.
χέεσθαι, as etymological source of χάος, 57, 60n.
Cherniss, H.: on τὸ ἄπειρον, 110 n., 114; on opposites in Anaximander, 119n.; on Pythagorean cosmogony, 341n.; on Aristotle's view of the soul in atomism, 427n.
Choerilus of Iasus, 97n.
χρεών, meaning of, 118
Chronos: oriental origin of cosmogonical concept, 22n., 57n.; represented as winged snake, 22n.; in Orphic

cosmogony, 22n., 22–8, 57n.; association with Kronos, 22n., 27–8, 57, 60, 67, 69; in cosmogony of Pherecydes, 51, 52n., 56–7, 57n.; initial creation from his seed, in Pherecydes, 58–60, 70; supplanted by Zas-Zeus, 67, 69; as father of Ophioneus, 70; *see also* Time
Χρόνου τάξις, in Anaximander, 57n., 118, 120–1
Chthonie: in cosmogony of Pherecydes, 51, 56–8; given the name of Ge, 56, 57n.; significance of, in relation to earth, 57, 61–2; as guardian of marriage, 61; marriage to Zas and gift of embroidered cloth, 60–3; the winged oak and the cloth, 63–5; as parent of Ophioneus, 70; equated with Hera, 70 (*cf.* 57n., 61)
Cicero: his use of the *Vetusta Placita*, 5; on god as mind, 97n.; on innumerable worlds, 124, 125n., 151n.
Cleanthes, 195n.; his work on Heraclitus, 6
Clement of Alexandria: as source for Presocratic thought, 2, 6; on Heraclitus, 198n.
Cleostratus of Tenedos, his *Astrologia*, 87
Clepsydra, 308n., 359n.
Colchis, identified with Aia, 56n.
Colophon: birthplace of Xenophanes, 75, 163, 164; capture of (546/5 B.C.), 164; foundation and alleged poem of Xenophanes, 166
Common sense: observation in Anaximander, 137; in philosophy before Parmenides, 195; who attacks it (as 'mortal opinion'), 241–2, 243–4, 247–8; as does Zeno, 276, 277–8; and Melissus, 398–400
Cornford, F. M.: his interpretation of χάος, 38–9, 41; on Diodorus, 42n.; on τὸ ἄπειρον, 110 *and* n.; on Anaximander, 122, 130n., 131, 142; on Pythagoreanism, 214; on Anaxagoras, 366, 373–4, 376n., 380
Cosmogony
    in mythic contexts, 7; Hesiod's attempt at systematization of legend, 7; rational investigations of the Milesians, 7, 8
    the naïve view of the world, 9–10
    the concept of Okeanos, 7, 10–17
    the concept of Night, 7, 17–20; in cosmogonical ideas associated with Orpheus, 18–20, 22–3, 25–6, 27–8, 31–2

Cosmogony (*cont.*)
similarities in near-eastern mythology,
7–8, 11–12, 16–17, 33, 41n., 43 4,
45–6, 57n., 58, 59, 65n., 68, 71
anthropomorphic image of growth of the
world, 8
Orphic, 21–33; Neoplatonic accounts,
22–6; the egg, 26–9; gold plates and
myth of Dionysus, 29–30; Derveni
papyrus, 30–3
Hesiodic, and separation of earth and
sky, 34–41; separation in Greek
literature, 42–3; in non-Greek sources,
43–4
mutilation myth in Hesiod, 44–6; Hittite
parallel, 45–6
Alcman, 47–9
Pherecydes of Syros, 50–71
in myth and philosophy, 72–4 (*cf.* 7–8)
of Thales, 88–94
of Anaximander, 106–10, 116–17,
118–19, 126–33
of Anaximenes, 151–3
denied in Heraclitus, 197–200
of Parmenides, 257–60
of Empedocles, 294–305 (*cf. also*
288n.)
of Philolaus and the Pythagoreans,
339–42
of Anaxagoras, 362–5, 371–4
of Archelaus, 387–8
of the atomists, 416–21
of Diogenes, 445–6
Cosmology
of Thales, 88–98
of Anaximander, 119–22, 133–40
of Anaximenes, 153–8
of Xenophanes, 172–8
of Heraclitus, 197–202
of Parmenides, 257–60
of Empedocles, 299–302
of the Pythagoreans, 330–1, 339–
45
of Anaxagoras, 378–82
of Archelaus, 386–8
of the atomists, 416–27
of Diogenes, 445–6
Cratylus: his Heracliteanism, 184, 185n.,
186; and the river-image, 195–6
Croesus, assisted by Thales in crossing of
Halys, 78
Croton: and Pythagoras, 222–8; medical
school, 224, 260, 339; and Philolaus,
323n.
Cyril of Alexandria, 5
Cyrus, King of Persia, 50, 164

Daimons: in Aetius' account of Thales,
97n.; in Heraclitus, 207–8, 211; in
Pythagoreanism, 236; in Empedocles,
314–17, 320–1; in Democritus, 433n.
Damascius, 19n., 20n.; on priority of Night
in Eudemus, 18–19, 22; on Orphic
cosmogonies, 22, 25nn.; πεντέμυχος, 52n.
Damasias, archonship of, 50, 76n.
Darius I, King of Persia, 164
Day: cosmogonical position of, 18;
generation from Erebos (Hesiod), 36;
in Parmenides' poem, 244; alternation
with night, in Anaximander, 120; in
Heraclitus, 189, 190; in Philolaus,
344; in Diogenes, 440–1; Empedocles'
diurnal and nocturnal hemispheres,
301; days of ten and seven months, 305
Decad, the, in Pythagorean doctrine, 233n.,
330, 332
Deichgräber, K.: on Xenophanes'
earth–sea cycle, 179; on his view of
knowledge, 180
Delos, 54, 55n.; in legend of Pherecydes, 52
Delphi: Heraclitus and the oracle at,
209–10, 211, 233; the oracle in
Pythagorean thought, 233 *and* n., 235
Demeter, 32, 314
Demetrius of Phaleron, on Thales, 74n.,
94n.; on Anaxagoras, 353
'Democrates', and ethical writings of
Democritus, 431
Democritus of Abdera, 123, 124, 132, 279,
294, 323, 329, 361, 385, 452; Stobaeus
as source, 2, 431; lost work by
Theophrastus, 4; in Diodorus, 42n.;
on the nationality of Thales, 76–7; on
Thales as astronomer, 82, 84n.; on the
drying-up of the sea and the end of the
world, 139 *and* n.; on the shape of the
earth, 152n., 153, 419; debt to
Milesians, 162; life and date, 404 (*cf.*
323, 329), 406n.; writings, 405–6;
individual contributions, 404, 405–6,
409n., 409–13, 415, 416n., 419, 420nn.,
421–3, 428–9, 429–33; epistemology,
409–13; on weight of atoms, 421–3;
theory of sensation, 428–9; ethics,
429–33; *see also* Atomists
Derveni papyrus, 19n., 26, 30–3
Descartes, R., 241
Deucalion, 140, 178
Διαδοχαί (accounts of philosophical
successions), 4, 5
Dicaearchus, on Pherecydes, 52; on
Pythagoras, 216, 226–7, 238
Dicks, D. R., 78n.

Diels, H., 143n., 169n., 175n., 178, 190, 193n., 202n., 228n., 243n., 284n., 287n., 291n., 303n., 388n., 399, 414, 423n., 425, 445; his *Doxographi Graeci*, 5, 80; on Pherecydes' book, 52n; on the winged oak, 63, 64n.; on Thales' star-guide, 87–8; on Anaximander's views on stars, 136; on πίλησις, 145; on Heraclitus' γνῶμαι, 184; on Empedocles' writings, 283n., 313; on Diogenes, 435

δίκη, in Heraclitus, 194; personified, 202

Diller, H., on Diogenes, 437n.

Diodorus Cronus, his debt to Zeno, 273, 279

Diodorus Siculus, cosmogony and anthropogony in Bk 1, 42n., 405n.

Diogenes of Apollonia, 115 *and* n., 116, 125, 144, 151n., 199n., 404
  date and life, 434
  writings, 434–6; his medical work, 436
  his eclecticism, 436–8; influence of other thinkers, 162, 351, 434, 437, 439, 441, 444–5, 445–6
  the basic substance, 438–40; contains divine intelligence, 440–1; teleological belief, 440
  air as basic form of matter, 441–5; life due to, 443; is soul and intelligence, 443 (*cf.* 161n.); divine, controls, 444; forms differ according to temperature, 444–5
  cosmogony and cosmology, 445–7; doctrine of plurality of worlds attributed to him, 126, 446; views on astronomy, 156, 157, 446
  physiology, 447–52; cognition, 447–50; anatomy and reproduction, 450–2 *and cf.* 58
  his influence on author of Derveni papyrus, 30; on *On the Sacred Disease*, 449n.; on Aristophanes' *Clouds*, 450n. (*cf.* 404)

Diogenes Laertius, as source for Presocratics, 2, 3, 4, 6; on Thales, 83–4, 85–8; on Anaximenes, 143; on Heraclitus, 184, 201, 202n.; on Pythagoras, 216 *and* n., 330n.; on Parmenides, 240–1; on Zeno, 263; on Empedocles, 281; on Philolaus, 323n., 325; on Archelaus, 385; on the atomists, 418n., 419, 420n.

Dion of Syracuse, 324

Dionysus, identified with Hades (Heraclitus), 209–10; in Orphic ritual and myth, 21, 29–30; Heraclitus and Orphic beliefs, 33, 208n., 210n.

Dodds, E. R., *The Greeks and the Irrational*, 8, 229n.

Dodona, Zeus' shrine at, 65

Douris, on nationality of Thales, 76–7

Dover, K. J., 354

Doxographical tradition: as source for Presocratic thought, 4–6; and views of Thales, 90; and 'innumerable worlds', 124–6; and Xenophanes' physical ideas, 173–5; and concept of plurality of worlds, 419; and of invisible celestial bodies, 156

Dualism: in Parmenides, 256; Pythagorean, 331, 339; in Anaxagoras, 365

Earth
  relation to sky and Tartaros, 9–10; solidly rooted, 9, 64; surrounded by Okeanos, 10–13; roots of, in Hesiod, 20, 64
  separation from sky: implies advent of Day and Night, 18; separation in Hesiodic cosmogony, 38–41; in Greek literature, 42–3; in non-Greek sources, 43–4; relevance of near-eastern cosmological ideas on, 11, 45–6, 92–3
  impregnated: by rain, 39n., 383; by severed member of god, 33, 45–6
  represented by winged oak in Pherecydes, 64
  Thales: floats on water, 88–93, 134; originates from water, 93–5
  Anaximander: free-swinging, 83, 128, 134; cylindrical, 132, 133–4; formation of, 131–3; drying up, 139–40, 178
  Anaximenes: flatness as cause of stability, 152n., 153–4, 155; tilted, 156–7, 420n., *and cf.* 446
  Xenophanes: has roots, 175 (*cf.* 90); becomes sea again, 176–8, 199
  relation to sea and fire in Heraclitean cosmos, 198–200
  in Pythagorean cosmology, 343–4; and counter-earth, 331, 343–4
  as one of Empedocles' four roots, 286; its place in cosmology, 298, 300, 301
  Anaxagoras' view, 381–2, 446 (*cf.* 152n.); heavenly bodies thrown off from, 382
  in cosmogony of Archelaus, 388
  the atomists: flat, tambourine-like, tilted, 419, 420n., 446; its composition, 427n.
  Diogenes: a tilted disc, 446
  See also Gaia (Ge)

Earthquakes, explanation of: Thales', 92n., 93n.; Anaximenes', 158; the Pythagoreans', 236

Echecrates, 323, 346 and n.

Echidna, 68nn.

Eclipses, 81–2, 84, 156, 174–5, 201, 344 and n., 381, 420n.

ecpyrosis, attributed by Stoics to Heraclitus, 185, 198n., 200n.

Egg: produced from union of two Titans, 19, 27, 59–60, 70; possibly mentioned in cosmogony attributed to Sanchuniathon, 41n.; in Orphic theogony, 24–6, 28–9; in non-Orphic sources, 26–8; produced by sharks (Plutarch), 141n.

Egypt, 75; the Nile floods and idea of Okeanos, 12; mythology of, similarities with Greek, 7, 11–12, 16–17, 43, 58, 68, 92–3; Thales' visit to, 79–80; astronomical observation in, 82; influence on Thales' cosmology, 92–3; supposed influence on Pythagoras, 219–21; Democritus' visit, 406n.

ἐκκρίνεσθαι, applied to opposites, 129–30

ἐκλεξάμενος, 217n.

ἐκροή, in Pherecydes, 60n.

Elea: Xenophanes' association with, 164, 165–6; foundation (540 B.C.), 164, 240, 263; and Zeno and Parmenides, 240, 263

Eleatic School, 213; Hippolytus as source for, 5; Xenophanes as founder, 164, 165–6; see also Melissus, Parmenides, Xenophanes, Zeno

Eleusis, 33, 236 (cf. 314), 357n.

Eliun, deity in theogony attributed to Sanchuniathon, 41n.

Elohim, replaced by Jahweh in Genesis i–ii, 45n.

Embryology: Anaximander's knowledge of, 141n., 142; and Parmenides, 259–60; Philolaus' theories on, 341n.; Empedocles' contribution, 452n.; Anaxagoras' theories, 382, 452n.; Diogenes' study, 452n.

Empedocles of Acragas, 111, 119, 128, 130n., 151n., 182, 200n., 218–19, 220, 234, 260, 261, 353–4, 359, 364, 369–70, 373–4, 384, 389, 398n., 400n., 429, 433, 439

  sources for: Simplicius, 1; Plato, 3; lost work by Theophrastus, 3–4; Hippolytus, 5

  influence of Parmenides, 213, 260, 261, 283, 285, 286, 287–8, 290–1, 295–6,

  297, 351; Pythagorean influence, 213, 218–19, 220, 234, 302, 313–14, 316, 320, 321; of Heraclitus, 285 and n., 288, 290; of Anaximander, 290; of Xenophanes, 295

  date and life, 280–2; political activities, 281–2; as doctor and orator, 282, 451

  writings, and relationship between the two poems, 282–3, 313–14, 320–1; poetic gifts, 283 and n.; On Nature addressed to Pausanias, 284, 312–13; Purifications to a hetaireia, 313

  defence of the senses, 284–5; the power of knowledge, 285–6

  the four roots, 286 (and cf. 72, 119); place in cycle of change, 289–91; in theory of mixture, 291–4; in cosmogony, 295–302; question of their natural motion, 307–8; in sensation and thought, 310–11, 321; in cycle of reincarnation, 314–15, 321; and Anaxagoras, 359, 369–70, 373–4; and Archelaus, 389; and Diogenes, 439; and Melissus, 400n.

  the cycle of change, 287–91, 294–304; and the cycle of reincarnation, 314–15, 320–1

  Love and Strife, motive forces of cycle of change, 287–90; in theory of mixture, 292–4; in cosmic cycle, 294–302; role of Love in zoogony, 297, 302, 305; explanatory properties, 307–8; place in cycle of incarnation, 314, 315, 318, 321; Love deified, 318 (cf. 290)

  'birth' and 'death': terms held to be philosophically unsound, 291–2 (and cf. 288n.); connexion with 'life' and theory of reincarnation, 292

  mixture, 292–4; in the cosmic cycle, 294–305

  cosmogony, 294–305; the Sphere, 294–6 (cf. also 311–12, 320–1); the Vortex, 296–9; problem of a supposed double cosmogony, 297–9 (cf. also 288n., 305n.); the first stages, 299–300; the present world, 300–2; zoogony, 302–5

  biology, 305–12; principles of explanation, 306–9; sense-perception, 309–10 (cf. 429); thought, 310–12

  theology, 311–12, 314–21 (cf. also 286, 290, 295–6)

  Purifications, 313–21; exploits theoretical framework of On Nature, 313–14; the cycle of incarnation, 314–17; the primal state, 318; bloodshed and cannibalism, 319–20; ritual

Empedocles of Acragas (*cont.*)
injunctions, 320; question of
compatibility of its doctrine with *On
Nature*, 320–1
views on respiration (the *clepsydra*),
359n.; on void, 398n.; on the fixed
stars, 155
Emperius, 141n.
Eos, 55n.
Ephesus, birthplace of Heraclitus, 75, 181–3
Epicharmus, 164, 165; on primeval deities,
56; and the Heraclitean tradition, 165
Epicureanism: influence on the
doxographical tradition, 6; Epicurean
interpretation of Democritus, 425
Epicurus, 124, 403; on the atomists, 403,
405; on shape and size of atoms,
415n.; parallel in phraseology with
atomists, 418n.; and weight of atoms,
22–3; his use of παλμός, 425
Epigenes, 221, 222n.
Epimenides, 163–4; cosmogony assigned to,
18–19, 21, 49; on production of
Tartaros by Night and Air, 19, 27;
writings attributed to, 21; comparison
with Pythagoras, 227, 229
Epistemology: Xenophanes on limitations
of human knowledge, 179–80; and
Heraclitus, 186–8, 193n., 202–3;
Parmenides' epistemological
arguments, 241, 244–9; his contrast of
truth and mortal opinion, 241–2,
243–4, 247–8, 254–6, 262;
Empedocles' views, 284–6, 290, 294,
311; and Philolaus', 326–8; and
Alcmaeon's, 339n.; and Anaxagoras',
384; Melissus' confutation of common
sense, 398–400; Democritus'
scepticism, 409–11; and theory of
confirmation, 411–13
ἐποχεῖσθαι, of the earth riding on air, 153
'Επτάμυχος, title of Pherecydes' book, 51
Eratosthenes, 4, 281; on cartography, 104
Erbse, H., on Homeric scholia, 59
Erebos: its relation to Hades and Tartaros,
9; possible Hittite etymology, 36;
place in Hesiodic cosmogony, 36; and
in Orphic, 24, 27–8; Aristophanes'
reference, 26
Eridu, Babylonian myth of, 92
Erinyes (Furies), 201
Eros: as rain/semen between sky and earth,
38; relation to Phanes, 24n., 28; Zeus,
as creator, changes into, 62
Esharra, the firmament of earth in
Babylonian Creation-epic, 43

estin, ambiguity of in Parmenides, 245–6
Ethics: of Heraclitus, 210–12; Pythagorean
acusmata, 229–32; Aristoxenus on
Pythagorean ethics, 348–9; of
Archelaus, 389n.; of Democritus,
429–33
Euclid, 85, 334–5
Eudemus, 3, 19n.; significance of Okeanos
and Tethys, 15; position of Night, 19;
Time as cosmogonical figure, 22n.; his
History of Theology, 22; account of
Orphic theogony, 22, 26; on Thales,
and astronomy, 82–3, 85–6, 87–8,
104n.; on the moon shining by
reflected light, 156n.; on periodic
recurrence of events, 238; on Zeno,
278n.; on Pythagorean mathematical
discoveries, 334–5; Proclus' summary,
336 *and* n.; on Empedocles' cycle of
change, 295
Euripides: on Okeanos as a circle around
the earth, 11; on immortality of
nature, 117n.; Xenophanes' influence
on, 168; and Anaxagoras, 355n.
Eurynome, daughter of Okeanos, 67
Eurytus of Croton, 323; his pebbles, 333–4
Eusebius: as source for Presocratic thought,
4, 5; his summary of cosmogony of
Sanchuniathon, 41n.
εὐθυμίη, in Democritean ethics, 431
Examyes, father of Thales, 76, 77n.

Farnell, L. R., 63
Favorinus, on Anaximander, 100
Fire: produced from seed of Chronos, 58,
60n.; in cosmogony of Anaximander,
131, 132–3, 135–7; of Anaximenes,
152; primary constituent in Heraclitus,
188, 441; and the world-order in
Heraclitus, 197–200; probably
identified with αἰθήρ, 198; in
Parmenides' cosmology, 258–9; in
Pythagorean cosmology, 342–4; in
Empedocles, 286, 293–4, 299–302, 304,
307–8; in Anaxagoras, 372; in
Archelaus, 388; atomist explanation,
427 *and* n.
Fish: in zoogony of Anaximander, 141,
142; Diogenes on their breathing, 450n.
Flux, Platonic interpretation of
Heraclitean, 185–6, 195–7, 200n.
Fossils, and Xenophanes' physical studies,
168, 177–8
Fränkel, H.: on Heraclitus fr. 92, 210n.; on
text of Zeno, 267nn.; on Parmenides'
cosmology, 259n.

Frankfort, H., and others, *Before Philosophy*, 8 (*cf.* 93n.)

Frankfort, H., on Nun, 93n.

Fritz, K. von: on Pherecydes, 63; on Xenophanes, 170n.; on Pythagoreans, 225n.

Furley, D. J.: on Parmenides, 256n.; on Zeno, 265; on the Pythagoreans, 333; on the atomists, 409nn., 415n.

Fusion, theory of, attributed to Anaxagoras, 367

Gaia, Ge
  her offspring, 18, 34–5 *and* n., 36; classed with Night, Okeanos and Ouranos in Hesiod, 18; in Hesiodic cosmogony, 18, 34–5; offspring of Night, 23n.; mutilation myth and her offspring, 44–5; mother of Typhoeus, 70; in Orphic cosmogony, 23, 25–6
  in Pherecydes: Chthonie receives her name, 56, 57n.; slanders Zeus to Hera, 59; represented on embroidered cloth, 61–2; her portion, 67–8

Galen, 2, 156n.

γαλεοί, 141n.

Ge, *see* Gaia

Genesis, cosmogony in, 43–4

γένεσις, whether genuine in Anaximander, 118

Geometry: Thales' alleged achievements, 78, 79, 83, 84–6; Anaximander as geometer, 101, Pythagorean contributions, 334–7

ginnunga-gap, in Nordic cosmogony, comparison with χάος, 38n.

γνώμη: Heraclitus' use of, 202n.; Democritean, 431

gnomon: used by Babylonians, 83; Anaximander's use, 83, 101, 103–4; use of notion in mathematics by Pythagoreans, 336–7

Gnosticism, and Ham–Zoroaster identification, 65n.

God, gods, the divine, ch. 1, *passim* (especially 7–8, 33, 34, 71, 72–4); in Thales, 95–8, 99; in Anaximander, 117; in Anaximenes, 150–1; in Xenophanes, 165–6, 167–72, 179–80; in Heraclitus, 190–1, 198–9, 202–3, 207, 209–10, 211–12; in Pythagoreanism, 235–8, 348–9 (*cf.* 343); in Parmenides, 242–4, 257–60; in Empedocles, 286, 295–6, 311–12, 313–21; in Diogenes, 440–4

Gold plates: eschatology of, 29–30, 33; and Orphism, 29–30; and Empedocles, 314

Gomme, A. W., on Stesimbrotus, 391n.

Gomperz, H., 53, 176; on ἐκρυή in Pherecydes, 60n.; on the oak and embroidered cloth, 63

γόνιμος, 131–2, 133n.

Gorgias: as pupil of Empedocles, 281; his book *On What is Not*, 103n., 279, 392n. (*cf.* 326n.)

Great Year, cycle of, 82, 200n., 208; in Hesiod, 315; and cosmic cycle of Empedocles, 315 (*cf.* 220)

Growth, Anaxagoras' theory of, 375–6

Gurney, O. R., *The Hittites*, 8, 43, 46n., 68

γυρόν, applied to the earth, 133n.

Güterbock, H. G., on the Kumarbi-tablet, 46n.

Guthrie, W. K. C.: on the Orphics, 21; on Anaximenes' theory of change, 148; on the use of ἧλος, 156n.; on Heraclitus fr. 51, 192n.; on his river fragment, 196; on Heraclitean fire, 200; on cosmic change in Heraclitus, 200n.; on Parmenides' account of thought, 262n.; on Empedocles as poet, 284n.; on Empedocles fr. 17, 289n.; on Pythagorean cosmogony, 341n.; on Bailey's view of the atomists, 404n.; on the indivisibility of atoms, 415n.

Hades: relation to Erebos and Tartaros, 9–10; share in division of the cosmos, 14n.; identified with Dionysus (Heraclitus), 209–10; in Pythagoreanism, 238; and Empedocles, 316; in Orphism, 221

Halys, river, diverted by Thales, 78

Ham: the prophecy of, and Pherecydes, 63, 65n.; identified with Zoroaster, 65n.

Harmonia, her marriage-gift from Cadmus, 62n.

harmonia (ἁρμονίη, ἁρμονία): in Heraclitus, 192–3; in Pythagoreanism, 232–5, 238, 331, 335–6, 344–5, 346; influence of Pythagorean concept on Heraclitus, Empedocles (*cf.* 290, 295, 302), Philolaus, 234; Philolaus' theory, 325, 327–8, 331 *and* n.; harmony of the spheres, 232–3, 330, 344–5; the soul a *harmonia*, 346

Harnack, A. von, on Ham–Zoroaster identification, 65n.

Hecataeus of Abdera, 405n.

Hecataeus of Miletus: his map, 104–5; rebuked by Heraclitus, 182, 188n.; his date, 182n.

Heidel, W. A., 202n.; on cosmogony of
    Anaximander, 133n.; on Pythagoreans
    and Greek mathematics, 336n.
Helen, 28n., 211
Hellanicus: on Orphic cosmogony, 24; his
    identity, 25n.
Hephaistos: depicts Okeanos on shield of
    Achilles, 10; in cosmology of
    Empedocles as fire, 302
Hera: her deception of Zeus, 14, 17;
    guardian of marriage, 57n., 61; and
    production of Typhoeus from egg,
    59–60, 70; represented by oaken statue
    in ἱερὸς γάμος, 62n.; equated with
    Chthonie, 70; in cosmology of
    Empedocles, 286
Heracles, Orphic name for Chronos, 24–5
Heraclides of Pontus, 281; his work on
    Heraclitus, 6
Heraclitus of Ephesus, 71, 72, 115 and n.,
    116, 118n., 120, 121, 123, 146, 147 and
    n., 151 and n., 162, 164, 179–80, 281,
    285
  sources for: Hippolytus, 2, 5–6; Plato, 3;
    non-Theophrastean influences in the
    doxographical tradition, 6
  relation to other thinkers, 75, 181–2;
    Xenophanes' influence, 167–8, 173–4,
    179–80; rebukes others, 181, 188n.,
    217; especially Pythagoras, 217–19;
    perhaps referred to by Parmenides, 182
    (cf. also 244); influence on
    Empedocles, 285, 288, 290; and
    Diogenes, 437, 440–1
  date and life, 181–3; fictitious anecdotes,
    182, 183; resignation of 'Kingship',
    183n., 211n.; the epithets 'obscure'
    and 'weeping', 183
  his book, 183–5
  his thought, 185–212
  distortion of his views and difficulty of
    interpretation, 185–6
  the Logos, 186–8, 199–200, 203; and the
    Delphic oracle, 209–10, 211; and
    human law, 212
  essential unity of opposites, 188–90; the
    'road up and down', 188, 189n.
  unity and plurality from opposites,
    190–1; god and the Logos, 191; god
    as connecting element in extremes,
    191; superiority of god to man, 191n.
  unity unapparent, dependent on balance
    between opposites, 192–3
  dominance of change, and strife between
    opposites, 193–4; fire as example,
    198–9

the river-image illustrates unity through
    balance in change, 194–7
fire and the world-order, 197–200, cf. 56,
    90, 440–1; his use of κόσμος, 159n.;
    the trade-image and world-order, 198,
    200n.
ecpyrosis attributed to, by Stoics, 185,
    198n., 200n.
views on astronomy, 200–2, and cf. 13,
    84n., 173–4; Simplicius assigns
    successive single worlds to, 125–6;
    heavenly bodies as bowls of fire, 201;
    fire nourished by exhalations from the
    sea, 201, 202n.; maintenance of
    measure in change, 201–2
the nature of wisdom, 202–3
views on the soul, 203–8, and cf. 8, 160,
    161, 445; waking, sleeping and death,
    205–7, 444n., 449; the soul and the
    Logos, 206; the fate of virtuous souls,
    207–8; survival after death, 207,
    208n.; suggestion of deification of some
    souls, 208n.
attitude to conventional religion, 209–10;
    and that of the Milesians, 150–1, 191
ethical and political advice, 210–12
summary of his position, 212
Hermippus of Smyrna, 324; as source for
    Presocratic thought, 4; on date of
    Pherecydes, 50n.; on Plato and
    Philolaus, 324
Hermodorus, exiled from Ephesus, 182,
    211n.
Herodotus: on Okeanos, 11; on Thales, 77,
    78, 81–2; on Babylonian use of gnomon,
    83; and anthropological approach to
    religion, 169; on Pythagoras, 217–18,
    219–20, 221; on Aristeas, 229
Hesiod, 17, 59; his attempt to systematize
    legend, 7; on relation of earth to
    Tartaros, 9–10, 175; and cosmogonical
    importance of Okeanos, 16; position of
    Night in his cosmogony, 18, 20, 36;
    rearrangement of the Hesiodic figures,
    19, 20; composition of Theogony, 34–6;
    methods of generation in, 36; primacy
    and meaning of χάος, 36–41;
    mutilation-myth, 44–6; non-Greek
    sources in Theogony, 45–6; comparison
    with Alcman, 49; influence on
    Orphics, 25–6, 33, 34, 222; and on
    Aristophanes' bird-cosmogony, 28;
    Phoenician affinities, 53–4, 68;
    contrasted with Pherecydes, 71;
    Xenophanes' attack on gods in, 168–9;
    rebuked by Heraclitus, 188n., 217;

Hesiod (*cont.*)
    and Heraclitus' views on the soul, 207,
    208; influence on Parmenides, 243–4,
    254, 255n., 257, 259, 262; and on
    Empedocles, 283, 315, 317, 318
[Hesiod], *Astronomia*, 87–8
Hesychius: on marriage of Zas and
    Chthonie, 62n.; on writings of Thales,
    86–7
hetaireia (ἑταιρεία), Pythagorean, 227–8, 313
Hieron, tyrant of Syracuse, 164
Hieronymus, source for Orphic theology,
    24, 25n.
Hieronymus of Rhodes, 4; on Thales, 85
Hippasus of Metapontum, 147n., 234–5,
    344n.
Hippias of Elis, 2; on Thales, 95, 96n.
Hippocratic works: use of γόνιμος, 131;
    and Archelaus' cosmogony, 389n.; and
    Diogenes, 436, 449n.
Hippolytus of Rome: as source for
    Presocratics, 2, 5–6, 95–6, 131;
    on Anaximander, 95–6, 131; on
    Xenophanes, 174, 178; on Heraclitus,
    192n.
Hippon of Samos (or Rhegium, etc.), on
    water as constituent material, 91nn.
Hipponion, and gold plate, 29
Hittite mythology, similarities with Greek
    theogonical and cosmogonical stories,
    7–8, 11, 33, 41n., 43–4, 45–6, 68
Hölscher, U.: on χάος in Hesiod, 41n.; on
    near-eastern parallels with Thales,
    93n.; on separation of opposites in
    Anaximander, 129–30; on Parmenides'
    cosmology, 259n.
Homer: naïve account of the world in, 7,
    9–10; on relation of earth to Tartaros,
    9–10, 88; on Okeanos as encircling
    river, 10–12, 13n.; Okeanos as origin
    of all things, 13–14; cosmological
    references in Διὸς ἀπάτη, 13–14, 17;
    Plato on, as forerunner of Heraclitean
    idea of flux, 15; personification of
    Night, 17; and the soul, 96, 159,
    443–4; animism in, 98n.; and the
    Heraclitean tradition, 165;
    Xenophanes and Homeric gods, 169,
    170 *and* n., 172; rebuked by
    Heraclitus, 188n.; poetic influence on
    Parmenides, 243; and Empedocles'
    poetic technique, 283 *and* n., 294, 308;
    Empedocles and descent to the
    underworld in *Odyssey*, 315
Homoeomeries: in Anaxagoras, 376–8; in
    Archelaus, 388

Hot and cold: in Anaximander, 132–3; in
    Anaximenes, 148–50; in Heraclitus,
    189; in Alcmaeon, 260; in
    Parmenides, 261; in Anaxagoras, 370,
    371, 373–4; in Archelaus, 387–8; in
    Melissus, 399; in Diogenes, 444–5
Humanism: humanist approach replaces
    cosmological, 452
Hussey, E. L., 112
'Hylozoism', and Thales' view of soul, 98

Iamblichus: as source for Presocratics, 2;
    for Pythagoreanism, 216; classification
    of *acusmata*, 233
ἰλύς: in Orphic cosmogony, 25; in zoogony
    of Anaximander, 140, 142
Indefinite, the, *see* Anaximander (τὸ
    ἄπειρον)
Infinity: Aristotle's attribution of specific
    quality to concepts of, 109, 111–12;
    Theophrastus on τὸ ἄπειρον as
    spatially infinite, 109; Aristotle and
    atomist arguments for, 123; Zeno's
    arguments, 265–72; and Anaxagoras'
    response, 357–9, 360–2, 367; Melissus
    on, 393–5; in atomism, 413–14, 415n.,
    417–19
Innumerable worlds: in Anaximander,
    122–6; in Anaximenes, 151n.; in
    Anaxagoras, 378–80; in the atomists,
    415n., 416–19; in Diogenes, 440n.,
    446
Intelligence (νόησις), and Diogenes' basic
    substance, 437, 440–5
Ion of Chios: on Pythagoras and
    Pherecydes, 53, 218; on Pythagoras
    and Orpheus, 220–1, 222n.; on
    Socrates and Archelaus, 386n.;
    relationship to Xuthus, 398n.; date,
    398n.
Ionia: development of thought in, 73–4,
    75; mainland colonists in, 77n.;
    contacts with Babylon, 82
Irenaeus, 4
Iris, 174, 380; *see also* Rainbows
Ishtar, 59
Isidorus the Gnostic, on the winged oak
    and embroidered cloth, 63, 65n.

Jacoby, F., on identification of Pherecydes
    of Syros, 50n.
Jaeger, W., *Theology of the Early Greek
    Philosophers*, 8; on title of Pherecydes'
    book, 52n.; on Xenophanes, 167
Jahweh, 92; contrasted with Elohim in
    Genesis, 45n.

Justice: and relation of opposites to τὸ ἄπειρον, 118–21, 139–40; Heraclitus' amendment of Anaximander's view, 193–4; personified by Heraclitus, 202; in Parmenides' poem, 244; and in his cosmology, 258

Kahn, C. H.: on Thales and Babylonian astronomy, 82; on the title Περὶ φύσεως, 103n.; on Anaximander's map, 105; on ἀρχή in Anaximander, 108; on Aristotle's 'intermediate' substance, 112; on κόσμος, 119n., 159n.; on Anaximander and innumerable worlds, 122; on his theory of the position of the earth, 134; and on his astronomy, 137; and meteorology, 138; and zoogony, 142n.; on Heraclitus' book, 184n.; on ἐκπύρωσις, 200n.; on νοεῖν in Parmenides, 247n.; on Pythagorean cosmogony, 341; on the relative chronology of Anaxagoras and Empedocles, 354n.
Keb, earth-god in Egyptian mythology, 43
Kerferd, G. B., on date of Anaximenes, 143n.
Kirk, G. S., Heraclitus, The Cosmic Fragments, 102n., 195n., 198n., 202n.; The Nature of Greek Myths, 8; on the Kumarbi tablet, 46n.; on τὸ ἄπειρον, 113; on Anaximander's innumerable worlds, 122
Kirk and Raven, The Presocratic Philosophers, 1st edition (KR): on Parmenides' estin, 246; on his fr. 8, 253, 256n.; on Zeno and the Pythagoreans, 278n.; on Pythagorean cosmogony, 241n.; on Zeno's moving rows, 276
Κοινή, dialect, 159n.
κόσμος, 159 and n.
κραδαίνει, in Xenophanes, 171n.
Kranz, W., 44n., 445
Kronos: Homer's reference to, 14n.; in Orphic, Homeric and Hesiodic cosmogony, 15–16; in mutilation-myth, 33, 35n., 38, 44–6, 58; parallel with Hittite Kumarbi–Anu story, 33, 45–6; and production of egg, 27, 59–60, 70 (see also Egg); in Orphic cosmogony, 27, 28n., 32–3; association with Chronos, 22n., 27, 28n., 57, 59–60, 67; fight with Ophioneus, 53–4, 66–9; and initial creation, in Pherecydes, 56–7; Pherecydes on etymology, 57; as first

king of the gods, 67; in Pythagorean eschatology, 236–7; in Empedocles' Purifications, 318
κυβερνᾶν, 115n.
Kumarbi, Hittite equivalent to Kronos, 33, 45–6
Kumarbi-tablet: as evidence of non-Greek elements in Theogony, 45–6; in Orphic cosmogony, 33
Kupris (Aphrodite): equated with cosmic Love (Empedocles), 302, 318; her rule, 318 (and cf. 294–9)

Lampsacus, Anaxagoras at, 353–4, 355n.
Law: in Heraclitus, 212; in Empedocles, 319–20; in Pythagoreanism, 349; in Archelaus, 389n.; in Democritus, 432; see also Justice
Lear, J. D., 274
Lee, H. D. P., 275n.
Leucippus, 123, 124; life and date, 402–4 (cf. 385, 437n.); writings, 404–5; inventor of atomism, 403–4; explanation of setting of heavenly bodies, 157, 446; debt to Milesians, 162, 419; to Anaxagoras' Mind, 405, 418; to Melissus, 398, 400, 403, 408–9, 414–15, 437n.; response to Zeno, 279, 361–2, 403–4, 408–9; metaphysical principles, 406–9; atoms and void, 413–16; cosmogony, 416–21; on the shape of the earth, 419, 446; on chance and necessity, 419n.; and weight of atoms, 422; and their motion, 424; on sensation, 429; see also Atomists (Leucippus and Democritus)
Leviathan, analogous with Tiamat, 92
Lewis, I. M., 229n.
Light: in Parmenides' cosmology, 255–62; in Pythagorean table of opposites, 338–9; see also Day, Eclipses, Fire, Moon, Sun
Lightning: Anaximander's explanation, 138; Anaximenes', 158; see also Meteorology, Thunder
Like-to-like principle: in Parmenides' theory of mortal thought, 261; in Empedocles, 307–8, 310–11, 313; in Anaxagoras, 373, 375–6; but denied in his theory of sense-perception, 383–4; in atomism, 417–18, 419n., 426–7; in Diogenes, 448–9
Limit: Parmenides' notion, 251–3 (cf. 259); Philolaus on limiters, 324–8; concept in Pythagoreanism, 329–31; Eurytus' development of it, 333–4; in theory of

Limit (*cont.*)
even and odd, 336 7; and in table of
opposites, 337–9; and in Pythagorean
cosmogony, 339–42; and astronomy,
342–4; in Melissus' dialectic, 393–4,
394n., 395
Linforth, I. M., on the Orphics, 21, 31
Lobon of Argos, 87, 166
Λόγος, in Heraclitus, 187–8, 191, 198n.,
199–200, 203, 205–6, 209–10, 212
Long, A. A., 256n.
Lorimer, H. L., on Syrie and τροπαὶ
ἠελίοιο, 55nn.
Love and Strife, *see* Empedocles
Lucretius, and Anaxagoras' homoeomeries,
377
Lysis, 224–5

Magnetism: Thales on, 95–7, 99; and
Empedocles, 310, 447n.; and
Diogenes, 447n.
Malta, fossils found at, 177
Mansfeld, J., 355n.
Maori mythology, similarities with Greek,
43, 45
Marcus Aurelius, 2
Marduk, in Babylonian Creation-epic, 33,
43, 68, 92
Marriage: Chthonie and Hera as guardians
of, 57n., 61; its Pythagorean number,
336
Mathematics: Thales' supposed discoveries,
84–6; neglected by other Milesians,
96; Pythagorean contribution, 334–7;
see also Geometry, Music, Pyramids
Matter: air as basic form of (Anaximenes),
144–8; (Diogenes), 441–5;
Anaxagoras' theory, 357–62, 365–71;
his dualism of mind and matter, 365;
atomists' theory, 413–15
Maximus of Tyre, 2
Mazdaism, and Iranian *Zvran Akarana*, 57n.
Medicine: influence of study of on
cosmology, 91; influence on
Parmenides' embryology, 260;
Alcmaeon's theory of health, 260;
Philolaus' interest, 341n.; Empedocles
as a doctor, 282; Diogenes' medical
work, 436
Melissus of Samos, 110, 165, 166, 171–2,
195n.
date and life, 390–1, 437n.; his naval
successes, 381; his book, 391–2
Aristotle's opinion of him, 392n., 394
deduction, 392–8; departures from
Parmenides, 393, 394, 395, 398;

influence of his monism, 395; debt to
Xenophanes, 397; influence of his
views on motion and void, 398
confutation of common sense, 398–400;
compared with Parmenides and Zeno,
400
the incorporeal, 400–1; possible
confusion with Zeno, 401nn. (*cf.* 268)
influence on atomists, 398, 400, 401, 403,
408–9, 414–15, 437n.; on Philolaus,
326n.
Menon, 3; on Philolaus, 323n., 324, 341n.
Mensuration, Thales' work in, 85–6
Merkelbach, R., 31
Mesopotamia, and development of idea of
Okeanos, 11
μετα-, implying change rather than
succession, 142
μετακοσμεῖσθαι, 437n.
Metapontum, 91n.; death of Pythagoras,
223 (*cf.* 228); miracles of Pythagoras,
228; cult of Aristeas, 229; and of
Apollo, 233n.
Meteorites: Diogenes' explanation, 156,
446; fall of, at Aegospotami (467 B.C.),
382, 446; Anaxagoras' alleged
prediction, 354, 382
Meteorology: Thales and 6th-century
interest in, 91, 92n.; Anaximander's
explanation of phenomena, 137–8;
and Anaximenes' choice of air as
material principle, 146; his
explanation, 157–8; Xenophanes',
174; function of the sea, in
Xenophanes, 176; Aristotle's
dual-exhalation theory, 202n.;
Anaxagoras' interest, 381–2;
Simplicius on Diogenes' book, 428;
influence on Diogenes' thought, 440–1;
see also Lightning, Meteorites, Rain,
Rainbows, Thunder
Metrodorus of Chios, 420n.
Milesian School, 75; rational approach to
cosmogony, 7, 8, 72–4; practical
activities, 73; and mathematical
theory, 86; contrasted with Heraclitus,
186; Pythagoreans and Eleatics, 213;
cosmogony contrasted with
Parmenides', 260; and with
Empedocles', 297; compared with
5th-century Ionian philosophers, 351;
see also Anaximander, Anaximenes,
Thales
Miletus: character of its society, 74;
birthplace of Thales, 75, 77; of
Anaximander and Anaximenes, 75;

Miletus (*cont.*)
possibly of Archelaus, 385; and of
Leucippus, 403; contact with Egypt,
79, 80; and geographical knowledge,
105; recession of the sea reflected in
cosmological ideas, 139, 140;
destruction of (494 B.C.), 143
Mind: in Anaxagoras, 362–5, 366, 383;
and single god of Xenophanes, 171–2;
regarded as a substance, 364;
substituted for Empedocles' Love and
Strife, 364; and motion, 364–5; Plato's
criticism, 374n., 388; Archelaus'
modification, 387; and Leucippus'
vortex-action, 418; adapted by
Diogenes, 437, 449
Moderatus, 215
μοῖρα, meaning in Anaxagoras, 367
Monism: material, of the Milesians, 75,
162; Heraclitus' position, 190–1;
Parmenidean monism, 249, 250–1;
Eleatic monism vulnerable to Zeno's
arguments, 269, 277; but Zeno
probably did not attack it explicitly,
278n.; Melissus' argument for monism,
395; Diogenes' reaffirmation of
material monism, 438–9
Moon: Thales' observations of, 83; in
cosmology of Anaximander, 135–6; of
Anaximenes, 155, 156; shines by
reflected light (Parmenides,
Empedocles, Anaxagoras), 156n.; in
Pythagorean eschatology, 232, 236;
Parmenides' view, 258–9; and
Empedocles', 301; and Philolaus',
343; the harmony of the spheres, 345;
Anaxagoras' view, 381–2
Morrison, J. S.: on Pythagoras at Croton,
227; on Parmenides' cosmology,
259n.
Mot (slime), in cosmogony attributed to
Sanchuniathon, 41n.
Motion: in Anaximander, 126–8, 129;
Anaximenes, 145, 147, 151, 152; cause
of ignition (Xenophanes, Anaxagoras),
152; the motionless god of
Xenophanes, 170–1; Parmenides on
Being as motionless, 251–2, *and cf.* 351;
Zeno's arguments against, 269–76;
Xuthus' argument, 398n.; Melissus'
disproof, 397–8; Anaxagoras on,
364–5; in Archelaus, 387–8; atomists'
theory of, 422–3, 423–5
Mourelatos, A. P. D.: on Parmenides fr. 1,
242n., 243n., 255n.; on fr. 8, 38,
252n.; on fr. 8, 54, 256n.

Musaeus, cosmogony assigned to, 18–20,
21, 26
Music: Pythagoras' 'discoveries', 234–5;
and Pythagorean number theory,
233–5, 331, 335; Philolaus on music,
331n.; and Archytas, 335; and
harmony of the spheres, 233, 238,
344–5
Muspellsheim, realm of fire in Nordic
cosmogony, 38n.
Mutilation-myth, in Hesiod, 32–3, 35n., 38,
44–6, 58; Hittite parallel, 33, 45–6
Myth: and philosophy, 7–8, 72–4;
systematizations, 7, 34, 71, 73;
near-eastern, similarities with Greek,
7–8, 11–12, 16–17, 33, 41n., 43–4,
45–6, 58, 59, 68, 71, 92–3, 98–9;
Maori, and earth–sky separation, 43,
45; as influence towards monism, 439

Naucratis, and Milesian contact with
Egypt, 79, 103n.
Navigation: Thales and use of the Little
Bear, 77, 84; his star-guide, 86–8
Neanthes of Cyzicus, 4
Necessity: in Anaximander, 118–19; in
Heraclitus, 193; in Parmenides, 246n.,
251–2, 258; in Empedocles, 315; in
atomism, 418, 419n.
Neoplatonists, 2; as sources for Orphic
cosmogonies, 22–6; for Pythagoras, 2,
215–16
Nestis (Water), in cosmology of
Empedocles, 286, 302
Neugebauer, O., 335
Nicolaus of Damascus, on Diogenes, 435n.,
436, 439n.
Niflheim, realm of ice in Nordic cosmogony,
38n.
Night: cosmogonical concept in Homer,
14n., 20; personification in Homer,
17; an archaic concept, according to
Aristotle, 18, 20; in Hesiod, 18, 19–20,
31–3, 35–6; in post-Hesiodic
cosmogonies, 18, 19–20; priority of, in
Orphic cosmogony, 19–20, 22–3, 25–6,
31–3; associated with Ἀήρ in
production of Tartaros, 19; gave birth
to Gaia and Ouranos, 23; daughter of
Phanes, 22–3; absolute priority not an
early concept, 20; mates with Erebos,
36; offspring of Chaos, 36, 40–1; the
halls of Night in Tartaros, 40; possible
affinity with Alcman's *skotos*, 48–9;
Heraclitus' connexion with day, 189;
in Parmenides, 244, 255–62; *see also* Day

Number: in Anaximander, 136; in
Pythagorean thought, 232–5, 238,
328–45; in Empedocles, 302; in
Philolaus, 326–8, 343–4; Zeno's
paradoxes of plurality, 265–9; and of
completion of an infinite series,
269–72; Anaxagoras' response, 360–2,
367
Numenius, 215
Nussbaum, M. C., 327n.

Oak tree: in Pherecydes, 63–5; at Plataea,
63n.; at Dodona, 65
O'Brien, D.: on Empedocles' cosmic cycle,
288n.; on the relative dates of
Empedocles and Anaxagoras, 354n.;
on Democritus' theory of weight, 423n.
Odd and Even: Pythagorean concept of,
328–32, 336–7, 337–9; in Philolaus,
326
Ogenos: a variant of Okeanos, 62n.;
problem of his position in
Kronos–Ophioneus fight, 69; see also
Okeanos
Oinopides of Chios, 82, 83, 104n.
Okeanos
surrounds the earth, source of all waters,
10–13, 91, 93, 103–4; a circular river,
11, 12; as broad outer sea, 11; concept
of, independent of experience, 11;
Homeric references and non-Greek
mythology, 11–12, 16–17; possible
connexion of concept with Nile floods
and Mesopotamia, 11–12, 16–17;
origin of the word and possible
etymology, 12n.; the sun's passage
round, 12–13; sun and stars and, in
Homer, 13n.
as source and origin of all things, 13–17;
slight indications of cosmogonical
importance in Homer, 14; significance
in Plato and Aristotle, 15–16; evidence
of Orphic poetry, 15–16; priority of,
not an early concept, 16, 20; archaic
cosmogonical position according to
Aristotle, 18; classed with Night, Gaia,
Ouranos, in Hesiod, 18, 36; in Orphic
cosmogony, 16, 31–2; in Hesiodic,
34–6
relation to Pontos, 36n.
provides contact between earth and sky,
36n.
treated as integral part of the earth's
surface, 64
in battle between Kronos and
Ophioneus, 66, 69

as Ogenos: in Pherecydes, 60–1;
represented on embroidered cloth
given to Chthonie, 61, 64–5; see also
Ogenos
Olbia, and Orphic tablets, 30
Onanism, in creation myths, 58–60, 70
Onomacritus, banished from Athens, 20n.
Ophioneus (Ophion), 63; battle with
Kronos, 53, 66–8, 69; analogous to
Typhon, 60; connected with ὄφις, 67;
problem of his parentage, 69–70
Ophionids, 68n.
Opposites: generation by, in Hesiodic
cosmogony, 36; in Anaximander,
108–9, 114–15, 119–21; separation
from the Indefinite, 128–30;
Anaximenes' attitude, 147, 149;
Heraclitus' theory of the essential unity
of opposites, 188–93 (cf. 2, 119); in
Parmenides' cosmology, 255–62; in
Pythagoreanism, 330–1, 337–9; in
Empedocles, 316; Anaxagoras' theory,
190, 359, 366, 368–74, 383–4; and
Archelaus', 388; in Melissus, 400n.; see
also Limit, Odd and Even
Oracle, see Delphi
Origen, 2, 5; quoting Celsus, on
Pherecydes, 64n.
Orpheus: non-Orphic elements attributed
to, in Apollonius' Argonautica, 43n.,
68n.; as supposed author, 221,
222n.
Orphics, 7, poetry as testimony for
cosmogonical importance of Okeanos,
15–16; priority of Night, 18–19; cult
and belief, 21–2; cult-societies and
Pythagorean communities, 21, 220–2;
elements derived from the Theogony,
33; oriental influences, 22n., 33; egg
in cosmogony, 23–9, 131–2, and see
Egg; Neoplatonist accounts of
Orphism, 22–6; Night and Phanes in
Orphic Rhapsodies, 22–3; date and
origin of the Rhapsodies, 23n.; the
'usual Orphic theology', 23–4;
Hieronymus and Hellanicus, 24–5;
Athenagoras, 25; recent discoveries,
29–33; gold plate eschatology, 30–1;
bone tablets, 30, 208n., 210n.; Derveni
papyrus, 19n., 26, 30–3; connexion of
Kronos with Chronos, 57n.;
Pythagorean and Orphic mythology,
222
Orthomenes, possibly father of
Xenophanes, 163
Ortygie, 54, 55nn.

οὐ μᾶλλον principle, 411, 415n.
οὐρανοί, as celestial spheres, 117, 125; *see also* 172
Ouranos: classed with Night, Okeanos, Gaia, in Hesiod, 18; an archaic cosmogonical concept, according to Aristotle, 18; offspring of Night, 19n.; successor of Phanes in Orphic Rhapsodies, 19n., 23; in Hesiodic cosmogony, 34–44; fertilizing the earth, 39n., 383n.; in Hesiodic mutilation-myth, 44–5, 58; as sky-god helping storm-god in Hesiod, 46; produced by Night in Orphic Rhapsodies, 23, 26; Athenagoras on production from egg, 25–6
Owen, G. E. L.: on Parmenides, fr. 8, 4, 248n.; on Zeno, 265

Pain: in Anaxagoras' theory of perception, 384; and pleasure, Empedocles' explanation, 311; Diogenes', 449; Melissus denies that what is feels pain, 396–7
παλίντονος, 192n., 193n.
παλίντροπος, 192n., 247–8
παλμός, of atoms, 424–5
Pamphile, on Thales as geometer, 86n.
Panathenaia, no connexion with Pherecydes' winged oak, 63, 64n.
Papa (earth), in Maori myth, 43, 45
Parmenides of Elea, 75, 115n., 119, 143, 213
  sources for, 1, 3, 241
  date and life, 239–41; early association with Pythagoreanism, 240; influenced by Xenophanes, 240–1 (*cf. also* 164, 165–6, 170n., 171)
  response to Hesiod, 243–4, 254, 255n., 257, 259, 262; debt to Anaximander, 244, 256, 259; possible echoes of Heraclitus, 182, 244 *and* n.; possible influence of Crotoniate medical tradition, 260
  his poem: contents, style, importance, 241–2; obscurity of connexion between its two parts, 241–2, 262; the whole summarized, 241–2
  the proem, 242–4; its epistemological point, 243–4; use of form of religious revelation, 179, 244
  the *Truth*, 244–54; the ways of enquiry, 244–7; interpretation of *estin*, 245–6; and of *noein*, 246n.; argument against negative existentials, 246; critique of mortal thought, 247–8; 'signs' of

truth, 248–9; Parmenides' deduction, 249–54; uncreated and unperishable, 249–50; use of principle of Sufficient Reason, 250; in what sense one and continuous, 250–1 (*cf.* 249); unchangeable, 251–2; obscurity of notion of *limit*, 251–3, 254n.; perfection, 252–3
  mortal opinions, 254–62 (*cf.* 241–2, 247–8); status of Parmenides' account, 254–5; light and night, 255–62; epistemological characterization of mortal belief, 254–7; cosmology, 254–5, 257–60; astronomy, 259; embryology, 259–60; theory of mortal thought, 260–2
Zeno's attitude to Parmenides, 239–40, 269, 277–9; Empedocles' response, 213, 260, 261, 283, 285, 286, 287–8, 290–1, 295–6, 297, 351; echoes in Philolaus, 258, 259, 327 *and* n., 328, 344n.; influence on Pythagorean table of opposites, 339; Anaxagoras' reaction, 351, 357–9, 364, 378; Melissus indebted to him but departs from him frequently, 351, 391, 393, 394, 395, 398, 400, 401; atomists' reaction, 351, 378, 406–9, 433; cosmology and Plato's myth of Er, 259
Paros, fossils found at, 177
Pausanias, and Empedocles' *On Nature*, 284, 313
πεντέμυχος, rejected as title of Pherecydes' book, 52n.
Pericles, and Anaxagoras, 352–5, 390; defeated at sea by Melissus, 390–1
περιέχω, used of air, 115 *and* n., 116, 159
περιπάλαξις, of atoms, 424–5
Persephone: in the Derveni papyrus, 32; in the gold plates, 314
Phaethon, 140
Phanes, in Orphic cosmogony, 19n., 22–3, 24 *and* n., 25n., 28n., 32–3; relation to Eros, 24n., 28
Pherecydes of Athens, 50, 51
Pherecydes of Leros, 50
Pherecydes of Syros, 7
  his approach to cosmogony, 50
  personification of Time, 22n., 28n., 57n.
  date and book, 50–2; the title, 51, 58
  life and legend, 52–6; miracles connected with Pythagoras, 50, 52–3 (*cf. also* 223–4); near-eastern affinities, 33, 53, 65n., 68, 71; the solstice-marker, 54–5, 83

492

Pherecydes of Syros (*cont.*)
contents of his book, 56–71; primeval
deities and creation, 56–60; his
addiction to etymology, 57, 60n., 62n.,
71; Chthonie-Ge, 57n., 58; connexion
of Chronos with Kronos, 57 *and* n., 58
(*cf.* 27, 28n.); initial creation by
Chronos, 58–60; the seven recesses, 51,
58–9; later interpretations of Chronos'
creation from his own seed, 58, 451;
Kronos–Chronos' impregnation of
eggs, 58–60; interpretation of χάος,
60n. (*cf.* 36–7)
wedding of Zeus and Chthonie and the
embroidered cloth, 60–2, 69, 71; the
embroidery an allegory of creation,
61–2, 69; Eros in the wedding, 62, 63n.
the winged oak and the cloth, 63–5;
interpretation of the oak, 63–5; the
oak as foundations of the earth, 64–5;
Pherecydes' world-picture, 64–5
the fight between Kronos and
Ophioneus, 66–8
similarities with Zeus–Typhoeus battle,
68; near-eastern parallels, 68
order of events, 69–71; division of the
cosmos, 69; missing incidents, 69, 71;
problem of parentage of Ophioneus,
69–70
summary of his position, 71; contrast
with Hesiod, 71
Philip, J. A.: on Philolaus and Aristotle's
account of Pythagoreanism, 304; on
Pythagorean mathematics, 335; on
Pythagorean cosmogony, 341
Philo of Byblus: and Sanchuniathon, 41n.;
on Pherecydes' borrowings from
Phoenicians, 68
Philodemus, 2, 19n.
Philolaus of Croton: date and life, 322–3;
problem of authenticity of writings,
216, 323–4; and of their relation to
Aristotle's account of Pythagoreanism,
324, 328, 330–1, 340–1, 343; theory of
limiters and unlimiteds, 324–8, 330–1;
concept of number, 326–7; notion of
harmonia, 234, 324–5, 327–8, 331 *and*
n.; epistemology, 326–8; cosmogony,
340–2; biology, 341 *and* n.; planetary
system, 342–4; on the sun, 344n.; on
eclipses, 344n.; possible contribution to
theory of the harmony of the spheres,
345; on suicide, 323, 349; influenced
by Eleatics, 258, 259, 326n., 327 *and*
n., 328, 344n.; and by earlier
physicists, 328, 344nn.

φθορά, whether genuine in Anaximander,
118
φιλόσοφος, in Heraclitus, perhaps with
allusion to Pythagoras, 218
φλοιός, in cosmogony of Anaximander,
133n., 142
Phoenicia: cosmogony of and Hesiod's
Chaos, 41n.; Phoenician affinities in
Hesiod, 53–4, 68; in Pherecydes, 53–4,
68; Thales' Phoenician ancestry, 77;
use of stars in navigation, 77, 84
Phokos of Samos, 86–7
φρήν, in Xenophanes, 170n.
Φυσικῶν δόξαι *see* Theophrastus
φύσις, conventional use in book-titles, 102
and n., 166, 184, 282, 391, 392n.
Physiology: influence of study of on
cosmology, 91 *and* n., 93; Philolaus'
theories, 341n.; Empedocles'
contribution, 302, 309–11; and
Diogenes, 438–9, 443, 447–52
πίλησις, applied to condensation of air,
145, 151
Pindar: on Chronos as πάντων πατήρ,
57n.; and Pythagoras' eschatology,
236–8; and Empedocles', 317
Placita: derived from Theophrastus, 4; of
Aetius, 5
Planets: in cosmology of Anaximander,
136–7; in Anaximenes, 155; in
Philolaus, 342–4
Plants: and doctrine of reincarnation in
Empedocles, 317, 319; in Anaxagoras,
383
Plato
as source for Presocratic thinkers: laxity
in quotation, 1; his comments and
references, 3
and cosmological significance of Okeanos,
14–15
on Homer as forerunner of Heraclitean
idea of flux, 15
on Orphic oracles and dispensations, 21
(*cf. also* 221–2)
concept of Time in *Timaeus*, 22n.; and of
space, 36
and Pherecydes, 71n.
on Thales, 81, 84, 95n.
on successive worlds, 122
motion in the *Timaeus*, 128
on the earth supported by air, 153
on Xenophanes, 165; the *Phaedo* myth
and, 174
on the Heraclitean school, 185n.
his interpretation of Heraclitus, 185–6,
195–6, 200n., 207n.

Plato (*cont.*)
on Pythagoras and the Pythagoreans, 214–16 (*cf.* 335); the *Phaedo's* Pythagoreanism, 215; numerology in *Timaeus*, *Philebus*, unwritten doctrines, 215; music of the spheres, 233; eschatology of the *Gorgias*, 238; *harmonia* theory of the soul, 346; and Aristoxenus' account of Pythagorean ethics, 347
ψυχή in the *Phaedo*, 220 (*cf. also* 346)
on Parmenides, 239–41; and cosmology of the Myth of Er, 259
on Zeno, 263–5, 277–9; his debt to Zeno, 279
on Philolaus, 323, 349; story of his plagiarism, 324
on Empedocles' theory of sense-perception, 309
and Alcmaeon's argument for the immortality of the soul, 347
criticism of Anaxagoras' use of Mind, 374n., 388
Pleasure and pain: Empedocles' explanation, 311; Diogenes', 448
πλήρης, meanings of, 97
Pliny, the Elder, 76n.; on early astronomy, 103n., 104n.
Plotinus, 2
Plurality, Pluralism: the target of Zeno's book, 263–5, 277–9; his surviving arguments against, 265–9; Melissus', 398–400; Empedocles' reaffirmation of pluralism, 287–9, 351; and Philolaus', 327; and Anaxagoras', 351, 357–9; and Zeno's attack, 360–2; types of, related to opposites, 359; in the atomists, 351, 406–9; Diogenes' rejection, 438–9
Plutarch
as source for Presocratic thought, 1, 6; false ascription to of the *Epitome of Physical Opinions*, 5; and of the pseudo-Plutarchean *Stromateis*, 5
on identification of Chronos with Kronos, 57n.
on Homer's conception of Okeanos, 15n.
on Parmenides' cosmology, 257
on the attribution to Thales of a star-guide, 87
his use of γόνιμος, 131
on Anaximenes, 148–9
on Heraclitus, 192n., 210n.
on Empedocles, 283, 284n., 292
[Plutarch] *Stromateis*, 5, 105–6, 119, 124, 129–30, 131–2

πνεῦμα, in Anaximenes, 146–7, 160; comparison with ψυχή, 158–62
Polycrates of Samos, 100, 101, 223–4
Pontos (sea), 16, 36
Poros, in Alcman's cosmogony, 47–9
Porphyry, 2
on Pherecydes, 52, 59n.; on his use of ἐκροή, 60n.
on Heraclitus, 191n.
on Pythagoras, 216, 232
on Diogenes, 435n.
Poseidon, 318; his share in the division of the world, 14n.
Posidonius: on Heraclitus, 207n.; on the atomists, 429n.
Presocratic thought, schools of (general summaries): Ionian, 75; Italian, 213; post-Parmenidean, 351; *see also* Succession-writers
Principles: of explanation, in Empedocles, 284–94; and in his biology, 306–9; metaphysical, in the atomists, 406–9; *see also* ἀρχή
Pritchard, J. B. (ed.), *Ancient Near Eastern Texts*, 8, 12n., 43, 45n., 58, 68
Proclus: as source for Presocratic thought, 2; on Thales as geometer, 85–6; likewise on the Pythagoreans, 334–5; his summary of Eudemus, 336
Protagoras, 404; his relativism, 411 *and* nn.; debt to Zeno, 279
ψυχή: compared with ἀήρ by Anaximenes, 158–62; distinguished from θυμός in Homer, 159, 433; in Pythagoras, 220; not in Empedocles, 321; *see also* Soul
Psychology, Heraclitus and rationalizing of, 204
Purification: ritual and Pythagorean rules, 229–32; and Empedocles' *Purifications*, 282–3, 318–20
Pyramids, measured by Thales, 83, 85
Pythagoras, 163, 164, 166, 215, 216, 281
sources for: Porphyry and Iamblichus, 2, 216; Hippolytus, 5; Diogenes Laertius, 216; Aristoxenus, 216, 222–5; Dicaearchus, 216, 226–7, 238; Timaeus, 216, 225–7; Aristotle, 215–16, 228–9, 230–2, 235–6; 5th-century evidence, 216–22; general problem of sources, 214–16
and Ionian thinkers, 75; possible influence of Anaximander, 136 (*cf.* 101n., 341)
his use of κόσμος, 159n.

Pythagoras (*cont.*)
  dubious reputation as sage, 216–19;
    scorned by Heraclitus, 181–2, 188n.,
    216–19; admired by Empedocles,
    218–19
  teaching on reincarnation, 219–20, 231,
    237–8, *and cf.* 292, 314–21, 347–8;
    mocked by Xenophanes, 180, 219–20;
    conception of ψυχή, 220; Day of
    Judgement, 220, 231, 235–8
  association with Orphic cults and
    writings, 21, 30, 220–2
  biography, according to Aristoxenus,
    222–5; political activities at Croton,
    224–8; formation of *hetaireiai*, 227–8;
    rise and fall of Pythagorean
    communities in South Italy, 223–5,
    227–8, 229; Pythagorean friendship,
    227–8
  miracle stories, 228–9; question of
    shamanism, 229 *and* n. *(cf.* 243)
  acusmata, 229–36; as catechism of
    doctrine and practice, 229; as *sumbola*,
    229; rules of abstinence, 222, 230–1,
    320; other prohibitions, 220–1, 231–2;
    three classes of *acusma*, 232–3; on the
    Delphic oracle, 223 *and* n. *(cf. also*
    228–9); on number and *harmonia*,
    232–5; the *tetractys*, 233 *and* n.;
    harmonic ratios, 233–5; *acusmatici* and
    mathematici, 234–5; the fate of the soul,
    235–8; mythic eschatology, 236–8;
    Pindar's testimony, 236–8
  conclusion: Pythagoras a sage, not a
    scientist, 238 *(cf.* 213, 235);
    Pythagorean silence, 238 *(cf.* 221, 228)
Pythagoreanism, in fifth century B.C.
  sources, general problem of, 214–16, 322,
    330n.; Aristotle's use of the fragments
    of Philolaus, 324, 328, 330–1, 340–1,
    343; Aristoxenus on Pythagorean
    ethics, 349
  communities, 215, 223–5, 227–8, 229,
    313, 323; their rules of life and
    doctrine, 220–2, 229–36, 238
  Philolaus' contribution to
    Pythagoreanism, 328, 330–1
  Aristotle's principal account, 328–32; his
    vagueness about antiquity and
    authorship of its doctrines, 330–1;
    their symbolic nature, 331–2
  Aristotle's principal criticism, 332–4;
    identification of numbers and things,
    333; Eurytus and his pebbles, 333–4
  mathematics and philosophy, 334–7;
    Pythagoreans made substantial

contribution to the development of
    mathematics, 335; but did not create
    it, 335–6; nor motivated by it to
    philosophize, 335–6; *gnomons* and
    theory of odd and even, 336–7;
  table of opposites, 337–8; possible
    connexion with Alcmaeon of Croton,
    339; and with Parmenides' cosmology,
    339
  cosmogony, 339–42; and respiration,
    341; and embryology, 341 *and* n.;
    Philolaus' theory, 340–1; question of
    its antiquity, 341; Platonizing
    developments, 341n.; merits of theory,
    342
  astronomy, 342–5; planetary system,
    342–4; theory of counter-earth, 343–4;
    its motivation and affinities, 344 *and*
    nn.; the harmony of the spheres, 344–5
  the soul, 346–8; theories of its nature,
    346; Alcmaeon on its immortality,
    347–8
  ethics, 348–9
  summary and evaluation of their
    systematic development of Pythagoras'
    ideas, 350

Rain: impregnating earth, 38, 383 *and* n.;
    Anaximander's explanation, 138, 139;
    Anaximenes', 158; Heraclitus on, 199
Rainbows: Anaximenes' explanation, 158,
    174; Xenophanes', 174; Anaxagoras',
    391, Pythagorean, 236, *see also* Iris
Rangi (sky) in Maori myth, 43, 45
Ras Shamra, 41n., 68
Rationality: of philosophy, contrasted with
    earlier accounts of the world, 7, 72–4,
    75, 99, 101, 142; quasi-rationalism of
    Hesiod, 7, 38, 44, 57, 71, 72–4;
    Pythagoras' irrationalism, 212, 219,
    228–9; his belief in the rationality of
    the universe, 235
Re, sun-god, 12n., 43, 58, 68
'Ρῆ, as name for Rhea, 57
Reale, G., on Melissus, 293nn.
Reason: in Parmenides, 171, 244, 248;
    Principle of Sufficient Reason, 250,
    420n., 424; οὐ μᾶλλον principle, 411,
    415n.; *a priori* reasoning, 85, 137, 294,
    325, 328, 413
Recesses, in cosmogony of Pherecydes, 51,
    58–9, 70
Reincarnation: as element of Orphic
    beliefs, 21; in Pythagoras, 219–20, 231,
    237–8; in Empedocles, 292, 314–21;
    perhaps in Alcmaeon, 347–8

Reinhardt, K., 259n.
Respiration: in Pythagorean cosmogony, 340–1; and Philolaus' embryology, 341 *and* n.; Empedocles' view, 359n.; Diogenes', 448–50
Rhapsodies, Orphic, 23n. *(cf.* 19n., 22–4, 28n., 30–3, 60)
Rhea: in Homeric, Hesiodic and Orphic cosmogony, 16, 27, 32; mother of Zeus, 6; and production of egg, 27; in Pherecydes, 57, 60n.; supplants Eurynome, 66–7, 69; in Pythagorean and Pindaric eschatology, 236, 237
Rhipaean mountains, 157
Ross, Sir D., 127n., 273n., 274n.; on Platonic theory of numbers, 215, 332n.; on Zeno's moving rows, 275n.; on Alcmaeon and Pythagoras, 338n.; on the relative chronology of Anaxagoras and Empedocles, 354n.
Russell, B., 279

St Elmo's fire, Xenophanes' explanation, 174
Salmoxis, said to be slave of Pythagoras, 217–18
Samos: birthplace of Pythagoras, 222–4; of Melissus, 390–1
Sanchuniathon, cosmogony attributed to, 25n., 41n.
Sardis, 75, 82, 98; capture of (546/5 B.C.), 4, 76n., 143, 144n.; (498 B.C.), 144n.
Scepticism: influence on the doxographical tradition, 6; and Sextus' interpretation of Heraclitus, 206; in Xenophanes, 180n.; in Philolaus, 327–8; in Democritus, 409–11, 412
Schofield, M., *An Essay on Anaxagoras*, ix, 361n., 368n., 372n.
Scythinus, metrical version of Heraclitus, 207
Sea: saltness attributed to earth, 11; as its sweat, by Empedocles, 301; Diogenes' explanation, 446; formation of, in Egyptian mythology, 92–3; cosmological idea of its drying up, 139–40, 446; function of, in Xenophanes, 175–6; his earth–sea transformation, 176–8; in Heraclitean cosmos, 199–200, 201–2; *see also* Okeanos, Pontos
Sedley, D. N., on atomist conception of void, 416n.
Semen, and early cosmogonical myths, 58–60, 70; in Stoic physiology, 58; Aristotle on, 94; Diogenes on, 443, 451

Semitic myths, and parallel with Greek, 43, 44n., 68, 92
Senses, and sensation: Heraclitus on correct interpretation, 188n.; Parmenides' disparagement, 248; Theophrastus on his theory in the cosmology, 261; Empedocles' defence, 284–5; his theory of sense-perception, 309–11; and Anaxagoras', 383–4; Melissus' attack on their validity, 398–400; Leucippus' response to his attack, 408; in Democritus' epistemology, 409–13; atomists' theory of sensation, 428–9; Diogenes on pleasure and pain, 448–9
Seth, equated with Typhoeus/Typhon, 68
Sethians, gnostic sect, 65n.
Seven Sages, 50, 76n., 84, 88
Sex, differentiation of: in Parmenides' embryology, 259–60; in Empedocles' evolutionary theory, 303–5; and Pythagorean numerology, 331, 336
Sextus Empiricus, 35n., 166, 243n., 284n; as source for Presocratic thought, 1; on Pherecydes, 60n.; on Heraclitus, 206 *and* n., 207n.; on Parmenides, 241, 243; on Anaxagoras, 384; on Democritus, 411
Shamanism, 229 *and* n., 243
Sharks, and zoogony of Anaximander, 141n.
Shield of Achilles: representation of Okeanos on, 10–11; contrasted with embroidered cloth given to Chthonie, 61–2
Shu (air god), in Egyptian mythology, 43
Sider, D., on Anaxagoras' chronology, 355n.
Σίλλοι, 166
Simplicius, as source for Presocratic thought, 1, 2, 3
  on Thales, 94n.
  on Anaximander, 127n., 130; his version of Theophrastus' account of τὸ ἄπειρον, 105–9, and Aristotle's attribution of an intermediate substance, 112; on reason for choice of primary substance, 113–14; and the extant fragment, 117–18; and application of atomist-type worlds, 124–5; on separation-off of opposites, 129–30
  on Anaximenes, 145, 151n.
  on Xenophanes, 166
  on Heraclitus, 198n.
  on Parmenides, 240, 243nn., 246n., 248n., 252n., 256n.; and preservation of his poem, 241

Simplicius (*cont.*)
on Zeno, 268, 278n.
on Empedocles, 287n., 295, 298
his preservation of the fragments of
Anaxagoras, 356, 358, 370; on
homoeomeries, 377; and question of
innumerable worlds, 380
his preservation of the fragments of
Melissus, 391; on the title of Melissus'
book, 391; his paraphrase, 392 *and* n.,
395n.; on fr. 7, 397n.; on the
incorporeal (fr. 9), 400–1 *and* nn.
on Xuthus, 398n.
on the atomists, 409n., 415n., 420n., 422
his preservation and information on the
ordering of the fragments of Diogenes,
435, 438, 440, 443; question of
number of Diogenes' writings, 435–6;
on the interpretation of Diogenes,
435n., 437, 439n., 440, 443n.
Sin, the primal, in Empedocles, 314–15,
318–21
σκιόθηρα, possibly name of natural feature,
100, 103, 104n.
Sky: like a bowl, 9, 155, 156; relation to
earth and Tartaros, 9–10; implies
advent of Night and Day, 18;
separation from earth, in Hesiodic
cosmogony, 34–41; in Greek literature,
42–3; in non-Greek sources, 43–4;
relation of Greek and Hittite versions
to a common archaic account, 45–6;
in Babylonian mythology, 92; *see also*
Ouranos
Snell, B., 96n., 190n.
Snow (and hail): Anaximenes' explanation,
158; in Anaxagoras' theory of
opposites, 371 *and* n.
Socrates, 212, 278, 323, 354, 357n., 374n.,
441, 452; and Parmenides, 239–40;
pupil of Archelaus, 395; and
Democritus' ethics, 431–2
Solon: on χρόνου δίκη, 57n., 121; visit to
Sardis, 83n.; possible anticipation of
Xenophanes, 171n.; on wisdom, 202n.;
on personal responsibility, 211–12
Sophists, xi; Archelaus and their view of
right and wrong, 389n.; use of book
titles, 392n.; Democritus as author of
sophistic age, 404; cosmology gives
way to study of man, 452
Sotion of Alexandria, 403; originator of
Διαδοχαί, 4, 102n.; Apollodorus of
Alexandria's debt to, 4–5; on
Heraclitus, 182; on Parmenides, 240;
on Anaxagoras, 353

Soul
pre-philosophical views: the Homeric
psyche, 8, 96, 204; the psyche and,
159, 443; Orphic instructions for souls
of the dead, 29, 30; and their view of
the body as its prison, 221–2
in Thales: souls as gods, 95; as motive, 96–
7; attributed to inanimate objects, 95–8
in Anaximenes, cosmic air and
breath–soul comparison, 158–62, 204
Heraclitus' view, 160, 161–2, 203–8, 212;
compared to spider, 205n.; *and cf.* 8
Pythagoras' doctrine of transmigration,
219–20; connexion with Orphic
teaching, 221–2; eschatology, 236–8
Parmenides on the fate of the soul, 240
Empedocles' views, 320–1
Pythagorean theories of nature of soul,
329, 346; Alcmaeon's argument for its
immortality, 347–8
in the theory of the atomists, 427 *and* n.,
429
Diogenes' view, 441–5
Sources for Presocratic thought, 1–6; direct
quotation, 1–3; *testimonia*, 3–6; the
doxographical tradition, 4–6; *see also*
Aristotle, Doxographical tradition,
Plato, Scepticism, Simplicius, Stoics,
Theophrastus
Space: as interpretation of χάος, 26; and
Parmenides' conception of reality, 246,
250–3; Zeno's paradox of place,
264–5; Melissus' argument for the
unlimited extension of reality, 393–5;
and atomist conception of void, 415,
416n.; *see also* Void
Sparta, Anaximander's association with, 49,
100, 103, 104n., 105 *and* n.
σπέρμα, meaning in Anaxagoras, 367–8
Speusippus, his Pythagorean tendencies,
215; on Parmenides, 240
Stars: bathe in Okeanos (Homer), 13n.;
archaic observations, 88; in cosmology
of Anaximander, 136–7; in
Anaximenes, 143, 154, 155;
Empedocles' view, 154; Parmenides',
258–9; Pythagoreans', 342–5;
Anaxagoras', 381–2; *see also*
Astronomy, Navigation
στεφάναι, in Parmenides' astronomy, 257–9
Stephanus of Byzantium, 62n.; on
Diogenes, 434n.
Stesimbrotus, 391 *and* n.
Stobaeus, John, 2; source for Aetius, 5,
124; on Xenophanes, 166; on ethics of
Democritus, 431

Stoics, Stoicism: influence on the
doxographical tradition, 6;
interpretation of χάος, 36–7, 57, 60n.;
influence on Orphic cosmogony, 26;
interpretation of Pherecydes' account
of creation, 58, 62; and interpretation
of Thales, 92n., 97nn.; and Heraclitus,
185, 198n., 200n., 202n., 204n., 206
and n., 207n.
Stokes, M. C.: on Anaxagoras, 372n.; on
the atomists, 404n., 409n., 415n.
Strabo, 2
Strang, C., on Anaxagoras, 368n.
Strife: personified in Hesiod, 35n.; as
justice in Heraclitus, 119, 193; as
Heraclitus' metaphor for change,
193–4; Strife and Love in Empedocles,
287–90, 294–302, 307–8, 314, 315, 318,
321, 364
Succession-writers: as sources of Presocratic
thought, 4, 102n.; on the date of
Anaximenes, 143
συλλάψιες, 190n.
Sumbola (σύμβολα), 229, 231
Sun
sails round Okeanos in a golden bowl,
12, 156, 201; as a bowl, 13, 201; rises
from Okeanos, 13; sails across the sky,
13, 92; Pythagorean *acusma*, 232, 236
solar observation: Thales', 76, 81–4;
Babylonian, 82–3; solstice-marker,
54–6, 83; establishment of cycle of
solstices, 82–4; discovery of obliquity
of the ecliptic, 83, 103, 104n.; ratio of
diameter to celestial path, 83n.;
archaic, 88; of Anaximander, 100,
103–4
in cosmology: Anaximander, 133, 135–7,
139, 142; Anaximenes, 154, 155–7;
Xenophanes, 172–5; Heraclitus, 201–2
(cf. 13); Parmenides, 257–8;
Empedocles, 301; Philolaus, 343–4;
Anaxagoras, 382 *(cf.* 152); atomists,
419, 420nn.; Diogenes, 446
see also Astronomy
Sundials, 100, 103–4; *see also Gnomon*
Syracuse, 164; connexion with Syrie
improbable, 55n.; fossils found at,
177
Syrie, in Homer's reference to the τροπαὶ
ἠελίοιο, 54–6
Syros, the solstice-marker at, 54–5, 83

Tannery, P.: on Thales' eclipse, 76n; on
motion in Anaximander, 128
τάξις, 120

Tartaros, 16; its relation to earth and sky,
9–10, 175; to Hades and Erebos,
9–10; Homer's references to, 14n.; in
Hesiodic cosmogony, 18; associated
with Night in Hesiodic and Orphic
cosmogonies, 19, 27–8, 35, 40–1;
produced by Night and 'Ἀήρ
(Epimenides), 19; Night surrounds the
'throat' of, 20; Aristophanes'
reference, 26–7; Pherecydes' account,
64, 65n., 66–7; Hesiod's description
related to Pherecydes' winged oak, 64
Taylor, A. E., on the trial of Anaxagoras,
354
Tekmor, in Alcman, 48–9
Teleology, of Diogenes, 437, 440
Tethys: cosmogonical position of, 14,
15–16, 67; Aristotle on, 15
Tetractys of the Decad, 233 *and* n.
Thales of Miletus, 3, 8, 15, 50, 75, 108,
163, 175, 177, 198
Hippolytus as source for, 5
life and practical activities, 76–86; date,
76, 101; nationality, 76–7;
astronomical and navigational work,
76, 77, 81–4, 87–8; as statesman and
engineer, 77–8; as type of practical
man, 78; as geometer, 79, 85–6, 98;
visit to Egypt, 79–81, 85, 86n.; on the
flooding of the Nile, 79–80; anecdotes
on, 80–1, 84, 86n.; measurement of
the pyramids, 83, 85; mathematical
discoveries, 84–6
writings, 86–8, 102n., 184
cosmology, 88–98; oriental influences
and similarities, 8, 11, 90, 91, 92–3,
98; water as principle of all things,
88–95, 98–9, 125; earth floats on
water, 89–91, 134 *(cf.* 11); theory of
earthquakes, 93n.; origin of
importance attached to water, 91–3;
earth originates from water, 93–4;
summary of his views on water, 94–5,
water as ἄπειρον, 94n., 110; life in the
apparently inanimate, 95–8, 127, 147;
the soul as motive, 95–7; 'all things
full of gods', 96–8
his work and thought summarized, 98–9;
'hylozoism', 98; as the first
philosopher, 99, 101
influence on Anaximenes, 162; and
Xenophanes' concept of god, 172
Theiler, W., on writings of Diogenes, 435
Themistius, 127n.
Themistocles, connexions with Anaxagoras
and Melissus, 390–1

Theodoretus, 4, 5
Theophrastus
  his Φυσικῶν δόξαι as source for
    Presocratic thought, 3–4, 6; his debt to
    Aristotle, 4–6; his place in the
    doxographical tradition, 4–6
  on Thales, 87, 91nn., 92n., 94 *and* n.,
    97n.
  on Anaximander: date, 101; versions of
    his account of the originative
    substance, 105–8; on ἀρχή and
    ἄπειρον, 108–9; and the extant
    fragment, 117–19, 121–2; question of
    plurality of worlds, 122–3; attribution
    of atomist argument, 123; attribution
    of atomist-type worlds, 124–6, 127–8,
    129, 151n., 419; on eternal motion,
    127, 128; on separation of opposites,
    129–30; the Indefinite likened to
    Anaxagoras' mixture, 130n.; formation
    of the cosmos, 131–3; meteorology,
    138; drying up of the sea, 139
  on Anaximenes: date, 143; book, 144;
    lost work on, 145; cosmology, 145–53;
    attribution of innumerable worlds,
    151n.
  on Xenophanes, 166–7; as Parmenides'
    master, 165; on his single god, 167n.,
    172; on his views on the sun, 173–4;
    on his relation to Anaximander, 240n.
  on Heraclitus: his μελαγχολία, 183; and
    Aristotle's interpretation, 185; on the
    'road up and down', 189n.; the
    trade-image, 200n.; the heavenly
    bodies, 201; exhalations, 202n.
  on Parmenides, as Xenophanes' pupil,
    240 *(cf. 165)*
  on Empedocles' philosophical affiliations,
    281; identification of the four roots,
    286; on his theory of sense-perception,
    310; and of thought, 311
  on Anaxagoras' theory of matter, 365n.,
    373n.
  on Archelaus' adaptation of Anaxagoras,
    387; his lost work on, 388n.
  on the atomists, 404, 405, 414; their
    theory of weight, 422; their account of
    sensation, 429
  on Diogenes' date, 434; theory of
    diagnosis, 436; his eclecticism, 437; his
    view of the basic substance, 437,
    439n.; and of void and innumerable
    worlds, 440n.; physiology, 448–9
Theopompus, on Pherecydes of Syros, 51
Theriomorphism, origin of in Greece, 22n.
  (cf. 220)

Theron of Acragas, 236
Thesleff, H., 216n.
Thetis, in Alcman, 47–9
Thought: and Xenophanes' god, 169–71;
    Heraclitus' theory of understanding,
    186–8; and of wisdom, 202–3; and of
    the intelligent soul, 203–7; Parmenides
    on thought and reality, 245–7, 248–9,
    253; on mortal error, 247–8, 254–5;
    theory of mortal thought, 260–2;
    Empedocles on understanding and the
    senses, 284–5; his account of thought,
    310–12; Philolaus on the necessary
    condition of thought, 326–7;
    Anaxagoras on mind, 362–5, 366;
    Archelaus' view, 387–8; the atomists
    on legitimate knowing, 412–13; their
    account of thought, 428–9; Diogenes'
    theory about intelligence, 437, 440–5;
    his account of thought, 448–50, 451
Thrasylus (Thrasyllus), and Democritus,
    405–6, 431
θυμός and ψυχή, distinction in Homer, 159,
    443
Thunder: Anaximander's account, 138;
    and Anaximenes', 158; Pythagorean
    maxim, 236; *see also* Meteorology
Thurii, foundation of, 4, 280–1
Tiamat, in Babylonian Creation-epic, 12n.,
    43, 68, 71, 92
Timaeus: on Xenophanes, 164; as source
    for Pythagoreanism, 216, 227; on
    Empedocles, 282
Time: as cosmogonical concept, 22n., 56–7,
    and see Chronos; 'assessment of Time'
    in Anaximander, 57n., 120–1;
    Pythagorean doctrine of cyclic
    recurrence, 238 *(cf.* 315); Parmenides'
    view, 250n., 251; in Zeno's arguments,
    272–6; Empedocles' conception of
    everlasting recurrence, 287–8; and of
    the fulfilment of time, 295; in
    Pythagorean cosmogony, 340, 342
Timon of Phlius and Xenophanes, 166,
    170n.; on Heraclitus, 183
Titans: Homer's references to, 14n.;
    parentage of, 16, 27; subjection of, 20,
    37–8; list of, in Hesiod, 34–5;
    Neoplatonist etymology of Τιτάν, 27n.
Transmigration: ridiculed by Xenophanes,
    180, 220; Herodotus on, 220;
    Pythagoras' teaching, 219–20, 237–8;
    teaching of Alcmaeon, 347–8; in
    Empedocles, 292, 314–21
Typhoeus (Typhon), 57n., 70; fight with
    Zeus, 54, 67–8; produced from egg,

Typhoeus (Typhon) (*cont.*)
59–60; snake-headed, 67; mates with
Echidna, 68nn.; equated with
Egyptian Seth, 68

Ugarit, 41n., 68
Ullikummi, Song of, 43–4, 46n.
Upelluri, in 'Song of Ullikummi', 43
ὑπόπτερος, 63

Varro, used the *Vetusta Placita*, 5
Verdenius, W. J., on Heraclitus' views on
soul, 208n.
Vernant, J. P., on Alcman, 48
Vetusta Placita, as source of doxographical
summaries, 5
Vlastos, G., 202n.; interpretation of χάος,
41n.; on opposites in Anaximander,
119n.; on the Indefinite as a mixture,
130n.; on cosmogonical process in
Anaximander, 132; on Heraclitus'
'road up and down', 189n.; on
παλίντροπος 192n.; on Heraclitean
flux, 196; interpretation of Heraclitus,
fr. 30, 198n.; on Heraclitus' views on
the soul, 204; on Anaxagoras, 366; on
Democritus, 405n.; on Anaxagoras
and Democritus, 420n.
deVogel, C. J., on Philolaus and the
Pythagoreans, 324
Void: in Pythagorean cosmogony, 340–1;
distinguished from air, and denied
existence, by Anaxagoras and
Empedocles, 359n., 398n., 409n.; void
denied existence by Melissus, 397–8;
and conceived by him as precondition
of motion, 397–8; atomists' theory,
406–9, 413–16; and account of
formation of worlds, 416–19; and
theory of weight, 422–3; and of motion,
423–4; and of formation of bodies,
425–6; Diogenes' view, 440n., 446
Vortex: Aristotle on, in Anaximander and
Anaximenes, 128, 130, 132, 134,
152n.; in Democritus, 132; in
Empedocles, 296–9; separating off
from vortex, in Anaxagoras, 132n.,
364–5, 372–3, 388, 445; in theory of
the atomists, 416–20, 422, 426–7; in
Diogenes, 445–6

Walzer, R., 202n.; (tr.) Galen, *On Medical
Experience*, 436
War, as Heraclitus' metaphor for change,
193–4
Wasserstein, A., on Babylonian measure-
ment of the ecliptic, 83n.

Water: earth floats on, 11, 89–91, 92–3,
98; male and female principles of, in
Babylonian Creation-epic, 12n.;
priority of, in Orphic cosmogony,
24–5; produced from seed of Chronos,
58, 60n.; in cosmology of Thales,
88–95, 98–9; and the soul, in
Heraclitus, 204, 449; Nestis, in
Empedocles, 286, 302; in Archelaus,
388; Aristotle on atomist theory of
composition of, 427n.; inhibits intelligence (Diogenes), 449; *see also* Okeanos
Webster, T. B. L., 65
Weight, concept of, and atomism, 421–3
West, M. L., 12nn.; on the bone tablets
from Olbia, 30; on Alcman, 48
Wiggins, D., on Heraclitean flux, 200n.
Wilamowitz, U. von, 50n., 57; on Time as
cosmogonical god, 57n.; on the
relation between Empedocles' two
poems, 313
Wind: produced from seed of Chronos, 57,
60n.; as cause of Nile floods, 79–80;
cause of movement of heavenly bodies,
of thunder (Anaximander,
Anaximenes), 137, 138, 155;
Xenophanes' explanation, 176
Wisdom: Heraclitus on, 202–3;
Pythagoras' pretensions, 216–19
Wright, M. R., 293n., 300n., 307n.; on the
assignment of fragments to
Empedocles' two poems, 283; on their
relative length, 283n.; attribution to
him of a double cosmogony, 288n.

Xenocrates, 408n.; his Pythagorizing
tendencies, 215; on Pythagoras'
supposed discovery of the harmonic
ratios, 234
Xenophanes of Colophon, 102n., 124, 152,
162, 193, 199, 206n.
Hippolytus as source for, 5
relation to other thinkers: references to,
and in, others, 163, 164; his place
among the Ionians, 75, 166; on Thales
as an astronomer, 82, 84n.; his
'hylozoism' compared with Thales',
98; as teacher of Parmenides, 164,
165, 240–1; rebuked by Heraclitus,
168, 181, 182n., 188n., 217; ridiculed
transmigration, 180, 219–20; influence
on epistemology, 178–80, 241, 327–8;
on Heraclitus, 167, 173–4, 179–80,
191, 193n., 198, 199, 206n.; on
Parmenides, 240–1 (*cf.* 165, 171); on
Empedocles, 295 (*cf.* 312); on
Melissus, 397

Xenophanes of Colophon (*cont.*)
date and life, 163–6, 182n.; poems, 163, 166–7; association with Elea, 164, 165–6
his physical studies, 167, 168
his importance and influence on religious thought, 167–8, 170
his theology, 168–72; theology his main interest, 167; attacks on conventional religion, 168–9, *and cf.* 150–1; reaction from Homeric idea of divine properties, 170–2, 180; single non-anthropomorphic deity, 169–71; his god and Parmenides' Being, 170n., 171–2 (*cf.* 165–6); corporeal and non-corporeal elements, 170, 171–2; wrongly identified with the whole world, 171–2; possible influence of Solon, 171n.
physical ideas, 172–8; heavenly bodies as concentrations of fire, 173–4; his ideas related to Heraclitus', 173–4; meteorological phenomena, 174–5, 177; theological motives in physical inquiries, 174; plurality of suns and moons, 174–5; explanation of eclipses, 174–5; the earth's roots, 175 6 (*cf.* 9–10, 90, 110); the earth becomes sea again, fossils as evidence, 177–8 (*cf.* 139n.)
on the limitations of human knowledge, 179–80
Xerxes, King of Persia, 353; and Democritus, 406n.
Xuthus, on motion, 398n.

Yggdrasil, Scandinavian world-tree, 65n.

Zas: in cosmogony of Pherecydes, 51, 56–7, 58; etymological connexion with Zeus, 57; marriage to Chthonie and presentation of embroidered cloth, 57n., 63, 69; as cosmogonical creator, 59n., 60–3; creates as Eros, 62–3; the winged oak and the cloth, 63–5; deposes Kronos-Chronos, 67; connexion with Zeus, 57, 67
Zeller, E., 151, 362, 388n.; on Pherecydes' winged oak, 64; on Anaximander's plural worlds, 122; on vortex action in cosmogony, 153n.; on Archelaus as ethical philosopher, 389n.
Zeno of Citium, 185; his interpretation of χάος, 36
Zeno of Elea, 110, 355, 392, 401 *and* nn., 403, 404

date and life, 239–40, 263, 361n.; alleged visit to Athens, 240; association with Parmenides, 240
book, 263–5; its form and plan, 264–5; paradox of the millet seed, 264; and of place, 264
extant antinomies against plurality, 265–9; question of conditions of discreteness, 266; problems of infinite series, 268–9; arguments undermine Parmenides' *Truth*, 269 (*cf.* 277, 278n.)
paradoxes of motion, 264–5, 269–76; question of their original form, 265; their assumptions about the structure of space and time, 265, 273, 276; their notoriety, 269; the stadium, 269–72; Aristotle's solution, 270–1; problems in completing an infinite series of acts, 272; the Achilles, 265, 272; the arrow, 272–4; Aristotle's criticism, 273; problems for philosophy of time, 273–4; the moving rows, 274–6; difficulties of interpretation, 275n., 276; problems for conception of motion, 276; comparison with the arrow, 276; Aristotle's objection, 276
Zeno's aims, 277–8; attacks common sense, 277; not the Pythagoreans, 278n.; nor monism, 278n.; as dialectician, 278
his influence, 279; Anaxagoras' reaction, 360–2, 367; and the atomists', 408
Zeus: deceived by Hera, 14, 17; his share in division of the cosmos, 14n., 67–8; subdues Titans, 20, 37, 58; in Orphic theogony, 31–3; paralleled by Hittite storm-god, 46; battle with Typhoeus, 53–4, 67; connexion with Zas, 57, 67; slandered by Ge, 54; his shrine at Dodona, 65; his childhood in Crete, 67; in Heraclitus, 202–3; in cosmology of Empedocles, 286; in Empedocles' *Purifications*, 318
Zodiac, discovery of obliquity of, 82, 83, 103n., 104n.
Zoogony: of Anaximander, 141–2; spontaneous generation, 142; of Empedocles, 302–5; of Archelaus, 388
Zoroaster: identified with Ham, 65n.; visited by Pythagoras, 65n.
Zoroastrianism: Pherecydes' connexion with, 53, 65n.; literature of, 65n.
Zuntz, G., 218n., 283n., 319n.; on Pythagoreanism and the Gold Plates, 30; on Empedocles' *daimones*, 315
Zvran Akarana (Iranian 'unending time'), 22n., 57n.

51,984

Kirk, G. S.
(Geoffrey
Stephen), 1921-

The presocratic
philosophers

DATE			
NOV - 5 1990			
APR			
APR 1 3 1995			
APR 1 9 1995			
DEC 0 3 1998			
OCT 3 1 2002			
NOV 2 1 2002			
DEC 0 4 2002			